Arndt

MONEY, INTEREST, AND PRICES

MONEY, INTEREST, AND PRICES

An Integration of Monetary and Value Theory

Second Edition

Don Patinkin

The Eliezer Kaplan School of Economics and Social Sciences
The Hebrew University of Jerusalem

Harper & Row, Publishers, New York

To My Mother and Father

Contents

Contents

Contents

Contents

Contents

Contents

Contents

BIBLIOGRAPHY AND INDEXES

Preface to the Second Edition

Though the basic approach and analytical framework of this book have remained the same, this new edition reflects countless minor changes and a significant number of major ones. The stimulus to these changes has come from the developments in the literature since the first edition of this book, from the specific criticisms that have been made of that edition, and finally, from my own dissatisfaction with various aspects of it.

This dissatisfaction has already expressed itself in part in articles published since the first edition of this book (see Bibliography) and cited at the appropriate points below. Most of the changes of this nature are, however, presented here for the first time.

Insofar as the aforementioned criticisms are concerned, in the many cases where I have accepted them, this fact has been indicated and explicit reference to the relevant criticism given. I have not, however, always been so explicit in the case of disagreement: for my primary objective in such cases has been the necessary clarification of substantive issues, and not polemics. I cannot, however, pretend that I have not on occasion strayed across the indefinite line that separates these two.

Despite—or, perhaps, because of—the extensive nature of the aforementioned changes, this book is not the one that would have emerged were I to be writing it today for the first time. For though considerable efforts have been made to carry these changes through consistently, it is inevitable—in a book as interwoven as this one—that there have remained undetected various passages which continue to reflect ways of thinking since superseded. I have, however, preferred to present a new book that may be somewhat blemished in this respect, rather than to leave unchanged the original, more integrated—and outdated—one.

The principal difference between this edition and the preceding one lies in the microeconomic theory of money of Chapters V–VII. The first of these chapters represents both a rewriting and noticeable expansion of the original treatment, while the last two (based on the work of Baumol, Markowitz, and Tobin) are entirely new. A common feature of all three chapters is the development of this theory within a multi-period Fisherine model. Chapter VI also demonstrates what had been contended only intuitively in the first edition: namely, that the demand functions used in this book hold—without basic modification—for a model in which money is held for the precautionary and speculative motives, as well as for the transactions motive.

The reader interested in further details of the revision of these chapters—and in an explanation of the other significant changes or additions that have been made in this book—is referred to Note N:2. Two of these changes are the addition of a section to Chapter III on the Archibald-Lipsey analysis of long-run equilibrium, and the radical revision—in both viewpoint and content—of Chapter XII. The last four sections of this chapter have been completely rewritten and, among other things, now make use of Gurley and Shaw's work to discuss the distinction between inside and outside money, and to show how the analysis of the functioning of a banking system (and other financial intermediaries) can be integrated into a macroeconomic model.

Three other major additions are Mathematical Appendix 2:b on the analysis of the real-balance effect in the context of the wealth effect, Mathematical Appendix 11 on the perennial problem of stocks and flows, and Note M on the empirical significance of the real-balance effect. This last reflects the generally increased concern of the present edition with relating the theoretical analysis to the empirical work that has been done in the field. Progress in this work has been particularly great during the past decade.

Preface to the Second Edition

In the long process of preparing this revised edition I have benefited from the help of many individuals. Some have pointed out errors in the first edition, and others have provided stimulating and helpful suggestions. Still others have read critically various parts of the new material. It is impractical to list all these individuals here (specific acknowledgments to some of them have been made at the relevant points in the book), but I would at least like to express my gratitude to both my nearby and more distant colleagues Kenneth Arrow, Yosef Attiyeh, Yoram Barzel, William J. Baumol, Robert Clower, Robert Eisner, Rendigs Fels, Milton Friedman, Zvi Griliches, John G. Gurley, Nissan Liviatan, Michael Michaely, Amotz Morag, and Tsvi Ophir. With sorrow, I also record my debt to the late Yehuda Grunfeld.

A good deal of work on this revision was carried out during a most pleasant and stimulating year (1961–62) spent at the University of California, Berkeley, as Ford Foundation Visiting Research Professor. I am deeply grateful to the Department of Economics at Berkeley for this opportunity and for all the facilities which it so generously made available. I also have a special debt to Dale Jorgenson, Robin Matthews and Thomas Mayer, who participated in an informal discussion group at Berkeley, and who subjected an earlier draft of Chapters V–VII to their searching and unrelenting criticism.

The material of Chapter V: 3–7 was in large part presented as a paper at the December 1961 meetings of the Econometric Society in New York, and I benefited from the discussion which took place at that time. I am also indebted to the participants in the International Economic Association "Conference on the Theory of Interest Rates," held at Royaumont, France, in March 1962, for their comments on a paper which was essentially an earlier draft of Chapters VI:1–2 and VII. The foregoing materials also formed the basis of several seminars given at various American universities in the fall of 1960 and winter of 1961, from which I derived many helpful suggestions.

Once again, it is a pleasure to express my gratitude to the students of the seminar in monetary theory at the Hebrew University during the past few years for their most valuable comments and suggestions. There is little in the new material of this book—and particularly that of Chapters V–VII—which has not been thrashed out with them. I am particularly indebted to Michael Bruno, Giora Hanoch, David Levhari, Naphtali Levi, Yosef Mai, Asher Shlain, and Eytan Sheshinsky. I am also grateful to the latter and to Shannon R. Brown (at the University of California) for the technical assistance which they have so conscientiously rendered. Susanne Freund has been of inestimable help in all the statistical work connected with Note M.

The typing of the various drafts of the manuscript has been carefully and most efficiently carried out by Mrs. Naomi Rosenblatt in Jerusalem and Mrs. Jan Seibert in Berkeley. Mrs. Hasida Nitzan and Moshe Felber have provided invaluable assistance at all stages of the work, and particularly in collating the various materials which make up this revision. Susanne Freund has helped greatly in the checking of proofs; her efficiency and thoroughness are much appreciated.

I wish finally to express my thanks to the Eliezer Kaplan School of Economics and Social Sciences of the Hebrew University and to the Department of Economics at the University of California, Berkeley, for research grants that made all this assistance possible.

DON PATINKIN

Jerusalem

Preface to the First Edition

This work is the outgrowth of ideas first presented in a doctoral dissertation submitted to the University of Chicago in 1947 and then further developed in a series of articles published in various journals and anthologies through the years 1948 to 1954. The reader interested in consulting these articles will find them listed in the Bibliography at the end of the book. The book itself, however, makes but few explicit references to them. Correspondingly, it makes practically no attempt to show how its argument is specifically related to that of these earlier articles. It must also be empasized that, with the exception of a few pages, the actual exposition of this book is entirely new. It represents an extensive reworking, elaboration, and refinement of the basic ideas of these articles within a much more systematic and comprehensive framework than was originally achieved.

Furthermore—and most gratifyingly—the text of the present book has been able to dispense with the apparently forbidding mathematical apparatus which marked the first of these articles. The argument is instead developed by the use of the more familiar literary and graphical techniques of modern economic analysis. There is an extensive Mathematical Appendix, which will, I hope, be of help and interest to the mathematically inclined reader. But this Appendix is not necessary for an understanding of the text. Indeed, the opposite is true: the text is necessary for a full understanding of the Appendix.

A similar statement holds for the Supplementary Notes and Studies in the Literature. These, too, are not necessary for the text, but the text is necessary for them. In particular, their full meaning can be understood only after reading Chapters VIII and XV, whereas these chapters can be understood without the Notes by the reader willing to accept their interpretations of doctrinal history without insisting upon detailed documentation from the literature.

The nature of the argument of this book has made it necessary to use numerous internal cross-references. These are of two types. First, there are those to the Mathematical Appendix and Supplementary Notes. Their purpose is to indicate to the reader the nature of the additional information that he can find in these places should he be interested in consulting them. Second, there are the cross-references to the text itself. Their main purpose is to remind the reader where—if need be—he can refresh his memory about an earlier conclusion which is being used as the basis for a further development in the argument. The reader who has no need for these reminders and who is interested only in the text itself can therefore ignore all cross-references and proceed with his reading undisturbed. On the other hand, anyone who wishes to follow up these references will find his task simplified by the fact that each page of this book carries the appropriate chapter-section number (in the case of the text), appendix-section number (in the case of the Mathematical Appendix), or note-section number (in the case of the Supplementary Notes).

In the process of working out the ideas of this book, I have been particularly fortunate in having had the opportunity of stimulating discussions—both oral and written, published and unpublished—with many individuals. I regret that it is impractical to name them all here. But I must make explicit my indebtedness to Kenneth J. Arrow, Leonid Hurwicz, and especially Trygve Haavelmo for the many illuminating informal discussions I enjoyed with each of them during the year (1946–47) I spent as a Social Science Research Council predoctoral fellow at the Cowles Commission for Research in Economics.

At a later stage I benefited greatly from the debate which developed in the journals as a consequence of the articles referred to above. With one or two minor exceptions, I have seen no point in returning in this book to these earlier polemics; the interested reader will, however, find the relevant critical articles and my replies to them listed in Supplementary Note N:1. Needless to say, the necessity for preparing these replies was an invaluable stimulus toward a constant reworking and improving of the argument and its exposition. I am particularly grateful in this respect to Herbert Stein, for clarifying the nature of open-market operations; to W. Braddock Hickman, for pointing out an incorrect usage of the concept "functional dependence" in one of the earlier articles; and to Frank H. Hahn, for showing the limitations of the one-period static model in terms of which the argument was initially developed.

I hope that without being presumptuous I may also indicate my general indebtedness to certain basic works in economic theory—an indebtedness which, by its very nature, cannot find adequate expression in mere footnote references. The analytical apparatus developed by J. R. Hicks in his *Value and Capital* is obviously fundamental to Part One. There is a correspondingly obvious dependence of Part Two on the macroeconomic concepts and techniques of J. M. Keynes' *General Theory* and the later Keynesian literature. Crucial use has been made at various points in the book of the dynamic stability analysis developed by P. A. Samuelson in his *Foundations of Economic Analysis.* The influence of A. W. Marget's *Theory of Prices* on some of the Supplementary Notes and Studies in the Literature will also be evident. And from the text the reader will likewise see how much my thinking has been colored by Knut Wicksell's classic *Interest and Prices.*

I have more immediate debts to Professor Martin Bronfenbrenner, Mr. Nadav Halevi, and Professor William Jaffé, for providing valuable criticisms of earlier drafts of the text; to my colleague Professor Aryeh Dvoretzky, for writing the very interesting Mathematical Appendix to Chapter V; and to many friends abroad for sending copies of materials that were not otherwise available.

It is a distinct pleasure also to express my deep gratitude and indebtedness to three successive classes of graduate students at the Hebrew University, Jerusalem. Stimulating contact with them—both in and out of seminars—has been a most valuable source of criticisms and suggestions. By their willingness to serve as critical "guinea pigs" for the earlier drafts of the text of this book, they have also helped repeatedly to indicate points of ambiguity and difficulty that needed further clarification. Once again, I regret that it is impractical to acknowledge all this help more explicitly. But I cannot let go unmentioned my special debts to Mr. Nissan Liviatan, whose valuable criticisms have been noted in Chapter XIII, and, in particular, to Mr. Tsvi Ophir (Goldberger), whose fruitful suggestions and penetrating remarks have been indicated at various points in the text. I have also benefited from Mr. Ophir's meticulous and conscientious assistance on various technical matters. Similarly, I am indebted to Mr. Azriel Levi, who has checked the computations of the Mathematical Appendix.

I wish finally to extend my thanks to Mrs. Aliza Argov, Mrs. Esther Copperman, and Mrs. Judith Schorr, for carefully seeing the typescript through its various drafts; to Miss Gila Abramowitz, for loyally providing technical assistance; and to the Eliezer Kaplan School of Economics and Social Sciences of the Hebrew University, for a research grant that made this technical and typing assistance possible.

DON PATINKIN

Acknowledgments

Appreciation is expressed to the following for permission to quote certain works in this book:

George Allen and Unwin Ltd. *and* Richard D. Irwin, Inc., *for*
L. Walras, *Elements of Pure Economics*, trans. and ed. W. Jaffé (London: George Allen and Unwin Ltd., 1954; Homewood, Illinois: Richard D. Irwin, Inc., 1954).

Ernest Benn Ltd. *and* Harcourt, Brace and Co., *for*
G. Cassel, *Fundamental Thoughts in Economics* (London: T. Fisher Unwin Ltd., 1925; New York: Harcourt, Brace and Co., 1925) *and* G. Cassel, *The Theory of Social Economy*, trans. S. L. Barron (new revised ed.; London: Ernest Benn Ltd., 1932; New York: Harcourt, Brace and Co., 1932).

The Brookings Institution, *for*
John G. Gurley and Edward S. Shaw, *Money in a Theory of Finance* (Washington, D.C.: The Brookings Institution, 1960).

Mr. Irving N. Fisher, *for*
I. Fisher, *The Purchasing Power of Money* (New York: The Macmillan Company, 1911).

Acknowledgments

Harcourt, Brace and Co. *and* Macmillan & Co. Ltd., *for*
  J. M. Keynes, *General Theory of Employment, Interest and Money*
  (New York: Harcourt, Brace and Co., 1936; London: Macmillan
  & Co. Ltd., 1936).

Longmans, Green & Co. Ltd., *for*
  J. S. Mill, *Principles of Political Economy*, ed. W. J. Ashley
  (London: Longmans, Green & Co. Ltd., 1909).

Macmillan & Co. Ltd., *for*
  A. Marshall, *Money Credit and Commerce* (London: Macmillan &
  Co. Ltd., 1923).

Routledge & Kegan Paul Ltd. *and* The Macmillan Company, *for*
  K. Wicksell, *Lectures on Political Economy*, trans. E. Classen
  (2 vols.; London: George Routledge and Sons Ltd., 1935; New
  York: The Macmillan Company, 1935).

The Royal Economic Society, *for*
  D. Patinkin, "Wicksell's 'Cumulative Process,'" *Economic Journal*,
  LXII (1952),
  K. Wicksell, *Interest and Prices*, trans. R. F. Kahn (Macmillan &
  Co. Ltd., 1936), *and*
  Works and Correspondence of David Ricardo, ed. P. Sraffa (Cam-
  bridge: Cambridge University Press, 1951).

Introduction

Money buys goods, and goods do not buy money. The natural place, then, to study the workings of monetary forces is directly in the markets for goods. This will be our central theme.

It cannot be claimed that the theme is a novel one. In a crude way it even appears in the transactions approach to the quantity theory of money. Specifically, the familiar $MV = PT$ can be looked upon as determining the equilibrium price level P as the resultant of forces represented by the aggregate demand for goods MV, on the one hand, and their aggregate supply T on the other. This equation, however, does little to exploit the full potentialities of the theme: It restricts monetary theory to the case of an aggregate demand function for goods which, to outward appearances, is independent of the rate of interest and directly proportionate to the quantity of money. This is as misleading as it is unrealistic, for it gives the false impression that the results obtained by analyzing this equation are necessarily dependent upon these extreme assumptions.

For some time, however, the transactions approach has been out of fashion. It has largely been replaced by monetary theories which shift the center of emphasis from the markets for goods to the market for money. The basic analytical tool of these theories—whether of the neoclassical or of the Keynesian variety—is the demand function for money. Correspondingly, their main concern is to describe this function and to apply it to the problems of monetary theory.

There is nothing logically wrong with this procedure. There is no reason why we should not enjoy the semantic liberty of saying that goods buy money and of describing, accordingly, a demand function for money. For if such a function is correctly described, it cannot but be the obverse image of the aggregate demand function for goods; hence, as we shall always be at pains to show, the side of the transaction from which the analysis is conducted cannot affect the conclusions reached.

Our criticism of these contemporary monetary theories is instead the pragmatic one that they fail to provide this obverse image. True, the neoclassical cash-balance equation is developed with particular regard for the alternative of spending money in the commodity market, and the Keynesian liquidity-preference equation with a corresponding regard for the bond market. Nevertheless, in neither case is there a systematic attempt to analyze the full implications of these markets for the respective monetary equation.

The alternative approach developed in this book begins with a description of the demand functions for commodities and bonds, with particular emphasis on the relatively neglected influence of money balances. These functions are then used to carry out a static and dynamic analysis of the central problems of monetary theory—the effects of changes in the quantity of money and shifts in liquidity preference on interest, prices, and employment. In this way we achieve an integration of monetary theory and value theory: the propositions of both theories are derived by applying the same analytical techniques to the same demand functions of the same markets. Such an integration is desirable, not only for showing these two theories to be special cases of a general theory of price, but also for enabling a simple and direct treatment of otherwise complicated problems.

Of necessity, our viewpoint is that of general-equilibrium analysis. For since monetary changes are assumed to affect all markets of the economy, their effects can be fully appreciated only by a simultaneous study of all these markets. Indeed, it will be seen that in most cases where we reach conclusions at variance with the accepted ones, it is a direct result of taking into account the dynamic interactions between price-level variations in the commodity market and interest-rate variations in the bond market. This interdependence of markets is a fundamental and recurring element of the argument.

For convenience, this argument is divided into two parts, according to the analytical technique used. In Part One the technique is that of microeconomics in the broad sense. That is, the market demand functions of this part continue to reflect the idiosyncrasies of the individuals' demand functions from which they are constructed. In Part Two the technique becomes that of macroeconomics. Here the idiosyncrasies disappear, and the market demand functions assume the aggregative forms familiar from Keynesian models.

It is, however, more instructive to outline the argument from the viewpoint of content rather than technique. Specifically, there is a major theme—running through both Parts One and Two—which deals with the monetary theory of an economy with full employment. This theme is developed by Chapters I–IV and IX–XII, and can be followed independently of the intervening chapters. In Part One, the only type of money considered is that which is based on the debt of some authority exogenous to the economic system ("outside money"); in Part Two, the analysis is extended to money based on the debt of endogenous units (*viz.*, banks) of the system ("inside money"). There is a second major theme which deals with the monetary theory of an economy with involuntary unemployment. This is developed by Chapters XIII–XIV. Then there are secondary themes, which the reader is free to follow or ignore in accordance with his interests. In particular, Chapters V and VI develop a marginal-utility theory of money and assets, and thus base the conclusions of the aforementioned chapters on the principle of utility maximization. Chapter VII, on the other hand, starts from the assumption that money should be considered as a producer's good (as contrasted with a utility-generating consumer's good) and rationalizes the individual's demand for money in the same terms used to describe a firm's demand for inventories as a factor of production. Finally, Chapters VIII and XV use the analytical results of this book as the background against which to develop a detailed critique of neoclassical and Keynesian monetary theory.

The more general conclusions of our argument can be summarized as follows: The propositions of the quantity theory of money hold under conditions much less restrictive than those usually considered necessary by its advocates and, *a fortiori*, its critics. Conversely, the propositions of Keynesian monetary theory are much less general than the *General Theory* and later expositions would lead us to believe. But this in no way diminishes the relevance of Keynesian unemployment theory for the formulation of a practicable full-employment policy.

One. MICROECONOMICS

I. The Theory of a Barter
Exchange Economy

*1. The nature of an exchange economy. The excess-demand curve.
2. The excess-demand function. 3. The determination of the equilibrium
price. 4. Individual-experiments and market-experiments.*

1. THE NATURE OF AN EXCHANGE ECONOMY.
THE EXCESS-DEMAND CURVE

The present part of this book is devoted to the rigorous development of the monetary theory of an exchange economy. By initially restricting ourselves to such a simple economy, we are able to concentrate on the essential features of the analysis with a minimum of distracting complications. The ultimate justification for this procedure will emerge from the argument of Part Two. This shows that the basic conclusions of the monetary theory here developed are equally valid for more complex, and more realistic, economies.

In order to review the analytical techniques of value theory that will be needed in the present part, we start with a practice-run over the familiar ground of an exchange economy which is also a barter economy. This is the ground covered by the Pareto-Slutzky-Hicks theory of consumer's behavior. Accordingly, this section and the two subsequent ones are devoted to summarizing Hicks' development of this theory.[1]

[1] J. R. Hicks, *Value and Capital* (Oxford, 1939), Chapters I, II, V, and IX.

The distinguishing mark of an exchange economy is the absence of production. That is, the goods available in this economy are produced in fixed quantities by extraneous forces which then arbitrarily and gratuitously distribute them among the individuals of the economy. Correspondingly, the sole economic problem of an exchange economy is the optimal redistribution of these goods among the various individuals. This is not quite as restrictive as it first sounds; for included among these goods are the personal services of the individuals themselves, and—in view of the possibility of leisure—the amount of these services can vary.

For simplicity, it is assumed that time in this economy is divided into discrete, uniform intervals called the "week." Each individual begins Monday morning of any given week with an initial collection of goods which, like the manna of the Children of Israel, has descended upon him "from the heavens" during the preceding night. On Monday afternoon he has the opportunity of bartering varying quantities of these initial goods for varying quantities of others which he prefers in their stead. The market in which these transactions take place is open only on Monday afternoon; no trading can take place at any other time during the week. It is assumed that the market is a perfectly competitive one.

The behavior of the individual in this market is now analyzed by use of an indifference map. In Figure I-1, indifference curves I, II, and III correspond, respectively, to different, and ascending, levels of utility. As will be recalled, the slope of these curves has particular economic significance. Assume, for example, that the individual consumes the collection Q, consisting of OG units of X and OH units of Y. Assume now that we reduce his consumption of X by EG units and wish to determine the amount of Y with which we must compensate him in order to keep him just as well off as he was at the point Q; that is, the amount by which we must now vary his consumption of Y in order to enable him to remain at the same, fixed level of utility represented by the indifference curve II. From Figure I-1 we see that this "compensating variation in Y" equals HA. The quotient HA/EG is thus the amount of Y, per unit of X taken away, with which we must compensate the individual. If we now take away smaller and smaller quantities of X from OG, this quotient approaches as a limit the slope of the line tangent to indifference curve II at $Q—HF/EG$. This slope measures "the marginal rate of substitution of *X* for *Y*" at the point *Q*. "It is the amount of *Y* which is needed by the individual in order to compensate him for the loss of a small unit of *X*."[2]

This slope also has meaning in terms of marginal utilities. Let the

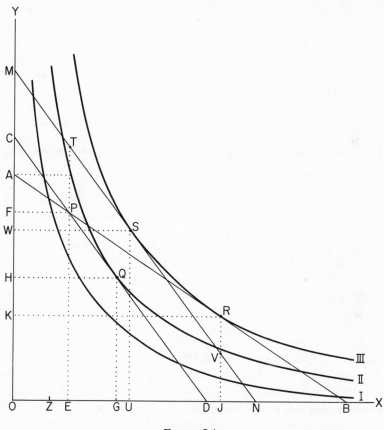

FIGURE I-1.

aforementioned "small unit" of *X* be the "marginal unit." Then, by definition, a decrease in the consumption of *X* by one such unit decreases the individual's total utility by an amount equal to the marginal utility of *X*. If, at the same time, his consumption of *Y* is increased

[2] *Ibid.*, pp. 14, 20.

5

by *HF/EG* units, there is an offsetting increase in total utility by an amount equal to the marginal utility of a unit of *Y times HF/EG* such units. By definition, the net effect of these compensating variations is to keep the individual's level of utility unchanged. That is, at the point *Q* the following relation must obtain:

the marginal utility of $X = \dfrac{HF}{EG} \cdot$ the marginal utility of *Y*.

From this it follows that

$$\frac{\text{the marginal utility of } X}{\text{the marginal utility of } Y} = \frac{HF}{EG}$$

= the marginal rate of substitution of *X* for *Y*.

This equality between the ratio of marginal utilities and the marginal rate of substitution will prove useful in Chapter V.

Let us now turn from the individual's subjective calculations to the given objective conditions under which he must operate in the market. Assume that his initial collection of goods consists of *OE* units of *X* and *OF* of *Y*. This will be referred to alternatively as his "initial endowment." Assume further that the price of *X* in terms of *Y* with which the individual is confronted corresponds to the slope of the line *CD*. Then *CD* is his budget line, or budget restraint. It describes all the possible collections of goods into which the individual can—by bartering *X* for *Y* at the given market price—convert his initial collection *P*.

Under the conditions of Figure I-1, the individual will obviously maximize his utility by bartering HF units of his initial endowment of *Y* in exchange for *EG* additional units of *X*. This brings him to the collection *Q*, for which the marginal rate of substitution of *X* for *Y* is equal to the price of *X* in terms of *Y*. The point *Q* thus denotes his "optimum collection" or "optimum position" under the given conditions. It describes the quantities of *X* and *Y* which the individual chooses to consume. Correspondingly, *OG* and *OH* are called the "amounts demanded" of *X* and *Y*, respectively, under the given conditions. They are to be contrasted with the "*excess* amounts demanded"—which are the respective differences between the amounts demanded and the amounts initially held of the various goods. A positive excess amount demanded means that the individual enters the market as a buyer; a negative one, as a seller. In our particular case the excess amounts demanded are, of course, *EG* of *X* and *minus HF* of *Y*. It will frequently be convenient to describe a *negative* amount of excess *demand* by the equivalent term "*positive* amount of excess *supply*." Thus we can in our case say that there is an excess supply of *HF* units of *Y*.[3]

Clearly, the optimum collection, hence the amounts demanded, and hence the excess amounts demanded, all depend on the given price ratio existing in the market. Thus if the individual's initial endowment remains *P* but he is now confronted with a lower price for *X*, his budget line becomes, say, *AB*. The corresponding optimum collection becomes *R*; the amounts demanded of *X* and *Y* become *OJ* and *OK*, respectively; and their excess amounts demanded become *EJ* and *minus KF*, respectively. Because of the cheapening of *X*, the individual is willing to barter a greater quantity of *Y* to acquire a corresponding greater quantity of *X*. This is represented in Figure I-1 as the joint result of the substitution effect and a reinforcing positive income effect.

By varying the relative price of *X* once again we obtain yet another budget line passing through *P* and, correspondingly, yet another optimum collection. Indeed, we can consider the individual—with his given indifference map and initial endowment *P*—to be a "utility-computor" into whom we "feed" a sequence of market prices and from whom we obtain a corresponding sequence of "solutions" in the form of specified optimum positions. In this way we can conceptually generate the individual's excess-demand curve for, say, *X*; this shows the excess amounts of *X* he demands at the various prices. Such a curve—for our given individual with his initial endowment *P*—is represented by *edh* in Figure I-2.

For reasons that will become evident in a moment, the origin of this diagram is designated as *E*. To its right are positive numbers, to its left, negative. The distances on the horizontal axis here represent the same quantities as in Figure I-1. The curve *edh* shows that at any price below *En* the amount of excess demand is positive. For example, if

---

[3] In order to avoid possible confusion it should be emphasized that our use of the term "amount demanded" does *not* correspond to its usual meaning, the amount an individual wishes to *buy* on the market at a given price. It is, instead, this amount *plus* the amount he wishes to retain out of his initial endowment. In other words, our "demand" is the ordinary demand *plus* Wicksteed's reservation demand.

we assume that the price *Em* is that represented by the slope of *CD* in Figure I-1, then both diagrams yield (as they must) the same information: the individual will want to buy in the market the quantity *EG*. On the other hand, at the price *En* the individual's initial and optimum collections coincide; hence he does not enter the market at all. Finally, prices above *En* are sufficiently attractive to induce him to sell part of his initial holdings. Thus at the price *Ep* his amount of excess demand is negative—or, alternatively, his amount of excess supply is positive—

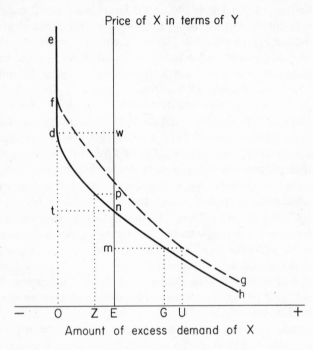

FIGURE I-2.

to the extent *ZE*. Indeed, should the price rise to *Ew* or above, the individual deems it worth his while to offer on the market his entire initial amount of *X*—*OE*—in exchange for *Y*.

We now note that by shifting the vertical axis to the point *O*, we convert this excess-demand curve into a demand curve. This relationship reflects the fact that, by definition, the amount demanded of *X equals* the amount of excess demand *plus* the initial amount of X. Thus the demand curve tells us how much X the individual demands at each price—without distinguishing between demand that is satisfied by resort to the market and demand that is satisfied out of initial holdings. This dual nature of Figure I-2 will subsequently prove useful.

2. THE EXCESS-DEMAND FUNCTION

In addition to depending on the market price with which he is confronted, the individual's optimum collection also clearly depends on his initial endowment. This is analogous to saying, in more familiar terms, that it depends on his income. Assume, for example, that for some unspecified reason the individual's initial quantity of Y is increased so that his initial position is now T instead of P in Figure I-1. If the market price is unchanged, the individual's budget line is then MN, parallel to CD. His optimum position shifts accordingly from Q to S. Thus the individual uses only part of his increased initial endowment of Y to increase the amount demanded of Y itself (by HW, less than PT); part is also used to increase the amount demanded of X (by GU).

Once again, we can conceptually confront the individual with a sequence of different market prices; rotate, accordingly, his budget line through T; and determine his corresponding sequence of optimum positions. In this way we generate his excess-demand curve connected with the initial endowment T. This is depicted as the curve *efg* in Figure I-2. Clearly, for X not an inferior good, this curve must lie to the right of *edh*. In particular, we see from this diagram—as we also see from Figure I-1—that at the price Em the excess amount demanded has increased from EG to EU. Since the individual's initial amount of X is unchanged, the curve *efg* also becomes vertical at the point O. However, in view of the fact that the individual's income is now higher, it does so at a higher price than does *edh*.

Even for X not an inferior good, one should not conclude that an increase in the value of the initial endowment always causes a rightward shift of the *excess*-demand curve. This is true, as we have just seen, for the case in which the initial quantity of *another* good is increased while that of X remains unchanged. It is not necessarily true for the case in which the initial quantity of X itself also changes. Thus assume that the initial endowment is increased from P to V, instead of P to T.

With the price ratio measured by the slope of *MN*, *V* and *T* clearly have the same value. It is also clear that the optimum collection remains *S*, so that the *amount* of *X* demanded remains *OU*. But now the *excess amount* demanded has changed from a *plus EU* to a *minus UJ*. It follows that at the price *Em* in Figure I-2 the excess-demand curve corresponding to the initial endowment *V* lies to the left of the vertical axis.

So far we have tacitly restricted the analysis to the case of an economy with only two goods. If there are more goods, the amount of excess demand for *X* is also influenced by the given prices at which the individual can barter *X* for these other goods. Thus, should the individual be confronted with a rise in the price of one of these goods, the whole excess-demand curve of Figure I-2 will shift: rightwards for a substitute good, leftwards for a complementary one.

We can summarize the discussion up to this point by saying that the individual's amount of excess demand for a given good is determined by the bartering ratios of all goods with which he is confronted on the market, the real value of his initial endowment, and his initial quantity of the good in question. Let us define the real value of his initial endowment of commodities as his real income. Then we can alternatively say that the individual's excess-demand function for a given good depends on the relative prices of all goods, his real income, and his initial quantity of the good in question. The excess-demand *curve* of Figure I-2 is clearly a cross-section of this *function* taken at fixed values of the relative prices other than that of *X*, a fixed level of real income, and a fixed initial quantity of *X*.[4]

So much for the excess-demand curve of a single individual. By aggregating those of all the individuals in the economy, we can then obtain the excess-demand curve of the market as a whole. For simplicity, assume that *edh* in Figure I-2 now represents this latter curve. The quantity *OE* then measures the sum of all the individuals' initial endowments of *X*. From the curve we also see that at the price *Em* there may be some individuals who wish to buy *X* and others who wish to sell but that in the aggregate the individuals of the economy wish to augment their initial endowments of *X* by the net amount *EG*. Similarly, at the price *Ep* they wish on balance to sell the amount *ZE*, while at the price *Ew* there is no one who can afford to consume the commodity *X*.[5]

----

[4] Following Slutsky, we can, of course, rigorously define "real income" in terms of a chosen basket of goods; see Mathematical Appendix 2:*b*, especially footnote 5.

[5] The reader can readily verify that the same market excess-demand curve *edh* is

3. The Determination of the Equilibrium Price

By continuing to consider *edh* as the market curve, we can also use Figure I-2 to explain the determination of the equilibrium market price of *X*. At any price below *En* there is a positive amount of excess demand in the market, driving the price up. At any price above *En* there is a negative amount of excess demand—or a positive amount of excess supply—driving it down. Only at the price *En*—where the amount of excess demand is zero, where, that is, the amount people want to buy is equal to the amount others want to sell—can equilibrium prevail.

By shifting the origin of Figure I-2 to *O*, this determination of the equilibrium price can alternatively be presented in terms of the more familiar supply-and-demand apparatus. The vertical line at *E* then becomes the supply curve, reflecting the fact that the total amount of *X* in the economy is absolutely fixed, and *edh* then becomes the demand curve. The equilibrium price is yielded in the usual manner by the intersection of these two curves at the quantity *OE* and price *Ot*.

This equilibrium price is assumed to be reached during the marketing period Monday afternoon. The details of this process are analyzed in Chapter III. For the moment it suffices to note that it presumes the existence of a recontracting arrangement. That is, individuals enter the market with offers to buy or sell varying quantities of *X* at the given price. If the market is not cleared, these offers are not binding. Instead, the price changes in response to the pressure of excess demand, and new offers are made accordingly. When the equilibrium price is finally reached, the marketing period is closed, contracts are made final, and arrangements are made for sellers to deliver the commodities to buyers during the ensuing week.

4. Individual-Experiments and Market-Experiments

There is a fundamental distinction between the analytical framework of the section just presented and of those that precede it. In the first two sections of this chapter, the economic unit under investigation is an individual or an aggregate of individuals. What we wish to explain

---

also yielded as the difference between demand and supply in the ordinary sense of the term—that is, as the difference between what individuals wish to buy and sell on the market at given prices. See p. 7, footnote 3. For a simple numerical example, see G. J. Stigler, *Theory of Price* (rev. ed.; New York, 1952), pp. 151–53.

—that is, the "dependent variables of the analysis"—are the amounts of excess demand of each individual. What we take as given and not subject to explanation—the "independent variables of the analysis"— are the individual's tastes and initial endowments, the prices with which he is confronted, and his desire to transform his initial endowment into an optimum one. The purpose of the analysis at this level is to conduct conceptual experiments with the individual—or group of individuals— in which arbitrary changes in one or more independent variables are made and the effects of these changes on the dependent variables observed. The results of one such "individual-experiment"—as we shall call them—are described by the excess-demand curve of Figure I-2— understood as referring either to one individual or to the aggregate of all of them. This curve shows how the amount of excess demand varies with changes in the price of X—other independent variables being assumed constant.

In the preceding section, the unit of investigation is different, and so, accordingly, are the dependent and independent variables of the analysis. Specifically, this unit now becomes the organized market operating under conditions of perfect competition. What we now wish to explain is that price which establishes equilibrium in this market. What we take as given are the structure of this market and the tastes, endowments, and desire for maximum utility of those individuals who appear in it. Within this analytical framework it is meaningless to inquire as to the effects of an arbitrary change in price, for, by assumption, such a change can now occur only as the result of a prior change in one of the independent variables. Indeed, it is the purpose of the analysis at this level to conduct conceptual "market-experiments" in which the effects of changes in these independent variables on the equilibrium price of the market are investigated.

The force of this distinction—and the reason for elaborating at such length on what is probably well known—will become clear in the discussion which follows.[6]

---

[6] For a precise description of this distinction, see Mathematical Appendix 1:*a*.

In "A Reconsideration of the General Equilibrium Theory of Money" [*Review of Economic Studies*, XVIII (1950–51), 55], I called individual-experiments "*ceteris paribus* experiments" and market-experiments "*mutatis mutandis* experiments." These terms have been replaced here because there are generally factors held in *ceteris paribus* even in market-experiments. Cf. equations (1.36)–(1.39) in Mathematical Appendix 1:*c*.

II. The Excess-Demand Functions
of a Money Economy

1. Introduction. The role of money. 2. Types of moneys and prices. 3. The individual's excess-demand functions for commodities: the wealth effect and the real-balance effect. 4. The concept of "money illusion." 5. The individual's excess-demand function for money. 6. The market excess-demand functions.

1. INTRODUCTION. THE ROLE OF MONEY

Let us now extend the foregoing analysis to the case of an exchange economy with money. Our method of approach has already been blocked out in the preceding chapter. We first describe the excess-demand functions of the economy; this is the task that will absorb us in the present chapter. We then use these functions to explain how equilibrium prices are determined in the market and how these prices are affected by changes in the quantity of money; this is the task to which we turn in the next chapter.

The individual's initial endowment of goods Monday morning is now assumed to fall into two mutually exclusive and exhaustive categories: commodities and money.[1] The former have reached him in the

---

[1] The terms "goods," "commodities," and "money" will be used henceforth only in the senses just indicated. This gives "goods" a different meaning than it has in the Introduction.

miraculous way described in the preceding chapter; the latter has been carried over from the preceding week. For the present we shall assume that the individual makes no consumption plans for any week beyond the current one. This enables us to postpone for later consideration the problems of borrowing, lending, and the rate of interest. The individual's sole concern with the future is assumed to be his desire to start next Monday morning with adequate money balances—where the adequacy of these balances is judged in the light of his expectation that next week's prices will be the same as this week's. This desire necessarily influences the commitments which the individual makes during the market period this Monday afternoon, for these determine his initial money balances on next Monday. With this exception, we deal exclusively with one-week-horizon men in a one-week-horizon world. We shall be able to relax these highly unrealistic—and, indeed, somewhat incompatible—assumptions only after we extend the analysis in Chapter IV to a multiweek economy.

One basic question immediately suggests itself: why does the individual of our economy plan to hold money balances? A rigorous answer to this question must await the discussion of Chapters V–VII. For the moment we merely assume—with full recognition that we have not yet provided the rigorous analytical framework which justifies such an assumption—that the individual finds it convenient to hold money as a reserve. In particular, we arbitrarily assume that payments on the final contracts of the Monday marketing period are made, not simultaneously at the close of this period, but at randomly determined hours of the ensuing week. It follows that the individual is uncertain both as to the hours he will receive payments for the commodities he has sold and as to the hours he will be called upon to make payments for the commodities he has bought. In other words, he is almost certain that these payments will not be perfectly synchronized during the week, and that there will therefore be generated discrepancies between the hourly inflows and outflows of money. Hence in order to have some means of meeting these discrepancies—and thereby to have some protection against the inconvenience and/or penalty costs of running out of cash—the individual will be interested in possessing at the beginning of each week reserves of money balances that will bear a certain relationship to the volume of his required payments. Clearly, the greater these reserves, the greater his security against running out of cash during the ensuing week. Thus the demand for money in our economy is explained in terms reminiscent of the familiar transactions and precautionary motives of the cash-balance approach to the quantity theory of money.[2] On the other hand, though we are abstracting here from the speculative motive, it will later be shown (Chapters VI:1 and XI:3) that the general implications of our analysis hold even after taking it into account.

2. Types of Moneys and Prices

Though we have spoken of "money" in the singular, we shall formally assume the presence of two distinct types of money in our economy. First, there is an abstract unit of account, which serves only for purposes of computation and record keeping. This unit has no physical existence; that is, it does not coincide with any of the goods which exist in the economy. Examples of such money in various societies are well known.[3] Perhaps the most familiar is the guinea in present-day England.

Second, there is a fiat paper money, which serves as the actual, physical medium of exchange and store of value. It is assumed to be an "outside money":[4] that is, one issued by some agency exogenous to the economic system itself. It is this money which was referred to in the preceding section. It is only of this money that balances can be held. We shall continue to denote it by the term "money," unmodified. The first type of money, on the other hand, will be referred to explicitly as "the abstract unit of account."

Corresponding to these two types of money there are two types of prices. Prices in terms of the abstract unit of account will be called "accounting prices." Prices in terms of the medium of exchange will

[2] Cf. K. Wicksell, *Interest and Prices* (London, 1936), p. 39; A. Marshall, *Money Credit and Commerce* (London, 1923), pp. 43–45; A. C. Pigou, "The Value of Money," *Quarterly Journal of Economics*, XXXII (1917–18), as reprinted in *Readings in Monetary Theory*, ed. F. A. Lutz and L. W. Mints (Philadelphia, 1951), pp. 164–65. For further references, see Chapter VIII:1 below.

[3] For a fascinating account of the nature and origin of some of these "ghost moneys," see Carlo M. Cipolla, *Money, Prices, and Civilization in the Mediterranean World: Fifth to Seventeenth Century* (Princeton, 1956), Chapter IV.

[4] The term is due to John G. Gurley and Edward S. Shaw, *Money in a Theory of Finance* (Washington, D.C., 1960), pp. 72–73. The discussion of its opposite, "inside money," will be deferred to Chapter XII:5 below.

be called "money prices," or, alternatively, "absolute prices," or, simply, "prices." In addition, there are "real" or, alternatively, "relative prices"; these represent the prices of commodities (as distinct from money) in terms of one another. In a corresponding way we can distinguish between the accounting, money, and real values of a collection of goods. These correspond, of course, to the aggregate value of these goods computed at their accounting, money, and real prices, respectively. Once again, the term "value," unmodified, will be taken to denote money value.

The accounting price of a given good is distinctive in having no operational significance for the market. The statement that "the money price of good X is 2" implies that the surrender of two pieces of paper money in the market procures in exchange one unit of X. Similarly the statement that "the real price of X in terms of Y is 3" implies that X can be bartered for Y in this proportion, or that the money obtained by selling one unit of X suffices to purchase three units of Y. But the statement that "the accounting price of X is 4"—in the absence of additional information on the accounting price of at least one other good—gives us no idea of what we must do to acquire a unit of X. Stated otherwise, empirical observation alone could not detect the, say, doubling of the accounting prices of all goods. In the market place we can observe only the manifestations of money, and hence real, prices.

It should be emphasized that paper money, like any other good, also has an accounting price. Thus, for example, the accounting price of the paper sterling pound is 20/21 guineas. Paper money also has a money price; but, unlike its accounting price, this, by definition, is always unity. Thus one can conceive of a change in the *accounting* prices of all *goods*. One can also conceive of a change in the *money* prices of all *commodities*. But it is a contradiction in terms to conceive of a change in the *money* prices of all *goods*. Similarly, it is a contradiction in terms to conceive of a change in the *relative* prices of all *commodities*.[5]

The reader may at this point feel that he has been unnecessarily encumbered with artificial distinctions. And it is true that from the

---

[5] The following notation may help fix these distinctions in the reader's mind: Consider an economy with n goods, the nth good being paper money. Let the respective prices of these goods in terms of an abstract unit of account be represented by

$$p_1, \ldots, p_{n-1}, p_n.$$

viewpoint of the analysis as such nothing would be lost—and simplicity would be gained—if we were to drop the assumption that the money which serves as the medium of exchange is distinct from the money which serves as the unit of account. Nevertheless, we shall have to carry this distinction throughout the following argument, for only in this way will we be able to understand the nature of certain confusions which have become entrenched in the literature on monetary theory.[6]

3. The Individual's Excess-Demand Functions for Commodities: The Wealth Effect and the Real-Balance Effect

Let us now consider the excess-demand functions. The rigorous derivation of these functions from utility analysis is deferred to Chapters V–VII. For the moment, we simply argue by analogy that in a money economy, as in a barter economy, the individual's excess demand for a given commodity depends on the relative prices with which he is confronted in the market and on the real value of his initial collection.[7] Now, however, this collection includes money as well as commodities. For the moment we continue to denote the real value of the latter by "real income." Correspondingly, we denote the real value of the initial money holdings—that is, the purchasing power over commodities which these holdings represent—by the term "real balances." In this way we reach the following formulation: The individual's excess-demand function for any given commodity depends on the array of

---

Then the respective money prices of the goods are

$$\frac{p_1}{p_n} , \dots , \frac{p_{n-1}}{p_n}, 1.$$

Finally, the relative prices of the $n - 1$ commodities in terms of the first one are

$$1, \frac{p_2}{p_1} , \dots , \frac{p_{n-1}}{p_1} .$$

We might, if we wish, also speak of the relative price of money, p_n/p_1; this represents the number of units of the first commodity that must be given up in order to acquire one unit of paper money.

[6] These will be discussed in Chapter VIII:3.

[7] See Chapter I:2. The third factor mentioned there—the initial quantity of the given commodity—is assumed constant throughout the present discussion; hence this factor is ignored both here and in what follows.

The excess demand for money is discussed in the next section.

relative prices of all commodities, his real income, and his real balances.[8]

This dependence on real balances is the crucial element of the following analysis. Though consistently overlooked in the standard theory of consumer's demand,[9] it is simply the obverse side of the familiar demand for money described above. For to say that an individual adjusts his money balances so as to maintain a desired relationship between them and his planned expenditures on commodities is at the same time to say that he adjusts these expenditures so as to maintain a desired relationship between them and his money balances. The exact nature of this relationship depends both on objective factors— the precise character of the random payment process and/or penalty costs referred to in Section 1—and on subjective factors—the individual's evaluation of the inconvenience and/or risk of running short of cash. The more probable the lack of synchronization between payments and receipts, and the greater this cost or inconvenience, the larger the reserves of money balances he will want to hold for a given volume of expenditures;[10] or, equivalently, the smaller the volume of expenditures he will be willing to undertake on the basis of a given level of money balances; or, to place our argument within a very familiar framework, the smaller the velocity of circulation of the money balances which he holds.[11]

It follows that if the individual's initial balances are for some reason increased above the level which he considers necessary, he will seek to remedy this situation by increasing his amounts demanded of the

---

[8] See Mathematical Appendix 2:*a*.

[9] To be more specific—and to anticipate for a moment our future discussion— though the dependence on real balances has usually (if implicitly) been recognized in the analysis of the demand for *bonds*, it has not been so recognized in the analysis of the demand for *commodities*. This failure will be analyzed in detail in Chapter VIII:3.

[10] I.e., in terms of the Cambridge cash-balance approach, the larger his K; cf. Pigou, "The Value of Money," *op. cit.*, pp. 166–70.

[11] The reader will recognize that this paragraph has been deliberately patterned after the traditional discussions of the determinants of V—or of K. These discussions are, however, much more general than the one presented here because the implicit model on which they are based is a much more complicated one. Nevertheless, it is clear that our "objective factors" are a special case of what Fisher—in his classification of the causes which affect V—subsumes under the heading "systems of payments in the community," and our "subjective factors" a special case of his "habits of the individual" [*Purchasing Power of Money* (New York, 1911), p. 79; cf. also the reference to Pigou in the preceding footnote].

various commodities, thereby increasing his planned expenditures, and thereby drawing down his balances. On the other hand, should they be decreased below the level he considers necessary, he will seek to remedy the situation by decreasing his amounts demanded, thereby decreasing his planned expenditures, and thereby building up his balances.[12]

Clearly, in judging the adequacy of these money balances—and hence in determining their influence on his demand for commodities— the individual can be guided only by their real value. For the magnitude of the discrepancies which these money reserves are designed to cover clearly depends on the prices which must be paid for commodities; hence the effective magnitude of these reserves can be determined only in relation to the level of prices. In the language of the cash-balance theorists, it is with the extent of his liquid command over *real* resources that the individual is concerned.

The foregoing represents the traditional explanation of the effect of a change in the real quantity of money on the demand for commodities— or what will henceforth be called the "real-balance effect."[13] This explanation can be rigorized—and the Slutzky-Hicks theory of consumer's behavior extended accordingly to a money economy—by first specifying a demand function which (in accordance with recent discussions[14]) depends *inter alia* on the total wealth of the individual; and by then noting that, in the one-period model with which we are now dealing, this wealth is measured as the sum of initial money holdings and the week's income.[15] It follows that an increase in the quantity of

[12] This paragraph paraphrases Wicksell, *Interest and Prices*, pp. 39–40. This passage is cited in full in Supplementary Note E:1. For similar references to other neoclassical advocates of the quantity theory, see Chapter VIII:1.

[13] The "real-balance effect" is identical with what I first called in "Price Flexibility and Full Employment" [*American Economic Review*, XXXVIII (1948), 556] the "Pigou effect." This was clearly a bad terminological choice.

[14] See the survey of the relevant writings by Friedman, Modigliani, Tobin, and others in Robert Ferber, "Research on Household Behavior," *American Economic Review*, LII (1962), 25–29, 37–38. See also the articles by Ackley, Ball and Drake, Crockett, and Spiro listed in the Bibliography. Cf. also the description of the empirical studies of a wealth-consumption relationship by Hamburger, Arena, and Ando and Modigliani, presented in Note M below, pp. 659–60.

[15] This definition differs from the usual one only by taking account of the fact that an individual's *stock* of wealth consists also of his *stock* of money balances. It should therefore be intuitively clear that there is no basis for H. G. Johnson's recent implication that this definition violates proper stock-flow relationships ["Monetary Theory and Policy," *American Economic Review*, LII (1962), 339].

From a more rigorous viewpoint, it should be emphasized that total income

money, other things being held constant, influences the demand for a commodity just like any other increase in wealth: if the commodity is a normal one (and this has been our tacit assumption above), the amount demanded will increase; if inferior, it will decrease. Even in the case of a normal commodity, nothing can be specified a priori as to the degree of the change in the amount of excess demand. In particular, if the initial money balances of the individual are increased, prices constant, there is no reason to expect the amount of excess demand for any commodity to increase in the same proportion as the quantity of money.

The demand function just specified can also be used to analyze the effect of price changes on the individual's demand function for any commodity. Thus consider an equiproportionate change in all prices—which is the type of price change that is our primary concern in monetary theory. This does not affect relative prices, and hence does not generate any substitution effect; it does, however, cause an opposite change in the real value of initial money holdings, and hence generates a wealth effect. Accordingly, we shall say that the price change in this case has only a wealth effect in the form of a real-balance effect. On the other hand, if only a single price changes, then there is a substitution effect in addition to the wealth effect—where the latter can be defined as consisting of a "nonmonetary-wealth effect" (reflecting the impact of the price change on the real value of the individual's nonmonetary wealth), as well as of a real-balance effect. However, for reasons explained at the end of Mathematical Appendix 2:*b*, the real-balance effect is not as economically meaningful an analytical entity in this case as in the case of an equiproportionate change in all money prices, where it coincides with the total wealth effect.[16]

---

receipts during the week (as distinct from the average *rate* of income prevailing during that period) are a time-dimensionless quantity: for they remain the same whether the week is called a week, or seven days, or 1/52 of a year. Correspondingly, no improper stock-flow relationships are involved in adding these receipts to initial money holdings, as in the preceding definition. For further details, see Mathematical Appendix 11, especially p. 519.

[16] For a demonstration—if it is necessary—that this paragraph uses "substitution effect" and "wealth effect" in the Slutzky-Hicks sense of the terms, see Mathematical Appendix 2:*b*, especially footnotes 5 and 6.

For a precise description of the Slutzky-Hicks wealth effect in the case of a change in a single price, see equation (2.14) on p. 408.

The "nonmonetary-wealth effect" is identical with what, in the first edition, was misleadingly called the "income effect."

As will readily become evident, the real-balance effect in the commodity markets plays a central role in the analysis of this book. It is therefore worth emphasizing at the outset that the fulfillment of this analytical (as distinct from policy) role depends not on the *strength* of this effect but only on its *existence*. And of this existence there seems to be fairly persuasive evidence—particularly from the postwar experience of the inflationary pressures generated by accumulated liquid assets, and of the subsequent dissipation of these pressures in a rising price level.[17]

It must also be emphasized that, for the simple exchange economy with which we are now dealing, the assumption that there exists a real-balance effect in the commodity markets is the *sine qua non* of monetary theory. For as we shall see below (p. 176), in the absence of this effect the absolute level of money prices in such an economy is indeterminate: that is, no market forces exist to stabilize it at a specific level. It follows that though approximations which neglect the real-balance effect may—because of the smallness of this effect—be useful in the theory of the determination of relative prices, such "approximations" ignore a basic analytical factor in the theory of the determination of the absolute price level. Thus, whatever the justification for neglecting the real-balance effect in value theory, there can be no justification for neglecting it in monetary theory.[18]

[17] Cf. A. J. Brown, *The Great Inflation 1939–1951* (London, 1955), Chapter X, especially pp. 236–37. For references to other empirical studies of the real-balance effect, see Note M below.

[18] In order to avoid any possible later misunderstanding—and in order to explain our hedging phrases "in the commodity markets" and "for the simple exchange economy"—it is worth while again anticipating our future discussion and pointing out that the determinacy of money prices in a pure outside-money economy (in contrast to a pure inside-money one—see Chapter XII:5) depends on the existence of a real-balance effect *somewhere* in the economy; but once we extend our analysis to an economy with bonds, this "somewhere" may be the bond market, and not necessarily the commodity markets. However, I can see neither theoretical nor empirical justification for basing the analysis on the one-sided view that the real-balance effect manifests itself *only* in the bond market. On the other hand, it should be emphasized that all of the conclusions of this book can be shown to hold even under this extreme assumption. So though the real-balance effect in the commodity market plays a "central role" in this book, this role—once bonds are introduced into the analysis—is *not* logically necessary for the validity of the argument.

I might also emphasize that the empirical evidence cited in the preceding footnote refers to the existence of a real-balance effect in the *commodity* markets. As already noted, its existence in the *bond* market has usually—if implicitly—been taken for

4. THE CONCEPT OF "MONEY ILLUSION"

We now define a concept which is fundamental to the following argument—the concept of "money illusion." An individual will be said to be suffering from such an illusion if his excess-demand functions for commodities do *not* have the property specified in the preceding section—that is, if they do *not* depend solely on relative prices and real wealth, inclusive of initial real balances. Conversely, an individual will be said to be "free of money illusion" if his excess-demand functions *do* have this property. It follows that if an illusion-free individual were confronted with an equiproportionate change in all *accounting* prices—including that of paper money—none of his amounts demanded of commodities would thereby be affected; for such a change would affect neither the array of relative prices confronting him, nor the level of his real wealth. To revert to the example of the preceding section, all guinea prices would, say, be doubled; but this would in no wise reduce the purchasing power of his pound holdings, for the guinea value of each of these pounds would also have doubled.

Similarly, if the initial paper-money endowment of an illusion-free individual were suddenly increased and he were simultaneously confronted in the market by new money prices, all of which had increased in the same proportion, he would once again have no reason for changing the amount demanded of any commodity. In fact, this case differs from the preceding one only in the method of maintaining the real value of initial money holdings invariant in the face of an equiproportionate change in the accounting prices of commodities: instead of accomplishing this by changing the accounting price of money too, holding its initial quantity constant, we do so by changing this quantity proportionately, holding its accounting price constant.

By way of contrast, consider the effects on the amounts of commodities demanded of simply confronting the individual with a proportionate increase in all *money* prices. Once again, there is no change in relative prices and hence no substitution effect. For the same reason,

---

granted, particularly by Keynesian interest theory. Indeed, it is sometimes referred to as the "Keynes effect"—an unfortunate term since, as we shall see below (pp. 239–40), this effect is an integral part of neoclassical theory too.

All these points will be discussed in further detail on pp. 180, 241–42 and 297–98. See also p. 635, footnote 5.

there is no nonmonetary wealth effect. But there is a wealth effect generated by the resulting decline in the real value of his fixed initial money balances. This negative real-balance effect causes the individual to decrease the amounts he demands of the various commodities. Thus an individual free of money illusion will definitely react to such a change.

We can summarize this discussion by saying that though the economic behavior of an individual free of money illusion depends solely on the *ratios* of the *accounting* prices, it does *not* depend solely on the *ratios* of the *money* prices. That is, such an individual does react to changes which affect only the *absolute level* of these *money* prices. On the other hand, an individual who *is* suffering from money illusion also reacts to changes which affect only the *absolute level* of *accounting* prices. That is, his economic behavior does *not* depend solely on the *ratios* of these prices.[19] [20]

Alternatively, we can make use of the familiar concept of elasticity to state these results in the following way: Absence of money illusion is marked by uniform zero elasticity of the individual's commodity excess-demand functions with respect to an equiproportionate change in all money prices and in initial money holdings. No such zero elasticity exists with reference to an equiproportionate change in all money prices alone; in general, this elasticity is negative, though in some cases it may be positive. This is equivalent to saying that no such zero elasticity exists with reference to a change in his initial money holdings alone and that, in general, this elasticity is positive, though it may be negative. Even when positive, there is no special reason for it to equal unity.[21]

[19] The reader will recall that the ratios of accounting prices are money prices, and the ratios of money prices relative prices; cf. p. 16, footnote 5.

[20] This paragraph makes it clear that our definition of "money illusion" differs fundamentally from the accepted one: the latter defines "money illusion" as sensitivity of the individual to changes in the absolute level of *money* prices. This will be discussed further in Chapter VIII:3.

[21] Absence of money illusion does, however, imply that the elasticity of Marshallian demand prices with respect to a change in initial money holdings is unity; see Mathematical Appendix 2:*a*.

From what has been said in Section 2, it should be clear that the phrase "all money prices" in the last three paragraphs is a shorthand expression for "all money prices that can change," i.e., "the money prices of all commodities."

5. THE INDIVIDUAL'S EXCESS-DEMAND FUNCTION FOR MONEY

Just as there are excess-demand functions for commodities, so is there one for the money which serves as the medium of exchange in our economy. The opening section of this chapter makes some observations on the general nature of this demand. We must now provide an exact description of its properties.

By the term "amount of money demanded" we mean the amount of money which the individual plans during the marketing period this Monday afternoon to hold in his possession next Monday morning—after he has, in the course of the week, made and received all the payments on the contracts into which he plans to enter this afternoon. By "amount of excess demand for money" we mean the difference between this amount demanded and the amount of his initial money holdings this Monday morning. The excess-demand function for money shows how this difference varies with changes in the conditions with which the individual is confronted. As noted above, we assume that the individual expects prices next week to be the same as those this week.

Actually, there is nothing that can be said about the excess-demand function for money which is not already implicit in the discussion of the preceding section. This is a direct consequence of the fact that the individual must formulate his marketing decisions within the framework of his budget restraint. In simplest terms, this restraint expresses the condition that the individual neither beg nor steal: instead, every expenditure for commodities must be financed either by the sale of part of his initial endowment of commodities or by the drawing down of his initial endowment of money balances. It follows that the amount of the individual's *excess demand* for money—at a given set of relative prices, real income, and real balances—is necessarily equal to the aggregate money value of the amounts of his *excess supplies* of commodities—corresponding to this same set of prices, income, and balances.[22]

Some examples will help clarify this basic relationship. Consider the simple case in which, in the light of the conditions confronting him, the individual plans to retain the initial quantities of all commodities but

---

[22] Recognition of this relationship can be found far back in the literature. See, for example, J. S. Mill, *Principles of Political Economy*, ed. Ashley (London, 1909), Book III, Chapter VIII, Section 2, pp. 490–91.

For the meaning of "excess supply," see above, p. 7.

one. That is, the excess amount demanded of every commodity but one is zero. Assume that this one amount of excess demand is positive. Clearly, the only way in which this additional quantity can be purchased is by drawing down initial cash balances to the extent of its money value. Thus when the individual formulates the preceding market plan for commodities, he is simultaneously formulating a plan for reducing his initial holdings of money. No additional independent decision on this score is involved.

More generally, assume that—at a given set of relative prices and real wealth—the individual plans to increase the holdings of some commodities and to decrease those of others. If the aggregate value of the increases is equal to the aggregate value of the decreases, the individual can carry out his plan without any change in his initial money balances. There is, however, no reason why such an equality need exist. If, instead, the value of the increases exceeds that of the decreases, the individual must of necessity be planning to draw on his initial money balances. Or, in other words, the amount of excess demand for money balances must be negative to exactly the same extent that the aggregate value of the amounts of excess supplies of commodities is negative. Conversely, if the value of the amounts of excess supplies of commodities is positive (i.e., the aggregate value of decreases exceeds that of increases), the individual must of necessity be planning an equal positive amount of excess demand for cash balances.

We should not conclude from this discussion that the excess-demand function for money is a purely passive ingredient of the individual's economic behavior, merely reflecting decisions initiated elsewhere. All the individual's decisions are made simultaneously. Hence we can just as well say that a decision for a positive amount of excess demand for money implies a decision for an equal positive aggregate value of excess supplies for commodities, or that the value of the amounts of excess demand for any one commodity is equal to the aggregate value of the amounts of excess supplies of all other commodities, plus the amount of excess supply of money; or we can adopt the completely neutral statement that the aggregate money value of the amounts of the individual's excess demands for all goods must be zero. All of these statements are equivalent expressions of the necessity for the individual's plans to be consistent with the restraint placed upon him by his budget.

Before going on, we should emphasize one point in order to avoid possible confusion. The equality that has been explained above is that between the *excess* demand for money and the value of the *excess* supply of goods. On the other hand, it is not true that there exists an equality between the amount of the individual's *demand* for money and the aggregate money value of the amounts of his *supplies* of commodities. In other words, there is obviously no necessary equality between the demand for money in the sense of the stock that the individual plans to hold at the end of the week, and the demand for money in the sense of the amount of money he plans to receive during the week by selling commodities. Similarly, there is no necessary equality between the supply of money in the sense of the individual's initial money holdings and the supply of money in the sense of the amount of money he plans to pay out during the week in buying commodities. On the other hand, it is clear that the excess demand for money in this latter sense— i.e., the planned net receipts of money during the week—is necessarily equal to the excess demand for money as defined above: this is simply an alternative statement of the relationship presented in the preceding paragraph. This alternative statement does, however, have the advantage of highlighting the fundamental fact that the only way to affect the level of the stock at the end of the week is by affecting the net receipts which accrue during the week. Correspondingly, an individual can be satisfied with the level of his planned stock of money at the end of the week if and only if he is satisfied with his planned net receipts of money during the week.[23]

Let us now examine some of the properties of the excess-demand function for money. Consider an individual free of money illusion who, at a certain set of relative prices and with a given real income and real balance, has a certain amount of excess demand for money. Assume that this individual is now confronted with an equiproportionate change in all money prices and in his initial endowment of money. According to the assumption of the last section, the amount of excess supply of each commodity is unaffected by this change. But the prices at which

[23] As can be inferred from footnote 15 above, these net receipts have the dimensions of a stock, and not a flow. On the other hand, the term "net receipts of money" in this last sentence can be replaced by "(average) rate of net inflow of money"—which, of course, does have the dimensions of a flow.

For further discussion of these questions see Mathematical Appendix 11, especially pp. 519–20.

these amounts of excess supplies are valued have all changed in the same proportion. Therefore the money value of the amounts of excess supplies of commodities, and hence the amount of excess demand for money, are also changed in the same proportion.

An alternative statement of the preceding result is that the *real* value of the amount of excess demand for money is not affected by a proportionate change in all money prices and in the initial amount of money. It follows, then, that the excess-demand function for *real* money balances depends only on relative prices and real wealth, inclusive of initial real balances. Thus the assumed absence of money illusion in the excess-demand functions for commodities implies the corresponding absence of money illusion in the excess-demand function for real money balances.

This dependence of the excess demand for money on the initial holdings of money should not arouse any fears that the argument is involved in circularity. The initial endowment of money is as much a datum of the problem as the initial endowment of any other good. There is no more circularity here than there is in the statement of Chapter I: 2 that the excess demand for X depends on the initial amount of X. Again in analogy to Chapter I: 2, an increase in the initial amount of money can be assumed to be used partly to augment the demand for money itself—the individual makes use of his increased wealth to improve his liquidity position—and partly to augment the demand for commodities. These increases are the manifestation of the wealth effect (in the form of the real-balance effect) in the money and commodity markets, respectively.

The foregoing argument can be presented in somewhat more familiar terms if we speak of the demand for money, instead of the excess demand. By definition, the amount of money demanded is equal to the initial holdings of money *plus* the amount of excess demand for money. It then follows immediately from the preceding analysis that an individual confronted with a proportionate change in money prices and in initial money holdings will always change his amount of money demanded in the same proportion. Once again, an alternative statement of this result is that the demand function for *real* money holdings depends only on relative prices and real wealth.

Graphically, we can present these conclusions in the following way. Since the present discussion is restricted to equiproportionate changes in prices, all commodities can be considered as a single composite with price p, to be denoted henceforth as the "absolute price level."[24] Clearly, p can also be considered as the price of the good *real* money holdings. For if the price of a unit of commodities-in-general is p dollars, the price of a unit of liquid command over a unit of commodities-in-general must also be p dollars. Correspondingly, we can in Figure II-1a draw a demand curve for real balances as a function of p. The verticality of this demand curve represents that, in the absence of money illusion, the demand for real money holdings—just as the demand for any other good (above, p. 23)—has uniform zero elasticity with respect to an equiproportionate increase in all money prices *and* in initial money holdings.

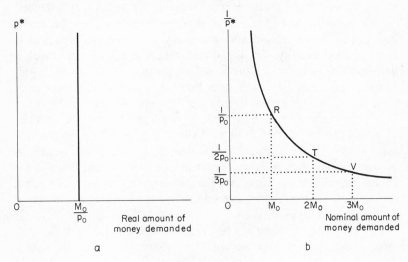

a b

FIGURE II-1.

*Changes in p are accompanied by proportionate changes in initial money balances.

On the other hand (and as already implied by footnote 5 above), the reciprocal of the price level $1/p$ can be considered as the "real" or "relative" price of the good *nominal* money holdings. Accordingly, we can conceive of a curve which describes the demand for these holdings as a function of this relative price. Such a curve is represented in Figure II-1b. The fact that it is a rectangular hyperbola—i.e., that it has

[24] For a rigorous presentation, see pp. 406 and 411–15 below.

uniform unitary elasticity—is the logical counterpart of the zero elasticity of the curve in Figure II-1a. For the *nominal* demand for money is the product of the price level and the *real* demand. Hence, since a doubling of all prices and initial money balances leaves the demand for real balances unaffected, it must cause a doubling of the demand for nominal balances. Conversely, at any point on the curve in Figure II-1b, the real value of the amount of money balances demanded —represented by the area of the subtended rectangle—is constant and equal to M_0/p_0.

All this changes as soon as the increase in money prices is *not* accompanied by an equiproportionate increase in nominal money holdings.

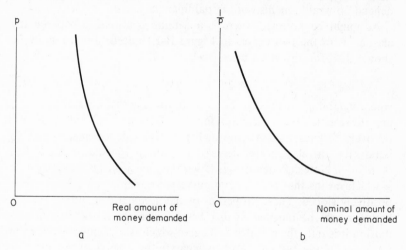

FIGURE II-2.

For then the price increase generates a real-balance effect which affects the demand for real balances and hence that for nominal. In particular, since real balances are a normal (as distinct from inferior) good,[25] its demand curve—represented in Figure II-2a—will now be negatively sloped instead of vertical. For the negative real-balance effect generated by the price increase causes the amount demanded of real balances to

[25] The empirical evidence on this point is clear. Cf. the studies cited by Johnson, "Monetary Theory and Policy," *op. cit.*, pp. 354–56; see also John Spraos, "An Engel-Type Curve for Cash," *Manchester School of Economics and Social Studies*, XXV (1957), 183–89.

decrease. Correspondingly, the amount of nominal balances demanded will increase less than in proportion to the price increase. This is shown by the demand curve in Figure II-2b. In general, this curve will have a different elasticity at each point. Only in the special case where the demand for real balances is a constant, independent of the wealth (and hence real-balance) effect—so that the demand curve in Figure II-2a would continue to have the same vertical form as that in Figure II-1a—would the demand curve for nominal money balances in Figure II-2b be of uniform unitary elasticity. In brief, the fact that the demand curve for money in Figure II-2b is not a rectangular hyperbola is simply a reflection of the fact that this demand is assumed to depend on wealth, inclusive of initial financial assets.

As might be expected, there is a definite relationship between the elasticities of the two curves in Figure II-2. Indeed, it can readily be shown that, for any given price level,

$$\eta_N = 1 - \eta_R,$$

where η_N and η_R (defined to be positive for a negatively sloped curve) are the elasticities of demand for nominal and real balances, respectively.[26] Thus, since the normality of real balances means that η_R is positive, the elasticity of demand for nominal balances will be less than unity. Note also that if η_R is larger than unity, η_N becomes negative —which means that the demand curve for nominal balances becomes positively sloped. These properties of the nominal demand curve will, however, not be pursued further here; for in the absence of money illusion it is only the real demand curve which is of significance for the workings of the system. And in what follows we shall assume this curve to have the negative slope of Figure II-2a.[27]

We should now note that what has been presented as a demand curve for real balances is more appropriately presented as a type of Engel curve for these balances. For, as we have seen, the negative slope of the curve in Figure II-2a is not a reflection of the traditional substitution

[26] This result is related to the familiar proposition that the elasticity of a product is the sum of the elasticities. A more detailed derivation is given in Mathematical Appendix 2:*d.*

[27] I am indebted to Philip W. Bell of Haverford College for pointing out an error in the originally published discussion of the nominal demand curve. The revised version presented here is based on a stimulated correspondence with Professor Bell on the points raised by him.

effect, but rather of the wealth effect (which in this case coincides with the real-balance effect) generated by the changing price level. The nature of this effect is described by the Engel curve of Figure II-3, whose positive slope is the logical counterpart of the negative slope of the demand curve in Figure II-2a.[28] In the special and unrealistic case where the demand for real balances is unaffected by changes in wealth, the curve in Figure II-3 would be a horizontal line. Obviously, this horizontal line would correspond to a vertical one in Figure II-2a, and to a rectangular hyperbola in Figure II-2b.

It might also be noted that the 45° line through the origin in Figure II-3 provides the same type of norm of comparison as in any other Engel-curve diagram. The point of intersection T of this line with the Engel curve represents that point at which the individual wishes to hold at the end of the week exactly the same amount of money he held at the beginning. On the other hand, at point R he wishes to draw down his money balances over the week by the amount RS—and at the point Q he wishes to add to them by the amount PQ. Note that under our present assumptions the individual's income during the week constitutes the maximum weekly addition he can make to his initial balances. Hence, if OA in Figure II-3 represents this income, the Engel curve is bounded from above by the 45° line AB.[29]

6. THE MARKET EXCESS-DEMAND FUNCTIONS

So far we have examined the excess-demand functions of a single individual. Let us now extend the analysis to the excess-demand functions of the economy as a whole.

---

[28] The meaning of the curve in Figure II-3 can be made clearer by considering the simple case in which the individual wishes to hold a constant proportion (k) of hi wealth (which in this case is measured by $\bar{G} + \bar{Z}_n/p$, representing, respectively, th initial holdings of commodities and real balances) in the form of real balances (Z_n/p). The curve is then the straight line described by the equation

$$\frac{Z_n}{p} = k\bar{G} + k\frac{\bar{Z}_n}{p},$$

where $k\bar{G}$ measures the Y-intercept.

[29] For use of Figure II-3 in a dynamic context—as well as in examining the implications of long-run equilibrium—see Chapter III:7 below.

On the argument of this section see Mathematical Appendix 2:d. This also deals with some criticisms recently made by H. G. Johnson (see footnote 16).

Consider, then, all the individuals of the economy, each free of money illusion, each with his given real income and real money balances, and each confronted with the same set of relative prices. These data enable us to determine the amount of excess demand of each individual for each commodity. By aggregating over all individuals, it is then possible

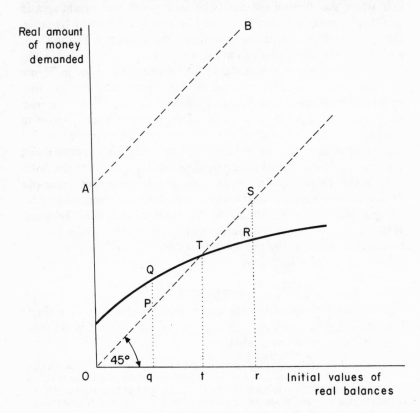

FIGURE II-3.

to determine the amount of excess demand in the market as a whole. By changing the given prices, we can then conceptually generate a market excess-demand function for each commodity. Each of these functions clearly depends upon relative prices and the *array* of the real wealth (inclusive of initial real balances) of the individuals of the economy. We can also define a market excess-demand function for money. For any given set of prices, this must yield an amount of excess demand for money equal to the value of the amounts of market excess supplies of commodities. This basic relationship thus holds for the market as a whole as well as for each individual.

There is, nevertheless, a clear lack of analogy between individual and market excess-demand functions. Specifically, the latter does not, in general, depend upon relative prices and the *total* real wealth of the economy. This form of dependence would be valid only under the unrealistic assumption that the distribution of wealth does not affect the amounts of market excess demand. By contrast, the form specified in the preceding paragraph makes it clear that the effect of, say, an increase in the total wealth of the economy on the amount of market excess demand for a good cannot be determined until the distribution of this increase among the members of the economy is first specified.

It follows that we cannot say that a proportionate change in all money prices and in the *total* initial quantity of money in the economy leaves unaffected the amounts of market excess demands for commodities and for real money balances. Instead, we must be satisfied with the more restricted statement that this invariance will exist if the initial money holdings of each and every individual in the economy are changed in the same proportion as prices. Correspondingly, there exists a uniform unitary elasticity of the market demand function for money only with respect to an equiproportionate change in all money prices and in the initial money holdings of each and every individual.[30]

---

[30] See Mathematical Appendix 2:*e*.

The analysis of this Chapter has been restricted to the short run. Its extension to the long run is deferred to Chapter III:7.

III. Money and Prices

1. The Problem Defined. Walras' Law

We now use the excess-demand functions developed in Chapter II to explain the determination of equilibrium prices in the market. Prices are thus no longer the given data of the analysis, subject to arbitrary change, but are instead the dependent variables, incapable of change without a prior shift in one of the independent variables. The latter now consist of the individuals' initial endowments, their tastes, and the structure of the market.[1] We shall be interested in presenting first a static analysis of our problem (the nature of the equilibrium position), then a dynamic analysis (the nature of the market forces which bring the economy to equilibrium from an initial position of disequilibrium), and finally a comparative-statics analysis (a comparison of equilibrium

---

[1] This paragraph makes the same distinction described at length in Chapter I:4.

positions before and after a specified change in one or more of the independent variables).

The concept of equilibrium in the market for a single good has already been defined (Chapter I: 3). The corresponding concept of equilibrium in the market as a whole—or, simply, in the market—is defined as the existence of equilibrium in the market for each and every good. A set of prices which brings the market as a whole into equilibrium will be called an equilibrium set.

In general, what is an equilibrium set of prices for one array of initial endowments will not be an equilibrium set for another. For assume that we begin with a market in equilibrium at a certain set of prices. Assume now that there occurs an arbitrary change in initial endowments, either in their distribution among individuals in the economy and/or in the sum total of initial endowments of one or more goods. From our discussion of the market excess-demand functions, we know that under these circumstances there will be changes in the amounts of excess demands. Hence, at the original set of prices, there will now exist positive or negative amounts of excess demands in at least some of the markets. Hence this original set is no longer an equilibrium one. Thus the term "equilibrium prices" must always be expressly or tacitly qualified by the phrase "at a given array of initial endowments." The same qualification must be made, *mutatis mutandis*, for the other independent variables of the analysis.

There is one fundamental property of equilibrium prices in our economy which must be noted at the outset. Assume that at a certain set of prices each of the commodity markets is in equilibrium. It follows that the money market must also be in equilibrium. For the amount of excess demand for money equals the aggregate value of the amounts of excess supplies of commodities. In equilibrium, the amount of excess supply in each commodity market is, by definition, zero. Hence the amount of excess demand for money must also be zero. Thus, in order to determine whether a certain set of prices is an equilibrium set for our economy, it is not necessary to examine the money market; instead, it suffices to show that this set of prices establishes equilibrium in each of the commodity markets alone. This relationship, which is a particular form of what is known as Walras' Law, is basic to the following analysis.[2]

[2] See L. Walras, *Elements of Pure Economics*, trans. and ed. W. Jaffé (definitive

It should be emphasized that there is no implication here that the equilibrating process in the money market is in any sense less significant than that in any other market. We could just as well have arbitrarily selected any one market and stated that equilibrium in all the other markets implies equilibrium in the chosen one too. This is the general form of Walras' Law, which follows from the general form of the budget restraint in our economy.[3] If we have chosen to work with the particular form of this law set out in the preceding paragraph, it is only out of considerations of symmetry and simplicity.

It should also be emphasized that though they are logically connected in our economy, Walras' Law and the budget restraint are conceptually distinct relations. To anticipate the terminology of the next section, the former deals with excess-demand *equations*, the latter with excess-demand *functions*. Indeed, we can conceive of an economy in which the existence of the restraint does *not* imply the existence of the law. This special case also makes clear the impropriety of referring to Walras' Law as an "identity" which must always be true.[4]

2. THE EQUALITY OF THE NUMBER OF EQUATIONS AND VARIABLES

Let us now examine the static meaning of the equilibrium set of prices. Define first the market excess-demand equation for a given good. This is a restriction which states that prices are such that the amount of market excess demand—that is, the value of the market excess-demand function for the good in question—is zero. By definition, this equation is satisfied if and only if the market for the good is in equilibrium.

Assume now that there are n goods in the economy: $n - 1$ commodities and paper money. As will be recalled, this money serves as the medium of exchange and store of value but not as the unit of account. To these n goods correspond, respectively, n market excess-demand equations. Actually, however, only $n - 1$ (at most) of these equations are independent. That is, only $n - 1$ of these equations place independent restrictions on the unknown equilibrium prices. For any set

---

ed.; London, 1954), pp. 162, 241, 281–82. This law was so named by O. Lange in "Say's Law: A Restatement and Criticism," *Studies in Mathematical Economics and Econometrics*, ed. O. Lange, *et al.* (Chicago, 1942), p. 50.

[3] See p. 25 above.

[4] This case is described in Note H, pp. 614–15.

of prices which satisfies $n - 1$ market excess-demand equations must also necessarily satisfy the nth. This, of course, is an alternative statement of Walras' Law.

Thus the equilibrium set of money prices can be regarded as the solution to a set of $n - 1$ independent, simultaneous equations in these $n - 1$ unknown prices. Now, equality between the number of unknowns and the number of independent equations is neither a necessary nor a sufficient condition for the existence of a solution. Nor does it insure that solutions, if they do exist, will be only finite in number. For our purposes, however, these highly complicated issues can be ignored. Instead, we shall accept such equality as justifying the reasonableness of the assumption that one and the same set of money prices can simultaneously create equilibrium in each and every market. We shall also assume that only one such set exists.[5]

Quite deliberately, we have omitted all discussion of the choice of the dependent equation to be "eliminated." Posing the question in this form might lead to misconceptions. It might be taken to imply that less is known about economic behavior in the "eliminated" market than in others or that the "eliminated" market is in some sense less significant. It might be taken to imply that there is a substantive choice involved and that different decisions as to which equation to "eliminate" will produce different results. Actually, of course, none of these statements is true. As can readily be deduced from the general form of the budget restraint,[6] the properties of the "eliminated" excess-demand equation are completely specified by those of the other $n - 1$ equations. The corresponding general form of Walras' Law then brings out the complete neutrality of the "elimination" process. It should also make clear that no matter what equation is eliminated, the solution for the equilibrium set of prices obtained from the remaining equations is always the same.

In order to avoid any such possible misconceptions, it is advisable not to "eliminate" explicitly any equation at all. Instead, the system is best considered as having n equations, equal in number to the n

[5] The discussion of this paragraph is obviously restricted to solutions in the real number system. On the second sentence, see the examples in my "Indeterminacy of Absolute Prices," *op. cit.*, p. 4. For discussions of the conditions under which the existence and uniqueness of a positive real solution can be assured, see the articles by Wald, Schlesinger, von Neumann, Arrow, and others cited in Note B, p. 538 below.
[6] Cf. p. 25.

goods in the economy. But the excess-demand equation for money should be written in the form dictated by the budget restraint. This makes clear the nature of the equational dependence described by Walras' Law.

The discussion has until now been concerned with the $n - 1$ money prices. A unique solution for these implies, of course, a unique solution for the $n - 2$ relative prices. On the other hand, it does not imply a unique solution for the n accounting prices. For if one set of accounting prices yields (after dividing through by the accounting price of money) a given set of money prices, any multiple of that set will also yield this given set. Thus there is an infinite number of sets of accounting prices corresponding to the same set of money prices. We might also explain this indeterminacy of equilibrium accounting prices by noting that there are n such prices and only $n - 1$ independent excess-demand equations. An economic interpretation of this indeterminacy is presented in what immediately follows.[7]

3. The Method of Successive Approximation: The Determinacy of Relative and Money Prices; the Indeterminacy of Accounting Prices

Who solves the equations?

The fact that the number of independent excess-demand equations is equal to the number of unknown money prices and that the system can be formally solved might some day interest a Central Planning Bureau, duly equipped with electronic computers and charged with setting equilibrium prices by decree. But what is the relevance of this fact for a free market functioning under conditions of perfect competition?

It was concern with this question which led Walras to formulate his celebrated theory of *tâtonnement*. This was a crucial element in his vision of the economy as reflecting the operations of a set of simultaneous equations. In simplest terms, this theory states that the free market itself acts like a vast computer. For start with any arbitrary set of prices—Walras' "*prix criés au hasard*." In general, it will not be an equilibrium one. That is, at this set of prices there will be some

---

[7] See on this section Mathematical Appendix 3:*a*. Note that this proves the indeterminacy of accounting prices *without* resorting to the mere counting of equations and unknowns.

markets with positive amounts of excess demand and others with negative amounts. Prices will then rise in the former markets and fall in the latter, bringing us to a new set of prices. In general, this set, too, will not be an equilibrium one. Once again prices will change in accordance with the state of excess demand in the various markets, a third set of prices will thereby be reached, and so the process will go on. It is by this continuous groping—*tâtonnement*—that the economy ultimately finds its way to the equilibrium position.

The principle by which the market automatically generates these successive approximations is admittedly a primitive one. Actual computors operate according to much more efficient principles. But what our imaginary computer lacks in the elegance of its principle it makes up by its size. Indeed, this size enables it to deal with systems of equations far beyond the practical capacity of any existing computer. Thus, not only is there no need for a conscious mind to solve our excess-demand equations, but it is also doubtful if any mind—human or electronic—could today be depended upon for such a solution.

So far we have followed Walras in failing to deal adequately with one fundamental issue. It is one thing to say that the process of *tâtonnement* prevents the market from remaining at a nonequilibrium set of prices and even exerts some sort of pressure in the direction of equilibrium. It is quite another to say that this process must ultimately bring the market to the equilibrium prices themselves. In other words, Walras' theory of *tâtonnement* depends for its ultimate and rigorous validation on the modern economic theory of dynamics. Conversely, the significance of this latter theory can best be appreciated within the framework provided by Walras. From this viewpoint, a stable system is one in which the process of *tâtonnement* will succeed in establishing equilibrium prices; an unstable system is one in which it will not.[8]

This whole process of successive approximation is assumed to take

[8] The implicit reference here is, of course, to the dynamic theory first presented by Samuelson and subsequently developed by Arrow, Block, Hurwicz, and others. See Mathematical Appendix 3:*b*.

For a discussion of the role of the theory of *tâtonnement* in Walras' *Elements*, and of the neglect it suffered in the later literature, see Note B.

Some time after the above was written, I discovered that R. M. Goodwin had presented the same concept of dynamic analysis in his "Iteration, Automatic Computers, and Economic Dynamics," *Metroeconomica*, III (1951), 1–2. But Goodwin misinterprets Walras and fails to see that this is precisely the role that Walras assigned to his *tâtonnement*. See the detailed discussion in Note B below.

place during the marketing period, Monday afternoon. To give it concrete embodiment, we might think of a central registry where all offers to buy and sell at the proclaimed prices are recorded. The registry is presided over by a chairman whose function is to raise the price of any commodity for which the registry shows an excess of buyers and to lower the price of any commodity for which it shows an excess of sellers. As indicated above, none of the offers are binding unless the proclaimed set of prices at which they were made turns out to be the equilibrium set. If it does not, individuals are free to recontract at the new set of prices proclaimed accordingly by the chairman. This Edgeworthian assumption[9] serves its usual purpose of precluding the completion of any prior purchases which might otherwise affect the final equilibrium position itself. In other words, this assumption assures that no matter which of the infinite number of paths open to it a convergent sequence of approximations takes, it must always reach the same equilibrium set of prices.

Let us use this assumption of recontract to show how the corresponding process of *tâtonnement* can be used to explain the two main results obtained in Section 2: the determinacy of equilibrium money prices and the indeterminacy of equilibrium accounting prices.[10]

Consider an economy during the marketing period. Assume first that the process of *tâtonnement* is at a stage where the absolute level of the presently proclaimed prices is the same as that in the ultimate equilibrium position but that the ratios between these proclaimed money prices differ from the corresponding equilibrium ratios. Then there are amounts of excess demand for those commodities whose relative prices are respectively lower than the corresponding equilibrium prices and amounts of excess supply for those commodities whose relative prices are respectively higher. Accordingly, in the next round of approximations, prices of the former goods will be raised and prices of the latter lowered. In brief, the existence of any discrepancy between the proclaimed relative prices and the equilibrium ones automatically generates

---

[9] For the specific references to Edgeworth and for the reason I have not followed the recent tendency to associate this assumption with Walras too, see Note B. See also N. Kaldor, "A Classificatory Note on the Determinateness of Equilibrium," *Review of Economic Studies*, I (1933–34), 126–29.

[10] The approach of the following three paragraphs is adapted from that of Wicksell, *Interest and Prices*, pp. 23–24, 39–40; the latter passage is cited in full in Note E:1. The discussion here admittedly ignores many difficulties. For a more rigorous statement, the reader is referred to Mathematical Appendix 3:*b*.

market forces which themselves tend to eliminate the initial discrepancy. Clearly, these same corrective forces are also automatically called into being by any accidental departure from equilibrium values, should they once be reached.

Assume now that the process is at a stage where relative prices are the same as in the ultimate equilibrium position, but the absolute level of money prices is, say, lower. This implies that the real value of money balances is higher than in the equilibrium position. Correspondingly, there exist amounts of excess demand in the various markets exerting corrective pressures on the prices. In this case the stability of the dynamic process need not be assumed, but can be readily established by graphical analysis. For since relative prices are assumed constant during the *tâtonnement*, all commodities can be considered as a single composite good with the price p. Assume (as is reasonable) that this good is not an inferior one. Then the positive real-balance effect generated by a decrease in p causes the amount demanded to increase. This is represented by the negatively sloped demand curve d in Figure III-1a. On the other hand, the supply of commodities in our exchange economy is fixed: hence this is represented by the vertical line s. It is clear from Figure III-1a that at any point below (above) p_0 there is an excess demand (supply) driving the price level upwards (downwards) again. Hence no matter what the initial level of p, the automatic functioning of the market will bring it to the equilibrium level p_0. Under the stated assumptions, the system is stable in the large as well as in the small.

By Walras' Law, this conclusion can alternatively (and equivalently) be demonstrated in terms of the demand (D) and supply (S) for nominal money holdings. This is done in Figure III-1b, the demand curve of which is reproduced from Figure II-2b. We saw in Chapter II:5 that the demand curve for these holdings is generally negatively sloped. Furthermore, it can be shown that even in the special case where this demand curve does have a positive slope in some regions, these regions must (if commodities are not inferior) lie leftwards of M_0. Hence we see from Figure III-1b that at any point above (below) $1/p_0$ there exists an excess supply (demand) for money driving the reciprocal of the absolute price level downwards (upwards) again.[11]

Let us now return to our process of *tâtonnement* and assume that it

[11] Note that the assumption of equiproportionate price movements effectively

has reached equilibrium but that the chairman accidentally continues to "cry out" prices. In particular, assume that he proclaims a new set of accounting prices, each of which exceeds the corresponding price of the equilibrium set by a constant percentage. As we saw in Chapter II: 4, this increase changes neither relative prices, nor real incomes, nor the real value of initial money balances. Hence none of the amounts of excess demand for commodities are thereby affected. Therefore, since the commodity markets were in equilibrium before this un-

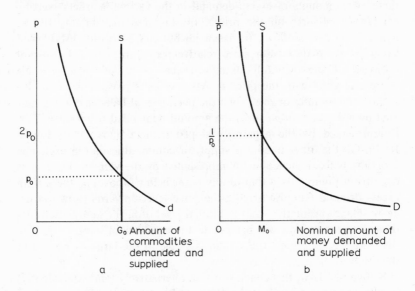

FIGURE III-1.

necessary *tâtonnement*, they must remain so afterwards too. By Walras' Law, the equilibrium of the money market must, therefore, also remain undisturbed. Thus the accidental proportionate departure of

---

reduces the stability problem to the relatively simple one of a two-good economy. Cf. Arrow, Block, and Hurwicz, *op. cit.*

Note also that the supply curve in Figure III-1a would remain a vertical line even if we were to drop the assumption of an exchange economy and assume that supply depends only upon relative prices. Nor would the argument be affected if we assumed supply to depend also on real balances—provided it was a decreasing function of such balances, so that the supply curve in Figure III-1b would have a positive slope.

accounting prices from an initial equilibrium position creates no amounts of excess demand for any good—and hence generates no market forces anywhere in the economy—which might operate to force these prices back to their original levels. Therefore, if one set of accounting prices is an equilibrium set, every multiple of that set must also be one. Accounting prices are indeterminate.

Actually, the existence of this indeterminacy is almost self-evident. As pointed out in Chapter II:2, accounting prices are not even observable market phenomena. Hence it is certainly not surprising that their equilibrium values cannot be determined by market forces. Instead, these forces must be supplemented by an external decree arbitrarily fixing the accounting price of one—and only one—of the goods in the economy. If equilibrium money prices are already determined, this suffices to determine the equilibrium accounting prices of all other goods. Thus, for example, if we know the pound prices of goods and are told that the accounting price of a paper pound is arbitrarily set at 20/21 guineas, we can immediately determine the corresponding guinea prices of all other goods by simply multiplying their pound prices by 20/21. Similarly, if the accounting price of the pound were to be arbitrarily doubled and set instead at 40/21 guineas, this would immediately fix the guinea prices of all other goods at levels which were also double those of the original case. Clearly, the money and relative prices of these two cases are, respectively, identical. Equally clearly, in the absence of such an arbitrary specification, equilibrium guinea prices cannot possibly be determined.

Thus equilibrium money prices and equilibrium accounting prices are determined by two distinct processes: the former by internal market forces, the latter by the arbitrary decree of a *deus ex machina*. No such distinction exists between money prices and relative prices. Both of these are simultaneously determined by market forces alone. Only conceptually can we decompose these forces into two components, one which operates through the real-balance effect and thereby determines the absolute level of money prices, and one which operates through the substitution effects and thereby determines the ratios of these prices.[12]

---

[12] See pp. 181–82 below.

4. THE EFFECTS OF AN INCREASE IN THE QUANTITY OF MONEY ANALYZED IN THE COMMODITY MARKETS

Let us now consider an economy in equilibrium and examine the effect of injecting into it an additional quantity of money. We continue with the assumption that to every set of given conditions there corresponds one and only one equilibrium position and that the process of successive approximation described in Section 3 always succeeds in reaching this position.

Assume that we stand at the close of the Monday marketing period with the set of equilibrium prices having just been reached. Let there now be some external force which, say, suddenly doubles the initial money holdings of each individual of the economy. The immediate implication of this increase is that the marketing period must be reopened and the *tâtonnement* recommenced, for what constituted the equilibrium set of prices before the increase cannot constitute one afterwards. In particular, at these prices real balances are now higher than in the original equilibrium position, whereas relative prices and nonmonetary wealth are the same. Hence at these prices a universal state of excess demand now replaces the original state of equilibrium.

In accordance with our accepted dynamic principle, these pressures of excess demand initiate a series of successive approximations which push proclaimed money prices upwards. Assume first, for simplicity, that these prices rise during the *tâtonnement* in an equiproportionate manner. Use can then be made of Figure III-1a to represent the effect of the doubling of the quantity of money on the demand for commodities by an upward shift in curve d which brings it to twice its original height at each and every quantity. On the other hand, the monetary increase does not affect the supply curve s. Hence the reopened *tâtonnement* will bring the price level to the new intersection point at $2p_0$.

Even if we drop the assumption about the nature of price movements during the *tâtonnement*, it can readily be seen that the equilibrium set of prices corresponding to the doubled quantity of money is one in which each and every price is doubled. For relative prices and real wealth (inclusive of initial money holdings) corresponding to this new set are the same as they were in the original equilibrium position; hence the amounts of market excess demand for each commodity and for real money holdings must respectively also be the same as in this position—that is, zero. Hence, if the system is stable, and if to every set of conditions there corresponds a unique equilibrium, the economy must reach the new equilibrium position just described.[13]

The validity of this conclusion clearly depends on the assumption that the individuals' initial money holdings are all increased in the same proportion, For consider a doubling of the total quantity of money in the economy which does not take place in this way. In such a case the economy need not be restored to equilibrium by a doubling of all prices. For the real value of the increased money holdings of *each* individual (and hence his real wealth) will then not be the same as in the original equilibrium position. Hence the amounts of market excess demands will also not be the same. In general, the new equilibrium position in this case will involve higher relative prices for those goods favored by individuals whose money holdings have more than doubled and lower relative prices for those goods favored by individuals whose holdings have less than doubled. This fact was duly emphasized by the classical and neoclassical advocates of the quantity theory of money.[14]

On the other hand, the preceding argument does not presume any restriction on the nature of the dependence of the commodity excess demands on real wealth, inclusive of real balances (see p. 20). As a corollary, neither does it presume that all individuals in the economy must react in the same way to changes in this wealth. For since real balances in the two equilibrium positions are identically the same, the question of what would happen to excess demands if these balances were changed can have no relevance for the comparative-static analysis. But it is very much relevant to the dynamic analysis, for the path followed by the economy during the period of dynamic adjustment is clearly dependent upon the way in which individuals react to the temporarily increased real balances which mark this period. These

[13] Note that the assumption that there exists an original equilibrium set of prices implies that there also exists a new one; no separate existence assumption on this score is required. Note also that even if we permit several solutions, one of them must be a multiple of the original set. But in this case an increase in the quantity of money need not increase prices proportionately; for prices may move to a new equilibrium set which is *not* this multiple. On these statements and the text in general, see Mathematical Appendix 3:*c*.

[14] For the analytical background of this paragraph, see Chapter II:6. For references in support of the last sentence, see Chapter VIII:1, p. 164, footnote 11.

observations hold even if we assume that some of the commodities are inferior. As just explained, this cannot affect the nature of the new equilibrium position itself, but it can and does affect the dynamic process by which this position is reached and in some cases might even prevent its being reached at all.

One further point might be noted. It is frequently said that a change in the quantity of money is equivalent to a change in the monetary unit. There is much truth in this statement—but it is also subject to two fundamental reservations. First, in the case of a change of the monetary unit everyone is aware that the change in the quantity of money has taken place in an equiproportionate way for all individuals. Hence— generalizing from their own behavior—they expect everyone's demand prices to change in the same proportion.[15] Second, when monetary authorities announce such a change, they also effectively announce the new set of equilibrium prices which corresponds to it: they effectively inform the public by how many places to move over the decimal point in the price quotations. Thus there is actually someone "solving the equations." For both these reasons there is no need for the new equilibrium prices in such cases to be determined by the workings of the dynamic market forces described above.

5. THE EFFECTS OF AN INCREASE IN THE QUANTITY OF MONEY ANALYZED IN THE MONEY MARKET

Let us now approach the problem from the viewpoint of the money market. Clearly, we must reach the same conclusions as in the preceding analysis, where the approach is from that of the commodity markets. Nevertheless, it is interesting to show explicitly the obverse relationship that exists between these two approaches.

Assume once again for simplicity that prices change during the *tâtonnement* in an equiproportionate manner. Then the demand and supply for nominal money holdings corresponding to the aggregate initial endowment of money M_0 (distributed in a given way among the individuals of the economy) can be represented respectively by the curves D and S of Figure III-1b, reproduced here in Figure III-2.

---

[15] Cf. above, p. 23, first paragraph of footnote 21.

As will be recalled from the discussion on p. 30, this demand curve is generally of less-than-unitary elasticity.

Assume now that the initial money endowments are all doubled, so that the total quantity of money in the economy rises to $2M_0$. This clearly causes a rightward shift of the supply curve to S' in Figure III-2. Consider now the demand curve. As will be recalled,[16] not all of the increased endowment is expended in the commodity markets. That is,

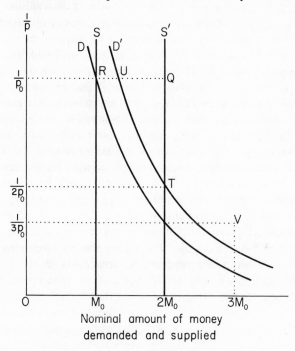

FIGURE III-2.

there is also a real-balance effect in the money market. This is reflected diagrammatically as a rightward shift from D to D': at the same level of absolute prices, individuals—because of their increased wealth—feel themselves able to indulge in a higher level of liquidity.

We now note that the form of D, together with the assumption that there is no money illusion, completely specify the form of D'. For if

16 P. 27.

according to curve D a certain amount of money is demanded at a given price level, then at twice that level—and twice the initial endowment of money—the curve D' will show twice that amount demanded (see Chapter II: 5). In particular, since point R in Figure III-2 lies on curve D, point T must lie on curve D'. But point T must obviously also lie on S'. Hence the form of D' is necessarily such that it intersects S' at the point T, corresponding to a price level of $2p_0$. Similarly, if the initial endowment of money were increased to $3M_0$, the new demand curve (not drawn in Figure III-2) must intersect the new supply curve at the point V, corresponding to the price level $3p_0$.

It remains to describe the dynamic process by which the market actually moves from R to T. It is here that we can see the advantage of the approach of the preceding section over that of this one. For the essential nature of the market forces which activate this process are neither directly nor concretely pictured in Figure III-2. Instead, we must resort to the reflection which this diagram casts on the state of demand in the commodity markets. Thus consider the price level p_0. After the quantity of money has been doubled, there exists at this price an amount of excess supply equal to UQ. But an excess supply of money means an excess demand for commodities. Therefore, at this price level pressures exist in the commodity markets to drive p up and hence $1/p$ down. Figure III-2 can thus be used only indirectly to explain the *tâtonnement* by which the point T is finally reached. Nevertheless, we do in this way ultimately reaffirm the conclusion of the preceding section: that an increase in the quantity of money causes a proportionate increase in equilibrium money prices.

6. Demand Curves and Market-Equilibrium Curves

Let us now consider the points R, T, and V in Figure III-2—and all other possible equilibrium points that can be generated by changing the quantity of money. The locus of these points is traced out in Figure III-3. It is obvious that the curve which emerges in this diagram is a rectangular hyperbola. It is equally obvious that it is *not* a demand curve. Indeed, by construction it is the locus of intersection points of demand curves and their corresponding supply curves.

To be more precise,[17] in back of Figure III-3 there is a conceptual

---

[17] See Chapter I:4 for an explanation of the concepts now to be used.

market-experiment in which we take an economy in equilibrium, introduce into it a disturbance in the form of an equiproportionate change in initial money holdings, and then let this disturbance work itself out in all its manifestations until the economy returns again to an equilibrium position. The results of this experiment give us one point in Figure III-3—a point which associates a quantity of money in the economy with its corresponding equilibrium level of money prices. By continuing to change the quantity of money in this way we generate

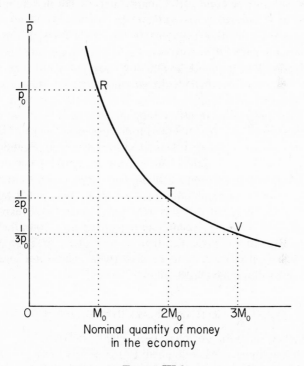

FIGURE III-3.

additional points. In accordance with the direct proportionate relationship that has been shown to hold between this quantity and the equilibrium price level, these points must trace out a rectangular hyperbola.

A curve generated in this way from market-experiments will be denoted henceforth by the term "market-equilibrium curve." It must be sharply distinguished conceptually from a demand curve—which, by definition, is generated by individual-experiments. In particular, it cannot be overemphasized that the market-equilibrium curve of Figure III-3 will have the form of a rectangular hyperbola regardless of the form of the demand curves of Figure III-2. This is evident from the graphical argument of the preceding section. In terms of our present terminology we can explain this independence by noting that these demand curves describe the outcome of an individual-experiment which is not at all relevant to the market-experiment under consideration. For at the close of this market-experiment, the individual finds himself confronted with an equiproportionate change in prices *and* in his initial money holdings; whereas any *given* demand curve of Figure III-2 describes the results of an individual-experiment in which prices are changed, but the individual's initial money holdings are kept constant.

This independence obviously disappears as soon as we consider a market-experiment and a *relevant* individual-experiment. Thus the market-equilibrium curve of Figure III-3 implies that in an individual-experiment in which the individual is confronted with an equiproportionate change in prices and initial money holdings, he increases the amount of money demanded proportionately. This information is clearly and consistently depicted either by Figure III-2 in the movement from the point *R* on one demand curve to the point *T* on another; or by Figure II-1b in the movement from *R* to *T* along a single demand curve which is itself a rectangular hyperbola. These are alternative descriptions of the same individual-experiment.[18]

7. LONG-RUN AND SHORT-RUN EQUILIBRIA

The discussion until now has been tacitly restricted to short-run equilibrium analysis: it has examined the forces that bring the economy to the equilibrium position that corresponds to the initial distribution of money endowments. But this equilibrium position will not generally be a long-run one in the sense that (other things equal) it will continue to prevail week after week. It is to this question that we now turn.[19]

[18] See Mathematical Appendix 3:*d*.
[19] On this distinction between short and long run, see D. W. Bushaw and R. W. Clower, *Introduction to Mathematical Economics* (Homewood, Ill., 1957), pp. 170–71.

The nature of the problem is most conveniently illustrated by Figure III-4—which is based on Figure II-3. For simplicity, assume that the economy consists of only two individuals—A and B—and that each has exactly the same Engel curve for real balances. Assume further that the equilibrium price level determined at the end of Week I is p_1—and that when evaluated at this price level the initial real balances of A and B are Oq and Or, respectively. Thus A has increased his cash balances over the week by an amount measured by $PQ = QV$, while B has drawn his down by $SR = RX$. (See the discussion of Figure II-3 above.) By the assumption that p_1 is the equilibrium price, $PQ = SR$; that is, A's excess demand for money *equals* B's excess supply.

Assume now that our individuals start Week II with the money balances carried over from the end of Week I—but with a new commodity endowment exactly equal to that received the preceding Monday. Two related things now happen: First, though the real incomes of the individuals in Week II are, by assumption, the same as in Week I, their initial value of real balances (evaluated at p_1) are different. Hence, the amounts they demand of commodities and real balances in Week II will also differ. In particular, A's initial balances are now Ou instead of Oq; correspondingly, the amount of balances he wishes to hold are uU instead of qQ. Similarly, B's initial balances are Ow instead

---

It is, however, not appropriate to describe this distinction as one between "flow equilibrium" and "stock equilibrium": for, as shown on p. 521, footnote 11 below, in the present context the variables of both the short- and long-run analyses have the dimensions of a stock.

I might also note that the distinction here between short- and long-run equilibrium is related to Hicks' distinction between "temporary equilibrium" and "equilibrium over time" (*Value and Capital*, p. 132). The latter, however, is defined by Hicks primarily in terms of constancy of prices, whereas (following Bushaw and Clower) we shall be interested in constancy of quantities as well.

The absence of any long-run analysis in the first edition of this book has been justly criticized by G. C. Archibald and R. G. Lipsey, "Monetary and Value Theory: A Critique of Lange and Patinkin," *Review of Economic Studies*, XXVI (1958), 2–9. Contrary to their implications, however, it will be seen that the filling of this lacuna does not require any fundamental changes in the analytical framework developed above.

The following is based on the Archibald–Lipsey treatment. We shall, however, present the argument in terms of Engel curves—whereas they have done so in terms of the indifference-curve analysis of Chapter V:4 of the original edition of this book. The Engel-curve approach is simpler and also lends itself more readily to a discussion of the determination and stability of the long-run equilibrium position.

of *Or*, and his amount demanded *wW* instead of *rR*. In terms of Figure III-1, shifts in the demand curves have taken place.

Second, the price level p_1 will generally no longer be an equilibrium one.[20] For it is clear from Figure III-4 that *A*'s excess demand (*UV*) exceeds *B*'s excess supply (*WX*). Hence there exists an excess supply in the commodity markets pushing prices down there. As the price

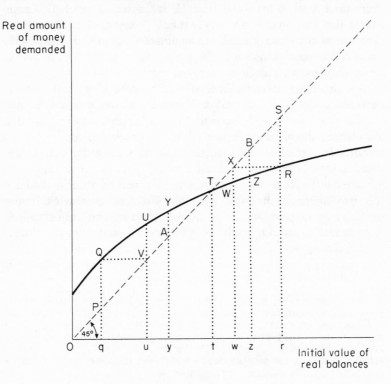

FIGURE III-4.

level falls, the initial balances of both *A* and *B* increase in value. This will continue until the resulting real-balance effect will once again equate *A*'s excess demand with *B*'s excess supply. This is portrayed in

[20] In principle, it is possible for the equilibrium level to remain the same. As can be seen from Figure III-4, this would be the case if the Engel curve were linear. Cf. Archibald and Lipsey, *op. cit.*, p. 6, footnote 1.

Figure III-4 as occurring when A and B's initial real balances are Oy and Oz, respectively. The equilibrium nature of this position is reflected in the fact that $AY = BZ$.

Obviously, this process will not stop at this point. Week III will find the individuals once again starting with different initial balances than they did in Week II—and this in turn will generally cause the equilibrium price level of Week III to differ from that of Week II. Let us assume that this process continues: that is, every week the individual starts anew with exactly the same commodity endowment—and with the cash balances carried over from the end of the preceding week. Let us also assume that the economy converges in this way to point T. At this point long-run equilibrium will have been reached: for an individual with the initial cash balances Ot will neither add to nor subtract from them over the week. Hence he will start every week with exactly the same cash balances as the preceding one; hence his amounts demanded will remain the same; and hence the equilibrium price level will remain the same.[21]

Note that the process of reaching long-run equilibrium is marked not only by changes in the price level, but also (and even more fundamentally) by a redistribution of money balances between A and B. More generally, the movement toward long-run equilibrium generates a unique distribution of initial balances among the individuals in the economy.[22] In other words, the initial balances of the individuals in their position of long-run equilibrium are not among the given conditions of the analysis (as is the case with the corresponding balances of the short run), but among the dependent variables determined by the analysis itself.

Let us now take a step backwards and construct demand curves within a long-run equilibrium framework. We shall say that an individual is in long-run equilibrium if he is neither adding to nor subtracting from his initial cash balances under the given endowment and price level conditions with which he is confronted. That is, the individual is at T in Figure III-5. Let us now take this individual and conduct the

[21] Clearly, the system need not necessarily converge to T. The determination of the conditions under which such convergence will take place (i.e., under which the system is stable) involves the solution of a system of nonlinear difference equations —something which cannot be attempted here. For some general remarks on the problem of convergence, see however Mathematical Appendix 3:e.

[22] *Ibid.*, p. 6.

following individual-experiment with him: We lower the price level, wait for him to return once again to a position of long-run equilibrium, and then compare the amount of money demanded in this new position with that in his original one.

The results of such an experiment can be traced out in Figure III-5. As a result of the price decrease with which he is confronted, the real value of the individual's initial real balances increases from *Ot* to *Oa*.

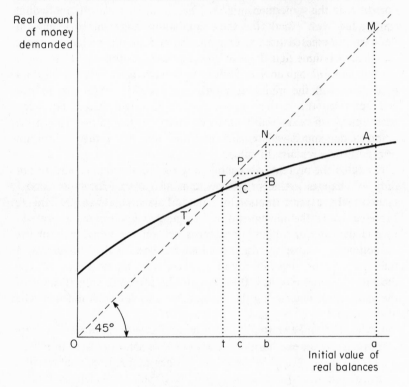

FIGURE III-5.

At this point the individual is drawing down his real balances by *AM = AN*—so that he starts the following week with balances of *Ob*. Here the individual continues to draw down his balances—this time by *BN = BP*. This process will continue until the individual returns once again to the same level of real balances—*Ot*—from which he started. Thus we see from Figure III-5 that the long-run demand for real cash balances is a constant, independent of the price level.[23]

There is a straightforward interpretation of this result. What Figure III-5 tells us is that the initial decline in the price level effectively presents the individual with a windfall gain which increases his wealth—and that within our simple model the individual will plan to make use of this gain entirely for the purpose of purchasing additional commodities in the subsequent weeks. This means that when the individual enters the "last" week (i.e., the one in which he reestablishes his state of long-run equilibrium), he does so with initial *real* cash balances equal to those of the original week of long-run equilibrium. That is, his initial *nominal* balances of this "last" week have been reduced (as compared with the original equilibrium position) in the same proportion as the price level. In this way the conceptual experiment just described must yield the same results as the one portrayed by Figure II-1 above: namely, the one in which the individual is confronted with an equiproportionate change in the price level *and* initial money holdings. In both cases the resulting absence of a real-balance effect on the demand for *real* balances means that this demand remains invariant under a change in the price level—which in turn means that the demand for *nominal* balances has the form of a rectangular hyperbola.[24]

Let us now conduct an alternative long-run conceptual individual-experiment. Consider an individual whose long-run equilibrium demand curve for nominal money balances is represented by the rectangular hyperbola D in Figure III-6 (for the moment ignore the vertical lines at M_0 and $2M_0$). Assume that the individual is at point A on this curve and let us make a once-and-for-all increase in his initial money holdings—while keeping the price level constant. From the

[23] *Ibid.*, p. 9. See also the reference to Leser on p. 435, footnote 17 below.

Though I have described the present individual-experiment as generating a "long-run demand curve"—and shall use the same description for Figure III-6—this is not a completely appropriate use of the term; for details, see pp. 436 ff. below.

[24] Note also the identity with the short-run individual-experiment (described as a special case on p. 30 above), in which the individual is confronted with a change in the price level only—but in which the resulting real-balance effect is used even in the short run entirely to increase the demand for commodities.

The quotation marks around "last" in this paragraph reflect the fact that—as can be seen from Figure III-5—the individual will converge to his new position of long-run equilibrium only after an infinite number of weeks.

On the nature of the convergence of the foregoing process, see once again Mathematical Appendix 3:*e*.

argument just presented, it is clear that the individual will choose to use up this windfall gain entirely in the acquisition of commodities during the ensuing weeks—so that in the long run he will return to nominal money holdings of M_0. This means that the increase in the quantity of money will not cause any shift in the long-run demand curve depicted in Figure III-6. This will obviously also be true if the curve D were to represent the long-run demand curve of the economy as a whole.

Let us now turn from individual-experiments to market-experiments.

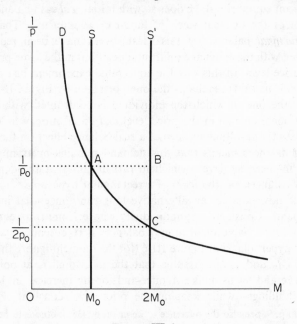

FIGURE III-6.

Consider an economy whose demand and supply curves for money are represented by D and S, respectively, in Figure III-6. Assume that the economy is in the initial position of long-run equilibrium represented by point A. Let the quantity of money in the economy now double. As we have just seen, this does not cause any shift in the demand curve D. On the other hand, it causes the supply curve to shift from S to S'—thus creating an excess supply of money equal to AB. Just as in our analysis of the short-run equilibrium (above, Figure III-2), this means that there is an excess demand for commodities—generated by the positive real-balance effect—driving prices upwards. This process will continue until the economy reaches the new position of long-run equilibrium *C* with a price level twice as high as the original one. Thus in the long run, as in the short run,[25] a mere comparison of the two equilibrium positions will not reveal any real-balance effect.[26] On the other hand, the stability of the equilibrium position in both "runs" is vitally dependent on the real-balance effect generated by any chance departure of the price level from it. Thus when we come to evaluate the significance of the real-balance effect for economic theory, the really important distinction that we must make is not between short run and long run, but between being concerned with the stability of an equilibrium position—with the possibility of its being reached by the automatic workings of a market economy[27]—and not being concerned.[28]

There is, however, one noteworthy difference between the short- and long-run analyses: namely, that the doubling of the price level in Figure III-6 is independent of the way the new quantity of money is injected into the economy.[29] In technical terms, since each individual's

---

[25] See p. 45 above; see also pp. 175–76 and 192 (footnote 62) below.

[26] But to infer from this that for "comparative statics the real-balance effect is irrelevant" (Archibald and Lipsey, *op. cit.*, p. 9) is like inferring from the equality of the equilibrium marginal rates of transformation in the increasing-cost case of international trade that the law of comparative advantage is then irrelevant for comparative-statics analysis. Cf. also F. H. Hahn, "The Patinkin Controversy," *Review of Economic Studies*, XXVIII (1960), pp. 40–41 and pp. 42, footnote 2.

To a certain extent, at least, the issues here have been complicated by semantic problems; see Mathematical Appendix 3:*e*, especially pp. 436–38.

[27] Cf. Chapter III:3 above, especially p. 38; see also p. 230 below.

[28] As Baumol has already indicated, Archibald and Lipsey's discussion of the real-balance effect (*op. cit.*, *passim*) is misleading because of its failure to see the dynamic stability context in which the role of this effect has been presented [W. J. Baumol, "Monetary and Value Theory: Comments," *Review of Economic Studies*, XXVIII (1960), 30].

[29] Archibald and Lipsey, *op. cit.*, pp. 8–9. On the short-run analysis, see above, p. 45.

Another difference between the short-run analysis of Figure III-2 and the long-run one of Figure III-6 is that the two equilibrium positions (*A* and *C*) of the latter correspond to two different weeks, whereas the two positions of the former (*R* and *T*) correspond to two alternative positions of the same week, one with the initial quantity of money M_0, and one, $2M_0$ (*ibid.*, p. 8). This is related to the discussion in the next paragraph of the text.

It might, however, be argued that Figure III-2 corresponds more closely to the true

long-run curve remains invariant under an increase in the quantity of money, so must the aggregate of these curves—irrespective of the way this increase is distributed among the individuals of the economy.

It might also be noted—though this is really inherent in all of the above—that if the quantity of money is doubled when the economy is *not* in long-run equilibrium, then the subsequent long-run equilibrium position will *not* be marked by a price level double that of the time of injection. For, as shown at the beginning of this section, the original short-run equilibrium price level would have changed over time even if no change in the quantity of money had taken place. Thus the effect of doubling the quantity of money can be measured only by comparing the actual price level in the long-run equilibrium position with the level which would have prevailed had the quantity of money remained constant. More generally, any change in price level between two periods must be decomposed into that part which would in any event have taken place in the course of the long-run equilibrating process—and that part which takes place as a result of a change in one or more of the exogenous variables.

In order not to leave a misleading impression, we must conclude this long-run analysis (and particularly the discussion of the rectangular-hyperbola demand curve of Figure III-6) by reminding the reader that it is actually restricted to a very special—and somewhat incongruous—case.[30] For though attempting to deal with long-run problems, the analysis has continued to be based on a model of one-week-horizon men whose real income (and wealth) is constant over time and who can hold their excess of income over consumption (i.e., their savings) only in the form of the sterile asset, money. As soon, however, as we extend the argument to the standard case in which savings can also be held in the form of an interest-yielding asset (say, the bond), the foregoing results will generally no longer obtain. In particular, it can then be

---

sense of the traditional quantity theory in showing that the changed quantity of money makes the price level different *from what it otherwise would have been*. For such a note in the writings of Ricardo, see J. Viner, *Studies in the Theory of International Trade* (New York, 1937), pp. 126–27, 176–77.

[30] Cf. p. 14 above.

Views similar to the following have already been expressed by R. J. Ball and R. Bodkin, "The Real Balance Effect and Orthodox Demand Theory: A Critique of Archibald and Lipsey," *Review of Economic Studies*, XXVIII (1960), 46–7; Hahn, *op. cit.*, p. 38.

shown that—under fairly reasonable assumptions about consumers' behavior—there does not exist a stable long-run equilibrium for the individual in the sense defined at the beginning of this section. Instead, the individual will make use of his interest earnings on savings to generate continuous growth in his levels of wealth, income, and consumption. Correspondingly, he will generally not consume all of the windfall gain represented by the real-balance effect,[31] but will devote part of it to increase his savings and thereby generate a permanent upward shift in the planned growth-path of his wealth holdings—including wealth in the form of money.[32] Thus the demand for money in this case will not be independent of the price level.[33]

In a similar way, the concept of long-run equilibrium loses its meaning in a production economy with investment—and even in the simplest of Keynesian models.[34] What becomes relevant instead is the equilibrium expansion-path of the system. And the nature of this path (particularly the price-level developments which characterize it) will generally be influenced by the real-balance effect. Similarly, the distribution effect of the increased quantity of money need no longer be neutral, but may influence the rate of capital accumulation and hence the rate of growth. This is the process of "forced savings" which constitutes an important element of certain theories of economic development.[35]

---

[31] Contrast this with the discussion on p. 55 above.

[32] See the forthcoming paper by Nissan Liviatan, "On the Long-Run Theory of Consumption and Real Balances," *Oxford Economic Papers*, XVII (1965). This also shows that the contrary implication of R. W. Clower and M. L. Burstem ["On the Invariance of Demand for Cash and Other Assets," *Review of Economic Studies*, XXVIII (1960), 32–36] is a consequence of their special assumptions.

[33] For empirical demand functions for money which meet this specification—by virtue of depending on real financial assets (either by themselves or as a component of wealth)—see the references to the studies by Bronfenbrenner and Mayer, and, especially, Meltzer on p. 652 below. This dependence is, of course, the counterpart of the real-balance effect in empirical consumption functions. On all this, see Note M below.

[34] This has been emphasized by Ball and Bodkin, *op. cit.*, p. 48.

[35] See especially Joseph A. Schumpeter, "Money and the Social Product," *Archiv für Sozialwissenschaft und Sozialpolitik*, XLIV (1917/18), as translated in *International Economic Papers*, No. 6 (London, 1956), pp. 191–92, 204–206; *Theory of Economic Development* (Cambridge, 1934), Chapter 3.

For further discussion of "forced savings," see Chapter XII:3 below.

IV. Money and Interest

1. Introduction. The meaning of time preference. The purpose and nature of bonds. 2–3. The excess-demand functions for commodities, bonds, and money. 4. The effects of an increase in the quantity of money. 5. The argument extended to a production economy.

1. INTRODUCTION. THE MEANING OF TIME PREFERENCE. THE PURPOSE AND NATURE OF BONDS

The foregoing analysis is based on the simplifying assumption that the individual's sole concern with the future is to meet it with adequate money reserves. The present chapter moves one step closer to reality by permitting the individual's economic horizon to extend over a period of time—say a "month"— which includes several weeks. It follows that the optimum collection of goods which he chooses in the current Monday marketing period specifies the amounts to be consumed, not only during the current week, but during future weeks as well. This in turn implies that the individual plans *now* how much to buy or sell of each commodity in each of the marketing periods of the month. It should, however, be clear that when in the course of time the individual comes to the marketing period in question, he will not generally act in accordance with the plans he now makes. For by that time new information will be available which will cause him to modify them. Thus, for example, he will by that time have information on a week—or on weeks—which is now beyond his economic horizon. In brief, we assume that every Monday each individual reconsiders the whole situation that will confront him during the ensuing month and formulates or revises his plans accordingly.[1]

An immediate implication of this extension of the economic horizon is that the money balances which the individual plans to hold at the end of, say, this week are intended to meet the transactions and precautionary needs of a clearly defined plan of expenditures for next week. Thus the demand for money in our present economy is a much more meaningful concept than the one to which we were logically restricted in the one-week-horizon case of preceding chapters.

By analogy with the argument of Chapters I and II, these plans are assumed to be determined by the individual's tastes, his endowment of commodities, his initial money holdings, and the prices with which he is confronted. But now the term "tastes" refers to future consumption as well as present; "endowment of commodities" includes the endowments which will descend upon him during future Sunday nights as well as that received this Sunday; and "prices" includes those with which he will be confronted in future marketing periods as well as in the present one. For simplicity, it is assumed that these future prices are expected—with certainty—to be identical with current ones. It is, however, generally assumed that future endowments are expected—again, with certainty—to differ from the current one.

This last assumption can be restated in more familiar terms if we remember that the value of any week's endowment of commodities is analogous to the income of that week.[2] We can then say that each individual takes the time shape of his anticipated income stream as

---

[1] The reader will recognize here the familiar technique of Hicks, *Value and Capital*, Chapters IX–X, especially p. 124. But whereas Hicks' main purpose in devising this technique is to analyze the origin and significance of discrepancies between planned and actual behavior, we have (except for the concluding section of the preceding chapter) ignored this problem. In the present chapter we use this technique only in order to rationalize the holding of money and to make room for transactions which involve a rate of interest. See below.

[2] This and the following paragraph are based on Irving Fisher, *The Rate of Interest* (New York, 1907), Chapters VI–VII; or, alternatively, his later *Theory of Interest* (New York, 1930), Chapters IV–V. Note, however, that our usage of "income" differs from Fisher's—though, for our present purposes, in an immaterial way.

Cf. also Friedman, *Theory of the Consumption Function* (Princeton, 1957), pp. 7–14.

certain and unalterable but, in general, not uniform. Diagrammatically, we have the situation shown in Figure IV-1. The numbers on the X-axis represent the weeks of the one-month economic horizon. This is assumed to extend, say, four weeks beyond the current one—represented by the number zero. The curves A, B, and C describe various possible income streams. The uniform income stream A represents the special case of an individual who expects to continue to receive exactly the same endowment of commodities in each future week. On the other hand, income stream B is that of an individual who expects his weekly income to decrease steadily during the month, while stream C is that of an individual with opposite expectations. Clearly, we can also have

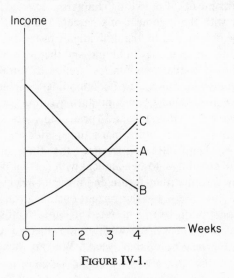

FIGURE IV-1.

more complicated cases in which the income stream is expected to rise during certain parts of the month and to fall during others. As already emphasized, the expectations in all these cases are held with certainty.

Though the individual's income stream is fixed, he can transfer purchasing power from one week to another either by changing the amount of money he carries over or by making appropriate transactions with a new good that we shall introduce—the bond. This is a note obligating the issuer to redeem it from the bearer one week after issue at the fixed price of one dollar. An individual who wants to consume more than his income (dissave) in any given week can sell such bonds during the Monday marketing period of that week; that is, he can borrow. An individual who wants to consume less (save) can buy such bonds; that is, he can lend. "Can," and not "must"; for, as just indicated, savings and dissavings may also express themselves in changes in money holdings. We assume further that there is no risk of default; hence the identity of the borrower is a matter of indifference to the lender. It follows that all bonds are economically indistinguishable from one another.

Thus the bond is just another good which is bought and sold on the market. Its price, like that of any other good, is also expected to be in the future exactly what it is today. This price, denoted by q, is clearly related to the rate of interest, $100r$ per cent. Specifically,

$$r = \frac{1-q}{q} \quad \text{or} \quad q = \frac{1}{1+r}.$$

As this relation shows, the higher the price of the bond, the lower the rate of interest, and conversely. Note that a bond price of unity corresponds to a zero rate of interest, and a price greater than unity to a negative rate.

It can also be seen from the preceding that, given the possibility of borrowing on future income, an individual will generally not choose to equate his consumption for any week with the arbitrarily given income of that week. Thus, for example, the individual with income stream C will prefer to dissave during the first part of the month and compensate for this by saving later; and conversely for the individual with income stream B. More precisely, it is the discounted value of his whole anticipated income stream—his wealth—which is relevant for the individual's consumption decisions of any given week; not the income of that week alone.[3]

The foregoing can be called a "time preference" theory of interest. If we have deliberately avoided doing so until now, it is because of the ambiguity which surrounds this term in the literature. As originally

[3] Cf. the references in the preceding footnote.

All this will be rigorously developed in Chapters V–VII, where it will also be shown that there may be circumstances under which the individual's demand is determined by the whole time shape of his income stream, and not only by its discounted value (cf. pp. 113–14 and 132).

used by Fisher it is merely a statement of the fact that individuals redistribute their consumption over time in an optimum way; it is not an explanation of the forces which bring them to feel that such a redistribution is desirable.[4] For such an explanation Fisher depends primarily—and in this we have followed him—on the time shape of the income stream. As a secondary explanation he brings in the possibility that, due to their lack of foresight and self-control, individuals may systematically prefer present over equivalent future consumption.[5] With or without awareness of their departure from Fisher's original meaning, later economists seem to have used the term "time preference" to refer only to this possibility.[6] Clearly, the foregoing analysis of borrowing and lending operations does not presuppose the existence of "time preference" in this sense of the term. But such a "preference" may—in an exchange economy—be logically necessary to explain why these operations generate an equilibrium rate of interest greater than zero. We shall return to this question again.[7]

2. THE EXCESS-DEMAND FUNCTIONS FOR COMMODITIES, BONDS, AND MONEY

The extension of the individual's economic horizon to more than one week and the concomitant introduction of bonds obviously call for modifications in the demand theory of the preceding chapters. First of all, there are hitherto undefined goods whose excess-demand functions must now be described. Second, even the excess-demand functions for goods already defined are no longer the same as they were. For these functions must now reflect two new influences—one representing the past, the other the future.[8]

Let us begin with a discussion of this second set of modifications. Consider the individual at the start of the Monday marketing period.

---

[4] See, e.g., Fisher, *Theory of Interest*, pp. 66–67.

[5] *Ibid.*, pp. 80 ff.

[6] Cf., e.g., K. E. Boulding, *Economic Analysis* (rev. ed.; New York, 1948), pp. 751–52; E. S. Shaw, *Money, Income, and Monetary Policy* (Chicago, 1950), pp. 322–23.

[7] Section 4.

For further discussion of the distinction between the two senses of "time preference," see p. 112, footnote 43.

[8] The rigorous development of what now follows is deferred to Chapters V–VII.

The assets which he has carried over from the preceding week now comprise matured bonds as well as money. Unlike any other good of the initial collection, these bond holdings can be negative in magnitude. This is the case for anyone who sold bonds the preceding Monday, that is, for anyone who starts the current marketing period as a debtor. Conversely, these holdings are positive for anyone who starts the period as a creditor.

These initial bond holdings must clearly affect the individual's net wealth and hence his current excess-demand functions for commodities. A debtor tends—*ceteris paribus*—to decrease his amounts of excess demand in order to be able to redeem—with interest—the bonds he sold last Monday. Conversely, by virtue of the repayment he receives on the bonds bought last week, a creditor tends to increase his amounts demanded. Clearly, the degree of the decrease or increase in the amounts of commodities demanded can rationally depend only on the *real* value of these initial, matured bond holdings.

So much for the influence of the past. Consider now the influence of the future. This is reflected first of all in the dependence of the current excess-demand functions on the time path of the future income stream. This has been sufficiently discussed in the preceding section. We need only add here that it is again the sequence of *real* values in this stream that is rationally significant for commodity demands.

The influence of the future is reflected, secondly, in the rate of interest. An increase in interest represents a cheapening of future commodities with respect to present ones. More specifically, it lowers the cost of the bonds necessary to provide purchasing power over a fixed quantity of future commodities. However, as is well known, it is impossible to specify a priori the effect of this change on the amount demanded of present commodities. If, for example, the demand for future commodities has only slight interest-elasticity, then the number of bonds which the individual demands in order to obtain purchasing power over them will increase only slightly; and in view of the lowered per-unit price of bonds, the individual's total expenditures on them will decrease. Hence funds will be released for additional expenditure on current commodities. If, however, the demand for future commodities is sufficiently interest-elastic, the total expenditure on bonds will increase, with a consequent decrease in the amount demanded of present commodities. We shall assume the latter possibility to hold. In other words, we shall assume that savings are positively related to the rate of interest.[9]

What is most significant for the following analysis is that the rate of interest is the analogue of a relative price. As we shall see in Chapter V: 7, just as the relative price measures the marginal rate of substitution between two different commodities consumed this week, so $1 + r$ (under certain circumstances) measures the marginal rate of substitution between a commodity this week and the same commodity next week. Similarly, the formula of the preceding section shows that r is equal to a fraction whose denominator is q (the money price of a bond at time of issue) and whose numerator is $1 - q$ (the difference between this price and the money price of a bond at time of maturity—by definition, equal to unity). Thus the rate of interest, like a relative price, is the quotient of two amounts, each of which has the dimensions of a money price. Correspondingly, we argue by analogy that wherever the term "relative prices" appears in the demand theory of preceding chapters, we must now write "relative prices and rate of interest."

To summarize, the excess-demand functions for current commodities of an individual with given tastes (including whatever preferences for present as against equivalent future consumption that he may possess) are now assumed to depend upon relative prices, the rate of interest, present and future real incomes, the real value of initial bond holdings, and the real value of initial money holdings. Alternatively, these functions can be said to depend upon relative prices, the rate of interest, and real wealth—where this last is measured inclusive of initial financial assets. However, for reasons that have already been noted, we shall not make use of this alternative formulation in this chapter.[10]

3. THE EXCESS-DEMAND FUNCTIONS FOR COMMODITIES, BONDS, AND MONEY (CONTINUED)

Consider now the new goods introduced in this chapter. There are, first of all, those commodities which will come into existence only in

[9] For simplicity, this paragraph abstracts from the additional influence of interest changes on the demand for money; this will be taken account of in our more detailed discussion of Chapter IX.

[10] Cf. footnote 3 above.

For simplicity, we continue to ignore the dependence on the initial endowment of the commodity in question; see p. 17, footnote 7.

On the argument of this section, see Mathematical Appendix 4:*a*.

the course of future weeks. Even though physically identical with the commodities now existing, they are more conveniently considered as analytically distinct.[11] Correspondingly, for each of these commodities there is a separate excess-demand function. This function describes the quantities which an individual decides this Monday to buy or sell of the commodity in question on some specified future Monday within his economic horizon. Now, by assumption, prices and interest in future weeks are expected—with certainty—to be identical with those currently prevailing. Hence the amount of excess demand for a future commodity depends on exactly the same relative prices, rate of interest, real income stream, and real value of initial bond and money holdings as does the amount of excess demand for a current commodity.

It should, however, be emphasized that the amounts of excess demand for a future commodity differ from those of a current one in *not* being registered on this Monday's market. That is, there is no futures market to provide a concrete manifestation of these plans. This "blackout" on the future lends somewhat more credibility to our assumption that the individual always expects prices and interest to continue unchanged. At the same time, we must remember that when the individual finally reaches the Monday in question, the prices which will then confront him will generally not be the same as those which he now envisages. But we shall have to abstract here from the complications generated by these discrepancies.[12]

The remaining new good is the bond. In order to prevent any possible confusion, it should be emphasized that we are now referring to the bonds currently issued and currently sold—or discounted—in the market. We are *not* referring to the bonds issued last week, which must now be redeemed at face value. From the viewpoint of the individual's behavior in the market this week, the latter are a datum; they are the initial holdings of matured bonds whose influence has already been discussed above. It is only with respect to currently issued bonds that different decisions can be made in accordance with the different

[11] See Hicks, *Value and Capital*, pp. 193–94.

[12] It should be clear that what we disregard here as a "complication" forms the basis of Hicks' dynamic analysis, *ibid.*, Chapters IX–X and Part IV. Conversely, what we—following Walras and Samuelson—have presented and shall continue to present under the caption "dynamic analysis" is more or less taken for granted by Hicks; see the Additional Note C which he appends to the second edition of *Value and Capital*. See also Note B below, especially p. 539.

given conditions of the market; hence it is only for these bonds that there can properly be said to exist a demand function.

By definition, the initial holdings of currently issued bonds are zero. Hence there is no difference between the *demand* for bonds and the *excess demand*. This amount demanded can be positive or negative— according to whether the individual decides, respectively, to lend or borrow during the current week. In the latter case we can say, alternatively, that the amount of bonds *supplied* is positive.

Before describing the properties of the demand function for bonds, we must first add restrictions which will keep it finite. In the absence of such restrictions, each individual would choose to borrow indefinitely large amounts each week and to provide for the payment of principal and interest on them by borrowing still larger amounts the following week. In this way he could continue interminably to refund his debt— no matter what its magnitude. This, in turn, would enable him to demand unlimited amounts of commodities each week.

The usual analysis bars this possibility by assuming that there is some type of "imperfection" in the capital market which prevents an individual from borrowing all he wants to at the going rate of interest. This is undoubtedly a realistic assumption. However, since it is desired to keep the analysis as simple as possible, we shall not employ it here. Instead, we shall accomplish the same result by assuming that the individual must formulate his present and future market plans under the additional restriction that on the final Monday of the month his planned holdings of bonds must be zero. Clearly, this Monday of reckoning recedes constantly into the future as time progresses. But as long as the individual acts on the assumption that it must ultimately come and that he must repay all his debts by the end of his economic horizon, he will curtail his planned borrowings accordingly.[13]

Like that for other goods, the demand function for bonds is assumed to depend upon relative prices, the rate of interest, present and future incomes, the value of initial bond holdings, and the value of initial money holdings. Unlike the case for other goods, however, the last three variables here cannot simply be replaced by the single variable, wealth. For since the demand for bonds reflects the difference between the optimum time pattern of consumption and the given time pattern

---

[13] Cf. p. 97 below.

of income, it is the whole shape of the latter—and not only its discounted value—which is obviously relevant. This is another reason why it has not been convenient to use in this chapter the alternative formulation described at the end of the preceding section.

An increase in initial money holdings increases the amount of bonds demanded; this, of course, is the basic assumption implicit in Keynesian interest theory.[14] Similarly, an increase in the initial holdings of bonds also increases the amount demanded of new bonds. In particular, the more pronounced the individual's initial creditor position, the more inclined he will be to buy new bonds and thereby replenish his portfolio; the more pronounced his debtor position, the more pressed he will be to sell new bonds and thereby renew the credit previously extended to him.

Consider now the influence of the rate of interest. It has already been assumed in the preceding section that a decrease in it will decrease the amount of bonds demanded. It is also clear that if there are no costs of carrying over money balances from one week to the next, the amount of bonds demanded at any negative rate of interest must be zero or negative. For no individual will pay more than one dollar for the right to a dollar's worth of purchasing power next week if he can obtain this same power by merely adding one dollar to his planned money balances. Indeed, this line of reasoning implies that the amount of bonds demanded will become zero at some positive rate of interest which measures the satisfaction which the individual derives from being liquid. At any rate below this, the individual will always choose to carry purchasing power over to next week in the form of liquid money holdings rather than illiquid bond holdings. This is merely Keynes' familiar argument translated into a form appropriate for the bond market.[15]

One property of the bond demand function is fundamental to the following analysis. Assume the individual to be confronted with a doubling of all money prices (expected to be permanent), initial bond holdings, and initial money holdings, while the rate of interest is kept constant. By the assumptions made above as to the form

[14] See Note K:1; this will be discussed further in Chapter XI:1.

[15] *The General Theory of Employment, Interest and Money* (New York, 1936), p. 207. This argument will be presented more precisely in Chapter IX:4. In general, it has been considered advisable to defer a more detailed discussion of the bond market until then.

of the excess-demand functions for commodities, there is no change in the amounts demanded of either present or future commodities. Thus there is no change in the extent to which the individual originally planned to reallocate his consumption between this week and future weeks. Neither, then, is there any change in the total amount of real purchasing power which the individual plans to hold at the end of the week. Finally, in view of the constancy of the interest rate, there is no change in the relative amounts of this purchasing power which the individual desires to hold in the form of bonds and in the form of money. Thus the preceding change does not affect the extent of command over next week's commodities which the individual plans to hold in the form of bonds. But the expected money prices of these future commodities have doubled. Hence, in order to maintain his originally planned level of future *real* purchasing power, the individual must also double his planned *nominal* holdings of bonds. That is, whatever he originally planned to lend or borrow, he must now plan to lend or borrow twice as much.

It remains to consider the excess-demand function for money. As in Chapter II:5, the form of this function is completely specified by the budget restraint. In particular, we can write

the amount of excess demand for current money holdings

= the (face) value of initial bond holdings

+ the aggregate values of the amounts of excess supplies of current commodities

− the (discounted) value of demand for current bond holdings.

From what has been said about the properties of the demand functions for commodities and bonds, we can immediately see from this formula that the change discussed in the immediately preceding paragraphs will also double the amount of money demanded.

More generally, an equiproportionate change in money prices, initial bond holdings, and initial money holdings, the rate of interest being held constant, will cause a proportionate change in the amounts demanded of bonds and of money. It follows that the demand functions for *real* bond holdings and *real* money holdings, like those for commodities, depend only on relative prices, the rate of interest, present and future real incomes, the real value of initial bond holdings, and the real value of initial money holdings.[16]

So far we have discussed the excess-demand functions of the individual. The corresponding functions of the market are derived by aggregation, as in Chapter II: 6. Once again, there is asymmetry in that the market functions depend on the *arrays* of initial real bond and money holdings of all individuals in the economy, and not generally on their respective *totals*. Another asymmetry appears in the form of the market excess-demand function for money. Since the economy is assumed to be closed, every existing debt must be owed by one of its members to another. Hence the value of *initial* bond holdings aggregated over all members of the economy must necessarily be zero: to every "positive" creditor there corresponds a "negative" debtor. On the other hand, as emphasized in the next section, this is not generally true of the amount of aggregate *demand* for *new* bonds. Thus we have

the amount of market excess demand for current money holdings

= the aggregate value of the amounts of market excess supplies of current commodities

− the (discounted) value of the amount of market demand for current bond holdings.

An immediate implication of the foregoing discussion is that the definition of money illusion presented in Chapter II: 4 is no longer appropriate. For consider an individual confronted with an equiproportionate increase in money prices and initial money holdings. If he is a debtor, such a change reduces the real burden of his initial debts and hence tends to increase his demands for goods; while if a creditor, the change reduces the real value of his initial bond assets and hence tends to decrease his demands. From the viewpoint of the self-interest of the individual, it is no more irrational for him to react to these changes in his real wealth than it is for debtor classes to support inflationary policies and creditor classes to oppose them. In other words, though the specified change does not have a wealth effect in the form of a real-balance effect (p. 20), it does have one in the form of what we shall call a "real-indebtedness effect." Only if the terms of past

[16] For a rigorous development, see Chapter V: 3–6.

indebtedness are adjusted to the new level of prices—or, what is equivalent, only if initial bond holdings are changed at the same time and in the same proportion as prices and initial money holdings—will this real-indebtedness effect disappear.

Accordingly, we must broaden the definition of money illusion in the following way: An individual is free of money illusion if the amount he demands of any real good (commodities, real bond holdings, and real money holdings) remains invariant under any change which does not affect relative prices, the rate of interest, the time stream of real incomes, and the real value of initial bond and money holdings. This definition clearly includes the earlier one as a special case.[17]

4. The Effects of an Increase in the Quantity of Money

In accordance with our usual procedure, let us now pass from market excess-demand functions to excess-demand equations and the nature of the equilibrium position.

Since it is new to the analysis, it is advisable first to devote particular attention to the bond market. From the preceding section it is clear that the bond demand and excess-demand equations are identical. We can then say that at the equilibrium set of prices and interest, the aggregate amount demanded in this market is zero—that is, the total amount of desired borrowings in the economy is equal to the total amount of desired lendings. At any other set it can be either positive—indicating an excess of willing lenders over borrowers—or negative—indicating the opposite.

It is also clear from the preceding section that the equilibrium rate of interest cannot be negative, for at such a rate there would always exist an excess of borrowers over lenders. On the other hand, there is no assurance that it must be positive. For if the only reason people lend or borrow is because of the time shape of their future income streams, and if it is just as likely that these streams show an increase over time as a decrease, then it may well be that at the minimum rate of interest needed to compensate lenders for their loss of liquidity, no one desires

---

[17] Once again, for commodities and money—though not for bonds—the last three variables here can, under our present assumptions, be replaced by the single variable, real wealth.

On the argument of this section, see Mathematical Appendix 4:*a*.

to borrow. Thus the bond market might be in a vacuous equilibrium in which neither borrowing nor lending takes place.[18]

In order to preclude this possibility it is necessary to strengthen the supply side of the bond market—that is, the desire to borrow. This can be done, for example, by attributing to the income streams a systematic upward bias. In such a progressive economy the desire to anticipate future income may understandably predominate. Alternatively, we can achieve the same result by assuming the prevalence of a systematic preference for present as against equivalent future consumption.[19] Actually, however—for reasons which will become evident in the final section of this chapter—we need not concern ourselves overmuch with this problem.

Let us now turn to the overall equilibrium position of the market. As emphasized at the beginning of the preceding section, this market deals exclusively with current goods. Correspondingly, its equilibrium set of prices and interest must equate to zero the amounts of market excess demand for current goods only. It would be sheer accident if this same set could also equate to zero the aggregate amounts of excess demand for future goods. Conversely, these potential future disequilibria cannot even cast a shadow on current market developments. They manifest themselves only in the course of time, as the future becomes the present.

Nothing, then, is essentially different from the analysis of Chapter III:2. Once again there are $n - 1$ unknown equilibrium values—now consisting of the $n - 2$ respective money prices of current commodities and the rate of interest on current bonds. Once again there are n excess-demand equations: $n - 2$ for current commodities, one for current bond holdings, and one for current money holdings. And once again only $n - 1$ of these equations are independent; for, as can be seen from the form of the excess-demand function for money in the preceding section, any set of prices and interest that equilibrates the commodity and bond markets must also equilibrate the money market; that is, Walras' Law is still valid. In brief, the extension of the economic horizon to future weeks—under our simplified assumptions—does not make it necessary

---

[18] Were it not for the liquidity factor, we could replace this by the simpler—and more familiar—statement that it may well be that at a zero rate of interest there is no excess of borrowers over lenders.

[19] See the end of Section 1 above.

to take into account the excess-demand equations for future goods. In our present analytical framework these equations do not exist: they place no additional restrictions on the equilibrium set of prices and interest. Let us assume for the present that the system is a stable one and investigate its comparative-statics properties. Let the economy be in equilibrium at a certain set of money prices and interest rate. Assume now that the initial money holdings of each individual are doubled. It is clear that the new equilibrium position corresponding to this increased quantity of money is *not* in general one in which prices have doubled and the rate of interest has remained unchanged. For such a doubling of prices creates real-indebtedness effects which increase the amounts demanded by debtors and decrease the amounts demanded by creditors. Only by chance would these exactly offset each other in each and every market. This exceptional case will be described as one in which the price change has a "neutral distribution effect."

Thus a doubling of the quantity of money can in general be expected to affect both equilibrium relative prices and the rate of interest. Specifically, the relative prices of those commodities favored by debtors will rise, while those favored by creditors will fall. Similarly, the interest rate will rise or fall, depending on which of two countervailing forces is stronger: the decrease in the demand for bonds, caused by the worsened real position of creditors; or the decrease in the supply of bonds, caused by the improved real position of debtors.[20]

Let us now assume that the equilibrium position of the economy is disturbed by a doubling of the initial money *and* bond holdings of each individual. In this case it is clear that equilibrium is reestablished with doubled money prices and an unchanged rate of interest: for relative prices, the interest rate, the arrays of real incomes, initial real bond holdings, and initial real money holdings are then exactly the same as in the original equilibrium position. Hence the amounts of excess demand for commodities, real bond holdings, and real money holdings must also be the same as in that position: each of them must be zero.

Thus we conclude: If there is no money illusion and if outstanding debts are revalued (or, alternatively, if there is a neutral distribution

[20] Note the similarity between this discussion and that on p. 45.

effect), then a uniformly introduced increase in the quantity of money causes a proportionate increase in the equilibrium prices of commodities and leaves the equilibrium rate of interest unaffected.[21]

This conclusion can be usefully restated in terms of the familiar concept of "neutral money." Strictly speaking, such neutrality obtains if the mere conversion of a barter economy to a money economy does not affect equilibrium relative prices and interest.[22] Now, because the systems of excess-demand equations of these two economies differ so fundamentally (in a barter economy there is obviously neither an excess-demand equation for money nor a dependence of commodity excess-demand equations on real balances), it is difficult, if not impossible, to make such a comparison in a general way. If, however, we conceive of a barter economy as the limiting position of a money economy whose nominal quantity of money is made smaller and smaller, we can obviate this difficulty. For we can then remain within the system of excess-demand equations of a money economy and note what happens to its equilibrium values of relative prices and interest as the quantity of money approaches zero as a limit. Under the conditions specified in the preceding paragraph, we see that we can in this way get as "close" as we want to a barter economy without affecting the equilibrium values of these variables. In this sense, the foregoing conditions are all that are needed in order to assure the neutrality of money.

This interpretation, however, has one serious drawback: As the nominal quantity of money approaches zero, so does the price level—and at the same rate. Hence the real quantity of money remains unaffected. Thus the limiting position that we have defined as a barter economy is one in which there exists the same *real* quantity of money as in a money economy! This drawback notwithstanding, there does not seem to be any other meaningful way of comparing the respective equilibrium positions of a barter and money economy.[23]

---

[21] See Mathematical Appendix 4:*b–c*.

[22] Cf. F. A. Hayek, *Prices and Production* (2nd ed.; London, 1935), pp. 129–30.

[23] On these two paragraphs, see Mathematical Appendix 4:*c*.

Without agreeing with his main contention, I have written this last paragraph under the stimulation of P. Wonnacott's comment on "Neutral Money in Patinkin's Money, Interest and Prices," *Review of Economic Studies*, XXVI (1958), 70–71.

5. The Argument Extended to a Production Economy

So far we have only the sketch of a theory of interest. We have not yet adequately described the markets for bonds and money; we have not discussed the dynamic process by which the economy reaches its equilibrium position; nor have we really explained the full meaning of the invariance of the equilibrium rate of interest under a change in the quantity of money. Furthermore, the theory itself is developed only for the case of a simple exchange economy. We must therefore extend it to the case of a production economy as well. At the same time, we must fill in the lacunae just listed. These are the tasks which await us in Part Two. The reader who is interested solely in these aspects of the argument can, then, continue directly with Chapter IX.

Even without the details of this later development, we can intuitively see that the assumption of an exchange economy is nowhere near as restrictive as it first appears. To speak somewhat loosely, the conclusion reached above—the invariance of relative prices and the rate of interest under a change in the quantity of money—flows from the assumption that there is no money illusion. Hence any change in the analytical framework which leaves this assumption intact must do the same for this conclusion.

Consider, in particular, the case of a production economy. Its differentia is that the amount supplied of any commodity is not constant —as it is in an exchange economy—but variable. That is, there exists in this economy the possibility of production. This means that firms can transform varying inputs of factor services into varying outputs of commodities. But the essential point is that—according to the marginal-productivity theory—once the technical conditions of production are specified, the decisions of a firm with respect to these inputs and outputs are based entirely on relative prices. Its decision on the optimum quantitative relationship between any two factors depends on the relative price of these factors as compared with their marginal rate of technical substitution; its decision on the optimum quantitative relationship between a factor and a commodity depends on the price of the former relative to the latter, as compared with the marginal productivity of the former in terms of the latter; finally, its decision on the optimum relationship between two commodities depends on their relative price as compared with the marginal rate of technical substitution between them.[24] If, in addition, we admit the possibility of investment, these decisions will also depend on the relationship between the rate of interest and the marginal productivity of capital. Finally, if we follow recent developments in the theory of the firm and assume it to be concerned with its balance sheet as well as its profit-and-loss statement, it will again be the *real* value of its assets and liabilities that the firm will take into account in reaching its decisions.

In brief, firms, no less than individuals, can be assumed to be free of money illusion. That is, in an economy with given technical conditions of production, firms enter the market with supply functions for commodities and demand functions for factor services, each of which is dependent upon relative prices, the rate of interest, and the real value of assets. From the earlier sections of this chapter, we know that, at the same time, households enter the market from the other side with demand functions for commodities and supply functions for factor services dependent upon exactly the same variables. Hence the market excess-demand equations of a production economy have exactly the same basic property—and reflect exactly the same absence of money illusion —as do those of our simple exchange economy: they depend solely on relative prices, the rate of interest, present and future real incomes, and the initial real value of financial assets. It follows that the invariance of relative prices and interest under a change in the quantity of money holds with equal validity for both types of economies.

This generalization of the argument eliminates one basic difficulty in the preceding interest theory. For as soon as we take into account the possibility of profitable investment in a production economy, we automatically provide that additional stimulus to the desire to borrow which was shown above to be necessary for the assurance of a positive equilibrium rate of interest. In fact, practically all of the borrowing in our economy can now be assumed to originate from entrepreneurs who require funds to finance investment and who are therefore willing to pay interest in keeping with its marginal productivity. Correspondingly, the supply side of the bond market is dominated by these entrepreneurs. In contrast, the consumption loans to which the analysis of this chapter has hitherto been restricted now exert only a minor influence on this side of the market.

[24] Cf. Hicks, *Value and Capital*, Chapter VI, especially p. 86.

V. A Utility Theory of Money, Assets, and Savings

1. THE NATURE OF THE UTILITY OF MONEY

The argument of the preceding chapter departs in one respect from the pattern set for it by Chapter I: instead of deriving the properties of the excess-demand functions from utility theory, it merely posits them by analogy. Actually, it is not at all clear that it is methodologically preferable to take utility functions—as against excess-demand functions —as the point of departure for the theory of demand. Furthermore, as will be shown below, the basic property of absence of money illusion can be derived without recourse to utility analysis, and by considering instead the revealed preferences of an individual assumed to be consistent in his choices. Nevertheless, in view of the fact that formal attempts to apply marginal-utility analysis to monetary theory are as old as the "subjective-value revolution" itself, it is worthwhile presenting a detailed description of how such an application can be carried out.

Before proceeding with this, we might note that the aforementioned attempts never actually achieved general acceptance. Indeed, their validity was for many years hotly debated among Continental followers of the marginal-utility school. Some of them even went so far as to provide mathematical demonstrations that money could not have any "utility." Others merely stated that money did not have any "direct utility." In neither case was the meaning of these contentions made clear. What is worse, even those who took the opposite side of the argument rarely based their analyses on a proper definition of the utility of money. As a result they were drawn into protracted, confused, and indecisive debates on a sham "circularity" issue which never should have arisen in the first place.[1]

It is thus essential to make clear at the outset the sense in which "utility of money" will be used in the present discussion. Clearly, it does not represent Marshall's use of this term.[2] Nor is it intended to denote the utility of the money commodity; indeed, we continue to assume a fiat paper money precisely in order to avoid any ambiguity on this score. Nor, finally, is it intended to denote "the marginal utility of the goods for which the money can be exchanged." Instead, our concern is with the utility of *holding* money, not with that of *spending* it. This is the concept implicit in all cash-balance approaches to the quantity theory of money; and it is the one that will be followed explicitly here.[3]

More specifically, assume that payments and receipts on commodity contracts occur randomly during the week in accordance with the stochastic process noted in Chapter II: 1 above. The redemption of bonds, on the other hand, is scheduled to take place at a fixed point of time: the end of the week. Assume also that an individual who runs out of cash during the week can meet the situation in one of two ways. Either he can default temporarily on any payment that he is called upon to make— a course of action that is assumed to generate some embarrassment for

[1] See below, Section 8.
[2] This too will be discussed in Section 8.
[3] The quotation in this paragraph is from L. von Mises, *The Theory of Money and Credit*, trans. H. E. Batson (New York, 1935), p. 109. On this and the preceding paragraphs, see the references to the literature in Note D below.

him; or he can replenish his balances by achieving an intraweek redemption (at their maturity value) of the bonds he holds—an action which is assumed to necessitate some extra bother on his part.[4] The security which money balances provide against either of these types of inconvenience is what is assumed to invest them with utility. It is also clear that the efficacy of money balances in providing this security is dependent on their real—and not nominal—value. Correspondingly, it is only the real value of money balances that is relevant for the individual's utility calculus.

Note that the foregoing implies the dropping of the assumption that all market activities take place on a single day of the week. Instead, we are now distinguishing between commodities (whose transactions are restricted to the Monday marketing period) and assets (which can be dealt with at any point during the week). This distinction gives expression to the recurrent theme in the literature that the individual can make more rapid adjustments in the composition of his stock of assets (particularly financial ones) than in his consumption of flows of commodities. At the same time it should be emphasized that we are now making the unrealistic assumption that these intraweek bond transactions do not affect the interest rate.

Three further comments might be made. First, our concern in this chapter is with the demand for money that would exist even if there were perfect certainty with respect to future prices and interest. Uncertainty does play a role in the analysis, but only uncertainty with respect to the timing of payments. Thus one by-product of the following argument is the demonstration that dynamic or uncertain price and/or interest expectations are not a *sine qua non* of a positive demand for money.[5]

Second, if our objective were solely to establish a rationale for such a positive demand, then there would be no need to assume uncertainties with respect to timing either. It would suffice to say that payments must be made at fixed and certain times during the week—and that it is

---

[4] Cf. Hicks, *Value and Capital*, pp. 164–66.

[5] The need for such a demonstration can most easily be seen from the survey of the literature in J. C. Gilbert, "The Demand for Money: The Development of an Economic Concept," *Journal of Political Economy*, LXI (1953), 144–59.

An individual with "static expectations" expects the prices and interest of future weeks to be the same as present ones; an individual with "dynamic expectations" expects them to be different. These expectations can be held with or without certainty.

impossible to effect any additional transactions (including those with bonds) during the week. But then—on the assumption that no individual will deliberately choose to default during the week—his demand for money would be a constant equal to the maximum cumulative discrepancy between payments and receipts that would be generated during the week. There would be no considerations of more or less—no weighing of alternatives.[6]

On the other hand, the introduction of uncertainties via the stochastic payment process readily enables us to analyze the problem of holding money by means of the traditional utility calculus. Correspondingly, it enables us to generate a demand curve for money which—like any other demand curve—has a smooth and negative slope with respect to its price. At the same time, it must be conceded that this result can be obtained even if we assume that the individual knows his payment dates with certainty—provided we also assume that he may deliberately plan to suffer the embarrassment of default for varying periods during the week in order to earn more interest on bonds.[7]

We note finally that though the emphasis of our remarks until now has been on the single asset, money, the general approach of the following argument is in the Keynesian spirit of analyzing the demand for this asset as one component of an optimally chosen portfolio of many assets.[8]

---

[6] Cf., the discussions of Walras and Schlesinger, pp. 549 and 576 below.

The impossibility of effecting transactions is an extreme instance of the type of "imperfections" in the bond market mentioned by Marget in this context; cf. pp. 548–49 below.

[7] This is K. J. Arrow's point in *Mathematical Reviews*, XVIII (1957), 706–707.

[8] *General Theory*, pp. 166–70, 222–29. In some ways, this portfolio approach to monetary theory is presented even more clearly in Keynes' *Treatise on Money* (London, 1930), Vol. 1, pp. 140–46. See also Hicks' basic article on "A Suggestion for Simplifying the Theory of Money," *Economica*, II (1935) as reprinted in *Readings in Monetary Theory*, pp. 13–32.

For the subsequent development of this approach at the hands of Marschak, Makower, Modigliani, Kahn, Robinson, Shackle, and Tobin, see the references in the Bibliography at the end of this book. A more recent—though somewhat mislabelled—contribution is Milton Friedman's "The Quantity Theory of Money—A Restatement," in *Studies in the Quantity Theory of Money* (ed. M. Friedman, Chicago, 1956), pp. 3–21. Its title notwithstanding, this is actually much closer to the Keynesian theory than to the quantity theory—or to the traditional Chicago theory—which Friedman claims to be restating. For whereas Keynesian theory emphasizes the optimal relationship among *stocks* of assets (which is Friedman's primary concern), neoclassical (and traditional Chicago) theory emphasized the optimal relationship

2. THE STOCHASTIC PAYMENT PROCESS

In view of our repeated references to the stochastic payment process, it is worthwhile—at the risk of some repetition—spelling out its nature in detail. The reader uninterested in these technical matters can, however, proceed directly to the utility analysis of the next section.

Assume that at the close of the Monday marketing period all the final contracts for commodities are placed in a common pool. Random drawings are then made from this pool in groups, say, of ten. Payments on the first ten contracts so drawn are then due at 8:00 A.M. Tuesday, payments on the second ten at 9:00 A.M., and so on for every business hour during the week. These random drawings are continued until the pool has been exhausted and every commodity contract tied up with a specific payment hour during the week. As already noted, payments on bonds are not randomly distributed, but are instead fixed for the last hour of the week.

It is possible that an individual will be called upon to make both payments and receipts at a given hour. To the extent that this happens he can offset one against the other. Clearly, however, the random process by which the payment hours for the various contracts are determined makes it irrational for the individual to depend upon a perfect hourly synchronization of his required payments and receipts. Hence, as noted in the preceding section, the only way the individual can avoid almost certain inconvenience at one or more payment hours during the week is to hold money reserves at its beginning.

This stochastic model not only rationalizes the demand for money, but also idealizes the traditional motives that have been associated with it. Thus the transactions motive is represented by the lack of synchronization between payments and receipts, and the precautionary motive by the uncertainty of the timing of these payments. Other aspects of the precautionary motive—say the desire to have a liquid reserve to be able to meet unexpected emergencies—can also be superimposed upon this model. Thus we might assume that there is a second random process which draws the names of individuals during the various payment hours,

---

between the *stock* of money and the *flow* of planned expenditures—where "stock" and "flow" are being used in the sense described on p. 521 below. Correspondingly, the latter paid little, if any, attention to the possible impact on the rate of interest of shifts in tastes relating to the form in which assets are held.

fines those individuals who are found with exhausted reserves, and distributes these fines as prizes to those found with positive reserves. However, in order to keep the argument as simple as possible, we shall not explore this possibility further here.

It should be clear that the monetary demand now being discussed is that for next week. The foreknowledge that the payments of that week will be randomly timed is assumed to make the individual adjust his commitments of the current marketing period so as to provide for the money reserves he will then need. True, temporary insolvency of some of his buyers may (if they decide against an intraweek conversion of bonds into money) delay payment on their purchasing contracts with him. But since no one can obligate himself in excess of his budget restraint, our individual can be sure that such delays can at most be intraweek ones. Hence his money balances at the end of this week—or, equivalently, the beginning of next week—must be exactly at the level implied by his final current marketing decisions.

Correspondingly, these decisions cannot affect the absolute level of the money balances with which the individual meets his liquidity needs of the current week, for these balances were in turn determined by the decisions of the preceding one. On the other hand, current decisions can very clearly affect the *relative* adequacy of these balances. This is nothing but the obverse side of the real-balance effect. In brief, at any given set of prices, the individual can alway adjust his amounts of excess demand so as to enable his given initial money balances to provide any desired degree of security against insolvency during the ensuing week. Indeed, in the limiting case, he can—by restricting the value of his purchases to the level of these given balances—assure their complete adequacy for any possible time pattern of payments that might be determined by the random process.[9]

We can sharpen these implications of our model by deriving (under simplifying assumptions) the probability distribution which is implicit in it. Consider, then, an individual who at the given market prices— expected with certainty to continue unchanged—currently plans to buy or sell certain amounts of commodities and bonds in next Monday's marketing period. Let us now consider the situation with which the individual would be confronted in the course of this next week should

[9] These last two paragraphs should be read against the background of pp. 17–19 and 24.

he enter it without any initial money balances at all, and should he also choose not to carry out an intraweek bond transaction.

Let the "excess payment due" at any given hour be the difference between the payments and receipts randomly selected as falling due at that hour. In addition to these payments, the individual is also assumed to be liable at this hour for any payment on which he might previously have defaulted because of insolvency. To take account of this factor we define his "net payment due" at any hour as the excess payment due for that hour *plus* the sum of excess payments due at all preceding hours. Both the excess and net payments due at any given hour can, of course, be negative; this will be the case when receipts exceed payments. We note also that the individual's net payment due at the last hour of the week is the sum of all planned payments during the week minus the sum of all planned receipts; by the budget restraint, this must equal his planned decrement in money balances over the week.

Clearly, the number representing the net payment due at any given hour during the week is a random number, for it is determined by a time sequence of payments and receipts which is itself the outcome of a random process. Only the number representing the net payment due at the last hour of the week is an exception; as just noted, this is uniquely fixed by the decisions of the individual. Consider now the maximum of all these numbers; obviously, this too must be a random number. Let us denote it by w and see what we can say about its probability distribution.[10]

For simplicity, assume that the individual plans to end the week with the same zero money balances with which he begins it. This planned constancy of money balances over the week implies that—regardless of the outcome of the random process—the net payment due at the

---

[10] Some readers may be helped by a mathematical statement of these definitions. Assume that there are m payment hours during the week. Let y_i $(i = 1, \dots, m)$ be the excess payment due at the ith hour. Similarly, let w_i be the net payment due at this hour. Then

$$w_1 = y_1,$$
$$w_2 = y_1 + y_2 = w_1 + y_2,$$
$$w_3 = y_1 + y_2 + y_3 = w_2 + y_3,$$
$$\dots\dots\dots\dots\dots\dots\dots\dots\dots\dots\dots\dots$$
$$w_m = y_1 + y_2 + \dots + y_m = w_{m-1} + y_m.$$

The random variable w is the maximum of the w_i.

last hour must be zero. Hence, under this assumption, the minimum value of *w* is also zero. This minimum is attained if there is a perfect hourly synchronization of payments and receipts, or if the early hours of the week are marked by negative excess payments which build up a reserve adequate to deal with the positive excess payments of later hours. Clearly, in either of these cases, the net payment due at each hour is either negative or zero.

At the other extreme, the maximum value of *w* is equal to the aggregate value of all the individual's *positive* amounts of excess demands for

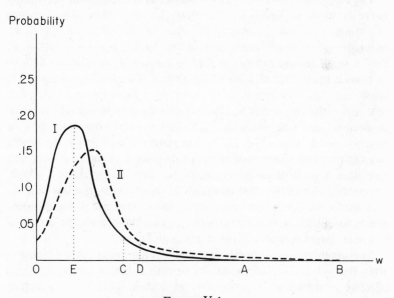

FIGURE V-1

commodities. It is attained if chance should decree that the individual must first pay for all his purchases before he receives payment for any of his sales. Let the sum of all these purchases be represented by *A*. Probability distribution I in Figure V-1 then reflects the fact that neither the minimum nor the maximum value of *w* is likely to occur.

The economic interpretation of this probability distribution is straightforward. Consider the point *C*. Assume that the total area underneath probability curve I from this point until *A* is, say, one-tenth of the total unit-area of the curve. This means that there is a probability of 90 per cent that the hourly net payments due during the week will not exceed C dollars. But this in turn means that if the individual had been equipped at the beginning of the week with money reserves of C dollars, there would have been a probability of 90 per cent that they would have sufficed to cover the timing discrepancies that might be generated by the random payment process. If these balances had been increased to D dollars, this probability would have been increased accordingly to, say, 95 per cent. And so on.

The long and attenuated right-hand tail of the foregoing probability curve is its most significant property. Let us define the "volume of transactions" as the aggregate value of the individual's planned purchases—represented in the present case by A. Then this tail shows us that a small reserve ratio of money to volume of transactions suffices to provide the individual with a large degree of security against possible insolvency. The intuitive basis of this property can be seen in the fact that high values of w can be attained only by long initial sequences of consecutive hours at which the individual must pay out more than he receives. At the same time, the budget restraint implies that the longer any such sequence, the smaller the probability that the next hour will also have a positive excess payment; for over the week as a whole, payments and receipts must be equal. In other words, the law of averages works here even more effectively than in the case of independent events to quickly reduce the probability that the cumulative excess of payments over receipts will reach any high value.

Another interesting property revealed by probability curve I is that—after the point E—equal additions to cash balances are decreasingly effective in reducing the probability of default. This is an important consideration for an individual on the margin of devoting additional resources to cash balances. It should, however, be noted that the increasing marginal effectiveness of cash balances up to the point E does not imply—for a world of measurable utility—increasing marginal utility of cash balances up to this point. For this increased effectiveness may be more than offset by the decreased marginal satisfaction the individual can be assumed to derive from additional security against the inconvenience of insolvency.

Let us now explore the possible effects of changes in the volume of transactions. Assume that for some reason the individual changes his excess demands so as to increase his planned volume of transactions to *B*. Let curve II in Figure V-1 represent the corresponding new probability distribution. We note first that the level of money reserves *A*—which previously provided complete security against any contingency—no longer does so. Conversely, if the individual had originally planned the volume of transactions *B* and had held money reserves equal to *A*, he could have assured the complete adequacy of these reserves by reducing his planned volume of transactions to *A*. This illustrates the already emphasized fact (p. 83) that the individual can affect the relative adequacy of his money reserves, even when he cannot affect their absolute level.

Assume that the individual's increased volume of transactions is generated by an increase, not in the *average value* of each of his contracts, but in their *number*. Then the increase in money reserves necessary to maintain a given level of financial security is less than proportionate to the increase in the volume of transactions. The intuitive basis for these "large-scale economies" in the relative size of money reserves is similar to that presented earlier for the long right-hand tail of the probability distribution. Indeed, it can be shown[11] that if *N* represents the number of one-dollar payments and receipts that must be made during the week, then the amount of money that must be held in order to maintain a given level of security increases in proportion to $\sqrt{N}$. The existence of these economies of scale is represented in Figure V-1 by the fact that though *C* on probability curve I and *D* on curve II correspond to the same 90 per cent level of security, the ratio of *C* to *D* is greater than that of *A* to *B*.[12]

The importance of the opening proviso of the preceding paragraph can be appreciated by considering the case in which the increase in

[11] See Mathematical Appendix 5 by Aryeh Dvoretzky, especially the table on p. 456.

[12] The analogue of this conclusion for a bank's reserve ratio has a long history. See the references to Edgeworth and Wicksell (*Interest and Prices*, pp. 66–68) in the stimulating article by W. J. Baumol, "The Transactions Demand for Cash: An Inventory Theoretic Approach," *Quarterly Journal of Economics*, LXVI (1952), 556. Baumol also points out that Fisher applied Edgeworth's theory to an individual's cash balances (*Purchasing Power of Money*, p. 167).

The reasoning of these writers differs, however, from that followed here. In particular, they based themselves on a stochastic model in which sampling from an infinite population generates a normal distribution. They also failed to bring out the distinction emphasized in the next two paragraphs of the text. See, however, the reference to Schlesinger in the next footnote.

the planned volume of transactions is the result of, say, a doubling of all prices and initial bond and money holdings. From Chapter IV we know that the amounts of the individual's excess demands are not thereby affected. He therefore continues to make the same number of contracts for the same amounts of commodities and real bonds. Hence the probability of drawing any particular time sequence of these contracts is also exactly the same as before. The only difference is that this same sequence will now call for payments and receipts twice as high as those it originally called for. It follows that the probability that the maximum net payment called for by this sequence will be, say, $2C$ is exactly the same as the original probability that it would have been C. Thus the new probability distribution is once again the solid curve of Figure V-1, with C, D, A, ... replaced by $2C$, $2D$, $2A$, ... , respectively.

In brief, the probability distribution corresponding to the individual's changed circumstances is obtained from the original one by merely changing the unit of measure of the X-axis. It follows that if the individual still wishes to maintain the same level of security against insolvency, he will have to hold twice the amount of money that he planned to before. Thus by another path we reach the already familiar conclusion that doubling prices and initial bond and money holdings doubles the amount of money demanded. But now this conclusion has the additional connotation that the resulting doubling of the individual's volume of transactions does not enable him to economize on the relative size of his cash balances.[13] [14]

[13] These two paragraphs also explain why inflationary expansions of demand deposits do not create opportunities for "large-scale economies" which might permit banks to lower their reserve ratios; see the preceding footnote.

After this section was written, I discovered that Karl Schlesinger—in a little-known monograph entitled *Theorie der Geld- und Kreditwirtschaft* (Munich, 1914)—makes use of similar probability concepts in his analysis of the demand for money (*ibid.*, especially p. 88, footnote 1). Schlesinger, however, does not develop the full implications of his model and, in particular, does not attempt to describe any probability-distribution curve. On the other hand, he repeatedly emphasizes that, because of the "law of large numbers," an increase in the volume of payments causes a less-than-proportionate increase in the demand for money; but, in contrast to the writers mentioned in the preceding footnote, he also emphasizes that this holds only subject to the distinction just made in the text. Schlesinger also presents an interesting marginal utility analysis of money. For further details, see Note D below.

[14] I am greatly indebted to my colleague Aryeh Dvoretzky for rigorously deriving the probability distribution here conjectured. His derivation is presented in Mathematical Appendix 5 below.

Kenneth Arrow has more recently noted that this distribution was also developed

3. The Conditions for Utility Maximization

Let us now determine the utility-maximizing conditions of an individual with a horizon of several weeks whose utility depends not only on the commodities which he will consume during each of these weeks, but also on the real value of the money holdings with which he will start them.[15] In order to concentrate attention on the problem of optimum intertemporal allocations which now concerns us, we shall henceforth assume that the individual expects relative commodity prices to remain constant for the duration of his planning period. This enables us to treat all the commodities consumed in the tth week as a single composite, say, Z_t.[16] For the present we shall make the further assumption that absolute commodity prices are also expected to remain constant over the economic horizon. Hence the price of the composite commodity in every week can be represented by the same symbol p.

In order for the individual to be in an optimum position subject to his budget restraints, it is necessary that he not be able to increase his utility by planning now to decrease his commodity expenditures in any week by one dollar, add it to the cash balances held at the end of that week, and use this dollar to increase his commodity expenditures the following week. That is, a condition for maximum utility is

(1)
$$\text{m.u. of a dollar's worth of } Z_t = \text{m.u. of a dollar's worth of } \frac{M_t}{p}$$
$$+ \text{m.u. of a dollar's worth of } Z_{t+1},$$

where m.u. denotes marginal utility, and where M_t represents the nominal—and M_t/p, the real—money balances which the individual plans to hold at the end of the tth week and thus carry over to the beginning of the $(t + 1)^{\text{th}}$.

Let us now take account of the fact that the individual also has the

---

by Swedish writers on insurance theory. See K. J. Arrow, S. Karlin, and H. Scarf, *Studies in the Mathematical Theory of Inventory and Production* (Stanford, 1958), p. 8.

[15] Some readers may prefer to follow the argument first for the two-period case presented graphically in Sections 4–5.

[16] Clearly, the individual in his optimum position will distribute his expenditures over commodities in any given week in such a way as to equalize the marginal utility of a dollar spent on each commodity. This, indeed, is the basic assumption of the composite-good theorem, whose simplifying consequences we are now exploiting. See Mathematical Appendix 2:*c*.

alternative of redistributing his consumption over time by buying or selling bonds. As will be recalled, these are notes issued one week and maturing the following—at the fixed maturity value of one dollar. The possibility of effecting these transactions implies that an individual with an optimum collection of goods must be in such a position that he cannot increase his total utility by planning now to decrease expenditures on commodities in any week by one dollar, buy bonds with the savings, and use the principal and interest he receives for these bonds the following week to buy commodities then. That is, the following familiar relationship must hold for any two successive weeks:

(2) m.u. of a dollar's worth of Z_t
$$= \text{m.u. of } (1 + r) \text{ dollars' worth of } Z_{t+1}.$$

The individual's optimum position is fully specified by the foregoing marginal conditions and his budget restraints.[17] Clearly, these marginal conditions imply that other intertemporal relations will also be satisfied. Thus, for example, repeated application of equation (1) yields

m.u. of a dollar's worth of $Z_t = $ m.u. of a dollar's worth of $\dfrac{M_t}{p}$

$+$ m.u. of a dollar's worth of $\dfrac{M_{t+1}}{p}$

(3) $+ \cdots + \cdots + \cdots$

$+$ m.u. of a dollar's worth of $\dfrac{M_{t+m}}{p}$

$+$ m.u. of a dollar's worth of $Z_{t+m+1}.$

That is, the individual in his optimum position will be indifferent between consuming a dollar in week t, on the one hand, and holding it for m weeks and consuming it then, on the other.[18] A corresponding

[17] In the case of "corner solutions," equalities (1) and (2) are replaced by inequalities; see, for example, pp. 103–104 and 121 below.

[18] Note that if the individual has an infinite horizon, this equation can be rewritten as

m.u. of a dollar's worth of Z_1
$$= \text{m.u. of a dollar held } permanently \text{ in real cash balances,}$$

where the right-hand term is the sum of the marginal utilities on the right-hand side of equation (3), with the last term there replaced by the appropriate infinite series.

statement can be made for holding a bond for m weeks, or, for that matter, for any time sequence of money and bond holdings.

Another intertemporal relationship implied by the foregoing marginal conditions is

(4)   m.u. of a dollar's worth of $\dfrac{M_t}{p}$ = m.u. of r dollar's worth of Z_{t+1},

which is obtained by substracting (2) from (1). In other words, the subjective opportunity cost of carrying over a dollar's purchasing power from one week to the next in the form of liquid cash balances, instead of doing so in the form of bonds, is the utility of the commodities that could have been bought the following week with the interest obtainable from the bonds. Hence, for an optimum collection, the marginal utility afforded by a dollar's worth of cash balances (the marginal "convenience yield" of these balances) must be equal to this marginal subjective cost.

Before leaving this world of measurable utility, let us note that in view of the assumed constancy of p, a dollar's worth of commodities or real balances in any week is represented by $1/p$ (p. 28). Substituting this into (1) and (2) then enables us to write these marginal conditions in the somewhat more familiar form

(5)   m.u. of Z_t = m.u. of $\dfrac{M_t}{p}$ + m.u. of Z_{t+1},

(6)   m.u. of Z_t = $(1 + r)$ m.u. of Z_{t+1}.

Let us now translate these last two marginal conditions into ordinal terms. The results of this translation can be made more meaningful by first considering the individual's budget restraints, which have so far been kept in the background of the analysis. There is one such restraint for every week within the individual's economic horizon. Each states that the real value of the individual's demand for commodities during the week plus his demands for bond and money holdings at its end must equal the income of that week plus the real value of the bond and money holdings which he demanded at the end of the preceding week and carried over from then.[19] By assumption, the individual's weekly

[19] Cf. p. 70 above.

income (his initial endowment of commodities) is exogenously given. Thus the budget restraint tells us that only four of the five demand-decisions which it relates for any week can be independently made. Alternatively, only two of the three decisions on commodity consumption, *change* in bond holdings, and *change* in money holdings during the week can be independently made.

Without loss of generality,[20] we can now adopt the simplifying assumption that the bond and money holdings for the end of (say) week $t + 1$ are independently chosen, so that the relevant budget restraint implies that the individual has only two independent decisions to make as amongst the three goods: commodities in week $t + 1$, bond holdings at the end of week t, and money holdings at the end of week t. It is then clear that the individual's decision on the marginal quantity of commodities to purchase in week $t + 1$ entails a decision on the marginal quantities of bonds and money to hold at the end of week t in order to finance this purchase. In other words, the marginal demand for commodities in any week is really a *joint demand* for these commodities and for the asset used to carry over the necessary marginal purchasing power from the preceding week.

The individual can accordingly be considered as independently deciding for any week upon his demands for two goods which we shall conceptualize, respectively, as "commodities via bonds" and "commodities via money." The quantity of each of these goods is measured as the real value of the relevant asset carried over from the preceding week. The marginal utility of each of these goods is the marginal utility of the asset in question for the liquidity it affords (zero, in the case of bonds) *plus* the marginal utility of its value-equivalent in commodities. Finally, the marginal rate of substitution (m.r.s.) between either of these goods and any other one—the rate at which the individual can substitute one good for the other without changing his level of total utility—is, as usual, equal to the ratio of the marginal utilities of the goods in question.

Applying these definitions to equations (5) and (6), we obtain, respectively, as the optimum conditions for the individual,

---

[20] In technical terms, an individual in his optimum position cannot increase his utility by any change in his demand decisions that accords with his budget restraints. Hence in deriving our necessary conditions for an optimum we can stipulate any such change. See Mathematical Appendix 6:*a*, especially p. 459.

(7)   m.r.s. of Z_t for Z_{t+1} via money $= \dfrac{\text{m.u. of } Z_t}{\text{m.u. of } M_t/p + \text{m.u. of } Z_{t+1}} = 1,$

and

(8)   m.r.s. of Z_t for Z_{t+1} via bonds $= \dfrac{\text{m.u. of } Z_t}{\text{m.u. of } Z_{t+1}} = 1 + r.$

Note that "m.u. of Z_{t+1}" in the denominator of (7) is necessarily equal to the corresponding term in the denominator of (8): for both refer to the marginal utility of the optimum quantity of commodities in week $t + 1$.

Alternatively, dividing (7) by (8) we can write

m.r.s. of Z_{t+1} via bonds for Z_{t+1} via money

(9)
$$= \frac{\text{m.u. of } Z_{t+1}}{\text{m.u. of } M_t/p + \text{m.u. of } Z_{t+1}}$$

$$= \frac{1}{1 + r}.$$

This last can properly be designated as the marginal rate of substitution of bonds for money.[21]

---

[21] The foregoing has been based on the assumption that bond holdings are not liquid, so that

(a)   m.u. of Z_{t+1} via bonds = m.u. of Z_{t+1}.

If, however, bonds are also assumed to have some degree of liquidity—and thus to provide direct utility similar to that of money balances—then we would have

(b)   m.u. of Z_{t+1} via bonds = m.u. of real bond holdings at end of week t
            + m.u. of Z_{t+1}.

The analysis can then be generalized to this case by simply substituting the right-hand side of (b) for that of (a) in equations (2), (6), (8), and (9).

This assumption has not been followed in the text because of the difficulties of giving it an economic interpretation in our present model. Thus, for example, since the bonds issued by the individual are identical with those he purchases, he need not hold bonds for liquidity purposes: he can instead simply issue a bond of his own during the week should he run out of cash. As we shall, however, see in Chapter VI:2, the assumption that bond holdings are directly represented in the utility function can be made economically meaningful in other cases. In any event, the detailed analysis of this assumption in the present case has been relegated to Mathematical Appendix 6:c–d.

Remembering that the price of both commodities and real money holdings is p, we see that the foregoing equations simply reflect the familiar necessary condition that the optimum marginal rate of substitution between any two goods equal the ratio of their prices. Indeed, the only reason for the somewhat unusual form this condition takes in equation (7) is the additional interdependence amongst demand-decisions caused by the fact that our individual is restricted by several budget restraints and not (as in the usual n-good case) just one.[22]

The foregoing development is particularly helpful for the insight it provides into the role of the rate of interest. The analogy of this rate to a relative price—already employed in Chapter IV: 2—is immediately apparent from equation (8) or (9). From these equations we also see that this rate operates simultaneously on the individual's margin of choice between present and future consumption—that is, on his saving decisions; and on his margin of choice between holding money and holding bonds—that is, on his liquidity decisions. Were we to extend our theory from an exchange to a production economy, this twofold margin would become a threefold one; for the rate of interest would then operate on the margin of investment decisions as well. This triple role of the rate of interest was duly recognized by neoclassical monetary theorists.[23]

In any event, we see from equations (7)–(8) and the budget restraints that the individual's optimum collection of real goods over his economic horizon depends on the rate of interest, the anticipated stream of real income over time, and the real value of initial bond and money holdings. In this way we have deduced the excess-demand functions of Chapter IV from the principle of utility maximization.[24] Similarly, the graphical analysis of the next three sections will show that these functions have the properties that have been attributed to them.

To return for a moment to the assumption of measurable utility, we might note that the foregoing derivation of illusion-free demand functions—and the consequent microeconomic validation of the quantity theory of money—does not depend on any assumed special

[22] For a geometric interpretation of this difference, see Mathematical Appendixes 6:a (especially footnote 6) and 6:d (especially footnote 23).

[23] For emphasis on this fact, see D. H. Robertson, *Essays in Monetary Theory* (London, 1940), pp. 16–17; "threefold margin" is, of course, his term. Nevertheless, neoclassical economists were guilty of some minor confusions on this matter; see Note D, especially p. 579.

[24] Cf. Mathematical Appendix 6:a.

relationship between the magnitude of real-money balances and their marginal utility. In particular, it does *not* depend on the assumption that the doubling of the nominal balances demanded, prices constant, is accompanied by the halving of the marginal utility of a dollar held in these balances.[25] All that is required for the validity of the quantity theory is that this marginal utility (like any other one) diminish. It then follows from marginal condition (5) that in order to return to an optimum position the individual will divert part of the aforementioned increase in balances to finance the increased purchase of commodities; that is, the real-balance effect will manifest itself. Nothing, however, need be specified about the extent of the diminution in the marginal utility of money, just as nothing need be specified about the magnitude of the real-balance effect (p. 45, above).

On the other hand, it is true that a doubling of nominal balances demanded *and* prices is accompanied by a halving of the marginal utility of a dollar held in cash balances. But this assumption is simply an expression of the fact that the doubling of the price level has halved the amount of *real* liquid purchasing power that is acquired by adding a dollar to money balances.[26] In other words, it is merely a reflection of the individual's freedom from money illusion.

Having displayed all the paraphernalia of the utility analysis, we must now assure ourselves that it is dispensable. The basic money-illusion property of the excess-demand functions can instead be derived by simply considering the individual's budget restraints from the viewpoint of revealed preferences. Any change which affects the real value of the individual's initial and future collections of goods or the terms on which he can exchange them for other goods will affect these restraints and hence the nature of the optimum collection. Clearly, however, an equiproportionate change in prices and initial bond and money holdings, interest being kept constant, leaves unaffected the collections of real goods from which the individual is free and able to

[25] This is emphasized here because of the allegation by Mises that the validity of the quantity theory depends on just this assumption; see Note D below, p. 575.

[26] That is, as noted above (p. 91),

$$\text{m.u. of a dollar's worth of } \frac{M_t}{p} = \frac{1}{p} \text{ m.u. of } \frac{M_t}{p} .$$

Hence the change just described in the text will halve $1/p$, while leaving M_t/p—and hence m.u. of M_t/p—unaffected.

choose. Hence, if he is consistent, he will again choose the same collection of real goods. Of such simple consistency is the absence of money illusion brewed.[27]

4. THE ARGUMENT PRESENTED GRAPHICALLY: THE BUDGET RESTRAINTS

The foregoing analysis can be made more concrete by presenting it in terms of a Fisherine individual with an economic horizon of two periods—designated, respectively, as "present" and "future".[28] We shall, however, depart from the usual Fisherine framework in two respects: first, in assuming that the individual carries over purchasing power from one period to the other by holding a portfolio which consists of money as well as bonds; second, in describing the individual's budgetary restriction not by a single wealth restraint relating to his economic horizon as a whole, but by two weekly restraints. The implications of these two assumptions for the Fisherine analysis will be examined in detail in Section 7 below.

The individual's budget restraints have the form

$$(10) \qquad Z_1 + \frac{1}{1+r}\frac{B_1}{p} + \frac{M_1}{p} = \bar{Z}_1 + \frac{B_0}{p} + \frac{M_0}{p} = R_1 ,$$

$$(11) \qquad Z_2 = \bar{Z}_2 + \frac{B_1}{p} + \frac{M_1}{p} ,$$

where Z_1 and Z_2 represent, respectively, present and future commodities demanded; $\bar{Z}_1$ and $\bar{Z}_2$, the given initial and future endowments of

---

[27] See Mathematical Appendix 6:*b*. Samuelson has provided a lucid explanation of his method of revealed preferences in "Consumption Theorems in Terms of Overconsumption Rather Than Indifference Comparisons," *Economica*, XX (1953), 1–9.

The validity of the present argument clearly depends on the assumption that the individual is concerned only with the real value of his money balances (above, p. 80). Correspondingly, the "distance" between the conclusion (absence of money illusion) and the assumption is indeed modest!

[28] The unrealism of this assumption could be attenuated by assuming that the "future" is longer than the "present." Indeed, as Leontief has shown, the Fisherine analysis can be extended to the case in which the future is infinitely long; see his "Theoretical Note on Time-Preference, Productivity of Capital, Stagnation and Economic Growth," *op. cit.*, pp. 104–105. For a more rigorous treatment, see Liviatan, "Multiperiod Future Consumption as an Aggregate," forthcoming.

these commodities; B_0 and M_0, the given initial endowments of bonds and money, respectively; R_1, the real value of the total initial endowment (for convenience, we shall also make use of the symbol $R_2 = \bar{Z}_2$); B_1, the number of one-dollar bonds the individual plans to carry over from the first to second week; and M_1, the corresponding amount of money.

The form of budget restraint (11) reflects the assumption that the individual's planned holdings of bonds and money at the end of the economic horizon are zero. This means that he must by that time have paid off any debts incurred in the first week. More generally, he will during the second week liquidate his entire portfolio $(B_1 + M_1)$ for the purpose of financing the purchases of commodities. In order to bring out this function of these assets, let us rewrite the foregoing restraints as

(12) $$Z_1 + \frac{1}{1+r}\, Z_{2B} + Z_{2M} = R_1 \, ,$$

(13) $$Z_2 = R_2 + Z_{2B} + Z_{2M} \, ,$$

where $Z_{2B} = B_1/p$ and $Z_{2M} = M_1/p$ represent future commodities via bonds and money, respectively (see p. 92).

Equations (12) and (13) describe the budgetary interrelationships of the individual's four decision variables: Z_1, Z_{2B}, Z_{2M}, and Z_2. Our first objective is to make use of the relatively simple transformations described by these equations in order to represent all four variables on a two-dimensional diagram. This is done in Figure V-2.

Since bonds can assume negative as well as positive values (the individual can borrow as well as lend), the horizontal axis of Figure V-2 extends into the negative quadrant. On the other hand, since money, by definition, can only be positive, the effective part of the vertical axis is only the positive segment; the negative segment has nevertheless been drawn (as a dashed line) for reasons that will become clear from what follows.

Every point in Figure V-2 represents a certain portfolio of bonds and money. In the right-hand quadrant, the quantities of both these financial assets are positive. In the left-hand quadrant, bonds are negative and money is positive; that is, the individual here is using at least part of his borrowings to finance the holding of cash balances.

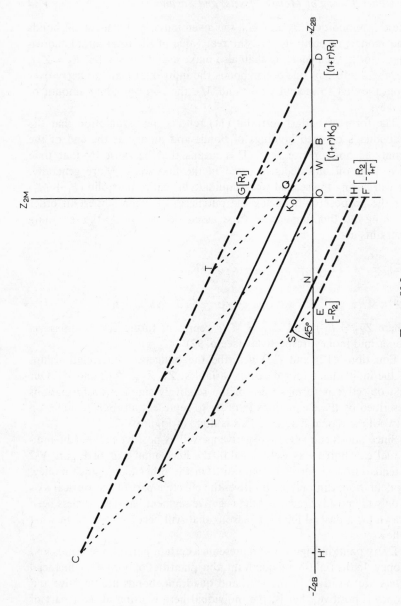

FIGURE V-2.

What must now be emphasized is that every point in Figure V-2 also represents a certain combination of present and future consumption. Thus consider the point Q. Pass through this point a straight line AB with the slope $-1/(1 + r)$.[29] Let the Y-intercept of this line be K_0. Then it is clear that the equation of this line is given by budget restraint (12), with Z_1 set equal to $Z_1^0 = R_1 - K_0$. Hence, if point G on the Y-axis represents R_1, the level of present consumption corresponding to portfolio Q can be read off Figure V-2 as the distance GK_0. Clearly, this same level corresponds to all the portfolios on line AB; for they all represent a net real current expenditure on financial assets of K_0.

Equation (12) thus rewritten also shows us that the lower Z_1, the higher the foregoing budget line. Indeed, since by definition consumption cannot be negative, this line is bounded from above by line CD, corresponding to $Z_1 = 0$. On the other hand, any budget line that lies below OL corresponds to a level of present consumption which exceeds present income (R_1). Thus SN corresponds to consumption which exceeds R_1 by the intercept on the Y-axis, OH. Similarly, point E corresponds to present consumption equal to $R_1 + R_2/(1 + r)$, which, for reasons that will become apparent in a moment, is the maximum level that can be achieved.

Though all the points on AB represent portfolios of the same *current* value K_0, their *maturity* values are clearly different. In particular, the heavier the bond composition of the portfolios described by AB, the greater their respective maturity values, and hence the larger the purchases of future commodities they can finance. In graphical terms, the more rightward a point on AB, the greater the value of Z_2 it represents. Indeed, we can see from (13) that constant levels of Z_2 are represented in Figure V-2 by the dotted straight lines of negative unitary slope; and that the lower Z_2, the more leftward these lines, until in the limit they reach the line CE representing a value of Z_2 equal to zero. In this way we also see that the constant value of Z_2 corresponding to the dotted line TW—and hence to point Q on budget line AB—can be read off Figure V-2 as EW. Similarly, ED represents the maximum possible level of Z_2, which equals $(1 + r)R_1 + R_2$.

Thus the relevant set of portfolios among which the individual must make his choice is defined by obtuse triangle CDE. Note that at every

[29] For clarity of the graphical representation, r has been chosen as equal to 0.5.

point in this triangle the individual is exhausting all his resources; thus the triangle as a whole corresponds to the budget line in the ordinary theory of consumer's choice. As we have already seen, vertices E and D of this triangle respectively represent the situations in which the individual devotes all of his resources to the purchase of present and future commodities. At vertex C, on the other hand, these purchases are both zero, and the individual devotes all his resources to the holding of cash balances. These balances are then used in the second period for debt repayment. In this way we can understand why vertex C also represents the maximum amount of debt that the individual can undertake: for, as we can see from equation (11), at any other point in triangle CDE he could always increase his future wherewithal for debt repayment either by decreasing Z_2, or by decreasing Z_1 and increasing M_1 accordingly.[30]

From this it is clear that the contrast between these results and the familiar Fisherine implication that the maximum amount that an individual can borrow is the discounted value of his future income stems from the existence in our model of a second asset, money, that the individual can carry into the future and use then for debt repayment. The present discussion can, however, be cast into Fisherine form by restating the limitation of the latter in terms of the net maturity value of the individual's portfolio as a whole. For, as is obvious from (13), this cannot exceed future income.

Our problem now is to determine the individual's optimum point within triangle CDE. Indeed, the first question that arises in this context is why this point must not necessarily lie on the line segment

---

[30] Mathematically, if we set $Z_1 = Z_2 = 0$ in equations (12) and (13) and solve them out, we obtain the coordinates of vertex C as

$$-\hat{Z}_{2B} = R_2 + \frac{(1+r)W_0}{r},$$

$$\hat{Z}_{2M} = \frac{(1+r)W_0}{r},$$

where $W_0 = R_1 + R_2/(1+r)$ is the individual's wealth. $\hat{Z}_{2M}$ thus represents the use by the individual of all of the resources that will be available to him at the beginning of next week [and these will by then have grown to $(1+r)W_0$] to pay for the liquidity services of money balances (whose imputed unit price is, of course, r). Correspondingly $-\hat{Z}_{2B}$ represents the use of these money balances as well as next week's receipts for the exclusive purpose of debt repayment.

Note too that geometrically $OH' = OE + EH' = OE + CH'$.

ED on the *X*-axis. For under the assumptions so far made, the dotted 45° lines constitute an indifference map in the sense that each such line represents a constant level of Z_2, and hence (given the level of Z_1) a constant level of utility. Hence the optimal position corresponding to any budget line parallel to *CD* (i.e., to any given level of Z_1) is at the corner on the *X*-axis where this line touches the highest attainable 45° line (i.e., the highest attainable level of Z_2). What is it, then, in the nature of money and bonds that makes them imperfect substitutes and thus creates the possibility that the individual may choose an interior point of triangle *CDE*? In more familiar terms, why should an individual be willing to hold money when he can instead hold interest-bearing bonds? This basic methodological question of monetary theory has been answered in Section 1 above in terms of an assumed bother of converting bonds into money. It remains to give graphical expression to this assumption.

5. The Argument Presented Graphically: The Indifference Maps. The Nature of the Optimum Position

Our graphical presentation proceeds in two stages. First we shall assume that the level of Z_1 is fixed and shall analyze the problem of choosing an optimum combination of Z_{2B} and Z_{2M}; then we shall take account of the fact that the individual is also free to choose his optimum level of Z_1.

The main geometrical implication of the assumed inconvenience of converting money into bonds is that the indifference map between Z_{2B} and Z_{2M} (as of a given level of Z_1) no longer consists of the family of 45° straight lines. For consider a southeast movement along such a line from (say) point *M* in Figure V-3. This will now clearly worsen the position of the individual: for though it will not affect the amount of Z_2 that he can buy, it will—by replacing money by an equivalent amount of bonds—increase the probability that he will run out of money reserves during the week and thus have to carry out a bond conversion. In brief, though not affecting his future commodity consumption, such a movement will decrease the liquidity of his portfolio. Hence, in order to keep the individual as well off as before, we must increase one or both of the components of his portfolio. Correspondingly, the slope of the indifference curve must be less than unity in absolute value.

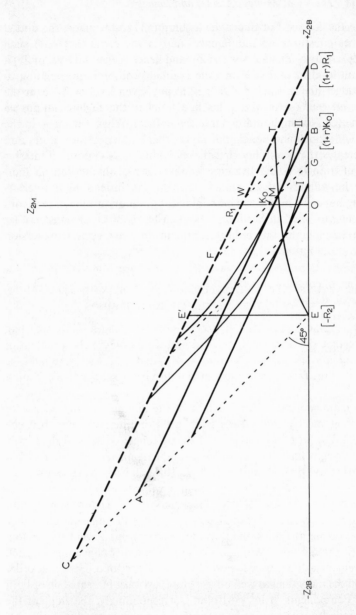

FIGURE V-3.

It should however be clear that this argument does not hold at any point within triangle $EE'C$ in Figure V-3. For any such point represents a portfolio whose money component Z_{2M} exceeds the planned volume of expenditures Z_2. Hence an exchange of bonds for money in this region of "money satiety" will still leave the individual's "reserve ratio" above 100 per cent and hence will not effectively alter his situation. Correspondingly, indifference curves I and II in Figure V-3 are drawn with a unitary slope in this region.[31]

It is clear from the foregoing that the utility index of any portfolio represented on these curves takes account both of the net liquidity of the portfolio and of the quantity of future commodities whose purchase it will finance.[32] Other special properties of this indifference map can be briefly noted as follows: First it must clearly lie within triangle CDE. Second, just like the budget lines, it extends into the negative quadrant of Figure V-3. At the same time we should recall that the relevant region here represents *positive* quantities of present and future commodities, as well as, of course, money. Finally, the slope of the indifference curves reflects the degree of illiquidity of bonds—the inconvenience involved in converting them into money during the week. The less this inconvenience, the closer the slope (in absolute value) to unity. In the limiting case in which this inconvenience disappears completely—in which, that is, bonds are completely liquid—money and bonds would be perfect

[31] Note that the vertical line EE' is the locus of portfolios whose money component exactly equals future expenditures: i.e., $Z_{2M} = Z_2$. This can accordingly be called the "satiety line."

The definitions of "satiety region" and "satiety line" here presented differ from those of my "Indirect Utility Approach to the Theory of Money, Assets, and Savings," *op. cit.*, p. 63.

[32] This can also readily be seen from the analytical derivation of these curves. Let the individual's utility function be

(a) $$U = f\left(Z_1, \frac{M_1}{p}, Z_2; \frac{M_0}{p}\right),$$

where, by assumption, M_0/p is a constant. Set $Z_1 = Z_1^0$ and substitute from (11) to yield—after changing our notation to accord with (12) and (13), and ignoring M_0/p because of its constancy—

(b) $$U = g(Z_1^0, Z_{2M}, R_2 + Z_{2B} + Z_{2M}).$$

The indifference map in Figure V-3 depicts this function as of different levels of utility U. The slope of any curve in this map is represented by the first equality in equation (9) (p. 93) above, after taking account of the fact that the marginal utility of cash balances is zero in the satiety region, and greater than zero rightwards of it.

substitutes, so that the indifference map would revert to the 45° lines which constituted the point of departure of this discussion (p. 101).

Assume that the fixed level of Z_1 on the basis of which the foregoing indifference map is drawn equals $R_1 - K_0$, so that—in accordance with budget restraint (12)—the relevant budget line in Figure V-3 is AB, with (absolute) slope $1/(1 + r)$. The corresponding optimum position is at point M, whose tangency conditions are described by

$$(14) \qquad \text{m.r.s. of } Z_{2B} \text{ for } Z_{2M} = \frac{1}{1 + r}.[33]$$

This, of course, is a particular instance of equation (9) above (p. 93). If r is positive, so that the (absolute) slope of the budget line and hence the optimum marginal rate of substitution is less than unity, this point of tangency must lie outside the satiety region $EE'C$. In the special case of a zero rate of interest, the slope of the budget line becomes unitary in absolute value, and the optimum position will be assumed to be on the satiety line EE' itself, though it could just as well be at any other point on the budget line in the satiety region. For under this assumption there is no budgetary limit on the individual's ability to borrow in order to finance the holding of cash balances—a fact which expresses itself graphically in the degeneration of triangle CDE into an infinite parallelogram.

An additional aspect of the optimum portfolio can be illustrated by considering the path generated by holding interest and the income stream constant and changing the level of current consumption Z_1 under the assumption that such changes leave the indifference map invariant. The locus of points of tangency traced out by the resulting parallel shifts in the budget line AB is represented in Figure V-3 by the curve ET. The positive slope of this curve reflects the assumption that the higher the level of planned future expenditure, the higher the demand for cash balances. On the other hand, the economies of scale which characterize money holdings (p. 87) are assumed to cause this demand to increase less than proportionately—and this despite the assumption that the increased income also increases the individual's desire to avoid

[33] Note that this result can be derived analytically by maximizing U in equation (b) of the preceding footnote, subject to budget restraint (12), with Z_1 set equal to $Z_1^0 = R_1 - K_0$. The conversion of (a) into (b) in this footnote is, of course, the way in which budget restraint (13) is also taken account of.

the inconvenience of running out of cash. The net implication of these assumptions reflects itself in the convexity and sharp leveling off of the path *ET*.

Let us now drop the assumption that the value of Z_1 is arbitrarily fixed and extend the analysis to explain the determination of the optimum value of this variable as well. The first step is to define the composite good[34]

$$(15) \qquad P = \frac{1}{1+r} Z_{2B} + Z_{2M}.$$

Thus *P* is the real value of the individual's portfolio in the first week: i.e., with bond holdings discounted at the going rate of interest. Clearly, higher values of *P* correspond to higher budget lines in Figure V-3. Accordingly, the maximum value of *P* corresponds to *CD*, and the minimum value to that budget line parallel to *CD* and passing through *E*: for any respectively higher or lower budget line would lie entirely outside the set of attainable points delimited by triangle *CDE*. Since budget line *CD* corresponds to $Z_1 = 0$, the maximum value of *P* determined by it is seen from (12) to be R_1. Similarly, since point *E* corresponds to $Z_1 = R_1 + R_2/(1 + r)$, the minimum value of *P* is determined from (12) as $-R_2/(1 + r)$. Note too that the budget line which corresponds to a zero value of *P* is *OL* in Figure V-2.

As already indicated, these results correspond in a broader sense to those of the usual Fisherine analysis. They reflect the intuitive observation that an individual makes the maximum addition to his portfolio by foregoing present consumption entirely and adding all of his current income to his asset holdings; and that he incurs maximum indebtedness—which by the necessity of future repayment is limited to the discounted value of future income—when he plans to forego all future consumption, including that of liquidity services. Note once again that the existence of a second asset, money, causes a divergence between a position of maximum *indebtedness* and one of maximum *borrowing*. Indeed, as we have already seen (p. 100), the latter position—which is depicted by point *C* in Figure V-3—represents the individual's devotion of all of his wealth to future consumption (of, namely, liquidity services); hence it corresponds to a *maximum* value of *P*.

[34] The following argument should be read against the background of the graphical presentation of the composite-good theorem in Mathematical Appendix 2:*c*.

The X-axis and the two dashed vertical lines in Figure V-4 thus mark off the limits within which the indifference map and budget line for P and Z_1 must lie. It is obvious from (12) that this budget line has the form

(16) $Z_1 + P = R_1.$

Hence at the optimum point T we must have

(17)   m.r.s. of Z_1 for $P = \dfrac{\text{m.u. of } Z_1}{\text{m.u. of } P} = 1.$

But the marginal utility of the composite good is, by definition,

(18)   m.u. of $P = \dfrac{\text{m.u. of } Z_{2B}}{1/(1 + r)} = \text{m.u. of } Z_{2M}.$

Substituting these into (17), we then obtain statements of our marginal conditions in the form of equations (7) and (8) above (p. 93).

The method of analysis is now clear. From Figure V-4 we determine the optimum quantities of Z_1 and P. This fixes the budget line and indifference map in Figure V-3 and thereby enables us to determine the optimum quantities of Z_{2M} and Z_{2B}, and thereby Z_2. This description, however, should not make us lose sight of the fact that the composite good P cannot be defined—and Figure V-4 cannot therefore be constructed—without a prior analysis of the indifference maps in Figure V-3.[35]

6. PROPERTIES OF THE DEMAND FUNCTIONS. THE INADEQUACY OF LIQUIDITY THEORIES OF INTEREST

Let us now use the foregoing diagrams to derive some of the properties of the excess-demand functions of Chapter IV. The absence of money illusion can immediately be inferred from the fact that an equiproportionate change in p, B_0, and M_0 does not shift the budget lines in Figures V-3 and V-4 and hence does not affect the individual's optimum position. On the other hand, an increase in M_0 or B_0 alone— or a decrease in p alone—causes the budget lines of both diagrams to shift to the right and hence (abstracting from the possibility of inferiority)

[35] Cf. again Mathematical Appendix 2:c.

increases the amounts demanded of commodities, bonds, and money.[36] Here, then, is the microeconomic rationale of the real-balance effect. It is also readily apparent that these conclusions actually stand free of any utility underpinning and follow directly from the revealed preferences of an assumedly consistent individual.[37]

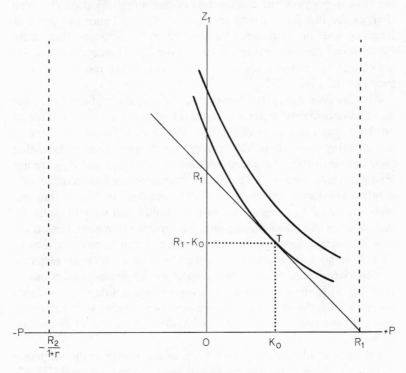

FIGURE V-4.

[36] There is, however, a complication here. Since the utility function depends on M_0/p (above, p. 103, footnote 32), a change in p will generally also cause a shift in the indifference maps of Figures V-3 and V-4. In order to determine the effects of a change in p, we must accordingly specify something about the nature of this shift. It is, however, possible to assume this problem away by assuming that the utility function in footnote 32 is separable (i.e., the sum of functions in which each of the arguments appears by itself), so that the marginal rates of substitution among Z_1, Z_{2B}, and Z_{2M} (and hence the aforementioned indifference maps) are unaffected by changes in M_0/p.

[37] Cf. end of Section 3 above.

Consider now the effects of a decrease in the rate of interest. This obviously causes the relevant budget line in Figure V-3 to become more steeply sloped. At the same time—by virtue of its effect on the optimum quantity of Z_1—it also changes the Y-intercept of this line. This latter shift is the consequence of the fact that the decrease in interest changes the relative prices of the components of the composite good P; hence changes the indifference map in Figure V-4; and hence the point of tangency with the unchanged budget line $R_1 R_1$. Note too that unless the marginal rate of substitution of Z_{2B} for Z_{2M} is independent of Z_1, the change in the latter will also cause a shift in the relevant indifference map of Figure V-3.

It is thus clear that in the absence of additional assumptions we cannot make an unequivocal statement about the effects of a change in interest on the demand functions of the individual and, *a fortiori*, of those of the economy as a whole. Accordingly, let us now assume, first, that there are no distribution effects and, second, that Z_{2B} and Z_{2M} are not Hicksian complements.[38] The latter assumption implies that the substitution effect of a reduction in interest manifests itself in a shift out of bonds and into money. The former implies that since the total net debt of our closed exchange economy is by definition zero, this reduction in interest does not in the aggregate generate any net income effect.[39] In brief, the reactions of debtors (who have been made better off by this change) are offset in this respect by the opposite reactions of creditors. Thus these two assumptions specify market demand functions for both money and bonds that are negatively sloped with respect to their relevant prices: r in the case of money, and $1/(1 + r)$ in the case of bonds.

Let us now analyze the implications of a decrease in the illiquidity of bonds—which in the present model means a decrease in the bother connected with converting them into money. Once again, in the absence

[38] The possibility of complementarity arises from the fact that there are three goods: Z_1, Z_{2B}, and Z_{2M}. See Hicks, *Value and Capital*, Chapter III; cf. also end of Mathematical Appendix 2:*c* below.

[39] Note that this argument does not hold in a production economy with investment; for then the fact that current consumption differs from current production (income) means that there will be an income effect even in the aggregate. We shall, however, assume that this effect is positive. See D. V. T. Bear, "The Relationship of Saving to the Rate of Interest, Real Income, and Expected Future Prices," *Review of Economics and Statistics*, XLIII (1961), 27–35.

of additional assumptions, no definite statements can be made: for the changed illiquidity of bonds causes a shift in the indifference map of Figure V-3, hence in that of Figure V-4, and hence also a shift of the budget line in Figure V-3. If, however, this last shift is assumed to be of a second order of magnitude as compared with that in the shapes of the indifference map in Figure V-3, and if, in addition, this map is assumed independent of the level of Z_1, then the effect of making bonds less illiquid will be to increase the demand for bonds and decrease that for money. This follows from the fact that the marginal rate of substitution of bonds for money at the original equilibrium point M in Figure V-3 is now increased. In graphical terms the new indifference curve through M will cut the original budget line from above. Hence—under the usual convexity assumption—the new point of tangency with a new budget line not too far from the original one must be southeast of M. Note, however, that even if the shift in the budget line is a significant one, it is reasonable to assume that there will at least take place a *relative* increase in the demand for bonds as compared with that for money.

It should be emphasized that we are dealing here only with the individual-experiment; the effects of a decrease in the illiquidity of bonds on the equilibrium levels of interest and prices must be analyzed within the framework of the relevant market-experiment. This must be deferred to Chapter X:4. There it will be shown that—under the assumptions of the preceding paragraph—decreasing the illiquidity of bonds decreases the equilibrium rate of interest; but that even in the case where bonds are completely monetized, there is no reason why this rate must fall to zero. To speak somewhat loosely, the primary manifestation of an increased liquidity for bonds is not a lowered rate of interest, but a decreased use of money as a medium of exchange. Correspondingly, the end result of making bonds completely liquid is to eliminate not the rate of interest but the use of money.[40] In this limiting case the medium of exchange would consist only of bonds, whose rate of interest would continue to reflect the traditional forces of thrift and capital productivity.

The foregoing discussion suffices to demonstrate the untenability of any theory which attempts to explain the rate of interest solely in terms of the imperfect liquidity of bonds. In particular, it shows that the basic proposition of Hicks' development of the Keynesian theory—

[40] Cf. pp. 103–104 above.

namely, that in the absence of such imperfections the rate of interest would disappear—is involved in a *non sequitur*.[41] Imperfect liquidity is an important element of interest theory—particularly for the explanation of interest differentials; but it is not a *sine qua non* of this theory. Correspondingly, the logical problem solved by Keynes and Hicks is not, as they believed, the existence of interest, but rather the peaceful coexistence of money and interest-bearing bonds.

7. The Relationship to the Fisherine Time-Preference Theory

The question which naturally arises at this point—and which has been adumbrated in part—is the relationship of the preceding to Fisher's "time-preference" theory. As is well known,[42] in its simplified form this analyzes the way in which a two-period individual allocates his expected income stream (R_1, R_2) optimally as between present (E_1) and future (E_2) consumption. If the individual should choose to concentrate his entire consumption in the present, he would borrow all he could on the basis of his future income and thus be able to consume currently his total wealth,

$$W_0 = R_1 + \frac{1}{1+r} R_2.$$

This is represented by point F in Figure V-5. Alternatively, if he should concentrate all his consumption in the future, he would use all of his current income to buy interest-bearing bonds and thus be able to consume $(1+r)W_0$. The line FH, whose equation is

$$(19) \qquad E_1 + \frac{1}{1+r} E_2 = W_0,$$

thus represents the individual's budget restraint over his economic horizon. Note that it must pass through the point S: for the individual

[41] Hicks, *Value and Capital*, p. 165. This *non sequitur* has already been noted by F. Modigliani, "Liquidity Preference and the Theory of Interest and Money," *Econometrica*, XXII (1944), as reprinted in *Readings in Monetary Theory*, pp. 233–35; and by P. A. Samuelson, *Foundations of Economic Analysis* (Cambridge, Mass., 1947), p. 123.

[42] See Fisher's *Theory of Interest*, especially Chapters V and X. See also Boulding, *Economic Analysis*, pp. 746–53.

can always choose a time pattern of consumption identical with his time pattern of income. Note too that, by construction, different points on this budget line represent different amounts of borrowing or lending —the magnitude of which is proportionate to the distance of the point in question from S. Thus in addition to the goods which appear explicitly on its axes, Figure V-5 also implicitly describes the quantity of bonds which the individual holds.

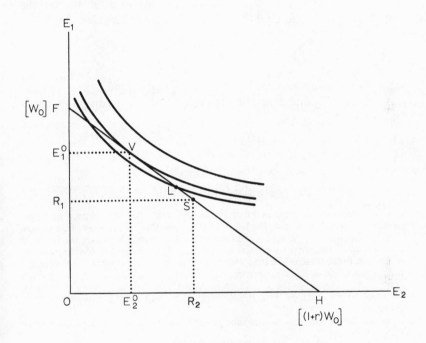

FIGURE V-5.

Each of the indifference curves in Figure V-5 represents equally satisfactory combinations of present and future consumption. As usual, the optimum combination is determined by the point of tangency (V) with the budget line and is described analytically by the familiar marginal condition

(20) $$\text{m.r.s. of } E_1 \text{ for } E_2 = \frac{\text{m.u. of } E_1}{\text{m.u. of } E_2} = 1 + r.$$

Simultaneously with this optimum combination of commodities, Figure V-5 also determines—as a residual—the optimum holdings of bonds. These can be measured at either their discounted $(R_1 - E_0^1)$ or maturity $(E_2^0 - R_2)$ value.[43]

It can now readily be shown that the Fisherine analysis can be extended so as to yield results identical with those of the preceding sections. First, present consumption E_1 is defined as equal to Z_1. On the other hand, future consumption is defined so as to include the imputed value of the liquidity services of money balances. That is,[44]

$$(21) \qquad E_2 = Z_2 + r\left(\frac{M_1}{p}\right).$$

Thus E_2 is a composite good defined as the real expenditure on optimal collections of Z_2 and M_1/p; that is, collections which satisfy the marginal condition

$$(22) \qquad \text{m.u. of } Z_2 = \frac{\text{m.u. of } M_1/p}{r},$$

which in turn is defined as the marginal utility of E_2. From the construction of this composite good it is clear that "m.u. of M_1/p" refers

[43] We can now distinguish more precisely between the two senses of "time preference" noted in Chapter IV:1. In Fisher's sense, this is a property of the excess-demand functions for present and future goods and merely expresses the fact that the optimal time pattern of consumption generally differs from the given time pattern of income. In the sense of the later literature, however, this is a property of the utility function: specifically, time preference in this sense exists if the value of this function is affected by changes in the time sequence in which the individual plans to consume given collections of goods. Thus these two senses correspond to two distinct levels of discourse.

In the case at hand, absence of time preference in the latter sense reflects itself in the identity

$$u(E_1, E_2) \equiv u(E_2, E_1),$$

where $u(\ )$ is the utility function. Graphically this means that the indifference curves are symmetric about the 45° line emanating from the origin.

[44] It might also be contended that E_1 should be defined analogously to E_2, so as to include the imputed liquidity services of M_0/p. Any such imputation, however, would have to be based on an arbitrary evaluation: for since initial balances are given and not optimally selected, the rate of interest does not measure the value of their services at the margin. Furthermore, even if we were to add an arbitrary evaluation of these liquidity services to E_1, it would not affect the analysis: for we should then also have to add it to R_1, so that wealth restraint (19) would remain unchanged.

The foregoing asymmetry between E_1 and E_2 would disappear if we were to assume that the individual does not carry over stocks of money from week to week,

only to the marginal utility of holding money; in contrast to "m.u. of Z_{2M}" it does not include the marginal utility of future goods.[45]

Making use of this fact—as well as the assumption that m.u. of $Z_{2B} =$ m.u. of Z_2—enables us to reduce (14) to (22). Similarly, substituting from (22) into (17)—while taking note of (18)—then yields the Fisherine marginal condition (20). Finally, multiplying the weekly budget restraint (11) by $1/(1 + r)$ and adding it to (10) yields—after substitution from (21) —the over-all wealth restraint (19).

The only difference between the two analyses is, then, one of emphasis. Whereas the Fisherine analysis highlights the choice between present and future consumption (and is thus particularly appropriate for the theory of saving), the analysis of Sections 4–6 highlights the choice between present consumption and the future portfolio of assets, as well as the choice of the components of this portfolio (and is thus particularly appropriate for the theory of asset-holding).[46]

We note, however, that this equivalence no longer obtains if bonds too can meaningfully be assumed to possess some degree of liquidity and thus to provide utility *per se*.[47] Indeed, if this assumption can be made, the Fisherine analysis—with its main implication that an individual's behavior depends only on the discounted value of his income stream and not on its specific time shape—is not longer valid. The simplest way of seeing this is to note that there would then exist no

---

but merely rents them at the rate of interest r. Note that in this case (which is akin to the pure-inside-money case described on p. 297 below) there are no initial money balances and hence no real-balance effect. If, however, the nature of the bond obligation continues to be defined as above (p. 90), there would remain a real-indebtedness effect.

[45] Graphically, E_2 is constructed from an indifference map for Z_2 and M_1/p drawn as of a fixed value of Z_1. This means that—in order not to violate budget restraint (10)—a unit increase in money balances along any curve in this map must be assumed to be accompanied by a compensating unit increase in the discounted value of outstanding bonds. This is tantamount to assuming that money balances are rented at the cost of the interest that must be paid on these compensating increases in debt. Correspondingly, the relevant budget line for this map is given by (21).

[46] Note too that, just like the analysis of the preceding section (pp. 106–109), the two-dimensional Fisherine analysis runs into complications when used to study the effect of a change in interest. For this changes the relative price of the components of the composite good E_2, and hence the indifference map in Figure V-5.

For an analytical statement of the argument of the text, see Mathematical Appendix 6:*c–d*.

[47] Technically, the transformations described two paragraphs above cannot be carried out if equation (b) of footnote 21 on p. 93 holds.

asset whose rate of return would measure the individual's marginal rate of substitution of present for future commodities and hence the rate at which he discounts future consumption and income. For the rate of return on any asset will also reflect the liquidity it provides while being used to effect the transfer of purchasing power. Correspondingly, there would be no way of deriving a single, relevant wealth restraint for the individual's economic horizon as a whole. Instead, the analysis would then have to take account of the weekly budget restraints, which in turn means that changes in R_1 and R_2—and even changes which leave their discounted value invariant—will generally affect demand. For reasons already indicated, however, further discussion of this case has been relegated to the Mathematical Appendix.[48] We might, however, note that a case which raises similar problems will be discussed in detail in Chapter VI: 1–2 below.

8. THE RELATIONSHIP TO MARSHALL'S "MARGINAL UTILITY OF MONEY." THE "CIRCULARITY CHARGE" REFUTED

With the analysis of Sections 1–5 as our background, we can now conveniently discuss the two points in the literature mentioned at the beginning of this chapter.

Consider first Marshall's "marginal utility of money"—which is more appropriately termed the "marginal utility of money income," or, even better, "of money wealth." Its differentia from the "marginal utility of money balances" as it has been used here can be brought out most easily by considering the conceptual experiments that respectively lie behind these two measures. Thus Marshall's concept measures the outcome of the following experiment: We take an individual with a collection of goods that is the *optimum* one for the given price level, interest rate, and wealth (inclusive of initial bond and money holdings); increase his wealth by one dollar; and permit him to spend it in the optimum way. Finally, we note the difference between the total utility from his new optimum collection of goods as compared with that from his original one. Consideration of equations (1)–(2) on pp. 89–90 above shows that the marginal utility of wealth so measured must equal the marginal utility of a dollar's worth of expenditure on commodities in the current week.

[48] See p. 93, footnote 21 and Mathematical Appendix 6: *c–d*.

The marginal utility of money balances held at the end of the current week is measured by a completely different experiment: We take an individual with a given collection of goods (in general, *not* the optimum one) and increase his holdings of money balances at the end of the week by one dollar, while keeping constant all other components of his collection, as well as the price level.[49] We then note the increase in his utility resulting from the increased liquidity thus made possible. Clearly, there is no necessity for this increase to equal the marginal utility of wealth.

On the other hand, if this last experiment were performed on a collection of goods which happened to be an optimum one, there would clearly be a relationship between the two concepts. Thus we can see from equations (5)–(6) that if under these circumstances money balances at the end of the first week alone were increased, then the additional utility thereby generated would equal $r/(1 + r)$ of the marginal utility of wealth.[50] [51]

Let us turn now to the "circularity charge." According to this charge, the value of money—that is, the price level—cannot be said to be determined by its marginal utility. For the utility of a given nominal quantity of money depends on its real value, and this cannot itself be known until the price level has first been determined. Hence in speaking of the marginal utility of money, we would already be implicitly assuming what we had undertaken to explain.[52]

The discussion of the preceding sections makes it clear that this charge originates in a basic misunderstanding of the theory of price determination. It is, of course, true that money differs from other goods (making the usual reservations for "snob goods" and the like)

[49] Note that this implies that the additional dollar is subsequently destroyed, so that it cannot be used to increase the consumption or money balances of later weeks.

[50] Note, however, that if in the optimum position there were to take place a *permanent* increase in money balances, then—for an individual with an infinite horizon—the additional utility would equal the marginal utility of wealth; cf. p. 90, footnote 18 above.

[51] On all the above, see Mathematical Appendix 6:*e*.

On Marshall, see his *Principles of Economics* (8th ed., London, 1920), pp. 95–96 and 838–39. Marshall's discussion here is restricted to a one-period individual; but it can readily be generalized to the multiperiod individual of the text.

The foregoing discussion is also relevant for Hicks' use of the term "marginal utility of money," which follows that of Marshall; cf. *Value and Capital*, pp. 33, 38 ff.

[52] This summarizes the argument of K. Helfferich, *Money*, trans. L. Infield (London, 1927), pp. 526–27. For further references to the literature, see Note D below.

in that its marginal utility cannot be determined unless prices are first specified. But, for the question at hand, this is a completely irrelevant distinction. For what interests us here is not the subjective utility calculus as such, but its implications for the properties of the demand functions. And for this purpose no more need be specified for the good money than for any other good.

Thus consider the indifference curve analysis of Sections 4–5. It is clear that the optimum quantities of neither commodities nor money balances can be determined in the absence of the relevant budget lines. But the position of these lines, in turn, cannot be determined unless prices are first specified.[53]

In brief, here again is a confusion between types of experiments.[54] In a market-experiment, money prices are the variables whose values must be determined. Hence it would truly be a case of *petitio principii* to assume that prices are already determined. But in an individual-experiment, the amounts of excess demands are the variables to be determined, and money prices are the independent variables whose values *must* be given in order to conduct the experiment. Clearly, there is no circularity in stating that the market excess-demand equations derived from such individual-experiments are then used to determine the equilibrium money prices of the market-experiment.

In more familiar terms, we have here a confusion of "demand" with "amount demanded." It is true that the amount demanded of money—as well as of any other good—depends upon prices. Nevertheless, it is also true that the equilibrium prices depend upon the demand functions. The "circularity charge" is simply a denial of this elementary distinction.[55]

[53] Actually, for reasons noted on p. 107, footnote 36 above, this is also generally true for the position of the indifference maps. As explained in that footnote, however, this complication can be assumed away; it is therefore not really relevant to the circularity issue.

[54] See Chapters I:4 and III:6.

[55] So A. W. Marget, *The Theory of Prices* (New York, 1938), Vol. I, p. 445, footnote 86.

VI. A Utility Theory of Money, Assets, and Savings (Continued)

1. *The precautionary and speculative motives.*   2. *The implications of the precautionary and speculative motives for the Fisherine analysis.*   3. *Commodities as an asset.*   4. *The influence of price expectations on the real-balance effect and on the demand for money.*

1. THE PRECAUTIONARY AND SPECULATIVE MOTIVES

This chapter extends the argument of the preceding one in two different directions. This and the following section provide an alternative rationale—in terms of the precautionary motive—for the imperfect substitutability of money and bonds. Sections 3 and 4, on the other hand, show how the optimum conditions of Chapter V:3 can be modified and supplemented so as to take account of the possibility of holding commodities, as well as bonds and money. In both cases the implications of the argument for the Fisherine analysis are investigated in detail.

As in the preceding chapter, we continue in the present section to assume that money provides the utility of a contingency reserve against uncertainties. But the uncertainties which will now concern us are not those connected with the timing of payments and receipts, but those connected with the future value of bonds. Correspondingly, the demand for money that will now be analyzed is not of a transactions type, but the precautionary demand of individuals who forego interest and hold money balances in order to mitigate the uncertainty—and hence disutility—of holding their wealth solely in the form of bonds.[1,2]

An immediate consequence of this approach is a change in the concept of liquidity. This no longer represents absence of inconvenience, but the absence of uncertainty with respect to the future real value of an asset. Thus the liquidity of an asset is now defined in terms of its riskiness as subjectively evaluated by the individual. In a world in which there is no uncertainty about the future price level, but there is uncertainty about future interest rates, money is therefore a perfectly liquid asset, while bonds are not.

As a consequence of his uncertainty about the value of his bond holdings, the individual is also uncertain about the levels of consumption his portfolio will enable him to finance. It follows that he is no longer able to choose these levels in a determinate manner, but must instead suffice with choosing (subject to his budget restraints) the optimum probability distribution of possible consumption levels. For simplicity we shall assume that the only aspects of this distribution which concern him—that is, which are involved in his utility calculus—are its central tendency (as measured by expected values) and degree of dispersion (as measured by standard deviations). This can be rationalized either on the basis of the assumption that these parameters alone suffice to describe the probability distribution in its entirety, or on the assumption that the individual maximizes expected utility under a

---

[1] This and the following section more or less reproduce the corresponding discussion in my paper on "An Indirect-Utility Approach to the Theory of Money, Assets, and Savings" presented before the International Economic Association "Conference on the Theory of Interest Rates" (1962) and published in a shortened form in the proceedings volume of that conference [*The Theory of Interest Rates* (ed. F. H. Hahn and F. Brechling, London, 1965) pp. 52–79].

The present section is a revision of Section 4 of the foregoing paper in its published form (cf. *ibid.*, p. 69, footnote 1). In carrying out this revision, I have benefited from stimulating discussions with my colleague Nissan Liviatan.

[2] As will become clear to the reader, the following discussion owes a basic debt to Tobin's "Liquidity Preference as Behavior Toward Risk," *Review of Economic Studies*, XXV (1958), 65–86. See also H. Markowitz, "Portfolio Selection," *Journal of Finance*, VII (1952), 77–91.

The inappropriateness of identifying the following demand with Keynes' speculative demand has been explained by Tobin (*ibid.*, pp. 70, 85). This point has been even more strongly emphasized by H. G. Johnson, "The *General Theory* after Twenty-Five Years," *American Economic Review: Papers and Proceedings*, LI (1961), 8. Cf. also pp. 125–26 below.

quadratic utility function.[3] Clearly, these are not mutually exclusive interpretations.

In order to make the argument more precise, let us once again consider the two-period individual of Chapter V: 4, now assumed to be uncertain as to the future "maturity value" of the bonds he purchases. In particular, assume that, in addition to its interest yield, each such bond is subject to a random capital gain or loss, represented by ε.[4] Correspondingly, budget restraints (10) and (11) of the preceding chapter (p. 96) are replaced, respectively, by

$$(1) \qquad Z_1 + \frac{1}{1+r}\frac{B_1}{p} + \frac{M_1}{p} = \bar{Z}_1 + \frac{B_0(1+\varepsilon_1)}{p} + \frac{M_0}{p} = R_1 + \frac{B_0\varepsilon_1}{p}$$

and

$$(2) \qquad Z_2 = \bar{Z}_2 + \frac{B_1(1+\varepsilon_2)}{p} + \frac{M_1}{p},$$

where ε_1 and ε_2 (assumed to be independently distributed) are, respectively, the values of ε in the first and second weeks.[5] The mean and standard deviation of ε are assumed to be zero and σ, respectively. In order to add an element of realism to the analysis, we shall also assume that the lowest value ε can assume is -1: that is, the greatest decline that can occur in the maturity value of the bond is one which makes it worthless.

By our assumption two paragraphs above, the individual is assumed to act as if he were maximizing a utility function dependent on four variables: $E[Z_1]$, $E[Z_2]$, $\sigma(Z_1)$, and $\sigma(Z_2)$, where $E[\ ]$ and $\sigma(\ )$ respectively represent the expected value (mean) and standard deviation of

[3] See Tobin, "Liquidity Preference as Behavior Toward Risk," *op. cit.*, pp. 74–77.

On the expected-utility hypothesis, see the well-known article by M. Friedman and L. J. Savage, "The Utility Analysis of Choices Involving Risk," *Journal of Political Economy*, LVI (1948) as reprinted in *Readings in Price Theory* (ed. G. J. Stigler and K. E. Boulding, Chicago, 1952), pp. 57–96. See also Markowitz, *Portfolio Selection* (New York, 1959), Chapter 10.

[4] The analysis could be made more realistic by assuming that the individual has a horizon of n weeks and that bonds are issued to mature in the nth week—or are even perpetuities. The "maturity value" of bonds in the second week would then be replaced in the analysis by the value of these bonds at the (uncertain) interest rate which would then prevail. Such a modification of the argument could be made without affecting its main results.

[5] I am indebted to Edmond Malinvaud for correcting an inaccuracy in the original form of these equations.

the variable in question.[6] It is also assumed that the higher the expected level of consumption, the greater the utility. On the other hand, the higher the standard deviation—i.e., the greater the degree of uncertainty attached to the consumption level—the smaller the utility. In other words, the individual is assumed to have an aversion to risk.

The random variations in the maturity value of his bond holdings will clearly force the individual to make adjustments in his other expenditure items in order to balance his budget. Assume for simplicity —and somewhat incongruously—that all such intraweek adjustments are made by the individual in his concurrent expenditure on commodities, and not in his holdings of bonds and money. This means that B_1/p and M_1/p are fixed variates, not subject to random fluctuation.[7] Correspondingly,

$$E\left[\frac{B_1}{p}\right] = \frac{B_1}{p}, \qquad E\left[\frac{B_1(1 + \varepsilon_2)}{p}\right] = \frac{B_1}{p} + \frac{B_1}{p}\,E[\varepsilon_2] = \frac{B_1}{p},$$

$$\text{and} \quad \sigma\left(\frac{B_1}{p}\right) = 0,$$

with similar relationships obtaining, *mutatis mutandis*, for M_1/p. It then follows from equations (1) and (2)—after taking account of the fact that $\bar{Z}_1$, $\bar{Z}_2$, B_0, and M_0 are all constants—that the variables which determine the individual's utility can be written as

$$(3) \qquad E[Z_1] = R_1 - \frac{1}{1 + r}\frac{B_1}{p} - \frac{M_1}{p},$$

$$(4) \qquad E[Z_2] = R_2 + \frac{B_1}{p} + \frac{M_1}{p},$$

$$(5) \qquad \sigma(Z_1) = \left|\frac{B_0}{p}\right|\sigma,$$

[6] In the more general case that accords with the foregoing assumptions, the utility function would also depend on the covariance of Z_1 and Z_2. In the case at hand, however, this covariance is zero as a result of the assumption of the next paragraph together with the assumption that ε_1 and ε_2 are independently distributed.

[7] At the same time it should be clear that the optimum values of these variables are dependent on the properties of the probability distribution of ε; see pp. 123 and 127 below.

and

(6) $$\sigma(Z_2) = \left| \frac{B_1}{p} \right| \sigma.$$

We now note that only three of these four variables are actually subject to the individual's choice: for since initial real bond holdings B_0/p are given, the standard deviation of current consumption—which by (5) is proportionate to these holdings—is also given. Our task, then, is to analyze the individual's optimum combination of his three decision variables $E[Z_1]$, $E[Z_2]$, and $\sigma(Z_2)$.

Using an approach analogous to that of Chapter V:5, we assume first that the level of $E[Z_1]$ is fixed at $E[Z_1]^0 = R_1 - K_0$, so that—by equation (3)—the relevant budget line in Figure VI-1 is once again represented by AB. Consider next the relevant indifference map. From equation (4) we note first that the dotted 45° lines in Figure VI-1 represent constant levels of $E[Z_2]$, whose values are read off as before (p. 99). On the other hand, equation (6) implies that the vertical lines in Figure VI-1 represent constant levels of $\sigma(Z_2)$, whose values are proportionate to the absolute distance of the particular line from the Y-axis. Thus the mean and standard deviation represented by point Q are EW and $|Oa|\sigma$, respectively. The corresponding values for point M are EU and $|Ob|\sigma$.

It follows that every point in Figure VI-1 represents not only a portfolio but also a probability distribution of future consumption Z_2. Correspondingly, the problem of constructing an indifference map in Figure VI-1 is the problem of determining—given the levels of $E[Z_1]$ and $\sigma(Z_1)$—the loci of equally satisfactory distributions of Z_2; that is, probability distributions generating the same level of expected utility. It is also clear from the preceding that if the individual were solely concerned with the expected value of these distributions, the indifference map would be represented by the 45° lines in Figure VI-1. Hence the optimum portfolio corresponding to any level of $E[Z_1]$ would be at that corner where the relevant budget line meets the X-axis: that is, the individual would hold only bonds. More generally, an individual concerned solely with the given expected rates of return on various assets will hold only that asset with the highest rate of return.[8]

[8] Markowitz, "Portfolio Selection," *op. cit.*, pp. 77–78.
Clearly the foregoing corner solution would also obtain if there were no

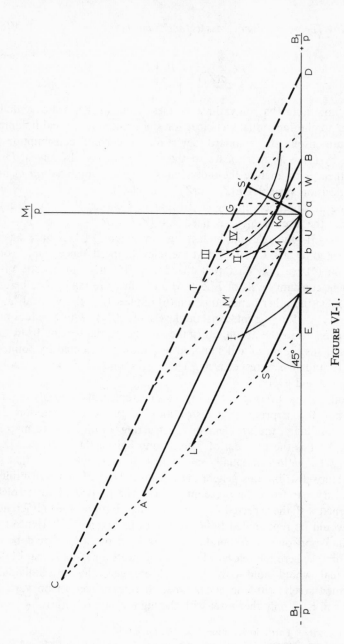

Figure VI-1.

Conversely, diversification of portfolio holdings in our present model can be rationalized only by attributing to the individual a concern with something more than expected returns. This "something more" in our analysis is the illiquidity of an asset as objectified by its riskiness. Correspondingly, the shape of an individual's indifference map depends both on the degree of this riskiness (as measured by σ) and the degree of his aversion to risk.[9]

The relevant properties of the indifference curves can now be deduced as follows. Consider first point Q and assume that bond holdings are increased, while the quantity of money is held constant. Since in the worst possible case these bond holdings will become worthless in the future, the individual has thereby been brought to a preferred position. Hence the indifference curve can at most be expected to be horizontal, while in general it can be assumed to be negatively sloped. This same conclusion can be reached by noting that a vertically upward displacement from Q represents a movement to a higher level of $E[Z_2]$ with an unchanged dispersion, and hence a movement to a preferred position.

Consider now a southeast movement along the 45° line through Q. This keeps the expected level of Z_2 constant, while increasing its dispersion. Hence our risk-averting individual has been made worse off and must therefore be compensated with an additional quantity of either bonds or money. Hence the absolute value of the slope of the indifference curve in the positive quadrant of Figure VI-1 must be less than unity. By a similar argument, the slope must be greater than unity in the negative quadrant. Finally, it will be assumed that the slope is exactly unity at the point where the curve crosses the Y-axis. Curves I–IV in Figure VI-1 display these properties, as well as that of convexity.[10]

---

certainty with respect to bond values; that is, if σ were zero. For under this assumption of perfectly liquid bonds the indifference map would once again be represented by the family of 45° straight lines. Cf. p. 101 above.

[9] As already noted (p. 120), the following discussion does not deal with the case of a risk-lover.

[10] On the convexity properties, cf. Tobin's discussion of the related curves in "Liquidity Preference as Behavior Toward Risk," *op. cit.*, p. 77.

Analytically, the argument of the text can be stated as follows: Let the individual's, (expected) utility function be represented by

(a) $$U = F\Big(E[Z_1], E[Z_2], \sigma(Z_2); \sigma(Z_1)\Big),$$

where, by assumption, $\sigma(Z_1)$ is a constant. Set $E[Z_1] = E[Z_1]^0$ and substitute from

It is clear from the foregoing that a risk-averter will never be at an interior point in the negative quadrant. For at any such point (say M') he can always improve his position by using his money balances to decrease his debt at the terms given by the budget line AB. For such a movement increases the expected value of future consumption (by virtue of the interest saved) while at the same time decreasing its dispersion. This does not mean that a risk-averter will never be a borrower. What it does mean, however, is that he will never borrow in order to increase present consumption as long as he can finance such purchases from existing money balances. A borrowing risk-averter must therefore be an individual whose expected level of current consumption exceeds his current receipts so that the relevant budget line in Figure VI-1 lies leftward of LO, at (say) SN. Such an individual will clearly be at the corner N on the X-axis, representing zero holdings of cash balances.

This same conclusion can be reached alternatively by noting that a risk-averter at an interior point in the negative quadrant is (at the margin) effectively borrowing and holding the proceeds in cash on the gamble that the redemption value of bonds will fall sufficiently (i.e., future interest rates will rise sufficiently) so as to enable him to repurchase his bonds at a profit. But due to the fact that the individual must pay interest in order to engage in this gamble, while at the same time his expected earnings from capital gains and losses are zero, the expected value of the gamble as a whole is negative. And a risk-averter, by definition, never takes such a gamble.[11]

---

equations (4)–(6) to yield

(b) $$U = F\left(E[Z_1]^0, \ R_2 + \frac{B_1}{p} + \frac{M_1}{p}, \ \left| \frac{B_1}{p} \right| \sigma; \left| \frac{B_0}{p} \right| \sigma \right).$$

By assumption, $F_2 > 0$ and $F_3 < 0$, where these represent the partial derivatives with respect to the second and third arguments of (b), respectively, and where the negative sign of F_3 reflects the aversion to risk. Differentiating this function implicitly as of a given level of U we then obtain

(c) $$-\frac{dM_1}{dB_1} = \frac{F_2 \pm F_3 \sigma}{F_2},$$

where the plus (minus) sign in the numerator obtains in the positive (negative) quadrant.

The analogy between this development and that of the preceding chapter is clear from a comparison with p. 103, footnote 32 above. See also Mathematical Appendix 6:*f*.

[11] I am indebted to Kenneth Arrow for this formulation.

The picture is, however, quite different in the positive quadrant: for by virtue of the interest which the individual receives on bond holdings here, he is effectively being paid for undertaking the risk of a change in maturity values. Hence he can be at an interior point (say, the point of tangency Q) at which this payment just induces him to gamble on the possibility of a future rise in the redemption value of bonds.

Even in this quadrant—where the individual can generally be assumed to hold a portfolio consisting of both bonds and money—there remains a fundamental difference between the precautionary and transactions demands: namely, there is no room in the present discussion for the notion of large-scale economies in the holding of money. For the sole function of money and bonds alike is to serve as a store of future purchasing power. Hence there is no reason to assume that their relative efficacy in fulfilling this function depends on their absolute levels. As a consequence there is no room for the notion of satiety of money holdings. Correspondingly, it is economically meaningful to assume in Figure VI-1—in contrast with Figure V-3—that the slope of any indifference curve (as of a given level of $E[Z_1]$) depends solely on the ratio of money to bonds. This, indeed, is the assumption that has been made in Figure VI-1.

In a manner analogous to that on p.104 above, let us now consider the locus of points of tangency generated in Figure VI-1 by changing the level of $E[Z_1]$, under the assumption that such changes leave the indifference map invariant.[12] It follows from the preceding argument that this path will have the form of the broken line EOS'. Clearly the slope of OS' depends on the rate of interest: the lower this rate, the lower the proportion of bonds. Indeed, in the special case of a zero rate of interest this part of the path will coincide with the line segment OG on the vertical axis. In brief, if bonds represent only risk, without compensating return, a risk-averter will hold any possible surplus of current income over consumption entirely in the form of cash.

As noted at the beginning of this section, the demand for money here described is of a precautionary nature: it stems from the individual's desire to mitigate the uncertainty of fluctuations in bond prices. This demand can, however, readily be combined analytically with that of a truly speculative nature, that is, with that stemming from the desire

[12] This path is clearly related to the "locus of efficient portfolios" defined by Markowitz, "Portfolio Selection," *op. cit.*, p. 82.

to hold money because of the expected capital loss from holding bonds.[13] In particular, assume that $E[\varepsilon_2] = q$, where q represents the average capital gain or loss which the individual expects on a bond. Correspondingly, budget equations (3) and (4) can be rewritten as

$$(7) \qquad E[Z_1] = R_1 - \frac{1}{1+i} \frac{B_1(1+q)}{p} - \frac{M_1}{p},$$

$$(8) \qquad E[Z_2] = R_2 + \frac{B_1(1+q)}{p} + \frac{M_1}{p},$$

where

$$(9) \qquad 1 + i = (1+r)(1+q).^{14}$$

If the X-axis in Figure VI-1 is relabeled "$B_1(1+q)/p$", the properties of the indifference curves are unchanged. On the other hand, the absolute slope of the budget line AB is now $1/(1+i)$. If this is greater than unity (which is the case for a Keynesian "bear" who expects a decline in bond prices large enough to wipe out interest earnings—i.e., for whom q is sufficiently negative to make the net expected yield on bonds i also negative), then the risk-averting individual will obviously never hold positive quantities of bonds. On the contrary, he will be at some point (generally, an interior one) in the negative quadrant where the expected decline in the value of his outstanding debt induces him to undertake the gamble of borrowing and holding cash balances.[15]

Before going on we must remind ourselves that money is one asset, not three. Hence even though the foregoing analysis has, for simplicity, followed the usual Keynesian distinction among transactions, precautionary, and speculative balances, it should be clear that every unit of money simultaneously satisfies all the motives for which it is held.[16]

[13] On the distinction between the two types of demand, see the references to Tobin and Johnson cited on p. 118, footnote 2 above.

[14] I am indebted to Dale Jorgenson for this formulation.

[15] Cf. p. 124 above. Note that in contrast with that discussion, even a boundary position is now impossible in the positive quadrant. This is a reflection of the fact that there are two assets through which purchasing power can be transferred from the present to the future, but only one through which the opposite can be done.

[16] Cf. J. G. Gurley and E. S. Shaw, *Money in a Theory of Finance* (Washington, D.C., 1960), p. 33; Friedman, "The Quantity Theory of Money: A Restatement," *op. cit.*, p. 14.

Correspondingly, the optimum portfolio is actually one obtained by confronting an indifference map which is some sort of "weighted average" of those of Figures V-3 and VI-1, with a budget line whose slope measures the net expected yield from bonds, inclusive of capital gains and losses. Without attempting a rigorous treatment of this comprehensive case, I should like briefly to indicate some of its general implications for our argument.

Clearly, the curves of the aforementioned indifference map are again negatively sloped. The absolute value of this slope is less than unity in the positive quadrant, and this can be assumed to be the case over at least part of the negative quadrant as well. Thus his transactions needs cause an individual to hold money even if he is a borrower who expects the average level of future bond prices to remain unchanged.

At the same time the influence of the precautionary motive will cause the individual to issue fewer bonds than he otherwise would. Indeed, if this influence is strong enough it might eventually cause the indifference curves in the negative quadrant to assume a slope greater than unity. In this case the individual might not be willing to go sufficiently into debt to finance satiety holdings of cash balances even at a zero rate of interest; that is, the optimum portfolio in this case might lie rightwards of *EE'* in Figure V-3.

It is also clear that, by the same argument used on p. 106 above, the excess demand functions generated by the foregoing general analysis will be free of money illusion and will reflect the influence of the real-balance effect. Again, by making assumptions similar to those on pp. 108–109, it can be shown that an increase in the rate of interest causes a shift out of money and into bonds. The same is true for an increase in the liquidity of bonds—in the sense of a decrease in either conversion inconvenience or riskiness (as measured by σ). In the limiting case of a perfectly liquid bond (in both of the foregoing senses) the demand for money disappears completely.[17]

One final comment that might be made is that we have analyzed the transactions, precautionary, and speculative motives in terms of a choice between the same pair of assets: money and bonds. It would, however, seem to be more realistic to distinguish between the nature of the choice in the various instances. In particular, there would seem to be

---

[17] Cf. pp. 103–104 and pp. 121–123, footnote 8 above.

a case for analyzing the transactions motive in terms of a choice between money and some asset whose value is certain or almost certain (say, savings deposits), and the precautionary and speculative motive as a choice between this asset and a much less certain one (say, bonds or, even more to the point, tangible assets of various kinds). We cannot develop this argument further here and will merely note that it would not change the essential nature of the analysis presented in Figures V-3 and VI-1—though it would imply that all money balances are, by definition, transactions balances.

2. The Implications of the Precautionary and Speculative Motives for the Fisherine Analysis[18]

As in the preceding chapter (p. 105), let us now drop the assumption that the value of $E[Z_1]$ is given and examine the determination of the optimum value of this variable as well. The primary purpose of this examination is to indicate some of the modifications that must be made in the usual Fisherine analysis as a consequence of the introduction of uncertainty. For this reason we shall, for simplicity, restrict the argument to the case in which money is held only for the precautionary motive. Again, for simplicity, we shall assume that the indifference map in Figure VI-1 is unaffected by changes in the value of $E[Z_1]$, and that the marginal rates of substitution of bonds for money which it represents depend solely on the ratio between these two assets. Even under these simplifying assumptions, a full treatment of the case is beyond the scope of the present discussion,[19] so that we shall have to suffice with some general observations.

Let us begin with the analog of the wealth restraint. As the discussion on p. 125 has shown, the preceding paragraph implies that the expansion path in Figure VI-1 has the form *EOS'*—representing the fact that the individual does not hold any money balances when he is a debtor, and that he holds a portfolio of bonds and money in a fixed proportion (dependent on the rate of interest) when he is a creditor. Denote the

---

[18] See p. 118, footnote 1 above.

[19] For an indication of the problems involved—though almost exclusively for the case in which an individual's wealth consists solely of his initial portfolio (i.e., $R_1 = R_2 = 0$)—see Markowitz, *Portfolio Selection* (New York, 1959), Chapter 13.

expected rate of return on this portfolio by $\bar{r}$, where

$$(10) \qquad 1 + \bar{r} = \frac{B_1 + M_1}{\left(\dfrac{1}{1+r}\right)B_1 + M_1},$$

so that

$$(11) \qquad \bar{r} = \frac{r\left(\dfrac{B_1}{1+r}\right)}{\dfrac{B_1}{1+r} + M_1} = \frac{r}{1 + \dfrac{M_1}{\dfrac{B_1}{1+r}}}.$$

That is, $\bar{r}$ is the weighted average of the expected rates of return on bonds (r) and money (0), and must therefore lie between these two values. An over-all wealth restraint can then be derived from (3) and (4) as

$$(12) \qquad E[Z_1] + \frac{1}{1+\bar{r}}E[Z_2] = R_1 + \frac{1}{1+\bar{r}}R_2.$$

If the individual is not a lender $(Z_1 \geq R_1)$, then $M_1 = 0$, so that $\bar{r} = r$; hence the restraint in this region coincides with the Fisherine one. If the individual is a lender,

$$(13) \qquad \bar{r} = \frac{r}{1+k} < r,$$

where $k > 0$ is the fixed proportion of money to discounted bonds. That is, the fact that part of the individual's portfolio consists of sterile money balances necessarily reduces its overall rate of return. Correspondingly, the expected marginal cost of substituting present for future consumption —when the transfer in purchasing power is made by changes in a portfolio of the aforementioned composition—is $1 + \bar{r}$, less than $1 + r$. Correspondingly, the budget restraint in this region must be more sharply sloped (with reference to the X-axis) than the Fisherine one, though still less than unity. This is the situation depicted by *FST* in Figure VI-2.[20] The horizontal distance between *SH* and *ST* thus represents the

---

[20] Note that we could have continued to follow here the approach of Chapter V:7 and written our budget restraint as

$$(a) \qquad E[Z_1] + \frac{1}{1+r}\left\{E[Z_2] + r\left(\frac{M_1}{p}\right)\right\} = R_1 + \frac{R_2}{1+r},$$

value (as measured by its cost in terms of expected future consumption) of the insurance which the individual obtains against the uncertainty of future bond values by virtue of his holding part of his portfolio in the form of money.

Consider now the relevant indifference map. The main point here is that since the individual is concerned with the whole probability distribution of Z_1 and Z_2—and not only its expected values—the marginal rate of substitution between $E[Z_1]$ and $E[Z_2]$ cannot be defined until the distributions respectively associated with these expected values are first specified.[21] In the case at hand—where the probability distribution depends only on the means and standard deviations—this means that the indifference map between $E[Z_1]$ and $E[Z_2]$ cannot be constructed until the degree of dispersion, $\sigma(Z_2)$, associated with any given level of $E[Z_2]$, is first specified.[22]

Let us, then, for simplicity associate with each value of $E[Z_2]$ that probability distribution specified by the standard deviation of the corresponding portfolio on budget restraint *FST*.[23] Thus the points on any vertical line in Figure VI-2 represent the same probability distribution of Z_2. In particular, the vertical line through S (where neither borrowing nor lending takes place) represents a distribution whose standard deviation is zero; that is, the level of future consumption at any point on this line is certain and equal to R_2. Similarly, any point on the vertical line through S' (where the individual's portfolio consists solely of AR_2 bonds outstanding) represents a distribution of Z_2 with mean OA and standard deviation $\overline{AR_2}\sigma$. Finally, the vertical line through

---

where

(b)

$$\frac{M_1}{p} = \frac{R_1 - E[Z_1]}{1 + (1/k)} \quad \text{for} \quad Z_1 < R_1$$

$$\frac{M_1}{p} = 0 \quad \text{for} \quad Z_1 \geqslant R_1.$$

Substituting from (b) into (a) then yields equation (12) of the text.

[21] See the stimulating remarks in Friedman, *A Theory of the Consumption Function*, pp. 14–15.

[22] As will be recalled from the discussion on p. 121 above, the value of $\sigma(Z_1)$ is, under our present assumptions, predetermined.

[23] Here is an additional way in which the introduction of uncertainty destroys "the sharp dichotomy between tastes and opportunities that is the central attraction of the indifference analysis under certainty" (Friedman, *Theory of the Consumption Function*, p. 15).

M represents a distribution with mean OB and standard deviation $R_2B\sigma/[1 + k/(1 + r)]$.

It is clear from this description that the indifference curves in Figure VI-2 will be negatively sloped. It is also possible to deduce the existence of a definite relationship between these curves and those that could be drawn in Figure VI-2 for an X-axis representing certain quantities of Z_2. In particular, the further away a point is from the vertical line R_2S, the greater the uncertainty which it represents. Hence, for a risk-averter,

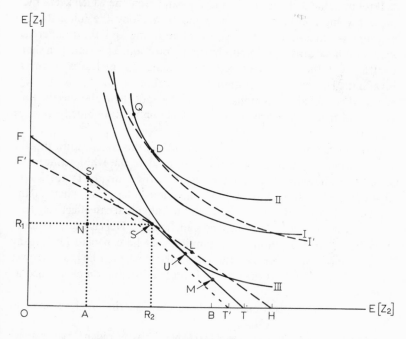

FIGURE VI-2.

the uncertain indifference curve (I) passing through any point on a certain one (I') will be more sharply sloped than the latter leftwards of the vertical line R_2S, and less sharply sloped rightwards. On this line itself (say, at point D) the two indifference curves will touch.

This implies that if under certainty the individual would have optimally been at point S', then under uncertainty he will be rightward of this point. Similarly, if his optimum position under certainty would have been at L, his position under uncertainty will be leftward of this point. Indeed, in this case the leftward movement generated by the change in the indifference curve is reinforced by the substitution and income effects generated by the shift of the budget restraint from SH to ST. In sum, the uncertainty generated by his bond operations makes the risk-averting individual less willing than under certainty to modify his given income stream by means of borrowing and lending.

It follows that a change in R_1 and R_2—and even one which keeps their present value constant (i.e., which moves S along the initial budget restraint)—will affect both the budget restraint and the indifference map, and hence the individual's optimum position. This stands in sharp contrast with the Fisherine case, where such a change leaves all curves invariant. The crucial operational implication of all this is that the commodity demand functions are now dependent on the specific time pattern of the income stream, and not only on its discounted value, or wealth.[24]

A somewhat more sophisticated statement of this conclusion is that the introduction of uncertainty in this way renders the whole concept of wealth—in the sense of a single measure of the individual's total anticipated resources over time—an ambiguous one. For what Figure VI-2 indicates is that the rate at which the individual can effectively lend is now less than that at which he can borrow. Hence the maximum amount of expected future consumption that he can plan on for any given level of present consumption depends on whether he is a borrower or a lender; and this is turn depends on the distribution of his income over time.[25]

Other familiar operational aspects of the Fisherine analysis are also

[24] In terms of the discussion on pp. 113–14 above, this implication is a consequence of our assumption that bond holdings enter the utility function; see equation (b) in footnote 10, p. 124 above.

[25] This dependence would be even more marked if instead of assuming $\bar{F}$ to remain constant, we were to assume it to vary with the extent of the lending. This would, of course, be the case if the composition of the portfolio changed with its size. Thus if the proportion of money decreased with size, $\bar{F}$ would increase with $E[Z_2]$. It is, however, clear from equation (11) that—unless money disappeared entirely from the portfolio—it would always remain less than r.

For the implication of differential borrowing and lending rates for the Fisherine analysis of investment, see J. Hirshleifer, "On the Theory of Optimal Investment Decision," *Journal of Political Economy*, LXVI (1958), 333–37.

affected by the introduction of uncertainty. Thus it is clear from Figure VI-2 that absence of time preference proper is no longer represented by symmetry of the relevant indifference curves about the 45° line through the origin. Intuitively, since the expected consumption of 5 units of Z_1 now and 10 units of Z_2 in the future involves a different degree of uncertainty than $10Z_1$ and $5Z_2$, there is no reason for the individual to be indifferent between these two alternatives.[26] Consequently (in contrast with the case of certainty), it is not true that absence of time preference and a positive rate of interest imply that (expected) present consumption will be less than (expected) future.

Similarly, even if we accept the assumption that the marginal rate of substitution of present for future consumption in the case of certainty depends only on the ratio of these two quantities, this does not carry over to the case of uncertainty. For doubling $E[Z_1]$ and $E[Z_2]$ will not generally also double the degree of uncertainty (as measured by the standard deviation). This reasoning suggests that the marginal rate of substitution might, however, remain invariant in Figure VI-2 under an equiproportionate change in $E[Z_1]$, $E[Z_2]$, and R_2. This in turn would imply that doubling the individual's wealth, the rate of interest being held constant, will double his demands for both $E[Z_1]$ and $E[Z_2]$ if this increase in wealth is effected by a doubling of both R_1 and R_2.

The foregoing analysis is based on a simple model indeed. But its fundamental conclusion—that the operational implications of the Fisherine analysis are changed by the introduction of bonds of uncertain value—would seem to hold all the more so in more complicated models. Thus let us now assume that the analysis of the preceding section is modified in such a way as to imply that a borrowing risk-averter can also hold money. At the same time let us assume that his aversion to risk is sufficiently strong to prevent him from borrowing only in order to hold precautionary money balances. In other words, if the individual is a borrower, then the net current value of his portfolio,

$$\frac{1}{1+r}\frac{B_1}{p} + \frac{M_1}{p},$$

---

[26] Cf. p. 112, footnote 43 above. In terms of the utility function described in p. 123, footnote 10 above, this change affects the value of $\sigma(Z_2)$ and hence the level of utility U.

will be negative.[27] Let us also assume for simplicity that the proportion of money to (the absolute value of) outstanding discounted bonds is constant and equal to $k_1 < 1$. Then it can readily be seen from (11) that

$$(14) \qquad \bar{r} = \frac{r}{1 - k_1} > r.$$

Thus the slope of the budget restraint leftward of S will be less in absolute value than that of the Fisherine restraint, so that the vital kink at S will be even sharper than before. This is the situation depicted by restraint $F'ST$ in Figure VI-2.

The economic interpretation of this result is straightforward. The fact that the individual's optimum response to uncertainty leads him to hold money under all conditions[28] means that the differential between his effective borrowing and lending rates of interest is actually widened. In particular, in computing from (11) this effective rate for a borrower we essentially divide his interest payments not by his outstanding debt, but by his smaller (in absolute value) net portfolio. All this is analogous to the higher interest rate effectively paid by a bank borrower who (in American fashion) is required to keep part of his loan on deposit.

Another way of extending the foregoing analysis is to assume that future, as contrasted with present, income is also subject to uncertainty. In particular, each dollar of future income is subject to a random error whose probability distribution is independent of that of the capital gains and losses on bonds. Let the mean and standard variation of this distribution be 0 and σ_2, respectively. Then the mean and standard deviation of future income are R_2 and $R_2\sigma_2$, respectively. Correspondingly, the standard deviation of future consumption now represented by point Q in Figure VI-1 is

$$(15) \qquad \sigma(Z_2) = \sqrt{R_2^2\sigma_2^2 + \left(\frac{B_1}{p}\right)_Q^2 \sigma^2},$$

where $(B_1/p)_Q$ is the amount of bonds outstanding at point Q.

The introduction of this additional uncertainty thus increases the standard deviation associated with every point of the indifference map

---

[27] In addition to being intuitively appealing, this assumption precludes the complication that $\bar{r}$ in equation (11) might have a negative value.
[28] Except when $Z_1 = R_1$.

in Figure VI-2, and therefore generally affects the specific slopes of these curves. On the other hand, it does not change their general properties, and particularly not their relationship to the certain indifference curves as described above. Similarly, it leaves intact the general shape of the budget restraint, though it will affect the slope of that part of this restraint rightward of point *S*.

The reason for this latter change is inherent in the discussion of the preceding section. The basic viewpoint of that discussion is that the individual chooses a portfolio of assets as as an instrument of achieving an optimum "probability mix" of future consumption. Now, other things equal, the fact that income is uncertain should not affect the nature of this optimum mix; but by this very fact it must affect the nature of the optimum portfolio. For this must now be chosen so as to complement the given probability distribution of future income so as to produce a "probability mix" of the desired properties. From this it follows that the existence of uncertainty with respect to future income will cause the given risk-averting individual to hold a portfolio with a larger proportion of money than before.[29] Hence $\bar{r}$ will be smaller, which means that *ST* will be more sharply sloped with respect to the *X*-axis than in Figure VI-2, though, of course, this slope must still be less than unity. It is also obvious that the risk-averting individual has been made worse off by this increased uncertainty: in graphical terms, even if the budget restraint has not changed, every point on it now represents a greater dispersion of future consumption.

We note finally that the dependence of the commodity demand functions of the individual on the time path of his income stream, and not only on its discounted value, is the consequence not of uncertainty *per se*, but of the fact that this uncertainty has been introduced in a way which effectively creates a discrepancy between the rates for borrowing and lending. Thus consider by way of contrast a model in which

[29] It would, however, be a *non sequitur* to deduce from this that an individual with a risky source of income will hold less cash than one with a more stable income. For if there is some freedom in the choice of income sources—some freedom in the choice of occupation—then these two individuals have revealed a basic difference in taste toward risk-taking. Correspondingly, it may well be that the individual with the stable income will hold more cash—or, more generally, hold a less risky portfolio—than his equally well-to-do compatriot with the unstable income. The civil servant with his gilt-edged securities is surely no rarer a bird than the oil-driller with his speculative stocks.

uncertainty exists only with respect to future income. Disregarding the transactions motive, the individual's portfolio will then consist exclusively of bonds whose future value is certain. Hence his budget restraint in Figure VI-2 is the straight line *FSH*. Correspondingly, the Fisherine conclusion that his demands depend only on tastes, the rate of interest, and wealth will once again be valid.[30]

Another property of this model is that the standard deviation of Z_2 at every point in the indifference map is the same and equal to $R_2\sigma_2$. Consequently, if the individual is concerned solely with the absolute level of this deviation (and not with its ratio to the expected level of Z_2); and if, furthermore, any two points which are indifferent under certainty remain indifferent when they are accompanied by the same absolute level of uncertainty (as measured by the standard deviation)—then absence of time preference proper will once again (p. 112) reflect itself in an indifference map symmetric about the 45° line. Similarly, the case for arguing that the marginal rate of substitution of present for future consumption depends only on the ratio of these two quantities is not affected by the introduction of uncertainty in the foregoing way.

3. COMMODITIES AS AN ASSET[31]

With the exception of the remarks at the end of Section 1 above, the analysis of the preceding chapter—as well as the present one until this point—has proceeded on the assumption that the only assets the individual can carry over from one week to the next are bonds and money. Let us now return to the analytical framework of the preceding chapter and assume that commodities too can be carried over, without incurring any additional costs. Assume further that the individual expects prices to rise by $s\%$ per week; it is this which makes him contemplate moving into commodities.[32]

---

[30] This model would seem to be the one implicit in Friedman's argument that the introduction of uncertainty will not affect the Fisherine analysis in any basic way; see *Theory of the Consumption Function*, pp. 14–15.

[31] The following is extensively revised and corrected from my "Secular Price Movements and Economic Development: Some Theoretical Aspects," in *The Challenge of Development* (ed. A. Bonné, Jerusalem, 1958), pp. 27–40.

[32] If there are carrying costs which are proportionate to the quantity of commodities, then *s* can be considered as measured net of these costs.

In terms of utility analysis, this means that if the individual does carry commodities over from week to week, then the marginal utility he obtains from a dollar's consumption of commodities in week t must equal that obtainable by holding these commodities until week $t + 1$, selling them for $1 + s$ dollars, and consuming the proceeds then. That is, the optimum conditions of Chapter V : 3 must be supplemented by

$$(16) \quad \begin{array}{l} \text{m.u. of a dollar's worth of } Z_t \\ \qquad = \text{m.u. of } (1 + s) \text{ dollar's worth of } Z_{t+1}. \end{array}$$

At the same time it is clear that if s and r are not equal, this equation and equation (2) on p. 90 cannot be simultaneously satisfied: one of them must be replaced by an inequality. We shall return to this point in a moment.

The translation of these conditions into ordinal terms proceeds as before. Effectively, the individual now has a new good which he can choose to hold—namely, future commodities via present commodities. If no utility attaches to the mere holding of commodities,[33] then the marginal utility of this good is equal to the marginal utility of future commodities. Our marginal conditions then become[34]

$$(17) \qquad \text{m.r.s. of } Z_t \text{ for } Z_{t+1} \text{ via money} = \frac{1}{1 + s},$$

$$(18) \qquad \text{m.r.s. of } Z_t \text{ for } Z_{t+1} \text{ via bonds} = \frac{1 + r}{1 + s} = 1 + m,$$

and

$$(19) \qquad \text{m.r.s. of } Z_t \text{ for } Z_{t+1} \text{ via commodities} = 1.$$

The right-hand sides of these equations are the relative prices of the relevant goods. Equation (19) reflects the fact that by simply carrying them over, the individual converts present commodities into an equal amount of future ones.

---

[33] This assumption is unlikely to be relevant in a period of continuous inflation in which commodities take on the functions of a medium of exchange; cf. the familiar example of "cigarette money" in postwar Germany.

[34] In deriving the following equations we make use of the fact that a dollar's worth of real money holdings or commodities in week $t + 1$ is represented by $1/(1 + s)p$. Cf. on all this Mathematical Appendix 6:g.

The variable m on the right-hand side of (18) is Fisher's real rate of interest: that is, the nominal rate corrected for the price increase.[35] Thus in choosing between present commodities and future commodities via bonds—and in choosing between holding bonds and holding commodities—it is only with this real rate that the rational individual is concerned. On the other hand, in choosing between holding bonds and holding money, it is only the nominal rate which is relevant: for the anticipated price increase will have the same effect on the real value of both these goods. This result can be derived formally by dividing equation (17) by (18), thereby obtaining once again equation (9) of the preceding chapter (p. 93).

As can be inferred from our earlier comment on equation (16), under our present assumptions marginal conditions (18) and (19) cannot both be satisfied. The nature of the corner solution which is involved here can most easily be illustrated by considering once again the two-period case. The budget restraints of this case now have the form

$$(20) \qquad Z_1 + Z_{2C} + \frac{1}{1+m} Z_{2B} + (1+s)Z_{2M} = R_1,$$

$$(21) \qquad Z_2 = R_2 + Z_{2C} + Z_{2B} + Z_{2M},$$

where Z_1 and Z_{2C} represent the amounts of present commodities *consumed* and *carried over*, respectively; and where Z_{2B} and Z_{2M} are now deflated by the higher price level that will prevail when they will be converted into commodities. That is,

$$(22) \qquad Z_{2B} = \frac{B_1}{(1+s)p} \quad \text{and} \quad Z_{2M} = \frac{M_1}{(1+s)p}.$$

If the Y-axis in Figure V-2 is relabeled "Z_{2C}," and "$1+r$" on the

---

[35] *The Rate of Interest*, pp. 358–60. See also *The Theory of Interest*, Chapters 2 and 19.

By cross-multiplying the last equation in (18) we obtain

$$m = r - s - ms = \frac{r-s}{1+s},$$

which, when s is small, can be reduced to the familiar approximation of the real rate as

$$m = r - s.$$

X-axis replaced by "$1 + m$", straight lines such as AB can now be taken as representations of budget restraint (20) as of fixed levels of Z_1 and Z_{2M}.

Consider now the relevant indifference map. Since we are assuming that the individual is concerned with bonds and commodity-inventories solely as embodiments of future purchasing power—and since in this respect they are assumed equivalent—this map is represented by the unitary-sloped dotted lines in Figure V-2. Hence if the real rate of interest is greater than zero, the individual optimum will be at a corner on the X-axis where he holds only bonds. If, however, m is negative, then the individual will want to borrow indefinitely large amounts for investment in commodity inventories. In graphical terms, he will move indefinitely leftward and upward along a budget line (not drawn in Figure V-2) whose slope is greater than unity, and which therefore never intersects the extension of boundary line EC.

All this is merely a specific instance of the general proposition already mentioned (p. 121) that if the individual is concerned solely with the rates of return on alternative assets, then he will hold only that asset with the highest rate of return. Conversely, he will hold more than one asset only if other attributes are also relevant to his decision-making. Thus he holds both money and bonds in our earlier discussion because of the liquidity of the former. Similarly, he would in the present case hold both bonds and commodity-inventories if they were assumed to have different attributes of convenience, safety, and so forth. Under such circumstances the indifference map between these assets would not be a family of straight lines, so that equations (18) and (19) could both be satisfied at some interior point of Figure V-2. Clearly, the marginal rates of substitution of these equations would then reflect the utility derived from the differing attributes of these assets, as well as from the future commodities to be purchased with them.

One further point that should be made is that the anticipation of a higher price level will influence the individual's behavior even if, for some reason or other, it is impossible to hold commodity inventories. In technical terms, this assumption eliminates only marginal condition (19) and the term Z_{2C} from budget restraints (20)–(21), while leaving conditions (17)–(18) intact. Note that from the budget restraints so modified we can then derive a wealth restraint which discounts future consumption and income by the real rate of interest. Its specific form is

(23) $$Z_1 + \frac{1}{1 + m}\left[Z_2 + r\,\frac{M_1}{(1 + s)p}\right] = R_1 + \frac{1}{1 + m}\,R_2 ,$$

whose bracketed expression is analogous to the right-hand side of equation (21) on p. 112 above. As in Chapter V:7, this wealth restraint can be used in Fisherine manner to determine the individual's optimum position.

Clearly, a wealth restraint can also be derived for our originally discussed case, in which commodities can be held. It will differ from the foregoing in measuring the individual's wealth inclusive of the discounted value of his anticipated inventory profits, net of interest charges. In mathematical terms, R_2 on the right-hand side of (23) will then be replaced by $R_2 - mZ_{2C}$. It should, however, be emphasized that Z_{2C} is not a constant but a function of (among other things) the magnitude of the anticipated price increase. This wealth restraint corresponds to Fisher's more general case in which the individual can modify his income stream by means other than loans and can therefore affect its present value.[36]

We note finally that the discussion of this section necessitates a change in the definition of absence of money illusion given above (p. 72). Such a state will now be said to exist if the demands for real goods remain invariant under any change which does not affect relative prices, the time stream of real incomes, the real value of initial bond and money holdings, and the respective rates of return on all the assets (commodities as well as bonds) which the individual can hold. This definition clearly includes our earlier one as a special case.

4. THE INFLUENCE OF PRICE EXPECTATIONS ON THE REAL-BALANCE EFFECT AND ON THE DEMAND FOR MONEY

The foregoing discussion provides a convenient point of departure for an analysis of the influence of price expectations on the strength of the real-balance effect.[37] In order to highlight the issue here let us write the wealth restraint of the preceding paragraph in nominal terms, distinguishing explicitly between present (p_1) and future (p_2) prices. Let us

[36] *The Theory of Interest*, Chapters 6–8, 11, and 13.

[37] It should, however, be noted that the following is actually independent of the utility assumptions of the preceding discussion and is based instead on the properties of the budget restraints.

also assume for simplicity that the individual will not receive any future endowment and that his present one consists solely of his initial money balances. His wealth restraint is then written as

$$(24) \quad p_1 Z_1 + \frac{p_2}{1+r}\left(Z_2 + r\,\frac{M_1}{p_2}\right) = M_0 + p_1\left(\frac{1}{1+r}\,\frac{p_2}{p_1} - 1\right)Z_{2C},$$

where the second term on the right-hand side represents inventory profits. Two additional assumptions made for the sake of simplicity are that (1) "the future" represents a much longer period of time than "the present," so that the optimum ratio of Z_1 to $Z_2 + r(M_1/p_2)$ will tend to be small; and (2) that this ratio will not be affected by changes in wealth unaccompanied by changes in relative prices.

Consider first the case in which inventories cannot be held, so that $Z_{2C} = 0$. The corresponding wealth restraint is represented by line AB in Figure VI-3a, on which the individual is assumed to choose P. If, now, p_1 declines while p_2 remains constant, this line shifts to CB on which the individual chooses, say, Q. If, however, both prices decline in the same proportion, the line shifts to CD on which, by assumption, the individual chooses S. Clearly, the wealth effect—which in the present case is synonymous with the real-balance effect—is stronger in the latter case (where, as measured by the Slutzky definition,[38] it is proportionate to PS) than in the former (proportionate to PR). And this discrepancy will be greater the longer the period of time represented by "the future" as compared to "the present."

Consider now the case in which inventories can be held so that (for p_2 sufficiently larger than p_1) Z_{2C} is positive. The original budget line is represented in Figure VI-3b by EF with its chosen point V. The intercepts on the Y-axis (E) and X-axis (F) equal, respectively,

$$(25) \quad \frac{M_0}{p_1} + \left(\frac{1}{1+r}\,\frac{p_2}{p_1} - 1\right)Z_{2C}$$

and

$$(26) \quad (1+r)\left[\frac{M_0}{p_2} + \frac{p_1}{p_2}\left(\frac{1}{1+r}\,\frac{p_2}{p_1} - 1\right)Z_{2C}\right].$$

Assume now that p_1 fails while p_2 remains constant. The resulting

[38] Cf. J. L. Mosak, "On the Interpretation of the Fundamental Equation of Value Theory," in *Studies in Mathematical Economics and Econometrics* (ed., O. Lange, *et al.*, Chicago, 1942), pp. 71–73; see also below, p. 407, footnote 5.

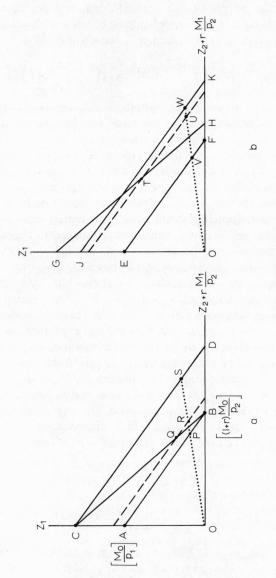

FIGURE VI-3.

shift in the budget line will reflect the operation of three conceptually distinct factors: (1) the changed real value of money balances in terms of p_1, as contrasted with its constancy in terms of p_2; (2) the increased real per unit profit on inventory holdings in terms of either p_1 (which equals $\dfrac{1}{1+r}\dfrac{p_2}{p_1} - 1$) or p_2 (which equals $\dfrac{p_1}{p_2}\left[\dfrac{1}{1+r}\dfrac{p_2}{p_1} - 1\right]$); and (3) the presumable consequent increase in the magnitude of these inventories themselves, Z_{2C}. The increased inventory profits generated by the second and third factors mean that—in contrast with the preceding case, in which only the first of the foregoing factors is at work—the individual benefits from the decline in p_1 even if he does not consume any of the cheapened commodity. This is the reason the new budget line GH (on which the individual chooses T) meets the X-axis rightwards of point F.

Note that what we are analyzing here is the effect of a price decline on the *consumption* of present goods. Hence inventory profits enter into the analysis only as part of the wealth effect influencing this consumption. If, however, we were to be concerned with the *purchases* of present goods, we would also have to take account of the increased speculative inventory holdings *per se*. That is, we would then have to analyze the effect of a price decline on $Z_1 + Z_{2C}$, and not only on Z_1.

Returning to the analysis of Figure VI-3b, assume now that p_2 declines in the same proportion as p_1. Then the budget line will shift parallel to itself to, say, JK, on which by assumption the individual chooses W. Furthermore, in view of the equiproportionate decline in price levels, there is no change in inventory profits (i.e., the second and third factors of the preceding paragraph are not at work); hence the intercept on the Y-axis, J, must be below G. On the other hand, the location of the intercept on the X-axis reflects the influence of two conflicting forces: the elimination of inventory profits, pushing the intercept leftwards of H; and the decline in p_2, pushing it rightwards. Thus the real-balance effect—the wealth effect of a price decline—is not necessarily greater in the case of a permanent decline as contrasted with a temporary one. In geometrical terms all depends on whether the budget line corresponding to an equiproportionate decline in prices lies above or below the dashed budget line in Figure VI-3b.

There is a simple, intuitive interpretation of these results. A decline in the current price level presents the individual with the potentialities of a capital gain on his initial money holdings. As in any other case, the extent of this gain depends on the nature of the alternative assets into which the individual can move in order to realize it. If the only such assets are future bond and money holdings, then the extent of the gain depends in a crucial way on the expected duration of the lower price level. If, however, commodities are also available, then this dependence is much attenuated: for even if the price decline is expected to be only temporary, the individual can realize his capital gain "in full" now by moving into commodities—or (if such should exist) into any other asset whose future real value will not be adversely affected by the expected relative rise in the future price level. In this way the individual can largely hedge against the effects of such a rise in prices on the real value of his future cash balances.

All this is analogous to the profit-taking operations that occur in the market in the case of any asset whose current real value rises relative to its expected future one. Clearly, such operations must affect the relation between these two prices; but this is another question.[39]

The discussion of the preceding section also enables us to generalize somewhat the theory of demand for money.[40] The basic—and familiar —point of this theory is that an individual's alternative cost of carrying over his wealth from one period to the next in the form of cash balances is the profit that he could obtain by carrying over this wealth in the form of other assets. Now, in the case under discussion there are two such possible assets: commodities and bonds. The profit that can be obtained by carrying over a bond is measured by the rate of interest. Similarly, the profit that can be obtained by carrying over commodities is measured by the anticipated rate of increase in prices. Hence just as we assume a negatively sloping demand curve for money as a function of the rate of

---

[39] The foregoing argument has been elaborated here because of the contrary contention of two recent writers that the real-balance effect of a price decline expected to be permanent is necessarily greater than that of a temporary one. See J. H. Power, "Price Expectations, Money Illusion, and the Real-Balance Effect," *Journal of Political Economy*, LXVII (1959), 133a and 135b; T. Mayer, "The Empirical Significance of the Real Balance Effect," *Quarterly Journal of Economics*, LXXIII (1959), 289.

[40] The following two paragraphs are based on the stimulating discussion in Phillip Cagan, "The Monetary Dynamics of Hyperinflation," in *Studies in the Quantity Theory of Money* (ed. Milton Friedman, Chicago, 1956), pp. 31–32. See also Milton Friedman, *Essays in Positive Economics* (Chicago, 1953), p. 255, and A. J. Brown, "Interest, Prices and the Demand Schedule for Idle Money," *Oxford Economic Papers*, II (1939), 46–69.

interest, so can we assume one as a function of the rate of price increase. In both cases the negative slope expresses the fact that the higher the alternative cost of holding cash balances, the smaller the amount demanded. On the other hand, it should be noted that though the rate of interest must be positive, the same is obviously not true of the rate of price increase. The more this is negative—that is, the greater the anticipated price decline—the greater the amount of money demanded.

This symmetry between the rate of interest and the rate of price increase brings out the fact that even the existence of certain anticipations of a price increase will not cause an absolute flight from cash. Instead, just as in the case of the interest rate, it will simply cause the individual to adjust his holdings of real cash balances so that the marginal utility of the liquidity they provide compensates him for the opportunity costs of holding these balances. In other words, what we should expect during a period of anticipated price increases is not that rational individuals will engage in an absolute flight from money, but that they will simply decrease their holdings of real money balances because of the increased cost involved. Thus the anticipation of further price increases during an inflationary process need not make it a self-perpetuating explosive one.[41] We shall return to this point in Chapter XII:7.

The obverse side of this argument is that during a deflationary period the rational individual will not necessarily continue to increase the volume of postponed purchases in order to benefit from the anticipated lower price level. In particular, we see from equations (17) and (18) that if the rate of decline in the price level remains constant, no additional substitution of future for present commodities will take place. The implications of this point will be further discussed in Chapter XIV:5.

[41] Cagan, *op. cit.*, pp. 64–73.

VII. Money as a Producer's Good[1]

*1. An inventory approach to the theory of money. The isoquants and
the optimum portfolio. 2. The implications for the Fisherine analysis.
3. The nature of the demand functions. Concluding remarks.*

1. AN INVENTORY APPROACH TO THE THEORY OF MONEY.
THE ISOQUANTS AND THE OPTIMUM PORTFOLIO

The two preceding chapters have approached the theory of money
from the viewpoint that money is a consumer's good, and that the demand for it—like the demand for any such good—should accordingly
be derived from a utility function which reflects the services which it
provides.[2] This, however, is not a methodologically necessary approach.
For the transactions demand for money can also be rationalized on the
basis of the assumption that the individual derives utility only from the
consumption of commodities, and that he holds money only as a
means of achieving a more desirable "basket" of these commodities.
This, indeed, is the kind of rationale which lies behind the demand for
bonds in Chapter V above: that is, despite the fact that bonds *per se*

---

[1] This chapter is based on both the published and unpublished portions of the
paper referred to on p. 118, footnote 1 above.

[2] Note that in the case of the precautionary demand, the utility function actually
reflects only the *dis*utility of *bond* holdings; cf. equation (b) in footnote 10 on p. 124
above.

do not provide any utility, they are held for their "indirect utility," i.e., for the interest they yield and for the improvement they make possible in the time shape of the consumption stream.[3]

In more formal terms, the alternative approach which will be presented in this chapter considers money and bonds to be producer's, and not consumer's, goods. Correspondingly, the individual's optimum portfolio of money and bonds will be analyzed from the same general viewpoint used in analyzing a firm's optimum combination of factors of production. And the particular aspect of the theory of the firm that will concern us is that dealing with the determination of its optimum inventory policy.[4]

The first change that will accordingly be introduced into the analysis of the transactions demand—*vis à vis* that of Chapter V—is that the imperfect substitutability of bonds and money is now assumed to follow not from the subjective bother of converting the former into the latter, but from the objective cost of so doing. In particular, it is now assumed that if in the course of the week the individual should run out of cash as a result of the stochastic payment process described in Chapter V: 2, he can always replenish his balances by selling bonds at a fixed price equal to $1/[1 + (1 - x)r]$, where x (which takes on values from 0 to 1) represents the proportion of the week which has elapsed at the time the transaction takes place. Such sales are accompanied by a double

---

[3] For earlier attempts (though along different lines than will be followed below) to rationalize the positive demand for money without putting financial assets into the utility function, see J. Marschak, "The Rationale of Money Demand and of 'Money Illusion,'" *Metroeconomica*, II (1950), 79–87, and K. Brunner, "Inconsistency and Indeterminacy in Classical Economics," *Econometrica*, XIX (1951), 169–71. These attempts have been discussed in my "Indirect-Utility Approach to the Theory of Money, Assets, and Savings," *op. cit.*, Section 1.

[4] The basic indebtedness of what follows to the fundamental contributions of Baumol and Tobin will be clear to all. See W. J. Baumol, "The Transactions Demand for Cash: An Inventory Theoretic Approach," *Quarterly Journal of Economics*, LXVI (1952), 545–56, and J. Tobin, "The Interest Elasticity of Transactions Demand for Cash," *Review of Economics and Statistics*, XXXVIII (1956), 241–47. I have also benefited from the introductory part of K. J. Arrow, S. Karlin, and H. Scarf, *Studies in the Mathematical Theory of Inventory and Production* (Stanford, 1958).

I should emphasize at the outset that a rigorous development of the following argument requires a far greater degree of mathematical competence than I possess. As a result this chapter relies heavily on intuitive argumentation and, indeed, at many points assumes properties which should be proved. Correspondingly, the discussion at these points can be taken only as illustrating the general approach followed—and as indicating the analytical problems yet to be solved.

"penalty cost." First, the individual forfeits that part of the interest he would have earned had he held the bond until the end of the week. Second, he must pay a fee to his brokers for their services in carrying out the transaction. This brokerage fee is assumed to consist of one element which is fixed regardless of the size of the sale, and one element which varies with it. Thus we might think of the fee as equalling $a + bY$, where Y represents the number of bonds sold, and a and b are strictly positive constants.[5] [6]

Conversely, should the individual find himself with a temporary excess of cash, he can purchase bonds during the week at the afore-mentioned price and hold them for their interest yield. Such a trans-action will obviously be carried out only if the expected yield to the end of the week exceeds the brokerage fee that must be paid in this case too.[7]

[5] This fee is the device employed by Baumol and Tobin in their analyses of the transactions demand; see the preceding footnote. Cf. also Schlesinger's reference to "the difference between net purchase and sales prices" as constituting part of the "friction" involved in converting assets into cash (*op. cit.*, p. 29 of the English translation).

Strictly speaking, before introducing brokerage services into the analysis we should extend the model to the case where incomes are not given, but are instead earned by the sale of goods and services. For simplicity, however, this complication is ignored.

[6] Note that in our oversimplified two-period model there is almost a certainty that the individual will have to sell all his bonds at various points during the second week: for the end of this week must find him with no assets. This element of unrealism could be eliminated by assuming that the individual wishes to hold a portfolio at the end of the second period (he wishes to leave an inheritance when he dies). In formal terms this means that this portfolio (though not the one at the end of the first week) enters his utility function.

Alternatively, we could eliminate the absolute necessity for selling bonds in the second week by extending the analysis to n periods. This would, of course, leave the problem for the last period. This problem, however, would also disappear as n approaches infinity: that is, as we consider an individual with an infinite horizon. In its operational implications such an assumption would seem to be very close to that of the preceding paragraph. For to assume that every generation wishes to leave an inheritance for the following generation is effectively to assume that the family is an infinitely-lived unit.

In any event, it can be conjectured that neither of the foregoing types of generaliza-tion would affect the basic outlines of the analysis which follows.

[7] If this transaction is carried out in the first week, it is conceivable that only one such fee will have to be paid. On the other hand, if it is planned for the second and final week of his horizon, the individual will almost certainly have to resell these bonds at a subsequent point in the week. Hence the expected yield in this case must cover a double brokerage fee ("in and out"). This necessity for a double fee would disappear under either of the generalizations described in the preceding footnote.

As is implied by the terminology used, the foregoing assumptions specify a problem in inventory theory. More specifically, denote the penalty costs of the first and second weeks, respectively, by P_1 and P_2. Clearly, these are random variables whose distribution depends on the nature of the stochastic payment process, as well as on the rate of interest and the brokerage fee. For simplicity, assume once again (p. 120) that the intraweek budgetary adjustments necessitated by the random incurrence of these penalty costs are made by the individual exclusively in terms of his concurrent expenditures on commodities. Thus the actual level of these expenditures is also a random variable. Finally, assume—in accordance with the usual approach of inventory theory— that the individual is concerned solely with the expected value of his stochastic decision variables.[8] This means that his utility function depends solely on

$$
(1) \qquad E[Z_1] = R_1 - \frac{1}{1+r} \frac{B_1}{p} - \frac{M_1}{p} - E[P_1]
$$

and

$$
(2) \qquad E[Z_2] = R_2 + \frac{B_1}{p} + \frac{M_1}{p} - E[P_2],
$$

respectively, where once again $E[\ \ ]$ represents the expected value of the variable in question, and where the nonstochastic nature of B_1/p and M_1/p is a consequence of the same argument presented on p. 120 above.

What can be said about $E[P_1]$ and $E[P_2]$? Clearly these depend on— among other things—the level of money balances with which the individual enters the week in question and the contracted-for volume of commodity purchases. For the larger this volume relative to cash balances, the greater the probability that the latter will prove inadequate

---

[8] Cf. Alan S. Manne, *Economic Analysis for Business Decisions* (New York, 1961), Chapter 8; T. M. Whitin, *The Theory of Inventory Management* (2nd ed., Princeton, 1957), Chapter 3.

The fact that, as we shall now see, the individual will nevertheless hold more than one asset is not a violation of the rule presented on p. 121 above: for in the present case the effective rate of return on bonds is not *given*, but depends instead on the magnitude of the penalty costs, which in turn depends on the size and composition of the portfolio. Cf. the next paragraph of the text.

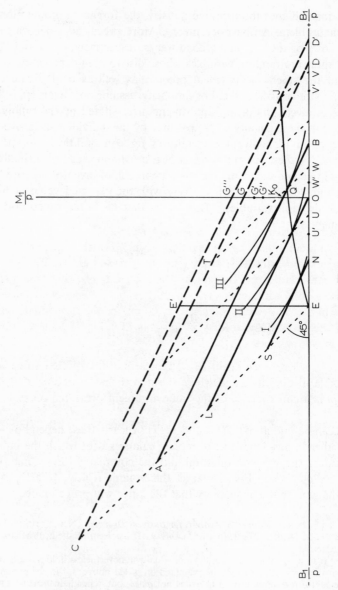

FIGURE VII-1.

and hence the higher the expected penalty costs. Now, the contracted-for purchases in the first and second week are represented, respectively, by

$$R_1 - \frac{1}{1+r}\frac{B_1}{p} - \frac{M_1}{p} \quad \text{and} \quad R_2 + \frac{B_1}{p} + \frac{M_1}{p}.$$

We can therefore write the penalty functions

(3) $$E[P_1] = F\left(R_1 - \frac{1}{1+r}\frac{B_1}{p} - \frac{M_1}{p}; \frac{M_0}{p}, r, a, b\right)$$

and

(4) $$E[P_2] = G\left(R_2 + \frac{B_1}{p} + \frac{M_1}{p}, \frac{M_1}{p}; r, a, b\right),$$

whose partial derivatives with respect to the second argument $F_2(\ )$ and $G_2(\ )$ are assumed to be negative, while all other partial derivatives are assumed positive. Note that in general neither $E[P_1]$ nor $E[P_2]$ is zero. Note too that money balances appear in these two functions in quite different ways. In particular, the money balances available in the first week, M_0/p, are a datum for the individual; but those of the second are a decision variable. The significance of this distinction will be made clear below.

With the aid of the foregoing discussion we can now provide an alternative rationale of the indifference map of Figure V-3, reproduced (with one slight modification to be noted in a moment) in Figure VII-1. In particular, equation (4) implies that—given the rate of interest and the brokerage fee—$E[P_2]$ is determined by the size and composition of the portfolio which the individual plans to hold at the beginning of the second week. It follows that every point in Figure VII-1 now represents a certain level of $E[P_2]$, and hence—by equation (2)—a certain level of $E[Z_2]$. Thus, for example, point Q represents the level of $E[Z_2]$ measured (say) by $EW' = EW - W'W$, where $W'W$ represents the relevant value of $E[P_2]$.[9]

Let curves I, II, and III in Figure VII-1 be loci of points representing, respectively, different fixed (and ascending) levels of $E[Z_2]$. Thus these curves correspond to the isoquants of a firm. By assumption (p. 149), given the level of $E[Z_1]$, the individual is indifferent as to the particular

---

[9] Cf. equation (2). Contrast this with the discussion on p. 99 above.

point on any such curve that he occupies. Thus the family of such isoquants can be termed an indifference map. Note, however, that in contrast with the map in Figure V-2, that of Figure VII-1 is by construction unaffected by changes in the level of $E[Z_1]$.[10]

The negative slope of the foregoing curves is a simple reflection of the fact that an increase in (say) the money-component of the individual's portfolio—while its bond-component is kept constant—will, by (4) and (2), increase $E[Z_2]$. By the same argument used in connection with Figure V-2, we can also see that the absolute value of this slope must be less than unity. For a southeast movement along a dotted 45° line in Figure VII-1 will decrease money balances while keeping the planned volume of future purchases constant. Hence it must increase $E[P_2]$ and thus decrease $E[Z_2]$.[11]

Indeed—and once again in contrast with the map of Figure V-3[12]— these curves retain their less-than-unitary slope leftwards of the satiety line EE'. This is a consequence of our present assumption that there can also take place intraweek conversions of money into bonds. Hence at any point in the satiety region where the expected interest earnings on such conversions exceed the brokerage fees, the expected penalty costs are negative, and, indeed, become increasingly negative as we move northwest along a 45° line. At the same time, it can be shown that the absolute value of the slope in this region must be larger than $1/(1 + r)$. For consider the aforementioned northwest movement. This replaces one dollar's worth of bonds (at their *maturity* value) by one dollar of cash which, because of his satiety, the individual will convert into

---

[10] Cf. p. 108 above.

[11] These properties can be deduced analytically as follows: Substituting from (4) into (2) and differentiating the resulting equation implicitly as of a given level of $E[Z_2]$, we obtain the absolute slope of any indifference curve in Figure VII-1 as

$$- \frac{dM_1}{dB_1} = \frac{1 - G_1(\ )}{1 - G_1(\ ) - G_2(\ )}.$$

Since by assumption $0 < G_1(\ ) < 1$ and $G_2(\ ) < 0$, this must be positive and less than unity.

The second derivative of the indifference curve can be obtained by differentiating the foregoing once again. However, in order to evaluate its sign—and thus determine the convexity of the curve—we must have more specific information about the signs of the second derivatives of $G(\ )$. Within our present oversimplified analysis, then, we shall suffice with the inference of convexity in the neighborhood of any observed interior point; see Hicks, *Value and Capital*, p. 22.

[12] Cf. p. 103 above. For yet another contrast, see p. 154 below.

interest-yielding bonds at the beginning of the second week. Hence this movement makes him better off. Due, however, to the brokerage fee and to the fact that these bonds will be held for less than a full week,[13] the net yield on this intraweek investment is necessarily less than the rate of interest. Hence the compensating change in his portfolio that will keep the individual at the same level of $E[Z_2]$ must involve a reduction in his cash balances which is less than $1/(1 + r)$ of the original increase represented by the northwest movement. Hence the inequality.[14]

In any event, given the expected level of present consumption represented by budget line AB in Figure VII-1,[15] the individual's optimum portfolio is determined by the point of tangency Q: for this portfolio enables him to achieve the highest level of $E[Z_2]$ consonant (from the viewpoint of the budget restraint) with the given level of $E[Z_1]$. Alternatively (in terms more in keeping with the treatment of money as a producer's good) Q is that portfolio for which the marginal revenue product of cash balances equals their marginal factor cost—for which the expected savings in penalty costs generated by the marginal unit of money held equals the interest that could have been earned on the marginal bond foregone.[16] [17]

---

[13] Cf. footnote 6 above. We can also assume that interest is lost because the intraweek conversion can be made only after a finite portion of the week has elapsed.

[14] In terms of the formula presented in footnote 11 above, the satiety region is characterized by $G_1(\ ) = 0$ and $-G_2(\ ) = k$, where $0 \leqslant k < r$. This immediately yields

$$-\frac{dM_1}{dB_1} = \frac{1}{1+k} < \frac{1}{1+r}.$$

If intraweek conversions of money into bonds are not permitted, $G_2(\ ) = 0$ in the satiety region, so that the slope is unity. This can also be seen directly from equation (2), after noting that $E[P_2]$ is now zero in this region.

[15] Note that (in contrast with the situation on p. 99 above) this is less than $K_0 G$ by (say) the distance $G'G$ on the Y-axis of Figure VII-1, where $G'G$ is assumed to measure the relevant value of $E[P_1]$. Hence the value of $E[Z_1]$ corresponding to AB is represented by $K_0 G'$ on the Y-axis. Cf. equation (1) above.

[16] Making use once again of the formula in footnote 11, we must have at a point of tangency

(a) $$-\frac{1 - G_1(\ )}{1 - G_1(\ ) - G_2(\ )} = -\frac{1}{1+r},$$

where $-1/(1 + r)$ is, of course, the slope of the budget line. This reduces to

(b) $$-G_2(\ ) + rG_1(\ ) = r.$$

The left-hand side is the marginal savings on penalty costs, decomposed into that

Note that under our present assumptions any two individuals with the same income stream must also have the same isoquant map in Figure VII-1. Hence if their levels of present consumption are the same, so will their optimum portfolios be. In brief, given the level of $E[Z_1]$, the individual's demand for financial assets in the foregoing model—like a firm's demand for inputs in the pure theory of production—is completely specified by technology (the nature of the stochastic payment process) and prices (the rate of interest and the brokerage fee). In contrast with the situation in Chapters V–VI, individual differences play no role.

Such differences can, however, be introduced into the analysis in the same way as in the theory of the firm: namely, by assuming that the maximizing units in question differ in their "efficiency." Alternatively, we could assume that different individuals must pay different brokerage fees. Within the framework of the preceding model, this is something of a *deus ex machina*. But as soon as we extend the notion of brokerage fees to include the imputed cost of the time involved in making an intraweek transaction; and as soon as we extend the analysis to a model in which income is not exogenous, but is earned by individuals who receive different wage rates for their labor services—then differing brokerage fees become a very meaningful assumption.[18] Note that in this way the disutility of carrying out an intraweek transaction (like the disutility of any other kind of work) must also be taken into account in determining the individual's optimum supply of labor services, so that the present analysis would merge into that of Chapter V.

2. The Implications for the Fisherine Analysis

In keeping with our usual practice, let us now drop the assumption that $E[Z_1]$ is arbitrarily fixed and examine the determination of its

---

part due to increased money holdings, and that part due to the fact that this increase reduces the contracted-for volume of future purchases by the interest foregone.

[17] It is clear from the preceding paragraph that Q must lie outside the satiety region.

[18] The more general question of the implications for demand theory of attributing differing transactions costs to individuals with different wage rates is discussed in Jacob Mincer, "Market Prices, Opportunity Costs, and Income Effects," in Carl Christ, *et al.*, *Measurement in Economics: Studies in Mathematical Economics and Econometrics in Memory of Yehuda Grunfeld* (Stanford, 1963), pp. 67–82.

optimum level. This is done in terms of the Fisherine analysis of Figure VII-2. In view of the assumption that the individual is concerned solely with the expected values of his consumption levels (p. 149), we can—in contrast with the situation in Figure VI-2—assume that there exists a unique indifference map between these levels.

Consider now the relevant budget restraint. This can be derived from Figure VII-1 by considering the locus of points of tangency generated by changing the level of $E[Z_1]$,[19] while keeping constant the rate of

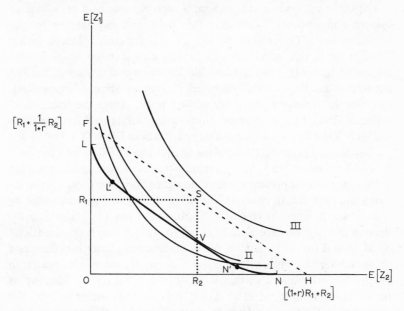

FIGURE VII-2.

interest and the stream of income: for such a locus enables us to define the maximum level of $E[Z_2]$ that the individual can afford for every given level of $E[Z_1]$. This path is represented in Figure VII-1 by *EJ*. By virtue of the assumptions of a positive relationship between money holdings and future consumption, and of economies of scale

---

[19] As will be recalled (p. 152), this leaves the isoquant map unaffected.

in such holdings,[20] it is similar in its slope[21] and convexity to ET in Figure V-3.

The origin of this path at point E reflects the fact that the planned volume of future purchases at this point—and hence $E[P_2]$—is zero. Note, however, that the (maximum) expected level of present consumption corresponding to E is less than $R_1 + R_2/(1 + r)$ by the expected penalty costs of the first period. At this point these are also at a maximum, represented in Figure VII-1 by the distance GG'' on the Y-axis.

The other extreme of the path, at J, corresponds to a zero level of present consumption. Note that this point lies beyond the former boundary line CD: for since he has no need for cash balances during the first week, the individual will convert all his initial holdings into bonds, so that $E[P_1]$ is negative. We have however assumed that the net interest earnings on this intraweek conversion are not large enough to offset the penalty costs of the second week. Hence the (maximum) expected level of future consumption corresponding to J is represented in Figure VII-1 by EV', which is less (by $V'D$) than $ED = (1 + r)R_1 + R_2$.

Note too the asymmetric behavior of $E[P_1]$ and $E[P_2]$ which has been assumed in Figure VII-1. $E[P_1]$ is represented as increasing steadily from $-GG'''$ to $+GG''$ as present consumption goes from zero to its maximum along the path EJ. In contrast, the magnitude of $E[P_2]$ represented by $V'V$ is not depicted as significantly different from $U'U$. This is a reflection of the difference already noted (p. 151) between the fixed level of M_0/p and the variable level of M_1/p. Since the latter is chosen as a component of an optimally composed portfolio, there is no reason to believe that—beyond a certain level—$E[P_2]$ will grow significantly as future consumption increases along the path. In other words, the individual will adjust his level of planned money holdings to his level of planned consumption. The proviso is however necessary in view of the earlier argument that $E[P_2]$ approaches zero together with future consumption.

[20] Cf. pp. 104–105 above.

It might be noted that these economies of scale would obtain even in the absence of a stochastic payment process. Indeed, the inventory models of Baumol and Tobin yield a "square-root formula" even though they assume that the timing of payments is known with certainty. On this interesting coincidence of inventory theory, see Manne, *op. cit.*, p. 130.

[21] There is an implicit assumption here that changes in $E[P_1]$ and $E[P_2]$ are of second-order importance.

As already indicated, these properties of the path *EJ* dictate the form of the relevant budget restraint *LN* in Figure VII-2. Thus they imply that *LN* must be negatively sloped[22] and below the Fisherine restraint.[23] In particular, the distances *FL* and *NH* in this diagram are respectively equal to *GG″* and *V′D* in Figure VII-1. Note too that the fact that every two individuals facing the same objective conditions must have the same path *EJ* (p. 154) now reflects itself in the more familiar guise that they must have the same budget restraint.

A less familiar aspect of the budget restraint *LN* is, however, the variability of its slope. This is a consequence of two differences between the present case and the usual Fisherine one. First, transfers of purchasing power from one period to another are now effected not exclusively by means of bond transactions at a constant rate of interest, but by shifts in the size and composition—and hence over-all rate of return—of optimally selected portfolios of bonds and money. Second, these transfers are also accompanied by changes in penalty costs.

By deriving the equation corresponding to *LN*, more detailed conjectures about this slope can be made. This equation is obtained by multiplying equations (2) on p. 149 by $1/(1 + r)$ and adding it to (1), so as to yield

(5)
$$E[Z_1] + \frac{1}{1 + r} E[Z_2] = R_1 + \frac{R_2}{1 + r} - \frac{1}{1 + r} r\left(\frac{M_1}{p}\right)$$
$$- \left\{E[P_1] + \frac{E[P_2]}{1 + r}\right\}.$$

The right-hand side of this equation can be interpreted as the wealth of an individual, net of the inherent costs of overcoming the frictions of a money economy. These costs are of two types, represented, respectively,

---

[22] Cf. the preceding footnote.

[23] It would, however, be an egregious *non sequitur* to infer from this fact that the individual has been made worse off by the use of money. For the latter has been introduced not into a frictionless Fisherine economy represented by budget restraint *FH*, but into a barter economy suffering from far more serious frictions than those represented by the brokerage fees of the money economy, and hence enjoying far fewer of the benefits of specialization and exchange. Correspondingly, the income stream of the individual in such a barter economy, and hence his wealth, would actually lie much below the level represented by wealth restraint *LN*.

by the third and fourth terms on the right-hand side of (5): first, the discounted value of the insurance premium which the individual pays (in terms of interest foregone) when he holds cash balances instead of bonds; second, the discounted value of the expected penalty costs that he incurs despite the holdings of these balances.[24] In other words, holding cash balances provides a type of "deductible" insurance policy: it diminishes the risk of losses without eliminating it entirely.

As usual, the slope of this restraint measures the cost of an additional unit of present consumption in terms of the marginal amount of future consumption that must be foregone. The greater the decrease in required money balances enabled by the decreased level of future consumption, the lower this marginal cost; hence the smaller the slope (in absolute value) with reference to the Y-axis. On the other hand, the greater the increased penalty costs of increasing present consumption, the greater the marginal cost, and hence the slope. Thus the behavior of this slope is the resultant of these two countervailing forces.

Consider now the situation that prevails in the region where the individual is planning "high" levels of consumption in both the present and the future, so that in both periods he is enjoying the economies of scale connected with money holdings. It can then intuitively be seen that a shift of consumption from one period to another will not significantly affect his total transaction costs for both periods and hence will not affect the marginal cost of this shift. In other words, the countervailing influences will then more or less offset each other, so that the marginal cost will be approximately constant at $1 + r$. This is the situation represented by the segment $L'N'$ of the budget restraint in Figure VII-2.

The situation is, however, quite different when one of the consumption levels is low. Thus consider the budget restraint in the neighbourhood of the Y-axis. To argue somewhat unrigorously, further increases in $E[Z_1]$ here will have little effect on present penalty costs; on the other hand, the corresponding decreases in $E[Z_2]$ will decrease future penalty costs at an increasing rate. Hence it would seem that segment LL' is convex with a slope (with respect to the Y-axis) less than $1 + r$.

---

[24] Graphically, these two costs are represented for (say) point Q in Figure VII-1 by WB and $G'G + \dfrac{W'W}{1+r}$, respectively. Cf. p. 151 and p. 153, footnote 15 above.

By a similar argument, segment $M'N$ is convex with a slope greater than $1 + r$.[25]

In this way we see that the existence of the foregoing monetary frictions does not require any essential changes in the usual Fisherine analysis.[26] Assuming that the individual is free of time preference proper, so that the indifference curves in Figure VII-2 are symmetric about the 45° ray through the origin; and assuming that the rate of interest is of the magnitude experienced in reality—then the individual will be consuming "large" quantities of both $E[Z_1]$ and $E[Z_2]$, so that the relevant part of the wealth restraint is the straight line $L'N'$, more or less parallel to FH. Thus once again the individual's optimum combination of present and future consumption is determined by his tastes, his wealth (net of the transactions costs of a money economy), and the rate of interest. Similarly, if the marginal rate of substitution of $E[Z_1]$ for $E[Z_2]$ is dependent only on the ratio between them, an increase in wealth, interest being held constant, will cause a proportionate increase in the demands for both present and future commodities.[27]

3. The Nature of the Demand Functions. Concluding Remarks

As in Chapter V:6 above, we can make use of the foregoing diagrammatic analysis to deduce properties of the excess-demand functions. Once again these can be shown to be free of money illusion and to reflect the real-balance effect. Consider now the effect of a decrease in the rate of interest. Here there is a double contrast with the indifference-curve analysis of Chapter V:6. On the one hand, the map in Figure VII-1 will not shift as a consequence of the change caused in the optimum level of present consumption;[28] on the other hand, it will shift as a consequence of the fact that this map is directly dependent on the rate of interest.[29] In particular, the indifference curve that was tangent at

[25] A rigorous derivation of these results requires knowledge about the second derivatives which arise when equation (5) is differentiated implicitly.

[26] Cf. especially the presentation of this analysis in Friedman, *Theory of the Consumption Function*, pp. 7–14.

[27] Compare this with the discussion of Chapter VI:2.

[28] Cf. pp. 108 and 152 above.

[29] Cf. equations (2) and (4) on pp. 149 and 151 above.

As a result of the reduction in $E[P_1]$ which such a decrease in interest generates, it also causes the point G' on the Y-axis of Figure VII-1 to move upwards, so that (say) the line AB now represents a higher level of $E[Z_1]$.

Q will now be replaced by one which cuts the original budget line at this point from above. Similarly, through every point on an indifference curve in the original map there will now pass a new indifference curve with a steeper slope. This shift in the indifference map tends thus to offset the increased steepness of the budget line.

The common sense interpretation of these two countervailing forces is that the reduction in interest decreases the marginal savings in penalty costs as well as the marginal cost of holding cash balances (cf. p. 153 above). This formulation also provides a justification for assuming that the latter force will predominate: for whereas interest is the whole of marginal cost, it is only one element of the penalty costs.[30] On the basis of the same type of consideration cited on p. 108 above, we shall therefore assume that on balance the decrease in interest causes a shift out of bonds and into money.

Consider now the effect of a decrease in the illiquidity of bonds— which in the present context means a decrease in brokerage fees. Once again it is necessary to make assumptions similar to those on pp. 108–109[31] in order to conclude that such a decrease causes a shift out of money and into bonds. Clearly, if the brokerage fee were to disappear completely, the individual would hold only bonds.

In sum, the analysis of money as a producer's good in this chapter yields demand functions of the same general properties as those yielded by the analysis in terms of a consumer's good in Chapter V. This means that—at the present level of generality[32]—these two approaches to the transactions demand are operationally equivalent: they cannot be identified, in the econometric sense of the term.[33]

From the viewpoint of welfare economics, however, there is a difference. For the treatment of money as a consumer's good implies that its services—like those of any other consumer's good—should be included in the national product. The approach of the present chapter, on the other hand, implies that these services are not a final product, but

[30] Cf. p. 153, footnote 16 above.

[31] Except for the now redundant assumption that the map in Figure VII-1 is not affected by changes in the level of current consumption; cf. the first paragraph of this section.

[32] Since, however, we can in principle specify the nature of the penalty function — in contrast with that of the utility function—the approach of this chapter is potentially capable of leading to a more precise specification of the demand functions.

[33] Note too the observation on p. 154 above, which indicates that even on a purely theoretical level these two approaches can merge.

one of the costs of increasing the economy's degree of specialization and exchange, and hence commodity output.[34] Correspondingly, the contribution of these money services to the total welfare of the economy is already reflected in this output, and it would be "double counting" to include them again. This is the meaning of our representing the services of money balances as a deduction from total wealth on the right-hand side of equation (5), and not as an addition to consumption on its left-hand side.[35]

---

[34] "Payments to banks, ... brokerage houses, etc., ... are payments not for final goods flowing to ultimate consumers, but libations of oil on the machinery of industrial society—activities intended to eliminate friction in the productive system, not net contributions to ultimate consumption" [Simon Kuznets, *Economic Change* (New York, 1953), p. 162].

As Kuznets has emphasized, this distinction between "intermediate" and "ultimate" consumption is one which leads to the exclusion from the national product of many other activities of a modern urban industrial society: intermediate government services, a good part of transportation, technical education, and the like. This problem, of course, becomes important only when making welfare comparisons in time or space between economies with highly different economic structures. [Cf. *ibid.*, pp. 161–63, 195–96. For a more general discussion of this distinction—and its implications for national-income accounting—see Kuznets, *National Income and Its Composition, 1919–1938* (New York, 1941), pp. 34–45.]

[35] Cf. equations (19) and (21) on pp. 110 and 112 above.

VIII. A Critique of Neoclassical Monetary Theory[1]

1. Introduction. The deficiencies of the traditional transactions and cash-balance approaches in analyzing the effects of a change in M. *The failure to test the stability of the equilibrium absolute price level and the significance thereof. 2. The cash-balance equation and the "uniform unitary elasticity of demand for money." 3. Valid and invalid dichotomies of the pricing process. The proper relation between monetary theory and value theory. 4. Conclusion: the failure of neoclassical monetary theory to fully understand the real-balance effect. 5. The effects of a change in* K. *6. The effects of a change in* T. *7. The implications of Say's Identity.*

1. INTRODUCTION. THE DEFICIENCIES OF THE TRADITIONAL TRANSACTIONS AND CASH-BALANCE APPROACHES IN ANALYZING THE EFFECTS OF A CHANGE IN M. THE FAILURE TO TEST THE STABILITY OF THE EQUILIBRIUM ABSOLUTE PRICE LEVEL AND THE SIGNIFICANCE THEREOF

Terminological disputes are rather sterile. Hence it is best to preclude them by making clear at the outset that "neoclassical" is being used here as a shorthand designation for the once widely accepted body of thought which organized monetary theory around a transactions

---

[1] This chapter concentrates on the theory of money and prices. The discussion of neoclassical interest theory is best deferred to Chapter XV:1.

or cash-balance type of equation, and which then used these equations to validate the classical quantity theory of money. Subsidiary—though, as we shall see, persistently recurring—components of this body of thought were a certain description of the demand function for money and a certain conception of the role of monetary theory *vis-à-vis* value theory.

In its cash-balance version—associated primarily with the names of Walras,[2] Marshall,[3] Wicksell,[4] and Pigou[5]—neoclassical theory assumed that, for their convenience, individuals wish to hold a certain proportion, K, of the real volume of their planned transactions, T, in the form of real money balances. The demand for these balances thus equals KT. Correspondingly, the demand for nominal money balances is KPT, where P is the price level of the commodities transacted. The equating of this demand to the supply of money, M, then produced the famous Cambridge equation, $M = KPT$. In the transactions version —associated primarily with the names of Newcomb and Fisher[6]—the velocity of circulation, V, replaced its reciprocal, K, to produce the equally famous equation of exchange, $MV = PT$. These equations were the parade-grounds on which neoclassical economists then put the classical quantity theory of money through its paces.[7]

The most persuasive formulations of this theory were developments of the following tripartite thesis: an increase in the quantity of money disturbs the optimum relation between the level of money balances and the individual's expenditures; this disturbance generates an increase

---

[2] But it will be argued in Note C:2 that though Walras definitely presented a cash-balance *equation*, he did not present a cash-balance *theory*.

[3] For references, see Note G:1.

[4] For references, see Note E:1.

[5] For references, see Note G:1.

[6] For references, see Note F:1.

[7] The reader will observe that $M = KPT$ and $MV = PT$ are treated here as *equations*, and not as *identities*. This interpretation is borne out by the works referred to in the preceding footnotes. It will also be observed that these two equations have been treated as analytically equivalent. Without committing ourselves on the attempts that have sometimes been made to distinguish substantively between them, we merely note that for our present purposes any such distinction can be disregarded. Cf. J. M. Keynes, *Treatise on Money* (London, 1930), Vol. I, pp. 237–39; Marget, *Theory of Prices*, Vol. I, pp. 424–33.

For good recent accounts of the two neoclassical equations and their respectively associated theories, see L. V. Chandler, *The Economics of Money and Banking* (rev. ed.; New York, 1953), Chapters XXIII–XXV; A. G. Hart, *Money, Debt, and Economic Activity* (rev. ed.; New York, 1953), Chapters X and XII.

in the planned volume of these expenditures (the real-balance effect); and this increase creates pressures on the price level which push it upwards until it has risen in the same proportion as the quantity of money. Among the writers mentioned above, only Wicksell[8] and Fisher[9] provided complete, systematic statements of this thesis. Nevertheless, the other writers made sufficient—if unintegrated—use of its individual components to justify our identifying these components with the general analytic background of neoclassical monetary theory.

Indeed, the basic fact underlined by the foregoing thesis—that the causal relationship between money and prices is not at all a mechanical one, but is instead the economic consequence of the prior effect of changes in the quantity of money on the demand for commodities—was already a commonplace of the classical quantity-theory tradition of Cantillon, Thornton, Ricardo, and Mill,[10] and was particularly vivid in the expositions of those writers who emphasized that the effects of an increase in the quantity of money on prices could not in general be said to be equiproportionate, but depended instead on whose money holdings, and hence whose demands, were increased.[11] This, after all, was the consideration which brought both classical and neoclassical economists to the recognition that a change in the quantity of money could generate "forced savings" and need not therefore always be neutral in its effects.[12]

On the other hand, it must be emphasized that, in contrast to the

---

[8] *Interest and Prices*, pp. 39–41. This is cited in full in Note E:1.

[9] *Purchasing Power of Money*, pp. 153–54. This is cited in full in Note F:1.

[10] For specific references, see Note A.

This is one of the central themes of Marget's study; see, in particular, *Theory of Prices*, Vol. I, pp. 307, 345 ff., and 500 ff. It also seems to me that a good part of H. Hegeland's monograph on the *Quantity Theory of Money* (Göteborg, 1951) suffers from the failure to recognize this fact; see *ibid.*, especially pp. 38–9, 57, 87–92.

[11] Cf., e.g., R. Cantillon, *Essay on the Nature of Trade* (1755), trans. and ed. H. Higgs (London, 1931), p. 179; Mill, *Principles*, pp. 491–2. Marget (*Theory of Prices*, Vol. I, p. 502) cites similar passages from Lubbock and Cairnes.

For this emphasis in later writers, see Walras, *Eléments d'économie politique pure* (first ed.; Lausanne, 1874), p. 181, who essentially repeats Mill; see also the definitive ed. of the *Elements*, ed. Jaffé, p. 328. See also Wicksell, *Interest and Prices*, p. 40; Schumpeter, "Money and the Social Product," *op. cit.*, pp. 191–2, 204–6; and Mises, *op. cit.*, pp. 139–40. But Mises carries himself away to an invalid extreme when he attempts to prove that even in the case of an equiproportionate increase in initial individual money balances, prices will not rise equiproportionately (*ibid.*, pp. 141–2). The nature of his error is best seen from the discussion on p. 45 above.

[12] This will be discussed further in Chapter XV:1.

neoclassical ones, none of these earlier expositions of the quantity theory should be regarded as having recognized the real-balance effect in the fullest sense of the term; for none of them brought out the crucial intermediary stage of the foregoing thesis in which people increase their *flow* of expenditures because they feel that their *stock* of money is too large for their needs. Instead, in a Keynesian-like fashion, these expositions more or less directly connected the increased *outflow* of money expenditures with the increased *inflow* of money receipts: people spend more money because they receive more money, not because their real cash balances as such have been augmented beyond the amount "which their convenience had taught them to keep on hand."[13] But it is precisely this augmentation—and the real-balance effect which it engenders—which helps explain why demand, and hence prices, remain at a higher level even in periods subsequent to the one in which the injection of new money into the economy takes place.[14]

Each part of the foregoing thesis clearly has its counterpart in the argument of Chapters II–IV. This parallelism not only brings out the traditional flavor of this argument—a flavor already accentuated by the suggestive footnotes referring to earlier writers with which it has been deliberately and justifiably seasoned—but it also shows that this argument provides the ultimate, rigorous validation of the classical quantity theory of money itself. Indeed—and this is the paradox—the only traditional elements missing from this demonstration are those very neoclassical equations which have become so strongly associated with the quantity theory as to become almost identified with it! But, as emphasized in the Introduction to this book, this omission, too, is deliberate; for the alternative approach followed here is at once more general, more rigorous, and less likely to mislead.

Thus, for example, the neoclassical equations suffer from the obvious disability that they assign no explicit role to the rate of interest and hence cannot deal with that whole body of theory which analyzes this rate. In particular, they cannot serve to validate the classical proposition that a change in the quantity of money leaves the rate of interest unaffected. Indeed, not only can they not help, they hinder.

---

[13] Fisher, *Purchasing Power of Money*, p. 153, with "his" changed to "their," and "him" to "them."

[14] The distinction made in this sentence will become clearer from the detailed period analysis of Chapter X:3.

For the omission of the rate of interest from the cash-balance equation creates the misleading impression that the classical invariance of this rate holds only in the special case where it does not affect the demand for money. As we have seen in Chapter IV:4, no such restriction is necessary. This is not to deny that in other contexts neoclassical economists did recognize the influence of the rate of interest on the demand for money, and did make other significant extensions of classical interest theory. But it is to stress that these contributions found no place in those fundamental equations which, more than anything else, are the hallmarks of neoclassical monetary theory.[15]

Again, our approach does not depend on the use of the cumbersome and frequently criticized aggregates K, V, P, T, but instead builds only on individual demands for individual commodities with their individual prices. And even when presented in an aggregative form—as it will be in Part Two—it does not needlessly cripple the quantity theory by implying—as does the MV of the transactions equation—that the validity of this theory holds only in the obviously unrealistic case where the aggregate demand for commodities is directly proportionate to the quantity of money. The preceding approach insists only that the demand functions be free of money illusion; otherwise it leaves them free to reflect the full range and variety of individual reactions to changes in the level of initial money balances.[16]

The cash-balance equation frequently replaced these unnecessary and vitiating restrictions on the commodity functions with equally unnecessary—and possibly invalid—restrictions on the money function. Since the details of these restrictions will be described in the next section, there is no need to discuss them further here. Aside from this substantive criticism, the neoclassical cash-balance approach is subject to the more general, pragmatic criticism that has already been voiced in the Introduction. In its neat description of the factors which lead individuals to hold money balances, this approach certainly accomplished its proclaimed objective of bringing these holdings "into relation with volition."[17] But all too often this "humanizing" of the demand for money led to an undue concentration on the money market,

---

[15] As already noted, the full discussion of neoclassical interest theory is deferred to Chapter XV:1.

[16] Cf. above, p. 45.

[17] Pigou, "The Value of Money," *op. cit.*, p. 174.

a corresponding neglect of the commodity markets, and a resulting "dehumanizing" of the analysis of the effects of monetary changes.

The force of this criticism can best be illustrated with the aid of Figure III-2 (p. 47) and its accompanying discussion—though, as will be emphasized in the next section, this figure differs significantly from the usual neoclassical one. What we are saying is that despite the already emphasized fact that adherents of the cash-balance approach recognized the real-balance effect, they frequently remained satisfied with the mechanical comparative-statics proposition that a doubling of the quantity of money shifted the equilibrium position in the money market from R to T; they frequently failed to provide a systematic dynamic analysis of the way in which the monetary increase generated real-balance effects in the commodity markets which propelled the economy from its original equilibrium position to its new one. Now, as the incisive counterexample of Wicksell proves, such an omission is *not* a necessary consequence of this approach. Nevertheless, it cannot be mere coincidence that it is precisely this dynamic analysis which was *not* integrated into the Cambridge cash-balance tradition of Marshall, Pigou, Keynes, and Robertson, with its deliberate emphasis on the money market. It thus appears that, in its analysis of the inflationary impact of a monetary increase, the Cambridge theory was actually less illumed by the spark of "volition" and individual behavior than the Fisherine transactions theory whose "mechanicalism" it was designed to correct![18]

As emphasized sufficiently above, it is one of the specific objectives of the alternative approach developed in this book to avoid this pitfall by taking the analysis directly into the commodity markets. A corollary advantage of this approach is that it enables a precise economic explanation of why, say, a doubling of the quantity of money causes a doubling—and just a doubling, neither more nor less—of the price level.

[18] It is for this reason that the foregoing Cambridge economists are not listed together with Wicksell and Fisher on p. 163 as having presented a full statement of the tripartite quantity-theory thesis. In order to evaluate the validity of this criticism, the reader must himself compare the expositions of the Cambridge school (as cited in Note G:1) with those of Wicksell and Fisher. It is similarly instructive to contrast the Cambridge expositions with those of such cash-balance theorists as Mises (*op. cit.*, pp. 132–5, 138–40, 147–9) and R. G. Hawtrey [*Currency and Credit* (3rd ed.; London, 1927), Chapters III–IV, especially pp. 35, 59–60; as can be seen from p. 35, Hawtrey's "unspent margin" is identical with what is usually referred to as a cash balance].

It shows the essence of the quantity theory to lie in the automatic, corrective market forces which continue to operate through the real-balance effect until this doubled price level is attained. Once again, there is no logical reason why these forces could not have been developed as a standard component of neoclassical monetary theory. Nevertheless, the stubborn fact seems to be that only Wicksell bestirred himself to ask what would happen if prices deviated from the equilibrium level called for by the quantity of money, and to describe how the dynamic forces thereby generated would return them to this level.[19]

The essence of the three preceding paragraphs can be summed up in one sentence: There is a basic chapter missing in practically all neoclassical monetary theory—the chapter which presents a precise dynamic analysis of the determination of the equilibrium absolute level of money prices through the workings of the real-balance effect. This is said, not for that aspect of dynamic analysis which describes the forces propelling the economy toward its new equilibrium position after an initial monetary increase—a problem adequately discussed by many neoclassical economists[20]—but for that aspect which describes the forces stabilizing the economy at this new position once it is reached—a problem separated by just a nuance from the preceding one, but nevertheless discussed only by Wicksell.

It would be a serious error to underestimate the significance of this nuance. The easiest way of convincing the reader of this is to bring him up sharply against the following facts: Walras was a man who never tired of establishing the stability of his system by elaborating on the corrective forces of excess supply that would be called into play should the price lie above its equilibrium value, and the forces of excess demand that would be called into play should it lie below. He did it when he explained how the market determines the equilibrium prices of commodities; he did it again when he explained how the market determines the equilibrium prices of productive services; and he did it a third time when he explained how the market determines the equilibrium prices of capital goods. But he did not do it when he attempted to explain how the market determines the equilibrium "price" of paper money. And Walras is the rule, not the exception. Precisely the same

[19] Cf. Chapter III:3 and the reference to Wicksell's *Interest and Prices*, pp. 39–40, there cited. As already noted, this crucial reference is reproduced in full in Note E:1.

[20] Cf. the references to Fisher, Wicksell, Mises, and Hawtrey in footnote 18 above.

asymmetry recurs among writers of the Cambridge tradition—with their standard supply-and-demand exercise of testing the stability of the equilibrium price in value theory and their standard omission of a corresponding exercise for testing the equilibrium absolute price level in monetary theory![21]

Thus in back of this nuance is the persistent failure of these economists to carry over to their monetary theory a simple, familiar technique of their value theory—and this despite their declared intention of integrating these two theories. We shall return to the significance of this fact in Section 4 below.

2. The Cash-Balance Equation and the "Uniform Unitary Elasticity of Demand for Money"

Another familiar proposition of the neoclassical cash-balance approach—one already alluded to in the preceding section—is that the demand for paper money has "uniform unitary elasticity" and is accordingly represented by a rectangular hyperbola. This theme recurs specifically in the writings of Walras, Marshall, and Pigou. In the case of the latter it is clear that it was considered to be a necessary condition for the validity of the quantity theory of money. In Pigou's words, "an increase in the supply of legal tender ought always, since the elasticity of demand [for legal tender] is equal to unity, to raise prices in the proportion in which the supply has increased." And there is the strong impression that this was also the intended context in which this proposition was advanced by other writers as well. Indeed, it is probably this assumed causal relationship which explains the importance that was attached to it.[22]

This makes it all the more essential to recall that not only is this

[21] On Walras, see Notes B and C:4, especially pp. 562f. On the Cambridge tradition, see Note G:2. See Note F:2 for a discussion of Fisher.

That the asymmetry just described has persisted down to the present can be seen by examining the more recent literature from the same viewpoint that has just been used for the neoclassical. On the other hand, there is not much point in trying to trace this inconsistency back to the classical literature: its value-theory discussions are of too different a nature. See end of Note A.

[22] Pigou, *Essays in Applied Economics* (London, 1923), p. 195. For references to the three writers mentioned here, see Note C (pp. 544 and 567–68) and Note G:3. The latter contains references to other writers too. For the existence of this assumption in the case of Cassel, see end of Note H.

proposition not necessary for the quantity theory, it is not even generally true. All this has been sufficiently explained in Chapters II: 5 and III: 5, with their demonstrations that the real-balance effect makes it generally impossible for the demand for money to be of uniform unitary elasticity, but that nevertheless an increase in the quantity of money causes a proportionate increase in prices. It should, however, be clear that the neoclassical contention about unitary elasticity is not inherent in the Cambridge function as such. Thus, if KPT is the demand for money and M its supply, the excess demand for money, $KPT - M$, correctly reflects the by-now familiar property than an equiproportionate change in P *and* in M causes a proportionate change in the excess amount of money demanded. On the other hand, a change in P alone generates a real-balance effect, hence a change in the planned volume of transactions, T, and hence a *non*proportionate change in the amount of money demanded, KPT. Thus, if properly interpreted, the Cambridge function does *not* imply uniform unitary elasticity.

There are two possible explanations for the failure of neoclassical economists to see this. First, they apparently never realized the need to pin down the meaning of T. Only occasionally did they give it the volitional connotation on which the argument of the preceding paragraph depends. At other times they treated it as something beyond the will of individuals—as the fixed "total resources ... enjoyed by the community." And at still other times they shifted unawares from one connotation to the next.[23] Second, even when they used T in its volitional sense—which is, of course, the only one that is consonant with the *raison d'etre* of the cash-balance approach—they never realized that the real-balance effect precludes T from remaining constant in the face of a change in P. Indeed, a standard lemma of the neoclassical proof of the quantity theory of money was that P and T were independent!

The force of the foregoing criticism is, however, highly attenuated by two considerations. First, if the Marshallian demand curve of value theory is interpreted as one from which the income effect has been eliminated; and if this interpretation is also extended to the Marshallian

---

[23] The quotation is from Pigou, *Essays*, p. 176. But just on the preceding page Pigou gives T a volitional connotation by connecting it with the volume of an individual's "payments" in his "ordinary transactions of life."

The reader will find it instructive to examine from this viewpoint the other expositions of the Cambridge equation referred to in Note G.

demand curve of monetary theory[24]—then the appropriate form of this curve is indeed the rectangular hyperbola of Figure II-1b, generated by confronting individuals with an equiproportionate change in both *P* and *M* (see pp. 27–28 above). Second, even if this interpretation is not accepted, it should in all fairness be said that some exponents of the cash-balance approach merely used "unitary elasticity of demand" as a complicated way of stating that an increase in the quantity of money causes a proportionate increase in prices. In other words, they had in mind the elasticity of the market-equilibrium curve of Figure III-3 (p. 49), not that of the demand curve of Figure II-2b (p. 29), so that they were not really referring to what Marshall denoted by "elasticity of demand." This, however, should not be taken as implying that these writers indicated any awareness of the existence of two conceptually distinct curves. Indeed, they shifted uninhibitedly from one meaning of elasticity to the other—sometimes even within the same sentence. This points up the general fuzziness from which neoclassical monetary theory suffered as a result of its failure to draw the fundamental distinction between individual-experiments, on the one hand, and market-experiments, on the other.[25]

3. Valid and Invalid Dichotomies of the Pricing Process. The Proper Relation Between Monetary Theory and Value Theory

Let us return to the analysis of the effects of a change in the quantity of money. Instead of carrying out this analysis in terms of the absolute level of money prices—which is, of course, the usual approach—we

[24] The reason for hinting that such an extension might not be appropriate is explained on p. 607 below.

The foregoing interpretation is, of course, that of Milton Friedman, who argues that Marshall assumed movements along his demand curve to be accompanied by compensating variations which keep real income constant ["The Marshallian Demand Curve," *Journal of Political Economy*, LVII (1949), as reprinted in *Essays in Positive Economics* (Chicago, 1953), pp. 50–3]. While not accepting the specifics of this argument, I do agree that Marshall's demand curve does not reflect the income effect; see my "Demand Curves and Consumer's Surplus," in Carl Christ, *et al.*, *Measurement in Economics: Studies in Mathematical Economics and Econometrics in Memory of Yehuda Grunfeld* (Stanford, 1963), pp. 104–8.

[25] For specific references to the literature, see Note G:3.

Once again Wicksell is an exception. For he makes it clear that the rectangular hyperbola he draws in his monetary theory is a market-equilibrium curve. See Note E:2.

can do it equivalently in terms of the *real* quantity of money; for once the nominal quantity of money is fixed, its real value varies in inverse proportion to the absolute level of money prices—or, in short, to the absolute price level. Such an approach can then proceed as follows: In the initial equilibrium position of our economy, the real quantity of money is just at that level which satisfies its transactions and precautionary needs. An exogenous increase in the nominal quantity of money then pushes the real quantity above this equilibrium value and thereby creates inflationary pressures in the various markets. The resulting price rise then reduces this real quantity and thereby lessens the disequilibrating inflationary pressures themselves. Now, by assumption, the initial monetary increase has not affected the economy's "taste" for real balances—that is, its desire to hold such balances in order to avoid the inconveniences, costs, and/or embarrassment of default. Hence the economy cannot achieve a new equilibrium position until the absolute price level has risen sufficiently to reduce the real quantity of money to its initial level once again.[26]

Let us now separate into two categories the given conditions (independent variables) which determine the nature of our exchange economy's equilibrium position. First, there are those which describe the economy's "real framework": namely, tastes (including those for *real* money balances) and initial holdings of commodities. Second, there are the conditions which describe its "monetary framework": namely, initial nominal holdings of money. Correspondingly, let us also separate the dependent variables of the analysis into two categories: "real variables," namely, the equilibrium values of relative prices, the rate of interest, and the real quantity of money; and the "monetary variable," namely, the equilibrium value of the absolute price level.[27]

Consider now the classical proposition that a change in the quantity of money merely causes an equiproportionate change in equilibrium money prices. The opening paragraph of this section enables us to

[26] Compare this with the change in the equilibrium real quantity of money that characterizes a shift in liquidity preference; see below, Section 5.

[27] On the distinction between dependent and independent variables, see Chapters I:4 and III:1 above.

Throughout the following analysis we abstract from distribution effects. This enables us to consider the total of initial nominal—and hence real—bond holdings as identically zero. Accordingly, neither one of these holdings appears in the preceding classificatory scheme.

replace this proposition by the equivalent one that such a change has no effect on the equilibrium values of relative prices, the rate of interest, and the real quantity of money. Now, to say that these values are independent of the nominal quantity of money is to say that they can be determined even without knowing this quantity. This permits us to conceive of the pricing process of our exchange economy as being divided into two successive stages: In the first one, specification of the real framework determines the equilibrium values of the real variables of the system. In the second, specification of the monetary framework then determines the equilibrium value of the monetary variable—for this value is simply the ratio between the specified nominal quantity of money and the equilibrium real quantity.[28]

It should be clear that this arbitrary and mechanical act of specifying the nominal quantity of money has nothing whatsoever to do with monetary theory. For, as we shall argue below, this theory is concerned, at the individual level, with the relation between commodity demands and real balances and, at the market level, with the causes of changes in the equilibrium value of these balances. And both of these problems are fully analyzed in the first stage of the foregoing dichotomy. Thus this stage is coterminous with economic analysis: it comprises both value theory and monetary theory. Correspondingly, the second stage of this dichotomy is beyond the pale of economic analysis: it deals with a completely adventitious act.

It should also be clear that the foregoing dichotomy is purely a conceptual one. The real and monetary frameworks of the actual market place are obviously "specified" simultaneously. Similarly, there are only money prices in this market, and these are simultaneously determined. In brief, our dichotomy has no operational significance other than that of the basic quantity-theory proposition from which it is derived.[29]

This dichotomy between relative and money prices must be sharply distinguished from that of Chapter III: 3 between money and accounting prices.[30] First of all, there is the obvious difference in the nature of the prices involved. Parallel to this difference is the one between the data

[28] See Mathematical Appendix 7:*a*(i).

[29] For echoes of the foregoing dichotomy in the literature, see Note I:1.

[30] Above, p. 43. For examples of this dichotomy in the writings of Wicksell, Fisher, Bowley, Cassel, and others, see Note I:2. For a mathematical statement, see Mathematical Appendix 7:*a*(ii).

respectively specified at the second stages of these dichotomies. In the dichotomy of Chapter III:3 this consists of the accounting price of one of the goods; in the present one it consists of the nominal quantity of money. Correspondingly, a change in the value of the supplementary datum in the present dichotomy affects money prices, whereas in that of Chapter III:3 it does not. Finally, the dichotomy of Chapter III:3 can have direct operational significance: there can be actual economics in which first money prices and then accounting prices are determined. Clearly, this additional set of prices is of no economic significance; but, in the present context, this is irrelevant.

Both of these dichotomies must be even more sharply distinguished from yet a third one which, though it has neoclassical roots in the works of Walras, Fisher, Pigou, and Cassel, did not achieve its most explicit form until the later expositions of Divisia, Lange, Modigliani, Schneider, and others. In this form it became undisputedly accepted as a statement of the proper relation between monetary theory, on the one hand, and value theory, on the other.

The point of departure of this familiar dichotomy (in practically every case in which it appears in the literature) is a pure outside-money economy (see p. 15) consisting of commodities and money, but not bonds. The dichotomy then begins by dividing the economy into two sectors: a real sector, described by the excess-demand functions for commodities, and a monetary sector, described by the excess-demand function for money. The former functions are assumed to depend only on relative prices; the latter, on these variables and the absolute price level as well. This assumed insensitivity of the demand functions of the real sector to changes in the absolute level of money prices is referred to as the "homogeneity postulate"[31] and is said to denote absence of "money illusion."[32]

[31] This term was first used by W. Leontief, "The Fundamental Assumption of Mr. Keynes' Monetary Theory of Unemployment," *Quarterly Journal of Economics*, LI (1936–37), 193. It originates in the fact that, in mathematical terms, demand functions which are not affected by an equiproportionate change in money prices are said to be "homogeneous of degree zero" in these prices.

[32] It should be clear to the reader that this does *not* correspond to our use of this term, which defines absence of money illusion as insensitivity to changes in the absolute level of *accounting*—and not *money*—prices; cf. p. 23.

In order to avoid any possible confusion, we might repeat that throughout this discussion "absolute price level" is a shorthand expression for "absolute level of *money* prices."

In a corresponding way, the market excess-demand equations corresponding to these functions are also separated into two groups. The equations of the real sector taken by themselves are then able to determine the equilibrium values of the only variables which appear in them—relative prices. These equations and the variables they determine thus constitute the domain of value theory. The equation of the monetary sector then determines the equilibrium value of the remaining variable—the absolute price level. And this equation and the variable it determines thus constitute the domain of monetary theory.[33]

As with the "unitary elasticity of demand," much of the attractiveness of this dichotomy lay in the belief that it was a necessary condition for the validity of the quantity theory of money.[34] It was felt that unless the demand functions were independent of the absolute price level, monetary increases—which necessarily affect this level—could not preserve their classical neutrality with respect to the real phenomena of the economy. But once again the truth of the matter is that not only is this dichotomy not necessary, not only is it not valid, but its basic assumption is even a denial of the quantity theory itself! For to say that the demand functions of the real sector are not affected by changes in the absolute price level—that is, to assert that they satisfy the "homogeneity postulate"—is to imply that they are not affected by changes in the real value of cash balances. But it is precisely on this real-balance effect that the quantity theory in our present model depends for the inflationary impact of a monetary increase! On the other hand, this dependence in no way violates the *final* neutrality of, say, a doubling of the quantity of money. For in the new equilibrium position the

[33] For the highly probable presence of the foregoing dichotomy in the writings of Walras, Fisher, Pigou, and Cassel, see Notes C:4 (end), F:3, G:4 and H (end), respectively. See also Note E:3 for a discussion of the ambiguities on this point in Wicksell.

For the explicit statement or endorsement of this dichotomy by Divisia, Lange, Modigliani, and Schneider—as well as by Marget, Rosenstein-Rodan, Myrdal, Hickman, and Hart—see Note I:3. This also discusses the case of Hicks and cites some additional examples from the more recent literature.

For examples of the usage of "homogeneity postulate" and/or "money illusion" in the sense cited here, see the references to Leontief, Haberler, Marschak, Samuelson, Tinbergen, and Boulding in Note I:3.

[34] This was explicitly claimed by, for example, Leontief, "The Fundamental Assumption of Mr. Keynes," *op. cit.*, p. 193, and Modigliani, "Liquidity Preference," *op. cit.*, p. 217. For further details, see Note I:3.

individual is confronted not only with a doubled price level, but also with a doubled initial holding of money. Hence—as compared with the initial equilibrium position—there is no real-balance effect; hence there is no change in behavior; and hence the classical neutrality of money is reaffirmed.[35]

More generally, if the function of monetary theory is to explain the determination of the absolute price level, then the "homogeneity postulate"—or, equivalently, absence of "money illusion" in the sense of the foregoing dichotomy—is the antithesis of all monetary theory within the simple model considered by the foregoing writers. For let the assumptions of the dichotomy obtain. Assume now that an initial position of equilibrium is disturbed in such a way as to cause an equi-proportionate change in all money prices. Since this does not change relative prices, the "homogeneity postulate" implies that none of the demand functions in the real sector are thereby affected. Hence, since the commodity markets of this sector were initially in equilibrium, they must continue to be so. By Walras' Law, so must the money market. Thus the equiproportionate departure of money prices from any given equilibrium level creates no market forces—that is, creates no amounts of excess demand anywhere in the system—which might cause money prices to return to their initial level. Hence if any set of money prices is an equilibrium set, any multiple of this set must also be an equilibrium set. The absolute price level is indeterminate.[36]

It follows that the foregoing dichotomy is involved in a basic internal contradiction. For if the demand functions of the real sector have the property it attributes to them, there cannot possibly be a "second stage" in which the absolute price level is determined.[37]

Since the foregoing argument has on occasion been misunderstood, it may be worth while elaborating upon it. The first thing that should be noted is that the contradiction with which it is concerned has nothing to do with the possible inconsistency of a system of static excess-demand equations in the sense that such a system may not have a formal

---

[35] Cf. Chapter III:4. On the concept of neutrality, see p. 75.

[36] Contrast this with the way determinacy is assured in the case where the real-balance effect does operate; above, p. 41.

[37] For a mathematical statement and critique of the foregoing dichotomy, see Mathematical Appendix 7:a(iii).

mathematical solution;[38] indeed, as has been emphasized above,[39] this type of question lies outside the interests of this book. Instead the notion of inconsistency with which the foregoing argument is concerned is the standard (and general) one of formal logic that a set of propositions is inconsistent if it simultaneously implies a proposition and its negative.[40]

The details of the foregoing argument can now be spelled out as follows: We start with the following three fairly reasonable assumptions: (1) Market forces will be generated to increase (decrease) the price of any given commodity if, and only if, there exists an excess demand (supply) for that commodity. (2) Market forces will be generated to increase (decrease) the absolute price level if, and only if, there exists an excess supply (demand) for money. (3) The absolute price level can change only if at least one commodity price changes.

Let the assumptions of the foregoing dichotomy now hold. For simplicity—and in accordance with the usual presentation of the dichotomy—assume also that the money equation is of the Cambridge form

$$KPT - M = 0.$$

Assume finally that the system is in an initial state of equilibrium which is disturbed in such a way as to cause a chance equiproportionate

---

[38] A fact that has been duly noted by various commentators on the dichotomy discussion; thus see Assar Lindbeck, "Den Klassiska 'Dichotomien,'" *Ekonomisk Tidskrift*, LXIII (1961), 32, 35, and 39; and H. G. Bieri, "Der Streit um die 'klassische Dichotomie,'" *Schweizerische Zeitschrift für Volkswirtschaft und Statistik*, II (1963), 177–78.

On the other hand—and as has already been indicated in a symposium participated in by Baumol ("Monetary and Value Theory," *op. cit.*, section I and p. 31, final paragraph), Hahn (*op. cit.*, p. 42), and Ball and Bodkin (*op. cit.*, p. 49, footnote 4)—the recent criticism of the foregoing argument by Archibald and Lipsey (*op. cit.*, pp. 9–17) stems from a failure to see this fact and is therefore beside the point.

Though relying on this symposium for his summing-up of the dichotomy discussion, Harry Johnson's recent survey also incorrectly implies that the foregoing argument deals with the inconsistency of a system of static equations ("Monetary Theory and Policy," *op. cit.*, p. 340, lines 13–20).

For further discussion, see end of Note I:3.

[39] Pp. 37–38. Cf. also pp. 230, 429–30, 531–32, 535–38, and especially p. 629, footnote 45 below.

[40] Cf., e.g., M. R. Cohen and E. Nagel, *An Introduction to Logic and the Scientific Method* (New York, 1934), p. 144; Patrick Suppes, *Introduction to Logic* (Princeton, 1957), pp. 36–7.

departure of commodity prices (and hence the absolute price level) from their equilibrium levels. As we have already seen, this does not generate any excess demands in any of the commodity markets. Hence by assumptions (1) and (3) above, there *will not* be generated market forces to cause a corrective change in the absolute price level; that is, this level is indeterminate.

Consider now the foregoing Cambridge equation—under the usual assumption that K, T, and M are kept constant during the discussion. Assume that the initial equiproportionate disturbance in commodity prices causes P to rise. It is then clear from the foregoing equation and assumption (3) that an excess demand for money is generated which *will* cause a corrective downward movement in the absolute price level; that is, this level is determinate. Hence a contradiction.

This contradiction can be expressed alternatively—and equivalently— in terms of an inconsistent system of *dynamic* market-adjustment equations (see p. 477). Graphically, the argument is as follows: Consider first the assumptions of the traditional dichotomy. These imply that the demand function for commodities is independent of real balances and hence the price level, and should therefore be represented in Figure III-1a (p. 42) by a vertical line. Now, if this vertical line does not coincide with the vertical supply curve, the *static* system of equations represented by Figure III-1a would be inconsistent: that is, it would have no equilibrium solution for a price level greater than zero. This, however, is *not* the inconsistency described in the three preceding paragraphs: for this continues to obtain even if the vertical commodity demand curve should coincide with the commodity supply curve as in Figure VIII-1a, so that the *static* system of equilibrium equations would have a (indeed, an infinite number of) positive solution(s).[41] In particular, the foregoing argument states that even in this case there would remain the inconsistency that Figure VIII-1a would show us that the system is in a state of *neutral* or *unstable* equilibrium, whereas Figure VIII-1b (which depicts the Cambridge equation, and which by the argument on p. 41 above must logically represent the obverse side of Figure VIII-1a) would show us that it is in a state of *stable* equilibrium.

[41] It is this coincidence of the demand and supply curves which is assured by the assumption of Say's Identity (cf. Section 7 below) made by Hickman, Archibald and Lipsey, and the other writers cited at the end of Note I : 3 below. For further discussion see p. 629, footnote 45.

Yet another expression of this contradiction is the following: Start once again from a position of equilibrium, and assume that the quantity of money is doubled. Since the commodity equations of the foregoing dichotomy are assumed to be independent of real balances, this does not disturb the initial equilibrium in these markets. Hence—by assumptions (1) and (3)—no market forces are generated by this monetary increase to push the price level upwards. From the Cambridge equation and assumption (2), on the other hand, we see that such market forces are created. Hence a contradiction.

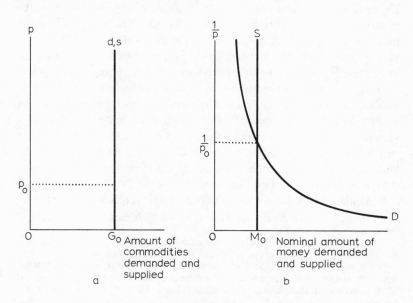

FIGURE VIII-1.

Actually, a much simpler way of dealing with this dichotomy is to note that it provides an operationally significant hypothesis—one capable of being tested by the facts of the real world. In particular, its basic "homogeneity postulate" implies that the behavior of consumers in commodity markets can never be affected by the real value of their money balances. But as shown in Note M below there is considerable empirical evidence that this behavior has been so affected. Hence this evidence alone suffices to refute this dichotomy. In brief, reality shows that there cannot be a money economy without a "money illusion."[42]

This empirical approach enables us to dispose of a certain variation of the foregoing dichotomy which—though it has never been advanced as such in the literature—can pass the test of internal consistency. Specifically, though continuing to consider an outside-money economy, we now assume the existence of bonds as well as commodities and money. We assume further that though the commodity equations continue to be independent of real balances, the bond equation is not. In such a Keynesian system, relative prices and the rate of interest can be determined in the commodity markets and the absolute price level in the bond or money market. In particular, the argument by which we previously established the indeterminacy of the absolute price level no longer holds. For an equiproportionate departure of money prices from their equilibrium level now disturbs the equilibrium of the bond market, and the resulting excess demand then acts through the rate of interest to force prices back to their original level. Nevertheless, this variation of the dichotomy is also unacceptable. For it implies that the real-balance effect never manifests itself in the commodity markets. Once again, this implication is refuted by the aforementioned empirical studies of the consumption function.[43]

It should also be noted that if the bond market, too, is assumed to be

[42] Once again, the reader is warned that this is *not* being used here in our sense of the term.

[43] See p. 572, footnote 103 below, for a criticism of Kuenne's recent contention that the dichotomy just described is the one Walras had in mind.

For a more precise statement of the argument in the text, see Mathematical Appendix 7 : a(iv). This "Keynesian case" will be discussed further on pp. 241–42 and 52. See also my "Indeterminacy of Absolute Prices in Classical Economic Theory," *Econometrica*, XVII (1949), 22.

I might also add the conjecture that it is impossible to derive the excess-demand functions of this Keynesian case from the microeconomic analyses of Chapters V–VII. For a common characteristic of these analyses is the symmetrical dependence of *all* the excess-demand functions on *all* the given factors with which the individual is confronted. Hence it is difficult to see how this analysis could be made to yield a system in which only the bond function, and none of the commodity functions, would be dependent on the individual's wealth in the form of initial real balances.

All this is said on the assumption that money is of the outside variety. However, as has recently been pointed out by Gurley and Shaw and by Modigliani, in a pure inside-money economy we can rationalize a system in which only the *excess* demand functions for bonds and money, though not commodities, depend on the supply of real balances, so that the system can be dichotomized. This is discussed in full in Chapter XII : 5 below.

independent of real balances, then the resulting model is not even internally consistent. In particular, it is involved in exactly the same type of indeterminacy already shown to hold for the invalid dichotomy. For once again an equiproportionate departure of money prices from an initial equilibrium position, the rate of interest being held constant, does not create any excess demands anywhere in the system. Hence no force is generated to bring prices back to their initial position.[44]

The conclusion to be drawn from the foregoing discussion is that, once the real and monetary data of an economy with outside money are specified, the equilibrium values of relative prices, the rate of interest, and the absolute price level are simultaneously determined by all the markets of the economy. It is generally impossible to isolate a subset of markets which can determine the equilibrium values of a subset of prices. In the true spirit of general-equilibrium economics, "everything depends on everything else."

In particular, as we have seen, it is fatal to succumb to the temptation to say that relative prices are determined in the commodity markets and absolute prices in the money market. This does not mean that value theory cannot be distinguished from monetary theory. Obviously, there is a distinction; but it is based on a dichotomization of *effects*, not on a dichotomization of *markets*. More specifically, both monetary theory and value theory consider *all* markets of the economy simultaneously. But, in each of these markets, value theory analyzes individual-experiments which measure the substitution effect and that part of the wealth effect which does not stem from changes in real balances; and monetary theory, individual-experiments which measure the real-balance effect. Correspondingly, value theory analyzes market-experiments which do not (significantly) affect the absolute price level and hence do not generate real-balance effects; and monetary theory, market-experiments which do not (significantly) affect relative prices and hence do not generate substitution and nonmonetary wealth effects. Thus shifts in tastes, changes in technology, and the like are in the domain of value theory. Changes in the quantity of money and—as we shall see—shifts in liquidity preference are in the domain of monetary theory.[45]

[44] See Mathematical Appendix 7:*a*(iii). For an example of this model in the literature, see the discussion of Lange in Note I:3.
[45] In accordance with the plan of the chapter as set out in its first footnote, the

If we now examine this classificatory scheme, we will discover the grain of truth in the intuitive feeling that in some sense value theory is connected with the determination of relative prices and monetary theory with the determination of absolute prices. In particular, assume that by a *tâtonnement* involving all prices and all markets the equilibrium values of money prices have been reached. We can now make use of this information to take a step backwards and approach the equilibrium position once again—but this time by a restricted *tâtonnement*. For example, holding the absolute price level constant at its already determined *equilibrium* value, we can arbitrarily shift relative prices from theirs, and then study the nature of the dynamic forces that—working simultaneously in *all* markets—return the economy to its original equilibrium position. By the very definition of this procedure, such a return can be accomplished without any change in the absolute price level. Hence the restricted *tâtonnement* by which equilibrium relative prices are thus redetermined need involve only these prices, need accordingly generate only substitution and nonmonetary wealth effects, and can therefore be studied entirely within the confines of value theory.

Similarly, we can define a restricted *tâtonnement* which—starting from a knowledge of the *equilibrium* values of relative prices and interest—works simultaneously through *all* the markets of the economy to redetermine the equilibrium value of the absolute price level. Such a *tâtonnement* can clearly succeed without requiring any changes in relative prices and interest; that is, it need generate only real-balance effects. Hence it can be studied entirely within the confines of monetary theory.

This decomposition of the overall *tâtonnement* into two components is a convenient expository device which has already been exploited in Chapter III:3. It can be used safely provided we are clear in our own minds that it separates out effects and not markets. In particular, we must guard against the apparent tendency to slip over from this valid device into the invalid proposition of the false dichotomy that, starting with an absolute price level held constant at an *arbitrary* level, a *tâtonnement* on relative prices in the *commodity markets alone* can determine these prices; that, holding these relative prices constant at

classification of the rate of interest as a real or monetary variable is deferred until Chapter XV.

the values so determined, a *tâtonnement* on the absolute price level in the *money market alone* can then determine this level; and that the absolute price level so determined, together with the relative prices determined by the first *tâtonnement* in the commodity markets, must *necessarily* preserve the equilibrium initially achieved in these markets. Clearly, this last statement will generally *not* be true unless the excess-demand equations of the commodity markets are actually independent of the absolute price level.[46]

This is the crucial point. The dynamic groping of the absolute price level towards its equilibrium value will—through the real-balance effect —react back on the commodity markets and hence on relative prices. And it is precisely the constant failure to find this point explicitly recognized—and, indeed, the constant sensation of being just on the verge of having it explicitly contradicted—that is the basis of our original contention that the roots of the invalid dichotomy are to be found in the neoclassical analyses of Walras, Fisher, Pigou, and Cassel.[47]

The preceding discussion not only analyzes the invalid dichotomy, but also brings out the many deceptive similarities between it and the valid ones. That these similarities have played a significant role in the etiology and persistence of the dichotomy is suggested by several instances in the literature. Thus there is at least one explicit example of the way in which the valid insensitivity of demand to equiproportionate changes in *accounting* prices shifts undetected into the invalid insensitivity to equiproportionate changes in *money* prices. That is, the valid dependence of demand solely on the ratios of accounting prices is

[46] The second half of this paragraph is an attempt—I hope not overelaborate—to give economic meaning to a simple mathematical proposition. For details, see Mathematical Appendix 7:a(v).

[47] The reader will find it particularly instructive to compare the last two paragraphs of the text with the passages from these analyses cited in full and discussed on pp. 560–63, 600–601, 609–10, and 618–20 respectively. See also the passage from Fisher cited at the end of the next section.

It should be clear that the criticism of these paragraphs is *not* directed against the frequent neoclassical practice of taking the absolute price level as given in the partial-equilibrium analysis of value theory. The same methodological considerations which permit this analysis to hold constant certain relative prices also permit it to do the same for the absolute price level. The purpose of this assumption is simply to enable the money price of a commodity to serve as a perfect index of its relative price. Cf. Marshall, *Principles* (eighth ed.), p. 62. This practice goes back at least to Mill, *Principles*, p. 439; cf. Marget, *Theory of Prices*, Vol. II, p. 281, footnote 128.

confused with the invalid dependence solely on the ratios of money prices. Indeed, this example considers this dependence to be a direct consequence of the "postulate...that the consumer's behavior is independent of the units in which prices are expressed...." But here again the same confusion is at work. For after a change in the monetary unit has worked itself out, the individual is confronted with an equiproportionate change in money prices *and* in his money holdings. Thus if the dollar is replaced by the half dollar as the unit of measure, all money prices will eventually double; but—as the very first result of this conversion itself—so will have the initial money holdings of each and every individual. Hence the proper analog of a change in the monetary unit is an equiproportionate change in *accounting* prices (which leaves the real value of initial money balances intact), not an equiproportionate change in *money* prices (which does not).[48]

Similarly, there are instances in which the valid dichotomy between accounting and money prices is confused with the invalid dichotomy between money and relative prices. Thus, in order to prove that *money* prices cannot be determined unless a special equation is added, it is argued that: "There are always just one *too few equations* to determine the unknown quantities involved. The equation of exchange [$MV = PT$] is needed in each case to supplement the equations of supply and demand"—and the first sentence is supported by an explicit reference to a mathematical development by the same author which, in order to determine *accounting* prices, adds an equation arbitrarily setting the accounting price of one of the goods equal to unity![49]

Examples in the literature of an alleged connection between the invalid dichotomy and the quantity theory of money have already been noted above.[50] As will be recalled, these allegations were based on a misunderstanding of the nature of the neutrality of money. It remains now to suggest that in its more sophisticated form this may have

---

[48] Cf. above, p. 22. The example referred to here is that of Samuelson; the quotation is also his. For details, see Note I:3.

The line of reasoning in the second half of this paragraph is one that I have frequently heard—though I have not succeeded in finding any additional example of it in the literature. Cf., however, Boulding, *Economic Analysis*, p. 320.

[49] Cf. above, pp. 173 f.

The passage cited is from Fisher, italics in original. Precisely the same confusion can be found in Cassel. For details, see Notes F:3 and H (pp. 617–18).

[50] See the references to Leontief and Modigliani above, p. 175, footnote 34.

expressed itself as a confusion between the invalid dichotomy and the first dichotomy described above (p. 173)—the one which is essentially a restatement of the quantity theory and which shows the valid sense in which relative and absolute prices are independently determined. In particular, we can find an example which states that "the proposition that the material set-up of our economic system determines only the *relative* and not the absolute prices of all commodities is so familiar that it hardly deserves further discussion"—and then justifies this statement with an implicit reference to the "homogeneity postulate" that demand remains unaffected by an equiproportionate change in money prices. Here we can almost see the exact point at which the line of reasoning slips off the correct path: Relative prices are determined independently of the absolute price level by the "material set-up of our economic system"—the valid dichotomy; "material set-up" means the conditions of demand in the commodity markets—the invalid dichotomy; but if these conditions alone determine relative prices, they can depend only on these prices—the "homogeneity postulate."[51]

Finally, we can find an example which—though not as clear as the preceding ones—seems to show how the valid intuitive feeling that different forces determine absolute and relative prices slips imperceptibly into the invalid identification of these forces with separate equations. How else can we interpret the train of thought revealed by the following passage: "...it is important to distinguish between the influences determining the general price level and the influences determining an individual price. The price level is determined by a comparatively simple mechanism, that of the equation of exchange. It is the result of the quantity of money and deposits, the velocities of their circulation, and the volume of trade. The general price level then helps to fix individual prices, although not interfering with relative variations among them...."[52]

This is admittedly a small number of examples. Nevertheless, the stature of the economists who provide them, the definitive aura of received doctrine that they all gave to the reasoning by which they

---

[51] The example referred to is that of Leontief, italics in original. It is discussed in Note I:3. As the reader will see from this discussion, I have interpreted Leontief's reference more specifically than he explicitly indicates. But I think it is quite clear that this is what he had in mind.

[52] The example is that of Fisher. It is discussed in Note F:3.

justified their statements, and the fact that this reasoning was never challenged—all this endows these few examples with a weight far out of proportion to their number. All this permits us to suggest that the explicit reasoning of these examples is representative of the general intellectual process that gave rise to the invalid dichotomy.

4. CONCLUSION: THE FAILURE OF NEOCLASSICAL MONETARY THEORY TO FULLY UNDERSTAND THE REAL-BALANCE EFFECT

In view of the continued discussion of the foregoing issues in the recent literature, it is worth while—even at the cost of some repetition—to summarize the argument of this chapter until this point. We must first of all emphasize that we are dealing with an *empirical* question: namely, the role of the real-balance effect in neoclassical monetary theory. Correspondingly, the universe from which our observations must be, and have been, drawn is the relevant body of neoclassical literature.

The specific empirical findings that have emerged from our study can be set out as follows:

1. In their discussion of value theory, neoclassical economists generally included an analysis of the stability of equilibrium. By this is meant nothing more complicated than the usual simple graphical exposition by which neoclassical economists showed that if the price of any given commodity were above (below) the intersection of the demand and supply curves, then there would exist an excess supply (demand) to drive it down (up) again.

2. Neoclassical economists consistently proclaimed their objective of integrating their monetary theory with their value theory; that is, of analyzing the former in the same manner as they had analyzed the latter.

3. Nevertheless, with one or two exceptions, neoclassical economists did not include a stability analysis in their monetary theory. That is, they did not explain the nature of the corrective market forces that would be brought into play should the absolute price level deviate from its equilibrium value.

4. Therefore, the omission of this analysis cannot be explained away as being the result of either a chance oversight, on the one hand, or a conscious lack of interest in monetary stability analysis, on the other.

5. An alternative hypothesis to explain this phenomenon is that though the neoclassical economists did recognize the real-balance effect, they did not achieve a full understanding of it and therefore did not carry out the monetary stability analysis which is so vitally dependent upon it.

6. Like any other empirical hypothesis, this one too achieves additional credibility from the fact that it explains some additional phenomena: namely, the fact that neoclassical economists supported both the rectangular-hyperbola demand curve for money and—in all probability—the invalid dichotomy.

    a. The evidence from the form of the demand curve is the weakest link in the chain. For it is not absolutely clear if neoclassical economists assumed the demand curve to have the form of a rectangular hyperbola because they failed to take into account the real-balance effect—or whether they did so because they assumed this effect to be eliminated as a result of compensating variations in initial money balances, or, alternatively, because they did not have in mind a demand curve at all, but instead a market-equilibrium curve. It is also possible that they had in mind the long-run rectangular hyperbola of Figure III-6 (p. 56).

    b. On the other hand, to the extent that we find indications of the invalid dichotomy in the neoclassical literature, the implications are straightforward. For this dichotomy reflects a failure to realize the direct contradiction between the real-balance effect, on the one hand, and the "homogeneity postulate" on the other; or, from an alternative viewpoint, a failure to realize the complete inappropriateness of denoting sensitivity of the individual to a change in the absolute price level by the term "money illusion," when in fact it is precisely this sensitivity which demonstrates the existence of a rational concern on the part of the individual with the surely nonillusory impact of such a change on the real value of his money holdings.

7. The foregoing hypothesis is on even stronger grounds with reference to the later literature, and this for two reasons. First, this literature explicitly accepts the invalid dichotomy as the undisputed statement of the relationship between monetary and value theory in an economy with outside-money;[53] indeed, this view has persisted in

[53] On an outside-money economy, see footnote 43 above.

some of the most recent writings.[54] Second, this literature provides yet another phenomenon which accords with our hypothesis: namely, the failure to see the equilibrating role that the real-balance effect can play in eliminating an inflationary gap.[55]

8. With reference to this later literature we might also note that the approach of Keynesian economics, with its emphasis on analyzing the demand for commodities as a function of the flow of income instead of the stock of assets, was hardly conducive to breaking down a mental block whose essence was the failure to see the significance of the effect of a change in the absolute price level on the real value of the *stock* of money.[56]

In concluding this critique of neoclassical monetary theory, I would like to emphasize once again[57] that not only does it not require the abandonment of any significant aspect of this theory, but it actually rigorizes and completes it.[58] Correspondingly, to the extent that it is meaningful to speculate about such matters, I have no doubt that neoclassical economists would have readily accepted the criticisms involved; would have declared the explicit introduction of the real-balance effect into the commodity demand functions to be a more precise reflection of their thinking on this matter all along and, indeed, a modification that could only strengthen their quantity-theory conclusions; and would accordingly have rejected the implication of some of their recent would-be defenders that they (neoclassical economists) had a vested intellectual interest in the "homogeneity postulate" and its related dichotomy.[59]

---

[54] Cf. footnote 38 above and end of Note I:3.

[55] Cf. the references cited in footnote 13, p. 637 below.

[56] See Note K:1.

[57] Cf. my "Indeterminacy of Absolute Prices in Classical Monetary Theory," *Econometrica*, XVII (1949), 23–7. Cf. also pp. 165–68 and 175–76 above.

[58] Above, pp. 40–41, 44–45, and 168.

[59] On these speculations, see again the reference cited in footnote 57.

It should also be clear from all this that there is no logical connection between the dichotomy issue and the classical-Keynesian controversy.

It might also be noted that the explicit use of the real-balance effect helps tie together other loose ends of the traditional theory. Thus see Amotz Morag's use of the real-balance effect in public finance theory to prove the long-debated equivalence of an income tax and a uniform sales tax ["Deflationary Effects of Outlay and Income Taxes," *Journal of Political Economy*, LXVII (1959), 266–74]. See also Michael Michaely's use of the real-balance effect in international trade theory to

5. The Effects of a Change in K

Let us now leave doctrinal history and return to analytical questions proper. Until now, this chapter has essentially been concerned with the relation between the quantity of money and the level of prices—that is, with the relation between M and P in the Cambridge equation $M = KPT$. But neoclassical monetary theory also used this equation to analyze the relation between K and P, on the one hand, and T and P, on the other. Since, unlike changes in M, the exact translation of changes in K and T into terms of our model is difficult to determine, the exact bearing of the following argument on the neoclassical one must also remain slightly unclear. Nevertheless, as the reader will see, the economic forces that appear in this argument have a distinctly neoclassical character.

We begin with the effects of a change in K. (Obviously, whatever will be said for these effects holds in the inverse for those of a change in the V of $MV = PT$.) Consider, in particular, an economy whose equilibrium is disturbed by a sudden increase in K. This is represented in our model by an increased desire for liquidity resulting from an increase in the probability of running out of cash, or an increase in the inconvenience or penalty costs of so doing. More specifically, this "change in tastes" reflects itself as an increase in the amount of money individuals demand at a given set of prices, interest, and initial endowments. By the budget restraint, this upward shift in the demand for money implies a simultaneous downward shift in the demand for commodities and real bond holdings. That is, because of their given incomes, individuals cannot demand more of one good unless they give up something of another. As a result of this latter shift, equilibrium prices will fall. The interesting question which now confronts us is whether the equilibrium rate of interest must also change.

As already noted, a full analysis of this question must await Chapter X:4. Nevertheless, there is a simple, intuitive answer that can be given

---

resolve the apparent contradiction between the "relative-price" and "absorption" approaches to the analysis of devaluation ["Relative-Prices and Income-Absorption Approaches to Devaluation: A Partial Reconciliation," *American Economic Review*, L (1960), 144–47].

at this point. To say that there has been an increase in the individuals' liquidity preferences is analytically equivalent to saying that the liquidity convenience of one dollar of cash balances is now less than it was before. And this, in turn, is equivalent to saying that the "subjective quantity" of money in the hands of individuals has decreased. Hence it seems only natural to argue that the conditions under which the rate of interest remains constant after an increase in liquidity preference are precisely those under which it remains constant after a decrease in the quantity of money.

Let us state this somewhat more exactly. As in the case of a decrease in the quantity of money, we abstract from distribution effects. We also assume the increase in liquidity preferences to be "uniformly distributed"; that is, the liquidity preference of each and every individual is assumed to change with the same "intensity." As explained above, this increase causes downward shifts in the demands of all markets and hence replaces their original state of equilibrium by one of excess supply. Consider now any one market. Clearly, the excess supply in this market can now be removed by an equiproportionate decline in prices, while the rate of interest remains constant. Specifically, this decline will continue until the real value of cash balances has increased sufficiently to satisfy the individuals' increased liquidity preferences and hence restore their demand in this market to its original level. Thus, in some subjective sense, the real quantity of money that influences this market is the same as it originally was. Now, by assumption, the initial shift in liquidity preferences is a "neutral" one: it changes only the relative desirability of money *vis-à-vis* all other goods, not the relative desirabilities of these other goods amongst themselves. Hence if this subjective quantity of money is "the same" with respect to the market for one of these goods, it must be "the same" with respect to that for any other. That is, the equiproportionate price decline needed to equilibrate one market must be equal to that needed to equilibrate any other. Hence equilibrium can be restored to the economy as a whole at a lowered price level and an unchanged rate of interest.[60]

Thus under these assumptions we obtain a reaffirmation of the classical position: An increase in K causes a decrease in P but leaves T and the rate of interest unaffected. By resorting to the device of carrying

[60] For details—and for explanation of all the phrases set off in quotation marks—see Mathematical Appendix 7:*b*.

out the analysis in terms of changes in the real quantity of money instead of changes in P,[61] we can bring out the deeper connotation that neoclassical economists ascribed to this proposition: An increase in K creates automatic market forces which themselves generate the increased equilibrium quantity of real balances desired by the community. The wonders of the "invisible hand" never cease.

6. THE EFFECTS OF A CHANGE IN T

Consider now an economy whose equilibrium is disturbed by a sudden increase in T. Let this be represented in our model by an exogenous doubling, say, of the individuals' initial commodity endowments. Such a change creates two opposing forces. On the one hand, there is, of course, an increase in the fixed supply of every commodity. On the other hand, there is an increase in wealth and a consequent increase in demand. If it should so happen that the increased demand for each and every commodity exactly offsets its increased supply, no further changes will occur, and the economy will remain in equilibrium at its original set of prices and interest rate. Clearly, this latter case implies a unitary marginal propensity to spend on commodities out of wealth. In general, however, this propensity can be assumed to be less than unity, for part of the increased wealth will be devoted to increasing the demand for money balances (p. 27). Hence it can be expected that the increases in the amounts of commodities demanded will be less than in the respective amounts supplied, thus generating a downward pressure on prices.

Let us now see if an equiproportionate decline in prices can return the economy as a whole to a position of equilibrium. Consider first the market for one particular commodity. Clearly, it is possible to conceive of the price decline continuing until the resulting positive real-balance effect together with the original positive wealth effect suffice to increase the amount demanded to the same extent that the amount supplied was originally increased. That is, it is possible that by an equiproportionate decline in prices, the rate of interest being held constant, the market for *any one* particular commodity can be brought back into equilibrium.

But the economy consists of many commodity markets, and each of them has been disturbed by the original increase in endowments.

[61] Above, beginning of Section 3.

In general, the resulting wealth effect will not be the same in all markets. Hence, in contrast with the preceding section, there is no reason why the equiproportionate decline in prices needed to bring one of these markets into equilibrium should be the same as that needed for any other one. That is, there is no reason why a given equiproportionate decline in prices should succeed in equilibrating all markets simultaneously. Hence, in order for such an over-all equilibrium to be restored, relative prices and interest will, in general, also have to change.[62]

Assume now that the exceptional occurs and that an equiproportionate decline in prices—interest constant—does succeed in restoring the economy as a whole to equilibrium. Clearly, even in this case there is no reason why this decline should be in inverse proportion to the original increase in commodity endowments. For the necessary magnitude of this decline depends on the strength of the wealth effect, as well as on the size of the increase in endowments.

Thus we can confirm the neoclassical position that an increase in T decreases P. Furthermore, we also confirm the neoclassical contention that (even when there is no change in the rate of interest) this decrease will, in general, *not* be an inversely proportionate one. In terms of the Cambridge equation, this contention rests on the assumption that K and T are *not* independent; that a change in the latter will affect the former. In particular, it assumes that an increase in the volume of transactions creates the possibility of economies in the relative magnitude of money balances necessary for a given level of security against insolvency. That is, it implies that an increase in T decreases K. Hence, $M = KPT$ can continue to be satisfied even though P does not change in inverse proportion to T.[63]

---

[62] The reason this argument is not relevant to the case of a decrease in M—and, by analogy, to the case of an increase in K as analyzed in the preceding section—can be seen from p. 45. In particular, the (subjective) quantity of real balances in these two cases is the same in the new equilibrium position as in the original one; hence no account need be taken of the fact that different demand functions show different sensitivities to changes in real balances. But in the present case the quantity of real balances is different in the two equilibrium positions; hence these different sensitivities now become significant.

[63] On these economies, cf. pp. 87–88, and particularly the reference to Fisher, *Purchasing Power of Money*, pp. 165–9. On this section as a whole, see Mathematical Appendix 7: c.

7. THE IMPLICATIONS OF SAY'S IDENTITY

We conclude this chapter with a discussion of Say's Identity. My own sympathies are with those who deny that this identity is a basic component of the classical and neoclassical position. Nevertheless, there are certain passages which can be cited in support of the opposite contention. Furthermore, whatever the proper interpretation, the attention that has been given to the identity since Keynes makes it desirable to analyze it in detail—particularly since some of its logical implications have not been correctly understood.[64]

Following Lange, we define Say's Identity as stating that—regardless of the prices and interest with which they are confronted—individuals always plan to use all of their proceeds from the sale of commodities and bonds for the purpose of purchasing other commodities and bonds. In other words, they never plan to change the amount of money they hold: its amount of excess demand is identically zero. In still other words—and as a direct consequence of the budget restraint—the aggregate value of the amounts of excess *supply* of commodities must always equal the value of the amount of *demand* for bonds: people divert any reduced expenditures on commodities to the purchase of bonds, never to the building up of money balances.[65]

It can readily be seen that this assumption implies that equilibrium money prices are indeterminate. For consider an economy with n goods: $n - 2$ commodities, bonds, and money. Assume that this economy is in equilibrium at a certain set of values for the rate of interest and for the $n - 2$ money prices. Let us now arbitrarily change one of

---

[64] On the literature—classical and Keynesian—see Note L.

"Say's Identity" is the useful term suggested by G. S. Becker and W. J. Baumol in order to emphasize that it may not really represent "Say's Law" in its classical and neoclassical meaning. But Becker and Baumol's attempt to give a classical connotation to the concept they call "Say's Equality" can only mislead. Cf. the discussion in Note L.

[65] The reader will recall that the budget restraint on p. 71 is

the amount of market excess demand for current money holdings

= the aggregate value of the amounts of market excess supplies of current commodities

— the (discounted) value of the amount of market demand for current bond holdings.

By Say's Identity, the left-hand side of this equation is identically zero, so that this yields the conclusion just stated in the text.

these prices. Consider first the $n - 2$ commodity markets. In general, it will be possible to find another set of $n - 2$ values for the rate of interest and for the remaining $n - 3$ money prices which will again equilibrate these $n - 2$ markets. But, by Say's Identity, any set of prices and interest which equilibrates these markets must also equilibrate the bond market, for, under this assumption, if the excess supplies of commodities are zero, so is the demand for bonds.[66] Finally, since the excess demand for money is identically zero, this market too is obviously in equilibrium. Thus the economy as a whole can be in equilibrium at an infinite number of sets of money prices. In mathematical terms, Say's Identity reduces the number of independent market excess-demand equations to $n - 2$, and these do not suffice to determine the equilibrium values of the $n - 1$ price and interest variables.[67]

Thus Say's Identity is inconsistent with the existence of a money economy with determinate prices. But this is the only type of money economy that has any economic meaning. Hence we can say that the existence of Say's Identity implies the existence of a barter economy. Conversely, the existence of a barter economy implies the existence of Say's Identity. For in such an economy it is physically impossible to "sell" one commodity or bond without "buying" another; thus Say's Identity in this economy is nothing but a statement of the budget restraint. In other words, people never plan to change their level of money balances in a barter economy, because, by definition, such balances are always zero.

Let us now return for a moment to the "homogeneity postulate." As was demonstrated above,[68] this postulate implies the absence of a real-balance effect and the consequent indeterminacy of money prices.

[66] The reader will recall that the demand and *excess* demand for bonds are identical, so that equilibrium exists in this market when either is zero; cf. p. 68.

[67] These two paragraphs essentially present Lange's analysis of Say's Identity, *op. cit.*, pp. 52–3. This analysis is also summarized in Mathematical Appendix 7:*d*. For generality, however, I have extended Lange's analysis to the case of an economy with bonds.

For a graphical analysis of the indeterminacy generated by Say's Identity in the case of an economy consisting only of commodities, see Figure VIII-1a and its related discussion on pp. 178–79 above.

[68] Pp. 180f. Note that the extension of the present argument to an economy with bonds has caused us to make a corresponding extension of the "homogeneity postulate" to include the bond market. However, the reader who prefers to retain the original sense of this term as applying only to the commodity markets can simply

By the same argument as in the preceding paragraph, we can then say that the existence of the "homogeneity postulate" implies the existence of a barter economy. Conversely, the existence of a barter economy implies the existence of the "homogeneity postulate." For in such an economy there are no money holdings, the "absolute price level" has no meaning, and hence there can be no real-balance effect.

Thus, contrary to the accepted opinion,[69] Say's Identity and the "homogeneity postulate" are logically equivalent properties: both are necessarily present in a barter economy; both are necessarily absent from a money economy. Thus the existence of the one implies the coexistence of the other.[70]

With this we have also said all that need be said for our purpose about a barter economy. Such an economy is the home—the necessary and only home—of the "homogeneity postulate" and Say's Identity. Prices in this economy can be measured either in terms of one of the commodities or—as in a Wicksellian "pure credit economy"—in terms of an abstract unit of account. Thus, at most, only relative and accounting prices are defined. The former are determined by the workings of market forces, the latter—as always[71]—by arbitrary decree. Money prices not even being defined, their determinacy or indeterminacy cannot be meaningfully discussed.[72]

---

ignore all references here to the bond market and the rate of interest and follow the analysis as if it applied to an economy with only commodities and money. This does not change the argument in any significant way. At the same time, this modification brings us back to the framework actually considered by Lange and Modigliani; cf. the preceding and following footnotes.

[69] Cf. Modigliani, *op. cit.*, p. 217, noting also the reference to Lange.

[70] Note that the proof of this proposition rests on the basic assumption that—from the viewpoint of meaningful economic analysis—the class of monetary economies with indeterminate price levels is an empty one. This fact has been overlooked in Archibald and Lipsey's recent criticism (*op. cit.*, p. 14, footnote 2).

[71] Cf. p. 43.

[72] As the reader has undoubtedly realized, here is another (cf. pp. 183ff. above) deceptive similarity which may have helped give rise to the invalid dichotomy: the "homogeneity postulate" *is* a correct description of rational behavior in a barter economy—but not in a money economy.

On Wicksell, see *Interest and Prices*, p. 68. Such a "pure credit economy" is described in detail in our discussion of Cassel's system in Note H.

On the general argument of this section, see Mathematical Appendix 7:*d*. This also points out a *non sequitur* that invalidates the accepted Lange proof of the proposition that Say's Identity implies the "homogeneity postulate." But, as the proof presented here in the text shows, the proposition itself is true.

Two. MACROECONOMICS

IX. The Model

1. Introduction.   2. The market for labor services.   3. The market for commodities.   4. The market for bonds.   5. The market for money.

1. INTRODUCTION

We go back now to pick up the thread of the argument interrupted at the end of Chapter IV. The task that awaits us has already been set out there. It is, in brief, to present both a static and a dynamic monetary theory of a production economy with outside money under conditions of perfect competition.

We gain information in this direction by giving up information in another. In particular, we forego microeconomic detail and work instead with an aggregative model which divides all the goods of the economy into four composite categories: labor services, commodities, bonds, and money. To each of these categories there corresponds a market, a price, an aggregate demand function, and an aggregate supply function. Conceptually, each of these functions is built up from the individual demand and supply functions of the relevant individual goods.[1] Thus, for example, the demand function for commodities is

---

[1] Note once again (cf. p. 160) that at the present level of generality it makes no difference whether these functions are assumed to be derived from a microeconomic analysis which considers money to be a consumer's good or from one which considers it a producer's good.

the aggregate of all the individual demand functions for each and every commodity. There is, however, no pretense of showing how this process of aggregation is actually carried out. As before, it is also assumed, unless otherwise noted, that the price of each good is expected with certainty to be the same in the future as it is in the present.

Each of the foregoing aggregate functions is assumed to reflect absence of money illusion. Each is also assumed to remain unaffected by any change in the distribution of real income or financial assets (bonds and money). Thus each of these functions can be represented as dependent upon—among other things—the real values of the *total* income and financial assets of the individuals or firms whose collective behavior it describes. In brief, the assumed absence of distribution effects makes it unnecessary to consider the *arrays* of the individual incomes and asset holdings in the economy (see pp. 33 and 71).

It should also be noted at the outset that in order to concentrate the analysis on the problems of monetary and employment theory which are of primary interest, I have made many additional simplifying assumptions. Thus despite the fact that we shall be considering an economy with investment, I have followed the usual Keynesian practice of ignoring the effects of the resulting increase in the nonfinancial assets of the economy on its various behavior functions. The only justification for this is the usual one that we shall be considering a period of time during which net investment in such assets is small relative to their existing stock. Thus with one or two exceptions[2] we shall not touch upon the interrelated problems of growth and business cycles.

Similarly, despite the detailed discussion of the wealth restraint in Chapters V:7, VI:2, and VII:2, I shall not enter any further into the crucial and much discussed question of the proper income variable to use in our functions. Similarly, I shall ignore the possibility that there may be circumstances under which no such single measure will suffice, and that instead the whole time shape of the income stream must be taken into account (pp. 113–14 and 132). Accordingly the variable *Y* in what follows can be interpreted as that average of present and past incomes which is considered relevant for current decisions. My main concern has been to specify these functions in such a way as to provide explicitly for the possible role of financial assets. For this reason these

[2] See especially Chapter XIV:5.

assets are represented by a separate argument. However, the reader who prefers to write these functions as dependent on wealth, inclusive of financial assets—and to drop, accordingly, the income variable—is free to do so.[3]

Our economy is inhabited by households, firms, and a government. Households sell their productive services to firms and use the proceeds to buy consumer commodities and bonds, to add to their cash balances, and to pay taxes. Firms sell consumer commodities to households and government, investment commodities to other firms, and bonds to households. They use the proceeds to pay for the productive services of households, to pay interest, to buy investment commodities, to repurchase the bonds they have issued, and to add to their cash balances. Any profit is appropriated by the entrepreneurs. Thus bonds are the sole item on the liability side of the firms' balance sheets.

The government receives taxes from households and uses the proceeds entirely for the purchase of consumer commodities from firms. These are then provided to the economy free of charge. For simplicity, it is assumed that the *real* value of these government expenditures is fixed at a constant level. It is also assumed that the government never holds cash balances and that it has no bonds outstanding. That is, except for the past occasions on which it has issued money, the government has always exactly balanced its budget with tax receipts.

These assumptions can be schematically summarized in the following "flow of funds" table, where the rows represent sales or money inflows, and the columns represent purchases or money outflows. The difference between the sum of a row and the sum of its corresponding column is, of course, equal to the change in the cash balances of the economic unit in question. The table thus provides a description of the budget restraint of each of the economic units.

The rest of this chapter is devoted to a detailed examination of each of our four composite markets. Subsequent chapters study the inter-relationships among these markets and explain the workings of the

---

[3] For references to discussions of the proper income variable to use in the consumption function, see p. 19, footnote 14 above.

It might be noted that some examples of empirical consumption functions dependent on both income and wealth—in the manner of equation (6) below—have recently appeared in the literature; cf. Spiro, *op. cit.*, p. 339. In a somewhat different fashion, Ando and Modigliani (*op. cit.*, pp. 57–58, 60–64) use as their two variables *nonproperty* income and *nonhuman* wealth, inclusive of net financial assets. For a detailed discussion, see Note M below.

Flow of Funds

Purchases from	Sales to		
	Households	Firms	Government
Households		Productive services Profits and interest Bonds (retirement)	
Firms	Consumer commodities Bonds (new issues)	Investment commodities	Consumer commodities
Government	Taxes		

system as a whole under varying conditions. All this will be done from the same general analytical viewpoint developed in Part One.

2. THE MARKET FOR LABOR SERVICES

It is most convenient to start with the market for labor services. Despite the heterogeneous nature of these services, they are considered as one composite good with a single price. By assumption, the demand for these services originates entirely in the firms of the economy.

Consider first the behavior of a single firm operating, as assumed, under conditions of perfect competition. It is confronted with a production function which specifies the given technological relationship between its inputs of factor services and the resulting outputs of commodities. For simplicity, it is assumed that the capital equipment of the firm is fixed, so that its sole problem is to choose its optimum input of labor services. For any real wage rate, this input will be that which yields a marginal product equal to the given rate. Thus the firm's demand curve for labor is the marginal-productivity curve derived from its production function.

If we transfer these concepts to the economy as a whole, we can conceive of an aggregate production function relating real gross national product Y to the total input of labor services in the economy N and to the total fixed capital equipment of the economy K_0:

(1) $$Y = \phi(N, K_0).$$

Let w represent the money wage rate and p the general price level of commodities. Then at any real wage rate w/p the total amount of labor demanded in the economy must satisfy the relationship

(2) $$\frac{w}{p} = \phi_N(N, K_0),$$

where $\phi_N(N, K_0)$ is the marginal productivity of labor.[4] Our aggregate demand curve for labor can then be obtained by inverting the preceding function and writing it as

(3) $$N^d = Q\left(\frac{w}{p}, K_0\right),$$

where N^d is the amount of labor demanded. Clearly, if the law of diminishing marginal productivity holds, this demand curve will be negatively sloped with respect to increases in the real wage rate.

Consider now the supply curve of labor. To the extent that an individual operates on the principle of utility maximization, the amount of labor he supplies will depend on the real wage rate. Therefore, we assume that the aggregate supply curve for labor also depends on this rate. Thus we write

(4) $$N^s = R\left(\frac{w}{p}\right),$$

where N^s is the aggregate amount of labor supplied. For simplicity, it is also assumed that this supply is an increasing function of the real wage rate, though there are well-known reservations on this score.

Finally, we have the condition that must be satisfied in order that this market be in equilibrium:

(5) $$N^d = N^s.$$

That is, the wage rate will not be an equilibrium one unless it equates the amounts demanded and supplied of labor. A graphical description of this market is presented in Figure IX-1. The equilibrium real wage rate is $(w/p)_0$, and to it corresponds the amount of labor, N_0. If the

---

[4] As usual, $\phi_N(\ )$ denotes the partial derivative of $\phi(\ )$ with respect to N.

wage rate were above this equilibrium level, there would be an excess supply of labor and the money wage rate would fall; if it were below, there would be an excess demand and money wages would rise.

It will immediately be recognized that we have greatly oversimplified the analysis of this market. Both the demand and supply functions for labor should actually be presented as dependent on the real value of bond and money holdings as well as on the real wage rate. Furthermore, if we were to permit the firm to vary its input of capital, its demand

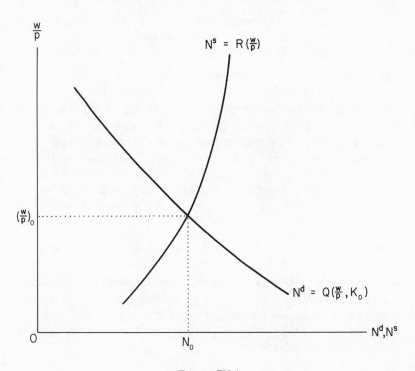

FIGURE IX-1.

for labor would depend also on the rate of interest. Finally, a full utility analysis of individual behavior would show the supply of labor also to depend on this rate.

If we have ignored these additional influences, it is because the labor market as such does not interest us in the following analysis; its sole function is to provide the bench mark of full employment. Hence it has been considered desirable to introduce this market in as simple a manner as possible. The full meaning of these remarks will become clear in Chapter XIII:1. For the moment, we merely note that—as the reader will be able to confirm for himself in the next chapter—the introduction of these additional influences would not affect the comparative-statics analysis, but it would greatly complicate the dynamic analysis and would preclude the use of the helpful graphical device by which this analysis will be carried out.

3. THE MARKET FOR COMMODITIES

Consider now the market for commodities. It is assumed that vertical integration of firms exists to such an extent that every firm is self-sufficient in raw materials. Thus the only commodities that appear in this market are finished ones. These are divided into two categories: consumer commodities and investment commodities. The prices of these two categories are assumed to change in the same proportion.

The demand of households for the first of these composite goods is the familiar consumption function, while the demand of firms for the second is the equally familiar marginal-efficiency-of-capital function. Each of these is conceptually aggregated from individual-experiments in which households and firms are confronted with varying combinations of real income, rate of interest, and initial real money balances and asked to indicate their corresponding optimum consumption and investment plans.[5] Thus these functions have, respectively, the forms

$$(6) \qquad C = g\left(Y, r, \frac{M_0^H}{p}\right)$$

and

$$(7) \qquad I = h\left(Y, r, \frac{M_0^F}{p}\right),$$

where C represents the real amount demanded by households of consumption commodities; I, the real amount demanded by firms of investment commodities; r, the rate of interest; M_0^H, the initial nominal money

[5] On the empirical significance of the real-balance effect on consumption, see again Note M.

holdings of households; M_0^F, the initial money holdings of firms; and p, the absolute price level of both investment and consumption commodities. The variable Y here represents gross real national income, necessarily equal, of course, to gross real national product. To these demands we add the constant demand of government for consumption commodities,

$$(8) \qquad\qquad\qquad G = G_0,$$

where G is the real level of government expenditures, and G_0 is a constant not affected by any of the economic variables of our system.

For our purposes, it is only the total real demand for commodities E which is of interest. Thus we combine the preceding three functions into an aggregate demand function for commodities:

$$(9) \qquad\qquad\qquad E = F\left(Y, r, \frac{M_0}{p}\right),$$

where

$$(10) \qquad F\left(Y, r, \frac{M_0}{p}\right) \equiv g\left(Y, r, \frac{M_0^H}{p}\right) + h\left(Y, r, \frac{M_0^F}{p}\right) + G_0,$$

and M_0 is the fixed total quantity of money in the economy, equal to the sum of M_0^H and M_0^F. For a given value of $r = r_0$ and $p = p_0$, this function has the familiar form indicated in Figure IX-2.

The curves labeled C, I, and G represent the consumption, investment, and government functions, respectively. As stated in equation (10), the aggregate demand curve E is the vertical sum of these three component curves. It shows the total amount demanded of commodities at varying levels of real income, assuming the rate of interest and price level to remain constant. It reflects the assumption that, *ceteris paribus*, an increase in income increases the amounts demanded of both consumption and investment commodities but that this joint increase is less than the increase in income. That is, the marginal propensity to demand commodities out of real income is assumed positive, but less than unity.

Before continuing with the description of this aggregate demand curve let us note three oversimplifications that have been made. First, there is the somewhat crude treatment of income and financial assets that has already been noted at the beginning of this chapter. Second, there is the exclusion of the bond holdings from the consumption and investment functions. Strictly speaking, the first of these functions should have been shown as dependent upon the real value of the initial net bond holdings of households, and the second, on the exactly offsetting negative value of the initial bond holdings of firms. But since we are primarily interested in the aggregate demand function and not in its individual components, and since by the assumed absence of distribution effects

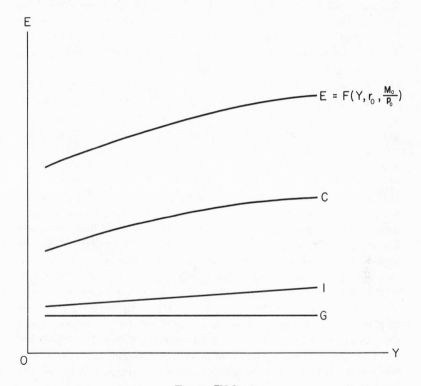

Figure IX-2.

this aggregate function depends only on the *total* of initial bond holdings in the economy, and since this total for a closed economy with no government borrowing is identically zero (for every creditor there is an offsetting debtor), we have also taken the liberty of omitting these holdings from the component functions as well (cf. p. 71 above).

A third oversimplification occurs in the stated dependence of consumption and investment on the level of gross real national income, Y. It is much more reasonable to assume that consumption, at least, depends on disposable income. However, under certain assumptions, Y can be taken as an index of disposable income too. First, we assume that depreciation charges are a constant proportion b of gross national product. Second, we assume that the government resorts only to income taxes to balance its budget. This implies that these taxes are fixed at the constant real level G_0. Hence Y can also represent the linearly related variable, real disposable income, equal to $(1 - b)Y - G_0$. This implicit assumption holds for the other markets of the economy too.

Let us now return to our aggregate demand function and examine the effects of an increase in the rate of interest. By assumption, the creditors' capital losses from such an increase exactly offset the debtors' capital gains. Hence the increase in interest cannot affect aggregate demand in this way. Instead, it exerts its influence through more traditional channels. In particular, by its influence on the margin of a household's choice between consuming and saving, it is assumed to decrease the amount of current commodities demanded. This has been sufficiently discussed above.[6] To this we now add its influence on the margin of a firm's choice between expanding its investment program and retiring one of its outstanding bonds. Let us adopt the usual assumption of a declining marginal efficiency of capital. Then, the higher the rate of interest, the fewer the investment projects the firm can undertake which yield (after taking into account risk factors) a rate of return greater than or equal to the rate it could earn in interest-savings by simply repurchasing its bonds. Hence the higher the interest rate, the smaller the amount demanded of investment commodities and the greater the tendency toward debt retirement. Conversely, the lower this rate, the greater the number of projects for which it pays the firm to borrow and invest. Thus, in graphical terms, an increase in the rate of interest above r_0 causes a downward shift in the whole aggregate demand curve of Figure IX-2: at the same level of national income, the total amount of commodities demanded is decreased. Conversely, a decrease in interest below r_0 causes an upward shift in this curve.

It remains only to refer briefly to the by-now familiar real-balance effect. The greater these balances, the greater the amounts demanded

[6] Pp. 65–66 and 94.

of both consumption and investment commodities. More specifically, the marginal propensity to spend on commodities out of real balances is assumed to be positive, but less than unity. It follows that, *ceteris paribus*, an increase in the price level above p_0 causes a decrease in the real value of cash balances M_0/p and a consequent downward shift in the aggregate demand curve of Figure IX-2: at each level of national income, the amount of commodities demanded is decreased. Conversely, a decrease in the price level below p_0 causes an upward shift in this curve. It should be emphasized that under our present assumptions of no government debt and no distribution effects, the real-balance effect of a change in p is once again (p. 20) identical with the wealth effect of such a change.

Obviously, each of the foregoing components of the aggregate demand function, and, consequently, the aggregate demand function itself, reflects the absence of money illusion: each shows that any change which affects neither real income, the rate of interest, nor real balances does not affect economic behavior. The significance of this property for the consumption function is clear from Part One. Its significance for the government function is simply that there is a concern only with the real content of the budget. Its significance for the investment function can be made equally clear. Consider, for example, a doubling of prices and wages accompanied by a doubling of the firms' initial money and bond holdings, the rate of interest being held constant. This does, indeed, double the costs of any given investment project. But, by assumption, there is a simultaneous doubling of the money returns anticipated from this project. Hence, by definition, the marginal efficiency of capital—its marginal rate of return—is not affected by the combined wage and price increase. At the same time, the real asset position of firms is unchanged. Hence any project which firms found worth while to undertake before will still be found worth while. That is, the real demand for investment commodities is not affected by the specified change. And this is precisely what investment function (7) shows.

Let us now turn to the supply side of the market. Consider first the supply function of a given firm under conditions of perfect competition. This function describes the outcome of a conceptual individual-experiment in which the firm is confronted (in a perfectly competitive market) with varying prices and costs and asked to specify the respective amounts of commodities it would like to supply in order to maximize its profits. It follows, under the simple assumptions of the preceding section, that the firm's supply function depends only on the technical conditions of production, its fixed amount of capital equipment, and the real wage rate. For, given the latter two, the firm's optimum input of labor is determined by its marginal productivity. And given this input and the firm's fixed capital equipment, the production function then determines the corresponding optimum output of commodities.

In a similar way we can conceive of an aggregate supply function for the economy as a whole which is dependent upon the real wage rate prevailing in the economy and on its fixed amount of capital. Write this function as

$$(11) \qquad Y = S\left(\frac{w}{p}, K_0\right),$$

where, in contrast to our description of the demand side of the market —but in accordance once again with our description of production function (1)—Y represents gross real national *product*, and not *income*. From the explanation of the preceding paragraph, it is clear that the output corresponding to a given real wage rate as given by this supply function must correspond to the output we would obtain by determining from the aggregate demand function for labor (3) the optimum amount of labor firms would employ at this given rate and then determining from the production function (1) the output corresponding to this input of labor. In other words, the supply function for commodities can be derived by substituting function (3) into function (1) to obtain

$$(12) \qquad \phi\left[Q\left(\frac{w}{p}, K_0\right), K_0\right] \equiv S\left(\frac{w}{p}, K_0\right).$$

Thus supply function (11)—like the more familiar one described in the preceding paragraph—indicates the amounts of commodities the firms of the economy would like to supply in order to maximize their profits at the given real wage rate with which they are confronted in the market.[7]

---

[7] It is obvious from equation (12) that if we were to abandon our oversimplified form of the labor demand function and, instead, represent it as dependent also on real balances and the rate of interest, the commodity supply function would also be so dependent.

It follows that, for any given real wage rate, the aggregate commodity supply function must appear in Figure IX-2—or IX-3—as a vertical line drawn at the level of gross national product yielded by equation (11) for that specified wage rate. As long as this rate remains unchanged, so, too, must this vertical line. If, however, the real wage rate should rise, then the optimum input of labor, and hence the optimum output of commodities, will decrease. Hence the aggregate supply curve—though still represented by a vertical line—will shift to the left in Figure IX-3 until it reaches the level of gross national output yielded by (11) for the increased real wage rate. In the opposite case of a decrease in the real wage, the vertical supply curve will shift to the right. But we shall for the most part not be interested in such shifts until we reach the analysis of involuntary unemployment in Chapter XIII; until then the aggregate commodity supply function will play a rather passive role in the argument.

We might note that the supply function assumes the more familiar form of an upward-sloping curve if it is drawn within the coordinate system of Figure III-1a (p. 42). For the higher the price level, the lower the real wage rate, the greater the input of labor, and the greater, therefore, the aggregate amount of commodities supplied.[8] Similarly, it is clear from the discussion on p. 41 that the aggregate demand function for commodities (9) can be represented in Figure III-1a (as of a given level of Y and r) by the negatively sloping curve which now appears there.

The equilibrium condition for the commodity market is the usual one: the amount demanded must equal the amount supplied. That is,

$$(13) \qquad\qquad E = Y.$$

Graphically, we have the situation represented in Figure IX-3, where $w_0/p_0 = (w/p)_0$ and where Y_0 is, of course, the commodity output resulting from the input of N_0 units of labor in Figure IX-1. Equilibrium exists when the demand and supply curves intersect on the 45° radius vector.

The meaning of this equilibrium condition can be seen as follows. Assume, for example, that the rate of interest remains r_0 but that the price and wage levels fall in the same proportion below w_0 and p_0,

---

[8] Contrast this with the vertical supply curve of an exchange economy, without production, now represented in Figure III-1a.

respectively. The real wage rate being unchanged, the supply curve
in Figure IX-3 is unaffected. But, due to the real-balance effect, the
demand function now rises above the solid curve of this diagram—say
to E_1. Hence, at the unchanged real income Y_0, there exists an excess
of commodities demanded over supplied equal to AB, inventories are
drawn down, and an upward pressure on prices is created. In the

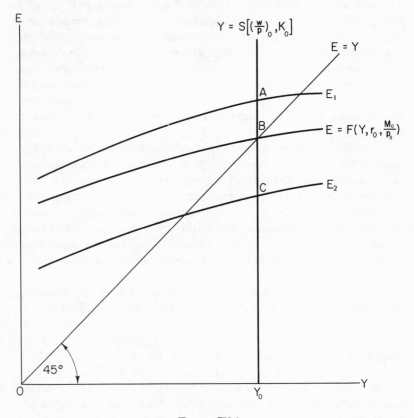

FIGURE IX-3.

opposite case, with a price level greater than p_0, the demand curve lies
below that of Figure IX-3—say at E_2. There then exists an excess of
commodities supplied over demanded equal to BC, inventories accumulate, and a downward pressure on prices is created. Equilibrium in

the commodity market can therefore exist only when the demand curve intersects the supply curve at the point *B*.

4. THE MARKET FOR BONDS

In the real world there are many kinds of bonds, of varying risks and maturities. We shall represent all of these by a composite perpetuity of representative risk paying one dollar per period. Thus the technical nature of this bond differs from that of Part One. For the purposes of the present analysis, however, this difference is unimportant; we can always consider the redemption of the one-period bond of Part One as being equivalent to the repurchase of a perpetuity.[9] The price of this perpetuity must obviously equal the reciprocal of the rate of interest.

It is assumed that the only demanders of bonds are households, whereas the primary suppliers are firms. Households can also supply bonds, but their relative importance on this side of the market is quite small. That is, the large majority of loans in our model are for production, and not consumption, purposes.

It should be noted that we are now using "demand for bonds" in a somewhat different sense than in Chapter IV. Specifically, this term now represents the demand for *positive* bond holdings; that is, it represents only the behavior of lenders. The behavior of borrowers, formerly described as a *demand* for *negative* bond holdings, is now represented separately as the "supply of bonds." Both the demand and the supply are for a *stock* of bonds. Households decide on the total stock of bonds they wish to hold; changes in these stocks represent their net lending during the period. Firms decide on the total stock they wish to have outstanding; changes in this stock represent their net borrowing during the period.

The demand side of the market has been sufficiently discussed in Chapters IV: 3 and V: 3. Letting B^d represent the number of bonds demanded and $1/r$ their per-unit price in dollars, we can summarize this discussion by writing

$$(14) \qquad \frac{B^d}{rp} = H\left(Y, \frac{1}{r}, \frac{M_0^H}{p}\right).$$

[9] Cf. Hicks, *Value and Capital*, pp. 144–45.

That is, the real value of bond holdings demanded depends only on real income, the rate of interest, and the real value of cash balances held by households. The form of the foregoing function makes explicit the assumed absence of money illusion: a doubling of prices and initial household money holdings, real income and the rate of interest being held constant, does not affect the amount demanded of *real*

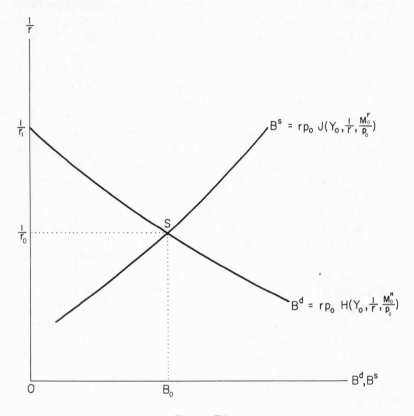

FIGURE IX-4.

bond holdings B^d/rp; that is, it causes a doubling of the amount demanded of *nominal* bond holdings B^d.

The demand curve for bonds, as of a fixed level of real income and prices, is represented by the curve B^d in Figure IX-4. As can be seen from equation (14), this curve abstracts from the influence of the initial bond holdings of households. Under this oversimplification, the internal consistency of our model then requires that the elasticity of this curve be both negative and greater than unity in absolute value. For it has already been assumed that an increase in interest—that is, a decrease in the price of bonds—decreases the amount demanded of consumption commodities; it will also be assumed below that it decreases the amount demanded of money balances; hence, by the households' budget restraint, their total expenditure on bond holdings must increase.

The demand curve B^d also depicts Keynes' basic proposition that there is a minimum positive rate of interest on which individuals insist in order to compensate themselves for the loss of liquidity involved in holding bonds instead of money. Figure IX-4 shows that—for the given real income Y_0, initial money balances M_0^H, and price level p_0—the rate at which the desired amount of bond holdings becomes zero is r_1. This is the economic meaning of the fact that above the price $1/r_1$ the demand curve for bonds is identical with the vertical axis.

Let us now examine the influence of changes in variables other than the rate of interest. Consider first an increase in real income or real balances. This is assumed to shift the whole demand curve to the right: at the same rate of interest individuals are willing to hold more bonds. As can be seen from the form of the demand function, an increase in the price level has no such clear-cut effect. *If* the real command over future commodities which the individual desires to hold in the form of bonds were to remain constant, then, clearly, the demand for bonds would increase in the same proportion that the anticipated costs of these future commodities had increased. But, under our assumptions, this desire cannot have remained constant, for the decrease in real cash balances occasioned by the price increase must exert a downward influence on this desire as well as on the demand for current commodities. Indeed, this real-balance effect may even be so strong as to cause a decrease in the demand for bonds. Disregarding this possibility, we conclude that, say, a doubling of the price level causes a less-than-proportionate rightward shift of the demand curve for bonds; that is, at a given interest rate, the amount of bonds demanded is increased, but not doubled.[10] Conversely, a decrease in prices causes a less-than-proportionate leftward shift in the demand curve.

[10] The reader will find it instructive to compare this case with that in which the

It should be emphasized that the shifts described in the preceding paragraph will, in general, also change the intersection point of the demand curve with the vertical axis. That is, the minimum rate of interest on which the individual insists is not generally an absolute constant of his behavior, but is itself influenced by his income and initial money holdings. It is, of course, possible that no matter how much, say, real income increases, this minimum rate cannot fall below a certain level; that is, as the demand curve rises, its intersection point with the vertical axis approaches a certain value as a limit. This assumption can be made, though it is not necessary for our argument.

Let us now consider the supply side of the market. To the extent that households are suppliers of bonds, no new element is added to the immediately preceding discussion. All that need be done is to substitute the phrase "decrease in amount supplied" wherever the phrase "increase in amount demanded" occurs. However, as has already been noted, the contribution of households to this side of the market is assumed to be negligible. Hence the major characteristics of the supply curve for bonds must be determined from a study of the behavior of firms.

As in the case of an exchange economy,[11] we must first assume that there is some market "imperfection" which prevents economic units from borrowing all they want at the prevailing interest rate. It is this "imperfection" which provides the ultimate restraint on the commodity demands of both firms and households. Let us now denote the number of bonds supplied by B^s and let

$$(15) \qquad \frac{B^s}{rp} = J\left(Y, \frac{1}{r}, \frac{M_0^F}{p}\right)$$

describe the real supply of bonds which firms deem it desirable to have outstanding under various conditions. Consider now the influence of changes in these conditions. An increase in gross real national product is assumed to increase the amount of bonds supplied; for the greater the volume of production, the greater the firms' requirements for loan capital with which to finance the necessary plant, equipment, and

---

initial holdings of bonds and money are also doubled, so that—by the absence of money illusion—the whole demand curve shifts over exactly twice as far to the right; cf. pp. 69–70.

[11] Cf. p. 68.

inventories. On the other hand, an increase in real balances decreases the amount supplied; for the decreased marginal value of the security against possible inconveniences and penalty costs provided by these increased balances will no longer compensate the firms for the interest-savings that can be achieved by using these balances for debt retirement.[12]

Let us now abstract from the influence of the firms' initially outstanding bonds and consider the effect of an increase in the rate of interest. The internal consistency of our model requires that this decrease the amount of *real* bonds supplied. For the higher the interest rate, the more firms will find it worth while to decrease their money balances and use the proceeds to retire debt. Similarly, the higher this rate, the smaller the demand for investment goods and the fewer, therefore, the number of projects that have to be financed. Hence the *real value* of bonds outstanding B^s/rp must decrease. But this does not mean that the *number* of bonds outstanding B^s must also decrease. For the rise in interest has lowered the price received for bonds and so may *increase* the number of bonds necessary to finance the firms' expenditures on investment commodities, even though these expenditures have *decreased*. We shall, however, assume that this latter tendency is outweighed by the first two, so that an increase in interest can be assumed to decrease both the real value and the number of bonds supplied.

The form of the foregoing supply function reflects the assumption that firms, too, are free of money illusion. A doubling of prices, wages, and initial money holdings, real income and interest held constant, does not change the firms' real positions and hence does not affect the real volume of their planned activities. Hence there is no change in the real value of bonds B^s/rp which firms deem it desirable to have outstanding. But, due to the increase in costs and prices, these same activities now require twice the nominal volume of bond financing as before. Hence B^s doubles.[13]

---

[12] Cf. pp. 79–80 and 147–48.

[13] There is an implicit assumption here that all the firms' capital equipment must be replaced during the period in question. Alternatively, we can assume that firms immediately write up their capital equipment in accordance with its increased market value, sell additional bonds to the extent of this increased value, and pass on the implicit capital gains to their respective entrepreneurs. Conversely, in the event of a decrease in prices, entrepreneurs must make good the implicit capital loss, and firms then use these funds to retire bonds. In this way the nominal amount of bonds outstanding can always be kept equal to the current value of the firms' assets.

The curve B^s in Figure IX-4 depicts the foregoing supply function of bonds as of a fixed level of real national product and prices. In accordance with the foregoing discussion, this curve is drawn with a positive slope. Again in accordance with this discussion, it is assumed that an increase in real national income or a decrease in firms' real balances shifts the whole curve to the right: at the same rate of interest, firms wish to have more bonds outstanding. As can be seen from the supply function (15), an increase in the price level also shifts the curve to the right. But, in contrast to the demand side of the picture, this shift is more than proportionate to the increase in prices. For here the real-balance effect reinforces the "cost effect." That is, firms have to increase their borrowing, not only to finance the increased costs of operations, but also to replenish their real balances. Conversely, a decrease in prices causes a more-than-proportionate leftward shift of the supply curve.

The condition for equilibrium in the bond market is, of course,

$$(16) \qquad\qquad\qquad B^d = B^s.$$

At the level of real national income Y_0 and prices p_0, such an equilibrium exists in Figure IX-4 at the rate of interest r_0. If, *ceteris paribus*, the rate of interest were less than this, there would be an excess supply of bonds, driving the price of bonds down (and, *ipso facto*, the rate of interest up). If it were greater, there would be an excess demand for bonds, driving the rate down again.

Throughout this section we have followed the practice of the preceding one and have disregarded the influence of the initial holdings of bonds. Let us now examine the significance of this omission. Strictly speaking, the demand for bonds should have been shown as depending also on the initial *positive* bond holdings of households, and the supply of bonds on the initial *negative* bond holdings of firms. If we were to take these additional influences into account in Figure IX-4, both the demand and supply curves would shift to the right: the former shift reflecting the fact that the stock of bonds demanded depends not only on the current income of households but also on the size of their initial bond portfolios; the latter shift reflecting the fact that the stock of bonds supplied depends not only on the need of firms to finance current activities but also on their need to keep on financing their initially outstanding debt. But if the assumption of neutral distribution effects holds, these two shifts would be exactly equal, so that the equilibrium rate of interest would not be affected. Thus, from the narrow viewpoint of the equilibrium interest rate, this omission is of no importance. On the other hand, this discussion makes it clear that no meaning can be attached to the amount B_0 at which the curves intersect in Figure IX-4; for the true intersection point—representing the equilibrium number of bonds outstanding—must be to the right of B_0.

This complication—as well as others that have arisen in the course of this section—can be avoided by conducting the analysis in terms of the demand for *real* bond holdings—where "demand" is now used in the sense of Chapter IV to refer to both positive and negative holdings.[14] The demand function for these real holdings is the difference between the real demand and supply functions of this section and can therefore be represented by

$$(17) \qquad D = B\left(Y, \frac{1}{r}, \frac{M_0}{p}\right),$$

where

$$(18) \qquad B\left(Y, \frac{1}{r}, \frac{M_0}{p}\right) \equiv H\left(Y, \frac{1}{r}, \frac{M_0^H}{p}\right) - J\left(Y, \frac{1}{r}, \frac{M_0^F}{p}\right).$$

As illustrated in Figure IX-5, at a rate of interest below r_0 the net demand for real bond holdings, D, is negative; that is, there is an excess of potential borrowers over lenders, and this drives the rate up. At a rate above r_0 the net demand is positive; there is an excess of potential lenders over borrowers, and this drives the rate down. Equilibrium exists in this market when

$$(19) \qquad B\left(Y, \frac{1}{r}, \frac{M_0}{p}\right) = 0,$$

that is, when the total amount of desired borrowings is equal to the total amount of desired lendings. Figure IX-5 shows that—for real income Y_0, price level p_0, and initial money holdings M_0—this condition is satisfied at the rate of interest r_0, at the price corresponding to which the demand curve for real bond holdings intersects the vertical axis.[15]

This alternative description of the bond market exploits to the full our simplifying assumption that what matters is only the total of any

---

[14] See third paragraph of this section.
[15] Cf. the similar argument at the beginning of Chapter IV:4.

item and not its distribution. In particular, since the demand curve of
Figure IX-5 describes the aggregate behavior of all the economic units
of our closed economy—whose total initial bond holdings are by definition zero—it can legitimately ignore these holdings. Similarly,
identity (18) makes use of the assumption that it is only the total of real
money balances that counts and not their distribution between households and firms. Correspondingly, Figure IX-5 implies that a redistribution of money holdings from, say, the latter to the former would

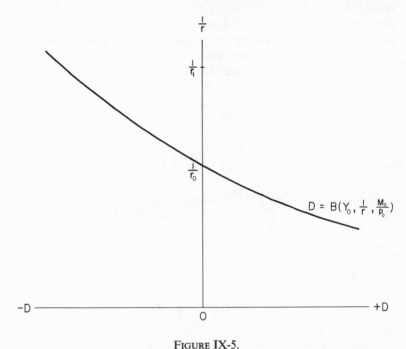

Figure IX-5.

affect neither the demand curve for bonds nor, consequently, the
equilibrium rate of interest. This is the counterpart of the more
complicated argument which would be needed to show that, in Figure
IX-4, such a redistribution shifts both the demand and supply curves
equal distances to the right.

But the most important advantage of Figure IX-5 derives not from its
use of "demand" in the sense of Chapter IV, but from its exclusive

concentration on real, as distinct from nominal, bond holdings. This procedure clearly and simply reveals the crucial relationship between the price level and the equilibrium rate of interest. It shows that in the bond market as a whole, an increase, say, in the price level has only a real-balance effect which unmistakably causes a downward shift in the demand curve of Figure IX-5 and therefore increases the equilibrium rate of interest.

These advantages are achieved at the cost of moving to a higher level of abstraction and thereby foregoing the fruitful contact with the more familiar language of the market and the literature. It also denies us a graphical representation of the meaning of Keynes' minimum rate of interest. For the purposes of the text, this price is too high to pay. Hence in what follows we shall work mainly with the more clumsy description of Figure IX-4, though we shall always indicate to the reader how he can simplify the argument by working instead with Figure IX-5.

5. The Market for Money

Let us turn finally to the market for money. We continue to restrict the discussion to a fiat paper money issued by the government. As in the case of bonds, the demand and supply in this market are for a stock and not a flow.

Actually, of course, the preceding discussion of the other three markets, together with the budget restraint, has already completely specified the form of the excess-demand function for money (p. 24). If we have assumed that an increase in real income or initial money balances (and hence real wealth) is devoted partly to increasing the demands for commodities and bonds, then we have also assumed that the remainder of this increase—and exactly the remainder—is devoted to increasing the demand for money. If we have assumed that the demand functions for labor, commodities, and real bond holdings are free of money illusion and are independent of the distribution of initial bond and money holdings, then we have also assumed this for the demand function for real money holdings. The function which reflects these assumptions can be written as

$$(20) \qquad M^d = p\,L\!\left(Y, r, \frac{M_0}{p}\right),$$

where M^d represents the amount of nominal money holdings demanded by households and firms taken together—the governmental demand being assumed zero.

By assuming the rate of interest and real income to remain constant, we can obtain from function (20) a demand curve for money which depends on the absolute price level. This has already been presented

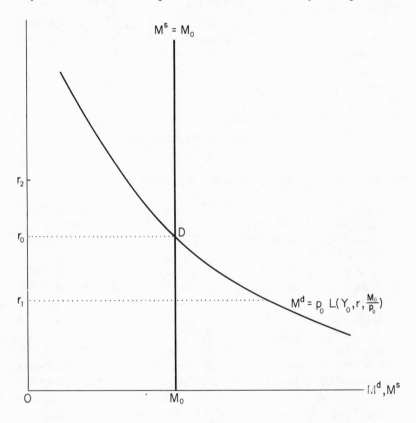

FIGURE IX-6.

in Figure II-2b (p. 29). However, in order to make our analysis graphically comparable to that of Keynesian interest theory, we choose instead to hold the price level and real income constant and to obtain accordingly a demand curve which depends on the rate of interest. Such a curve is presented in Figure IX-6. It should be clear that the choice between

Figures II-2b and IX-6 is not a substantive one; the same analysis can be carried out in terms of either diagram, as convenience indicates.

The negative slope of the following demand curve reflects the joint operation of the transactions and speculative motives as analyzed in Chapters V–VII above. More generally, it reflects the assumption that money holdings are not an inferior good. Hence a decrease in the price that must be paid for such holdings—in terms of interest foregone —causes an increase in the amount demanded. On the other hand, an increase in either real income or initial money balances causes a rightward shift in the curve as a whole: at the same rate of interest, the amount of money demanded is greater than it was before. Finally, an increase in the price level is assumed to cause a less-than-proportionate rightward shift in the curve as a whole. This, of course, is implicit in what has already been said about the shape of the demand curve in Figure II-2b (p. 30).[16]

As the reader can immediately see, the demand curve of Figure IX-6 differs in one respect from the usual Keynesian one. Specifically, our curve does not become indefinitely horizontal at the rate of interest r_1 at which, by Figure IX-4, no one is any longer willing to hold bonds. This conclusion emerges directly from the budget restraint after feeding into it the assumptions already made as to the effects of, say, a decrease in interest on the other markets of the economy. In particular, a decrease in the rate of interest has been assumed to affect the planned inflow and outflow of money by causing an

increase in the total planned expenditures of households on consumer commodities, an

increase in the total planned expenditures of firms on investment commodities, a

decrease in the total planned holdings by households of the bonds of firms and other households (i.e., total planned lendings of households), an

[16] Much empirical work has been done in recent years on the interest and income (or, alternatively, wealth) elasticity of the demand for money. For a critical survey of the work of James Tobin, Henry Latané, R. T. Selden, Milton Friedman, and others, see Johnson, "Monetary Theory and Policy," *op. cit.*, pp. 354–57. See also the articles by Bronfenbrenner and Mayer, Robert Eisner, and Allan Meltzer referred to on p. 349, footnote 24 below. See also the discussion of the empirical evidence on the real-balance effect in the demand function for money cited on p. 652 below.

> *increase* in the total planned issuance by households of their own bonds (i.e., total planned borrowings of households), and an
>
> *increase* in the total planned issuance by firms of their own bonds (i.e., total planned borrowings of firms).

Let us designate a money inflow as a positive amount and a money outflow as a negative one. Then to say that a decrease in the rate of interest increases the amount of money demanded is to say that the algebraic sum of the above five items is positive. That is, the planned inflow of money exceeds the planned outflow, so that—by the budget restraint—there is a planned increase in the stock of money holdings.[17]

It is clear from Chapters V:5 and VII:1 that there is nothing unrealistic about assuming that households may increase their borrowings in order to increase their money holdings. For the liquidity services of these holdings are a good like any other one. Indeed (to turn for a moment to the real world) any economic unit which is both a creditor and a debtor of a bank—which holds demand deposits at the same time that it is indebted to the bank for loans received—is in this position. If the economic unit wanted to, it could obviously reduce its debt by drawing down its demand deposits; and the fact that it does not do so means

---

[17] It may help the reader to see this if we write the budget restraint for the economy as a whole in the following form:

the amount of money demanded (that is, the stock of money planned for the end of the period)

= the given holdings (stock) of money at the beginning of the period

+ the planned money inflow from the sale of labor services, commodities, and bonds during the period

− the planned money outflow on the purchase of labor services, commodities, and bonds during the period.

Since this restraint views the economy as a whole, it does not include a term representing the interest payments made and received each period on bonds: by assumption, the net aggregate amount of these payments is zero. [Cf. my "Reconsideration of the General Equilibrium Theory of Money," *op. cit.*, equations (2.1), (2.2), and (5.3).] Note also that in the text we have ignored the influence of labor services; this follows from our assumption that the demand and supply for these services are independent of the rate of interest.

On the stock–flow aspect of this restraint, see Mathematical Appendix 11, especially equations (11.14)–(11.15).

that it is effectively borrowing in order to maintain its desired level of cash balances.

Assume now that the rate of interest has been reduced to r_1 and consider the effects of a still further reduction. The only significance of having reached this minimum rate of interest is that the third item in the preceding list becomes zero: individuals no longer plan to convert bond holdings into money holdings for the simple reason that they no longer have any such bonds to sell. But if money is still a noninferior good, the planned inflows of the last two items continue to overbalance the outflows of the first two, so that planned money holdings continue to grow. Thus, in general, the rate of interest r_1 does not manifest itself in any particular way in the demand curve for money.[18]

The only case in which the demand curve could become indefinitely horizontal at r_1 is the one in which the supply of bonds in Figure IX-4 becomes infinite at this rate. But an individual who plans an infinite supply of bonds is for some reason unconcerned with his obligation to make interest payments on these bonds. Hence if the amount supplied is infinite at any positive rate of interest, it must be so at all rates. Under this assumption, it follows that the demand for money would also be infinite at all positive rates. Indeed, the same must hold true for the demand for commodities. These unrealistic implications explain why we ignore this possibility and retain our original assumption that the institutional framework of the economy keeps the supply of bonds finite.[19]

On the other hand, the demand curve for money could have a limited horizontal stretch at the rate r_1. This would be the counterpart of such a stretch at the beginning of the demand curve for bonds. This situation is shown in Figure IX-7, where the horizontal segment FG in panel (b) represents the money value of the bonds held at point C in panel (a). Once the individual has disposed of these bonds, his demand curve for money will, in general, resume its negative slope (segment GJ). On the other hand, in the special case where the inflows of the last two items on

---

[18] This is the counterpart of its failure to manifest itself in any particular way in Figure IX-5.

[19] See p. 216.

Note that by the argument on p. 126 above, even a "bear" will generally not borrow an infinite amount in order to hold money balances on the expectation of a future rise in interest rates—if (as is realistic to assume) these expectations are not held with certainty.

pp. 223–24 exactly offset the outflows of the first two, the curve will become vertical (segment *GE*).[20]

It should be emphasized that in order for the foregoing horizontal segment to appear in the market demand curve too, it is necessary that there exist unanimity of opinion as to the interest rate which is minimal. For if there does not, then in the process of aggregating the individual demand curves, these horizontal segments will become smoothed out, so that the market curve will have the usual negative slope.[21] On the other hand, unanimity is not a sufficient condition for the existence of a horizontal segment. Thus, for example, if the bond demand curve of every individual were represented by that of Figure IX-4, the aggregate

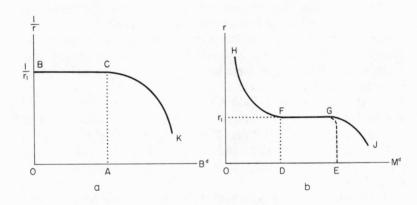

FIGURE IX-7.

money demand curve would have the continuous negative slope of Figure IX-6.

Let us turn now to the supply side of the market. We have assumed throughout our analysis that the quantity of money in circulation is constant. Thus our supply function is simply

$$(21) \qquad\qquad M^s = M_0,$$

---

[20] The foregoing argument is clearly not specific to the rate of interest r_1: the demand curve for money will have a horizontal segment at whatever rate the demand curve for bonds has one.

[21] Cf. Tobin, "Liquidity Preference as Behavior Toward Risk," *op. cit.*, pp. 67–69.

where M^s is the nominal amount of money supplied and M_0 is a constant. The equilibrium condition is

(22) $$M^d = M^s,$$

and this is shown to obtain in Figure IX-6 at the rate of interest r_0. Alternatively, in Figure III-2 (p. 47), equilibrium could have been shown to obtain at $1/p_0$ for a demand curve drawn for constant real income Y_0 and interest r_0. In either diagram we can see that if the rate of interest were below r_0 or the price level above p_0, then there would be an excess demand for money; by the budget restraint, this implies the existence of an excess supply of bonds and/or commodities. Hence the rate of interest would rise and the price level fall. Conversely, if the rate of interest were above r_0 and the price level below p_0, automatic market forces would be generated to lower the former and raise the latter.

We note finally that the way in which the budget restraint specifies the form of the demand function for money can now be precisely described by the identity

(23)
$$\frac{M_0}{p} - L\left(Y_0, r, \frac{M_0}{p}\right)$$
$$\equiv \left[Q\left(\frac{w}{p}, K_0\right) - R\left(\frac{w}{p}\right)\right] + \left[F\left(Y_0, r, \frac{M_0}{p}\right) - Y_0\right]$$
$$+ B\left(Y_0, \frac{1}{r}, \frac{M_0}{p}\right),$$

where use has been made of equation (19) on p. 219. An immediate implication of this identity—and one of which we have already made implicit use—is that the sum of the marginal propensities to spend out of initial real balances on all goods—including money—is unity.[22] A corresponding statement holds, of course, for the marginal propensities to spend out of income or wealth.

---

[22] Mathematically, taking the partial derivative of (23) with respect to M_0/p we obtain

$$1 \equiv F_3(\ ) + B_3(\ ) + L_3(\ ),$$

where $F_3(\ )$ represents the partial derivative of $F(\ )$ with respect to M_0/p—and a corresponding interpretation holds for $B_3(\ )$ and $L_3(\ )$.

X. The Workings of the Model:
Full Employment

1. The equality of the number of equations and variables. 2. The stability of the system: the method of successive approximation. 3. The effects of an increase in the quantity of money. 4. The effects of a shift in liquidity preference.

1. The Equality of the Number of Equations and Variables

The preceding chapter provides a description of each market of the economy. This chapter and the next one integrate these separate descriptions into an overall one of the functioning of the economy as a whole on the assumption of full employment. The meaning of this assumption and the implications of dropping it will be discussed at length in Chapter XIII. For the moment we shall simply understand it as implying that the level of real national product remains fixed at Y_0 throughout the analysis. Correspondingly, the level of employment remains fixed at N_0, the labor input necessary to produce Y_0.

Let us now describe our model in formal mathematical terms. There are four markets. For each market there are three equations: a demand equation, a supply equation, and an equilibrium equation. For each market there are also three variables: the amount demanded, the amount supplied, and the price of the good in question. The price of money is, by definition, unity. Hence there is a total of only eleven variables to be determined. On the other hand, Walras' Law as expressed by equation (23) on the preceding page shows that if any three equilibrium equations are satisfied, the remaining one must also be satisfied. Hence there is also a total of only eleven independent equations with which to determine these variables.

By substituting these demand and supply equations into their respective equilibrium equations, we can reduce the foregoing system to the following one:

	Condition for Equilibrium	*Market*

(1) $$Q\left(\frac{w}{p}, K_0\right) = R\left(\frac{w}{p}\right)$$ Labor services,

(2) $$F\left(Y_0, r, \frac{M_0}{p}\right) = Y_0$$ Commodities,

(3) $$rp \cdot H\left(Y_0, \frac{1}{r}, \frac{M_0^H}{p}\right) = rp \cdot J\left(Y_0, \frac{1}{r}, \frac{M_0^F}{p}\right)$$ Bonds,

(4) $$p \cdot L\left(Y_0, r, \frac{M_0}{p}\right) = M_0$$ Money.

Here we have made use of the assumption that the level of output is fixed at Y_0. By Walras' Law, only three of these equations are independent. Correspondingly, there are only three unknown variables to be determined: the money wage rate, the price level, and the rate of interest. As before,[1] we then take this equality between the number of equations and unknowns as justifying the reasonableness of the assumption that this system of equations does have a solution. Indeed, this assumption is already implicit in Figures IX-1, IX-3, IX-4, and IX-6. For these posit the existence of a single set of values for the variables w_0, p_0, and r_0 which can simultaneously equilibrate each and every one of the four markets of the economy.

---

[1] See Chapters III:2 and IV:4.

2. THE STABILITY OF THE SYSTEM: THE METHOD OF SUCCESSIVE APPROXIMATION

As emphasized in Chapter III: 3, it is not enough to argue that a system of excess-demand equations has a solution; it must also be shown that the market, by its normal functioning, will itself reach this solution —that, in other words, the market is stable. Let us then examine the dynamic process of successive approximation—Walras' *tâtonnement*— by which the market "solves" the system of equations just set out. Taking advantage of Walras' Law, we need only trace this process for the first three markets. We further simplify our task by assuming that there is an instantaneous reaction to the pressure of excess demand or supply in the labor market. Specifically, any increase in the price level lowers the real wage rate, thereby creates an excess demand for labor, thereby generates an immediate proportionate increase in the money wage rate, and thus uninterruptedly maintains the equilibrium of the labor market. Hence we can restrict our dynamic analysis to the commodity and bond markets.

The nature of the dynamic forces in these two markets has already been described in the preceding chapter. There it was shown that if there were an equilibrium rate of interest but a less-than-equilibrium price level, then there would exist a state of excess demand in the commodity market driving prices up. Similarly, if there were an equilibrium price level but a less-than-equilibrium rate of interest, then there would exist a state of excess supply in the bond market driving the rate of interest up.

In each of these cases it was assumed that initially only one variable differed from its equilibrium value. Let us now consider a case in which both do. Assume, for example, that we start from a position in which the price level is at p_2, less than p_0. Other things equal, this implies that the aggregate demand curve for commodities is at a position like that of E_1 in Figure IX-3 (p. 212). There would then exist upward pressures on the price level. But assume that the rate of interest happens to lie at r_2, greater than r_0 just to the extent necessary to bring the aggregate demand curve down to an equilibrium level once again. This situation is depicted in Figure X-1, which, for the sake of comparison, also reproduces the demand curve of Figure IX-3. By assumption, both of these demand curves intersect the supply curve on the 45° radius vector. This is the only necessary relation between them.

Clearly, under these circumstances, no corrective force emanates from the commodity market. But consider now the bond market as described by Figure IX-4 (p. 214). By assumption, the lowering of the price

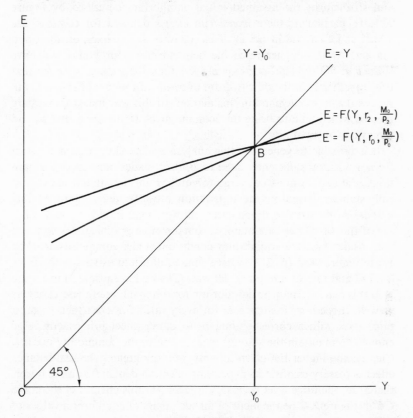

FIGURE X-1.

level below p_0 has—at the price $1/r_0$—shifted the supply curve further to the left than the demand curve. Hence, even if the rate of interest were to remain r_0, a state of excess demand would now replace the former state of equilibrium. And this is *a fortiori* the case for r_2, a rate of interest greater than r_0. Alternatively, in terms of Figure IX-5

p. 220), the lowered price level has raised the excess-demand curve and thereby increased the excess demand existing at any rate of interest greater than r_0.

As a result of this excess demand, the rate of interest begins to fall. But this fall causes an upward shift in the commodity demand curve and so disturbs the assumed initial equilibrium described by Figure X-1. In particular, there is now an excess demand for commodities which causes a rise in prices. This, in turn, reacts back on the bond market. At this higher price the demand curve for bonds will have shifted to the right proportionately less than the supply curve, so that this, together with the downward movement of the rate of interest, will reduce the excess demand in this market. In this way market forces are created which tend to bring the economy back to the price level p_0 and the rate of interest r_0.

It is possible to generalize this analysis and to show that if we start from a position sufficiently close to B, then, under our simple assumptions, the system must converge to equilibrium; i.e., that it is dynamically stable. A rigorous demonstration must be deferred to Mathematical Appendix 8:a. Fortunately, however, an intuitive understanding of this proof can be obtained from a simple graphical device.[2]

Consider first the equilibrium condition of the commodity market. From Figure IX-3 (p. 212) we see that equilibrium exists for the price level p_0 and rate of interest r_0. However, as we have just seen in Figure X-1, this market can be in equilibrium for other values of these variables as well. Indeed, we assume that for every rate of interest there exists a price level with a corresponding real-balance effect just exactly large enough to maintain the state of equilibrium in the commodity market. Clearly, the higher the given interest rate, the greater the real-balance effect necessary to offset its depressing effect on demand, and the lower, therefore, the price level necessary to generate this effect. Let the curve CC in Figure X-2 be the locus of all such pairs of equilibrium values of the rate of interest and price level. It follows from what has just been said that this curve must have a negative slope throughout. It also follows that whenever the joint values of the price level and interest rate that happen to prevail in the commodity market correspond to a point

[2] Adapted from the ingenious graph of Lloyd A. Metzler, "Wealth, Saving, and the Rate of Interest," *Journal of Political Economy*, LIX (1951), 104. Note that what is demonstrated here is stability in the small, and not stability of the Walrasian *tâtonnement* in the large. See the end of Mathematical Appendix 3:b.

to the right of *CC*, there will exist a state of excess supply in this market driving the price level downwards. Conversely, at any point to its left there will exist a state of excess demand driving it upwards.

In a similar way it is possible to construct a curve *BB* which is the locus of all pairs of values of the rate of interest and price level for which the bond market is in equilibrium. Clearly, this curve passes through

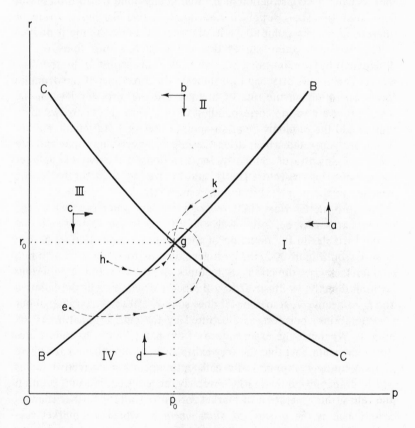

FIGURE X-2.

the point (p_0, r_0) and has a positive slope. For consider a rate of interest higher than r_0. From Figure IX-4 (p. 214) we see that at such a rate there will be an excess demand for bonds. But this excess demand can be eliminated and equilibrium restored by a sufficient increase in the price level. For such an increase causes a greater rightward shift of the supply curve than of the demand curve. Alternatively, in terms of Figure IX-5 (p. 220), a rise in the price level shifts the excess-demand curve downwards, hence lowers its intersection point with the vertical axis, and thus causes the equilibrium rate of interest to rise too. It follows from the construction of *BB* that at any point below it there will be a state of excess supply in the bond market driving the rate of interest up; at any point above it, an excess demand driving it down.[3]

The two intersecting curves divide Figure X-2 into four sectors, designated by roman numerals. Consider any point *a* in the first sector. The arrows attached to it indicate the directions of the dynamic forces operating on the rate of interest and the price level when the market is at a position corresponding to this point. These arrows show that should the economy be at any point in sector I, automatic market forces are generated which drive the rate of interest upwards and the price level downwards. Similarly, the directions of the dynamic market forces operating in sectors II, III, and IV are indicated by the arrows attached to the points *b*, *c*, and *d*, respectively.

Thus, no matter what the levels of prices and interest at which the market happens to be, there always exist forces which push at least one of the variables in the direction of the equilibrium position *g*. As can be seen from Figure X-2, the path generated by these forces moves in a counterclockwise direction. Sometimes it reaches the equilibrium position directly, as illustrated by the paths originating at the points *h* and *k*, respectively; sometimes it does so only after first spiraling about the equilibrium position, as illustrated by the path originating at the point *e*. Whatever the exact nature of the path, Figure X-2 illustrates the fundamental fact that the very existence of disequilibrium anywhere in the economy automatically calls into operation corrective forces which ultimately eliminate it. Conversely, once the equilibrium position is reached, the generation of market forces making for further changes ceases. This is the process of *tâtonnement* by which the market successfully gropes its way toward the solution of the system of equations of the preceding section.

---

[3] Mathematically, *CC* and *BB* are the graphs of equations (2) and (3), respectively, considered as implicit functions of r and p. Clearly, $B(Y_0, 1/r, M_0/p) = 0$ is equivalent to (3) for this purpose.

We must now bring to the fore one tacit assumption on which the foregoing proof of stability rests: namely, that excess demand in one market affects only the price of that market. For the most part, this assumption is uncritically taken for granted in the contemporary theory of economic dynamics.[4] Nevertheless, a moment's reflection shows that it is really an atavistic vestige of partial-equilibrium analysis which cannot be justified in a general-equilibrium framework. For just as this framework emphasizes that a change in the price of one good affects the amounts demanded of all other goods, so does it suggest that the pressure of excess demand in one market affects the price movements of all other markets. Thus, for example, an individual who does not succeed in buying all he wants of a given good will not only bid up its price but will also divert part of the money he was originally planning to spend on that good to bidding up the prices of other goods as well. Such interrelated market pressures are particularly noticeable during periods of suppressed inflation. Here the pent-up excess demand in the controlled markets spills over into the uncontrolled ones and pushes their prices upwards. Our contention is simply that this familiar characteristic of periods of "permanent disequilibrium" also manifests itself—even if in a milder form—during the periods of temporary disequilibrium which are necessarily inherent in the dynamic process of *tâtonnement*.

Let us then assume that households which do not succeed in buying all the commodities they want at the existing price level use part of their resulting excess purchasing power to bid up the price of bonds as well as of commodities. Similarly, firms which do not succeed in selling all the bonds they wish at the current rate of interest attempt to alleviate their resulting shortage of funds by offering commodities as well as bonds at a lower price. These assumptions do not change the nature of the market forces at work in the first and third sectors of Figure X-2. Indeed, in these sectors the forces emanating from one market reinforce those from the other. But they do cause a basic change in the forces at work in the two remaining sectors.

Consider, for example, the fourth sector. Here there is an excess demand for commodities, exerting an upward pressure on both commodity and bond prices. At the same time, there is an excess supply

---

[4] Its inappropriateness was first pointed out to me by Milton Friedman. See also Samuelson, *Foundations*, p. 274.

of bonds, exerting a downward pressure on both these prices. Hence the movement of a point in this sector depends on the relative strengths of these two opposing sets of pressures. If we assume that the forces generated in one market always predominate in determining the price movement of the other market, then the direction of the arrows attached to point *d* must be reversed. A similar statement holds for point *b*. Thus, under this assumption, the automatic market forces of sectors II and IV propel both the price level and the rate of interest away from their equilibrium values. It follows that the *tâtonnement* will not necessarily succeed in reaching the equilibrium values of the economy; that, in other words, the system is not necessarily stable.[5]

In what follows we shall disregard this possibility. Though recognizing the interrelationships just emphasized, we shall always assume that they are never strong enough to change the directions of the market forces described by Figure X-2. Hence the system remains stable. But this stability is now a matter of assumption—not of proof.

3. The Effects of an Increase in the Quantity of Money

Let us now investigate the effects of, say, a doubling of the quantity of money. Essentially, our present model can be considered to be a special case of the more general one developed in Chapter IV; hence the conclusions of that chapter are immediately applicable. Even without this, equations (1) through (4) readily show that *if* for the quantity of money M_0 the system is in equilibrium at the wage rate w_0, price level p_0, and rate of interest r_0, *then* for the amount $2M_0$ it is in equilibrium at $2w_0$, $2p_0$, and r_0. The reader can confirm this by substituting these values directly into these equations. It might also be noted that this conclusion holds even if the demand and supply functions for labor are assumed to depend on the rate of interest and real balances as well as on the real wage rate.[6]

So much for the comparative-statics analysis. Let us turn now to the dynamic analysis. The basic elements of this analysis have already been presented in the preceding section, and it remains only to apply them to the case at hand. In order to avoid repetition, we shall carry out this application in a somewhat mechanical way. The reader can

[5] See Mathematical Appendix 8:*a*.
[6] Cf. end of Chapter IX:2.

breathe more economic life into it by referring back to the relevant discussions of the preceding chapter.

The dynamic impact of an increase in the quantity of money depends on the way in which it is introduced into the economy. Consider first the case in which the government suddenly decides to increase its purchases of commodities during a certain period and to finance these purchases by printing new money. It is also assumed that in subsequent periods the government reverts to its usual level of purchases and to its policy of balancing the budget, so that no further additions to the money supply take place.

In the first period, then, there are two forces exerting an upward pressure on the aggregate demand curve for commodities. First, the government component of this curve has increased. Second, the total real value of cash balances has increased, with resulting increases in the consumption and investment components (see p. 207, Figure IX-2). As a result, the aggregate demand curve is pushed above its equilibrium level in Figure IX-3 (p. 212) to, say, the position represented by E_1. Since real output remains fixed at the full-employment level Y_0, an inflationary gap equal to AB is accordingly created; but, for simplicity, we assume that this does not yet express itself in a rise in prices.

In the next period, and in all subsequent ones, only the second of these forces can—at most—be at work; for, by assumption, government expenditures now return to their original level. Hence the aggregate demand curve drops back somewhat toward its original position— though, because of the continued presence of the second force, not all the way. Thus it is only the real-balance effect which prolongs the inflationary pressure in the commodity market in periods subsequent to the one in which the new money is injected into the economy. It might also be noted that the aggregate demand curve is now at the level to which it would have initially been pushed up if the original injection of money had taken place through government transfer payments instead of commodity purchases. For under this alternative assumption, the first force described in the preceding paragraph would clearly never have existed. Correspondingly, under this assumption, no inflationary pressure would ever have existed in the commodity market were it not for the real-balance effect.[7]

[7] As will be noted in a moment, we are at this point of the argument abstracting from the bond market and hence assuming that the rate of interest is as yet unchanged.

In any event, at this stage an inflationary gap continues to prevail in the commodity market. We now take account of the fact that this gap drives the price level upwards, thereby reduces the real value of cash balances, and thus causes the demand curve to shift downwards. Clearly, this process must continue until, and just until, prices have also doubled. For, to repeat the argument of Chapter III:4, at any lower price level the real value of the doubled cash balances will still be greater than the real value of the original balances; correspondingly, the aggregate demand curve will still be higher than it originally was; and therefore an inflationary gap will continue to prevail in the commodity market driving prices further upwards. Conversely, should prices more than double, the real value of the doubled cash balances will be less than the real value of the original ones, so that a deflationary gap will be created to push prices downwards again. Only when the price level has exactly doubled will the real value of the doubled cash balances have been exactly reduced to the real value of the original ones; that is, only then will the real wealth of the economy return to its original level. Correspondingly, only then will the aggregate demand curve have returned exactly to its original position, so that the inflationary gap will finally have been closed and equilibrium reestablished in the commodity market. In this way we see how the inflationary process itself sets into operation an equilibrating force—the price rise—which ultimately brings it to an end.

So far we have tacitly assumed that during this dynamic process the rate of interest remains constant. Actually, of course, this is not to be expected. The initial doubling of the quantity of money shifts the bond demand curve to the right and the supply curve to the left, so that the rate of interest initially falls. This situation is represented by the dashed curves in Figure X-3, where the unlabeled dot-dash curves are those of the original equilibrium position. Alternatively, in terms of Figure IX-5 (p. 220), the monetary increase raises the bond excess-demand curve and, consequently, its intersection point with the vertical axis. In terms of either diagram, the basic fact is the increase in the *real* quantity of money in the economy and its consequent real-balance effect in the bond market. This causes an increase in the supply of loans and a decrease in the demand, with a consequent decline in the rate of interest.

What must now be emphasized (and what classical and neoclassical economists did emphasize) is that this fall in interest is a transitory—but crucial—element of the dynamic adjustment process by which the economy eventually returns to a new equilibrium position at an unchanged rate of interest r_0 and a doubled price level $2p_0$. In Wicksell's familiar terms, this initial decline in interest creates a discrepancy between the market rate and the natural rate; for in view of the unchanged marginal productivity of capital to which it is equal, the natural rate is still r_0. Hence the investment component of the aggregate demand curve rises, further strengthening the inflationary pressures of the commodity market. But as these pressures push the price level upwards, there is a reaction back on the bond market. Specifically, the price rise causes the dashed demand curve in Figure X-3 to shift to the right less than the corresponding supply curve. (In terms of Figure IX-5, the price rise causes a real-balance effect which pushes the excess-demand function down again.) Hence the downward movement of the interest rate must eventually be reversed. In particular, when the price level has finally doubled, this rate will have necessarily climbed back to its original value r_0. For, as shown by the dot-dash curves of Figure X-3, at this rate individuals originally demanded B_0 units bonds and supplied the same amount; hence, now, at a doubled price level and quantity of money, they must—by the absence of money illusion—demand $2B_0$ units of bonds and again supply the same amount. Therefore, the demand and supply curves must again intersect at the price corresponding to the rate of interest r_0—as is represented by the solid curves in Figure X-3. In brief, as the rising price level eliminates the initial increase in the *real* quantity of money in the economy, it also eliminates the excess demand for bonds (excess supply of loans) which temporarily depressed the rate of interest.[8]

Here is the essence of the classical and neoclassical view. If, for any reason, there is an increase in the quantity of legal-tender notes in the economy, then—in Ricardo's words—these "notes would be sent into every market, and would everywhere raise the prices of commodities, till

[8] In terms of Figure IX-5 (p. 220), when the price level has finally doubled, real balances are back to their original value; hence the demand curve again occupies the position it originally did; hence its intersection with the vertical axis again corresponds to r_0.

they were absorbed in the general circulation. It is only during the interval of the issue [of the new notes], and their effect on prices, that we should be sensible of an abundance of money; interest would, during that interval, be under its natural level; but as soon as the additional sum of notes or of money became absorbed in the general circulation,

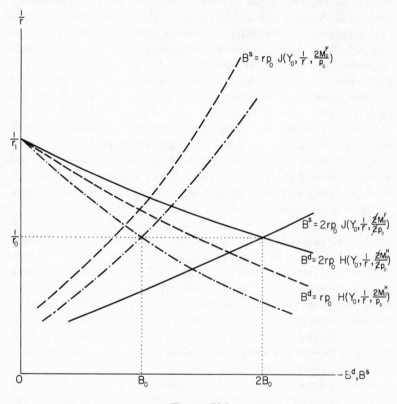

FIGURE X-3.

the rate of interest would be as high, and new loans would be demanded with as much eagerness as before the additional issue."[9]

[9] David Ricardo, *The High Price of Bullion* (1810), *Works*, ed. Sraffa (Cambridge, 1951–52), Vol. III, p. 91. In the original, "issues" appears, and not "issue."

Similar passages from many other classical—and neoclassical—economists will be cited in Chapter XV:1.

We can sharpen the classical flavor of our argument by assuming that the monetary increase originates in the banking system; this, indeed, is the case considered by Ricardo in the preceding passage. In particular, let us assume that the government gratuitously distributes the newly printed money to the banks.[10] Since banks do not themselves appear as buyers or sellers on the commodity market, this does not directly affect the aggregate demand in this market. However, as a result of this increase, banks find themselves with excess reserves. Hence their demand for bonds (supply of loans) increases, with a consequent downward pressure on the rate of interest. This, in turn, causes the investment curve to rise and thus disrupts the equilibrium of the commodity market. And now the argument proceeds along the lines already familiar from our discussion of Figure X-3.

It is, however, worth emphasizing—since this is the crucial point emphasized by classical monetary theory—that in the final equilibrium position banks no longer have to offer a lower interest rate in order to entice additional borrowers. For with costs twice what they originally were, any given project requires the borrowing of twice as much money. At the same time, any project that was worth financing before is worth financing now too. For the anticipated money returns from the project have also doubled, so that the rate of return upon it remains unchanged and equal to the original equilibrium rate of interest. Hence, after the additional quantity of money has, through the price increase, been "absorbed in the general circulation," individuals increase their demand for loans to the same extent that the banks originally increased their supply—so that the equilibrium rate of interest is ultimately unaffected.

From this discussion it can immediately be seen that the invariance of the rate of interest and doubling of the price level holds even under the extreme Keynesian assumption that changes in the quantity of money directly affect only the bond, and not the commodity, market; that, in other words, the latter market is completely free of the real-balance effect.[11] Here, too, the effects of a monetary increase work themselves out through an initial reduction in the rate of interest and subsequent dynamic interactions between price movements in the commodity market and interest movements in the bond market. More

[10] More in keeping with Ricardo's discussion, we can assume an influx of gold into a gold-standard banking system; cf. pp. 299–300 below.

[11] For specific references to the *General Theory*, see Note K:1.

formally, we can readily see that the comparative-statics argument of this section's opening paragraph is equally valid for the case in which the term M_0/p is omitted from equation (2) on p. 229, so that this equation becomes

$$(5) \qquad \psi(Y_0, r) = Y_0,$$

where $E = \psi(Y, r)$ is our new aggregate demand function for commodities. Nor does this omission affect the stability of the system. In particular, equation (5) states that the level of aggregate demand is independent of the price level and that, accordingly—under the assumption of full employment—there is only one possible rate of interest at which the commodity market can be in equilibrium. Hence the curve CC in Figure X-2 becomes a straight horizontal line at the height r_0. At any point above this line there exists a deflationary pressure in the commodity market; at any point below, an inflationary one. Hence the directions of the arrows attached to the points a, b, c, and d in Figure X-2 are not affected. Hence the system must continue to converge to the equilibrium position.[12]

In this way we have finally and rigorously demonstrated the fact set out at the beginning of this book (p. 21, footnote 18): that despite our systematic and repeated emphasis on the role of the real-balance effect in the commodity market, such a role is *not* logically necessary for the validity of our conclusions. In particular, these conclusions can be shown to hold even when this effect is restricted to the bond market. On the other hand, this restriction is—within our present model—an unreasonable one; for the real-balance effect now coincides with the wealth effect (p. 209) and should therefore operate in a similar fashion in all markets.[13]

The general argument of this section can be conveniently summarized in terms of the concepts used in Figure X-2.[14] As will be recalled, the curves CC and BB of this diagram are drawn for the quantity of money

---

[12] For a more rigorous statement, see the end of Mathematical Appendix 8:*a*.

[13] Cf. p. 180, footnote 43 above.

As will, however, be shown below (pp. 297–98), the assumption that changes in the quantity of money directly affect only the bond and money markets can in principle be rationalized in terms of a pure inside-money economy, in which by definition the real-balance effect does not operate in any market. At the same time, there are good reasons not to interpret Keynes in this way; see p. 339, footnote 9.

[14] I am indebted to Mr. Tsvi Ophir for suggesting this additional use of Figure X-2.

M_0. Let us see what happens to these curves as a result of increasing this quantity to $2M_0$. Clearly, absence of money illusion implies that, for any given rate of interest, the price level must now be twice as high as before in order to restore equilibrium to any given market: for only then will the real value of the doubled money holdings be equal once

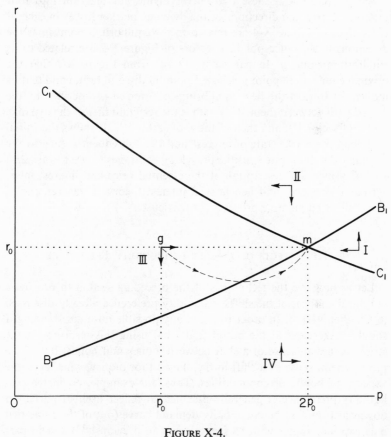

FIGURE X-4.

again to the real value of the original ones, thereby insuring the disappearance of the inflationary pressures that—at an unchanged rate of interest—would otherwise prevail in the market. Hence the curves corresponding to $2M_0$ must each be twice as far to the right as those of

Figure X-2. These curves are represented in Figure X-4 by C_1C_1 and B_1B_1, respectively. From what has just been said, it is clear that they must intersect at the point m, corresponding to the rate of interest r_0 and price level $2p_0$. This is accordingly the new equilibrium position of the economy as a whole.

As in Figure X-2, these two curves divide our diagram into four sectors. Clearly, the directions of the dynamic market forces in each of the sectors of Figure X-4 are related to the equilibrium point m as the directions in the corresponding sectors of Figure X-2 are related to its equilibrium point g. In particular, we see from Figure X-4 that the original equilibrium point g is now a point of disequilibrium and that its movement toward the new equilibrium position m is described by the dotted path between them. This path is the resultant first of the dynamic forces of sector III, and then of those of sector IV. It shows the initial decline in the market rate of interest and the subsequent return to the unchanged natural rate r_0 as the price level continues to rise toward $2p_0$. It thus provides a description of the essential price and interest interactions of classical and neoclassical interest theory, in general, and of Wicksell's "cumulative process," in particular.[15]

4. THE EFFECTS OF A SHIFT IN LIQUIDITY PREFERENCE

Let us now use the techniques of the preceding section to provide a graphical analysis of the shifts in liquidity preference already discussed in Chapter VIII:5. In order to avoid any possible misunderstanding, I should make clear at the outset that I am using this term not in the strict Keynesian sense of a shift between money and bonds, but in the more general sense of a shift in the demand for money, whether at the expense of bonds or commodities. Thus, for example, an increase in liquidity preference is generally assumed to reflect itself in part by a downward shift in the commodity demand curve (out of the same real balances individuals wish to spend less than previously[16]) and in part by a leftward shift in the demand for bonds and a rightward one in the supply (individuals feel an increased need for liquidity and therefore

---

[15] These doctrinal implications will be discussed further in Chapter XV:1.
[16] I.e., there is an increase in K—or, alternatively, a decrease in V.

move out of bonds and into money: they are less willing to lend and more inclined to borrow).

This situation can be described graphically in the following way. Assume that we begin from an equilibrium position in which the aggregate demand curve is represented by $E = F(Y, r_0, M_0/p_0)$ in Figure IX-3 (p. 212). As a result of the increased demand for money,

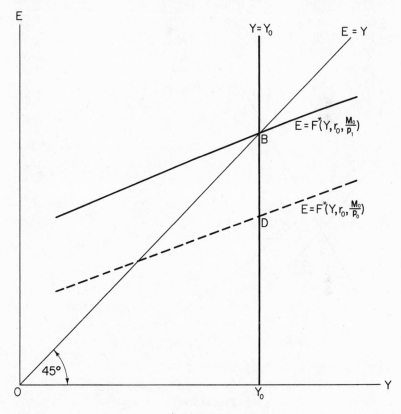

FIGURE X-5.

this curve now shifts downwards to, say, $E = F^*(Y, r_0, M_0/p_0)$ in Figure X-5. The asterisk denotes the fact that a change in tastes has taken place: at the same rate of interest and price level, individuals wish now to spend less than they did before. Thus the curves in Figures

X-5 and IX-3 are cross sections of two different demand functions. Similarly, the bond market is represented in the initial equilibrium position by the curves of Figure IX-4 (p. 214—not reproduced in the following diagram), and, as a result of the increase in liquidity preference, these then assume the form of the dashed curves in Figure X-6.

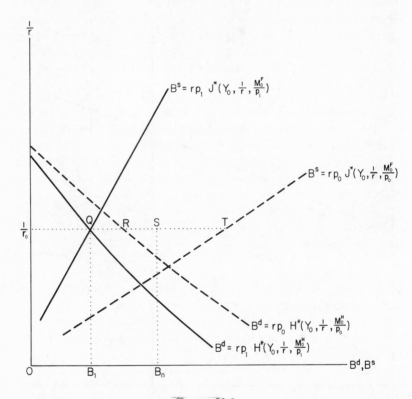

FIGURE X-6.

Clearly, the initial effect of this shift is to generate a downward pressure on the price level, reflected by the deflationary gap *BD* in Figure X-5, and an upward pressure on the rate of interest, reflected by the excess supply *RT* in Figure X-6. Now, as the price level falls, the real-balance effect pushes the commodity demand curve upwards. At the same time, it pushes the bond supply curve further leftwards than the demand curve. In this way the price decrease must ultimately more than eliminate the excess supply in the bond market and thus reverse the initial upward movement of the rate of interest.

Assume that this eventual downward movement of the rate of interest continues until it returns to r_0. Assume also that, at the same time, prices fall to p_1 and that at this level the stimulation of the real-balance effect is sufficiently strong to close the initial deflationary gap in the commodity market. The demand curve corresponding to the new equilibrium position in this market is then represented by the solid line in Figure X-5. It remains to examine the concurrent situation in the bond market.

We must first be a little more specific about the nature of the shift in liquidity preference. In particular, we assume that this shift has been a "neutral" one—that it has affected only the desirability of bonds-and-commodities relative to money, not that of bonds and commodities relative to each other. Now, from Figure X-5 we see that at the price level p_1 and rate of interest r_0 the individuals of the economy demand the same *real* amount of commodities as they did in the original equilibrium position. From the assumption of neutrality it then follows that at these prices they must now also demand and supply the same *real* holdings of bonds as they did originally. But since these respective real holdings were equal in the original equilibrium position, they must be so now too. That is, at the price p_1 and interest r_0 the bond market must also be in equilibrium. In other words, the nominal amounts demanded and supplied of bonds at the price $1/r_0$ are again equal, though less than they were in the original equilibrium position in the same proportion that p_1 is less than p_0. This is the situation represented by the solid lines in Figure X-6.[17]

Thus, under these assumptions the neoclassical position is vindicated. The increase in liquidity preference depresses the equilibrium price level but leaves the equilibrium rate of interest unaffected. Indeed, it is precisely this price decline which manufactures the additional *real* quantity of money that the economy is desirous of holding.

---

[17] Actually, the explanation is more restrictive than the diagram. The latter requires only that, at the price $1/r_0$, the amounts demanded and supplied decrease equiproportionately, but not necessarily in the same proportion as the price decline. However, only the case considered in the text has economic meaning, for only in this case are the *real* demand and supply for bonds the same as they originally were.

By way of contrast, consider the case in which the increase in liquidity preference is only at the expense of bond holdings: this is the implicit assumption of Keynesian interest theory. At first such an increase disturbs neither the demand for commodities nor, consequently, the initial state of equilibrium which prevails in this market. But as soon as the excess supply in the bond market begins to press the rate of interest upwards, it also generates a deflationary gap in the commodity market. As before, the resulting decrease in price then reacts back on the bond market and eventually reverses the upward movement of the interest rate. But this time, over-all equilibrium cannot be restored at the rate of interest r_0. For due to the price decrease and unchanged tastes in the commodity market, this level now corresponds to an inflationary gap. Hence, in order to remove this gap, the new equilibrium position must be marked by an interest rate which is higher than the original one.

It must be emphasized that this effect on the rate of interest is not a consequence of the change in the relative desirability of bonds and money *per se*. For such a change in desirability occurs in the case of a neutral shift too. Furthermore, as the reader can readily establish for himself, a shift in liquidity preference which is entirely at the expense of commodities and does not at all affect the relative desirability of bonds and money also affects the rate of interest—though in a downward direction. In brief, an increase in liquidity preference which raises the rate of interest must be one which—in some sense—is at the expense of bond holdings *more than* at the expense of commodities.

In any event, it is clear from the foregoing presentation that the different views of neoclassical and Keynesian economics on the effects of a shift in liquidity preference are due not to a difference in analysis, but to a difference in what is implicitly assumed about the nature of the shift.

Once again the argument can be conveniently summarized in terms of Figure X-2. An increased demand for money at the expense of both commodities and bonds (the neoclassical case) shifts both CC and BB to the left: at any rate of interest, a lower price level is needed in each market in order to generate the stimulatory real-balance effect necessary to eliminate the initial excess supply created by the shift in liquidity preference. If the relative desirability of commodities and bonds is not affected by this shift, then, by the argument just presented, the new curves—represented by C_2C_2 and B_2B_2 in Figure X-7—must intersect at the point n, corresponding to the price p_1 and the rate of interest r_0. The original equilibrium point g is now one of disequilibrium, and the dashed path between g and n shows the movement toward the new equilibrium position. Clearly, this path reflects the directions of the dynamic market forces at work in sectors I and II. It shows the initial

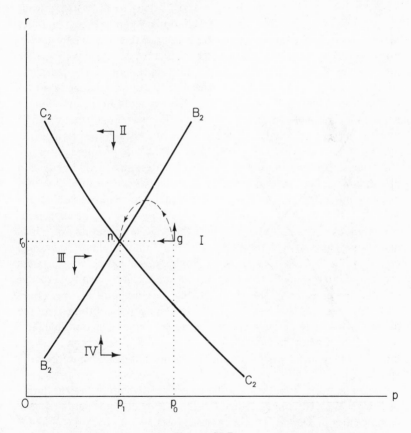

FIGURE X-7.

rise in interest and the subsequent decline generated by the continuously falling price level.

Consider now the Keynesian case in which the increase in liquidity preference is only at the expense of bonds. In this case the curve CC

remains unaffected, so that we obtain Figure X-8. The intersection of the unchanged *CC* with the leftward-shifted B_2B_2 must clearly be at a lower price level and higher rate of interest than the original equilibrium point *g*. As the path *gw* indicates, the movement to this new equilibrium position *w* can be a direct one. On the other hand, as the path *gtw*

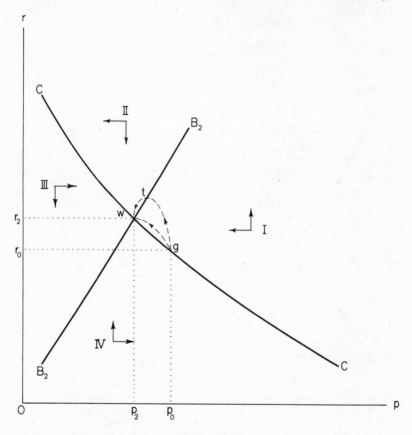

FIGURE X-8.

indicates, it too may involve an initial rise in the rate of interest above its new equilibrium value and a subsequent decline. Thus, in this case too, the price level may exert a moderating influence on a temporarily overreacting interest rate.

From this we can also see that the impact of this Keynesian shift in liquidity preference on the rate of interest depends on the strength of the real-balance effect in the commodity market. The weaker this effect, the shallower the slope of *CC*, and hence the less the effect on the rate of interest. Indeed, in the extreme Keynesian case where this real-balance effect is entirely absent, the curve *CC* becomes a horizontal line, so that the rate of interest is not affected at all.[18] This is simply a reflection of the already mentioned fact (p. 242) that under this assumption the commodity market can be in equilibrium at only one rate of interest. Hence no exogenous change that occurs solely in the bond and money markets can affect this rate.[19]

The case of an increased demand for money solely at the expense of commodities is equally clear. Here *BB* remains constant, while *CC* shifts to the left. Hence the new equilibrium price and interest levels must both be lower than the original ones.

It is left as an exercise for the reader to show how the foregoing analysis can, *mutatis mutandis*, be applied to the case of a decrease in liquidity preference. A neutral shift of this type can clearly be represented by Figure X-4. Of particular interest to us, however, is the case in which the shift in liquidity preference is primarily in favor of bonds and little if at all at the expense of commodities. As will be recalled,[20] such a change in tastes is analytically equivalent to a technical change in the nature of the bond which in some way makes it more liquid—more readily convertible into money. Both of these changes express themselves in Figure X-2 as a downward shift in *BB*, with *CC* remaining more or less constant: for, by assumption, both leave demand in the commodity market relatively unchanged, while increasing demand in the bond market,[21] and thereby—for any given price level—lowering the rate of

---

[18] This somewhat (for Keynesian economics) paradoxical conclusion is due to our un-Keynesian assumption of full employment; cf. Chapter XIII:4.

[19] In other words, under the foregoing assumption the system is validly dichotomized; cf. p. 180 above. See also F. Modigliani, "The Monetary Mechanism and Its Interaction with Real Phenomena," *Review of Economics and Statistics*, XLV (1963), Supplement, 84.

[20] See Chapters V:6 and VII:3.

[21] There is an implicit assumption here that the increase in the liquidity which the bond represents to the creditor is not offset by an increase in the illiquidity which it represents to the debtor. On the other hand, this assumption would not be necessary in an economy whose private sector has net positive bond holdings (e.g., one in which there exists government debt, as in Chapter XII:4).

interest that must prevail in order to maintain equilibrium in this market. Hence the new intersection of *BB* and *CC*—and thus the new equilibrium position—is at a rate of interest below r_0 and a price level above p_0. The more we make bonds liquid, the more *BB* shifts to the right, the more, therefore, the rate of interest falls and the price level rises, and the smaller, therefore, the *real* quantity of money in the economy becomes.[22]

[22] For an analytical treatment of the argument of this section, see Mathematical Appendix 8:c.

XI. The Workings of the Model:
Full Employment (Continued)

1. The argument in terms of the money market. The speculative motive for holding money and the validity of the quantity theory. 2–3. The full general-equilibrium analysis: statics and dynamics. The assumptions of Keynesian interest theory. 4. Demand curves and market-equilibrium curves once again. 5. The analytical technique applied to other problems. 6. Savings and investment.

1. The Argument in Terms of the Money Market. The Speculative Motive for Holding Money and the Validity of the Quantity Theory

We shall now show that the conclusions reached in the preceding chapters by an analysis of the commodity and bond markets can also be reached—in a somewhat more familiar way—by an analysis of the money market. This equivalence is, of course, a simple implication of Walras' Law. Nevertheless, we shall find it instructive to illustrate it in detail.

As already noted in our description of Figure IX-6,[1] the negative slope of the demand curve for money with respect to interest reflects the joint operation of the transactions and speculative motives. In order, however, to bring the following discussion as close as possible

[1] Above, p. 222. Cf. also Chapters V:6, VI:1 (end), and VII:3.

to the original Keynesian one, let us assume that the latter is the sole source of interest elasticity. For the same reason let us assume that there is no real-balance effect in the money market. The equilibrium condition in this market—equation (4) on p. 229—is accordingly rewritten in the special Keynesian form[2]

$$(1) \qquad p \cdot L_1(Y_0) + p \cdot L_2(r) = M_0,$$

where $L_1(Y)$ represents the demand for *real* transactions balances, and $L_2(r)$ the demand for *real* speculative balances.

The argument in Part One of this book, however, has caused us to write this equation in a form which differs in one significant respect from that of the *General Theory*. As is shown in Note K:2, this equation has—in our notation—the form

$$(2) \qquad p \cdot L_1(Y_0) + L_2(r) = M_0.$$

The p which multiplies $L_2(r)$ in (1)—and which is absent from (2)—reflects the assumption that there is no money illusion in the demand for nominal speculative balances. As we shall see, it is this difference which assures the classical invariance of the rate of interest.

Since it will prove to be so crucial to the following argument, it is worth dwelling at somewhat greater length on the meaning of this money illusion. According to equation (1), if individuals are confronted with a doubled price level, they will respond by doubling their demand for *nominal* speculative balances $p \cdot L_2(r)$; that is, their demand for *real* speculative balances will remain invariant. On the other hand, equation (2) implies that their demand for *nominal* speculative balances, $L_2(r)$, will remain invariant, so that their demand for *real* speculative balances will decrease. In other words, it implies that the demand for *real* speculative balances is at one level when the monetary unit is called the dollar and at quite another level when it is called the peseta. And this is the essence of money illusion.[3]

---

[2] *General Theory*, pp. 168–69, 199–202. In his later writings Keynes did permit the rate of interest to affect $L_1(\quad)$ as well as $L_2(\quad)$; see his "Theory of the Rate of Interest" (1937), as reprinted in *Readings in the Theory of Income Distribution*, ed. W. Fellner and B. F. Haley (Philadelphia, 1946), p. 422.

[3] The reader will recall that changing the monetary unit is analytically equivalent to confronting individuals with an equiproportionate change in prices *and* initial money holdings; cf. p. 184.

We can put this in yet another way. Just as the nominal transactions-precautionary demand represents the desire to hold liquid command over a *real* quantity of commodities, so the nominal speculative demand represents the desire to hold liquid command over a *real* quantity of bonds. Hence just as an increase in the price level affects the first of these demands, so must it affect the second. This is the symmetry underlined by equation (1). And this is precisely the symmetry denied by equation (2)—with its insistence that though the demand for nominal transactions-precautionary balances is dependent on the absolute price level, that for nominal speculative balances is not.

Deferring the remaining discussion of equation (2) and Keynesian interest theory to the next chapter, let us now return to the task of analyzing the money market from the viewpoint of equation (1). Assume, then, that this market is in the equilibrium position D determined by the intersection of the dashed demand and supply curves in Figure XI-1. Let this state of equilibrium now be disturbed by a doubling of the quantity of money. This shifts the supply curve rightwards to $M^s = 2M_0$. Hence an excess supply of money is created at the original equilibrium rate of interest r_0. This is represented in Figure XI-1 by the line segment DF. (Curve II in this diagram should for the present be ignored.)

If prices were to remain the same, equilibrium could be reestablished in this market only at a rate of interest lower than r_0; for only by such a reduction could individuals be induced to hold the additional money now available. But prices cannot and do not remain the same. For the excess supply DF is indicative of an excess demand in the commodity market, and this excess demand must drive prices upwards. This in turn reacts back on the money market and shifts its demand curve rightwards. For, as sufficiently emphasized above, at a higher price level individuals must hold larger money balances in order to meet their various needs. In particular, when the price level has finally doubled, they will double the amount of money they demand at any given rate of interest. Hence their new demand curve—occupying position III in Figure XI-1—must intersect the new supply curve at the same rate of interest that originally prevailed. This is the crucial point: the dependence of demand on the absolute price level (as implied by the absence of money illusion) insures that the transactions, precautionary, *and* speculative demands for money can together ultimately absorb *all* of the additional supply—even at an unchanged rate of interest.

Similarly, an increase in liquidity preference causes an initial rightward shift in the demand curve for money and thereby generates an excess demand for money at the original rate of interest r_0. But this excess demand is indicative of an excess supply of commodities which

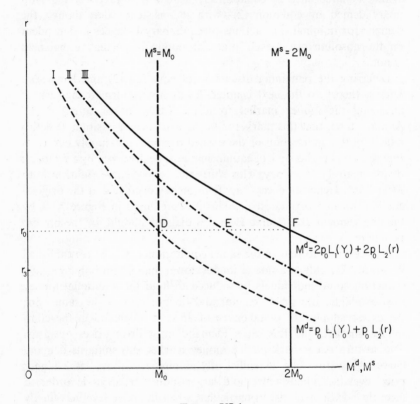

FIGURE XI-1.

drives prices downwards; and this downward movement, in turn, shifts the demand curve for money back to the left. If the increase in liquidity preference is a neutral one, this price decline and consequent leftward shift will continue until, and just until, the demand curve once again intersects the original and unchanged supply curve at the rate of interest r_0. If the increase is not a neutral one, then the rate of interest will be affected.

One advantage of the foregoing analysis is its underlining of the fact that—Keynes notwithstanding—the classical invariance of the interest rate under a change in the quantity of money does not depend on the assumption that the speculative demand "always be zero in equilibrium":[4] at no point in the preceding argument has it been necessary to assume that $L_2(r) = 0$. Thus the quantity theory can be valid when money is also held as a store of value for speculative purposes, as well as when it is held only as a medium of exchange for transactions purposes. All that the speculative motive does is to introduce another reason for the negative slope of the demand for money with respect to the rate of interest; but since we have assumed such a negative slope to exist anyway within the classical model (for transactions purposes), this cannot affect the foregoing conclusion. This illustrates our general contention that no matter why individuals hold money, it can only be the real value of these holdings that concerns them, and that the absence of money illusion which this reflects then insures the validity of the classical analysis.

At the same time it should be noted that within a broader context the Keynesian speculative motive does call for a significant change in the neoclassical approach. For in concentrating on the choice between holding bonds as against money, Keynesian theory also highlights the possibility (not considered by neoclassical economists) of a shift in liquidity preference as between these two assets alone—with its consequent effect on the rate of interest. We shall return to this question in Chapter XV:2.

We might also note that the assumption that the demand for money is motivated in part by dynamic expectations can sometimes invalidate the classical invariance of interest even with respect to changes in the quantity of money. This should certainly not surprise us. For in introducing these elements into the analysis we also introduce many additional "degrees of freedom." Hence as long as these elements are not in some way tied down, we can—by endowing them with the appropriate properties—obtain any conclusion we might desire.

---

[4] *General Theory*, pp. 208–9. Note that Keynes considers this assumption to be necessary in addition to that of full employment.

Only after we have specified the way in which individuals formulate their expectations can the analysis become determinate. We shall return to this question in Chapter XII: 7.

2. THE FULL GENERAL-EQUILIBRIUM ANALYSIS: STATICS AND DYNAMICS. THE ASSUMPTIONS OF KEYNESIAN INTEREST THEORY

Let us now carry out the analysis in a truly general-equilibrium way by extending Figure X-2 so as to provide a simultaneous description of all three markets of the model.[5] This is done in Figure XI-2. The curve *LL* in this diagram is the locus of all pairs of values of the rate of interest and the price level for which the demand and supply for money are equal. Its positive slope reflects the fact that an increase in the price level shifts the demand curve for money in Figure IX-6 (p. 222) to the right and thus raises the level of the rate of interest necessary to maintain equilibrium in this market.

We can, however, say even more about the curve *LL*. From Walras' Law (and the assumption made on p. 230 above that the labor market is always in equilibrium) we know that *LL* must pass through the intersection of *CC* and *BB*: for any price-interest combination which equilibrates the commodity and bond markets must also equilibrate the remaining market. From the budget restraint we know in addition that it must pass through sectors II and IV of Figure X-2. For the nature of *LL* is such that it divides any area through which it passes into two: an area to the right, consisting of points representing a state of excess demand in the money market ($L > 0$); and an area to the left, consisting of points representing excess supply ($L < 0$). Hence *LL* cannot pass through either sectors I or III of Figure XI-2. For in sector I there is an excess supply of both commodities ($C < 0$) and bonds ($B < 0$), so that by the budget restraint *every* point in this sector corresponds to a state of excess demand in the money market. Similarly, *every* point in sector III corresponds to a state of excess supply in this market. In sectors II and IV, on the other hand, there is an excess demand for one of the two goods, commodities and bonds, and an excess supply of the other.

[5] I am indebted to Mr. Tsvi Ophir for pointing out the possibility of this elaboration. The following is based on his suggestion and was originally presented in my "Liquidity Preference and Loanable Funds: Stock and Flow Analysis," *Economica*, XXV (1958), 308–14.

Depending on which of these two forces predominates, there will be an excess demand or an excess supply for money. The details of these relationships are presented in the accompanying table on p. 260.

The general-equilibrium interpretation of the comparative-statics analysis of the preceding chapter is now clear. A doubling of the

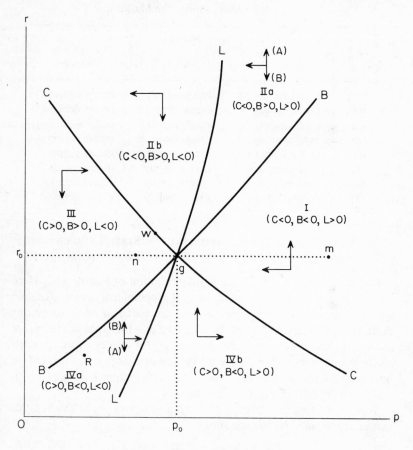

FIGURE XI-2.

quantity of money shifts all three curves in Figure XI-2 twice as far to the right so that they intersect at the point *m* (compare Figure X-4). Similarly, a neutral increase in liquidity preference shifts all three to the left so as to intersect at n (compare Figure X-7). Finally, a Keynesian increase in liquidity preference which is solely at the expense of bonds will leave CC unaffected, while shifting BB and LL leftwards so as to intersect at w (compare Figure X-8).

Interrelationships Among the Markets

Sector or Curve	Market		
	Commodities	Bonds	Money
I	excess supply	excess supply	excess demand
IIa	excess supply $>$	excess demand	excess demand
LL	excess supply $=$	excess demand	equilibrium
IIb	excess supply $<$	excess demand	excess supply
III	excess demand	excess demand	excess supply
IVa	excess demand $>$	excess supply	excess supply
LL	excess demand $=$	excess supply	equilibrium
IVb	excess demand $<$	excess supply	excess demand

3. The Full General-Equilibrium Analysis: Statics and Dynamics. The Assumptions of Keynesian Interest Theory (Continued)

Let us turn now to the dynamic interpretation of Figure XI-2. Here we are immediately confronted with the complications of dynamic intermarket pressures which we at first succeeded in avoiding in our discussion of Figure X-2. In particular, even as a first approximation we cannot say that an excess demand or supply for money expresses itself solely in one market. For the very function of money is to be spent on both commodities and bonds. Indeed, this is the implicit assumption on which the analysis of Figure X-2 is based.

This can be seen as follows. The dynamic assumptions of this analysis can be represented by the equations

$$(3) \qquad \frac{dp}{dt} = k_1 \left[F\left(Y_0, r, \frac{M_0}{p}\right) - Y_0 \right]$$

and

$$(4) \qquad \frac{dr}{dt} = -k_2 B\left(Y_0, \frac{1}{r}, \frac{M_0}{p}\right),$$

where k_1 and k_2 are positive constants. Under the assumption of an always-equilibrated labor market, budget restraint (23) on p. 227 can be written as

(5) $\left[F\left(Y_0, r, \frac{M_0}{p}\right) - Y_0 \right] + B\left(Y_0, \frac{1}{r}, \frac{M_0}{p}\right) \equiv \frac{M_0}{p} - L\left(Y_0, r, \frac{M_0}{p}\right).$

Substituting from (3) and (4) into (5) then yields

(6) $\frac{1}{k_1}\frac{dp}{dt} - \frac{1}{k_2}\frac{dr}{dt} = \frac{M_0}{p} - L\left(Y_0, r, \frac{M_0}{p}\right).$

Thus the dynamic assumptions of Figure X-2 imply that an excess supply of money affects both the price level and the rate of interest.

By way of contrast, consider the Keynesian assumption that an excess demand for money affects only the interest rate. This involves replacing (4) by

(7) $\frac{dr}{dt} = k_3 \left[L\left(Y_0, r, \frac{M_0}{p}\right) - \frac{M_0}{p} \right].$

Except for sectors IIa and IVa in Figure XI-2, this does not require changing the direction of the arrows specified by equation (4)—though it will, of course, generally affect the intensity of the movement represented by these arrows: for in all these sectors an excess demand for money is accompanied by an excess supply of bonds and vice versa. On the other hand, at, say, point R in sector IVa, interest will fall according to (7) (represented by the arrow marked "A") and will rise according to (4) (arrow "B"). A corresponding statement holds for any point in sector IIa.

We now note that whether we accept assumption (4) or (7), the system will converge: for in either case market forces exist to propel at least one of the variables towards its equilibrium value. Obviously, however, the exact nature of the adjustment paths in the two cases will differ. But it also obvious that this difference is not the result of our carrying out the analysis in different markets, but of our making different assumptions as to the dynamic operations of the *same* market. Specifically, the movements of the money market described by the system of dynamic equations (3), (6) differ in general from those described by (3), (7). On the other hand, systems (3), (4); (3), (6); and (4), (6) are all equivalent, even though they refer to different markets. Thus the market in which the dynamic analysis is carried out cannot *per se* affect the outcome.

Let us now return to assumption (7) and note its a priori implausibility. For this assumption implies that an excess supply of money drives interest down in the bond market, regardless of the state of excess demand there! Assumption (4), on the other hand, implies that under certain circumstances (and point *R* is an example) an excess supply of money may be accompanied by such a large excess demand for commodities that individuals will attempt to finance their additional purchases not only by using up all their excess cash but also by selling part of their bond holdings. In this way, an excess supply of money might be accompanied by an excess supply of bonds and hence by an increase in interest.

At first sight it might appear that this implausibility can be avoided by adding to equation (7) the further assumption that the excess supply of money is identical with the excess demand for bonds; i.e.,

$$(8) \qquad B\left(Y_0, \frac{1}{r}, \frac{M_0}{p}\right) \equiv \frac{M_0}{p} - L\left(Y_0, r, \frac{M_0}{p}\right).$$

It then follows that a point of excess supply (demand) for money is necessarily a point of excess demand (supply) for bonds; hence the curves *BB* and *LL* in Figure XI-2 coincide; and hence sectors IIa and IVa, with their troublesome points, simply disappear.

But this is to jump from the frying pan into the fire: for equation (8) really implies that the system is unstable! This can readily be shown in the following way. We know—by virtue of Walras' Law—that the analysis of Figure XI-2 can be carried out in terms of any two of the three markets. Now, there is no reason why the two markets so chosen should not be the bond and money markets. Hence—since we are ignoring the commodity market—Figure XI-2 reduces to Figure XI-3, where the single curve represents both *LL* and *BB*. Assume now that the system is in equilibrium at the point *P* and that a random disturbance moves it to *Q*. Clearly, the dynamic pressures which exist in the system (denoted by the arrows) can at best succeed in bringing the system back to some point (say T) on curve BB (or LL). They cannot assure its return to the original position P. Thus the system is not stable. It is in a state of neutral equilibrium.

The same conclusion can be reached, though in a somewhat more complicated way, even if we carry out the analysis in terms of the commodity and bond (or money) markets. Substituting from (8) into (5) we obtain

$$(9) \qquad F\left(Y_0, r, \frac{M_0}{p}\right) - Y_0 \equiv 0.$$

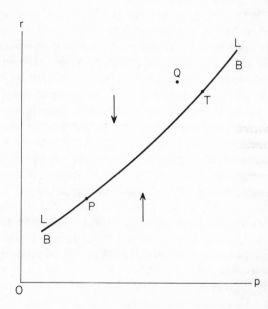

FIGURE XI-3.

That is, the excess demand for commodities is zero *no matter what the rate of interest or price level.* Thus under the present assumptions the curve CC of Figure XI-2 becomes blown up until it comprises the entire area of Figure XI-3. Correspondingly, the "intersection" of this special form of CC with curve BB (or LL) is the latter curve in its entirety. Thus the indeterminacy of the equilibrium position is again demonstrated.

Before concluding this section, I should clarify the implications of the conclusion just reached for Keynesian monetary theory. At first sight this conclusion seems to invalidate the familiar contention of many Keynesian economists that an excess supply of money creates a corresponding excess demand for bonds. Actually, however, I do not think that these economists had in mind the troublesome identity described by equation (8). Instead, all they wanted to assume is that there exists an identity *with respect to certain kinds of changes.* In particular, all they wanted to say is that an excess supply of money *generated by an increase in the quantity of money in the system* is diverted completely to the bond market and is thus identical with the excess demand thereby generated in that market. This is completely different from saying (as is said in equation (8) and Figure XI-3) that an excess supply of money *generated by any cause whatsoever* is identical with the excess demand for bonds so generated. Indeed, this latter statement contradicts the fundamental Keynesian assumption that an excess supply of money generated by an increase in the rate of interest will be accompanied by a decreased demand for investment goods—a fact which must necessarily also affect the extent of the excess demand for bonds. Thus under this assumption the excess supply of money could *not* be identical with the excess demand for bonds in the sense of equation (8).

More simply, the aforementioned contention would seem to be intended only as an alternative formulation of the familiar—though usually implicit—Keynesian hypothesis that changes in the quantity of money directly affect only the bond and money markets, as contrasted with those for commodities and labor. From this it immediately follows that a change in real balances which creates an excess demand in the money market must create an exactly equal excess supply in the bond market. This assumed absence of a real-balance effect in the commodity market may or may not be empirically true: but—unlike equation (8)—it represents a logically tenable position.[6]

[6] In terms of the equation in footnote 22 on p. 227 above, the Keynesian assumption is that

$$F_3(\quad) \equiv 0,$$

so that

$$L_3(\quad) - 1 \equiv -B_3(\quad).$$

On all of this section, see Mathematical Appendix 8:*b*.

It should once again be noted (see p. 242, footnote 13) that the Keynesian assumption of a direct monetary effect restricted to the bond and money markets is a

4. DEMAND CURVES AND MARKET-EQUILIBRIUM CURVES ONCE AGAIN

The preceding argument has shown that though the amount of money demanded depends upon the rate of interest, the rate of interest does not depend upon the amount of money. Superficially, there seems to be a paradox here. But it is one that is immediately resolved by noting that the word "depend" is being used in two different senses to describe the outcomes of two distinct conceptual experiments. More specifically, the solution to this paradox lies in distinguishing once again between individual-experiments and demand curves, on the one hand, and market-experiments and market-equilibrium curves, on the other.[7]

Consider first the following individual-experiment. We confront the individual with a lowered rate of interest, holding other things constant, and observe the variation in the amount of money he demands. Alternatively, adopting a Marshallian approach,[8] we force the individual to increase his planned money holdings and then record the reduction in interest upon which he insists, *ceteris paribus*, in order to be just willing to maintain these increased holdings. Either of these experiments yields the familiar negatively sloped individual demand curve for money from which the market demand curves of Figures IX-6 and XI-1 are aggregated. It is the slope of these curves that we have in mind when we say that the demand for money depends on the rate of interest.

These individual-experiments can be contrasted with another, less familiar one. Once again we force the individual to, say, double his planned money holdings; but this time we simultaneously confront him with a doubling in the price level *and* in his initial money holdings. It follows from the absence of money illusion that in these circumstances the individual will indicate his willingness to maintain these larger holdings without any reduction in the interest rate. A corresponding result will hold for the aggregate of individuals in the economy should they all be simultaneously confronted with the change just described.

---

reasonable one only in the context of a pure inside-money economy (cf. pp. 297–98 below; cf., however, p. 635).

[7] On the meaning of this distinction, cf. Chapter III:6.

In what follows we abstract from the real-indebtedness effect.

[8] *Principles* (8th ed.), pp. 94–95.

This is represented graphically by the movement from the point *D* to the point *F* in Figure XI-1.

So much for individual-experiments. Consider now the following market-experiment. Into an economy in equilibrium we introduce a disturbance in the form of a doubling of the quantity of money. We then let this disturbance work itself out in all its manifestations until the economy returns once again to an equilibrium position. Finally, we compare the rate of interest in the new market equilibrium position with that of the original one. As we have seen in our analysis of Figure XI-1, this rate is unchanged.

This result is completely consistent, as it must be, with those of the preceding individual-experiments. At the close of the market-experiment each individual finds himself confronted with a doubling of the price level and his initial money holdings. Hence the first individual-experiment—in which both these factors are held constant—can be of no relevance for the market-experiment. On the other hand, these increases are precisely those with which the individual is confronted in the second individual-experiment. Indeed, the willingness of the individuals in the economy to double their planned holdings of money without any decrease in the interest rate, as revealed in this experiment, is the explanation of the invariance of the equilibrium interest rate, as revealed by the market-experiment.

Let us now consider *D*, *F*, and all other possible supply-and-demand intersection points that can be generated in Figure XI-1 by market-experiments of the foregoing type. From what has just been said, it is clear that the locus of these points must be the horizontal line of Figure XI-4. Each point on this line thus associates a quantity of money with its corresponding, unchanged equilibrium level of interest. Obviously, then, this line is a special case of what we have called a market-equilibrium curve. It is also clear that, regardless of the slopes of the demand curves in Figure XI-1, this market-equilibrium curve must have the horizontal form specified in Figure XI-4. It is this horizontality that we have in mind when we say that the rate of interest does not depend on the quantity of money.

It is tempting to replace these complicated distinctions with the simple statement that just as the *real* quantity of money demanded depends on the rate of interest, so the equilibrium rate of interest depends on the *real* quantity of money; and that in the case at hand this rate remains constant because this real quantity does also. Tempting—but, strictly speaking, meaningless. For both the rate of interest and the real quantity of money in the economy are dependent variables of the analysis; hence their equilibrium values cannot be dependent on each other, but only on the independent variables.[9]

This might tempt us alternatively to say that—within our simple model, in which the quantity of net bond holdings and nonfinancial assets is by assumption constant (pp. 200 and 207)—any change in independent variables which leaves unaffected the equilibrium real quantity of money (and hence the real size and composition of the

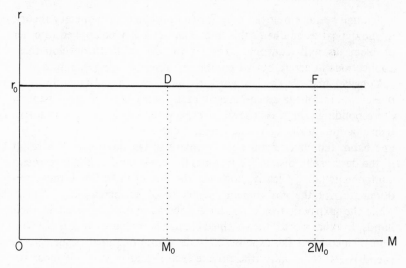

FIGURE XI-4.

economy's equilibrium portfolio of assets) must also leave the equilibrium rate of interest unaffected, and conversely. This is a meaningful proposition; but, though it happens to hold for the case of a change in the nominal quantity of money, it need not always be true. This is evident from Chapter X:4—where, as we have seen, a neutral shift in

[9] This is the distinction between dependent and independent variables already drawn on pp. 12 and 34. The reader will also recall the argument of pp. 171–72 that, since one moves in inverse proportion to the other, the price level and the real quantity of money are analytically equivalent, so that either one can be considered as the dependent variable of the analysis.

liquidity preference changes the price level and hence the real quantity of money in the economy, though not the equilibrium rate of interest. It will also be evident from the two additional cases discussed at the end of the next section, which show that the equilibrium rate of interest can change though the real quantity of money does not. Nevertheless, whenever valid, it is suggestive to speak in these terms. Hence, though keeping in mind the pitfall inherent in them, we shall occasionally do so.[10]

5. The Analytical Technique Applied to Other Problems

Though so far employed only for the problems of monetary theory the analytical technique of this book can obviously be applied to other problems as well. It would carry us too far afield to develop these applications in detail, but we can briefly describe a few examples.

Consider first the case in which the government permanently raises the level of income taxes and uses all of its increased receipts to finance a correspondingly increased level of expenditures. Two opposing forces then operate on the aggregate demand curve for commodities. On the one hand, the government component rises. On the other, as a result of the decrease in disposable income, the consumption and investment components fall.[11] Clearly, however, the first of these forces must predominate: for the government spends all of its increased "income," while the taxpayers would not have done so had it remained in their hands. In other words, the specified change is analogous to a redistribution of income at the expense of those whose marginal propensity to spend is less than unity (the private sector) and in favor of those for whom it equals unity (the government sector).[12]

Once we have determined that the effect of the specified change is to raise the aggregate demand curve for commodities, the analysis proceeds along familiar lines. As a result of the upward shift in this curve, an inflationary gap is created. The resulting price rise then generates a

[10] Actually, use has already been made of these terms on p. 239. See, on all of this section, Mathematical Appendix 4:d.

[11] Cf. above, p. 208.

[12] Note the clear parallelism to the analysis—under conditions of unemployment—of the multiplier effect of a balanced budget. Cf., e.g., P. A. Samuelson, "The Simple Mathematics of Income Determination," in *Income, Employment and Public Policy: Essays in Honor of Alvin H. Hansen* (New York, 1948), pp. 140–42.

negative real-balance effect which pushes the demand curve down again. At the same time, the price rise also disturbs the equilibrium of the bond market and causes the rate of interest to rise. This too helps close the inflationary gap in the commodity market. Equilibrium will finally be reestablished at a higher price level and higher rate of interest.

Deriving this result alternatively from Figure XI-2 (p. 259), we note first that if the exogenous change in disposable income has no net effect on the bond market (i.e., it decreases lending and borrowing to the same extent), then the foregoing change will leave *BB* invariant.[13] On the other hand, as we have just seen, it will shift *CC* rightwards. Similarly, the decrease in disposable income will cause a downward shift in the demand for money and hence generate a rightward shift in *LL*. Hence the intersection point in Figure XI-2 must move northeast.

Consider next the case in which a wave of technological inventions increases the productivity of capital. Let us restrict the analysis to a period of time too short for the resulting increase in commodity output to affect the market. Then this technological change has two initial effects. First, it increases the desire of firms to undertake investment projects. This raises the investment component of the aggregate demand curve and thus generates an inflationary gap in the commodity market. Secondly, and concurrently, it increases the need of firms for loan capital with which to finance these new projects. This shifts the supply curve of bonds to the right and thus drives interest upwards. Assume for simplicity that all of the additional financing comes in this way, and none from any drawing down of cash balances. Then, in terms of Figure XI-2, *CC* shifts rightwards and *BB* leftwards, while *LL* remains constant; hence the new intersection point is at a higher price level and interest rate.

It should be emphasized that this represents the short-run impact of the technological advance. In the long run the increased output made possible by this advance will reflect itself in a higher full-employment level of *Y*. Hence the *CC* curve will begin to shift leftwards and the *LL* curve rightwards. Correspondingly, the price level and interest rate will decline once again.

[13] Cf. above, pp. 215–16.

It might, however, be argued that whereas the supply of bonds depends on national income or product (which is assumed to remain unchanged at the full-employment level) the demand for them depends on disposable income (which decreases as a result of the increased tax burden; cf. p. 208 above). In this event *BB* will shift upwards.

Consider finally the case of an increase in savings—or, in our terminology, a decrease in the demand for consumption commodities. If this is accompanied by a corresponding increase in the demand for money holdings, then we have an increase in liquidity preference at the sole expense of commodities. The depressing effect of this change on both interest and the price level has already been analyzed in Chapter X:4. If, instead, this increase in savings is accompanied by a corresponding increase in the demand for bonds, the depressing effect on interest is reinforced. In terms of Figure XI-2, *CC* shifts leftwards while *LL* remains constant, so that a new equilibrium position is established at a lower price level and interest rate. A particularly interesting instance of this case is one in which the increased savings and lendings are both engendered by an increase in the liquidity of bonds: an increase in the safety and convenience with which savings can be held.

The reader can work out additional cases for himself. We might, however, note that the foregoing analysis of changes in investment and savings yields results completely in accordance with those of the classical and neoclassical theory of interest.[14]

6. Savings and Investment

With the immediately preceding exception, we have throughout this book deliberately avoided the concept "savings" and its familiar accompaniment, the "savings = investment" condition. This decision has been based on the fact that such a concept is out of place in an analytical framework which views the economy as consisting of a number of goods, each with a price, and each with a market. For savings are clearly not a good, they have no price, and they are not themselves transacted on a market.[15]

This need not, however, prevent us from defining gross real savings, S, as the difference between gross income after taxes and consumption. We can then write the savings function

$$(10) \qquad\qquad S = f\left(Y, r, \frac{M_0^H}{p}\right),$$

[14] Cf. Mathematical Appendix 8:*e*.

[15] Cf. B. Ohlin, "Alternative Theories of the Rate of Interest," *Economic Journal*, XLVII (1937), 424.

where

(11) $$f\left(Y, r, \frac{M_0^H}{p}\right) \equiv Y - G_0 - g\left(Y, r, \frac{M_0^H}{p}\right).$$

As the reader can see from equations (6) and (8) on pp. 205–206, $g(\ )$ is the consumption function and G_0 is the fixed real level of government expenditures, assumed to be financed entirely by taxes. The savings-investment equality can then be written as

(12) $$f\left(Y, r, \frac{M_0^H}{p}\right) = h\left(Y, r, \frac{M_0^F}{p}\right),$$

where $h(\ )$ is the investment function presented in equation (7) on p. 205.

By substituting from identity (11) and rearranging terms, equation (12) becomes

(13) $$g\left(Y, r, \frac{M_0^H}{p}\right) + h\left(Y, r, \frac{M_0^F}{p}\right) + G_0 = Y.$$

But, by equation (10) on p. 206, this is precisely the equilibrium condition for the commodity market described by equation (2) on p. 229. In graphical terms, if the savings and investment functions were to be superimposed on Figure IX-3 (p. 212), they would necessarily intersect at the level of real income Y_0. In brief, the level of real income at which the aggregate amount of commodities the economy demands is equal to the amount it supplies is necessarily the level at which the amount the economy wishes to save is equal to the amount it wishes to invest. Similarly, a level of income at which the amount of commodities demanded is greater than the amount supplied is necessarily one in which the propensity to invest is greater than the propensity to save, and conversely. A corresponding statement holds for a level of real income at which an excess supply of commodities exists.

Thus the savings-investment equality is an alternative statement of the equilibrium condition in the commodity market. As such, it is best replaced by the direct statement of this condition itself. This, of course, has been the procedure followed in the preceding argument.

Clearly, however, any statement involving savings can readily be translated into terms of our model. Consider, for example, the Austrian "monetary over-investment" school's familiar classification of the three alternative ways an increase in investment can be financed.[16] First, there is the case of "financing out of savings." Here the upward shift in the investment function is accompanied by an offsetting downward shift in the consumption function; hence the aggregate demand curve does not rise, so that no upward pressure on prices is created. Then there is the opposite case in which no initial offsetting shift in the consumption function takes place. This must be further classified as follows. First, the investment may be "financed out of hoards"; that is, the increased demand for investment commodities may be financed by a decrease in the demand for money. In this case—to use the shorthand device of Figure XI-2 (p. 259)—*CC* and *LL* shift to the right, while *BB* remains constant. Second, the investment may be "financed out of inflationary bank credit"; that is, by an increased willingness of banks to buy the bonds of firms. In this case, all three curves in Figure XI-2 shift to the right. The common feature of both these cases—and the one which distinguishes them from the case of "financing out of savings"— is the inflationary price development which marks the movement toward the new equilibrium position. It should however be recalled that this price rise will reverse itself as the increased output made possible by the increased investment begins to appear on the market.[17]

It must finally be emphasized that the savings = investment condition is *not* an alternative statement of the equilibrium condition in the bond market. In particular, an act of saving is not necessarily an act of demanding bonds; for the funds withdrawn from consumption might be added instead to cash balances. Conversely, the demand for bonds might be at the expense of cash balances, instead of at the expense of consumption. Similarly, an act of investment is not necessarily an act of supplying bonds; for the funds for the investment program might be forthcoming instead from cash balances. Conversely, the supply of bonds might be for the purpose of adding to cash balances and not for financing investment.

Indeed, the very existence of a money economy precludes the simultaneous identity of savings with the demand for bonds, and investment

[16] Cf., e.g., G. Haberler, *Prosperity and Depression* (3rd ed.; Geneva, 1941) Chapters 3A and 10A.

[17] Above, p. 269.
Note that the increase in investment analyzed in the preceding section falls in none of the foregoing three categories.
Cf. on this paragraph Mathematical Appendix 8:*e*.

with their supply. For we have already seen that the excess of investment over savings is necessarily equal to the excess of commodities demanded over supply. Hence if this simultaneous identity were to hold, the excess demand for commodities would then necessarily equal the excess supply of bonds. That is, individuals would always plan to finance the additional purchase of commodities by the sale of bonds, and vice versa. Accordingly, they would never plan to change the level of their cash balances; that is, their excess demand for these balances would be identically zero; or, in still other words, Say's Identity would hold. But then—to repeat the argument of Chapter VIII: 7—this would mean that any arbitrary departure of prices from their equilibrium level would not create any excess demand or supply of money, and hence would not generate any corrective market forces to return the economy to its original equilibrium position. Hence the equilibrium level of money prices would be indeterminate—a contradiction in terms for a money economy.

As in Section 2 above, this indeterminacy can be demonstrated by use of Figure XI-2. Since the savings = investment condition is equivalent to the equilibrium condition for the commodity market, it too is represented by the curve *CC* in this diagram. Now, if in addition the savings = investment condition were also equivalent to the equilibrium condition for the bond market (as is implied by the simultaneous identity above), then *CC* and *BB* would necessarily coincide. The curve *LL*, on the other hand, would become blown up until it comprised the whole diagram. Thus there would be only one curve in Figure XI-2. That is, there would exist no market forces to stabilize the economy at a determinate level of prices.

XII. The Model Extended: Full Employment

1. WAGE AND PRICE RIGIDITY. MONEY ILLUSION IN THE BOND MARKET. ADDITIONAL ASPECTS OF KEYNES' INTEREST THEORY

The preceding argument has succeeded in freeing the neoclassical quantity theory from two highly restrictive assumptions which have frequently been considered necessary for its validity. In particular, it has shown that this theory presupposes neither a proportionate dependence of commodity demand on cash balances nor a completely interest-inelastic demand curve for money. It is nevertheless obvious that the theory is significantly circumscribed by its other assumptions. It is the purpose of this chapter to relax some of these and to show how the model can be modified and extended to deal with the additional factors thus introduced into the analysis. In this way we shall be able to approach a few steps closer to reality.[1]

---

[1] Because it drops their simplifying assumptions, this chapter is considerably more complicated than preceding ones. The more general reader might, therefore, find it convenient to restrict himself initially to Sections 1 and 7.

In order to avoid any possible misunderstanding, it should be emphasized that this relaxing of assumptions will not be cumulative; instead, each section of this chapter will start anew from the basic model developed above and will show how this model is affected by dropping one, and only one, of its assumptions. The discussion will be carried out only for changes in the quantity of money; the reader can readily establish that it holds also for shifts in liquidity preference.

There is, first of all, the assumption of wage and price flexibility. If this is absent, the dynamic process of Chapter X:3 by which an increasing price level causes a negative real-balance effect in both the commodity and bond markets—and thus ultimately eliminates the inflationary pressures created there by the initial monetary increase—clearly cannot operate. Hence the economy cannot be brought to a new equilibrium position. Thus, for example, assume that the government accompanies its printing of new money by the institution of a system of absolute wage and price controls. Under these circumstances no real-balance effect can be generated, and hence no force can operate to press the aggregate demand curve down again from the level E_1 in Figure IX-3 (p. 212). Accordingly, the inflationary gap AB continues undiminished. In brief, the commodity market is marked by the state of "permanent disequilibrium" so familiar from the suppressed inflation that manifested itself in many countries during and after World War II. Similarly, if, in the face of a monetary decrease, wages and prices do not fall, no force can be at work to raise the aggregate demand curve again. We shall discuss this case further in Chapter XIII:4.

We turn next to the fundamental assumption concerning money illusion. Let us for once assume that such an illusion does manifest itself in our system. For example, assume that the bond demand and supply curves are not affected by changes in the price level but are affected by changes in nominal money balances. Then the original equilibrium position of this market is represented by the solid curves in Figure XII-1. The functional descriptions attached to these curves imply that the demand and supply for *real* bond holdings *are* affected by a change which varies neither real income, the rate of interest, nor the real value of initial money holdings. For example, consider the effect of confronting individuals with a doubling of the price level and initial money holdings. This causes the demand for bonds to increase. But there is now no reason for it to increase in the same proportion as the quantity of money; hence the *real* amount demanded will change. *Mutatis mutandis*, the same is true for the *real* amount supplied. And this distinguishing characteristic is, of course, the manifestation of money illusion.[2]

Assume now that this initial equilibrium is disturbed by a doubling of the quantity of money. This causes the demand and supply curves to shift over to the positions indicated by the dashed curves in Figure XII-1: in view of their increased balances, individuals wish to lend more and borrow less. Hence at the original rate of interest there now exists an excess demand for bonds, and this begins to press the rate of interest downwards. But this time—unlike Chapter X:3—no force operates to bring about an eventual reversal of this movement. For, due

---

[2] The argument of this paragraph can be made clearer if we convert the demand function of Figure XII-1 into one for real bond holdings by dividing through by rp. This yields

$$\frac{B^d}{rp} = \frac{W\left(Y_0, \frac{1}{r}, M_0^H\right)}{p},$$

which can be instructively contrasted with the form of the demand function for real bond holdings when there is no money illusion—

$$\frac{B^d}{rp} = H\left(Y_0, \frac{1}{r}, \frac{M_0^H}{p}\right)$$

(see p. 213).

It might also be noted that there are many other ways in which we can introduce money illusion into the bond market. Thus any of the following demand functions reflects such an illusion:

$$\frac{B^d}{rp} = H\left(pY_0, \frac{1}{r}, \frac{M_0^H}{p}\right),$$

$$B^d = H\left(Y_0, \frac{1}{r}, \frac{M_0^H}{p}\right),$$

$$\frac{B^d}{r} = H\left(Y_0, \frac{1}{r}, \frac{M_0^H}{p}\right).$$

The first of these functions states that the demand for real bond holdings depends on *nominal*, and not *real*, income. The second function states that the demand for *nominal* bond holdings depends on the *real* economic variables. The third function states the same thing for the money value of the demand for bond holdings.

Note, however, that if, in the last two cases, the bond supply function is of exactly the same form, then the two illusions "cancel out." That is, the *excess*-demand function for bonds is free of money illusion.

to the fact that it depends only on the *nominal* level of money holdings (our money-illusion assumption), the bond market does not react to the reduction in the *real* value of these holdings caused by the price rise in the commodity market. Hence the rate of interest continues to decline undisturbed to the new equilibrium level r_3 in Figure XII-1. At the same time, in order to achieve equilibrium in the commodity

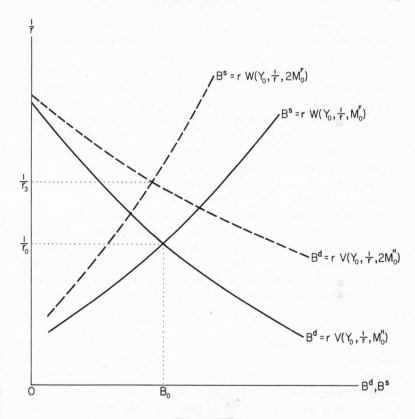

$$B^s = r\ W(Y_0, \tfrac{1}{r}, 2M_0^F)$$

$$B^s = r\ W(Y_0, \tfrac{1}{r}, M_0^F)$$

$$B^d = r\ V(Y_0, \tfrac{1}{r}, 2M_0^H)$$

$$B^d = r\ V(Y_0, \tfrac{1}{r}, M_0^H)$$

FIGURE XII-1.

market, prices must more than double in order to offset the stimulatory effects of a lower rate of interest on aggregate demand in this market. Thus the new equilibrium position is marked by a rate of interest less than r_0 and a price level greater than $2p_0$.

By presenting this argument in terms of the commodity and money markets instead of the commodity and bond markets, we can at one and the same time illustrate the validity of Walras' Law and throw light on certain aspects of Keynes' interest theory. As will be recalled from Chapter XI:1, Keynes' liquidity equation has the form

$$(1) \qquad p \cdot L_1(Y_0) + L_2(r) = M_0.$$

Now, as already emphasized (pp. 125f.), Keynes' speculative demand for money $L_2(r)$ is a reflection of the bond market: it represents the amount of money held as an immediate alternative to holding bonds. Hence the assumption of the preceding equation that this demand is independent of the absolute price level is the obverse side of the assumption that the demand for bonds is so independent. That is, Keynes' assumption (intentional or not) that there is money illusion in the speculative demand for money (which, as shown on pp. 254f., is what its independence of the price level implies) is the obverse side of the foregoing assumption that there is money illusion in the bond market.[3]

Once we accept the money illusion of his liquidity equation, Keynes' analysis of the effects of an increase in the quantity of money follows as a matter of course. A doubling of this quantity cannot merely double the price level and leave the equilibrium rate of interest unaffected. For—as equation (1) shows—the price rise generated by such a doubling affects only the transactions-precautionary demand for money and *not* the speculative demand. This is the crucial point. From it, it follows that—unlike the situation described by the illusion-free equation

$$(2) \qquad p \cdot L_1(Y_0) + p \cdot L_2(r) = M_0$$

of the preceding chapter (p. 254)—the doubling of the quantity of money and the price level doubles only the demand for nominal transactions balances and leaves unaffected that for nominal speculative balances; hence it can *not* double the *total* demand for nominal money holdings. In terms of Figure XI-1, such a change shifts the demand curve for money from position I to II; it cannot shift it to position III. In other words—and in sharp contrast to the basic property of equation

---

[3] That the foregoing equation reflects money illusion in the speculative demand for money can be made clearer by writing this demand in real terms as $L_2(r)/p$. This shows that, say, a doubling of the quantity of money and the level of prices decreases the real demand for these speculative balances.

(2) (see pp. 255f.)—such a change cannot bring about the absorption of the doubled money supply *at an unchanged rate of interest*; it leaves instead an excess supply equal to *EF*. Hence—to paraphrase the *General Theory*—some proportion of the increased money supply will seek an outlet in the purchase of securities. And this will continue until these purchases have depressed the rate of interest to such an extent that the resulting increase in the speculative demand, together with the increase in the transactions demand brought about by the price rise, suffices to absorb all of the new money. The new equilibrium position is represented in Figure XI-1 by the intersection of demand curve II with the supply curve $M^s = 2M_0$ at the rate of interest r_3.[4]

Nor can the invariance of the rate of interest be preserved by a sufficiently more-than-proportionate price increase which causes the transactions demand alone to absorb all of the increased money supply. For under these assumptions equilibrium could not prevail in the commodity market. In particular, the aggregate demand for commodities is still represented by $E = F(Y, r, M_0/p)$. Hence, at an unchanged rate of interest r_0, quantity of money $2M_0$, and price level greater than $2p_0$, the demand curve in Figure IX-3 (p. 212) will—because of the real-balance effect—be at a level like that of E_2. Hence a deflationary gap will prevail, forcing the price level down. This will react back on the money market, force interest down too, and thus reverse the movement of the price level. In this way we are again brought to the conclusion that interest must fall.

This analysis, too, can be summarized in terms of Figure XI-2 (p. 259). The curve *CC* in this diagram remains the same. But, under the conditions described by Figure XII-1, the bond market is unaffected by the price level and can therefore be in equilibrium at only one rate of interest. Hence *BB* is initially a horizontal line at r_0 and is accordingly represented by B_3B_3 in Figure XII-2. As in Figure X-4 (p. 243), a doubling in the quantity of money then shifts the curve *CC* twice as far to the right to C_1C_1. By Figure XII-1, it also shifts the curve B_3B_3 downwards to B_4B_4, at the height corresponding to the new equilibrium

---

[4] *General Theory*, pp. 200–201. I have taken the passage out of its less-than-full-employment context and represented it as dealing with a price level which is not explicitly mentioned. For proof that the interpretation in the text nevertheless identifies the crucial element of Keynes' argument, see the detailed evidence in Note K:2. All this will be discussed further in Chapter XV.

rate, r_3. Hence the equilibrium point in Figure XII-2 moves from g to q
—at which point the price level is more than twice as high as it originally
was, but the rate of interest is lower.

The same result must, of course, be reached by an analysis of the
money market. Let L_3L_3 represent the locus of equilibrium points for
Keynes' liquidity equation (1). Consider now the effects of a doubling
of the quantity of money. As already emphasized, the distinguishing
characteristic of equation (1) is that a doubling of the quantity of money
and the price level will *not* affect the speculative demand and hence will

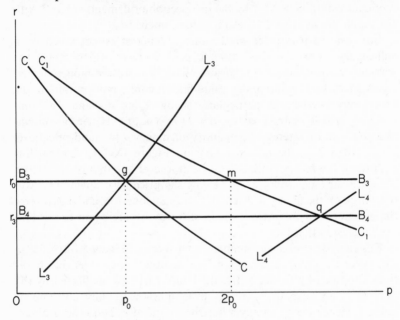

FIGURE XII-2.

not double the *total* nominal demand for money. This means that, at the
unchanged rate of interest r_0, the price level will have to more than
double in order to increase total demand sufficiently to maintain
equilibrium in the money market. Hence at this rate of interest the
curve L_3L_3 must shift over further to the right than the point m, which
corresponds to the price level $2p_0$. The curve corresponding to the
quantity of money $2M_0$ is accordingly represented by L_4L_4 in Figure

XII-2. Clearly, the intersection of this curve with C_1C_1 must be at a rate of interest less than r_0 and a price level greater than $2p_0$.[5]

2. Money Illusion in the Labor Market

Let us now analyze the implications of money illusion in the labor market, instead of the bond or money market. Assume, in particular, that though the demand for labor continues to depend on the real wage rate, the supply depends only on the nominal one. The original equilibrium position is now described by the solid curves in Figure XII-3. Since the vertical axis now represents the nominal wage rate, the demand curve must be drawn as of a given price level. Obviously, money illusion would exist even if the supply curve depended on the price level as well as on the money wage rate—so long as it did not depend on the ratio between them. For simplicity, however, we have drawn the supply curve as dependent solely on the latter.

Assume again that the economy's equilibrium position is disturbed by a doubling of the quantity of money. The resulting pressures in the commodity and bond markets start upward movements in the prices of both these goods. As the price level rises, the demand curve in Figure XII-3 shifts over to the right; for the same money wage rate now corresponds to a lower real one. Thus for the price level p_2, greater than p_0, the equilibrium money wage rate and level of employment are w_2 and N_2, respectively. Clearly, the real wage rate w_2/p_2 must be less than w_0/p_0; for otherwise the amount of labor demanded could not be greater than N_0.

As a result of this decrease in the real wage rate and consequent increase in employment, the supply curve of commodities also shifts to the right. Let the new equilibrium position in this market now be represented by the solid curves in Figure XII-4, where the output Y_2 corresponds to the input of labor N_2. Thus the increase in the quantity of money changes the bench mark of full employment itself.[6]

It remains to determine the relationship between the new equilibrium values—w_2, p_2, and r_2—and the original ones. Consider first the situation in the bond market. By the assumptions made above (pp. 215

[5] The analytical derivation of these results is left as an exercise for the mathematically inclined reader.

[6] The variability of this bench mark will be discussed further in Chapter XIII:1.

and 216f.), the increase in real national output to Y_2 shifts both
the demand and supply curves for bonds to the right. Assume that these
shifts always exactly offset each other. Then—in the absence of any
other change—the situation in the bond market is as indicated in
Figure XII-5. That is, the increase in real income does not affect the
equilibrium rate of interest. But now we must take account of the fact

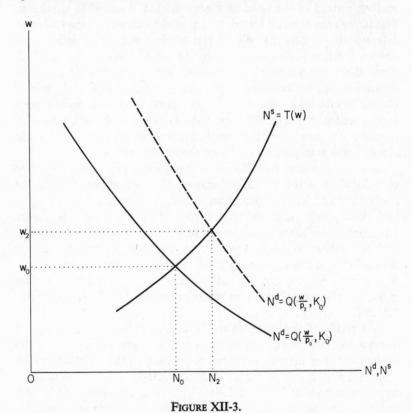

FIGURE XII-3.

which is inherent in the initial assumption of our present analysis:
namely, that the original doubling of the quantity of money has generated a real-balance effect in the bond market which has shifted the demand
curve to the right and the supply curve to the left. Hence the interest
rate must decrease.

Let us now return to the commodity market. At first sight it appears from Figure XII-4 as if the increased supply creates a downward pressure on the price level which might ultimately offset the initial upward pressure generated by the monetary increase. But a moment's reflection shows that equilibrium could not exist at such a lowered price level. For if the price level were to fall, the real wage rate would rise;

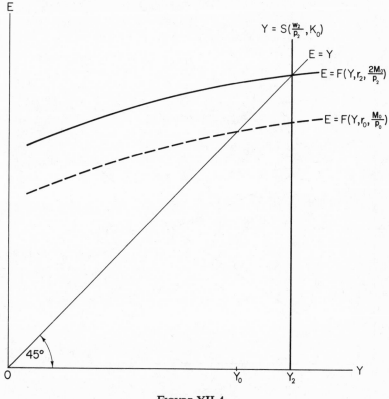

FIGURE XII-4.

and this would replace the increase in the input of labor and consequent increase in the supply of commodities by a decrease in both these items. On the other hand, the lowered price level would reinforce the initial downward pressure on interest in the bond market, and hence raise the aggregate demand curve for commodities. Hence an inflationary gap

283

would exist in the commodity market. It follows that the new equilibrium price level must lie above p_0.

Assume now that the price level has doubled. Then, since there is no money illusion there, the bond market is once again in equilibrium at the original rate of interest r_0. But the commodity market cannot be in equilibrium. For the real value of cash balances is now once again

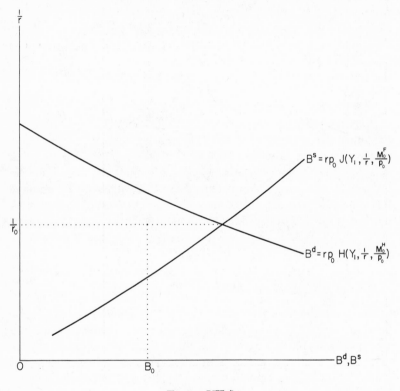

FIGURE XII-5.

equal to its original value; hence the aggregate demand curve must now coincide with the original dashed one in Figure XII-4. At the same time, the doubling of the price level and consequent reduction of the real wage rate has increased the input of labor and thus shifted the commodity supply curve to the right. Hence a deflationary gap exists in this market. This would be so *a fortiori* if the price level had more than doubled and the rate of interest had accordingly risen in the bond market.

Thus consideration of all the markets in our economy brings us to the following conclusion: If there is money illusion on the supply side of the labor market, an increase in the quantity of money decreases the rate of interest and causes a less-than-proportionate increase in the price level. The validity of this conclusion is clearly based on the assumption that the increase in real income has a neutral effect on the bond market; that is, that it generates offsetting shifts in the demand and supply curves of this market.

As usual, the argument can be summarized in terms of Figure XI-2. The assumption of the neutrality of income effects in the bond market implies that doubling the quantity of money shifts BB twice as far over to the right—as represented by B_1B_1 in Figure X-4 (p. 243). On the other hand, because of the increased supply in the commodity market, the curve CC shifts over less than twice as far to the right. That is, at any given rate of interest, the price level must less than double in order to leave a positive real-balance effect that will enable the demand for commodities to absorb the additional supply. Hence the new curve must lie to the left of C_1C_1 in Figure X-4. The intersection of this new curve with B_1B_1 must clearly be at a rate of interest less than r_0 and a price level less than $2p_0$.[7]

3. Distribution Effects. "Forced Savings"

The preceding argument has assumed throughout that aggregate behavior depends on the *total* of real incomes, bond holdings, and money holdings in the economy, and not on their distribution among the individuals. Similarly, it has assumed that any monetary increase is uniformly introduced among these individuals. Let us now see how we can analyze certain cases which do not make these simplifying assumptions.

Assume, for example, that the redistribution of real incomes generated by a price increase is such as to decrease the demand for consumption commodities and increase the demand for bonds and money. That is, the individuals whose real incomes are increased by the price change

[7] For an analytical treatment, see Mathematical Appendix 9:*a*.

have a higher propensity to save and lend than those whose real incomes are decreased. Then a doubling of the quantity of money will no longer leave the rate of interest invariant. For the "forced savings" created by the price rise will cause the rate of interest to decline. The level of national income will remain the same, but its composition will change in favor of investment, as against consumption, commodities. Cor-

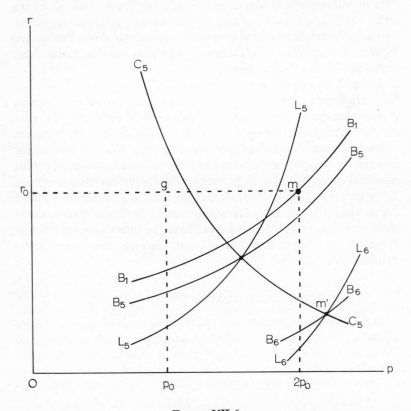

FIGURE XII-6.

respondingly, the rates of capital accumulation and hence growth will increase: money is no longer neutral. This possibility was duly recognized and emphasized by classical and neoclassical economists.[8]

---

[8] These doctrinal issues will be discussed further in Chapter XV.

In terms of Figure XI-2, the specified change shifts CC over to the right; but, because of the initial downward shift in the propensity to consume (upward shift in the propensity to save), not twice as far to the right. That is, it must lie to the left of C_1C_1 in Figure X-4 (p. 243). The resulting curve is represented by the curve C_5C_5 in Figure XII-6. By the same reasoning, BB shifts further to the right than B_1B_1; for, at any given rate of interest, the price level must more than double in order to create a negative real-balance effect that will offset the initial upward shift in the demand for bonds. The resulting curve is represented by B_5B_5 in Figure XII-6. Finally, LL must shift less than twice as far to the right, to L_5L_5. The intersection of the new curves must clearly be at a rate of interest below r_0.[9]

Figure XII-6 also shows that the rate of interest would decline even if there were no shift in the demand function for bonds, that is, even if the "forced savings" were used entirely to augment money balances in order to satisfy a suddenly increased preference for liquidity. Under this assumption, the new LL curve (not drawn) would pass through the intersection of C_5C_5 and B_1B_1, which would represent the new equilibrium position. As before, the price level must necessarily be less than $2p_0$; hence the real quantity of money must be higher than in the original equilibrium position. It is the pressure of this real-balance effect in the bond market which explains the fact that the rate of interest is reduced, even though there is no initial shift in the demand and supply conditions of this market.[10]

Clearly, similar arguments hold for the effects of a price change on the distribution of real bond and money holdings. For example, creditors and debtors need not react in offsetting ways to changes in the real value of outstanding debt. Hence, even if the monetary increase is

[9] For the moment the other curves in this diagram should be ignored.

I am indebted to J. G. Gurley for pointing out an error in the original presentation of this argument.

[10] The reader will recall that this type of argument in terms of an alleged relationship between the real quantity of money and the rate of interest is beset with analytical pitfalls and so must be used with care; see the end of Chapter XI:4.

The discussion of this and the preceding paragraphs slurs over a certain difficulty. Once distribution effects are introduced, the slope of BB might become negative. If this should cut CC from above, an increase in the quantity of money would then lead to an increase in the rate of interest. It can, however, be shown that, under certain simple dynamic assumptions, the stability of the system precludes this possibility. For a full discussion, see Mathematical Appendix 9:c–d.

uniformly introduced, there will be net real-indebtedness effects (pp. 45 and 74). The analysis of these effects—in terms of Figure XII-6— is carried out as in the preceding case.

We note finally that, in a certain sense, the real-balance effect is itself a distribution effect. For our fiat paper money is the debt of the government; and if the government were to react to changes in the real value of this debt as do households and firms to theirs, there could be no net real-balance effect in the economy as a whole. Any, say, decrease in the price level would generate a positive real-balance effect for households and firms and an exactly offsetting negative one for the government. Thus the preceding analysis has been based on the tacit—though realistic—assumption that the government, alone of all economic units, is unconcerned with the real value of its outstanding (noninterest-bearing) debt, and plans its demand for commodities accordingly.[11]

4. GOVERNMENT DEBT AND OPEN-MARKET OPERATIONS[12]

Let us now drop the assumption that the only form of government debt is money and introduce government bonds into the analysis. These bonds are assumed identical with those issued by firms and, like the latter, are held only by households. The government is also assumed to engage in open-market operations, the consequences of which will be one of our primary concerns in what follows.[13]

[11] As Arnold Collery has recently emphasized, the foregoing interpretation does not hold for an economy in which money is not the debt of government, but (say) gold. See his "Note on the Saving-Wealth Relation and the Rate of Interest," *Journal of Political Economy*, LXVIII (1960), 509–10.

[12] Most of the changes in the emphasis and contents of this section have been stimulated by the explicit and implicit criticisms of the original treatment in Carl Christ, "Patinkin on Money, Interest, and Prices," *Journal of Political Economy*, LXV (1957), 349–50; Shaw and Gurley, *op. cit.*; and R. A. Mundell, "The Public Debt, Corporate Income Taxes, and the Rate of Interest," *Journal of Political Economy*, LXVIII (1960), 622–26.

The section as a whole continues to reflect the influence of Lloyd Metzler's basic article on "Wealth, Saving, and the Rate of Interest," *Journal of Political Economy*, LIX (1951), 93–116, and particularly of its emphasis on the difference between monetary changes generated by deficit financing, on the one hand, and open-market operations, on the other.

[13] Actually, as has been emphasized by Gurley and Shaw (*op. cit.*, pp. 144 ff.; see also Alain Enthoven's remark on p. 305 of his mathematical appendix to this book), analogous consequences would be forthcoming (*mutatis mutandis*) even if the government were to carry out its open-market operations on bonds of the private sector. The

The first question that arises is whether account must be taken of the real value of outstanding government bonds for the purpose of analyzing the wealth effect. One possibility is to treat bonds just like money in this respect, and thus write our excess-demand functions as dependent upon $V_0/rp + M_0/p$, where V_0 represents the number of government bonds outstanding. The difficulty with this approach is that the interest burden on these bonds must presumably be financed by future taxes. Hence if the private sector discounts its further tax liabilities in the same way that it discounts future interest receipts, the existence of government bonds will not generate any net wealth effect.[14] In brief, the net financial assets of the private sector will still be represented by M_0/p.[15]

For generality, let us not adopt either of the foregoing two extremes but assume instead that the proper wealth variable for our excess-demand functions is $kV_0/rp + M_0/p$, where k is a constant (greater than zero and less than one) reflecting the degree to which individuals do *not* discount the future tax liabilities connected with government bonds. Accordingly, the system of equations in Chapter X:1 is replaced by:

Condition for Equilibrium		*Market*
(3)	$Q\left(\dfrac{w}{p}, K_0\right) = R\left(\dfrac{w}{p}\right)$	Labor services,
(4)	$F\left(Y_0, r, \dfrac{kV_0}{rp} + \dfrac{M_0}{p}\right) = Y_0$	Commodities,

---

existence of government bonds as the object of these operations has, however, been assumed here in order to make the analysis more realistic.

[14] This point is due to Carl Christ, who cites in turn discussions with Milton Friedman. Christ's own view, however, is that bonds should be treated like money. See the reference to his article cited in footnote 12, above.

[15] The fact that government debt in the form of money does not generate any tax burden rules out the possibility (recently suggested by H. G. Johnson) that the logic of the foregoing argument be applied to such debt as well, so that on a priori grounds money balances (just like interest-bearing government debt under our present assumptions) could not be the source of a net wealth effect ("Monetary Theory and Policy," *op. cit.*, p. 343; see also end of preceding section).

In addition to this theoretical objection to Johnson's suggestion, there is, of course, the empirical one implicit in the many studies which have yielded a statistically significant real-balance effect. For details, see Note M below.

Condition for Equilibrium   *Market*

(5) $B\left(Y_0, \dfrac{1}{r}, \dfrac{kV_0}{rp} + \dfrac{M_0}{p}\right) = \dfrac{kV_0}{rp}$ Bonds,

(6) $L\left(Y_0, r, \dfrac{kV_0}{rp} + \dfrac{M_0}{p}\right) = \dfrac{M_0}{p}$ Money,

where the excess-demand function for bonds has been written in the form of equation (19) on p. 219 above.

The fact that k differs from zero causes the foregoing system to differ from that of Chapter X:1 in three related respects. First, the positive net bond holdings of the private sector must be reflected on the supply side of equation (5). Note that here too their real quantity is premultiplied by k. For to the extent that the private sector discounts its tax liabilities, the government bonds it holds represent a liability as well as an asset. Hence the net effective addition of these bonds to the supply side must be represented by kV_0/rp.[16]

Second, since the net financial assets of the private sector no longer coincide with its real money holdings, the wealth effect of a change in the price level no longer coincides with the real-balance effect.[17] Correspondingly, the impact of such a change on the demands for various goods should no longer be analyzed in terms of this latter effect, but in terms of an analogous "net-real-financial-asset effect."

Third, there is now a new way in which an increase in the rate of interest affects the demand for goods. For now that net bond holdings are positive, we can no longer assume—as we did on p. 207—that the capital losses and gains created by such an increase will cancel out.

---

[16] The rationale of this argument can be made clearer by restating it in terms of the demand and supply functions which lie behind equation (5) (see Chapter IX : 4). If the total amount of debt which the private sector is willing to have outstanding is represented by $J(\ \ )$, and if it considers government debt in part as its own, then the amount of bonds which the private sector will issue in its own name is

$$J(\ \ ) - (1 - k)\dfrac{V_0}{rp}.$$

The total supply of bonds (inclusive of those issued by government) is then

$$\left[J(\ \ ) - (1 - k)\dfrac{V_0}{rp}\right] + \dfrac{V_0}{rp} = J(\ \ ) + \dfrac{kV_0}{rp}.$$

Subtracting this from the demand for bonds $H(\ \ )$ then yields (5).

[17] Cf. p. 209.

Instead, there is a net capital loss—represented by the decrease in kV_0/rp—which makes its depressing influence felt throughout the economy. In the commodity and money markets, this negative wealth effect reinforces the substitution effect of an increase in interest; in the bond market, however, these two effects work in opposite directions. Indeed, if the capital loss effect is sufficiently strong, the slope of the demand curve for bonds in Figure IX-4 (p. 214) might become positive.

Even in this case, however, the *excess*-demand curve represented by equation (5) above must retain its negative slope of Figure IX-5. For since we assume that the marginal propensity to spend out of wealth is less than unity, the decrease in the real demand for bonds generated by the capital loss is necessarily less than the decrease in its net real supply kV_0/rp. Hence the excess supply of real bond holdings must decrease—which means that the excess demand must increase. Correspondingly, the positive slope of the *BB* curve in Figures X-2 and XI-2 is not affected by the foregoing considerations.[18]

Let us now analyze the effects of changing the quantity of money in the foregoing system—first by means of deficit financing, and then by open-market operations. In the first case it can readily be seen that, say, a doubling of the quantity of money will not merely double equilibrium wages and prices, while leaving the rate of interest unaffected. For under such circumstances the real value of government-bond holdings kV_0/rp would be less than in the original equilibrium position, whereas other influences on commodity demand would be the same. Hence, by equation (4), there would at point m in Figure XII-6 exist a deflationary gap in the commodity market. Nor would the bond market be in equilibrium at this point: for the decrease in the real value of government bonds must reduce both demand and supply, but, as argued in the preceding paragraph, the latter decrease must be greater than the former. Hence point m in Figure XII-6 would correspond to a state of excess demand in the bond market. By a similar argument, it would correspond to a state of excess supply in the money market. In brief, the new *CC* curve (represented once again by C_5C_5 in Figure XII-6) must lie leftwards of point m, and the new *BB* (B_6B_6) and *LL* (L_6L_6) curves rightwards.

---

[18] The slope of *BB* could however become negative because of the type of considerations referred to in footnote 10, p. 287 above. For a full discussion, see Mathematical Appendix 9:*e*.

Hence the new equilibrium rate of interest (defined in Figure XII-6 by the point m') must be lower than the original one. This failure of interest to remain invariant can be interpreted in either neoclassical or Keynesian terms. From the neoclassical viewpoint the assumption that there are incompletely discounted government bonds introduces into the analysis elements which are analogous to the presence of both money illusion and distribution effects (see Sections 2–3 above). The former is reflected on the supply side of the bond market—which shows that the government wishes to maintain V_0 bonds outstanding regardless of the price level, so that its real supply of bonds varies inversely with this level. The latter is reflected on the demand side of the respective markets—which shows that in contrast with our earlier analysis (p. 207), the indebtedness effects do not in the aggregate cancel out and are, indeed, represented by the term kV_0/rp. For both of these reasons the total real value of the portfolio (and hence total wealth) at point m is less than at point g, so that equilibrium cannot prevail. Alternatively, from a Keynesian viewpoint, the aggregate portfolio corresponding to point m cannot be an optimum one for the simple reason that its real composition differs from the one at point g, while the rate of interest is the same.[19]

This interpretation suggests that if the existence of government bonds were not to generate any of the foregoing influences, then the rate of interest would remain unchanged. This would indeed be the case if these bonds carried an escalator clause tying their interest payment to the price level, and thus leaving their real value unaffected by movements of the latter.[20] In technical terms, this would imply that V_0 in the preceding equations would be replaced everywhere by pV_0, so that kV_0/rp is replaced by kV_0/r. As can readily be verified by direct substitution into this modified system of equations, a doubling of the quantity of money by deficit financing then brings the economy to a new equilibrium position in which prices and wages double, while the rate of

[19] Compare this with the situation described on p. 238; cf. also pp. 266–67.

[20] Such bonds have become increasingly common in the inflationary economies of postwar years. For some descriptions, see David Finch, "Purchasing Power Guarantees for Deferred Payment," *International Monetary Fund: Staff Papers,* V (1956), 1–22; Bank of Israel, *Annual Report: 1958* (Jerusalem, 1959), pp. 277–80; Peter Robson, "Index-Linked Bonds," *Review of Economic Studies,* XXVIII (1960), 57–68. Cf. also J. Viner, *Studies in the Theory of International Trade* (New York, 1937), pp. 282 ff. for instances of the advocacy of such bonds in England at the beginning of the nineteenth century.

interest remains invariant. Diagrammatically, the *CC*, *BB*, and *LL* curves which originally went through point *g* in Figure XII-6 all shift twice as far to the right and intersect at point *m*. Correspondingly—and unlike the preceding case—the real quantities of bonds and money at this point are the same as at the original equilibrium point *g*. Thus the invariance of the interest rate reflects the fact that once again (see pp. 266–67) the monetary change affects neither the composition nor real magnitude of the economy's equilibrium portfolio of money, bonds, and nonfinancial assets.

This invariance of the interest rate, however, no longer obtains if the quantity of money doubles as a result of open-market operations.[21] For even in the case of an escalated bond, the real portfolio at point *m* differs from that at point *g*. In particular, though real money balances are the same, the real quantity of government debt has been decreased as a consequence of the open-market purchase. Correspondingly, by an argument analogous to that on pp. 291–92 above, the new *CC* curve must lie leftwards of point *m*, and the new *BB* and *LL* curves rightwards, so that the equilibrium rate of interest is reduced. Once again, this decline in interest can be interpreted in either neoclassical or Keynesian terms.[22]

Clearly, the foregoing argument holds for the case of a nonescalated bond as well. Indeed, in this case the new curves must respectively lie below those corresponding to the case in which the increased quantity of money is injected into the system by deficit financing. For consider any point on, say, B_6B_6. This clearly cannot be an equilibrium point after an equivalent open-market purchase. For, in accordance with our earlier argument, the amount of bonds supplied at this point is less than in the deficit-financing case by the extent of the open-market purchase, while the amount demanded is less by a smaller amount. Hence any point on B_6B_6 now represents a state of excess demand in the bond market. Similarly, any point on C_6C_6 or L_6L_6 now represents

[21] In order to restrict the discussion to once-and-for-all changes in the money supply, it is assumed that the government's savings on interest payments made possible by the reacquisition of its own debt is accompanied by a corresponding reduction in taxes, so that its budget continues to be balanced. Cf. Metzler, "Wealth, Saving and the Rate of Interest," *op. cit.*, p. 109, footnote 15; Mundell, *op. cit.*, p. 624.

[22] In the present case there is, of course, nothing corresponding to a money illusion; accordingly, the neutrality of money is disturbed only by the analog of a distribution effect. Cf. also G. Haberler, "The Pigou Effect Once More," *Journal of Political Economy*, LX (1952), 245.

a state of excess supply in the commodity or money market, respectively. It follows that the new equilibrium position resulting from an open-market purchase must correspond to a lower rate of interest than that resulting from an equivalent monetary increase through deficit financing. A parallel statement holds in a trivial way for an escalated bond: for, as already noted, in this case interest remains invariant under a monetary increase of the latter type.[23]

Two final comments are in order. First, just as in the case of a shift in liquidity preference (p. 251), the decline in interest generated by an open-market purchase will be smaller the less the importance of the financial-asset effect in the commodity market. Second, the foregoing analysis of open-market operations has been based on the crucial—though reasonable—assumption that there is an imperfect discounting of the tax liability associated with the bonds which are the object of these operations. In the absence of such an imperfection (that is, if $k = 0$), system (3)–(6) above reduces to the already familiar one of Chapter X:1. This in turn implies that the effect of a change in the quantity of money on the economy is the same whether this change originates in deficit financing or in open-market operations.[24] In brief, if government so perfectly represents the corporate will, then its exogenous supply of bonds simultaneously represents an offsetting exogenous demand. Government is a veil.[25]

[23] One special case of interest with reference to open-market operations is that in which individuals do not discount their future tax liability at all, so that $k = 1$ in system (3)–(6). An open-market purchase in this case does not *initially* (i.e., before any change in interest or prices) generate a wealth effect, and hence does not shift the demands for any of the goods in the system: for it merely replaces bonds by an equivalent amount of money in the portfolios of individuals. Correspondingly, it does not initially disturb the equilibrium of the commodity market. On the other hand, it does create a portfolio imbalance in the form of an *excess* supply of money and an *excess* demand for bonds, thus leading to the same kind of result as that described in the text.

Graphically, the *BB* and *LL* curves in this case continue to shift as in Figure XII-6; but the *CC* curve rotates in a clockwise direction about the point *g*, for the open-market purchase has diminished the base (i.e., the number of bonds V_0) on which the wealth effect of a change in interest is exerted.

[24] Cf. Mundell, *op. cit.*, p. 625.

From the viewpoint of the discussion on pp. 292–93 above, note that in this case an open-market operation too will not affect the real size or composition of the equilibrium portfolio of nonfinancial assets, net bond holdings [now once again (p. 267) assumed to be zero], and real money holdings.

[25] Cf. p. 290 above, especially footnote 16.

On the argument of this section, see Mathematical Appendix 9:*e–f*.

5. The Existence of a Banking System and of Financial Intermediaries [26]

Our entire argument until this point has been based on the assumption that money is of the outside variety: that is, representing or based on the debt of a unit (the government) exogenous to the economic system itself. Let us now take account of the fact that in reality most money in a modern economy is of the inside type: that is, based on the debt of endogenous economic units. This in turn is a consequence of the fact that money in such an economy is largely the creation of a private banking system.

In order to fix our ideas, let us divide the economy into three sectors: the private nonfinancial sector (households and firms), the private banking sector, and the government sector. As the first step in the analysis, assume that the respective balance sheets of these sectors are as shown on p. 296.

For the sake of concreteness, the first balance sheet records the gross amounts of bonds issued and held, though it would be more elegant merely to designate on the debit side the net amount issued by the nonfinancial sector ($B^f - B^h$). Bonds are assumed to be the sole asset of the banking system and money the sole debt of government. By definition, M' and M'' are the respective quantities (assumed to be exogenously determined) of inside and outside money. The nonfinancial sector is assumed to be indifferent as to which of these moneys it holds. The net real wealth of this sector is

$$(7) \qquad W = A + \frac{M + \dfrac{B^h}{r} - \dfrac{B^f}{r}}{p},$$

where tangible assets A are assumed to remain constant (and hence ignored) throughout the subsequent discussion. Making use of the definitions

$$(8) \qquad M = M' + M'' \quad \text{and} \quad B^f = B^h + B^b,$$

as well as the fact that $B^b/r = M'$, this reduces to

[26] The basic indebtedness of this and the following section to Gurley and Shaw's pathbreaking work on *Money in a Theory of Finance* (*op. cit.*) will be evident to all. I have also drawn freely on my review article of this book in the *American Economic Review*, LI (1961), 95–116.

$$(9) \qquad W = A + \frac{M''}{p}.$$

In other words, the net financial assets of the private sector consist only of the outside money which it holds: its inside money is offset

Private Nonfinancial Sector			
Money	M	Bonds issued by firms	$\dfrac{B^f}{r}$
Bonds held by households	$\dfrac{B^h}{r}$	Net worth	pW
Tangible assets	pA		
	$M + \dfrac{B^h}{r} + pA$		$\dfrac{B^f}{r} + pW$

Private Banking Sector			
Bonds held by banks	$\dfrac{B^b}{r}$	Money (demand deposits)	M'
	$\dfrac{B^b}{r}$		M'

Government Sector			
Cumulated deficits on current account	D	Money (hand-to-hand currency)	M''
	D		M''

by a corresponding debt to the banking system.[27] In accordance with our usual practice—and disregarding the equilibrated labor market—we must then rewrite the system of equations of Chapter X:1 as

$$(10) \qquad F\left(Y_0, r, \frac{M_0''}{p}\right) = Y_0,$$

---

[27] This was first pointed out by M. Kalecki, "Professor Pigou on the 'Classical Stationary State'—A Comment," *Economic Journal*, LIV (1944), 131–32.

(11)
$$B\left(Y_0, \frac{1}{r}, \frac{M_0''}{p}\right) + \frac{M_0'}{p} = 0,$$

(12)
$$L\left(Y_0, r, \frac{M_0''}{p}\right) = \frac{M_0''}{p} + \frac{M_0'}{p},$$

where the zero subscripts indicate those quantities which are exogenously determined, and where the two terms in equation (11) represent the net demand for bonds on the part of the nonfinancial and banking sectors, respectively.

The foregoing model assigns a separate role to each of the three money quantities: outside, inside, and total. The nature of these roles is, however, different. The total quantity of money appears in its own right on the supply side of (12). In contrast, the quantities of outside and inside money are not themselves primary analytical entities: that is, they appear as separate variables only because they happen to coincide in the foregoing system with the sum of net financial assets and with the banks' demand for bonds, respectively. We shall return to this distinction in the next section (pp. 307f.).

Clearly, if all money is of the outside type, then $M_0'' = M_0$ and $M_0' = 0$, so that system (10)–(12) reduces to that of the preceding chapters. Of more interest to us in the present context is the opposite extreme in which all money is of the inside type, so that $M_0'' = 0$ and the foregoing system reduces to

(13)
$$F(Y_0, r) = Y_0,$$

(14)
$$B\left(Y_0, \frac{1}{r}\right) + \frac{M_0'}{p} = 0,$$

(15)
$$L(Y_0, r) = \frac{M_0'}{p}.$$

A significant property of this system is that it is dichotomized: the equilibrium rate of interest is determined solely in the real (commodity) sector and is therefore unaffected by any exogenous change which takes place solely in the monetary (bond and money) sector. Furthermore—and in contrast with our discussion heretofore (pp. 180, 242, and 251)—this dichotomization now stems from the assumption that the wealth effect in the form of the real-balance effect is consistently absent from *all* markets. But despite the fact that this implies that changes in p do not affect the private real *demands* for any of the goods, the level of *p* is still determinate by virtue of its impact on the *excess* demands for bonds and money. Thus an upward (say) departure of the price level from its equilibrium level will generate an excess supply of bonds— matched by an equal excess demand for money—which will raise interest, hence reduce the demand for commodities, and hence cause the price level to decline again to its original level. In terms of Figure XI-2, system (13)–(15) is a stable one in which *CC* is a horizontal line, while the *BB* and *LL* curves remain as there depicted. Similarly, and again in contrast with our main discussion (pp. 19–20, 44, 237), a (say) decrease in the quantity of money influences the system (13)–(15) not through the wealth effect, but through the opposite and matching changes directly generated in the excess supplies of bonds and money. Graphically, these changes appear as equal leftward shifts in *BB* and *LL*, which again intersect on an unchanged, horizontal *CC*.[28][29]

Needless to say, money is neutral in both of the foregoing cases. This neutrality need not hold, however, in an economy with both inside and outside money. For, as the reader can readily verify, an increase in only one of these types of money in system (10)–(12) will not yield a proportionately increased price level at an unchanged rate of interest. These results would obtain only if outside and inside money happen to increase in the same proportion.[30]

[28] Note how this paragraph rationalizes the interpretation of Keynes on p. 264.

[29] The foregoing properties of a pure inside-money economy have been described by Gurley and Shaw, though without explicit reference to the dichotomy issue (*op. cit.*, pp. 72–75, 81–82). See also the recent emphasis on the validity of the dichotomy in this case in the postscript attached by Modigliani to the reprinting of his well-known article on "Liquidity Preference and the Theory of Interest and Money" in *The Critics of Keynesian Economics* (ed. H. Hazlitt, Princeton, 1960), pp. 183–84. This has been further elaborated by Modigliani in his "Monetary Mechanism and Its Interaction with Real Phenomena," *Review of Economics and Statistics*, XLV (1963), Supplement, pp. 81, 83–88.

Note how the type of dynamic inconsistency described in our discussion of the invalid dichotomy (pp. 177–79) does not exist in the present case: for no matter in which two of the three markets we carry out the analysis, the stability of the system is consistently attested.

Note too that even under our present assumptions there is an element of artificiality about the dichotomy: for it would disappear simply as a result of assuming that there are two types of bonds, each with its own rate of return, and that the demand for commodities depends on both these rates. Cf. footnote 39 below.

[30] Gurley and Shaw, *op. cit.*, pp. 82–86. Cf. also Johnson, "Monetary Theory and Policy," *op. cit.*, p. 342 and Modigliani, "Monetary Mechanism and Its Interaction with Real Phenomena," *op. cit.*, p. 87.

In terms of Figure XI-2, a doubling of inside money alone will leave *CC* unaffected

Within the framework of the foregoing model—which assumes that the respective quantities of these two types of money are independently determined—such an equiproportionate increase would be highly coincidental indeed. What has not, however, been recognized is that this assumption of independence is generally an unrealistic one. Thus, for example, in many banking systems these two quantities of money are significantly related by virtue of the fact that outside money also fulfils the function of reserves (or reserve-substitutes) for the demand deposits which constitute the inside money. Indeed, this was a major characteristic of the gold-standard world in which the neoclassical economists were writing. Correspondingly, it might well be that an equiproportionate change in outside and inside money in such a system is not the chance happening implied by the preceding paragraph, but the determinate consequence of structural relationships.

In order to bring out this point let us reconsider the balance sheet of the banking sector and assume that, in addition to holding bonds, this sector also holds reserves in the form of outside money M_b'' as a fixed ratio c of its demand deposits; that is,

$$(16) \qquad M' = \frac{1}{c} M_b''.$$

Let us also assume that the nonfinancial sector maintains a constant ratio t between its holdings of outside money (hand-to-hand currency) M_n'' and demand deposits; that is,[31]

$$(17) \qquad M_n'' = tM'.$$

As the reader can readily verify, this does not affect the representation of net financial assets in system (10)–(12). On the other hand, the

---

while shifting BB and LL less than twice as far to the right; hence it will depress the equilibrium interest rate and increase prices less than proportionately. On the other hand, a doubling of outside money alone will shift CC twice as far to the right, while shifting BB and LL rightwards to a lesser extent; hence it will raise interest while again increasing the price level less than proportionately.

[31] Both of these assumptions are made by Fisher, *Purchasing Power of Money* (rev. ed., New York, 1913), pp. 50–51, and by Pigou, "The Value of Money," *op. cit.*, pp. 165–66.

The assumption of a constant ratio between hand-to-hand currency and demand deposits is, of course, highly unrealistic. For a theoretical and empirical study of the actual relationship, see Phillip Cagan, "The Demand for Currency Relative to the Total Money Supply," *Journal of Political Economy*, LXVI (1958), 303–28.

demand of the banking system for bonds in equation (11) is now represented by $M'/p - M_b''/p$, and the supply of money in equation (12) by $M_n''/p + M'/p$. Furthermore, the foregoing assumptions effectively introduce a new good into the analysis, hand-to-hand currency, demanded by both banks and the nonfinancial sector. By equations (16) and (17), the equilibrium condition for this good is

$$(18) \qquad (t + c)M' = M_0''.$$

Assume for simplicity that equilibrium always prevails in the market for hand-to-hand currency. Then—substituting from equation (18), and taking account also of the argument of the preceding paragraph—the system of equations (13)–(15) becomes

$$(19) \qquad F\left(Y_0, r, \frac{M_0''}{p}, \alpha\right) = Y_0,$$

$$(20) \qquad B\left(Y_0, \frac{1}{r}, \frac{M_0''}{p}, \alpha\right) + \frac{1 - c}{t + c} \frac{M_0''}{p} = 0,$$

$$(21) \qquad L\left(Y_0, r, \frac{M_0''}{p}, \alpha\right) = \frac{1 + t}{t + c} \frac{M_0''}{p},$$

where the parameter α should for the moment be ignored.

The foregoing equations bring out the crucial fact that, under the neoclassical assumptions of a fractional-reserve banking system which is always "loaned up," neither the volume of bank credit nor that of demand deposits is exogenously determined. Correspondingly, it is meaningless to inquire about the effects of (say) an expansion in M' upon the system. The only exogenous variables of the model—ignoring again the parameter α—are the quantity of outside money M''; the required reserve ratio c; and the currency-demand-deposit ratio t. As can readily be determined from (19)–(21), a change in M'' will cause a proportionate change in p, while leaving r unaffected; from (18) we also see that it will change M' in the same proportion. On the other hand, it should be emphasized that a change in either c or t—which by its very nature does not cause an equiproportionate change in inside and outside money—will not have this neutral impact on the system.[32]

[32] This is essentially the kind of change considered by Gurley and Shaw, *op. cit.*, pp. 82–86.

Before leaving this subject we should note that the neutrality associated with a change in the quantity of outside money is not dependent on the fixity of the ratios described by equations (16) and (17). It suffices instead that the functional relationships between bank reserves and demand deposits, on the one hand, and currency and demand deposits, on the other, be free of money illusion. This will become clearer from the discussion of the next section.[33]

Until now banks have been assumed to be the only kind of financial institution. With the help of the foregoing system the argument can, however, be extended to other kinds of financial intermediaries: insurance companies, savings and loan associations, mutual funds, and so forth. These intermediaries can fruitfully be conceived as processing plants whose effective function it is to transform the bonds issued by firms into securities which the ultimate lenders (i.e., households) consider more suitable for their needs. Intermediaries are able to profit from this transformation process by exploiting "economies of scale in lending and borrowing. On the lending side, the intermediary can invest and manage investments in primary securities at unit costs far below the experience of most individual lenders. The sheer size of its portfolio permits a significant reduction in risks through diversification. It can schedule maturities so that chances of liquidity crises are minimized. The mutual or cooperative is sometimes favored with tax benefits that are not available to the individual saver. On the borrowing side, the intermediary with a large number of depositors can normally rely on a predictable schedule of claims for repayment and so can get along with a portfolio that is relatively illiquid."[34]

In other words, the result of developing nonbanking financial intermediaries (like that of improving distributive techniques in the securities market) is to provide ultimate lenders with the possibility of purchasing

---

Needless to say, neither system (19)–(21)—nor the more general one (10)–(12)—is dichotomized.

[33] The problems of a banking system have also been formally analyzed by Leif Johansen, "The Role of the Banking System in a Macroeconomic Model," *Statsokonomisk Tidsskrift* (1956) as translated in *International Economic Papers*, No. 8 (1958), pp. 91–110. Johansen's concern, however, is with a system whose absolute price level is fixed. Correspondingly, his analysis deals largely with different questions.

See also Karl Brunner, "A Schema for the Supply Theory of Money," *International Economic Review*, II (1961), 79–109, and the references there cited on p. 79 footnote 2; and Assar Lindbeck, *A Study in Monetary Analysis* (Stockholm, 1963), Chapters IV–VI.

[34] Gurley and Shaw, *op. cit.*, p. 194.

a security which is more attractive (more "liquid") than the primary securities issued by the ultimate borrowers. This increased liquidity can be represented in system (19)–(20) by an increase in the parameter α which is assumed to shift the demand for bonds upwards, and that for money downwards. If the direct effect of the change in α on the demand for commodities is assumed to be small, the impact of financial intermediaries in reducing the interest rate can then be analyzed as on pp. 251–52 above.

In this way it is also possible to bring out the essential similarity between banking and nonbanking intermediaries.[35] To speak somewhat loosely, both of these intermediaries influence the economy by affecting the terms on which bonds are demanded and supplied. But, from the viewpoint of bond equation (20) above, the banking system does this through the second component of this demand (as a result of an exogenous change in either the absolute level of reserves or the reserve ratio); whereas nonbanking intermediaries do so through the liquidity of bonds, and hence the first component. Alternatively, in somewhat more familiar terms, we can make the comparison in terms of the money equation (21) and say that the banking system affects the economy by changing the supply of money; whereas nonbanking intermediaries do so by changing α, hence the demand for money, and hence the velocity of circulation. Note, however, that in both cases there are further endogenous changes in velocity caused by the resulting change in the interest rate.

6. The Existence of a Banking System and of Financial Intermediaries (Continued)

Let us now return, for simplicity, to a pure inside-money economy and explore some further aspects of the banking system.

In system (13)–(15) above it was assumed that the quantity of inside money is exogenously given. Such an assumption is hardly consistent with the supposed operations of a *laissez faire* banking system, interested in maximizing profits. Instead it should be assumed that this system has a supply function for money dependent on the real wage rate and the rate of interest. Since the former is considered constant in the present

---

[35] This is one of Gurley and Shaw's central theses; cf., *op. cit.*, pp. 198–99, 202.

discussion, we can then simply write

$$(22) \qquad \qquad \frac{M'}{p} = S(r).$$

If we substitute this function in equations (14) and (15), we see that the price level no longer appears as a variable of system (13)–(15), and hence obviously cannot be determined by it. Indeed, what we have here is the indeterminacy of Wicksell's "pure credit" economy in which all transactions are carried out by checks, while banks hold no reserves.[36] The economic interpretation of this indeterminacy is straightforward: In order for the absolute price level to be determined by market-equilibrating forces, changes in it must impinge on *real* behavior in *some* market—i.e., must create excess demands in some market. Now, the joint assumptions of a pure inside-money economy and the absence of distribution effects implies that there is no such impingement on the real demands of the private sector for commodities, bonds, money, respectively. Similarly, the absence of reserve requirements (either legal or economic) implies that there is no impingement on the real demand and supply functions of the banking sector. Hence the economy does not generate resistance to any arbitrary change in the price level. Accordingly, there is nothing to prevent the frictionless flow of prices from one level to another.

In contrast, the price level in system (19)–(21) above is determinate because changes in it impinge on the real value of the fixed nominal quantity of outside money in the system and hence on the behavior of both the nonfinancial and banking sectors. An analogous result can be derived for the pure inside-money economy with which we are now dealing by simply assuming that the banking system holds reserves, and that the nominal quantity of these reserves is exogenously fixed.[37] In particular, assume that there exists a central bank which creates reserves solely by purchasing bonds issued by firms. Assume also that these reserves—which, by assumption, are more liquid than bonds—yield a rate of return d' (less than r) and are held only by member banks in order to meet temporary discrepancies between the flows of checks to

---

[36] See p. 594 below.

[37] The following is adapted from the highly stimulating analysis developed by Gurley and Shaw, *op. cit.*, pp. 247–64.

and from depositors in other banks. Thus reserves can be considered as a type of security supplied by one financial institution and demanded only by another, yielding a return determined by the free play of these market forces.[38] Correspondingly, the balance sheet of the banking sector in the preceding section should now be separated into two, as follows:

Member Banks

Reserves	R	Money (demand deposits)	M'
Bonds	$\dfrac{B^b}{r}$		
	$R + \dfrac{B^b}{r}$		M'

Central Bank

Bonds	$\dfrac{B^c}{r}$	Reserves	R
	$\dfrac{B^c}{r}$		R

Assume finally that member banks are not subject to any legal reserve requirements, but are instead free to choose their optimum portfolio of assets and liabilities, inclusive of reserves. As in the case of any other economic unit, this decision is based on a comparison of the relative liquidity (and illiquidity) of the assets and liabilities in question with their alternative rates of return. Since in the present case demand deposits are not assumed to bear any interest, this means that the portfolio decisions of the banking system depend on r and d', as well as on other real variables (e.g., the real wage rate) which in the present discussion are assumed constant and hence ignored. Correspondingly, the system's real supply function of money can now be written as

$$(23) \qquad\qquad\qquad S(r, d'),$$

[38] *Ibid,*. pp. 257–58.

and its real demand function for reserves,

(24) $$G(r, d').$$

At the same time, the private banking system's supply of money is clearly no longer identical with its demand for bonds. The latter is instead now represented by, say, $U(1/r, d')$ where, by the banks' consolidated balance sheet,

(25) $$U\left(\frac{1}{r}, d'\right) \equiv S(r, d') - G(r, d').$$

Note that, in contrast with (16) above, the supply of money does not explicitly depend on the quantity of reserves. Instead, both the money supply function and the reserve demand function depend on the same variables r and d'. By assumption, an increase in r—or a decrease in d'—increases the banks' supply of money and demand for bonds, while decreasing their demand for reserves. In brief, the greater the differential between the rates of return on bonds and reserves, the more banks will want to shift out of the latter and into the former. Correspondingly, the reserve ratio maintained by banks depends inversely on this differential rate of return.

The remaining element of our model is the central bank's real supply of reserves, which is also its real demand for bonds. By assumption, this is simply

(26) $$\frac{R_0}{p},$$

where R_0 is the fixed nominal quantity of reserves. Correspondingly, system (13)–(15) becomes

(27) $$F(Y_0, r) = Y_0,$$

(28) $$B\left(Y_0, \frac{1}{r}\right) + U\left(\frac{1}{r}, d'\right) + \frac{R_0}{p} = 0,$$

(29) $$L(Y_0, r) = S(r, d'),$$

(30) $$G(r, d') = \frac{R_0}{p},$$

where the equations refer respectively to the markets for commodities, bonds, money, and reserves. Note that the quantity of money is not exogenous to this system, but is determined endogenously by supply function (23). Correspondingly, an expansion or contraction of bank credit (and hence money) in this model can take place only as a result of a prior change in one of the given conditions of the system.

From a somewhat unrigorous examination of the foregoing system it can be seen that any arbitrary departure of the price level from its equilibrium level will generate corrective market forces. Thus, for example, an arbitrary increase in p will decrease the real supply of reserves and thus create an excess supply of bonds in equation (28) and an excess demand for reserves in equation (30). Correspondingly, r will rise, thus decreasing the demand for commodities and driving the price level down once again. Thus the system is presumably stable.

Some of the comparative-statics properties of the system can also be readily established. Thus if the central bank were to double the volume of reserves in the system, this would increase the demand for bonds, hence temporarily depress the interest rate and thereby stimulate the demand for commodities, and hence push the price level upwards. Final equilibrium would be established at a doubled price level, but with a rate of interest and yield on reserves which had returned to their original levels. The nominal quantity of money in the new equilibrium position would, of course, also be doubled.

A similar result would obtain if the private banking system should experience a "change in tastes" which would make it willing to work with a smaller reserve ratio: if, that is, there occurs a shift in the liquidity preference of the banking system in the form of an upward shift in its demand for bonds and supply of money, while its demand for reserves shifts downwards or remains unchanged. In somewhat more familiar terms, all that the foregoing describes is a sudden expansion of bank credit which creates additional money in the system. Once again, the new equilibrium position generated by such an expansion is marked by a higher price level and nominal quantity of money, but an unchanged rate of interest. Because of the shift in the supply function of (29)—as well, possibly, as in the demand function of (30)—the rate of return on reserves will, however, generally not remain unchanged.

The invariance of the equilibrium interest rate in both the preceding cases reflects the fact that system (27)–(30) describes a pure inside-money economy in which—assuming full employment—the commodity market can be in equilibrium at only one rate of interest. Hence no exogenous change which occurs solely in other parts of the economy can affect this rate. In brief, the system is dichotomized.[39]

It is, however, clear from the analysis of Section 4 that this dichotomy would disappear if the system were also to contain government bonds. In particular, if we assume that the central bank returns to the treasury the interest on the government bonds which it holds—so that these bonds do not effectively represent a future tax liability—the net real financial assets of the private sector are then

$$\frac{kV_0^h}{rp} + \frac{kV_0^b}{rp} + \frac{V_0^c}{rp},$$

where the three terms refer to the government bonds held respectively by the nonfinancial sector, member banks, and the central bank. These net bond holdings then appear on the supply side of equation (28) and as an additional argument (representing the real-financial-asset effect described on p. 290) of the demand functions $F(\ )$, $B(\ )$, and $L(\ )$ in equations (27), (28), and (29), respectively. Correspondingly, the commodity market can be in equilibrium at an infinite number of combinations of interest rates and price levels, as exemplified by our usual *CC* curve.

This more general system has several additional properties which should be noted. First, it is obviously not a pure inside-money economy. For despite the fact that all money still consists of bank debt in the form of demand deposits, these deposits are now in part "backed" by government debt and to this extent represent outside money. To be exact, the quantity of such money in the economy equals $kV_0^b/rp + V_0^c/rp$. Second, the foregoing model gives expression to the already noted fact (p. 297) that the quantities of outside and inside money are not primary analytical entities. Thus in contrast to the situation in model (10)–(12) on pp. 296–97 above, neither of these quantities appears as a

---

[39] Cf. pp. 297–98 above.

Note, however, that this dichotomy would disappear if the nonfinancial sector also held reserves, so that the demand for commodities depended on d' as well as r (cf. end of footnote 29 above). On the other hand, system (27)–(30) reflects a second dichotomy—of quite a different nature—which would continue to prevail in this case too. In particular, the equilibrium values of r and d' would continue to be determined solely in the markets for commodities and money, while the price level is determined in the market for bonds and reserves.

separate variable of the system: the former, because it no longer coincides with the sum of net financial assets;[40] the latter, because it no longer coincides with the demand of the banking system for bonds.

Finally, a change in the quantity of reserves in the foregoing system will generally no longer have neutral effects. Such neutrality will, however, obtain if (a) there is complete discounting of the tax liability connected with government bonds (i.e., $k = 0$), and (b) these bonds are the sole asset held by the central bank. There are, of course, clear parallels between the system corresponding to these assumptions and the gold-standard system described by equations (19)–(21) above.

Let us now return to the pure inside-money economy described by equations (27)–(30). It is clear that the determinacy of the price level in this system is a consequence of our assumption that the nominal supply of reserves is fixed at R_0. The simplest way of demonstrating this is to assume instead that the central bank, just like private banks, is interested in maximizing profits, and hence provides reserves in accordance with a supply function which (as usual) depends on the alternative rates of return; that is,

$$(31) \qquad \frac{R}{p} = T(r, d').$$

Just as in the case of equation (22) above, substituting this supply function into (27)–(30) would yield a system in which the price level would not be assigned any role, and hence could not be determined.

In terms of our earlier argument (p. 303), all that this means is that since in the aggregate no other economic unit in system (27)–(30) reacts to changes in absolute prices, then, in order to assure the determinacy of the price level, the central bank must do so. This is the behavior denied by equation (31) but affirmed by equation (26). For the latter implies that the central bank's supply of real reserves is inversely proportionate to the price level. On the other hand, it is clear that this is not a necessary condition for determinacy. It suffices instead that the central bank act in accordance with any supply function for real reserves which depends on absolute prices—say,

$$(32) \qquad \frac{R}{p} = W(r, d', p).$$

[40] Note that this is also true of model (3)–(6) on pp. 289–90.

As a special case of the foregoing generalization we might consider the situation in a pure gold-standard economy. Here the central bank creates reserves by buying gold instead of bonds. Indeed its demand for gold—and hence its supply of reserves—is infinitely elastic at the absolute price of gold which it arbitrarily fixes. Correspondingly, the quantity of gold—and hence the nominal value of bank reserves in the system—is not fixed by the central bank, but is endogenously determined by the cost structure of the domestic gold industry and by the international specie-flow mechanism (which in turn depends on the relation between domestic and foreign prices).

In brief, a necessary condition for the determinacy of the absolute price level in the foregoing system (or, equivalently, a necessary condition for money to play a meaningful role in this system) is that the central bank concern itself with some money value—and in this sense be willing to suffer from money illusion. But this is a somewhat overdramatic statement of the obvious and already emphasized fact that in order for money prices to have economic significance, someone's real behavior must be dependent upon one or more of them.

The foregoing argument has been presented in a somewhat formal fashion. It is therefore worth emphasizing in conclusion that it also reflects some simple truths about monetary policy. Thus, for example, the price indeterminacy which characterizes some of the foregoing systems can be interpreted as reflecting the vicious cycle of inflation (or deflation) generated by a policy based on the "real bills doctrine." For the essence of this doctrine is that the banking system should expand credit in accordance with the "legitimate needs of business"—where these "needs" are measured in money terms, and thus increase proportionately with the price level. Correspondingly, the nominal money supply function inherent in this doctrine is also directly proportionate to the price level—as is explicit in equation (22), and implicit in equation (31). Hence the indeterminacy of the absolute price level in systems containing these equations is simply a reflection of the fact that any (say) upward price movement in such a system will—in accordance with the "real bills doctrine"—generate an increased supply of money which will enable the movement to continue indefinitely.[41]

Another—and related—interpretation of money supply function (22)

[41] For a theoretical and historical discussion of the "real bills doctrine," see L. W. Mints, *A History of Banking Theory* (Chicago, 1945), Chapter III. See also J. Viner,

is in terms of an economy with a strong labor-union movement, and with the declared policy of maintaining an absolutely continuous state of full employment. If the unions were then to disturb an initial state of equilibrium by an upward movement of the money wage rate, the monetary authorities would be forced to expand the money supply in the same proportion. In brief, in such an economy the money wage rate would be exogenously determined by the unions, while the money supply would be endogenously adapted by the monetary authorities so as to maintain full employment. This, of course, is one possible way in which the much discussed phenomenon of "cost inflation" can take place.[42]

7. THE INFLUENCE OF EXPECTATIONS

Let us now return to the analysis of Chapters X–XI and see how it is affected by taking account of expectations. Our contention is that, though these expectations must obviously affect the dynamic adjustment path of the system, they will not generally prevent it from stabilizing itself at the new equilibrium position.

In judging the reasonableness of this contention, we must emphasize that the analysis of preceding chapters deals with the effects of a once-and-for-all increase in the quantity of money. The significance of this remark can best be appreciated by noting that most of the traditionally

---

Studies in the Theory of International Trade (New York, 1937), pp. 148–54, 234–43.

It might be noted that the pressures on the monetary authorities to act in accordance with the "real bills doctrine" are likely to be strongest just at that stage of an inflationary process where the increasing price level would otherwise cause a decrease in the real supply of money which would tend to bring the process to an end. Needless to say, in its battle to offset these "disinflationary pressures" by a further expansion of the money supply, the business community would be joined by the labor unions, concerned with the possible threat to full employment. And, under certain circumstances, it might even be joined by the treasury itself. For the price rise may increase government expenditures more than tax receipts, and thus confront the treasury with a budgetary deficit.

[42] The literature on this subject is already voluminous. See, e.g., Charles L. Schultze, *Recent Inflation in the United States* (Washington, D.C., 1959), and the references there cited.

On the difficulties of distinguishing empirically between a "cost inflation" and a "demand inflation" once the inflation has proceeded for some time, see A.C. Harberger, "The Dynamics of Inflation in Chile," in *Measurement in Economics: Studies in Mathematical Economics and Econometrics in Memory of Yehuda Grunfeld* (C. Christ, *et al.*, Stanford, 1963), pp. 219–50.

cited hyperinflations have been marked by continuously increasing injections of new money into the system.[43] In the absence of such renewed injections, it does seem reasonable to assume that the negative real-balance effects of a rising price level must ultimately become strong enough to more than offset any possible speculative expansionary effects on current demand that it might generate. Individuals may anticipate further price increases; but, in the absence of adequate real money balances, they just do not have the means by which they can indefinitely increase their demands in accordance with their expectations. Hence, after a certain point, these expectations will cease to be self-justifying; and accordingly, after a still further point, they will be replaced by more stable ones which will reflect the leveling-off of prices. In brief, the presence of inflationary expectations may well make the price level rise above its new equilibrium level at some stage of the dynamic process; but the real-balance effect (or, more generally, the real-financial-asset effect[44]) will ultimately push it downwards again.

The plausibility of this argument is reinforced by the analysis at the end of Chapter VI:4 which shows that the degree to which an individual wishes to anticipate future purchases of commodities is determined not by the mere expectation that prices will rise, but by the expected rate of increase of this rise. Thus if prices should rise at a constant rate, there will be no further increase in current demand as a result of inter-temporal substitution; at the same time this demand would be subjected to the ever-growing dampening pressure of a negative real-financial-asset effect. And in this way the stability of the system would be assured.[45]

More generally, if we take account of the fact that expectations are not pulled out of the air, but are related to past price experience; and if we further assume that this relation expresses itself in the fact that the expected price is a weighted average of past ones (where the weights decline as one goes back in time)—then it can be shown that a system

---

[43] Cf. F. D. Graham, *Exchange, Prices, and Production in Hyper-Inflation: Germany 1920–23* (Princeton, 1930), pp. 104–107; Cagan, "The Monetary Dynamics of Hyperinflation," *op. cit.*, p. 26; A. J. Brown, *The Great Inflation*, p. 179.

[44] Cf. p. 290 above.

[45] The relevant macroeconomic system is described in Chapter XIV:5 below.

For simplicity, we have assumed here that the expected rate of increase equals the actual current rate. In the real world, however, the relationship is undoubtedly more complicated. See the next paragraph in the text.

stable under static expectations will remain so even after these are replaced by dynamic ones.[46] Of particular interest to us is the fact that such a stability seems to have characterized even some of the most violent of modern hyperinflations. As might be expected (pp. 144–45), the increasing rate of price increase of these inflations did cause sharp decreases in the amount of real balances demanded—and hence in the amount actually existing in these economies. But at the same time the expectations generated were not in all cases "explosive": that is, the inflationary process continued only because of the uninterrupted pumping of additional money into the system; expectations alone in these cases could not have converted the inflationary process into a self-perpetuating one.[47, 48]

[46] K. J. Arrow and M. Nerlove, "A Note on Expectations and Stability," *Econometrica*, XXVI (1958), 297–305; K. J. Arrow and L. Hurwicz, "Competitive Stability under Weak Gross Substitutability: Nonlinear Price Adjustment and Adaptive Expectations," *International Economic Review*, III (1962), 233–55.

An expectation function will meet the conditions here described if "the expected rate of change in prices is revised per period of time in proportion to the difference between the actual rate of change in prices and the rate of change that was expected" (Cagan, "Monetary Dynamics of Hyperinflation," *op. cit.*, p. 37).

See also A. C. Enthoven, "Monetary Disequilibrium and the Dynamics of Inflation," *Economic Journal*, LXVI (1956), 256–70. On the other hand, see J. Marchal, "La restauration de la théorie quantitative de la monnaie," *Revue d'économie politique*, LXIX (1959), 897–903, and E. James, *Problèmes monétaires d'aujourd'hui*, (Paris, 1963), pp. 133–34, 136–37, for the contention (which, however, overlooks the argument just presented in the text) that the existence of expectations invalidates the quantity theory.

On the definition of "static" and "dynamic" expectations, see p. 80, footnote 5 above.

[47] Cagan, "Monetary Dynamics of Hyperinflation," *op. cit*,. pp. 64–73.

[48] An additional—and fundamental—direction in which the argument of the preceding chapters should be extended is in that of providing an analysis of the monetary properties of the system under the assumption that real income is growing, instead of remaining constant. Some aspects of this question are discussed in Chapter XIV:5 below.

XIII. The Workings of the Model:
Involuntary Unemployment

1. The concept of involuntary unemployment. 2–3. A theory of involuntary unemployment. 4. Monetary theory under conditions of involuntary unemployment.

1. THE CONCEPT OF INVOLUNTARY UNEMPLOYMENT

Throughout the static and dynamic analysis of this part, one assumption has remained untouched: namely, that the economy is and remains at a position of full employment. It is high time to investigate the meaning of this assumption and the implications of dropping it.

We approach the concept "full employment" through its opposite, "involuntary unemployment." The crucial attribute of this concept is its relativity. In the absolute sense, the whole notion of "involuntariness" must disappear: for everyone "wants" to do whatever he is doing at the moment; otherwise he would not do it.[1] It is only by comparing an individual's reactions under given circumstances with his corresponding reactions under arbitrarily designated "ideal" circumstances that we are able to define the element of "involuntariness" which may

[1] I cannot help citing here the Talmudic dictum that—in certain cases of private law where the formal consent of an individual is required—the court is permitted "to coerce him until he says 'I am willing.'"

be involved. Thus our first task in defining "involuntary unemployment" is to define that behavior which is to be taken as the norm of voluntariness.

Unfortunately, a precise description of this norm is, by its very nature, an impossibility. In the present context, however, it suffices to define it in general terms as the economic behavior of an individual maximizing utility in the "normal" environment of a free, peacetime, democratic society, subject to the restraints imposed by the given market prices and his budget. An individual subjected to any additional restraints will be said to be acting involuntarily. Voluntariness, however, is not to be equated with either happiness or justice. For example, an individual acting in accordance with a severe budget restriction may be both poor and unhappy. Thus no moral approbation is necessarily attached to the maintenance of voluntariness in the sense here defined.[2]

The reader will immediately recognize that the behavior corresponding to the "normal" restraints of the preceding paragraph is precisely that behavior described by the ordinary demand and supply curves of economic analysis. Hence, as long as an economic unit is "on" such a curve, it will be said to be acting voluntarily. It follows that the individuals of a given economy cannot all be acting voluntarily at one and the same time unless the economy is in a position of general equilibrium. For, by definition, only in such a position can all the demand and supply functions of the economy simultaneously be satisfied. Conversely, in such a position no one will be acting involuntarily. Indeed, for classical and neoclassical economists, this was precisely the beauty of the equilibrating process of a free market economy. This was the harmony of interests and compatibility of desires achieved by the "invisible hand" which guided such an economy.[3]

The application of this general definition to the specific problem at hand is immediate: The norm of reference to be used in defining involuntary unemployment is the supply curve of labor; for this curve shows the amount of employment which the workers of the economy want to obtain in the light of the money wage, price level, and budget restraints with which they are confronted. Hence as long as workers are "on their

[2] Cf. F. H. Knight, *The Ethics of Competition* (New York, 1935), pp. 45–58.
[3] This is the harmony of the Paretian optimum. Its full social significance cannot, of course, be judged apart from considerations of distributive justice. See end of preceding paragraph and reference there cited.
The notion of involuntariness will be discussed further at the end of Section 3.

supply curve"—that is, as long as they succeed in selling all the labor they want to at the prevailing real wage rate—a state of full employment will be said to exist in the economy. It follows that a state of general equilibrium in the economy as a whole, or even a state of partial equilibrium in the labor market by itself, is *ipso facto* a state of full employment. It also follows that the bench mark of full employment is not an absolute constant, but something which itself varies with every change in the real wage rate or in the subjective or objective determinants of the labor supply curve. Chapter XII:2 has already provided us with an example of this variability.

Conversely, if workers are not on this curve, they are acting involuntarily. Thus, if they are at the point A in Figure XIII-1 (a reproduction of Figure IX-1), involuntary unemployment to the extent $N_3 - N_1$ exists. On the other hand, if they are at the point E, there exists involuntary *over*employment to the extent $N_0 - N_2$. Such a situation prevails when, for example, wartime workers are exhorted by patriotic appeals to work longer hours than they would normally choose.

Thus, by definition, the extent of involuntary unemployment is identical with the extent of the excess supply of labor which exists at the prevailing real wage rate. It follows that if the terms are understood in their usual, strict sense, the coexistence of involuntary unemployment and flexible money wages precludes the existence of equilibrium. For "flexibility" means that the money wage rate tends to fall with excess supply, and "equilibrium" means that nothing tends to change in the system. Hence, by definition, the foregoing "coexistence theorem" must be true.

But like any other theorem which is tautologically true, this one too is uninteresting, unimportant, and completely uninformative about the real problems of economic analysis. It tells us nothing about the nature of the forces which generate unemployment. It tells us nothing about the relationship between the height of the real wage rate and the existence of unemployment. It tells us nothing about the proper policies to follow in order to combat unemployment. And—most important of all—it tells us nothing about the central question which divides classical and Keynesian economics: the efficacy of an automatically functioning market system with flexible money wages in eliminating involuntary unemployment. It is to this question that we now turn.[4]

[4] For textual proof that Keynes' references to "unemployment equilibrium" were

2. A THEORY OF INVOLUNTARY UNEMPLOYMENT

Assume that the position of full-employment equilibrium described in Chapter IX is disturbed by a downward shift in the consumption or investment functions. Let this be represented in Figure XIII-2 (a reproduction of Figure IX-3) by the movement of the aggregate demand curve

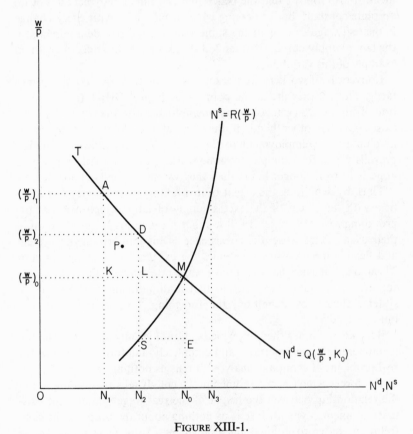

FIGURE XIII-1.

not intended as denials of this innocuous tautology, but were simply based on a usage of "equilibrium" which differs from the usual one—see Note K:3.

From this we can see that much of the heated and still continuing debate on whether there can or cannot be a state of "unemployment equilibrium" is a sterile terminological debate which never would have started had either side bothered to define its terms precisely.

from E to E_2. This movement creates a deflationary gap in the commodity market equal to BC. Our task now is to examine the nature of the self-corrective market forces which this initial disturbance sets into operation. For simplicity, we shall deal with a pure outside-money economy; the argument can, however, readily be generalized to an

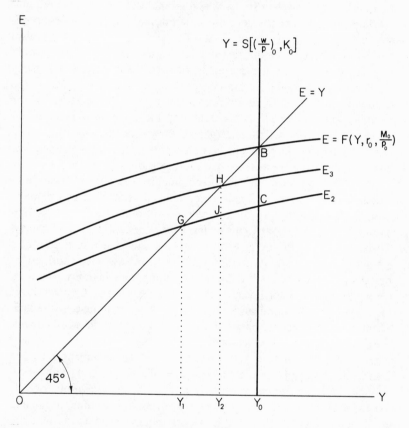

FIGURE XIII-2.

economy with both outside and inside money, as well as interest-bearing government debt, as described on p. 307. In this case the term "real-balance effect" in what follows should be understood as referring to the analogous real-financial-asset effect.

To the extent that the decreased demand for commodities is accompanied by and finances an increased demand for bonds, an excess demand is created in the latter market, driving the rate of interest down. This, in turn, reacts back on the commodity market and tends to push the aggregate demand curve up again. Here is the familiar classical and neoclassical mechanism by which an increase in savings flows into the loan market, thereby depresses interest, and thus stimulates an offsetting increase in investment. It should be noted that this mechanism will operate even if the obverse side of this increase in savings should consist initially of an increase in the demand for money, without any shift whatsoever in the demand for bonds. In this case, however, the decline in interest must await the impact on the bond market of the positive real-balance effect generated by the downward pressure on prices of the initial deflationary gap. Clearly, in addition to providing this indirect stimulus through the bond market, the real-balance effect also stimulates the commodity market directly.

Thus the downward shift in the commodity demand function automatically creates market forces which tend to offset it. If this demand is sufficiently sensitive to these forces, it will quickly return to a full-employment position at a lower level of wages, prices, and interest. Throughout this period of adjustment there will exist a state of excess supply in the commodity market. But due to the assumed shortness of this period, producers will react to their temporary inability to sell by simply permitting their inventories to build up. That is, they will leave their level of production unchanged at Y_0. This, of course, is the tacit assumption on which we have heretofore analyzed the effects of a downward shift in commodity demand.[5]

Once this assumption is dropped, the whole argument must be drastically modified. In the absence of sufficient interest- and price-elasticity, the adjustment process becomes a long, drawn-out one. It cannot then realistically be assumed that firms will continue producing at an unchanged level, for this would require them to accumulate inventories at ever increasing levels. Hence they must eventually take some step to bring current output—and consequently current input—into line with current sales. And this is the beginning of involuntary unemployment.

[5] Namely, in the case of an increase in liquidity preference in Chapter X:4 and in the case of an increase in the propensity to save on p. 270.

We must now translate this common-sense conclusion into the more precise terms of our model. Unfortunately, this translation can be neither simple nor immediate. For though it is obvious that there must be some connection between the firms' output of commodities and their input of labor, this connection is not explicit in our demand function for labor in Figure XIII-1.[6] Indeed, to all outward appearances, this function depends only on the real wage rate, and not on the volume of output. Furthermore, it must be emphasized that this absence of an express dependence on the volume of output is not a property peculiar to our function, but one that holds for any labor demand function derived in the standard way from the principle of profit maximization. Nevertheless, if we look more closely into the tacit assumptions on which this standard derivation is based, we shall find the vital dependence that we seek.

In particular, our demand function for labor describes the behavior of firms maximizing profits within a framework of perfect competition. This means that the planned labor input it specifies for any given real wage rate reflects the firms' assumptions *that they will be able to sell all of their resulting output at the prevailing market price.* Hence any development in the commodity market which invalidates this crucial assumption must also invalidate these plans. In particular, the continued forced accumulation of unsold outputs described above must eventually make firms drop both their assumption of an unlimited market and, consequently, their plans for labor inputs as described by the demand curve in Figure XIII-1. In other words, the accumulation of these unsold inventories must in some sense eventually cause a leftward shift of this demand curve. Thus the influence of commodity output on labor input reflects itself, not in the *variables* on which the labor demand function is dependent, but in its *form*.

More specifically, the influence of commodity output on labor input expresses itself in our model through the dynamic intermarket pressures discussed at the end of Chapter X:2. As will be recalled from that discussion, if individuals do not succeed in buying all they want of a given good, they will use part of the unspent funds that accumulate in their hands to bid up the prices of other goods as well. Similarly, if

---

[6] But it is explicit in the commodity supply function when written in the form $Y = \phi[Q(w/p, K_0)]$, where $\phi(\ )$ is the production function, and $Q(\ )$ is the demand function for labor; cf. equation (12) on p. 210.

firms do not succeed in selling all they want of a given good, they will attempt to alleviate their resulting shortage of funds by reducing the prices of other goods as well. The application of this principle to the case at hand is immediate. As a result of the initial decrease in demand, a "glut" is created on the commodity market. In particular, we see from Figure XIII-2 that firms' sales fall short of their Y_0 output by BC units. The pressure of this excess output then causes firms to bid down not only the price of commodities, but also the price of labor. Indeed, this pressure manifests itself in a most concrete way. For when firms planned the inputs of labor described by the demand curve in Figure XIII-1, they assumed that they would be able to pay for these inputs with the sales proceeds of the resulting outputs. Therefore, when these sales fail to materialize, firms find themselves with their funds tied up in illiquid inventories and hence financially unable to carry out their original plans.[7] Accordingly, for the input of labor N_0 they now offer a real wage rate below that indicated by the demand curve of Figure XIII-1; or, alternatively, at the real wage rate $(w/p)_0$ they now demand a smaller input.

Thus the initial decrease in commodity demand causes a corresponding decrease in the input of labor. Clearly, the magnitudes of these decreases must be related. In particular, assume that as a result of the market pressures just described, firms find themselves at the point L in Figure XIII-1. That is, at an unchanged real wage rate their labor input consists of N_2 units instead of N_0. Let the corresponding commodity output [as given by the production function $Y = \phi(N, K_0)$ of p. 203] be Y_2 in Figure XIII-2. Then we can see from this diagram that the firms' output will still exceed their sales by HJ units. Hence the same market pressures of excess output and accumulating inventories which pushed labor input down from N_0 to N_2 will continue to push this input even further downwards. Only when this input has been reduced to N_1, with a corresponding reduction in output to Y_1, will these pressures cease; for only then will firms finally succeed in selling all that they produce.

In this way the economy is brought to a position described by the point K in Figure XIII-1 and its corresponding point G in Figure XIII-2. But what must now be emphasized is that this position is *not* one of equilibrium: for at point K there is an excess supply of labor, $N_0 - N_1$,

---

[7] I am indebted for this observation to Mr. Nissan Liviatan.

which continues to press down on the money wage rate, and at point G there is an excess supply of commodities, $Y_0 - Y_1$, which continues to press down on the price level.

The nature of both these dynamic pressures requires further clarification. Consider first the point G. Even though this point is not marked by an excess of *output*—firms are selling all they are producing—it is marked by an excess of *supply*. That is, despite the fact that firms have decreased their *actual* output to Y_1, the fact remains that the *optimum* output they *desire* to supply at the real wage rate $(w/p)_0$—*should the market be willing to absorb this output*—is still Y_0. In other words, since the real wage rate has, by assumption, remained unchanged, so has the vertical commodity supply curve. Hence at the point G there is an excess of desired over actual supply equal to $Y_0 - Y_1$ units of commodities. This manifests itself as an excess in the productive capacity of firms. And this idle capacity continues to induce firms to lower their prices in an attempt to increase their volume of sales and thereby return to the optimum output designated by their commodity supply curve.[8]

Consider now the point K in Figure XIII-1. At first sight, $N_0 - N_1$ would seem to represent an excess demand for labor as well as an excess supply, for K is just as much to the left of the demand curve as to the supply curve. Accordingly, the point K would seem to be associated just as much with an upward pressure on the money wage rate as a downward one! But this absurdity is removed as soon as we recall that at the present stage of the analysis the demand curve in Figure XIII-1 does *not* describe the actual behavior of firms; hence the input of labor which this curve specifies—N_0—is *not* really that which firms now attempt to purchase. On the other hand, nothing has happened to invalidate the supply curve of Figure XIII-1 as a description of the actual behavior of workers. Hence the point K is effectively marked only by an excess supply of labor.

[8] Once again, I am indebted to Mr. Liviatan for calling my attention to the possible role of excess productive capacity in the dynamic process.

It might be useful at this point to remind the reader about the dual meaning of "Y" in Figure XIII-2. As related to the demand side of the commodity market, it represents the alternative levels of real national *income* which may *actually prevail* in the economy. As related to the supply side, it represents the alternative optimum levels of real national *product* which firms *desire* to produce at different real wage rates. Accordingly, the numbers $Y_0, Y_1, Y_2, \ldots$ on the X-axis of Figure XIII-2 represent now the former, now the latter—and now simply the output of firms, whether optimum or not.

Nevertheless, this simultaneous departure of K from both the demand and supply curves does seem unduly bizarre. But a moment's reflection shows that it really expresses another simple—though usually neglected —fact. Specifically, it expresses the involuntariness with which firms, no less than workers, must be acting during periods of unemployment. For just as the latter are then not receiving as much employment as they would normally like at the prevailing real wage rate, so the former are not providing as much as they would normally like. Both firms and workers are being coerced by the same *force majeure* of insufficient demand in the commodity market. Both are thereby being prevented from achieving their optimum mode of behavior. In particular, the involuntary departure of firms from their labor demand curve as revealed by point K in Figure XIII-1 is the simple counterpart of their involuntary departure from their commodity supply curve as revealed by point G in Figure XIII-2. Not being able to sell all they want, they cannot employ all they want. This is the neglected obverse side of involuntary unemployment.

We might, however, note that at the point K there no longer exist the unsold inventories and resulting illiquidity which we used above to explain why the input of labor is pushed leftwards from the points M and L of Figure XIII-1. Nevertheless, the pressures of these unsold inventories continue to exist in potentiality. For should firms attempt to increase their input beyond N_1, they will immediately re-create these inventories and hence will be pushed back again to point K.

It might help to represent these ideas graphically by saying that as long as the demand conditions in the commodity market continue to be described by the curve E_2 in Figure XIII-2, the corresponding "demand" conditions in the labor market are described by the kinked curve TAN_1 in Figure XIII-1. Though this is not a demand curve in the strict sense of the term, it does make clear that the input of labor is—under these conditions—effectively limited to N_1 units. Correspondingly, it underlines the fact already noted that the solid demand curve of Figure XIII-1 no longer describes the behavior of firms and that, accordingly, no effective excess demand for labor exists at the point K.

Alternatively, such a kinked demand curve underlines the fact that at the point K the marginal product of labor is *not* represented by N_1A and hence does *not* exceed the real wage rate N_1K. In brief, the kink at point A emphasizes that should firms increase their input beyond

N_1, they will not be able to sell the resulting additional output. Hence the marginal product of labor at this point is indeterminate.[9]

We can now return to our main discussion and emphasize that it is within the foregoing framework of dynamic disequilibrium—and resulting downward pressures on both the price level and the money wage rate—that we must study the problem of involuntary unemployment. This is the real import of the innocuous tautology of the preceding section: not that involuntary unemployment can be defined away, but that it can have no meaning within the confines of static equilibrium analysis. Conversely, the essence of dynamic analysis is involuntariness: its domain consists only of positions *off* the demand or supply curves. Indeed, it is this very departure from these curves, and the resulting striving of individuals to return to the optimum behavior which they represent, which provides the motive power of the dynamic process itself.

Thus our first task in studying involuntary unemployment is to free ourselves of the mental habit—long ingrained by the methods of static analysis—of seeing only the points *on* the demand or supply curve. Once we do this, we find ourselves able to give precise expression to many intuitive, common-sense ideas which have all too frequently been unjustifiably rejected as violating the precepts of rigorous economic analysis. First we see that involuntary unemployment can exist even

[9] There is, nevertheless, a basic analytical problem here whose full solution is still not clear to me: The kink in the curve TAN_1 is one that exists from the viewpoint of the economy as a whole; but, by definition of perfect competition, this kink cannot be taken into account by any individual firm. Now, as already emphasized, at the point K there no longer exist the liquidity pressures of unsold inventories. What, then, keeps each individual firm from expanding its input until it reaches its demand curve for labor?

The answer may be that already implied in the text: each firm does indeed attempt to do this, but some of them then find themselves with unsold inventories which force them to contract input again. Thus K does not represent a static situation, but one in which there are always some firms expanding input and output, and others contracting —though, as long as commodity demand conditions remain unchanged, never in the aggregate succeeding in moving to the right of K.

Another possibility is that these repeated frustrating experiences lead firms to disregard completely their ordinary demand curves as guides to optimum behavior. But this then leaves the question as to how they do determine their behavior. It may be that, as Mr. Liviatan has suggested, a complete answer to this question depends on the development of a theory of the firm operating under conditions of uncertainty with respect to the size of its market.

For references to some recent attempts to deal with the foregoing logical difficulty, see p. 670 below.

in a system of perfect competition and wage and price flexibility. In particular, the departure of K from the labor supply curve reflects the existence of involuntary unemployment to the extent $N_0 - N_1$. Second, we see that a deficiency in commodity demand can generate a decrease in labor input without requiring a prior increase in the real wage rate. For since the point K is not on the demand curve for labor either, it is not bound by the standard inverse relation between labor input and the real wage rate which this curve specifies.[10] Both of these implications will be discussed further in the next chapter.

3. A Theory of Involuntary Unemployment (Continued)

As just emphasized, the position represented by point K in Figure XIII-1 and point G in Figure XIII-2 is not an equilibrium one. In particular, the excess supplies of the two markets described by these diagrams reinforce each other in exerting a downward pressure on both wages and prices. Let us assume for the moment that these decline in the same proportion (so that the real wage rate is not affected) and examine the implications of this movement for the magnitude of involuntary unemployment.

As explained at the beginning of the preceding section, this price decline creates a positive real-balance effect which exerts both a direct and (through its depressing effect on interest in the bond market) indirect upward pressure on the aggregate demand curve for commodities. Assume that as a result of these pressures this curve rises to, say, E_3 in Figure XIII-2. If firms continued with their output of Y_1, they would find their inventories being drawn down below the desirable level. Hence, by the reverse of the argument of the preceding section, they will increase their labor input above N_1 and, accordingly, their commodity output above Y_1. Clearly, this process will continue until employment has risen to N_2 and output to Y_2. At these levels there will once again be neither a deficiency nor an excess of actual output—though, as we shall emphasize in a moment, this output is still less than that which firms would like to produce.

This possibility of an automatic decrease in the extent of involuntary unemployment is what is denied by the usual oversimplified statement

[10] It might be noted that this inverse relation characterizes the Keynesian theory of employment no less than the classical. Cf. the *General Theory*, pp. 17–18.

of the Keynesian position. According to it, any attempt of firms to increase their labor input to N_2 would result in an output Y_2, which could not be sold. Indeed, at such an output there would, in Figure XIII-2, be a deflationary gap of HJ which would compel firms to reduce output and, accordingly, input until they had once again returned to Y_1 and N_1, respectively.[11] This argument is clearly based on the tacit assumption that the aggregate commodity demand curve remains unchanged at E_2. In brief, here, as elsewhere, Keynesian economics overlooks the direct influence of the real-balance effect on this demand.[12] Similarly, it overlooks the supply side of the commodity market which, by its excess over the demand, generates this effect.

Leaving this doctrinal issue behind, we now apply the argument of the preceding section to show that the dynamic process cannot stop at the stage represented by the output Y_2 and input N_2. For with the real wage rate unchanged at $(w/p)_0$, there is still at the point L in Figure XIII-1 an excess supply of labor exerting a downward pressure on wages. Similarly, there is still at the point H in Figure XIII-2 an excess of desired over actual supply of commodities; for since the real wage rate has remained unchanged, so too has the vertical supply curve at Y_0. Hence there remains an excess supply of $Y_0 - Y_2$ (which manifests itself once again in the form of excess productive capacity) exerting a downward pressure on the price level.

Let us continue with our assumption that wages and prices always decline in exactly the same proportion. Then the dynamic process in its entirety can be summarized in the following terms: The initial decrease in commodity demand creates a state of involuntary unemployment. But it also generates a price decline and a consequent real-balance effect which—both directly and indirectly—tends to force this demand up again. As the demand curve rises, it pulls commodity output up after it. And this pulls labor input up concurrently. In particular, as output is pulled diagonally upwards along the 45° radius vector in Figure XIII-2, input is pulled correspondingly rightwards along the horizontal dotted line corresponding to the unchanged real wage rate $(w/p)_0$ in Figure XIII-1. In this way the extent of involuntary unemployment is continuously diminished.

[11] Cf. *General Theory*, pp. 261–62.
[12] See Note K:1 and p. 339, footnote 9 below. On the overlooking of the supply side, see end of Note N:1.

If this process is successful, it will continue until the aggregate demand curve is raised sufficiently to be able once again to absorb the output Y_0. That is, it will bring the economy once again to point B in Figure XIII-2. The resulting disappearance of the excess supply of commodities will have two simultaneous effects. First, it will eliminate the downward pressure on the price level which previously emanated from this market. Second, it will eliminate the dynamic cross-pressure on the labor market which prevented firms from being on their demand curve there. That is, since firms will be able to sell Y_0 units of commodities, they will be willing once again to employ the N_0 workers represented by the point M on the demand curve in Figure XIII-1. Hence involuntary unemployment will disappear from this market and with it the downward pressure on the wage level. Thus both activating forces of the preceding dynamic process will be removed. Correspondingly, the economy will have been brought to a new equilibrium position. By definition (p. 315)—and like any other over-all equilibrium position—this position is one of full employment. It differs from the original one only in having lower levels of wages, prices, and interest.[13]

The essential nature of this equilibrating process is not changed if wages and prices do not initially fall in the same proportion. The major difference will be that the real wage rate, and hence the commodity supply curve, will no longer remain constant during the period of adjustment. This means that the system will pass through such points as P in Figure XIII-1. Consider, however, the special case in which the price decline that raises the demand curve in Figure XIII-2 to E_3 is accompanied by a wage decline which lags behind just sufficiently to raise the real wage rate to $(w/p)_2$. At this rate nothing prevents firms from employing the N_2 units specified by the demand curve in Figure XIII-1. For, as can be seen from Figure XIII-2, the conditions of demand in the commodity market are such that firms will be able to sell the full output of Y_2 corresponding to the input of N_2.

In brief, under these assumptions the economy will reach the position described by the point D in Figure XIII-1 and the point H in Figure XIII-2. What distinguishes this position from the one described in the preceding section is that the commodity market is no longer in disequilibrium. For, as already indicated, the rise in the real wage rate

---

[13] For a diagrammatic presentation of that part of this argument which deals with the commodity market, see final paragraph of this chapter.

has decreased the optimum output of firms. In particular, it has shifted the vertical supply curve as a whole from Y_0 leftwards to Y_2 (a movement *not* shown in Figure XIII-2).[14] Hence there is no excess of either actual or desired output in the commodity market. In other words, there is neither excess output nor excess capacity: firms are producing and selling exactly the optimum output corresponding to the real wage rate $(w/p)_2$. Hence no downward pressure on prices emanates from this market.

On the other hand, the labor market is obviously *not* in equilibrium. In particular, the involuntary unemployment (excess supply of labor) which exists at the real wage rate $(w/p)_2$ will continue pressing the money wage rate downwards. This will reduce the real wage rate, thereby push the optimum labor input and hence the commodity supply curve rightwards again, and thereby renew the downward pressure of excess capacity on the price level. The real-balance effect resulting from the price decline will then renew the upward push on the aggregate demand curve. In this way the economy will once again be propelled back toward the same full-employment equilibrium position of the preceding case. The primary effect of the initial "stickiness" in money wages will thus be a prolongation of the dynamic adjustment process into which the economy is thrown by the initial decrease in demand.

Consider now the opposite case in which the wage rate falls faster than the price level, so that the labor market is brought, say, to the point S in Figure XIII-1. Here, by definition, full employment prevails. But this reduction in the real wage rate has shifted the vertical supply curve in Figure XIII-2 to the right of Y_0 (again, not shown in the diagram) and has thereby increased the pressures of excess capacity in the commodity market. Hence the price level will continue to fall, the real wage rate will accordingly rise, and involuntary unemployment will accordingly be re-created. In this way the economy will continue moving toward its over-all equilibrium position.[15]

If, however, either the wage rate or the price level is absolutely rigid,

[14] For further details on such shifts, see p. 211.

[15] The preceding argument has assumed throughout that an excess supply of labor always causes a decline in the wage rate. In the real world, however, nominal wages begin to rise after unemployment falls to a certain level. This, indeed, is one of the characteristics of cost inflation. For an extension of the foregoing analysis to this case, see A. P. Lerner, "On Generalizing the General Theory," *American Economic Review*, L (1960), 133–42.

this dynamic process cannot work itself through to a successful culmination. In particular, if there were absolute wage rigidity, the process described two paragraphs above would be arrested at the point D in Figure XIII-1 and its related point H in Figure XIII-2. Because of the failure of the real wage rate to fall below $(w/p)_2$, firms would have no inducement to expand input and hence output. Correspondingly, the commodity supply curves would not shift rightwards again. Similarly, if the price level were absolutely rigid, there could be no real-balance effect to stimulate aggregate demand either directly or indirectly. Hence there would be no force to pull output and input back to their full-employment levels. Thus as long as either of these rigidities prevails, the system must remain in a state of unemployment disequilibrium.

The argument of this chapter can now be summarized in the following terms: Equilibrium means full employment, or, equivalently, unemployment means disequilibrium. Hence our study of the corrective market forces automatically generated by the presence of involuntary unemployment is a study of the dynamic workings of an economy in disequilibrium. And the assumption made until now, that, granted flexibility, these forces will restore the economy to a state of full employment, is an assumption that the economy is consistent and stable; that, in other words, an equilibrium position always exists and that the economy will always converge to it. More specifically, it is an assumption that just as the market can "solve" the system of excess-demand equations in Chapter X:1 when the level of real income is held constant during the *tâtonnement*, so can it solve it when the level of real income (and hence employment) is also permitted to vary. This is the conceptual framework within which we must analyze the problem of involuntary unemployment.

4. MONETARY THEORY UNDER CONDITIONS OF INVOLUNTARY UNEMPLOYMENT

Deferring further examination of the case of flexible wages and prices to the next chapter, let us now analyze a case of absolute rigidity which has special importance for monetary theory. Assume that such a rigidity has persisted from the very inception of the dynamic process. Then after the downward shift in demand from E to E_2 in Figure XIII-2 has brought the economy to the position described by point G in this diagram and its related point K in Figure XIII-1, no corrective force will operate to move it back to a full-employment position again. More specifically, whatever reduction in interest has been directly caused by the increased demand for bonds which may have accompanied the decreased demand for commodities is already reflected in the curve E_2. And, in the absence of a price decline, there will be no real-balance effect to exert any further influence—direct or indirect—upon it.[16]

Into an economy in this position let us now introduce an increase in the quantity of money or a neutral decrease in liquidity preference. Either of these changes generates an upward shift in the commodity demand curve and rightward and leftward shifts, respectively, in the bond demand and supply curves. This causes a fall in the rate of interest, which pushes the aggregate demand curve even further upwards. Assume that as a result of both of these pressures the demand curve is raised to the position represented by E_3 in Figure XIII-2. Accordingly, just as in the preceding section, firms will increase their commodity output to Y_2 and hence their labor input to N_2. That is, the economy will move to—and remain at—the position described by point L in Figure XIII-1 and point H in Figure XIII-2.

Thus we have here a form of comparative-statics analysis—with the difference that neither the initial nor final position is one of general equilibrium. In particular, our "comparative-statics" theorem states that if we begin from a situation of involuntary unemployment, and if wages and prices are absolutely rigid, then an increase in the quantity of money—or a neutral decrease in liquidity preference—causes an increase in real national product and employment and a decrease in the rate of interest. Clearly, this result holds for a Keynesian decrease in liquidity preference as well.[17]

The argument can, of course, be presented alternatively in terms of the money market. As in Chapter XI:1, write the equilibrium condition of this market in the special form

$$(1) \qquad p \cdot L_1(Y) + p \cdot L_2(r) = M_0,$$

where p is now assumed constant. A doubling of the quantity of money

---

[16] Cf. beginning of Section 2 above.

[17] Cf. p. 248 above. Note the tacit assumption that the increase in real income increases demand and supply equally in the bond market; cf. pp. 281–82. Note also that a change in the quantity of money affects interest whether used to finance budgetary expenditures or open-market operations; cf. Chapter XII:4.

will cause an increase in the transactions demand through its effect in raising real income, Y. But—to paraphrase Keynes—there is clearly no reason to expect these increases to absorb all of the additional money. In terms of Figure XI-1 they will shift the demand curve over from position I to II and the supply curve over from $M^s = M_0$ to $M^s = 2M_0$, leaving the excess supply EF. Hence part of the monetary increase will find an outlet in the purchase of securities. And these purchases will continue until they have depressed the rate of interest sufficiently to bring about such an increase in the speculative demand that it, together with the increase in the transactions demand brought about by the rise in real income, suffices to absorb all the new money. This new equilibrium position is represented in Figure XI-1 by the intersection of demand curve II with the supply curve $M^s = 2M_0$ at the rate of interest r_3.[18]

The analysis of this section can be instructively summarized in terms of a diagram which is conceptually analogous to Figure XI-2.[19] Let us first construct the general-equilibrium system of equations which corresponds to our present set of assumptions. This can be set out as follows:

Condition for Equilibrium   *Market*

(2) $F\left(Y, r, \dfrac{M_0}{p_0}\right) = Y$ Commodities,

(3) $H\left(Y, \dfrac{1}{r}, \dfrac{M_0^H}{p_0}\right) = J\left(Y, \dfrac{1}{r}, \dfrac{M_0^F}{p_0}\right)$ Real bond holdings,

(4) $L\left(Y, r, \dfrac{M_0}{p_0}\right) = \dfrac{M_0}{p_0}$ Real money holdings.

---

[18] I have deliberately phrased the discussion here to parallel that on pp. 278–79 above in order to bring out the similarities and differences of the two interpretations of the same passage in the *General Theory* (p. 200) which they respectively offer. This passage by itself is sufficiently ambiguous to admit of either interpretation. But, as implied on p. 279 above, the evidence of cognate passages makes it clear that the interpretation presented there is the one which really identifies the crucial element in Keynesian interest theory. For further discussion, see Chapter XV below.

[19] The following diagrammatic analysis is adapted from the well-known one which Hicks first presented in his "Mr. Keynes and the 'Classics': A Suggested Interpretation," *Econometrica*, V (1937), as reprinted in *Readings in the Theory of Income Distribution*, ed. W. Fellner and B. F. Haley (Philadelphia, 1946), p. 469. Cf. also Modigliani, "Liquidity Preference," *op. cit.*, pp. 198–204.

Here we have dropped the special form of the demand function for money specified in (1) and returned to the general one of Chapter IX:5. The basic differentia of the foregoing system—as contrasted with that of Chapter X:1—is that Y and p have reversed their roles: the former is now a variable and the latter a constant. Because of this assumed absolute price—and wage—rigidity, we also ignore the labor market, which, as already noted, is assumed to remain unchanged in a state of disequilibrium. Similarly, we ignore the aggregate supply function in the commodity market, which no longer can cause the price level to vary. Correspondingly, the "equilibrium" in the commodity market is one of *output*, not of *supply* (p. 321). For simplicity, we have also rewritten the bond and money equations of Chapter X:1 in real terms.

Consider now the commodity market and assume it to be in a state of equilibrium of the type just described. Let real national product, Y, now increase. Because of the assumed less-than-unity marginal propensity to spend, this increases the demand for commodities by a smaller amount. Hence an excess output is created in the commodity market. In order to restore equilibrium to this market, demand must therefore be stimulated by a decrease in interest. We can in this way generate the curve GG in Figure XIII-3. This curve is the diagrammatic representation of equilibrium condition (2): it is the locus of all pairs of r and Y at which the commodity market can be in equilibrium. By the argument just presented, it must have a negative slope throughout.[20]

At any point to the right of GG, there is an excess of output, hence an accumulation of unwanted inventories, and hence a pressure on firms to decrease their output. Conversely, at any point to the left of GG, there is an excess of demand, hence a drawing down of inventories below their optimum level, and hence a pressure on firms to increase their output. These dynamic pressures are represented by the horizontal arrows of Figure XIII-3.

Let us now turn to the bond market and assume it also to be in an initial state of equilibrium at the rate of interest r_0. Let Y now increase. Under the assumption that this increases the demand and supply for

---

[20] Except for the fact that the X-axis represents real—and not money—income, this is Hicks' *IS* curve; for, as emphasized in Chapter XI:6, the savings = investment condition (from which Hicks derives his curve) is equivalent to the equilibrium condition in the commodity market.

bonds equally, the state of equilibrium in this market continues undisturbed at the unchanged rate of interest r_0. Hence the curve *PP*—which represents the locus of all equilibrium points in the bond market—is a horizontal line at the corresponding height. This line is, of course, the diagrammatic representation of equilibrium condition (3) under our stated assumption. At any point above *PP*, there is an excess

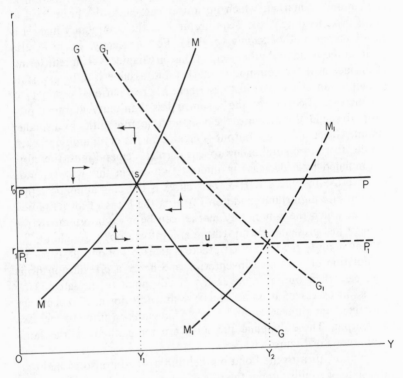

FIGURE XIII-3.

demand for bonds, driving the rate of interest down again; at any point below, an excess supply, driving it up. These dynamic pressures are represented by the vertical arrows of Figure XIII-3.

Finally, *MM* in Figure XIII-3 is the diagrammatic presentation of equation (4): it is the locus of points at which the money market can be

332

in equilibrium. Its positive slope represents the fact that an increase in Y increases the amount of money demanded for transactions purposes; hence in order to maintain equilibrium in this market this increase must be offset by an increase in interest.[21] By Walras' Law, the curve MM must also pass through the point s.[22] Furthermore, if the dynamic assumptions with respect to MM are consistent with those just made with respect to GG and PP,[23] the directions of the arrows in Figure XIII-3 remain as depicted.

The intersection of GG, PP, and MM at point s indicates the rate of interest and level of real national income—r_0 and Y_1—which can simultaneously equilibrate the commodity and bond markets. The arrows of Figure XIII-3 then show us that there always exist automatic market forces to drive at least one of the variables in the direction of its equilibrium value. Hence the system is stable and converges to the equilibrium point s.[24]

The curves GG, PP, and MM correspond to the initial quantity of money M_0. Let this now be increased to $2M_0$. Then GG shifts upwards to, say, G_1G_1: at any given level of real income, the rate of interest must be higher in order to eliminate the inflationary gap otherwise created by the positive real-balance effect of the monetary increase. Similarly, this real-balance effect causes PP and MM to shift downwards to, say, P_1P_1 and M_1M_1, respectively. The intersection of G_1G_1, P_1P_1, and M_1M_1 at point t then indicates the new equilibrium position

[21] This curve is identical in conception with Hicks' LL. But unlike his curve, ours does not have a horizontal section near the Y-axis. This is a direct consequence of the fact that—in contrast to Hicks'—our demand curve for money does not become a horizontal line at a minimum rate of interest, but instead retains its negative slope throughout (p. 223). On the other hand, it is clear from the construction of PP that it cannot fall below this minimum rate in Figure XIII-3.

These points will be further discussed in Chapter XIV:3, where it will be shown that the foregoing difference in the presentation of LL is not really a substantive one.

[22] Actually, this application of Walras' Law is not at all self-evident: for the existence of an excess supply in the labor market means that there can exist excess demands elsewhere in the system, so that all three curves need not pass through s. We can, however, dodge this difficulty by attributing to workers a completely passive behavior pattern according to which they adjust their planned supply of labor to the amount demanded by employers. Hence, by definition, "equilibrium" always exists in the labor market.

For further discussion of this point, see my "Liquidity Preference and Loanable Funds," *op. cit.*, pp. 314–15.

[23] Cf. Chapter XI:3.

[24] For a more rigorous demonstration, see Mathematical Appendix 10:a.

corresponding to the lower rate of interest r_1 and the higher level of real national income Y_2. It can also be shown that an equivalent increase in money via open-market operations will depress interest even more.[25]

Figure XIII-3 can also be used to analyze the effects of shifts in liquidity preference. Thus the effects of a Keynesian decrease in liquidity preference is represented by a downward shift in *PP* and a rightward shift in *MM*, while *GG* remains unchanged. Hence the new equilibrium position is marked once again by a lower rate of interest and higher real national income.[26]

We might now note that the variability of the equilibrium rate of interest in the analysis of the present section, as compared to its invariance in the case of flexible prices, has a heuristic explanation. In the latter case, an increase in the nominal quantity of money does not in the long run affect its real quantity; hence it does not permanently affect the rate of interest. In the present case, however, because of the price rigidity, the real quantity does permanently increase; hence the rate of interest must generally be affected. From this we can see that to the extent that the price level rises instead of remaining fixed, the effect of a monetary increase on interest and employment is accordingly diminished. In any event, it is clear that the assumptions of the present section carry us into a Keynesian world of unemployment in which monetary changes express themselves primarily in changes in the level of real national income and the rate of interest, and only secondarily —if at all—in changes in the level of prices.

We note finally that Figure XIII-3 can also be used to illustrate the argument of the preceding section. Assume for this purpose that wages and prices are once again flexible, and that Y_1 represents a position of unemployment. Then the downward pressure on the price level that will exist at point *s* will generate positive real-balance effects that will shift the *GG* and *MM* curves rightwards and the *PP* curve downwards. This process will continue until the system returns to the full-employment position (say) Y_2.

---

[25] Cf. Mathematical Appendix 10:*a*, equations (10.18)–(10.19).

[26] Note that this result obtains even if there is no real-balance effect in the commodity market; cf. p. 251, footnote 18 above.

XIV. Keynesian versus Classical Theories of Employment: An Interpretation

1. KEYNESIAN AND CLASSICAL THEORIES OF INVOLUNTARY UNEMPLOYMENT

Let us now develop the argument of the preceding chapter into an analytical framework for interpreting the debate between Keynesian and classical theories of employment.

As the reader has undoubtedly noticed, the stable dynamic process assumed to operate in Chapter XIII:3 is, in a significant sense, the counterpart of the one described in Chapter X:3. In both instances the price movement itself ultimately eliminates the pressures (of inflation or deflation—as the case may be) which initiated it. It is precisely this necessity for a major price decline in the present case which makes this process unacceptable as a primary ingredient of a modern full-employment policy.[1]

Let us, then, temper this process by supplementing it with the traditional discretionary open-market and rediscounting operations of a central bank. The immediate implication of such operations is that a

---

[1] This will be discussed further below.

decline in the rate of interest need no longer wait, as it did in Chapter XIII:2, for a decline in prices. Instead, open-market purchases replace the real-balance effect as the source of increased demand in the bond market. In this way, by primary reliance on a manipulated lowering of the rate of interest, aggregate demand might be raised to its full-employment level without any prior decline in prices. Indeed, in this Wicksellian world, such a decline would itself be taken as evidence that the rate of interest had not been lowered sufficiently.[2]

It is the belief in the efficacy of this monetary policy which will be identified here with the neoclassical position. Correspondingly, it is the denial of this efficacy which will be identified with the Keynesian one. According to this position, the great degree of uncertainty which surrounds any investment plan makes it unlikely that interest variations of a practical magnitude can be depended upon to stimulate such activity significantly.[3] Hence, though working in the proper direction, interest reductions are too weak to justify the reliance placed upon them by monetary policy. For this reason such a policy will not be able to close a deflationary gap with the speed necessary to prevent a protracted price decline.

Thus the success of monetary policy depends ultimately on the stability of the dynamic process initiated by this decline. This brings us back to the analysis of Chapter XIII:3. But now—in order to present the Keynesian position in its entirety—we shall have to introduce into this analysis two hitherto neglected factors.[4]

There is, first of all, the question of distribution effects. As emphasized in Chapter XII:3, we cannot assume that the negative indebtedness effects of debtors are simply canceled by the positive effects of creditors. More specifically—and in Keynes' words—"if the fall of wages and prices goes far, the embarrassment of those entrepreneurs who are heavily indebted may soon reach the point of insolvency,—with severely adverse effects on investment." In brief, a protracted price

---

[2] *Interest and Prices*, pp. 189 *et passim*.

[3] On this insensitivity, see Oscar Lange, *Price Flexibility and Employment* (Bloomington, Ind., 1945), p. 85, and the references to empirical studies there cited. For an excellent theoretical discussion, see G. L. S. Shackle, "Interest Rates and the Pace of Investment," *Economic Journal*, LVI (1946), 1–17. See also Hicks, *Value and Capital*, pp. 225–26.

[4] The following interpretation of Keynes takes as its point of departure the stimulating discussion of L. R. Klein, *The Keynesian Revolution* (New York, 1947), pp. 80–90, 206–13.

decline will cause a wave of bankruptcies which will eliminate both the firms' liabilities and the households' assets, and leave only a seriously impaired state of business confidence.

Second, there is the influence of expectations. To the extent that the monetary authorities reduce interest only by slow stages, potential investors may delay carrying out their plans in anticipation of benefiting from still lower rates. Similarly, the decline in prices and wages may create the expectation of still more rapid declines, and thus lead both households and firms to postpone their purchases. Furthermore, the anticipation of a lower future price level has the same effects on the amount of labor demanded as a rise in the current real wage rate. For, in making their plans, firms will compare the wage paid for current input with the lower price that will subsequently be received for its resulting output. Due to these factors, the stimulating real-balance effect of a price decline may be more than offset by its depressing expectation effects.[5]

The contrast between the present emphasis on expectations and their deemphasis in Chapter XII:7 can be justified. In Chapter XII:7 we were concerned with an inflationary process. Hence there was reason to believe that the continuous contraction in the real quantity of money held by individuals would ultimately make it impossible for them to finance the increased demand for goods called for by their expectations, and would thus eventually compel them to modify these expectations themselves. No such restrictive—and hence corrective—influence operates in the case of deflationary expectations; for the passive postponement of expenditures encouraged by them does not have to be financed. This asymmetry is analogous to the one frequently emphasized in connection with the activities of a central bank: the attempts of such a bank to combat inflation by contracting member-bank reserves are more likely to succeed than its attempts to combat deflation by expanding them.

Thus Keynesian economics is the economics of unemployment

---

[5] This and the preceding paragraph are largely adapted from Keynes' discussion in the *General Theory* of the effects to be expected from a protracted decline in money wages and prices. See, in particular, *ibid.*, pp. 205–8, 232–34, and 260–69. The quotation in the preceding paragraph is from p. 264.

Note that though in comparing future with present prices it is the *rate* of decline which is relevant (Chapter VI:3 above), in comparing future prices with the present wage rate it is the *level* of these prices that must be considered.

*dis*equilibrium. It argues that as a result of interest-inelasticity, on the one hand, and distribution and expectation effects, on the other, the dynamic process of Chapter XIII:3—even when aided by monetary policy—is unlikely to converge either smoothly or rapidly to the full-employment equilibrium position. Indeed, if these influences are sufficiently strong, they may even render this process unstable. In such a case the return to full employment would have to await the fortunate advent of some exogenous force that would expand aggregate demand sufficiently.

A more extreme possibility is that, even without taking into account the discouraging effects of adverse expectations, the stimulating effects of interest and price declines may be too weak ever to generate an aggregate demand strong enough to absorb the output of full employment. That is, these effects may succeed only in raising the aggregate demand curve asymptotically to a less-than-full-employment level. This will be true if the indefinitely increasing real balances generated by the decreasing price level are dissipated to an ever increasing extent in the money market—until, indeed (by the budget restraint), the real demand in this market becomes infinite.[6] Such a possibility involves a denial of the hitherto unquestioned assumption that our basic system of excess-demand equations in Chapter X:1 is consistent. In other words, it contends that, apart from all dynamic considerations, there may exist no set of wages, prices, and interest that can simultaneously equilibrate all the markets of this system. Note that in the limit this contention rests on the unreasonable assumption that the wealth effect in the form of the real-balance effect does not influence all markets in a similar fashion (above, p. 242). Note too that the inconsistency which it proposes is operationally equivalent to the instability of a consistent system: in neither case do the dynamic forces of the economy succeed in bringing it to an equilibrium position; but in the former case this failure is inherent in the simple fact that no such position exists.[7]

[6] Cf. p. 352, footnote 27 below. The reason the increase in real balances cannot alternatively find an infinite outlet in the bond market will become clear from that discussion.

In terms of Figure XIII-3, the argument of the text implies that GG asymptotically approaches some intermediate position leftward of G_1G_1. For further details see Mathematical Appendix 10:b below.

[7] Note the economic interpretation this paragraph gives to an inconsistent system. Such a system can be described by one of the following three equivalent statements: It is impossible for everyone simultaneously to be on his demand and/or supply curve. It is impossible for everyone simultaneously to act voluntarily. It is impossible

But it is not necessary to go to either of these analytical extremes. As already indicated, even if monetary policy could definitely restore the economy to full employment, there would still remain the crucial question of the length of time it would need. There would still remain the very real possibility that it would necessitate subjecting the economy to an intolerably long period of dynamic adjustment: a period during which wages, prices, and interest would continue to fall, and—what is most important—a period during which varying numbers of workers would continue to suffer from involuntary unemployment. Though I am not aware that he expressed himself in this way, this is the essence of Keynes' position. This is all that need be established in order to justify his fundamental policy conclusion that the "self-adjusting quality of the economic system"—even when reinforced by central-bank policy—is not enough.[8]

This interpretation forces upon Keynesian economics the abandonment of the once-revolutionary "diagonal-cross" diagram with which it swept its way into the textbooks. It compels it to recognize that this diagram takes account neither of the supply side of the commodity market nor of the real-balance effect which its excess over the demand side generates. It therefore compels it to concede that (in terms of Figure XIII-2) the intersection of the aggregate demand curve E_2 with the 45° diagonal at G does not imply that there exist no automatic market forces to push real income up from the unemployment level Y_1. Indeed, it compels it to accept the classical contention that such forces not only exist, but even succeed eventually in raising income to the full-employment level Y_0.[9]

---

for the system ever to be in equilibrium; for there must always exist excess demands or supplies to propel it away from whatever position it happens to be at.

[8] *General Theory*, pp. 266–67 and 378. These passages are cited in full in Note K:3.

[9] These limitations of the standard Keynesian diagram have already been noted on pp. 324–25. On its overlooking of the supply side, see again end of note N:1.

One might be tempted to rationalize Keynes' neglect of the real-balance effect—or, more generally, real-financial-asset effect—on the grounds that he was concerned with a pure inside-money economy without government bonds [cf. pp. 297 and 305–307]. I do not, however, believe that textual evidence can be adduced in favor of this conjecture (cf. p. 635). More important in the present context, there is no reason to restrict the Keynesian argument in this way; for, as we have just seen, its essential point holds for an economy in which outside-money—and hence a real-balance effect—also exist. And, as implied above (p. 317), a corresponding generalization can be made, *mutatis mutandis*, for an economy which also has government bonds.

But this narrowing of the analytical distance between Keynesian and classical economics does not generate a corresponding narrowing of the policy distance. It still leaves Keynes insisting that the inefficacy of the automatic adjusting process is so great as to be remediable only by a program of direct government investment in public works. And it still leaves modern-day adherents of the classical view conceding the inefficacy of monetary policy by itself, but insisting that it need only be supplemented by an automatic system of contracyclical tax remissions and transfer payments.[10] In brief, our interpretation takes the debate on the degree of government intervention necessary for a practicable full-employment policy out of the realm of those questions that can be decided by a priori considerations of internal consistency and logical validity, and into the realm of those questions that can be decided only by empirical consideration of the actual magnitudes of the relevant economic parameters.[11]

While our interpretation takes off the analytical edge of Keynesian economics in one direction, it sharpens it in another, more vital one. It makes unmistakably clear—what should always have been clear[12]— that the involuntary unemployment of the *General Theory* need *not* have its origin in wage rigidities. Indeed, in this respect we are more Keynesian than Keynes. For by unequivocally placing the center of emphasis on the inadequacy of aggregate demand in the commodity market, and by recognizing the resulting involuntary unemployment to be a pheno- menon of economic dynamics, we have freed ourselves from the neces- sity of static analysis to connect decreases in employment with increases in the real wage rate. We have been able to explain the existence of

[10] Thus contrast the *General Theory*, p. 378, with the views of the "Chicago school" as expressed by H. C. Simons, *Economic Policy for a Free Society* (Chicago, 1948), pp. 40–77, 160–83; L. W. Mints, *Monetary Policy for a Competitive Society* (New York, 1950); Milton Friedman, *Essays in Positive Economics* (Chicago, 1953), pp. 133–56.

[11] For a survey of relevant empirical studies, see Johnson, "Monetary Theory and Policy," *op. cit.*, pp. 365–77. See also Michio Morishima and Mitsuo Saito, "A Dynamic Analysis of the American Economy, 1902–1952," *International Economic Review*, V (1964), 138–51, and Franco Modigliani, "Some Empirical Tests of Monetary Management and of Rules versus Discretion," *Journal of Political Economy*, LXXII (1964), 211–45.

In this connection see also the empirical evidence on the real-balance effect cited in Note M below, which shows that the elasticity of consumption with respect to the price level is low, and may well be less than 0.10 (see especially p. 660 below).

[12] For supporting references, see Note K:3.

involuntary unemployment without placing any restrictions on the movement of the real wage rate.[13] Conversely, we have shown that reductions in this rate are neither a necessary nor a sufficient condition for the rapid reestablishment of full-employment equilibrium in the economy.

Correspondingly, our interpretation does not tie the Keynesian theory of unemployment to any special form of the supply function for labor. In particular, it is independent of the all-too-frequent assumption that this theory presupposes a supply curve for labor as represented in Figure XIV-1. The crucial characteristic of this curve is that it remains infinitely elastic at the prevailing—and presumed rigid—money wage rate w_0 until the point N_0. Accordingly, writers who make use of this curve identify the maximum amount of employment that workers are willing to offer at the rate w_0 with the level of "full employment," and define involuntary unemployment as the difference between this level and the one actually existing in the economy, say N_1.[14]

In fact, one cannot escape the impression that Figure XIV-1 is another reflection of the ingrained habit already mentioned (p. 323) of seeing only the points *on* the supply curve. More specifically, the line of reasoning which brought writers to posit a supply curve of the shape specified in Figure XIV-1 seems to have been the following: If the curve did not have this shape, but instead always rose (no matter how slowly), and if at every wage rate workers were always at the uniquely corresponding point upon the curve, then, by definition, no involuntary unemployment could ever exist in the system: workers would always be receiving as much employment as they desired at the prevailing wage rate. Hence in order to be able to speak of such unemployment and yet retain the assumption that workers are on their curve, it is necessary to drop the habitual assumption that the supply curve is single-valued and to represent it, instead, as specifying more than one amount supplied at a given wage rate. Involuntary unemployment can then be defined as the difference between two points—both of which lie on the same supply

[13] As pointed out on p. 324, footnote 10, Keynes does accept this restriction; cf. *General Theory*, pp. 17–18.

[14] Cf., e.g., Modigliani, "Liquidity Preference," *op. cit.*, p. 189. This also seems to be Keynes' view in the *General Theory*, pp. 8–9, 295, 301–3, and 336. In any event, it is definitely the way Lange interprets him (*Price Flexibility and Employment*, p. 6, footnote 4).

curve and correspond to the same wage rate. This is clearly the significance of the horizontal line segment $N_1 N_0$ in Figure XIV-1.

Correspondingly, once we free ourselves of this inhibition against seeing points *off* the supply curve, and once we recognize that the essence of involuntary unemployment is, indeed, being off this curve, the necessity for positing any special shape of the labor supply curve in order to be able to speak of involuntary unemployment disappears. This should be clear from the whole argument of Chapter XIII:1–3.

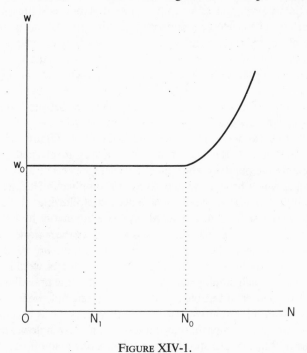

FIGURE XIV-1.

This is not to say that money wage rigidities do not aggravate the depth and duration of involuntary unemployment. Clearly—as the analysis at the end of Chapter XIII:3 shows—they do. But it is to deny that such rigidities are logically necessary for the genesis or even persistence of involuntary unemployment. And it is to deny that even the complete absence of such rigidities would assure the elimination of this unemployment within a socially acceptable period of time.

Nevertheless, our theory does depend on rigidities. For, by definition, any system which fails to respond quickly and smoothly to equilibrating market forces is suffering from rigidities. But the offending rigidities are not those of extraneous monopolistic elements interfering with the otherwise smooth functioning of a capitalist economy, but those inherent in the very fact that the level of aggregate commodity demand in such an economy is the resultant of individual decisions to consume and to invest, and that these decisions respond only "stickily" to market changes in interest and prices. They are the rigidities of sovereign consumers and investors unwilling to modify their expenditure habits on short notice.

2. THE MULTIPLIER

The preceding interpretation omits two familiar elements of Keynesian economics: the multiplier and the "liquidity trap." With the aid of some modifications, the first of these, as we shall now see, can be introduced into the argument. Similarly, we shall in the next section see the proper meaning that can be attached to the "trap."

We must first distinguish between the "instantaneous" multiplier of comparative-statics analysis and the "successive-period" multiplier of dynamic analysis.[15] The former describes the outcome of a conceptual experiment in which we take an economy at rest in an initial position of unemployment; exogenously inject into it a *permanent* increase in, say, annual government expenditure (that is, one that will continue to remain in force for every future year too); permit this change to work itself out in all its manifestations until the economy once again reaches a position of rest; and then compare the increase in the level of annual national income as between the new and original positions (denoted by ΔY) with the exogenous increase in annual government expenditures (denoted by ΔG).

The graphical technique by which the formula for this multiplier can be derived is quite familiar. Consider the description of the commodity market in Figure XIV-2, where, for simplicity, the aggregate demand curves are assumed to be straight lines. Let the initial position of this curve be represented by E_4. The intersection of this curve with the 45°

[15] For a clear discussion of this distinction, see Haberler, *Prosperity and Depression*, pp. 456–58, and the references to J. M. Clark and F. Machlup there cited.

radius vector determines the initial level of real income in this economy, *OA*. Assume now that the government component of aggregate demand is suddenly increased by *GH* units. This pushes up the aggregate demand curve to E_5, generates accordingly the new intersection point *F*, and thereby determines the new level of real income *OC*, which is *AC* units greater than the preceding level.

The comparative-statics multiplier is the ratio of these two increases. Specifically, it is

(1)
$$\frac{\Delta Y}{\Delta G} = \frac{AC}{GH} = \frac{1}{\dfrac{GH}{AC}} = \frac{1}{\dfrac{JF}{AC}} = \frac{1}{\dfrac{DF - DJ}{AC}} = \frac{1}{1 - \dfrac{DJ}{AC}},$$

or

(2)
$$\frac{\Delta Y}{\Delta G} = \frac{1}{1 - \text{the marginal propensity to spend}}.$$

Here we have made use of the parallelism of E_4 and E_5 to equate *GH* and *JF*, and of the 45° angle of the radius vector to equate *AC* and *DF*. In this way we obtain the standard formula expressed by (2). This shows the traditional greater-than-unity multiplier that is a direct consequence of a marginal propensity to spend that lies between 0 and 1.

Strictly speaking, however, this multiplier has no place in our model. It is part and parcel of the Keynesian "diagonal-cross" analysis that has already been rejected (p. 339). Specifically, by ignoring the supply side of the market, this analysis overlooks the fact that neither point *G* nor point *F* is one of equilibrium. Thus it applies the concepts and techniques of comparative statics to a case where they are not really valid. More specifically, it fails to show that even without the assistance of an adventitious increase in government expenditures, automatic market forces will continuously be pushing the level of real income upwards from its original *OA* level.[16]

To diagnose this difficulty is to suggest the cure. A valid framework for this multiplier within our model can be created by resorting to the pseudo comparative statics of Chapter XIII:4. In particular, if we assume that both wages and prices are absolutely rigid, then the economy will have no automatic tendency to move away from either

[16] Yet another misleading aspect of this multiplier will be discussed in Section 4 below.

of its unemployment positions *G* or *F*. Hence comparisons such as those conceived by the instantaneous multiplier can be made.

It should, however, be emphasized that even under these assumptions the preceding formula will usually prove to be oversimplified. Thus, for example, it does not take into account that changes in government

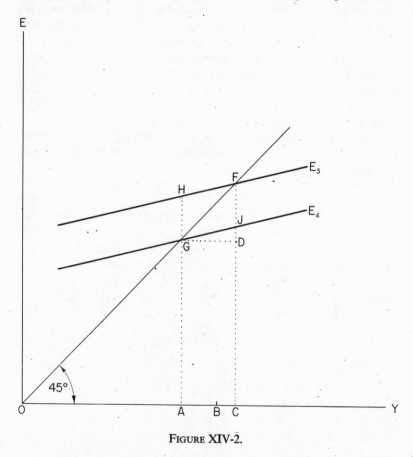

FIGURE XIV-2.

expenditure might also affect the rate of interest and hence the level of aggregate demand. Nor does it allow for the possible direct—and discouraging—effect of increased government expenditures on the private propensity to spend—and the propensity to invest in particular.

More generally, there is no such thing as "the" multiplier. Every model has its own multiplier. And this can be greater or less than unity—or even negative—in accordance with the assumptions of the model.[17]

Consider now the dynamic successive-period multiplier. This is based on a completely different conceptual experiment. Once again we begin with an exogenous increase in government expenditures; but this time it is assumed to be a once-and-for-all increase during one year only. We then trace through the expansionary effect of this increase on the real incomes of all subsequent years. Finally, the multiplier is defined as the ratio between the aggregate value of the latter increase and the value of the initial one.

The standard derivation of the formula for this multiplier starts from the assumption that individuals' expenditures during one year are determined by their incomes of the preceding one. Indeed, the expenditure function is assumed for simplicity to have the linear form

$$(3) \qquad E_t = a + bY_{t-1},$$

where E_t represents real expenditures in year t, Y_{t-1} represents real national income in year $t-1$, and a and b are constants. Assume now that the government makes a once-and-for-all increase of R dollars (of constant purchasing power) in its expenditures of goods and services. This causes the real income of the initial year to grow by R dollars. By (3), it also causes an increase of bR in real expenditures—and hence real income—in the next year. And this in turn causes an increase in real expenditures of $b(bR) = b^2R$ in the following year, and so on. Hence the final result of the initial increase of R dollars is to increase real national income over all years by

$$R + bR + b^2R + b^3R + \cdots + b^nR + \cdots$$
$$= R(1 + b + b^2 + b^3 + \cdots + b^n + \cdots)$$
$$(4) \qquad = R \cdot \frac{1}{1-b}.$$

---

[17] Some instructive examples have recently been provided by Martin J. Bailey, *National Income and the Price Level* (New York, 1962), pp. 71–80. See also A. S. Goldberger, *Impact Multipliers and Dynamic Properties of the Klein-Goldberger Model* (Amsterdam, 1959), Chapters III and V, for quantitative estimates of various multipliers in the U. S. economy.

By definition, the formula for the dynamic multiplier is then obtained by dividing through by R to yield

$$(5) \quad \frac{R \cdot \dfrac{1}{1-b}}{R} = \frac{1}{1-b} = \frac{1}{1 - \text{the marginal propensity to spend}},$$

which is seen to be identical with the formula for the comparative-statics multiplier in equation (2) above.

There is, of course, nothing coincidental about this identity. For consider our comparative-statics experiment. As already emphasized, this assumes that the government increases its expenditures relative to those of the original equilibrium position, not only in the first year, but in each and every subsequent one as well. Hence, in the year when equilibrium is finally reestablished, real income is at a higher level, first, because of the increase of R dollars in government expenditures during that year; second, because of the increase of R dollars in government expenditures during the preceding year—which causes income in the final equilibrium year to be higher by bR; third, because of the increase of R dollars in government expenditures two years earlier—which causes income in the final equilibrium year to be higher by $b(bR) = b^2 R$; and so on. Thus the total increase in real income between the two equilibrium positions can be decomposed into precisely the same geometric series presented in equation (4). Hence the comparative-statics multiplier, like the dynamic one, must be the sum of this series divided by R.

From this it is also clear that formula (5) is subject to the same reservations already voiced in connection with formula (2). What interests us now, however, is not the exact magnitude of the dynamic multiplier, but its general conceptual validity for our model. We therefore emphasize that since the dynamic multiplier is not dependent on the assumption of equilibrium, it can be introduced into our model with much less difficulty than the comparative-statics one. All that must be remembered is that part of the increase in income which occurs after the once-and-for-all increase in government expenditures cannot be ascribed to this increase, but to the automatic equilibrating process of the economy, which would in any case operate to push the level of income upwards. Thus the dynamic multiplier can be credited only with those income increases which would not have occurred in the absence of the government's "pump-priming."

Graphically, we can conceive of this multiplier in our model in the following terms: The curve *KLQN* in Figure XIV-3 shows what would have happened to the level of real national income over time had the economy been subjected to a sudden decrease in demand at time t_0, and had it then been required to work this deflationary pressure off through the automatic equilibrating process. By way of contrast, the curve *KLM* shows the corresponding time path of real national income

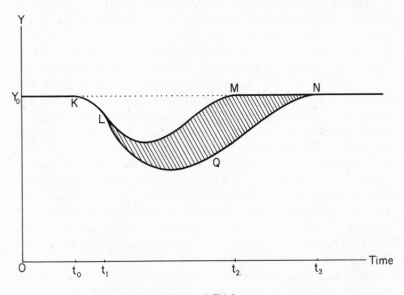

FIGURE XIV-3.

had the government "primed the pump" by a once-and-for-all expenditure at time t_1. It shows how this expenditure speeds up the equilibrating process and brings the economy to full employment at time t_2 instead of t_3. The real national income whose potential loss this government expenditure has prevented is thus represented by the shaded area in Figure XIV-3, and the multiplier is accordingly measured by the ratio between this income and the original once-and-for-all expenditure.[18]

[18] This diagram abstracts from the fact that by time t_2 or t_3 the full-employment level of income will have risen.

3. THE "LIQUIDITY TRAP"

Noticeable by its omission from the preceding interpretation of Keynesian economics is the contention that there is a minimum level below which the rate of interest cannot fall—the "liquidity trap." If this contention were true, then—completely aside from the question of interest-inelasticity which we have emphasized—monetary policy would be confronted with an absolute limitation on its powers to stimulate economic activity. Keynes himself did not seem to attach much importance to this possibility.[19] But later critics—both sympathetic and adverse—have raised it to a key position in the Keynesian argument.[20]

These critics rationalized this limitation by ascribing a special form to their demand curve for money. In particular, they assumed this curve to become an indefinitely extending horizontal line at that minimum level at which "almost everyone prefers cash to holding a debt which yields so low a rate of interest."[21] Accordingly, they presented this curve as in Figure XIV-4 and argued that it demonstrated the impossibility of driving interest below r_1.

Now, as has been emphasized in Chapter IX:5, this cannot be the form of the demand curve for money in the ordinary sense of the term.[22] For when due account is taken of the individuals' planned behavior in all markets, this curve must retain its negative slope throughout.[23] In particular, the amount of money demanded cannot become infinite unless the supply of bonds does so; but, as shown on p. 126 above, the presence of uncertainty makes it irrational even for a "bear" to supply such an infinite amount.[24] Nevertheless, as we shall now see, there is a

[19] *General Theory*, pp. 203 and 207.

[20] Cf., e.g., J. R. Hicks, "Mr. Keynes and the 'Classics,'" *op. cit.*, pp. 469–70; Modigliani, "Liquidity Preference," *op. cit.*, pp. 196 and 198–99; A. H. Hansen, *A Guide to Keynes* (New York, 1953), pp. 132–33.

[21] *General Theory*, p. 207.

[22] The reason for this proviso is explained in footnote 27 below.

[23] Note, however, the discussion on pp. 225–26 above of the conditions under which our demand curve could also have a horizontal segment.

[24] See also p. 225, footnote 19 above.

To these a priori considerations can now be added the empirical findings of Bronfenbrenner and Mayer (*op. cit.*, pp. 831–33) and Meltzer (*op. cit.*, p. 245), who fail to find evidence that the elasticity of demand for money increases as the rate of interest declines. See, however, the dissenting opinion of Robert Eisner in his exchange with the foregoing writers in *Econometrica*, XXXI (1963), 531–50. See also the criticisms by Bronfenbrenner and Mayer (*op. cit.*, pp. 812–13) and by Johnson ("Monetary Theory and Policy," *op. cit.*, p. 354) of the early, influential study by

very real limitation on the downward influence that monetary policy—
in its usual sense—can exert on the rate of interest. But it is a limitation
that flows from the significance of the minimum rate r_1 in the bond
market, and not in the money market.[25]

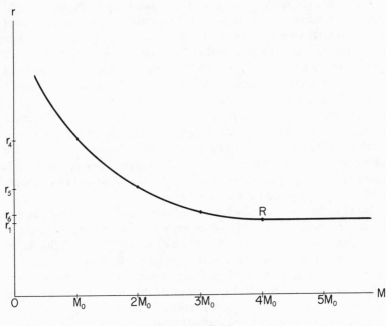

FIGURE XIV-4.

In order to show this let us revert to the analysis of absolute wage and
price rigidity under conditions of unemployment as presented in Chapter
XIII:4 above. In this analysis, an increase in the quantity of money
permanently shifts the demand curve for bonds rightwards and the supply curve leftwards and thus reduces the equilibrium rate of interest.[26]
In terms of Figure XIV-5, the successive increases in the quantity of

---

Tobin which found evidence of a "trap" ["Liquidity Preference and Monetary
Policy," *Review of Economic Statistics*, XXIX (1947), 130–31].

[25] Cf. Chapter IX:4, particularly Figure IX-4 (p. 214).

[26] The term "equilibrium" is applied to the case of rigidities subject to the reservations already noted in the pseudo "comparative-statics" analysis of p. 329 above.

money from M_0 to $2M_0$, $3M_0$, and $4M_0$ shift the demand and supply curves from position *I* to *II, III,* and *IV,* respectively, and thus cause the point of equilibrium to move from *A* to *B, C,* and *D,* respectively.

Figure XIV-5 also reflects the crucial additional assumption that as the demand curve for bonds shifts upwards, its intersection point with the vertical axis approaches the price $1/r_1$ as a limit. That is, no matter

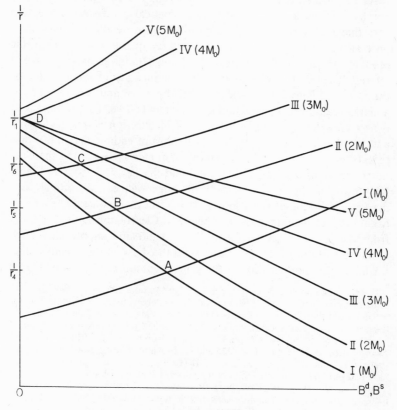

FIGURE XIV-5.

how large the value of their initial money holdings, individuals will never agree to hold bonds at a rate of interest below r_1. At such low rates they will always prefer to hold money instead (see p. 215). At the same time, the higher the initial money holdings of firms, the less pressed they are to borrow, and the lower, accordingly, the maximum rate of interest they are willing to pay. It follows that after the monetary expansion has reached a certain point—$4M_0$ in our diagram—the bond market will become inactive: no borrower will be willing to pay the minimum rate of interest on which lenders insist. This situation is represented by the demand and supply curves of position V.

As the reader has undoubtedly realized, the two preceding paragraphs describe a market-experiment identical in general conception with that of Chapter XI:4, though differing in details. In particular, once again we are exogenously changing the quantity of money in the economy and noting the effects of this change on the equilibrium rate of interest. The results of this conceptual experiment can be represented by the curve of Figure XIV-4—now cut off at point R and considered to be a market-equilibrium curve, and not a demand curve. That is, this curve is now considered to be the locus of all intersection points of demand and supply curves in Figure XIV-5. Its abrupt ending at point R thus reflects the fact that when the quantity of money exceeds $4M_0$, there are no transactions taking place in the bond market described by Figure XIV-5, so that the rate of interest is no longer defined. Accordingly, our market-equilibrium curve also reflects the fact that monetary expansion cannot reduce the rate of interest below r_1. Clearly, this limitation flows from the assumed properties of the demand and supply curves for bonds; it therefore holds no matter what the shape of the demand curve for money.[27] Alternatively, in the general-equilibrium terms of Figure

[27] Returning now to the proviso mentioned in footnote 22 above, I would like to suggest that Keynesian economists have not been referring to the demand curve in the usual sense of the term, but to a curve generated by changes in the quantity of money, thus see the references to such changes in Hicks, *Trade Cycle*, pp. 141–42; Modigliani; "Liquidity Preference," *op. cit.*, pp. 198–99; Joan Robinson, "The Rate of Interest," *Econometrica*, XIX (1951), 101–102; and R. F. Kahn, "Some Notes on Liquidity Preference," *The Manchester School*, XXII (1954), 247. These writers might, then, have had in mind the market-equilibrium curve of Figure XIV-4.

Alternatively, they may have been thinking of a demand curve generated by increasing the individual's *initial endowment* of money and asking him what the rate of interest would have to be in order to be willing to hold this increased quantity. Now, at the minimum rate r_1 there is no real-balance effect in the bond market; nor (according to the usual Keynesian assumption) is there ever such an effect in the commodity market; it follows that at the rate r_1 the real-balance effect expends itself entirely on increasing the demand for money, so that the curve which describes the outcome of this experiment becomes a horizontal line at r_1 (see p. 514 below).

I doubt, however, if this is a proper interpretation of Keynesian thinking, for the notion of a real-balance effect in the demand function for money is quite foreign to it

XIII-3, this limitation reflects the assumption that—regardless of the shape of *MM*—the curve *PP* cannot be driven below r_1.

At the same time, it is clear from Figure XIII-3 that even if monetary policy cannot drive interest below r_1, the economy will not remain "trapped" at a less-than-full-employment level (denoted, say, by point *u*). For this policy also creates a real-balance effect which shifts *GG* rightwards until full employment is reached (cf. p. 334 above).[28] This, however, does not negate the "Keynesian Revolution," but only requires us to interpret it as in Section 1 above. Indeed, since this interpretation is free of the special assumptions on which the "liquidity trap" is based, it actually increases the generality of the Keynesian theory of unemployment.

It must now be emphasized that the foregoing limitation on monetary policy exists only in the case where the increased quantity of money is generated by deficit financing. For such an increase can then influence the bond market only through its being spent there by individuals; and individuals refuse to buy at prices greater than $1/r_1$. But once the monetary increase is generated by open-market purchases, this limitation obviously disappears. For then the government need not wait for individuals, but can enter the bond market itself and bid up bond prices as high as it wants. In brief, government, unlike individuals, is not inhibited by liquidity considerations; hence it is willing to hold bonds even at rates of interest below r_1. It follows that if the government is willing to pursue a sufficiently vigorous open-market policy—one that encompasses private as well as government bonds—there is no reason why it should not be able to drive interest down as low as it wants.

But things are not quite so simple. By driving interest down below the "minimum" rate, the government also drives all private individuals

---

(cf. above, p. 254). Note too that this interpretation is inconsistent with any attempt to interpret Keynes in terms of a pure inside-money economy (see above, p. 339, footnote 9). Clearly, it is also inconsistent with our view of the real-balance effect as a wealth effect operating in a similar fashion in all markets (above p. 242).

[28] It is this rightward shift in *GG* which is overlooked by Hicks in his discussion of the "liquidity trap" in "A Rehabilitation of 'Classical' Economics?," *Economic Journal*, LXVII (1957), 286–8. For further details, see my "Keynesian Economics Rehabilitated: A Rejoinder to Professor Hicks," *Economic Journal*, LXIX (1959), 584–85.

Note that the argument of the text holds even if we accept the Keynesian presentation of the "liquidity trap" and assume accordingly that the *MM* curve in Figure XIII-3 has the shape P_1tM_1.

out of the bond market. In brief, it succeeds in pushing interest below the level at which "almost everyone prefers cash to holding a debt" only by itself becoming the sole debt-holder—and, by that very fact, the sole lender—in the economy. It thus negates the whole institutional meaning of a policy designed to enable government to influence the over-all level of activity in the economy with a minimum of direct intervention.

Thus there is a limitation on the ability of monetary policy to reduce interest. But it is a limitation which originates in political, and not economic, factors. Furthermore, it is highly unlikely that this limitation has ever yet endangered the efficacy of monetary policy.[29] These conclusions hold even in the special case of a money demand curve with a horizontal segment (Figure IX-7b). Here, too, only political limitations would prevent the government from choosing (if necessary) any desired rate of interest between r_1 and zero and then offering loans at this rate to firms desirous of undertaking investment.

Before leaving this subject we might digress briefly to note that the minimum rate of interest in the foregoing sense is not an absolute constant, but reflects instead the public's state of expectations at the point of time in question. Since these expectations, in turn, are based on historical experience, it follows (somewhat paradoxically) that the minimum rate of interest—which is frequently considered to be the keystone of a Keynesian *monetary* theory of interest—can more appropriately be interpreted as reflecting a *real* phenomenon: namely, the fact that the productivity of capital has historically been higher than (say) 2 per cent, so that when interest falls to the neighbourhood of this level the public anticipates a subsequent rise and acts accordingly.[30]

---

[29] Keynes' presentation of this view has already been cited in footnote 19 above. In this context it might be noted that even during the British "cheap-money" episode of 1931–39 the monetary authorities never acquired more than 15 per cent of outstanding government securities [see E. Nevin, *The Mechanism of Cheap Money* (Cardiff, 1955), p. 180]. A similar statement holds for the Federal Reserve authorities in the United States [see *Banking and Monetary Statistics* (Washington, D.C.: Board of Governors of the Federal Reserve System, 1943), p. 512, Table 149]. In view of this fact—and the general deflationary situation existing in the thirties—it is difficult to believe that the monetary authorities then could not have driven interest down even further by increasing their holdings of government securities. Cf. also Nevin, *op. cit.*, pp. 73–74, 96–98, 113; and F. W. Paish, "Cheap Money Policy," *Economica*, XIV (1947), 167–68.

[30] "Unless reasons are believed to exist why future experience will be very different from past experience, a long-term rate of interest of (say) 2 per cent leaves more to

In the light of these considerations we should expect that the powers of monetary authorities to drive interest down within the normal framework of open-market operations will be greatest in times of protracted unemployment and deep depression. For then the dangers of inflation (which might cause a reversal of policy) do not exist, while the stagnation of industry makes the productivity of capital only a dim memory. If the public can see the return of prosperity only as a vague eventuality, and if the monetary authorities make it clear that in the intervening period they will persist in their cheap money policy, then there would seem to be good chances for its success.[31]

At the other extreme we have the case of an economy operating in the shadow—or in the reality—of full-employment boom conditions. Even under such circumstances the government may be interested in promoting a cheap-money policy; for example, it may in this way want to achieve a more equal distribution of income. But in this case it is unlikely that the public will be willing to believe that the monetary authorities will not ultimately have to take account of the inflationary consequences of their policy. It is also unlikely that the relative scarcity of real capital that usually exists under such circumstances will permit the public to accept the view that a low rate of interest can be maintained. Correspondingly, it is unlikely that monetary authorities could succeed much in depressing interest under these conditions.[32]

4. Say's Identity Again

Just as there are some familiar elements missing from our interpretation of Keynes, so are there some missing from our interpretation of the classics. In particular, Section 1 above has presented the classical position without even a mention of Say's Identity.

The usual macroeconomic interpretation of this identity is that,

---

fear than to hope, and offers at the same time a running yield which is only sufficient to offset a very small measure of fear" (*General Theory*, p. 202).

Cf. also Joan Robinson, *The Rate of Interest* (London, 1952), pp. 93 and 110.

[31] Cf. the references to Paish, Nevin, and Robinson in the preceding two footnotes.

[32] The classic example here is, of course, the Dalton experiment in postwar England. See C. M. Kennedy, "Monetary Policy," in *The British Economy: 1945–1950* (ed. G. D. N. Worswick and P. H. Ady, Oxford, 1952), pp. 188–206; Paish, *op. cit.*, pp. 174–75; R. S. Sayers, "British and American Experience in the Early Post-War Years," as reprinted in *Central Banking After Bagehot* (Oxford, 1957), pp. 26–28.

regardless of the rate of interest and level of prices, the total demand of household and firms for commodities is always equal to the total income of the economy.[33] Graphically this means that the aggregate demand curve must coincide with the 45° radius vector. Figure XIII-2 on p. 317 is accordingly replaced by Figure XIV-6. As this diagram

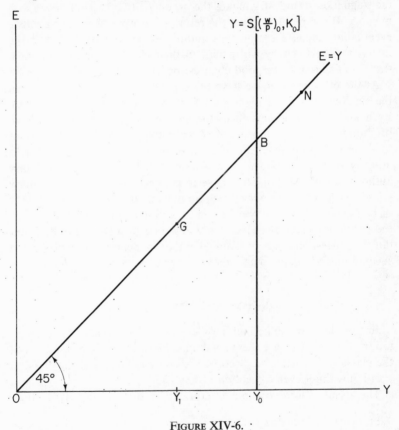

FIGURE XIV-6.

shows, the special form which Say's Identity imposes upon the aggregate demand curve requires it to intersect the aggregate supply curve

[33] This is actually stricter than the statement of Say's Identity on pp. 193 and 273 above; for it requires receipts from commodities *alone* always to be spent on commodities *alone*.

at, and only at, the full-employment point *B*. Furthermore, as long as this identity holds, there can never be any shift in the aggregate demand curve to disturb this equilibrium position even momentarily.

This is a statement of the classical position—as seen with Keynesian eyes.[34] It is another by-product of the oversimplified "diagonal-cross" approach (p. 339). For if one starts from the Keynesian assumption that there is neither a real-balance effect nor an aggregate supply curve in the commodity market—and hence no automatic tendency for a state of involuntary unemployment to generate corrective equilibrating forces—then the only way one can conceive of an economy which must necessarily be brought to a position of full employment is in terms of an aggregate demand curve of the special shape depicted by Figure XIV-6. Conversely, once one recognizes the existence of these equilibrating forces, one can also recognize that the classical position is logically dependent, not on any special form of the aggregate demand function, but only on the assumption that this function— whatever its form—is sufficiently sensitive to price and interest variations to assure the rapid convergence to full employment of the equilibrating process described by Chapter XIII:3. Though there is no evidence that classical economists ever expressed themselves in these terms—and though there is a little evidence that they may sometimes actually have thought in the Say's-Identity terms ascribed to them by Keynes[35]— this is all that need logically be said in order to rationalize their policy conclusions.

The foregoing discussion of Say's Identity also serves to clarify a frequent misunderstanding of its true nature. It is evident from Figure XIV-6 that this identity necessarily involves a marginal propensity to spend equal to one. This has sometimes led to the mechanical application of the standard

$$\frac{1}{1 - \text{the marginal propensity to spend}}$$

formula to produce the conclusion that Say's Identity makes the multiplier infinite and thus renders the system unstable. Additional support for this conclusion seems to come from the apparent existence

---

[34] *General Theory*, pp. 18–21, 25–26.
[35] See the discussion of the literature in Note L.

of a "diagonal-cross" diagram in which only the 45° diagonal appears, and in which, therefore, there seems to be no force pinning national income down to one specific level.

It can readily be shown that this line of reasoning is yet another fallacious by-product of the usual Keynesian neglect of the supply side of the commodity market. In particular, once the standard "diagonal-cross" diagram is supplemented by a supply curve—as it is in Figure XIV-6—the nature of the automatic stabilizing forces which bring the economy to the full-employment position B becomes evident. Thus, if the economy were at point G in Figure XIV-6, firms would be operating with an excess capacity measured by $Y_0 - Y_1$. Hence they would be under pressure to expand their output. But now—unlike the situation that exists in the case of the usual aggregate demand curve with a marginal propensity to spend of less than unity—this tendency would not be aborted by a deficiency in the demand necessary to absorb this additional output.[36] Hence firms would continue to expand production until they brought the economy to the full-employment position B. Conversely, if the economy were at N, firms would be producing more than the optimum output indicated by their supply curve.[37] Hence they would contract production and thereby return the economy once again to B. Thus equilibrium position B is a stable one. Figure XIV-6 also shows how, under the assumption of Say's Identity, the only limit on the ability of the economy to produce is that imposed by the technological and subjective conditions of supply; never that of an inadequacy of demand.

Similarly, the supply side of the commodity market is overlooked in the standard derivation of the multiplier formula. Thus the graphical analysis of Figure XIV-2 takes no account of the possibility that the vertical supply curve may intersect the X-axis at point B and therefore prevent the multiplier from carrying real income beyond this point. This suffices to demonstrate the general inapplicability of the standard multiplier formula to any case in which the expansionary effects of an exogenous increase in expenditures may be brought up short against the ceiling of full employment. In particular, it is clear that once we

[36] Cf. especially pp. 324–25.

[37] The reader will recall that the aggregate supply curve is not a technological curve describing physically possible outputs, but a behavior curve describing economically optimum ones. Hence it is quite possible that firms may sometimes inadvertently find themselves to the right of their supply curve.

take account of this ceiling, the multiplier in the case of Say's Identity will (if it is defined) not be infinite.

Nevertheless, Say's Identity is connected with instability; but it is an instability of money wages and prices, not of real income. Specifically, let us assume—in a minor variation on the argument of Chapter VIII:7—that with the economy at the equilibrium position *B* in Figure XIV-6, a sudden disturbance causes the price level to rise. By assumption, this has no effect on the aggregate demand curve and hence none on the equilibrium of the commodity market. But it reduces the real wage rate and thus creates an excess demand in the labor market. This in turn pushes the money wage rate upwards until the original real wage is restored. In this way the economy is brought to a new equilibrium position in which wages and prices are proportionately higher than they originally were, while real national income remains the same.

But as indicated in Chapter VIII:7, this is a somewhat misleading description. For Say's Identity implies the existence of a barter economy. Hence what manifests itself here as "instability" of the money wage and price levels is actually the reflection of the simple fact that in such an economy these magnitudes are not even defined. From this we can also see that, within its appropriate framework of a barter economy, Say's Identity does not generate any instability.

5. SECULAR GROWTH VERSUS SECULAR STAGNATION

The discussion of the preceding section takes place in what is most conveniently described as a cyclical framework: one in which an excess supply of commodities is generated by a downward shift on the demand side of the market. Actually, however, the excess supply which really absorbed the attention of classical economists is that generated by an upward shift on the supply side. Specifically, their primary interest lay in the long-run capability of a capitalist economy to absorb the output of a continuously expanding productive capacity. In modern terms, their main concern was to disprove the possibility of secular stagnation, not that of cyclical unemployment. Accordingly, they argued the impossibility of a "general glut on the market," not under the chapter heading "Commercial Crises," but under the heading "Effects of Accumulation."[38]

[38] On this and all that follows, see discussion of the literature in Note L.

Let us, then, complete the discussion of the preceding section by interpreting the classical position within this secular framework. Assume that due to the growth of population the supply curve for labor shifts continuously to the right; or that due to capital accumulation or technological progress there is a corresponding shift in the demand curve for labor. Either of these changes causes firms to increase their labor inputs and, consequently, their commodity outputs. That is, either of them causes the commodity supply curve to shift continuously to the right and thereby disturb any existing equilibrium in that market.

If, now, the situation of Figure XIV-6 obtains, this disturbance is immediately eliminated; for due to the unitary marginal propensity to spend, the continuous increase in supply is accompanied by an equal increase in the amount demanded. Thus a "general glut" on the commodity market cannot even momentarily exist. Supply always and instantaneously creates its own demand.

This is one interpretation of the classical position; but, as can be surmised from the preceding section, not a necessary one. In particular, this position can be rationalized without resorting to Say's Identity and by assuming instead that the aggregate demand for commodities is sufficiently sensitive to the stimulating effects of the interest and price changes generated by the expanding supply so as to increase at the same pace as the latter. In brief, a permanent glut is an impossibility because of the corrective market forces set into operation by the existence of temporary ones.

A rigorous analysis of this moving equilibrium can not be attempted here. All that will be provided is a tentative indication of some of the problems posed by this analysis, particularly with respect to the neutrality of money.[39] Let us first make use of the microeconomic analysis of Chapter VI:3–4 to describe the commodity, bond, and money markets of our expanding economy by the equations

$$(6) \qquad F\left[Y, m, s, \frac{M}{(1 + s)p}\right] = Y,$$

[39] The following has been revised and corrected from the original treatment so as to take account of the valid criticisms of Power, "Price Expectations, Money Illusion, and the Real Balance Effect," *op. cit.*, pp. 138–43.

(7) $$B\left[Y, \frac{1}{m}, s, \frac{M}{(1+s)p}\right] = 0,$$

(8) $$L\left[Y, m, s, \frac{M}{(1+s)p}\right] = \frac{M}{(1+s)p},$$

where the full-employment level of Y is assumed to be continuously increasing, and where m represents Fisher's real rate of interest and s the expected rate of change in the price level. In what follows, this level will be assumed constant or declining, so that s is either zero or negative. Thus we can say that each of our equations depends (*inter alia*) upon the alternative yields that can respectively be earned on the assets, bonds and money.[40]

The dependence of the foregoing functions on m parallels that on r in the stationary economy discussed heretofore. The dependence on s is of a double nature: on the one hand, changes in s generate a substitution effect, and this is represented by the fact that this variable appears as a separate argument in the preceding functions; on the other, such changes affect the real value of cash balances, and hence the strength of the wealth effect. Insofar as the substitution effect is concerned, this is assumed to be positive in the case of commodities and negative in the case of bonds and money. That is, the smaller s algebraically—i.e., the greater the expected rate of decline in the price level—the smaller the current demand for commodities, and the greater the demands for bonds and money, as of a given level of wealth. Insofar as the wealth effect is concerned, however, the greater the rate of decline in prices, the greater the rate of increase in real balances, and hence the greater the rate of increase in the demands for all goods. Thus in a secular growth context, as well as a cyclical one (see pp. 336–37), a change in the rate of decline in the price level exerts opposing influences on commodity demand.

Let us now assume that the growth in real output is accompanied by a continuous expansion of the money supply at such a rate as to prevent the emergence of a deflationary gap. Since the price level is thus constant,

---

[40] From the fact that m is approximately equal to $r - s$ (p. 138, footnote 35) it is clear that the foregoing equations also depend implicitly on the nominal rate of interest r.

Once again (cf. p. 311, footnote 45), we are assuming that whatever process is under discussion has continued sufficiently long to cause the expected rate of change in prices to equal the actual one.

s in the foregoing equations is zero. Thus the ever-increasing real-balance effect is in this way assumed to maintain the economy on a full-employment growth path.

At the other extreme is the case in which the increasing real-balance effect is generated by a continuously declining price level while the nominal quantity of money remains constant. Here such a growth path may be impossible of achievement. For assume that demand is not increasing at a sufficient rate to absorb the increasing supply, and that as a result the price level begins to fall at an even faster rate. Then if the substitution effect of this (algebraic) decrease in s outweighs the wealth effect, the economy will be driven even further from the full-employment path. The system is secularly unstable.[41]

On the other hand, stability will exist if the wealth effect predominates. For then a net increase in commodity demand can always be generated by a price level which falls sufficiently fast. Note, however, that the full-employment path thus generated will not generally be the same as the one corresponding to an expanding monetary supply at a constant price level. For the fact that s in system (6)–(8) is no longer zero means that the growth path of commodity demand is also different. This is particularly likely to be true if the different equilibrium value of s is accompanied by a different value of m, which in turn generates different investment plans. In brief, money in this secular context is not neutral: different policies as to the rate of expansion of its nominal supply will generate different growth paths.[42]

The likelihood of neutrality is, however, increased if we make assumptions analogous to those which characterized our dichotomized system in Chapter XII : 5 above. In particular, assume that we have a pure inside-money economy, so that there is no real-balance effect in any market. Assume also—and more importantly—that commodity demand depends only on the real rate of return m, so that (6) is replaced by

$$(9) \qquad\qquad F(Y, m) = Y.$$

Assume finally that, in accordance with the properties of a "balanced-growth" model, a proportionate increase in Y—m constant—will cause

[41] *Ibid.*, p. 141.

[42] See A. L. Marty, "Gurley and Shaw on Money in a Theory of Finance," *Journal of Political Economy*, LXIX (1961), 57.

a proportionate increase in commodity demand. Then the same constant rate of expansion in output will be maintained regardless of what happens to the nominal money supply and hence the price level.[43]

Three comments should, however, be made in this context. First, since m is approximately equal to $r - s$, the constancy of the real rate of interest implies that the nominal rate falls by an extent equal to the rate of decline in the price level. It is the necessary existence of these offsetting movements in equation (9) which leaves unchanged the real equilibrium volume of investment and saving, and hence the rate of growth.

Second, in a money economy r cannot assume negative values. Hence the foregoing tacitly assumes that the rate of decline in the price level is less than the real rate of interest.[44] This is likely to be the case in growth models whose real rate of return on capital equals the rate of growth of output,[45] and whose real demand for money increases, *ceteris paribus*, less than proportionately than the latter because of "economies of scale."[46] Correspondingly, equilibrium can be maintained in the money market of such an economy by means of a price level which declines at a lower rate than that at which output increases.

Finally, the preceding analysis has tacitly assumed away another possible cause of the non-neutrality of money. For in the case where the private sector's real quantity of money is increased solely by virtue of a declining price level, all of the increased output of the economy is acquired in the first instance by this sector. However, if this increased real quantity is generated by an increased nominal supply of money at an unchanged price level, this is obviously not so. For the government's issuance of money in this case is essentially an exploitation of the

[43] These assumptions more or less bring us back to the Gurley-Shaw model (*op. cit.*, p. 337 of Alain Enthoven's appendix; cf. also preceding footnote). See in addition J. Tobin, "A Dynamic Aggregative Model," *Journal of Political Economy*, LXIII (1955), 103–15, and A. W. Phillips, "A Simple Model of Employment, Money and Prices in a Growing Economy," *Economica*, XXVIII (1961), 360–70.

Our present assumptions should be viewed within the context of the argument in the final paragraph of footnote 29 on p. 298.

[44] Cf. W. Fellner, *Trends and Cycles in Economic Activity* (New York, 1956), pp. 171–73.

[45] This is a property of the balanced-growth model presented by J. von Neumann, "A Model of General Economic Equilibrium," *Review of Economic Studies*, XIII (1945–46), 1–9.

[46] Cf. p. 87.

private sector's willingness to hold increasing real balances so as to "float" an interest-free "loan" in perpetuity. Correspondingly, the economy's growth path will generally be influenced by the way in which the government makes use of this "loan," and particularly as to its disposal as between consumption and investment commodities. Thus the preceding paragraph has tacitly assumed that the government in this case does not make use of its increased purchasing power to disturb the existing pattern of demand for current output.[47]

In any event, we see from the discussion of system (6)–(8) that the real-balance effect can play an important analytical role on the classical side of the Great Debate on the internal consistency of an ever expanding capitalist economy.[48] We must, however, emphasize that here, as in the preceding section, our concern has been not with what classical economists "really" said but with what is logically sufficient to validate their conclusions. As usual, it is much more difficult to give a definitive answer to the first of these questions than to the second. As already noted, there is a little evidence that classical economists may actually have thought in terms of Say's Identity; but there is more evidence that they did not. On the other hand, there is no evidence that they thought in the precise terms of the dynamic adjustment process with which we have rationalized their position here. Indeed, it seems quite likely that

[47] Gurley and Shaw, *op. cit.*, p. 41.
Note that the amount of money the government can thus "borrow" at an unchanged price level is determined by the income elasticity of the demand for money. The greater this elasticity, the greater such borrowings.

[48] The operative word here is "analytical." For the main way demand has *historically* absorbed an expanding supply has been through the development of new products, new tastes, and new and unremitting demands for higher standards of living—and surely not through the real-balance effect. Similarly, the fact that the classical position is *analytically* consistent does not mean that one must adopt its *policy* attitude toward the problem of secular expansion. This should be clear from the argument of the preceding section.

The emphasis here on the secular aspect of the real-balance effect follows that of the well-known articles by A. C. Pigou on "The Classical Stationary State," *Economic Journal*, LIII (1943), 343–51, and "Economic Progress in a Stable Environment," *Economica*, XIV (1947), as reprinted in *Readings in Monetary Theory*, pp. 241–51. See also the emphasis on this role in the *Journal of Political Economy* articles by G. Ackley, "The Wealth-Saving Relationship," LIX (1951), 155; A. Hansen, "The Pigouvian Effect," the same volume, pp. 535–36; and G. Haberler, "The Pigou Effect Once More," LX (1952), 240–46.

The present discussion is, of course, concerned with the theory of employment and growth; the significance of the real-balance effect for monetary theory is much more immediate. Cf. Chapters II:3 and VIII:3.

they never faced up to this problem at all. It seems as if their valid and vigorous insistence that increased production generates increased "means of purchasing" and hence increased demand, coupled with their absolute faith in the "wants and tastes of mankind as unlimited," blinded classical economists to the need for analyzing the exact details of the automatic market mechanism by which demand supposedly keeps pace with supply. What is worse, they transferred this neglect of detail to the short-run cyclical problem as well. And for this analytical lacuna they were rightly and forcefully criticized by Malthus and Sismondi, in their times, and by Keynes, in ours.[49]

[49] The first quotation is from J. B. Say, *A Treatise on Political Economy*, trans. C. R. Prinsep (4th ed.; Philadelphia, 1834), p. 137, first paragraph. See also Say's *Letters to Malthus* (1821, reprinted London, 1936), p. 4. The theme of this quotation is most explicit in Mill, *Principles*, pp. 557–58; this passage is discussed in detail in Note L below.

The second quotation is from a letter by Ricardo to Malthus in *Works and Correspondence of David Ricardo*, ed. Sraffa, Vol. VI, p. 134, bottom. See also *Notes on Malthus*, *Works*, Vol. II, p. 311, and Malthus' letter to Ricardo, *Works*, Vol. VII, p. 122; this last passage is cited in full on p. 648, footnote 18 below.

Further background material for this paragraph is provided by Note L.

XV. A Critique of Classical and Keynesian Interest Theory

1. The nature of classical and neoclassical interest theory.   2. Keynesian interest theory.   3. Loanable-funds versus liquidity-preference theories of interest.   The real and the monetary in the rate of interest.

1. THE NATURE OF CLASSICAL AND NEOCLASSICAL INTEREST THEORY

On various occasions in this book—and in Part Two in particular —we have digressed briefly on the implications of the argument for classical or Keynesian interest theory. The task of this final chapter is to pick up the loose ends of these digressions and—at the risk of some repetition—integrate them into a systematic critique of these two theories.

Let us begin with the classical and neoclassical theory. In modern terms this is best described as a loanable-funds theory. Its point of departure is that "the rate of interest . . . depends essentially and permanently on the comparative amount of real capital offered and demanded in the way of loan." Accordingly, "fluctuations in the rate of interest arise from variations either in the demand for loans or in the supply." These words happen to be those of J. S. Mill. But they represent the thinking of such writers as Hume, Thornton, and Ricardo, before him, and Sidgwick, Marshall, Pigou, Wicksell, and Fisher, after.[1]

[1] Mill, *Principles*, pp. 647 and 641, respectively; the reader is strongly urged to

At first sight this bears little resemblance to Keynes' picture of a classical theory which in some mysterious way determines the rate of interest at that level which equates savings and investment.[2] But it would be unfair to press this criticism of Keynes too far. For there was no precise attempt in the classical literature to distinguish between savings and the supply of loans, on the one hand, and between investment and the demand for loans, on the other. There was no recognition of the fact that this distinction is logically inherent in the assumption that a money economy exists; that, more specifically, the existence of a simultaneous identity between savings and lending, and investing and borrowing, implies Say's Identity and hence a barter economy.[3]

Though determining the rate of interest in the loan market—which is obviously identical with what we have called the bond market—classical and neoclassical theory always emphasized the crucial interdependence that exists between this market and the commodity market. This, indeed, is the real significance of its celebrated distinction between the "money rate" and the "natural rate." These terms are, of course, Wicksell's. But, as he himself was the first to concede,[4] the theory in back of them had already been sketched out by Ricardo. And much the same sketch can be found in Thornton and Mill as well.[5]

The essence of this theory—and of the interdependence which it stresses—can be set out briefly. By the "money rate" is meant the

study for himself the whole of Book III, Chapter XXIII, from which these passages are taken. For specific references to the other writers, see Note J below.

[2] *General Theory*, Chapter XIV.

[3] See end of Chapter XI:6.

This distinction is, of course, a basic point of the *General Theory* (cf., e.g., p. 166), though there is no indication that Keynes saw it as logically inherent in a money economy.

It might also be noted that this distinction is explicit in the modern versions of the loanable-funds theory as presented by Bertil Ohlin, "Alternative Theories of the Rate of Interest," *op. cit.*, pp. 424–26; Robertson, *Essays in Monetary Theory*, p. 3; and Haberler, *Prosperity and Depression*, Part II, especially pp. 292–96.

[4] *Lectures on Political Economy*, trans. E. Classen (London, 1935), Vol. II, p. 200.

[5] Wicksell's concession was made to David Davidson, who had brought his attention to the passage which appears in Ricardo's *Principles of Political Economy*, ed. Sraffa, pp. 363–64. To this can be added the passage from *The High Price of Bullion* cited in full on pp. 239–40 above.

On Henry Thornton, see his *Enquiry into the Nature and Effects of the Paper Credit of Great Britain* (London, 1802), pp. 261–62 and, especially, pp. 287–91 (pp. 237–38, 253–56 of the 1939 reprint). On Mill, cf. his *Principles*, pp. 645–47, especially p. 647, lines 10–15.

rate of interest actually prevailing in the loan market. By the "natural rate" is meant not a rate quoted upon a market, but the investors' rate of return on capital in the commodity market. Equilibrium can exist only when these two rates are equal; conversely, any discrepancy between these two rates automatically generates equilibrating forces which bring them to equality. In particular, if the money rate happens to lie below the natural rate, then individuals can profit by expanding their borrowings and using the proceeds to increase their demand for investment goods; assuming full employment, this generates an inflationary gap in the commodity market which drives prices upwards; and this in turn reacts back on the bond market and causes the rate of interest to rise.

Nowhere is this stated more precisely and with fuller appreciation of its deeper significance than in the striking words with which Wicksell defined the major problem to which he addressed himself and indicated the nature of the famed "cumulative process" by which he proposed to solve it: "The money rate of interest depends in the first instance on the excess or scarcity of *money*. How then does it come about that it is eventually determined by the excess or scarcity of *real capital*?... The only possible explanation lies in the influence which is exerted on *prices* by the difference between the two rates of interest. When the money rate of interest is relatively too low all prices rise. The demand for money loans is consequently increased, and as a result of a greater need for cash holdings, the supply is diminished. The consequence is that the rate of interest is soon restored to its normal level, so that it again coincides with the natural rate."[6]

Thus Wicksell's "cumulative process" is not the unstable explosive process that almost all later commentators have tried to make of it, but a stable equilibrating process whose function it is to achieve the long-run equality of the money and natural rates of interest. This is not a quibble. For the commonly accepted interpretation of Wicksell completely overlooks the central problem with which he was concerned.

---

[6] *Interest and Prices*, pp. 108–11, italics in the original. From the context it is clear that the first sentence refers to "excess or scarcity of money *loans*." For an explanation of why "the greater need for cash holdings" causes the supply of loans to diminish, see top of p. 370.

For other examples of this theme in Wicksell's work, see *ibid.*, pp. xxvi–xxvii and p. 75; *Lectures in Political Economy*, Vol. II, pp. 194, 200, and, especially, 206.

And it thereby also overlooks the vital key which he provides to an understanding of one of the central themes of classical interest theory.[7]

It was within the foregoing framework that classical economists carried out their analysis of the effects of an increase in the quantity of money. Such an increase could influence the rate of interest only through its prior effect on the demand or supply function in the loan market. Hence if this increase were not expended in this market at all—if, that is, it were directed entirely to the commodity market—interest would not be affected.[8] But in the classical scheme this was generally not the case. For the increased money supply was usually assumed to be injected into the economy through the banking system and thus to result in an increased supply of loans. Hence the rate of interest declined. But even in this case the decline was only a transitory one. In the long run, interest would generally return to its original equilibrium level.

This distinction between the short-run variability of interest in the face of a monetary increase and its long-run invariability in no way represents the "unbridged conflict" in classical theorizing that Keynes made it out to be.[9] It represents instead the well-reasoned conclusion of the analysis which has already been described above: the analysis which takes account of the effect of a rising price level in the commodity market on the rate of interest in the loan market. For Hume, Thornton, Ricardo, Mill, and Fisher, this effect works its way through the demand side of the latter market: the monetary increase causes a rise in the price of investment goods and thereby increases the volume of borrowing necessary to finance their purchase. In this way the demand for loans begins to overtake the initially expanded supply. For Marshall, this increased demand for loans results instead from the "confident spirit in the business world" which the price increase generates. For Giffen and Wicksell, the reaction works its way instead through the

---

[7] For examples of this misinterpretation of Wicksell, see Hicks, *Value and Capital*, pp. 251–54; L. A. Metzler, "Business Cycles and the Modern Theory of Employment," *American Economic Review*, XXXVI (1946), 280, footnote 4; and the additional references cited in my "Wicksell's 'Cumulative Process,'" *Economic Journal*, LXII (1952), 835, footnote 2.

For a detailed discussion of Wicksell's "cumulative process," see Note E : 4 below. This also explains what Wicksell meant by the term "cumulative" and shows that he had almost no interest in the unstable case.

[8] See the discussion of Wicksell on p. 589 below.

[9] *General Theory*, pp. 182–83.

supply side of the market: the price increase generates an internal drain which draws bank reserves down and hence forces them to raise their rates again—or, what is the same thing, to decrease again their supply of loans. This, indeed, is what Wicksell relies upon for the stability of his "cumulative process." The common theme of all these writers is that at the same time that the monetary increase pushes interest down, it also pushes prices up; and that the latter movement must ultimately cause a reversal of the former one.[10]

It was this interaction between the commodity and loan markets—in any one of the three preceding forms—which provided the explicit rationale of the classical argument that in the long run, as distinct from the short run, a monetary increase will have a symmetrical effect on the demand and supply of loans, and will therefore leave interest invariant. Or, alternatively, approaching the problem from the viewpoint of the commodity market, classical economists argued that the monetary increase does not change any of the real characteristics of the economy; that, in particular, it does not change the marginal productivity of capital; and that, therefore, it does not change the natural rate of interest. More specifically, the monetary increase causes an equi-proportionate increase in the money cost of any investment project and in the money value of its anticipated returns; hence it leaves the rate of profit—and hence the long-run equilibrium rate of interest—unchanged.[11]

It is clear from this discussion that the invariance of interest was not the dogmatic First Principle of Faith of the classical school that its latter-day critics—and defenders—have made of it. It was instead the rational conclusion which emerged from the application of ordinary

[10] See the specific references in Note J.

It might be worth noting that, say, Mill's exposition is decidedly more precise and systematic than Marshall's. More generally, it is difficult to understand why, in its analysis of a monetary increase, the Cambridge school as a whole failed to make use of the specific interrelationship between price and interest movements that Mill and his predecessors had consistently employed.

One cannot also help wondering how Keynes' chapter on "The Classical Theory of the Rate of Interest"—and how, accordingly, the views of a generation which has learned its classical economics from this chapter—would have been affected if Keynes had taken his basic texts from Mill, instead of Marshall and Pigou.

[11] Cf. the references to Thornton and Mill in footnote 5, p. 367 above. Cf. also J. S. Nicholson, *Principles of Political Economy* (London, 1897), Vol. II, p. 231; and—in a somewhat different context—W. S. Jevons, *Investigations in Currency and Finance* (London, 1884), p. 22.

supply-and-demand analysis to the loan and commodity markets. Furthermore, what strikes one immediately in reading the classical literature is the flexibility with which this conclusion was modified whenever there was reason to believe that, even in the long run, a monetary increase might have an asymmetrical influence on the demand and supply of loans, and might therefore permanently affect the rate of interest.[12]

As a case in point, consider the celebrated classical and neoclassical doctrine of "forced savings." The essence of this doctrine is that an exogenous increase in the quantity of money which accrues initially to entrepreneurs, or to those who lend to them, will increase the proportion of an economy's expenditures going into investment, and that the necessary corresponding increase in savings will be forced upon workers and fixed-income recipients by the inflationary price movement which the monetary expansion generates. In this way such an expansion can increase the amount of real capital in the economy. But if it can do this, it can also lower the marginal productivity of capital and thereby the long-run equilibrium rate of interest. This conclusion was explicitly drawn—without a trace of self-consciousness—by such writers as Mill, Wicksell, Nicholson, and Pigou. It is but a special case of the general awareness of classical economists that a monetary increase cannot be neutral in its effects unless it is initially distributed among all members of the economy in a uniform way.[13]

On the other hand, classical and neoclassical monetary theorists did not see that shifts in liquidity preference could affect the long-run equilibrium rate of interest. Nor did they see that such an effect might also be directly generated by open-market operations. But it should be clear that these propositions do not strike at any vital foundations of the classical theory. More specifically, if classical economists could recognize the permanent effect on interest of a monetary change in the case of "forced savings," there is no reason why they should not have been equally willing to accept the Keynesian argument about the corresponding effects of shifts in liquidity preference and open-market operations. At the same time they would probably have questioned

[12] Cf., e.g., Mill, *Principles*, p. 642.
[13] The passages referred to in the preceding sentence are cited in full in Note J. On the last sentence, see pp. 45 and 164.

the historical importance of these factors in explaining changes in the average long-run interest rate.[14]

2. KEYNESIAN INTEREST THEORY

The basic proposition of Keynes' interest theory is that the rate of interest must operate on the margin of liquidity decisions as well as on those of savings and investment, and that accordingly there is an inverse dependence between the amount of money demanded and this rate. It is true that references to such a dependence can be found earlier in the monetary writings of Walras, Wicksell, Fisher, and Lavington.[15] But these writers essentially ascribed it to the precautionary motive; whereas Keynes, though recognizing this influence, ascribed it primarily to the speculative motive.[16] Furthermore, and more important, each of the above writers—with the exception of Walras—made only passing reference to this dependence; it was left for Keynes to bring it to the fore of monetary theory.

Unfortunately, Keynes' analysis of the implications of this dependence is repeatedly marred by a confusion (which characterizes the later Keynesian literature as well) between his basic proposition that the amount of money demanded is inversely dependent upon the rate of interest and the completely different proposition that the equilibrium rate of interest is inversely dependent upon the amount of money. His discussion of liquidity preference in the *General Theory*[17] shifts uninhibitedly from one proposition to the other with never an indication that they are in any way not identical. More specifically, there is never a recognition that, in our terminology, the first of these propositions describes an individual-experiment and the second a market-experiment, and that the truth of the first need not imply the truth of the second.[18]

[14] Cf. concluding paragraphs of this chapter.
This section presupposes as its background the analysis of Chapters X:3, X:4, and XII:3–4.
[15] For specific references, see pp. 545, 556, 579–80.
An even more explicit anticipator of Keynes is the almost completely forgotten Karl Schlesinger. In 1914 this writer presented a two-component demand function for money which bears striking similarity to Keynes' $L_1(\ ) + L_2(\ )$. See pp. 577–78 below.
[16] Cf. above, p. 254, footnote 2.
[17] Chapters XIII and XV.
[18] Cf. Chapter XI:4 above.

Leaving this behind, let us now examine the reason why a change in the quantity of money generated by deficit financing affects interest in the Keynesian system. Two interpretations have been presented in this book: Chapter XII: 1 attributes this variability to the assumption of money illusion in the speculative demand for money, and Chapter XIII: 4—in accordance with more standard interpretations—to the assumption of price and wage rigidities under conditions of unemployment. Clearly, these two interpretations are not mutually exclusive. Correspondingly, most cases in which the *General Theory* analyzes the depressing effect on interest of a monetary increase reflect the joint and reinforcing influence of money illusion and rigidity. On the other hand, I find it difficult to believe that all Keynes wanted to say is that the quantity of money can affect interest under conditions of wage and price rigidity—for classical and neoclassical economists would never have disagreed with such a proposition. This is clearly implied by their repeated emphasis that—under conditions of price flexibility—the injection of new money into the economy will depress interest as long as prices have not yet risen in proportion to the quantity of money.[19]

It should, however, be emphasized that neither of the foregoing assumptions was systematically set out by Keynes in his monetary theory. Nor is there even evidence that he was aware of their presence in his argument. This is particularly true for the assumption of money illusion. But against our failure to find this assumption explicitly recognized, we must place the evidence of the passages in the *General Theory* in which it is all too unconsciously exploited. More specifically, Keynesian monetary theory never permits the speculative demand to absorb an increased supply of money except at a lower rate of interest. It never allows for the fact that, provided the price level rises, such an absorption may take place even at an unchanged rate. Nor can this omission be explained as itself proving that the analysis of the *General Theory* proceeds on the assumption of absolute price rigidity. For there are passages in this work in which Keynes explicitly assumes the wage

[19] See the preceding section and, especially, pp. 369–70.

For an example of the interpretation of Keynes in terms of rigidities, see W. Leontief, "Postulates: Keynes' *General Theory* and the Classicists," *The New Economics*, ed. S. E. Harris (New York, 1948), pp. 238–39. See also Leontief's earlier "Fundamental Assumption of Mr. Keynes' Monetary Theory of Unemployment," *op. cit.* This is also the well-known interpretation of Modigliani, "Liquidity Preference," *op. cit.*, especially p. 223.

or price level to rise, in which he explains how this rise affects the transactions and precautionary demands, and in which he overlooks the fact that it may also affect the speculative demand. And, to the best of my knowledge, this significant omission has continued to characterize the later Keynesian—and non-Keynesian—literature as well.[20]

On the other hand, to the extent that Keynesian monetary theory is concerned with shifts in liquidity preference and with monetary changes generated by open-market operations, its conclusions are independent of the foregoing assumptions. At the same time it is difficult to interpret Keynesian theory solely in these terms: for then its conclusions are also independent of Keynes' much-stressed proposition that the demand for money is a function of the rate of interest.[21]

To summarize: The over-all tone of the *General Theory* leaves little doubt that Keynes intended his liquidity-preference theory to be a fundamental challenge to classical and neoclassical monetary theory. But if this challenge is to meet the latter theory on its own grounds—those of full employment and price flexibility[22]—then Keynes' position cannot be vindicated except by attributing to him the assumption of money illusion in the speculative demand for money. In particular, his extended demonstration that the demand for money depends on the rate of interest does not itself constitute proof that the equilibrium rate of interest depends on the quantity of money.

But since Keynes never explicitly pointed out that his speculative demand was independent of the price level—and *a fortiori* never attempted to rationalize the money illusion implicit in such an assumption—it is difficult to believe that what has turned out here to be a

[20] The significance of the speculative motive's insensitivity to price changes—and the reason this implies the presence of money illusion—can best be appreciated from a comparison of Chapters XI:1 and XII:1. See especially pp. 254–55 and 278–79.
The passages from the *General Theory* referred to in the preceding sentence are cited in full and analyzed in Note K:2.

[21] The reader can readily verify this by noting that the analyses in Chapters X:4, XII:4, and XIII:4 would not be affected (insofar as the direction of the change in interest is concerned) by assuming that the equilibrium curve for the money market is a straight line parallel to the Y-axis.

[22] For evidence that Keynes did offer such a challenge, see *General Theory*, pp. 208–209; this is discussed at the end of Chapter XI:1 above. There is, however, the contradictory evidence of p. 191 where Keynes concedes that "assuming flexible money-wages, the quantity of money as such is, indeed, nugatory in the long period." This contradiction and a suggestion for resolving it are discussed in detail in Note K:2, pp. 641–42.

crucial assumption of the liquidity-preference theory has its origin in anything more than a simple—but vital—oversight. Correspondingly, once this oversight is corrected, Keynesian theory must give up its claim to have demonstrated the existence of a basic logical fallacy in classical and neoclassical monetary theory. What it has instead demonstrated is the existence in this theory of several significant lacunae. Accordingly, the Keynesian contribution lies in filling these lacunae by analyzing the speculative motive and interest differentials, by emphasizing the dependence of the demand for money on the rate of interest, and by stressing that shifts in liquidity preference as between money and bonds affect this rate. At the same time, Keynes should also have taken account of the fact that shifts in liquidity preference can, in principle, also affect the demand for commodities; that this is, indeed, the implicit neoclassical assumption; and that in such a case the rate of interest need not be affected (see Chapters X: 4 and XI: 1-2).

It should finally be emphasized that the foregoing criticism of Keynes' liquidity-preference theory in no way affects the basic validity of his theory of unemployment. This should be clear from the interpretation of the latter theory in Chaper XIV: 1. It is even clearer from Keynes' own statement that "the initial novelty [of the *General Theory*] lies in my maintaining that it is not the rate of interest, but the level of incomes which ensures equality between saving and investment. The arguments which lead up to this initial conclusion are independent of my subsequent theory of the rate of interest, and in fact I reached it before I had reached the latter theory."[23]

3. LOANABLE-FUNDS VERSUS LIQUIDITY-PREFERENCE THEORIES OF INTEREST. THE REAL AND THE MONETARY IN THE RATE OF INTEREST

One question which has so far been deliberately avoided in this book is that which has been hotly and prolongedly debated under the heading "loanable-funds versus liquidity-preference theories." The first of these theories, of course, maintains that the rate of interest is determined in the loan market, while the second maintains that it is determined in the

---

[23] "Alternative Theories of the Rate of Interest," *Economic Journal*, XLVII (1937), 250.

money market. Despite Hicks' demonstration many years ago that these theories are logically equivalent, this pointless debate has continued to recrudesce sporadically in the literature.[24]

The best way of approaching this debate is to try to pin down the meaning of "determined in the loan (money) market." Clearly, this cannot mean that the rate of interest influences only one of the markets. Nor can it mean that the demand and supply functions of one of these markets are solely dependent on the rate of interest, so that a *tâtonnement* in this market alone can determine its equilibrium value. For, as shown in Chapter IX:4–5, the functions of all markets depend on both the rate of interest and the price level, not to speak of the level of real national income. In brief, the very conception of general-equilibrium analysis requires us to recognize that each market is influenced by all the prices of the system, and each price influences all markets.

A more sophisticated approach would have the phrase "determined in the loan (money) market" mean that the dynamic movement of interest is determined by the excess demand which exists in the loan (money) market. But as has been repeatedly emphasized above, this, too, is a vestige of partial-equilibrium analysis. In a general-equilibrium framework we cannot logically justify any argument which is based on the assumption that the dynamic pressures for changing a given price can emanate from one, and only one, market.[25] Conversely, we cannot justify any argument which restricts the dynamic influence of excess demand in a given market to one, and only one, price. And, in particular, we cannot possibly justify such a restriction in the case of the money market. For it is the essential nature of money to be spent on all goods —and not just on one.[26]

There still remains the possibility of having the phrase in question refer, not to the actual processes of the market, but to the analytical procedure of the theorist. Specifically, it might refer to the freedom given him by Walras' Law to "drop" one of the market excess-demand

---

[24] For a good critical survey of this debate, see B. F. Haley, "Value and Distribution," *Survey of Contemporary Economics*, ed. H. S. Ellis (Philadelphia, 1948), pp. 39–44. See also the discussion by L. R. Klein, W. Fellner, H. M. Somers, and K. Brunner on "Stock and Flow Analysis in Economics," *Econometrica*, XVIII (1950), 236–52. The literature has been more recently surveyed in the articles cited in footnote 31 below.

[25] Cf. end of Chapter X:2.

[26] Cf. p. 260.

equations. If, then, he "drops" the money equation, he has a "loanable-funds" theory; and if the bond equation, a "liquidity-preference" theory. But how shall we classify his theory if he "drops" neither of these equations, but a commodity equation instead?[27] More fundamentally, what can be the entire point of such a distinction if, by the very nature of Walras' Law, it can make no difference which equation he "drops"?[28] And, even more fundamentally, how shall we classify his theory if he "drops" no equation at all, but carries out his analysis in terms of the complete system of equations—with one of them written in a form which makes explicit the equational dependence?[29]

The irrelevance of this classifactory scheme is, indeed, one of the conclusions that emerges most explicitly from the argument of this book. If a system is stable—or has certain comparative-statics properties—when analyzed from the viewpoint of the commodity and bond markets, then it must also be stable—or have these properties—when analyzed from the viewpoint of the commodity and money markets. Every set of assumptions in the former framework has its exact counterpart in the latter. And if this counterpart is correctly specified, then—as we have repeatedly seen[30]—an analysis which concentrates on the bond market must always reach the same conclusions as one which concentrates on the money market. Correspondingly, no logical significance can be attached to any distinction between these two analytical frameworks.

Similarly, there is no validity to the contention that the loan equation refers to a flow and the money equation to a stock, so that (it is alleged) a substantive "stock-flow" difference exists between these two equations. For, first of all, there is the primarily semantic point that the demand for or supply of loanable funds during a given period has the dimensions of a stock and not a flow. Second, it is clear from all the preceding chapters that the analysis of the loan market can be carried out just as well in terms of the demand for and supply of the total stock of bonds outstanding. Finally, it has also been shown above that in the one-period model with which the literature has largely been concerned the

---

[27] In the mischievous words of Abba P. Lerner, what happens if he drops the equation for peanuts?

[28] Cf. the classic demonstration by Hicks, *Value and Capital*, pp. 158–62. Cf. also above, pp. 37–38, and Mathematical Appendix 3:*a*.

[29] This is the procedure advocated in Chapter III:2 and adopted on pp. 44 and 236.

[30] In Chapters XI:2–3 and XII:1.

demand and supply for the flow of money will be equal if and only if the demand and supply for the stock of money is.[31]

The approach of the opening paragraphs of this section can also be applied to the related and much discussed question as to whether interest is a "real" or "monetary" phenomenon. There are certain tautological ways of settling this debate. Thus if "monetary" means being matched with the bond or money markets in the same sense that the price of shoes is matched with the shoe market, then the rate of interest—or rather its reciprocal—is clearly matched with the bond market and is therefore a monetary phenomenon. On the other hand, if "real" means having the dimensions of a relative price and "monetary" the dimensions of a money price, then the rate of interest is obviously a real phenomenon: it is the quotient of two quantities, each of which has the dimensions of a money price.[32]

This is classification by definition, and hence classification without analytical importance. Let us turn, then, to operationally significant classifications. Thus, for example, we might say interest is a "real" phenomenon if it influences only the commodity markets; and a "monetary" one if it influences only the bond and/or money markets. But the general-equilibrium considerations already noted force most contemporary theories to reject such extreme positions and to recognize that interest exerts its influence in all markets and that, in particular, it operates simultaneously on the "threefold margin" of time preference (consumption decisions), marginal productivity of capital (investment

---

[31] Cf. above p. 20 footnote 15, and p. 26. See Mathematical Appendix 11, especially pp. 519–20.

This is not to deny that significant distinctions can be made among interest theories according to the role which they assign to the existing stock of various assets; nor is it to deny the desirability of casting monetary theory within the framework of a so-called "stock-flow model" (see p. 521, footnote 11). My main point is that these issues are not related to the choice of the market in which to carry out this analysis; nor in many cases are they really related to the distinction between stocks and flows.

For a survey of the relevant literature, see Johnson, "Monetary and Value Theory," *op. cit.*, pp. 360–65 and G. L. S. Shackle, "Recent Theories Concerning the Nature and Role of Interest," *Economic Journal*, LXXI (1961), 222–35. See also W. J. Baumol, "Stocks, Flows, and Monetary Theory," *Quarterly Journal of Economics*, LXXVI (1962), 46–56; and L. R. Klein, "Stocks and Flows in the Theory of Interest," in *The Theory of Interest Rates* (ed. F. H. Hahn and F. Brechling, London, 1965).

[32] Cf. p. 66.

decisions), and liquidity preference (decisions as to the relative sizes of bond and money holdings).[33] Similarly, we should not try to classify the rate of interest as "real" or "monetary" according to the excess demand which determines its dynamic movements, for, from the general-equilibrium viewpoint, these are determined by the excess demands of all markets.[34]

This leaves the familiar criterion that the rate of interest is a "real" phenomenon if it is determined in the commodity markets and a "monetary" phenomenon if it is determined in the bond or money market.[35] Its continued acceptance notwithstanding, this classificatory scheme is not very useful; for it restricts the "realness" of the interest rate to the special cases in which the economy can be validly dichotomized into real and monetary sectors.[36] In general, however, the equilibrium values of relative prices, the rate of interest, and the absolute price level are simultaneously determined by *all* the markets of the economy; that is, it is generally impossible to break off a subset of markets which can by itself—i.e., by a self-contained *tâtonnement*[37] —determine a subset of variables. And the rate of interest is no exception.

Nevertheless, we can usefully distinguish between the real and the monetary in the rate of interest. But, once again,[38] this distinction cannot proceed along market lines. Instead we shall say that interest is a real phenomenon if it behaves like a relative price, and a monetary phenomenon if it behaves like the absolute price level. More specifically, it is a real phenomenon if its long-run equilibrium value is not affected by exogenous changes which do not affect relative prices, and is affected by those that do. And it is a monetary phenomenon if its long-run value is affected by exogenous changes which affect only the absolute price level. From this viewpoint, one of the obvious conclusions of this book is that interest is a real phenomenon: changes in the quantity of money and shifts in liquidity preference which leave relative

[33] Cf. p. 94.
[34] Cf. p. 376.
[35] The best-known presentation of this view is that of Modigliani, "Liquidity Preference," *op. cit.*
[36] Cf. pp. 180 and 297–98 above.
[37] Cf. pp. 182–83.
[38] Cf. p. 181.

prices invariant also leave it invariant;[39] while changes in tastes and in technological conditions of production, whose nature it is to cause relative prices to vary, also cause it to vary.[40]

Clearly, this is not a hard and fast criterion. As has been sufficiently emphasized above, changes in the quantity of money and shifts in liquidity preference can affect interest;[41] but so can they sometimes affect relative prices.[42] Thus our distinction must remain a matter of degree. Nevertheless, it does enable us to formulate the classical view on the "realness" of interest in terms of the following meaningful hypothesis: Variations in the average long-term rate of interest—in time and space—have originated primarily in technological changes which have affected the marginal productivity of capital, and in time-preference changes which have affected the desire to save; they have not originated primarily—or even significantly—in changes in the quantity of money or shifts in liquidity preference. Keynes thought that he had found a logical error in classical reasoning which justified the immediate rejection of this hypothesis; but, as has been emphasized in the preceding section, it was Keynes' reasoning itself which was in error. Correspondingly, the acceptability of this hypothesis cannot be determined except by detailed historical studies. Thus we have reached the limits of what can be done within the purely theoretical framework of this book. But I might be permitted to express the prejudgment that such studies would give more support to the classical view than to the Keynesian.

I might finally also express the conjecture (based on an even more hesitant venture into the "sociology of knowledge") that it is no accident that the Keynesian monetary theory of interest originated in—and gained acceptance during—a deep depression which had rendered the productivity of capital a dim memory, and that it has lost ground during the postwar boom period of "capital shortage." Nor do I think it accidental that it has found few adherents among economists from

---

[39] Cf. Chapters IV:4, VIII:5, X:3–4, and XII:5–6, and their related Mathematical Appendixes.

Note that according to the present definition interest can be a real phenomenon even in a nondichotomized system.

[40] Cf. Chapter XI:5–6. Note in particular the analysis of shifts in the savings and investment functions.

[41] Cf. Chapters X:4 and XII:1–6.

[42] Cf. pp. 45 and 74 above.

young nations engaged in intensive development programs, for whom the productivity of capital is one of the major variables of policy formulation.

Mathematical Appendix

Introduction

As emphasized in the Preface, this Appendix is not intended to be read independently of the text. Indeed, the reader is specifically warned that it rarely draws the economic implications of the mathematical argument which it presents. Thus in order to obtain these intended implications the reader must in each case study the Appendix together with the sections of the text to which it is explicitly attached. Appendixes 1 and 11 are, however, exceptions. Though they too are directly related— and, indeed, basic—to the text, they can be read independently of it. They deal with subjects of wider significance which have nevertheless been inadequately treated in the standard textbooks on mathematics for economists. This is the reason for their inclusion here.

The main purposes of this Mathematical Appendix are two in number. First, it proves conclusions that the reader of the text is asked to take on faith. Second—and quantitatively more important—it develops the argument with a rigor and precision which the reader has the right to demand, but which the literary and graphical presentations of the text cannot achieve. In particular, it makes clear the full meaning and significance of the crucial distinction between demand curves and market-equilibrium curves, as well as of the fine, though fundamental, distinctions among the various dichotomies of Chapter VIII: 3.

It might also be noted that the somewhat extended treatment of Appendixes 8–10 is intended to serve the additional purpose of illustrating the mathematical technique of comparative-statics and dynamic analysis by applying it to specific problems of Part Two of the text. In particular, they illustrate and elaborate upon the application—and limitations—of Samuelson's "correspondence principle" in analyzing these problems. It has also been considered desirable to use Appendixes 8–10 to illustrate the detailed workings of Walras' Law in assuring that neither the comparative-statics nor the dynamic analysis of any problem can be affected by the choice of the markets in which this analysis is carried out. This, of course, is a fundamental and recurrent theme of the text.

1. Derivatives in Economic Analysis[1]

a. THE MEANING OF A DERIVATIVE

The purpose of the discussion now to be presented is to make precise the basic conceptual framework which frequently lies behind the argument of the text and of the Mathematical Appendix. Though this framework is implicit in any of the standard expositions of comparative-statics analysis,[2] it has nevertheless remained the center of much confusion in the literature. The following exposition makes no pretense at full mathematical rigor. Nevertheless, it does clarify the nature of this confusion and shows how it can be avoided.[3]

Our primary concern is with the fundamental distinction made in the text between individual-experiments and market-experiments.[4] Mathematically speaking, this is a distinction between derivatives. More generally, it is a reflection of the fact that, by definition, a derivative measures the effect on a dependent variable of a change in an independent variable which is functionally related to it. Hence no derivative

---

[1] I am indebted to my colleague Dr. Shmuel Agmon (Department of Mathematics) for reading over Appendix 1. Needless to say, he is in no way responsible for its style or lack of rigor.

[2] See, in particular, P. A. Samuelson, *Foundations of Economic Analysis*, pp. 258–60, 276–78.

[3] My own understanding of these points began with the lucid explanation I heard many years ago from Trygve Haavelmo. I should like to take this opportunity to express again my indebtedness to him.

[4] Cf. Chapters I:4 and III:6.

has any meaning until this functional relationship is first specified and its variables classified as dependent or independent. The remainder of this discussion is essentially an elaboration of these two sentences.[5]

Consider, for example, the demand function

(1.1) $$q^D = \phi(p),$$

where q^D represents the amount demanded of a certain commodity, and p, its price. Here p is taken as the independent variable, and q^D as the dependent. That is, this function describes the outcome of a conceptual individual-experiment in which an individual (or group of individuals) is confronted with a price over which he has no control and is asked to indicate the amount of the commodity he demands at that price. Correspondingly, the derivative

(1.2) $$\frac{dq^D}{dp} = \phi'(p)$$

describes the change in this amount demanded resulting from an arbitrarily imposed unitary change in the price with which the individual is confronted. By assumption, this derivative is negative.

Alternatively, we can write the demand function in the form

(1.3) $$p^D = \psi(q),$$

where $\psi(\ \ )$ is the inverse function of $\phi(\ \ )$. This function describes a conceptual experiment in which an individual is arbitrarily confronted with a certain amount q of a commodity and asked to indicate the highest per-unit price he is willing to pay for that amount. That is, p^D is Marshall's "demand price."[6] Correspondingly, the derivative

(1.4) $$\frac{dp^D}{dq} = \psi'(q)$$

describes the change in this demand price resulting from an arbitrarily imposed unitary change in the quantity of the commodity with which the individual is confronted. This derivative, too, is assumed to be negative.

[5] Cf. on this whole discussion W. F. Osgood, *Advanced Calculus* (New York, 1925), Chapter V, especially pp. 140–41.

[6] *Principles*, p. 95.

Thus the derivatives $\phi'(p)$ and $\psi'(q)$ describe, respectively, the outcomes of two conceptually distinct individual-experiments. Indeed, by their very nature these two experiments cannot be conducted simultaneously. It is, of course, true that

$$(1.5) \qquad \psi'(q) = \frac{1}{\phi'(p)};$$

but this "inverse function rule"[7] should be understood as stating that the effect of an arbitrary variation in price on the quantity demanded also gives us information about the outcome of an alternative experiment which measures the effect of an arbitrary variation in quantity on the demand price.

So much for individual-experiments; let us now turn to market-experiments. Let $q^S = g(p)$ represent the supply function of the market, and equation (1.1) the corresponding demand function. Then the equilibrium position of this market is described by the following system of equations:

$$q^D = \phi(p),$$
$$(1.6) \qquad q^S = g(p),$$
$$q^D = q^S = q.$$

From the viewpoint of the system as a whole, neither dq/dp nor dp/dq has any meaning. For, by assumption, this system describes one point—the equilibrium point (q_0, p_0) in Figure A-1—and the derivative of a point is not defined. In other words, system (1.6) fixes a unique, constant value for p and a unique, constant value for q. Hence it is meaningless to inquire as to the effect of a change in one of these variables on the other. But this, after all, is what is meant by a derivative.

Let us now assume that demand depends also on population, which is assumed to be uninfluenced by the economic forces of our market. Denote this variable by t. Then the foregoing system is replaced by

$$q^D = f(p, t),$$
$$(1.7) \qquad q^S = g(p),$$
$$q^D = q^S = q.$$

[7] Cf. R. G. D. Allen, *Mathematical Analysis for Economists* (London, 1938), pp. 171–72.

Instead of (1.2), we now have the partial derivatives denoted by

(1.8)
$$\frac{\partial q^D}{\partial p} = \frac{\partial f(p, t)}{\partial p} \equiv f_1(p, t)$$

and

(1.9)
$$\frac{\partial q^D}{\partial t} = \frac{\partial f(p, t)}{\partial t} \equiv f_2(p, t),$$

where the numbers 1 and 2 denote, respectively, the first and second arguments of $f(p, t)$. The derivative (1.8) measures the same individual-experiment as (1.2); hence it too is negative. The derivative (1.9)

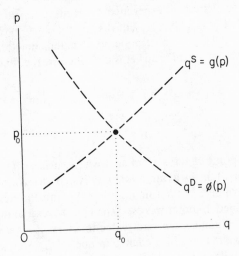

FIGURE A-1.

measures an individual-experiment in which the population of the economy is suddenly increased, the price being kept constant, and the effect of this increase on the amount demanded is noted. This partial derivative is assumed to be positive.

Let us now consider system (1.7) as a whole. This consists of four equations in the four dependent variables q^D, q^S, q, and p, and the single independent variable t. Assume that it can accordingly be solved for the dependent variables as functions of the independent one to yield the system of functions

(1.10)
$$p = J(t),$$
$$q^D = q^S = q = K(t).$$

For any given value of t, systems (1.7) and (1.10) must, by definition, yield the same values for q^D, q^S, q, and p, respectively. In this sense these two systems are equivalent.

From system (1.10) we can immediately see that as long as t remains constant there can be no change in either p or q. Hence in system (1.7) as a whole, as in system (1.6), it remains meaningless[8] to inquire as to the effect of a change in p on q, or vice versa. For p and q are the dependent variables of the system: they cannot change unless the independent variable t changes first. All that we can meaningfully ask about is the effects of a change in t on p or on q. These effects are described, respectively, by the following derivatives:

(1.11)
$$\frac{dp}{dt} = J'(t),$$

(1.12)
$$\frac{dq}{dt} = K'(t).$$

Though, as just emphasized, systems (1.7) and (1.10) as a whole are equivalent, their individual functions are obviously distinct. In particular, those of (1.7) are demand and supply functions, conceptually generated by individual-experiments whose purpose it is to relate amounts demanded and supplied to arbitrarily given price and population levels; while those of (1.10) are market-equilibrium functions, conceptually generated by market-experiments whose purpose it is to relate equilibrium levels of price and quantity to arbitrarily given levels of population.[9] Correspondingly, the derivative of (1.9) is distinct from that of (1.12). The former describes the outcome of the individual-experiment sketched out on the preceding page. The latter describes the outcome of a market-experiment which begins with the

[8] Meaningless, that is, as long as the dependent and independent variables are defined as they are above. Mathematically, however, there is no reason why p or q could not be designated as an independent variable and t as a dependent one. But this possibility has been excluded by our economic assumption about the exogenous nature of population growth.
[9] Cf. Chapter III:6.

market in a position of equilibrium, disturbs this position by an arbitrary change in population, and then measures the effect of this change on the equilibrium quantity of the market. Clearly, there is no necessity for these two derivatives to be equal.

It is precisely its failure to underline this fundamental distinction that makes the usual notation of differential calculus so undesirable for economic analysis. Thus the symbol dq/dt leaves it dangerously ambiguous as to whether the reference is to $f_2(p, t)$ of equation (1.9) or to $K'(t)$ of equation (1.12). Indeed, it fails to draw attention to the fact that such a distinction even exists. Chapters VIII:2 and XV:2 afford examples of the possible confusions to which this imprecision can lead.

Correspondingly, it is this ambiguity which has led to the adoption in this Appendix of the admittedly cumbersome notation which denotes the derivative of a function of a single variable by adding a prime to the function [see, e.g., equations (1.2) and (1.11)], and the partial derivative of a function of several variables by adding a subscript to the function to designate the argument with respect to which the partial derivative is being taken [see, e.g., equations (1.8) and (1.9)]. This notation has the additional advantage of emphasizing that the derivative itself is a function—though, of course, a different one—of the same variables on which the originally derived function depends.

We note finally that the distinction made here between demand functions and market-equilibrium functions is the same one made in the econometric literature between "structural relations" and the "reduced form."[10]

b. THE MULTIPLIER AS AN EXAMPLE

Before continuing, let us briefly consider another example which illustrates the importance of the distinction just made. This example is drawn from the familiar field of multiplier analysis.

[10] Cf., e.g., Jacob Marschak, "Economic Measurements for Policy and Prediction," in *Studies in Econometric Method* (ed. W. C. Hood and T. C. Koopmans, New York, 1953), pp. 3–4; L. R. Klein, *Econometrics* (Evanston, Ill., 1953), p. 113. The classic discussion of this distinction is, of course, Trygve Haavelmo's "The Probability Approach in Econometrics," *Econometrica*, XII, Supplement (1944), Chapters III and V.

The econometric literature has been concerned mainly with the implications of this distinction for the problem of achieving unbiased estimates of the structural parameters.

Let C, I, and Y represent consumption, investment, and national income, respectively. Assume the equilibrium position of the economy to be described by the following simple equations:

(1.13) $C = H(Y),$

(1.14) $C + I = Y,$

where $H(Y)$ is the consumption function and I is assumed to be exogenous. That is,

(1.15) $I = I_0,$

where the level I_0 is determined by forces outside the economic system. The well-known formula for the multiplier, in its usual notation, is then

(1.16) $$\frac{dY}{dI} = \frac{1}{1 - \dfrac{dC}{dY}}.$$

At first sight this is somewhat puzzling. For, by (1.15), dI/dY is obviously zero; yet by the formula of (1.16), its apparent reciprocal, dY/dI, is just as obviously not infinite. One cannot dismiss this seeming inconsistency by merely saying that derivatives cannot be treated as fractions. For with respect to the issue at stake, the inverse function rule[11] seems to imply that they can be so treated and that one can validly write

(1.17) $$\frac{dI}{dY} = \frac{1}{\dfrac{dY}{dI}}.$$

We can, however, readily solve this puzzle by resorting to the notation advocated at the end of the preceding section. Consider (1.13)–(1.14). These are two equations in the two dependent variables—C and Y— and the one independent variable—I. Solving for the dependent variables as functions of the independent one, we obtain

(1.18) $Y = M(I),$

(1.19) $C = N(I).$

---

[11] Cf. above, equation (1.5).

These functions relate a given level of investment to the corresponding equilibrium levels of income and consumption. They are, in our terminology, market-equilibrium functions, in contradistinction to the aggregate demand function represented in (1.13).

Now, by definition, the multiplier is the derivative of (1.18) with respect to I: it describes the outcome of a market-experiment in which the level of investment is arbitrarily changed, and the effect of this change on the equilibrium level of national income is noted. Clearly, this derivative need bear no relationship to the derivative of (1.15) with respect to Y: this describes the outcome of an individual-experiment in which the level of national income is arbitrarily changed, and the effect of this change on the planned level of investment is noted. By the assumption that investment is exogenous, this effect must, of course, be identically zero.

Let us now substitute from (1.13) into (1.14) to yield

$$(1.20) \qquad\qquad H(Y) + I = Y.$$

Substituting from (1.18), we then have, by definition of a solution,

$$(1.21) \qquad\qquad H[M(I)] + I \equiv M(I).$$

Making use of the "function of a function" rule,[12] and differentiating both sides of this identity with respect to I, we obtain

$$(1.22) \qquad\qquad H'(Y)M'(I) + 1 = M'(I).$$

This yields

$$(1.23) \qquad\qquad M'(I) = \frac{1}{1 - H'(Y)},$$

where $H'(Y)$ is evaluated at the point of equilibrium.

This is the formula for the multiplier in its most explicit form. It makes unmistakably clear that the derivative on the left-hand side of (1.16) is related to the function (1.18), and not to the investment function (1.15). Thus it also makes clear that our original "puzzle" is merely the result of the failure to distinguish between the derivatives of these two completely different functions.

---

[12] Allen, *op. cit.*, p. 169.

c. The Meaning of Implicit Differentiation

Let us now return to our discussion in Section *a*. This assumes that the derivatives of the market-equilibrium functions in (1.11)–(1.12) are computed directly from these functions after they have been explicitly solved out from the system of demand and supply equations (1.7). Actually, however, we can obtain these derivatives without first working out this solution. In brief, we can instead make use of the technique of implicit differentiation.[13]

In order to understand this technique—which is used throughout the Appendix—we shall first define the "total differential." Consider, for example, the function $u = H(x, y)$. Let there now be arbitrary incremental changes in the independent variables. Denote these changes by the differentials dx and dy, respectively. These changes must clearly cause a corresponding incremental change in the value of the dependent variable u. Denote this by du or $dH(\ \ )$, where $H(\ \ )$ represents the function $H(x, y)$. Then it can be shown—and this is the fundamental theorem—that

(1.24) $$du = H_1(x, y)dx + H_2(x, y)dy,$$

where, as already noted, the subscripts indicate the argument with respect to which partial differentiation is being carried out.

Assume now that x and y are themselves the functions of other variables,

(1.25) $$x = \phi(v, w) \quad \text{and} \quad y = \psi(v, w).$$

Then, by the fundamental theorem,

(1.26) $$dx = \phi_1(v, w)dv + \phi_2(v, w)dw,$$
$$dy = \psi_1(v, w)dv + \psi_2(v, w)dw.$$

Substituting in (1.24), we then obtain

(1.27) $$du = H_1(\ \ )[\phi_1(\ \ )dv + \phi_2(\ \ )dw]$$
$$+ H_2(\ \ )[\psi_1(\ \ )dv + \psi_2(\ \ )dw].$$

[13] The following is a somewhat amateurish version of the relevant parts of Osgood, *op. cit.*, Chapter V. See also Allen, *op. cit.*, Chapter XIII, and R. Courant, *Differential and Integral Calculus* (2nd ed.; London, 1937), Vol. I, pp. 457–85; Vol. II, pp. 59–69, 72–73.

Actually, the end of the preceding section has already made use of the technique of implicit differentiation.

This is the "function of a function" rule for differentials. It should be emphasized that it holds no matter what the nature of the transformation (1.25). In particular, it holds also when we use the transformation $x = x$ and $y = f(x)$. In this case (1.27) becomes

(1.28) $$du = H_1[x, f(x)]dx + H_2[x, f(x)]f'(x)dx.$$

Before applying these equations to the example of the first section, let us make this discussion somewhat more general by assuming that just as there is an exogenous variable influencing the demand side, so is there one on the supply side. In particular, let m be an index of climatic factors, and let an increase in m increase the amount supplied. System (1.7) is thus replaced by

(1.29)
$$q^D = f(p, t),$$
$$q^S = h(p, m),$$
$$q^D = q^S = q.$$

By assumption, the partial derivatives of these functions have the signs $f_1(p, t) < 0$, $f_2(p, t) > 0$, $h_1(p, m) > 0$, and $h_2(p, m) > 0$.

Now, system (1.29) is one of four equations in the four dependent variables—q^D, q^S, q, and p—and the two independent variables—t and m. Assume, then, that it can be solved for the dependent variables in terms of the independent ones to yield the market-equilibrium functions (or reduced form)

(1.30)
$$p = F(t, m),$$
$$q^D = q^S = q = G(t, m).$$

It is desired to determine the signs and magnitudes of the partial derivatives of these functions with respect to t and m without explicitly solving for the functions $F(\quad)$ and $G(\quad)$ themselves.

The first step is to substitute the unspecified solutions (1.30) into (1.29) to yield—by definition of a solution—

(1.31)
$$G(t, m) \equiv f[F(t, m), t],$$
$$G(t, m) \equiv h[F(t, m), m].$$

We next apply the fundamental theorem (1.24) in order to take the total differential of both sides of these identities and to obtain

(1.32)
$$dG(t, m) = f_1(p, t)dF(t, m) + f_2(p, t)dt,$$
$$dG(t, m) = h_1(p, m)dF(t, m) + h_2(p, m)dm,$$

where the partial derivatives of $f(\quad)$ and $h(\quad)$ are evaluated at the point of equilibrium. Upon expansion, this yields

(1.33)
$$G_1(t, m)dt + G_2(t, m)dm = f_1(p, t)[F_1(t, m)dt + F_2(t, m)dm]$$
$$+ f_2(p, t)dt,$$
$$G_1(t, m)dt + G_2(t, m)dm = h_1(p, m)[F_1(t, m)dt + F_2(t, m)dm]$$
$$+ h_2(p, m)dm.$$

In this system of equations, $f_i(\quad)$ and $h_i(\quad)$ $(i = 1, 2)$ are the known partial derivatives of the specified functions $f(\quad)$ and $h(\quad)$; while $F_i(\quad)$ and $G_i(\quad)$ are the unknown partial derivatives of the unspecified functions $F(\quad)$ and $G(\quad)$.

Let us first assume that only t varies, while m remains constant. That is, $dm = 0$. Substituting this into (1.33) and dividing through by dt, we obtain

(1.34)
$$G_1(t, m) = f_1(p, t)F_1(t, m) + f_2(p, t),$$
$$G_1(t, m) = h_1(p, m)F_1(t, m).$$

Rewrite this as

(1.35)
$$f_1(p, t)F_1(t, m) - G_1(t, m) = -f_2(p, t),$$
$$h_1(p, m)F_1(t, m) - G_1(t, m) = 0.$$

This can be considered as a system of two equations in the two unknowns $F_1(t, m)$ and $G_1(t, m)$. Solving this system by the use of determinants, we obtain

(1.36) $\quad F_1(t, m) = \dfrac{\begin{vmatrix} -f_2(p, t) & -1 \\ 0 & -1 \end{vmatrix}}{\begin{vmatrix} f_1(p, t) & -1 \\ h_1(p, m) & -1 \end{vmatrix}} = \dfrac{f_2(p, t)}{-f_1(p, t) + h_1(p, m)}.$

According to the assumptions made above as to the signs of $f_i(\ )$ and $h_i(\ )$ $(i = 1, 2)$, we see that $F_1(t, m)$ is always positive. Similarly, we obtain

$$(1.37) \qquad G_1(t, m) = \frac{h_1(p, m)f_2(p, t)}{-f_1(p, t) + h_1(p, m)},$$

which must also be positive. That is, a positive shift in tastes increases both the equilibrium price and quantity: a rightward shift of the demand curve intersects the unchanged supply curve at a higher price and quantity.

In a corresponding way, by permitting only m to vary, and setting $dt = 0$, we obtain

$$(1.38) \qquad F_2(t, m) = \frac{-h_2(p, m)}{-f_1(p, t) + h_1(p, m)} < 0$$

and

$$(1.39) \qquad G_2(t, m) = \frac{-f_1(p, t)h_2(p, m)}{-f_1(p, t) + h_1(p, m)} > 0.$$

That is, favorable climatic conditions increase the equilibrium quantity, but decrease the equilibrium price: a rightward shift of the supply curve intersects the fixed demand curve at a higher quantity, but lower price.

Thus the properties of the unknown derivatives can be specified in terms of the known derivatives—without explicitly solving for the functions $F(\ )$ and $G(\ )$. This, of course, is the meaning of implicit differentiation.

We note finally that equation (1.37) clearly shows the distinction emphasized at the end of Section a above. In terms of systems (1.7) and (1.10) discussed there, this equation takes the form

$$(1.40) \qquad K'(t) = \frac{g'(p)f_2(p, t)}{-f_1(p, t) + g'(p)}$$

Here we explicitly see that $K'(t)$ and $f_2(p, t)$ are two distinct derivatives. True, the former does depend upon the latter; but it depends just as well upon $g'(p)$ and $f_1(p, t)$.

d. MAXIMIZATION SUBJECT TO SIDE RESTRAINTS.
THE TECHNIQUE OF LAGRANGE MULTIPLIERS

Another important application of the total differential—and one used repeatedly in this Appendix—is that connected with maximization subject to side restraints. For rigorous treatments of this question the reader is referred elsewhere.[14] Our present purpose is to provide an intuitive understanding of the problems involved.

Assume, for example, that it is desired to maximize

$$(1.41) \qquad w = f(x, y).$$

This, of course, is accomplished by choosing those values of x and y which satisfy the system of equations

$$(1.42) \qquad \begin{aligned} f_1(x, y) &= 0, \\ f_2(x, y) &= 0, \end{aligned}$$

where $f_i(\quad)$ $(i = 1, 2)$ is the partial derivative of $f(\quad)$ with respect to its ith argument.[15] Let us now assume that the maximization of $f(\quad)$ is to be carried out subject to the additional restriction

$$(1.43) \qquad y = g(x).$$

Then we are no longer free to choose both x and y as in (1.42); for (1.43) tells us that once the value of x is chosen, that of y is specified. In effect, then, we are no longer maximizing a function of two variables —x and y—but a function of one variable only. In particular, substituting (1.43) into (1.41), our problem reduces to the ordinary maximization of

$$(1.44) \qquad w = f[x, g(x)] \equiv h(x)$$

with respect to x.

It might help to visualize this problem if we think of $w = f(x, y)$ as describing the height of a hill at each of its points.[16] If we wish to find the maximum point of this hill, we obviously choose those values of x

---

[14] Osgood, *op. cit.*, pp. 180–82. A more detailed treatment can be found in T. Chaundy, *Differential Calculus* (Oxford, 1935), pp. 256 ff.

[15] We assume throughout this section—and the Mathematical Appendix in general —that the second-order conditions for a maximum are satisfied.

[16] The following illustration is due to Allen, *op. cit.*, p. 365.

and y which correspond to its peak. But our task may be limited instead to finding the highest point on the path on this hill which is cut out by its intersection with the vertical surface described by $y = g(x)$. This is what is involved in the maximization of $w = h(x)$. Clearly, there is no reason why this path should pass through the peak; hence there is also no reason why the value of x yielded by the maximization of $w = h(x)$ should be the same as that yielded by the unrestricted maximization of $w = f(x, y)$.

More generally, assume that we wish to maximize

$$(1.45) \qquad u = \psi(x_1, \dots, x_n),$$

subject to the m side restraints,

$$(1.46) \qquad \phi^j(x_1, \dots, x_n) = 0 \qquad (j = 1, \dots, m < n).$$

Assume that we can solve out the m equations of (1.46) for $x_1, \dots, x_m$ as explicit functions of the remaining x_i:

$$(1.47) \qquad x_j = F^j(x_{m+1}, \dots, x_n) \qquad (j = 1, \dots, m).$$

Then the desired maximization is achieved by substituting from (1.47) into (1.45) to yield

$$(1.48) \qquad \begin{aligned} u &= \psi[F^1(x_{m+1}, \dots, x_n), \dots, F^m(x_{m+1}, \dots, x_n), x_{m+1}, \dots, x_n] \\ &\equiv G(x_{m+1}, \dots, x_n), \end{aligned}$$

and by maximizing $G(\quad)$ with respect to its $n - m$ variables.[17]

As in the case of implicit differentiation, however, it is desirable to find a method by which we can find this maximum position without the necessity of carrying out the foregoing substitution explicitly. This is the method of Lagrange multipliers. Let us first see how it is applied to the simple case discussed in (1.41)–(1.44) above.

We form first the sum

$$(1.49) \qquad v = f(x, y) - \lambda[y - g(x)],$$

where λ—the so-called Lagrange multiplier—is a new variable arbitrarily introduced into the analysis. Let us now find the values of x

---

[17] Note that if $m = n$, the function $G(\quad)$ becomes a constant, so that the problem of maximization disappears. More specifically, under this assumption, system (1.46) has n equations which are assumed to be sufficient to determine specific values for each of the n variables, x_i ($i = 1, \dots, n$). Hence no freedom is left to choose values of these variables that enable $G(\quad)$ to satisfy some maximization criterion.

and y which maximize this sum for a given value of λ. Differentiating partially with respect to x and y, we obtain the maximum conditions

(1.50) $$f_1(x, y) + \lambda g'(x) = 0,$$

(1.51) $$f_2(x, y) - \lambda = 0.$$

To these we add the side restriction (1.43),

(1.52) $$y = g(x).$$

Thus (1.50)–(1.52) are three equations in the three variables—x, y, and λ. It now remains to show that the value of x determined by this system of equations is necessarily that value which maximizes $w = h(x)$ in (1.44).

In order for $h(x)$ to be at a maximum, its total differential must be zero. That is, it must be impossible to increase $h(x)$ by any incremental displacement dx in the value of x. Using the identity of (1.44), we express this condition as

(1.53) $$dh(x) \equiv df[x, g(x)] = 0.$$

Expanding by (1.28), we then obtain

(1.54) $$f_1[x, g(x)]dx + f_2[x, g(x)]g'(x)dx = 0.$$

Dividing through by dx this reduces to

(1.55) $$f_1[x, g(x)] + f_2[x, g(x)]g'(x) = 0.$$

But substituting from (1.51) and (1.52) into (1.50), we see that this is precisely the condition which emerges from the use of the Lagrange multiplier. Thus both methods determine the same value of x, and hence—by (1.43)—the same value of y.

Let us now consider the more general case described in (1.45)–(1.48). We introduce into the analysis the Lagrange multipliers λ_j ($j = 1, \dots, m$) and form the sum

(1.56) $$V = \psi(x_1, \dots, x_n) - \sum_{j=1}^{m} \lambda_j[x_j - F^j(x_{m+1}, \dots, x_n)].$$

Let us now find the values of the x_i ($i = 1, \dots, n$) which maximize this sum for given values of the λ_j. Differentiating partially with respect to the x_i, we obtain

$$(1.57) \qquad \psi_j(x_1, \dots, x_n) - \lambda_j = 0 \qquad (j = 1, \dots, m),$$

$$(1.58) \qquad \psi_r(x_1, \dots, x_n) + \sum_{j=1}^{m} \lambda_j F_r^j(x_{m+1}, \dots, x_n) = 0$$
$$(r = m + 1, \dots, n).$$

Add now the side conditions (1.47),

$$(1.59) \qquad x_j = F^j(x_{m+1}, \dots, x_n) \qquad (j = 1, \dots, m).$$

Altogether, then, we have $n + m$ equations in the $n + m$ variables— x_i $(i = 1, \dots, m, m + 1, \dots, n)$ and λ_j $(j = 1, \dots, m)$. It remains to show that the values of the x_r $(r = m + 1, \dots, n)$ determined by this system of equations are necessarily those which maximize $u = G(x_{m+1}, \dots, x_n)$ in equation (1.48).

In order for $G(\quad)$ to be at a maximum, its total differential,

$$(1.60) \qquad du = \sum_{r=m+1}^{n} G_r(x_{m+1}, \dots, x_n)dx_r,$$

must be zero no matter what the nature of the displacements dx_r.[18] In particular, setting all but one of the dx_r equal to zero by turn, we obtain the $n - m$ maximum conditions

$$(1.61) \qquad G_r(x_{m+1}, \dots, x_n)dx_r = 0 \qquad (r = m + 1, \dots, n).$$

By (1.27) and identity (1.48), these can be written as[19]

$$(1.62) \qquad \sum_{j=1}^{m} \psi_j[\quad]F_r^j(\quad)dx_r + \psi_r[\quad]dx_r = 0$$
$$(r = m + 1, \dots, n).$$

Dividing through by dx_r, we obtain the conditions that must be satisfied by the x_r $(r = m + 1, \dots, n)$ in order to maximize $G(\quad)$. But substituting from (1.57) and (1.59) into (1.58), we see that these are precisely the conditions which emerge from the use of the Lagrange multipliers. Thus both methods determine the same values of the x_r $(r = m + 1, \dots, n)$, and hence—by (1.47)—the same values of the x_j $(j = 1, \dots, m)$.

[18] Cf. Courant, *op. cit.*, Vol. II, p. 185.
[19] The brackets in the following expression emphasize the fact that we are considering the function ψ after substitution—that is, in the form described by (1.48).

2. Appendix to Chapter II

a. THE DEMAND AND EXCESS-DEMAND FUNCTIONS FOR COMMODITIES[1]

Consider an economy with n goods, the nth being paper money. Let $p_1, \ldots, p_n$ be the prices of these goods in terms of an abstract unit of account. The corresponding money prices are, then, $p_1/p_n, \ldots, p_{n-1}/p_n, 1$. Finally, the relative prices of the $n-1$ commodities are $p_1/p_k, \ldots, p_{n-1}/p_k$. Define now the absolute level of commodity prices as

$$(2.1) \qquad p = \sum_{j=1}^{n-1} w_j p_j,$$

where the w_j are known weights whose nature will be explained in the next section. The relative prices can then be written $p_1/p, \ldots, p_{n-1}/p$.

Consider a particular individual, the ath. Let $\bar{Z}_1^a, \ldots, \bar{Z}_{n-1}^a$ represent the respective quantities of his initial holdings of the $n-1$ commodities. Similarly, let $\bar{Z}_n^a$ represent his initial quantity of money. Then his real nonmonetary wealth is represented by $\sum_{j=1}^{n-1} p_j \bar{Z}_j^a/p$; his real money balances, by $p_n \bar{Z}_n^a/p$; and his real wealth, by the sum of these two items (above, pp. 19–20). Let $Z_1^a, \ldots, Z_{n-1}^a$ represent the respective quantities of his optimum collection of commodities. Then the demand functions are assumed to have the forms[2]

---

[1] Attached to Chapter II:3–4.

[2] In view of the comments at the end of Mathematical Appendix 1:a above, it might be well to point out that the $F_j(\ )$ are *not* partial derivatives.

$$(2.2) \qquad Z_j^a = F_j^a\left(\frac{p_1}{p}, \dots, \frac{p_{n-1}}{p}, \frac{\sum_{r=1}^{n-1} p_r \bar{Z}_r^a}{p} + \frac{p_n \bar{Z}_n^a}{p}\right) \qquad (j = 1, \dots, n-1).$$

Define now the excess demand for a commodity

$$(2.3) \qquad\qquad X_j^a = Z_j^a - \bar{Z}_j^a \qquad\qquad (j = 1, \dots, n-1).$$

Then the commodity excess-demand functions of the ath individual can be written as

$$(2.4) \qquad X_j^a = F_j^a\left(\frac{p_1}{p}, \dots, \frac{p_{n-1}}{p}, \frac{\sum_{r=1}^{n-1} p_r \bar{Z}_r^a}{p} + \frac{p_n \bar{Z}_n^a}{p}\right) - \bar{Z}_j^a$$
$$(j = 1, \dots, n-1).$$

These functions clearly have the properties attributed to them in the text: they depend on relative prices and real wealth, inclusive of the real value of initial money balances (see, however, p. 17, footnote 7). In technical terms, they are homogeneous of degree zero in accounting prices—or, alternatively, in money prices and money wealth.[3]

The demand functions (2.2) treat the p_i $(i = 1, \dots, n)$ as the independent variables and the Z_j^a as the dependent ones. Let us now reverse the roles of these variables and form accordingly the inverse functions of (2.2). We first rewrite (2.1) as

$$(2.5) \qquad\qquad \sum_{j=1}^{n-1} w_j \frac{p_j}{p} = 1.$$

Consider now equations (2.2) and (2.5) as n equations in the n variables p_j/p $(j = 1, \dots, n-1)$ and $p_n \bar{Z}_n^a/p$. Assume that we can solve these equations for the inverse functions

$$(2.6) \qquad \frac{p_j}{p} = \phi_j^a(Z_1^a, \dots, Z_{n-1}^a; \bar{Z}_1^a, \dots, \bar{Z}_{n-1}^a)$$
$$(j = 1, \dots, n-1),$$

$$(2.7) \qquad \frac{p_n \bar{Z}_n^a}{p} = \phi_n^a(Z_1^a, \dots, Z_{n-1}^a; \bar{Z}_1^a, \dots, \bar{Z}_{n-1}^a).$$

[3] On the properties of homogeneous functions, see K. J. Arrow, "Homogeneous Systems in Mathematical Economics: A Comment," *Econometrica*, XVIII (1950), 60–62.

Dividing (2.6) by (2.7), we then obtain

$$(2.8) \qquad \frac{p_j}{p_n} = \frac{\bar{Z}_n^a \phi_j^a(Z_1^a, \ldots, Z_{n-1}^a; \bar{Z}_1^a, \ldots, \bar{Z}_{n-1}^a)}{\phi_n^a(Z_1^a, \ldots, Z_{n-1}^a; \bar{Z}_1^a, \ldots, \bar{Z}_{n-1}^a)}$$

$$(j = 1, \ldots, n-1).$$

These are Marshallian demand functions: they express the money demand prices an individual is willing to pay, p_j/p_n, as functions of the Z_j^a and $\bar{Z}_j^a (j = 1, \ldots, n-1)$ (cf. p. 388 above). As can be seen from (2.8) an increase in $\bar{Z}_n^a$ causes a proportionate increase in these demand prices.

b. The Wealth Effect and the Real-Balance Effect[4]

For simplicity, drop the index a in functions (2.2) and set $p_n = 1$. Let $T = \sum_{j=1}^{n-1} p_j \bar{Z}_j$ and $W = T + \bar{Z}_n$ respectively represent the individual's nonmonetary and total wealth in money terms. Consider an individual who at the given prices $p_1^0, \ldots, p_{n-1}^0$ and wealth $W^0 = \sum_{j=1}^{n-1} p_j^0 \bar{Z}_j + \bar{Z}_n = T^0 + \bar{Z}_n$ chooses—in accordance with demand functions (2.2) and (2.19)—Collection Zero consisting of commodity-basket $(Z_1^0, \ldots, Z_{n-1}^0)$ and real money holdings Z_n^0/p^0, where $p^0 = \sum_{j=1}^{n-1} p_j^0 Z_j^0$ is the total cost of the commodity-basket. Denote the cost of this basket at any set of prices p_j by $p = \sum_{j=1}^{n-1} p_j Z_j^0$ and the corresponding total cost of Collection Zero by

$$P = p + p\left(\frac{Z_n^0}{p^0}\right) = p\left(1 + \frac{Z_n^0}{p^0}\right).$$

[4] Attached to Chapter II:3, *et passim.*

Essential background material for this section is provided by Mosak's (*op. cit.*). well-known and illuminating comparison of the Slutzky and Hicks definitions of the substitution effect. Note in particular the proof (due to A. Wald) that in the limit these definitions (and hence the corresponding definitions of the wealth effect) are equivalent (*ibid.*, p. 73, footnote 5).

For a Hicksian analysis of the problem of this section see Per Meinich's stimulating discussion in his "Money Illusion and the Real Balance Effect", *Statsøknomisk Tidsskrift*, LXXVIII (1964), 9–16, 20–21. Note, however, that Meinich's definition of the real-balance effect (*ibid.*, p. 16) differs from the ones presented at the end of this section. The reader is also referred to Meinich's well-taken criticisms (*ibid.*, pp. 13–14, 23–26) of Cliff Lloyd's recent "The Real-Balance Effect: *Sine Qua What?*," *op. cit.*, and "The Real-Balance Effect and the Slutzky Equation," *op. cit.*

The first—and, from certain viewpoints, still most general—development of the Slutzky equation for a monetary economy is to be found in Leser's 1943 *Econometrica* paper described on p. 574 below.

I am indebted to Nissan Liviatan for helpful discussions of various points in this section.

Finally, let

$$P^0 = p^0\left(1 + \frac{Z_n^0}{p^0}\right)$$

be the total money cost of Collection Zero at the given prices. By the budget restraint, $P^0 = W^0$.

The variable p is what we define as the absolute price level. Note that it is *not* an average of prices. It is clear from the definition of P that p can also be considered as the price of real money holdings (cf. p. 28 above).

The effect of a unit increase in money wealth on the amount demanded of Z_j can now be described as

$$(2.9) \qquad \frac{\partial Z_j}{\partial W} = F_{jn}(\quad) \frac{\partial(W/p)}{\partial W} = \frac{F_{jn}}{p},$$

where $F_{jn}(\quad)$ is the partial derivative of $F_j(\quad)$ with respect to its nth argument. Clearly,

$$(2.10) \qquad \frac{\partial Z_j}{\partial W} = \frac{\partial Z_j}{\partial T} = \frac{\partial Z_j}{\partial \bar{Z}_n};$$

that is, since every dollar of money wealth is like any other one, it can make no difference whether the aforementioned unit increase takes place in nonmonetary wealth or in initial money balances.

Assume now that the individual at Collection Zero is confronted with an equiproportionate increase in money prices from p_j^0 to $p_j^0 + dp_j$, where $dp_j^0/p^0 = m$ $(j = 1, \ldots, n - 1)$ is the common factor of proportion. Correspondingly, p increases to $p^0 + dp = p^0 + mp^0 = p^0(1 + m)$. Similarly, the cost of Collection Zero increases to $(1 + m)P^0$. At the same time, the nonmonetary component of wealth increases to $(1 + m)T^0$. Hence the compensating variation in money wealth necessary to enable the individual to continue purchasing Collection Zero after the price increase is $dW = m\bar{Z}_n$; for the money wealth of an individual so compensated is $(1 + m)T^0 + (1 + m)\bar{Z}_n = (1 + m)W^0 = (1 + m)P^0$. In brief, in order to leave the individual as well off (in Slutzky's sense of the term) as he was before, we must increase his originally chosen money balances in the same proportion that the absolute price level has increased.

Continuing to follow Slutzky, let us define the wealth effect of this equiproportionate price change as the effect on the demand for Z_j (per unit change in p) of the *failure* to make the foregoing compensating variation in money wealth. That is, the wealth effect is

$$(2.11) \qquad -\frac{\partial Z_j}{\partial W}\frac{dW}{dp} = -\frac{\bar{Z}_n}{p}\frac{\partial Z_j}{\partial W},$$

where use has been made of the fact that the compensating variation $dW = m\bar{Z}_n = (dp/p)\bar{Z}_n$. Note further that since the equiproportionate change in prices leaves the p_j/p ($j = 1, \ldots, n-1$) constant in demand function (2.2), the partial derivative of this function with respect to this price change stems only from the argument representing real wealth, W/p.[5] That is,

$$\frac{\partial Z_j}{\partial p} = \frac{\partial Z_j}{\partial (W/p)} \cdot \frac{\partial (W/p)}{\partial (\bar{Z}_n/p)} \cdot \frac{\partial (\bar{Z}_n/p)}{\partial p}$$

$$(2.12) \qquad = F_{jn} \cdot 1 \cdot \left(-\frac{\bar{Z}_n}{p^2} \right)$$

$$= -\frac{\bar{Z}_n}{p}\frac{F_{jn}}{p} = -\frac{\bar{Z}_n}{p}\frac{\partial Z_j}{\partial W},$$

where use has been made of (2.9). Comparing (2.12) with (2.11) we then see that an equiproportionate change in money prices has only a wealth effect; in Slutzky's terms, there is no "residual variation" to manifest itself as a substitution effect. Furthermore, it is clear from (2.12) that the wealth effect stems entirely from the existence of wealth in the form of initial money balances, $\bar{Z}_n$, as distinct from nonmonetary

[5] Actually, from a Slutzky viewpoint, the proper deflator of W [and hence the p_j in demand function (2.2)] is P, and not p: for W/P represents the number of Collections Zero that can be purchased with the given money wealth at the given array of prices, and is therefore a more appropriate definition of "real wealth". Since, however, P is proportionate to p, this does not affect the analysis.

We can however, make use of this interpretation of W/P to note that that part of the partial derivative of (2.2) that stems from the $n-1$ arguments representing relative prices can be described as

$$\left(\frac{\partial Z_j}{\partial p} \right)\frac{W}{P} = \frac{W^0}{P^0} = 1,$$

where the derivative is evaluated at Collection Zero. Thus this part of the partial derivative represents the change in the amount demanded of Z_j caused by the change in p, under the condition that the individual is still able to purchase Collection Zero. Hence it can be identified with the Slutzky substitution effect. The constancy of relative prices in the present case then makes it clear that this effect is zero—which is an alternative demonstration of the argument which now follows.

wealth, T. That is, there is a real-balance effect, but no nonmonetary-wealth effect (cf. p. 20 above).

Consider now the case of a change in a single price p_k to $p_k^0 + dp_k$, all other commodity prices remaining constant. The compensating variation in money wealth necessary to enable the individual to continue purchasing Collection Zero is

$$(2.13) \qquad dW = (Z_k^0 - \bar{Z}_k)\, dp_k + Z_n^0 \frac{dp}{p^0},$$

where the first term is the familiar Slutzky compensation that must be made in order to enable the individual to buy the same net amount of Z_k as he originally did, and the second term is once again the proportionate increase in nominal money holdings that must take place in order to preserve their real purchasing power in terms of the commodity-basket $(Z_1^0, \ldots, Z_{n-1}^0)$. In the present case, however, the cost of this basket has increased by $dp = Z_k^0 dp_k$. Hence the Slutzky equation has the form

$$(2.14) \qquad \frac{\partial Z_j}{\partial p_k} = S_{jk} - \left[(Z_k^0 - \bar{Z}_k) + Z_k^0 \frac{Z_n^0}{p^0} \right] \frac{\partial Z_j}{\partial W},$$

where the second term is the wealth effect and the first one, S_{jk}, is the substitution effect.[6] Equation (2.14) clearly includes the usual Slutzky equation as the special case of a barter economy, in which by definition $Z_n^0 = 0$.

As Meinich has pointed out (see footnote 6 below), the seemingly strange form of the wealth effect in (2.14) simply reflects the fact that—in contrast with the standard Slutzky-Hicks case—$\partial Z_j / \partial p_k$ in this

[6] For an explicit definition of S_{jk} in terms of a bordered utility determinant, see Meinich, *op. cit.*, p. 14. As Meinich points out (*ibid.*, p. 15, footnote 10), in contrast with the usual Slutzky-Hicks substitution term, S_{kk} is not necessarily negative. An interpretation of this fact will be presented in the paragraph which follows.

In order to reduce Meinich's definition of the wealth effect (*ibid.*, pp. 16, 20–21) to the one presented in (2.14), we need only replace the general weights w_j which he uses to define the price level p [see equation (2.1) above] by the specific ones Z_j^0. However, Meinich's decomposition of the Slutzky equation into a "direct effect" (due to the change in p_k) and "indirect effect" (due to the change in p)—a decomposition also made by Leser (*op. cit.*, pp. 130–31)—is of doubtful meaning, for reasons indicated below.

The reader can readily establish that the second term in (2.14) represents that part of the partial derivative of (2.2) stemming from the realwealth argument W/p; i.e., it is $F_{jn}[\partial(W/p)/\partial p_j]$. Hence, using again the approach of the second paragraph of the preceding footnote, the first term S_{jk} represents that part of the partial derivative of (2.2) stemming from the relative-price arguments p_j/p.

equation actually measures the effect on the demand for Z_j of a change in the prices of *two* goods: the kth, with price p_k; and real money holdings, with price p. This is clear from (2.13). Correspondingly, a wealth effect analogous to that of (2.14) would be obtained even in the standard case of a barter economy—provided there were to take place a simultaneous change in two commodity prices, say, p_k and p_t. From this we can also understand the fact, again noted by Meinich, that the substitution term S_{kk} in (2.14) is not necessarily negative. For, to return to our analogy, even if p_k and p_t were to change in the same proportion—so that the kth and t^{th} commodities would be considered as a single composite—there would be no assurance that the substitution effect would be negative for (say) the kth commodity alone (see end of next section). And this is *a fortiori* so when—as in the present case of a change in p_k and p—the two prices do not change in the same proportion.

We have yet to distinguish a real-balance effect as a component part of the total wealth effect in (2.14). As already indicated in the text (p. 20), any such distinction is arbitrary. The natural tendency would be to follow the line of reasoning represented by equations (2.13)–(2.14) and to define the real-balance effect as

$$- \left(Z_k \frac{Z_n}{p} \right) \frac{\partial Z_j}{\partial W}.$$

This definition, however, yields a real-balance effect of

$$- \frac{Z_n}{p} \frac{\partial Z_j}{\partial W}$$

for the case of an equiproportionate change in all money prices, which is inconsistent with the definition used in the discussion of equation (2.12) above. This definition (which is the one used throughout this book) takes as its point of departure not the *originally chosen* quantity of money, but the *initially endowed* one. It follows that the corresponding definition of the real-balance effect of a change in a single price p_k is

$$- \left(Z_k \frac{\bar{Z}_n}{p} \right) \frac{\partial Z_j}{\partial W}.$$

This, of course, equals that part of the partial derivative in (2.14) which stems from $\bar{Z}_n/p$ in demand function (2.2); that is, it equals

$$\frac{\partial Z_j}{\partial (W/p)} \frac{\partial (W/p)}{\partial (\bar{Z}_n/p)} \frac{\partial (\bar{Z}_n/p)}{\partial p_k},$$

which is to be compared with the first line of equation (2.12) above.

Another arbitrary aspect of our definition is reflected in the fact that the total wealth effect of a change in p_k is invariant under a shift in the composition of the initial endowment of the individual as between money and commodities other than the kth. From this viewpoint, then, the significant distinction is not between the monetary and nonmonetary assets of the initial endowment, but between the asset whose price has changed and all other initially held assets.

An even more fundamental question arises if we attempt (as we should) to interpret each of the two terms of the wealth effect from the viewpoint of the compensating variation necessary to keep the individual as well off as he was before. As noted in our discussion of (2.13), these two terms reflect the changes in p_k and p, respectively. Accordingly, since a change in the former necessarily causes one in the latter, there would not seem to be much meaning (from the foregoing viewpoint) in treating them as separate entities. This problem clearly does not arise for the case of simultaneous and independent changes in commodity prices p_k and p_t described above. On the other hand, if the price changes in question are discrete instead of infinitesimal, then it is impossible (again, from the viewpoint of compensating variations) to decompose the overall wealth effect into meaningful component parts in either of the foregoing cases.[7]

It should also be emphasized that the entire argument of this section has been predicated on the assumption that, from the viewpoint of the individual's utility calculus, the proper deflator of nominal money balances is $p = \sum p_j Z_j^0$; that is, that the individual measures the liquidity of his money holdings in terms of the number of commodity-baskets $(Z_1^0, \ldots, Z_{n-1}^0)$ that he can purchase with them. Clearly, this assumption is a reasonable one only if the individual's optimum position is in the neighborhood of this basket. More general results can, however, be achieved by assuming that there exists for each individual a "deflating function" $p = \pi(p_1, \ldots, p_{n-1})$, valid for the entire commodity space and homogeneous of degree one in $p_1, \ldots, p_{n-1}$. In this case, dp in equation (2.13) equals $\pi_k dp_k$, where π_k is the partial derivative of $\pi(\quad)$

[7] The reason is the same as that which makes it meaningless to talk of a cost-of-living allowance to compensate an individual for a discrete change in only one price when he is confronted with simultaneous discrete changes in two or more prices. For an explanation, see Liviatan and Patinkin, "On the Economic Theory of Price Indexes," *op. cit.*, pp. 532 and 535–36.

with respect to p_k. The corresponding Slutzky equation is then obtained from (2.14) by substituting π_k for Z_k^0 as the coefficient of Z_n^0/p^0. Note that the wealth effect in this case differs fundamentally from the usual one in that it cannot be defined solely on the basis of observable quantities(namely, Collection Zero and $\partial Z_j/\partial W$), but requires additional information on the individual's subjective function $\pi(p_1, \ldots, p_{n-1})$. The necessity for information on subjective preferences would be even greater if one were to assume that the individual does not measure the "realness" of his nominal money balances in terms of any overall deflator, but is instead concerned with the separate quantities $\bar{Z}_n/p_1, \ldots, \bar{Z}_n/p_{n-1}$. As will be seen below (pp. 550–51 and 574), this was indeed the assumption adopted by Walras in his pioneering utility analysis of money—and subsequently used by Leser and Samuelson as well.

Two final comments are in order. First, the difficulties in giving economic meaning to a separate real-balance effect in the case of a change in a single price do not affect the basic proposition that the wealth effect in a money economy must reflect the presence of financial assets, and hence the impact of a change in the absolute price level on the real value of such assets. Second, none of the foregoing difficulties arise in the case which is the primary concern of monetary theory, and the only one with which we shall henceforth deal: namely, the case of an equiproportionate change in the p_j ($j = 1, \ldots, n - 1$). Note in particular that even under the general Walrasian assumption that the individual is concerned with the separate quantities $\bar{Z}_n/p_1, \ldots, \bar{Z}_n/p_{n-1}$, the proportions among these "goods" remain fixed in this case, so that they can, following Leontief (see footnote 8 below), be considered as a single composite, $\bar{Z}_n/p$—where p is defined as in (2.1) with arbitrary weights w_j. In any event, it is clear that the real-balance effect in the case of an equiproportionate change in all money prices coincides with the wealth effect and can be unambiguously defined as in (2.12).

c. THE HICKS COMPOSITE-GOOD THEOREM

It will frequently be convenient to be able to treat a group of consumers' goods as a single, composite one. Let us then digress in order to describe certain conditions under which this can be done.

One obvious case is that in which the goods must—for technical reasons—be consumed in fixed proportions. A less obvious case—and one much more important for our purposes—is the one in which not the relative quantities, but the relative prices of the group of goods remain fixed.[8] For convenience—and without effectively restricting the argument—let us assume that there are only three goods, X_1, X_2, and Y, whose respective prices are p_1, p_2, and p_y. Consider a certain combination of X_1 and X_2—say, X_1^0, X_2^0—which is chosen at certain base prices, p_1^0, p_2^0, p_y^0. Let the cost of acquiring this combination at any set of prices be

$$(2.15) \qquad p_x = p_1 X_1^0 + p_2 X_2^0.$$

Finally, represent any other combination of X_1 and X_2 by the quantity index

$$(2.16) \qquad X = \frac{p_1 X_1 + p_2 X_2}{p_1 X_1^0 + p_2 X_2^0}.$$

Thus X is the "real expenditure" on X_1 and X_2. We wish to show that X can be treated analytically as a single good if the ratio of p_1 to p_2 remains constant and equal to p_1^0/p_2^0. Note that this is precisely the condition under which (2.16) will be a "true" quantity index of an observed shift from (X_1^0, X_2^0) to (X_1, X_2): that is, one which measures the magnitude of this shift by the ratio of the respective minimum costs of acquiring the utility levels of these two combinations at a specified set of prices.[9]

Let us first rewrite (2.16) as

$$(2.17) \qquad X = \frac{p_1}{p_x} X_1 + \frac{p_2}{p_x} X_2.$$

The solid lines in Figure A-2 are representations of this equation for different levels of real expenditure X. For convenience, we shall refer to them as "semibudget lines." Their parallelism follows from the assumed constancy of p_1/p_2. Clearly, the higher X, the higher the semibudget line; and conversely. Thus t_1, t_2, t_3, ... in Figure A-2 represent a decreasing sequence of numbers.

[8] See Hicks, *Value and Capital*, pp. 33–34, 312–13. The following demonstration is based on Herman Wold, *Demand Analysis* (Stockholm, 1952), pp. 108–10.

Wold refers to the following as the "Leontief-Hicks theorem." This, however, is a misnomer, for Leontief's discussion refers only to the case of fixed proportions. See W. Leontief, "Composite Commodities and the Problem of Index Numbers," *Econometrica*, IV (1936), Section III, 53–59.

[9] On the properties of quantity indexes referred to here and below, see Samuelson, *Foundations*, pp. 160–63, and N. Liviatan and D. Patinkin, "On the Economic Theory of Price Indexes," *Economic Development and Cultural Change*, IX (1961), 507–9.

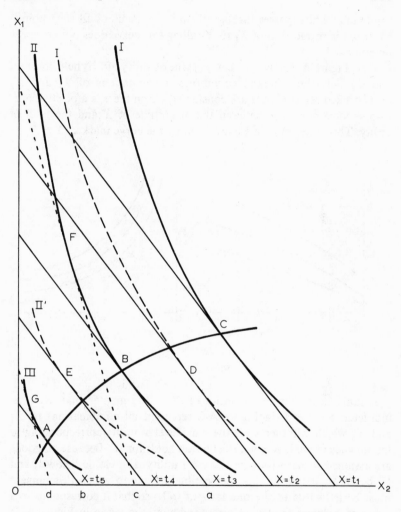

FIGURE A-2.

The solid indifference curves in Figure A-2 are drawn as of a given quantity of $Y = K_1$. (For the moment disregard the dashed curves.) Let us now restrict our attention to those points at which the individual might ultimately be in his optimum position. This means that the only points which interest us are the points of tangency A, B, C, ... The solid curve which passes through them is the locus of all such points. Clearly, the proportion of X_1 to X_2 along this curve does not generally remain fixed.

Thus Figure A-2 shows us that if (1) the quantity of Y is held constant and (2) only the potential equilibrium combinations of X_1 and X_2 at their fixed relative price are considered—then there is a positive one-to-one correspondence between the magnitude of X and the level of utility. This is depicted in Figure A-3a by the curve marked $Y = K_1$.

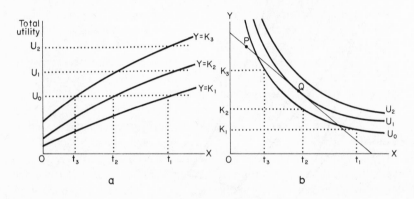

FIGURE A-3.

Assume next that the quantity of Y is K_2, greater than K_1. Let indifference curve I′ in Figure A-2 represent all combinations of X_1 and X_2 which will then yield the same level of utility corresponding to indifference curve I. A similar definition holds for II′. Because all goods are assumed to have positive marginal utility, I′ must lie below I, and II′ below II. It follows that the semibudget line to which I′ is tangent must be leftwards of the one tangent to I—so that it corresponds to a value of X lower than t_1. Correspondingly, the curve in Figure A-3a referring to $Y = K_2$ must lie leftwards of that corresponding to $Y = K_1$. A similar statement holds for the curve referring to $Y = K_3 > K_2$.

Let us now hold the level of utility in Figure A-3a constant at U_0. This yields the usual negatively-sloped indifference curve denoted by U_0 in Figure A-3b. By changing the level of utility, we obtain a family of such curves. Clearly, they cannot intersect. Finally, since the price of X is p_x, we can write a budget equation

(2.18) $p_x X + p_y Y = $ constant,

depicted by the straight line in Figure A-3b. Note in particular that the point P on this line can represent an initial endowment of Y and X, where the exact value of the latter is computed in accordance with (2.16). The curves in Figure A-3b are thus identical in their properties with those of Figure I-1 (p. 5) above, and so can conceptually be used to derive demand and Engel curves for X.[10]

From the foregoing presentation we can also see the necessity of assuming that the relative price p_1/p_2 remains fixed. In brief, at different relative prices, the same indifference curve will correspond to different values of X. Thus assume that indifference curve III in Figure A-2 is our base of reference. Then the utility level represented by curve II will correspond to a value of X equal to Oa/Ob if the price ratio represented by the solid semibudget lines prevails—but to Oc/Od if the dashed lines prevail. (This is the counterpart of the simple fact that the value of a "true" quantity index depends on the prices used as weights.) Thus the indifference map between X and Y will generally not remain invariant under a change in the relative price of X_1 and X_2. Correspondingly, the demand and Engel curves for X derived under one set of relative prices cannot be used to analyze any problem which involves another set.

In somewhat more intuitive terms, the demand curve for X derived above provides information about the individual's behavior—particularly his total money expenditure on X_1 and X_2—only along the expansion path ABC in Figure A-2. If the relative price of X_1 and X_2 changes, the individual will no longer be on this path. Hence the foregoing demand curve will no longer be relevant.

In certain special cases, however, knowledge about one expansion

---

[10] The convexity of the indifference curve in the neighborhood of observation is established in the same way as in the ordinary case: namely, by the observed stability of such a point. See Hicks, *Value and Capital* p. 22; the rigorous proof is presented *ibid.*, pp. 312–13.

Note that the technique just presented can be applied to other problems too. Thus, for example, all the inputs of a competitive firm (which, by definition, takes its factor prices as given) can be considered as a composite input which can be related in a monotonically increasing manner to the output of the firm. The argument proceeds exactly as above—with the curves in Figure A-2 now representing isoquants, and "total utility" in Figure A-3 replaced by "total production."

path provides information about others too. An obvious example is the one in which all expansion paths in Figure A-2 are straight lines through the origin: that is, in which the income elasticities of X_1 and X_2 are constant regardless of the price ratio. Correspondingly, the Engel curves for X in this case would have the same slope (on a double-logarithmic scale) no matter what the price ratio used to define the composite good. This is the counterpart of the fact that under this assumption (in technical terms, the assumption of a homogeneous utility function) the "true" quantity index of a shift between one indifference curve and another is the same regardless of the prices used as weights. On the other hand, the height of the Engel curve for X would vary in accordance with the relative price of X_1 and X_2. Hence even in this case we could not determine from one Engel curve the amount of money an individual would spend on X_1 and X_2 under a different set of relative prices.

In brief, though eliminating the ambiguity with reference to the "true" quantity index, the assumption of homogeneity does not help to measure the "true" price index. Hence, in the case of a change in relative prices, it does not help us to predict total expenditures on X_1 and X_2.[11]

As a final aside, we might note that the foregoing diagrams can also be usefully employed to demonstrate the nature of Hicksian complementarity. Thus assume that the individual is initially at Q in Figure A-3b. Assume now that the price of Y is increased and that the resulting substitution effect brings the individual to another point on curve U_1, rightward of Q. This represents an increased quantity of X, and hence a higher semibudget line in Figure A-2. But this higher line need not correspond to a point of tangency with a larger quantity of both X_1 and X_2 (though in Figure A-2 as drawn it does). Thus one of these commodities (though not both) can be complementary to Y.

From this line of reasoning we can also see that complementarity will not exist if (1) the indifference map between X_1 and X_2 is not affected by changes in Y (i.e., the utility function is separable in this sense) and (2) neither X_1 nor X_2 is an inferior good.

---

[11] I am indebted for this observation to Dale Jorgenson, who has also called my attention to the more general discussion of this question (with respect to production) in Ronald W. Shephard, *Cost and Production Functions* (Princeton, 1953), pp. 61 ff.

Cf. also Liviatan and Patinkin, "On the Economic Theory of Price Indexes," *op. cit.*, pp. 504–9.

d. The Demand and Excess-Demand Functions for Money[12]

Let us now return to our main discussion. Let Z_n^a represent the individual's optimum amount of money. Write the demand function for money as

$$(2.19) \qquad Z_n^a = F_n^a \left(p_1, \dots, p_{n-1}, p, \sum_{j=1}^{n-1} p_j \bar{Z}_j^a + p_n \bar{Z}_n^a \right).$$

Let $X_n^a = Z_n^a - \bar{Z}_n^a$ be the excess demand for money. Then the excess-demand function is

$$(2.20) \qquad X_n^a = F_n^a \left(p_1, \dots, p_{n-1}, p, \sum_{j=1}^{n-1} p_j \bar{Z}_j^a + p_n \bar{Z}_n^a \right) - \bar{Z}_n^a.$$

Here the form of the function is only generally indicated. However, as emphasized in the text, the budget restraint enables us to write this function in a more specific way, one which clearly shows its relationship to the corresponding commodity functions.

In particular, this restraint states that the money value of the individual's optimum collection must equal the money value of his initial one. That is,

$$(2.21) \qquad \sum_{j=1}^{n-1} \frac{p_j}{p_n} Z_j^a + Z_n^a = \sum_{j=1}^{n-1} \frac{p_j}{p_n} \bar{Z}_j^a + \bar{Z}_n^a.$$

This can be rewritten as

$$(2.22) \qquad X_n^a = Z_n^a - \bar{Z}_n^a = - \sum_{j=1}^{n-1} \frac{p_j}{p_n} (Z_j^a - \bar{Z}_j^a) = - \sum_{j=1}^{n-1} \frac{p_j}{p_n} X_j^a.$$

Substituting from (2.4) into (2.22), we then see that the excess demand function for money (2.20) has the specific form

$$(2.23) \qquad \begin{aligned} &F_n^a \left(p_1, \dots, p_{n-1}, p, \sum_{j=1}^{n-1} p_j \bar{Z}_j^a + p_n \bar{Z}_n^a \right) - \bar{Z}_n^a \\ &\equiv - \sum_{j=1}^{n-1} \frac{p_j}{p_n} \left[F_j^a \left(\frac{p_1}{p}, \dots, \frac{p_{n-1}}{p}, \frac{\sum_{r=1}^{n-1} p_r \bar{Z}_r^a}{p} + \frac{p_n \bar{Z}_n^a}{p} \right) - \bar{Z}_j^a \right] \end{aligned}$$

---

[12] Attached to Chapter II:5.

$$(2.24) \qquad \equiv \sum_{j=1}^{n-1} \frac{p_j}{p_n} \left[\bar{Z}_j^a - F_j^a \left(\frac{p_1}{p}, \dots, \frac{p_{n-1}}{p}, \frac{\sum_{r=1}^{n-1} p_r \bar{Z}_r^a}{p} + \frac{p_n \bar{Z}_n^a}{p} \right) \right].$$

As can readily be seen, this function has the properties attributed to it in the text. An equiproportionate increase in the money prices of commodities *and* in the initial quantity of money leaves unchanged each of the bracketed terms in the above summation. But these terms are now, respectively, premultiplied by a proportionately higher money price p_j/p_n. Hence the right-hand side of (2.23)—or (2.24)—must increase in the same proportion. Hence so must the amount of excess demand for money X_n^a. In other words, the excess demand for *real* holdings remains constant. This result can be obtained alternatively from (2.20) and (2.24) by multiplying through by p_n and then dividing by p. This yields the excess-demand function for *real* money holdings,

$$(2.25) \qquad \frac{p_n X_n^a}{p} = \sum_{j=1}^{n-1} \frac{p_j}{p} \left[\bar{Z}_j^a - F_j^a \left(\frac{p_1}{p}, \dots, \frac{p_{n-1}}{p}, \frac{\sum_{r=1}^{n-1} p_r \bar{Z}_r^a}{p} + \frac{p_n \bar{Z}_n^a}{p} \right) \right].$$

This function clearly depends only on relative prices and real wealth.

Let us turn now from the excess-demand to the demand functions. From (2.25) we obtain the demand function for *real* money holdings,

$$(2.26) \qquad \frac{p_n Z_n^a}{p} = \sum_{j=1}^{n-1} \frac{p_j}{p} [\bar{Z}_j^a - F_j^a(\ )] + \frac{p_n \bar{Z}_n^a}{p}.$$

Rewrite this for convenience as

$$(2.27) \qquad \frac{p_n Z_n^a}{p} = \psi^a \left(\frac{p_1}{p}, \dots, \frac{p_{n-1}}{p}, \frac{\sum_{r=1}^{n-1} p_r \bar{Z}_r^a}{p} + \frac{p_n \bar{Z}_n^a}{p} \right).$$

Correspondingly, the demand function for *nominal* money holdings can be obtained either by transposing the term $\bar{Z}_n^a$ to the right in equation (2.23)—or (what is more revealing) by multiplying both sides of the preceding equation by p/p_n.[13]

Let us now examine some properties of these functions. Since in the following discussion we shall be dealing with responses to equiproportionate changes in money prices, all the ratios on the right-hand side of (2.27) will remain constant except for $p_n \bar{Z}_n^a / p$. The functions can therefore be rewritten as dependent solely on this variable. Furthermore, the constancy of relative prices enables us to consider commodities as a single composite—say, G—with the price p (see the preceding section). Dropping the index a and setting $p_n = 1$ for simplicity, we can then write the demand for real balances and commodities as

$$(2.28) \qquad \frac{Z_n}{p} = H\left(\frac{\bar{Z}_n}{p}\right)$$

and

$$(2.29) \qquad G = G\left(\frac{\bar{Z}_n}{p}\right),$$

respectively. These are related by the budget restraint

$$(2.30) \qquad G + \frac{Z_n}{p} = \bar{G} + \frac{\bar{Z}_n}{p},$$

where $\bar{G}$ represents the initial endowment of commodities. From this it follows that

$$(2.31) \qquad G'(\ ) + H'(\ ) = 1;$$

that is, the sum of real-balance effects is unity. From this and from our assumption that neither commodities nor real balances are inferior goods, it follows that

$$(2.32) \qquad 0 < G'(\ ) < 1$$

$$(2.33) \qquad 0 < H'(\ ) < 1.$$

Note now that unlike any other good, real money holdings have the property that the slopes of the demand and excess-demand functions

---

[13] Here and in the following section, I have denoted the excess demand for nominal money holdings by X_n and X_n^a, respectively. The reader might instead prefer to denote such holdings by $p_n X_n$ and $p_n X_n^a$, respectively. This in no way affects the essentials of the argument. A similar statement holds for Z_n^a and $p_n Z_n^a$.

are different. In particular, though the demand for real balances is negatively sloped with respect to p, the *excess* demand is positively sloped. For

$$(2.34) \qquad \frac{X_n}{p} = H\!\left(\frac{\bar{Z}_n}{p}\right) - \frac{\bar{Z}_n}{p}.$$

Hence

$$(2.35) \qquad \frac{d\!\left(\dfrac{X_n}{p}\right)}{dp} = -H'(\quad)\frac{\bar{Z}_n}{p^2} + \frac{\bar{Z}_n}{p^2} = \frac{\bar{Z}_n}{p^2}[1 - H'(\quad)] > 0.$$

The reason for this peculiar property is that real money holdings are distinguished from every other good by the fact that a change in their price necessarily causes a change in their *initial* quantity. Furthermore, since $H'(\ ) < 1$, the increase in demand will always be less than the increase in the initial quantity. This is the reason for the positive slope in (2.35).

Let us turn now to elasticities.[14] The elasticity of demand for real balances with respect to p is

$$(2.36) \qquad \eta_R = -\frac{dH\!\left(\dfrac{\bar{Z}_n}{p}\right)}{dp} \cdot \frac{p}{\dfrac{\bar{Z}_n}{p}}$$

$$= H'\!\left(\frac{\bar{Z}_n}{p}\right) \cdot \frac{\bar{Z}_n}{Z_n}.$$

In order to determine the elasticity of demand of *nominal* balances, we first write the demand function

$$(2.37) \qquad Z_n = pH\!\left(\frac{\bar{Z}_n}{p}\right) = \frac{1}{\left(\dfrac{1}{p}\right)}\,H\!\left(\frac{\bar{Z}_n}{p}\right).$$

---

[14] The original version of this discussion has been revised as a result of criticisms by Philip W. Bell; cf. above, p. 30, footnote 27.

The elasticity of Z_n with respect to $1/p$ is

$$\eta_N = - \frac{d\left[pH\left(\frac{\overline{Z}_n}{p}\right)\right]}{d\left(\frac{1}{p}\right)} \cdot \frac{\frac{1}{p}}{Z_n}$$

(2.38)
$$= -\left[p\overline{Z}_n H'\left(\frac{\overline{Z}_n}{p}\right) - p^2 H\left(\frac{\overline{Z}_n}{p}\right)\right]\frac{1}{pZ_n}$$

$$= -H'\left(\frac{\overline{Z}_n}{p}\right)\frac{\overline{Z}_n}{Z_n} + 1$$

$$= 1 - \eta_R.$$

Note that the price elasticity η_R is equal to the wealth elasticity[15]

(2.39)
$$\frac{dH\left(\frac{\overline{Z}_n}{p}\right)}{d\left(\frac{\overline{Z}_n}{p}\right)}\frac{\frac{\overline{Z}_n}{p}}{\frac{Z_n}{p}} = H'\left(\frac{\overline{Z}_n}{p}\right)\frac{\overline{Z}_n}{Z_n}.$$

This brings out the essential equivalence between Figures II-2a and II-3 in the text (pp. 29 and 32).

From (2.36) together with (2.33), we see that as long as the individual is maintaining or adding to his initial money holdings (i.e., $Z_n \geqslant \overline{Z}_n$) then η_R is positive and less than unity. Hence, by (2.38), η_N must also be positive and less than unity—which means that the demand curve for nominal balances must be negatively sloped in this region. On the

---

[15] Since the only form of wealth that can change under our present assumptions are real money balances, the derivative here is taken with respect to this variable. This procedure can be made clearer by rewriting demand functions (2.28) and (2.29) in the more explicit form

$$\frac{Z_n}{p} = H\left(\overline{G} + \frac{Z_n}{p}\right)$$

and

$$G = G\left(\overline{G} + \frac{Z_n}{p}\right),$$

and noting that $\overline{G}$ is a constant.

other hand, if the individual is drawing down sufficiently on his money holdings $(Z_n < \bar{Z}_n)$, η_R can become greater than unity, so that η_N can become negative and the slope of the nominal demand curve accordingly positive.

These two possibilities are represented in Figure A-4. Note that even in the case where the demand curve becomes positively sloped at some point left of $\bar{Z}_n$ (the dashed curve), it cannot bend backwards sufficiently to intersect the vertical line at $\bar{Z}_n$. This has implications for our

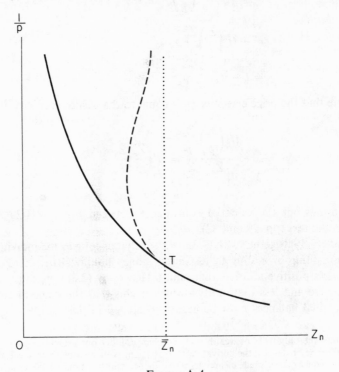

FIGURE A-4.

later discussion of market equilibrium: for it shows that even if the demand curve is positively sloped, it cannot be so sloped in the neighborhood of the equilibrium point T. Hence, under our present assumptions the possible positive slope of the nominal demand curve cannot be a source of short-run instability in the system.

For the sake of completeness, we might also briefly note the implications of the assumption that either commodities or real balances are inferior goods (obviously, both cannot simultaneously be so). In the latter case, $\eta_R < 0$, so that it follows from (2.38) that the demand for nominal balances has a greater-than-unity elasticity. This is also clear from (2.37), which would under these circumstances show that a price increase causes an increase in both of the factors $[p$ and $H(\ )]$ whose product makes up the demand for nominal balances. On the other hand, if commodities are inferior, then by (2.31), $H'(\ ) > 1$, so that by (2.36) the elasticity of real balances η_R can be greater than unity even when $Z_n > \bar{Z}_n$. Hence, the demand for nominal money holdings can then be positively sloped even in the neighborhood of $\bar{Z}_n$ and to its right. In other words, the decline in the demand for real balances resulting from a price increase in this case may be so sharp as to cause a corresponding decline in nominal balances. Owing to the economic implausibility of these assumptions there is little point in exploring their implications any further.[16]

[16] Cf., however, Mathematical Appendix $3:e$.

Though the inferior-money-holdings case is of no economic significance, it is nevertheless worth noting that it is not involved in the alleged logical difficulties which H. G. Johnson (who bases himself in turn on the "oral tradition of the University of Chicago Money and Banking Workshop") describes in the following terms: "By shortening the week and reducing the individual's weekly endowment of commodities proportionally, a procedure which leaves the rate of flow of the individual's income unchanged, it can be made impossible for the individual to cut his commodity consumption sufficiently to increase his planned balances. 'Inferiority' of real balances is therefore not invariant with respect to the time-unit of the analysis" ("Monetary Theory and Policy," *op. cit.*, p. 339, footnote 2).

Its last sentence notwithstanding, the question with which the foregoing passage is really concerned is not the consequence of a change in the "time-unit of the analysis" (which, as shown on p. 19, footnote 15 and p. 26, footnote 23, leaves the money demand function invariant), but the consequence of shortening the length of time during which a given rate of flow of income is expected to prevail. Correspondingly, it is obvious from the very definition of wealth that there is no validity to the foregoing implication that such a change should leave the individual's behavior invariant. For reducing the individual's economic horizon from (say) a week to a day—and reducing his initial commodity endowment accordingly to one-seventh its original level—also reduces the individual's wealth to (roughly) one-seventh its preceding level: for now the other six days—with their anticipated income—have from the economic point of view been eliminated. Correspondingly, all that is implied by the foregoing passage is the reasonable statement that by reducing an individual's wealth sufficiently, one can in general eventually force him to reduce his demand for cash balances.

If, on the other hand, we consider the case in which the individual's *horizon* remains

Finally, let us investigate the relationship between the wealth elasticities of demand for real balances and commodities. Under our present assumption the latter can be written as

$$(2.40) \qquad \eta_G = \frac{dG\left(\dfrac{\overline{Z}_n}{p}\right)}{d\left(\dfrac{\overline{Z}_n}{p}\right)} \cdot \frac{\dfrac{\overline{Z}_n}{p}}{G}.$$

From (2.31) and (2.36) we then obtain

$$(2.41) \qquad \eta_R = (1 - G')\frac{\overline{Z}_n}{Z_n} = \frac{\overline{Z}_n}{Z_n} - \frac{pG}{Z_n}\,\eta_G.$$

This can be rewritten in a somewhat more suggestive way as

$$(2.42) \qquad \frac{Z_n\eta_R + pG\eta_G}{\overline{Z}_n + p\overline{G}} = \frac{\overline{Z}_n}{\overline{Z}_n + p\overline{G}};$$

that is, the average of the elasticities weighted by their relative expenditures is equal to the proportion of the initial endowment which consists of money holdings. This is analogous to the familiar proposition that the weighted sum of income elasticities is unity.[17] In the present case, however, a change in price causes a proportionate change only in the real value of initial balances, and not in total wealth $\overline{G} + \overline{Z}_n/p$. Hence, the

---

unchanged at one week (now relabeled "seven days"), while his *income period* is reduced to a day—then it is obviously no longer true that his maximum addition to cash balances during any given day is limited to the income of that day. For we would then have a multiperiod model (cf. Chapters V–VII) in which the shortening of the current income period simply shifts income from the "present" to the "future," and thus leaves the individual's total wealth intact. Correspondingly, the individual can then finance his present increment to real balances by borrowing on the basis of his future income. This, after all, is a simple implication of the "permanent income hypothesis": namely, that the individual's demand during any given period depends not on the income actually received during that period, but on the discounted value of his income stream during all periods within his economic horizon (i.e., on his wealth).

[Though not relevant for the present discussion, it should be noted that while the change just described does not affect the individual's *maximum* addition to cash balances, it will generally affect the amount he actually demands: for this is clearly dependent on the nature of the income (or payment) period.]

For a more rigorous treatment of some of the issues raised here, see Mathematical Appendix 11, especially p. 522, footnote 12.

[17] Cf., e.g., Herman Wold, *Demand Analysis* (Stockholm, 1952), p. 112.

sum of the elasticities with respect to this price change is equal to the relative weight of the initial real balances.

e. The Market Functions[18]

Assume that there are A individuals in the economy. Let the market demand for any good be represented by $Z_i = \sum_{a=1}^{A} Z_i^a$. Similarly, let the total initial endowment of a good be represented by $\bar{Z}_i = \sum_{a=1}^{A} \bar{Z}_i^a$. Then—to return to the notion of Section a—the market excess-demand function for the jth commodity can be aggregated from (2.4) as

$$
(2.43) \qquad
\begin{aligned}
X_j &= Z_j - \bar{Z}_j \\
&= \sum_{a=1}^{A} \left[F_j^a\left(\frac{p_1}{p}, \dots, \frac{p_{n-1}}{p}, \frac{\sum_{r=1}^{n-1} p_r \bar{Z}_r^a}{p} + \frac{p_n \bar{Z}_n^a}{p} \right) - \bar{Z}_j^a \right].
\end{aligned}
$$

For convenience, this will be written as

$$
(2.44) \qquad
\begin{aligned}
X_j = F_j\Bigg(&\frac{p_1}{p}, \dots, \frac{p_{n-1}}{p}, \frac{\sum_{r=1}^{n-1} p_r \bar{Z}_r^1}{p} + \frac{p_n \bar{Z}_n^1}{p}, \dots \\
&\dots, \frac{\sum_{r=1}^{n-1} p_r \bar{Z}_r^A}{p} + \frac{p_n \bar{Z}_n^A}{p} \Bigg) - \bar{Z}_j \\
&\qquad\qquad\qquad\qquad (j = 1, \dots, n-1).
\end{aligned}
$$

The excess-demand function for money then has the form

$$
(2.45) \qquad
\begin{aligned}
X_n = -\sum_{j=1}^{n-1} \frac{p_j}{p_n} \Bigg[F_j\Bigg(&\frac{p_1}{p}, \dots, \frac{p_{n-1}}{p}, \frac{\sum_{r=1}^{n-1} p_r \bar{Z}_r^1}{p} + \frac{p_n \bar{Z}_n^1}{p}, \dots \\
&\dots, \frac{\sum_{r=1}^{n-1} p_r \bar{Z}_r^A}{p} + \frac{p_n \bar{Z}_n^A}{p} \Bigg) - \bar{Z}_j \Bigg].
\end{aligned}
$$

If the marginal propensity to spend out of wealth on any good were always equal for any two individuals, then (2.44) and (2.45) could be

[18] Attached to Chapter II:6.

rewritten, respectively, as

$$(2.46) \qquad X_j = F_j\left(\frac{p_1}{p}, \dots, \frac{p_{n-1}}{p}, \frac{\sum\limits_{r=1}^{n-1} p_r \overline{Z}_r}{p} + \frac{p_n \overline{Z}_n}{p}\right) - \overline{Z}_j$$

$$(j = 1, \dots, n - 1)$$

and

$$(2.47) \qquad X_n = -\sum_{j=1}^{n-1} \frac{p_j}{p_n}\left[F_j\left(\frac{p_1}{p}, \dots, \frac{p_{n-1}}{p}, \frac{\sum\limits_{r=1}^{n-1} p_r \overline{Z}_r}{p} + \frac{p_n \overline{Z}_n}{p}\right) - \overline{Z}_j\right].$$

Thus only under these assumptions are the market excess-demand functions analogous to the individual excess-demand functions.

3. Appendix to Chapter III

a. The System of Excess-Demand Equations[1]

From (2.44) and (2.45) we obtain the n market excess-demand equations

$$(3.1) \quad F_j\left(\frac{p_1}{p}, \ldots, \frac{p_{n-1}}{p}, \frac{\sum_{r=1}^{n-1} p_r \bar{Z}_r^1}{p} + \frac{p_n \bar{Z}_n^1}{p}, \ldots, \frac{\sum_{r=1}^{n-1} p_r \bar{Z}_r^A}{p} + \frac{p_n \bar{Z}_n^A}{p}\right) - \bar{Z}_j = 0$$

$$(j = 1, \ldots, n-1),$$

$$(3.2) \quad \sum_{j=1}^{n-1} \frac{p_j}{p_n}\left[F_j\left(\frac{p_1}{p}, \ldots, \frac{p_{n-1}}{p}, \frac{\sum_{r=1}^{n-1} p_r \bar{Z}_r^1}{p} + \frac{p_n \bar{Z}_n^1}{p}, \ldots\right.\right.$$

$$\left.\left. \ldots, \frac{\sum_{r=1}^{n-1} p_r \bar{Z}_r^A}{p} + \frac{p_n \bar{Z}_n^A}{p}\right) - \bar{Z}_j\right] = 0.$$

To these must be added the definition of the absolute price level, rewritten from (2.1) as

$$(3.3) \quad \sum_{j=1}^{n-1} w_j \frac{p_j}{p} = 1.$$

[1] Attached to Chapter III:2.

The dependence which exists among the market equations is clear from the way in which the excess-demand equation for money (3.2) has been written. There are, thus, a total of n independent equations in the system of $n + 1$ equations (3.1)–(3.3).

The independent variables of this system are the nA initial endowments $\bar{Z}_i^a$ ($i = 1, \dots, n;\ a = 1, \dots, A$) and the $n - 1$ weights w_j ($j = 1, \dots, n - 1$). We note that the $n + 1$ dependent variables $p_1, \dots, p_n, p$ appear only in the form of the n ratios $p_1/p, \dots, p_{n-1}/p, p_n/p$. Hence system (3.1)–(3.3) can at most be solved out for these ratios, in contradistinction to their individual components, the p_i ($i = 1, \dots, n$) and p. Assume now that a solution in terms of these ratios has been determined. Divide through the first $n - 1$ of them by the last one p_n/p—which is the reciprocal of the average money-price level. This yields the specific money prices $p_1/p_n, \dots, p_{n-1}/p_n$. It follows that system (3.1)–(3.3) can at most determine money prices. Accounting prices p_i must remain indeterminate until the value of one of them is arbitrarily set. This then enables us to determine all of the p_i.[2]

The choice of the dependent equation to be "eliminated" clearly does not affect the solution of the preceding system. Consider, for example, the following two possibilities. First, the equilibrium money prices are solved out from the subset of n equations consisting of (3.1) and (3.3). Second, these prices are, instead, solved out from the subset of n equations consisting of (3.2)–(3.3) and all of equations (3.1) but, say, the first. Let us now multiply each of the $n - 2$ remaining commodity equations by its respective money price, and subtract the sum of these $n - 2$ products from (3.2). Equation (3.2) is then reduced to

$$(3.4) \qquad \frac{p_1}{p_n} [F_1(\ ) - \bar{Z}_1] = 0.$$

If p_1/p_n is nonzero and finite, this reduces to the excess-demand equation for the first commodity—the equation which was originally eliminated.

Thus no matter which of the commodity equations is eliminated, we can—by the standard operations applicable to sets of simultaneous

[2] Note that the indeterminacy of accounting prices is established without making use of the fact that there are $n + 1$ accounting prices and only n independent equations.

equations—transform the resulting subset of equations into that obtained by eliminating the money equation. It follows that no matter which of the excess-demand equations is eliminated, the resulting subsets all yield the same solution for the equilibrium set of money prices.

The distinction between accounting and money prices having served its purpose, it can now be dispensed with. Henceforth we shall assume that the good whose accounting price is arbitrarily fixed is money, and that the price so fixed is equal to unity. That is, we set $p_n = 1$. Hence the money and accounting prices of any good must now always be equal.

b. Assumptions of the Dynamic System[3]

The task of the economist is not complete until he has shown how the market goes about solving the set of equations (3.1)–(3.3). For this purpose Walras formulated his theory of *tâtonnement*, which can be represented by the following system of differential equations:[4]

$$(3.5) \qquad \frac{dp_j}{dt} = K_j[F_j(\ ) - \bar{Z}_j] \qquad (j = 1, \ldots, n-1),$$

$$(3.6) \qquad \sum_{j=1}^{n-1} \frac{p_j}{K_j} \frac{dp_j}{dt} = -X_n,$$

$$(3.7) \qquad \frac{dp}{dt} = \sum_{j=1}^{n-1} w_j \frac{dp_j}{dt},$$

where t represents time and the K_j are positive constants.

Equations (3.5) state that a positive amount of excess demand in the jth market causes the price of the jth commodity p_j to rise over time. The extent of this rise is directly proportionate to the constant K_j, which thus represents the rapidity with which prices react to amounts of excess demand. Equation (3.7) states that the rate of change in the average price level is the weighted average of the rates of change of the individual prices. Equation (3.6) is obtained by substituting from (3.5) into (2.45). It states that, "on the average," an excess supply of money

---

[3] Attached to Chapter III:3.
[4] The following is based on the well-known dynamic analysis of Samuelson, *Foundations*, Chapter IX, especially pp. 260–61. On Walras, see Note B, below.

causes the prices p_j to rise. It clearly adds no information to (3.5) and can therefore be ignored.[5]

Starting from any initial set of prices, equations (3.5) and (3.7) describe the movements in prices generated by the resulting excess demands. In this way they trace out the variation over time of each of the price variables. Assume that we can obtain explicit descriptions of these time paths by solving equations (3.5) and (3.7) for the money prices as functions of time, t,

$$(3.8) \qquad\qquad p_j = q_j(t) \qquad\qquad (j = 1, \dots, n - 1),$$

$$(3.9) \qquad\qquad p = q(t).$$

Clearly, the functions $q_j(\ \ )$ and $q(\ \ )$ are those whose derivatives are dp_j/dt and dp/dt, respectively.

Assume that p_j^0 $(j = 1, \dots, n - 1)$ and p^0 are the equilibrium values of the system (3.1) to (3.3) Then the system (3.5)–(3.7) is defined as stable if

$$(3.10) \qquad\qquad \lim_{t=\infty} q_j(t) = p_j^0,$$

$$(3.11) \qquad\qquad \lim_{t=\infty} q(t) = p^0.$$

Thus stability means that the method of successive approximation described by equations (3.5) and (3.7) ultimately succeeds in solving the system of simultaneous equations (3.1)–(3.3).

One point should now be emphasized. Walras' *tâtonnement* presumably refers to stability in the large: that is, it attempts to describe the process by which the economy reaches equilibrium from any point whatsoever. Samuelson's original work, however, provided a detailed analysis only of stability in the small: that is, in the neighborhood of the equilibrium point. In the case of a unique equilibrium point, such stability is a necessary—but not sufficient—condition for the stability of Walras' *tâtonnement*.[6]

[5] For an example in which equation (3.6) is used, see Chapter XI:3, equation (6).

[6] I am indebted to R. F. Miller for pointing out to me that Walras' *tâtonnement* deals with stability in the large.

For the explicit form of functions (3.8)–(3.9) and for the conditions under which they converge in the small, see Samuelson, *Foundations*, pp. 270–72. See also below, Mathematical Appendix 9:*b*.

More recently, however, conditions have been developed for stability in the large as well. In particular, it has been shown that if all goods are gross substitutes, then such stability will obtain under the dynamic adjustment equations described by (3.5)–(3.7).[7]

c. THE EFFECT OF A CHANGE IN THE QUANTITY OF MONEY[8]

Consider the system (3.1)–(3.3), with p_n now replaced by unity wherever it appears. Assume that for $\bar{Z}_i^a = \bar{Z}_i^{a0}$ $(i = 1, \ldots, n; a = 1, \ldots, A)$ this system has the solution $p_j = p_j^0$ $(j = 1, \ldots, n - 1)$ and $p = p^0$. Consider now the solution for $\bar{Z}_j^a = \bar{Z}_j^{a0}$ $(j = 1, \ldots, n - 1; a = 1, \ldots, A)$ and $\bar{Z}_n^a = t\bar{Z}_n^{a0}$ $(a = 1, \ldots, A)$, where t is a positive constant. That is, consider the effects of an equiproportionate increase in the initial money holdings of each and every individual. By inspection of (3.1)–(3.3) one can readily see that there must exist a new solution $p_j = tp_j^0$ $(j = 1, \ldots, n - 1)$ and $p = tp_0$.

d. DEMAND CURVES AND MARKET-EQUILIBRIUM CURVES[9]

Since the analysis is restricted to changes which do not affect the relative magnitudes of the $\bar{Z}_n^a$ $(a = 1, \ldots, A)$, we can express each of these initial quantities as a fixed proportion of the total quantity of money in the economy,

$$(3.12) \qquad \bar{Z}_n^a = k_a \bar{Z}_n \qquad (a = 1, \ldots, A),$$

where the k_a are given constants. Making use of these equations and of the fact that the $\bar{Z}_j^a$ $(j = 1, \ldots, n - 1; a = 1, \ldots, A)$ are also constants

---

[7] For this and other results see K. J. Arrow and L. Hurwicz, "On the Stability of the Competitive Equilibrium I," *Econometrica*, XXVI (1958), 522–52; K. J. Arrow, H. D. Block, and L. Hurwicz, "On the Stability of the Competitive Equilibrium II," *Econometrica*, XXVII (1959), 82–109.

For a critical discussion of the recent literature, see Takashi Negishi, "The Stability of a Competitive Economy: A Survey Article," *Econometrica*, XXX (1962), 635–69. See also K. J. Arrow and L. Hurwicz, "Competitive Stability under Weak Gross Substitutability: Nonlinear Price Adjustment and Adaptive Expectations," *International Economic Review*, III (1962), 233–55. Cf. also the articles by F. H. Hahn, M. Morishima, and H. Uzawa in the same issue.

[8] Attached to Chapter III:4.

[9] Attached to Chapter III:6.

in the present discussion, and remembering that we have set $p_n = 1$, we can rewrite (3.1) and (3.3) as

(3.13)
$$G_j\left(\frac{p_1}{p}, \ldots, \frac{p_{n-1}}{p}, \frac{\bar{Z}_n}{p}\right) - \bar{Z}_j = 0$$

$$(j = 1, \ldots, n - 1)$$

(3.14)
$$\sum_{j=1}^{n-1} w_j \frac{p_j}{p} = 1.$$

Let us now consider (3.13)–(3.14) as constituting a set of n equations in the n variables p_j/p and $\bar{Z}_n/p$. Solving for these variables, we obtain

(3.15)
$$\frac{p_j}{p} = \alpha_j \qquad (j = 1, \ldots, n - 1),$$

(3.16)
$$\frac{\bar{Z}_n}{p} = \alpha_n,$$

where the α_j and α_n are constants for any fixed set of the w_j, $\bar{Z}_j^a$, and k_a. Rewriting (3.16) as

(3.17)
$$p = \frac{1}{\alpha_n} \bar{Z}_n,$$

we see the directly proportionate dependence of the dependent variable p on the independent variable $\bar{Z}_n$. Substituting from (3.17) into (3.15), we obtain

(3.18)
$$p_j = \frac{\alpha_j}{\alpha_n} \bar{Z}_n \qquad (j = 1, \ldots, n - 1).$$

That is, this direct dependence also characterizes each of the individual money prices. In this way we have reaffirmed the conclusion of the preceding section.[10]

The distinction between individual-experiments and demand curves, on the one hand, and market-experiments and market-equilibrium curves, on the other, is now most explicit. The demand curves in Figure III-2 of the text are representations of equation (2.37) above. The slopes of these curves are the derivatives of the right-hand side of

[10] The present development is obviously related to the derivation of the inverse (Marshallian) demand functions in (2.6)–(2.8) above.

(2.37) with respect to $1/p$. In contrast, the market-equilibrium curve in Figure III-3 is a graphical representation of equation (3.17) rewritten as

(3.19)
$$\frac{1}{p} = \frac{\alpha_n}{\bar{Z}_n}.$$

Obviously, equation (3.19) is distinct from equation (2.37). More specifically, the market-equilibrium function will have the form of the rectangular hyperbola described by equation (3.19), regardless of the form of the demand function described by equation (2.37).

This also makes it clear that equation (3.19)—or (3.17)—is *not* a variant of a cash-balance equation. For the latter was intended as an excess-demand equation, and not a market-equilibrium equation— though, as indicated in the text, it is precisely on this point that there existed some confusion among proponents of the cash-balance approach.[11]

Finally, we note again (p. 392) that the foregoing distinction corresponds to the econometric one between a structural equation [(2.37) above] and a reduced-form equation [(3.17)].

e. THE LONG-RUN DEMAND FUNCTIONS[12]

The geometrical analysis of the individual's adjustment process in Figure III-5 (p. 54) actually represents the solution of the first-order difference equation

(3.20)
$$\frac{Z_{nt}}{p} = F\left(\bar{G} + \frac{Z_{n,t-1}}{p} \right),$$

where Z_{nt} represents cash balances at the end of the tth period, p is the *given* price level, and where we have used the form of the demand function described on p. 421, footnote 15 above. From the general properties of such an equation[13] we know that convergence will take place if—as in Figure III-5—the Engel curve is positively sloped and cuts the 45° line from above. If, however, it cuts it from below (as

---

[11] Cf. Chapter VIII:2.

[12] Attached to Chapter III:7.

The argument of this section has been greatly improved as a result of Nissan Liviatan's invaluable criticisms and suggestions.

[13] See W. J. Baumol, *Economic Dynamics* (2nd ed., New York, 1959), pp. 257–62.

will be the case when commodities are an inferior good[14]), then the system will diverge. Finally, if the Engel curve should be negatively sloped at its intersection with the 45° line (as will be the case when real balances are an inferior good), then the system will oscillate—converging to the equilibrium position or not according as the slope at the point of intersection is respectively less than or greater than unity in absolute value. Thus in the former case the individual's approach to his equilibrium position will be marked by alternate "undershooting" and "overshooting." That is, unlike the situation in Figure III-5—in which the individual either continuously adds to or draws down on his cash balances—the individual under these circumstances will follow a "cobweb" pattern of adding to his balances (and hence wealth) in one week, and drawing down upon them in the following one, until he reaches equilibrium.[15]

Since it is clear from other economic considerations that neither commodities-in-general nor money balances are inferior, both of these cases—with their peculiar implications—can safely be ignored. Restricting ourselves accordingly to the case of stability, we note that the assumptions of the graphical analysis of the text[16] imply that the long-run equilibrium solution of (3.20) has the form of the single-valued function

$$(3.21) \qquad \frac{Z_n^*}{p} = f(\bar{G}).$$

Thus under the stated assumptions there is for every value of $\bar{G}$ a unique long-run (or stationary) level of demand for real balances that will be reached regardless of the initial value of Z_{nt}/p.[17]

---

[14] See Mathematical Appendix 2:*d*.

[15] It should be noted that this "overshooting"—and the difficult-to-rationalize "cobweb" pattern which it generates (cf. Johnson, "Monetary Theory and Policy," *op. cit.*, p. 339, footnote 2)—would disappear if we were to analyze the individual's behavior in terms of a first-order differential equation, instead of difference equation. In intuitive terms, if the individual's long-run equilibrium depends solely on the stock of money he holds—and not on the rate of change of this stock—then his instantaneous adjustment process will come to an end whenever he reaches his equilibrium stock. I am indebted to Milton Friedman for this observation.

[16] See p. 31, footnote 28, and pp. 54–55.

[17] This is one of the major conclusions of Archibald and Lipsey, "Monetary and Value Theory," *op. cit.*, pp. 5–6, 9. For a more rigorous statement, see Clower and Burstein, *op. cit.*, pp. 32–34, who attribute priority for this result to Leser, *op. cit.*, pp. 133–34. See also Ball and Bodkin, *op. cit.*, pp. 45–46.

Alternatively, the adjustment process can be analyzed by means of the first-order difference equation

$$(3.22) \qquad G_t = G\left(\bar{G} + \frac{Z_{n, t-1}}{p}\right),$$

which describes the demand function for commodities. This is related to (3.20) by budget restraint (2.30) above, rewritten as

$$(3.23) \qquad G_t + \frac{Z_{nt}}{p} = \bar{G} + \frac{Z_{n, t-1}}{p}.$$

Since by definition of long-run equilibrium $Z_{nt} = Z_{n, t-1}$, equation (3.23) implies that the corresponding demand function for commodities is

$$(3.24) \qquad G^* = \bar{G}.$$

This brings us to what is essentially a semantic point. The long-run demand functions (3.21) and (3.24) have on occasion been described as being independent of real balances.[18] This statement seems to me to be somewhat misleading. For, as has been emphasized on p. 53 above, in the long-run analysis of individual demand the level of real balances is an endogenous, and not exogenous, variable; hence by definition it has no place in the corresponding demand functions.[19] In other words, the correct description of the role of the real-balance effect in the long-run analysis of demand is not that this effect is then zero, but that it cannot then properly be designated as an independent variable of the demand functions.

There is a second, and more significant, semantic point. The foregoing refers to (3.21) and (3.24) as "demand functions." From one viewpoint, this is a legitimate use of the term: for these equations express a quantity demanded as a function of the exogenous variable of a certain process. In a deeper sense of the term, however, this usage is misleading: for even after the individual reaches long-run equilibrium, he continues to determine his behavior in the light of his wealth restraint (3.23);

---

[18] See again the reference to Archibald and Lipsey in the preceding footnote. See also the statement in Griliches *et al*, that "the coefficient of liquid assets [in the consumption function] should be zero in long-run equilibrium *if* income is measured correctly" ["Notes on Estimated Aggregate Quarterly Consumption Functions," *Econometrica*, XXX (1962), p. 496, footnote 8, italics in original].

[19] Cf. Chapter I:4 above.

accordingly his demand functions in the usual sense of the term continue to depend on wealth as defined by the right-hand side of this restraint.[20] In other words, the individual demanding Z_n^*/p and G^* in long-run equilibrium does not conceive himself as acting in accordance with (3.21) and (3.24), but as buying the optimum amounts indicated by (3.20) and (3.22) for the level of wealth $\bar{G} + Z_n^*/p$.[21]

Now, as long as the individual remains in long-run equilibrium, it is obviously impossible to distinguish operationally between these two alternatives. However, once he departs from this position (say, as a result of an exogenous change in real money holdings), it not only becomes possible, but it is then immediately evident that only equations (3.20) and (3.22) provide correct descriptions of the individual's behavior. Thus these equations—unlike (3.21) and (3.24)—are valid whether or not the individual is in long-run equilibrium.

This disadvantage of equations (3.21) and (3.24)—the necessity of replacing them by completely different equations the moment we depart ever so slightly from long-run equilibrium—is probably what has led some writers to contend that the real-balance effect should be reflected in the consumption function not by the level of existing balances, but by the difference between this level and the long-run equilibrium one, so that this effect is automatically "removed from the equation" once long-run equilibrium is reached.[22] Under our present simple assumptions this means that, for example, consumption function (3.22) should

[20] This point is spelled out in greater detail in Mathematical Appendix 6:a below.

[21] In this way we can also infer the relationship between the functions (3.20) and (3.21). Specifically, from

$$\frac{Z_n^*}{p} = F\left(\bar{G} + \frac{Z_n^*}{p}\right),$$

we obtain

$$d\left(\frac{Z_n^*}{p}\right) = F'(\ )d\bar{G} + F'(\ )d\left(\frac{Z_n^*}{p}\right),$$

which yields

$$\frac{d(Z_n^*/p)}{d\bar{G}} = f'(\ ) = \frac{F'(\ )}{1 - F'(\ )}.$$

[22] See E. J. Mishan, "A Fallacy in the Interpretation of the Cash Balance Effect," *Economica*, XXV (1958), 107, 110. Mishan's "cash balance effect" is actually expressed in terms of the difference between the amount of money demanded and supplied. The following comments are, however, relevant (*mutatis mutandis*) to this contention as well.

For an attempt to estimate an equation of the type described in the text, see Jean

be rewritten as

$$(3.25) \qquad G_t = \bar{G} + g\left(\frac{Z_{n,\,t-1}}{p} - \frac{Z_n^*}{p}\right),$$

where $g(0) = 0$, so that in long-run equilibrium (3.25) reduces to (3.24).

This procedure is subject to both of the semantic criticisms just noted: Z_n^* cannot properly appear in a demand function, and the form of (3.25) does not reflect the dependence on total wealth which characterizes a demand function derived in the usual manner from utility maximization. The nature of these criticisms can be exemplified by noting that if Z_{nt} is (say) greater than Z_n^*, then $Z_{n,\,t-1}$ is less than Z_{nt}; hence by (3.23) G_t is greater than G^*. But this argument can just as easily be reversed. In other words, the positive deviation of Z_{nt} from Z_n^* is not a *cause* of the corresponding deviation of G_t from G^*, but both deviations are simultaneous *consequences* of the same dynamic process operating with the specified exogenous variables.[23, 24]

Crockett, "Income and Asset Effects on Consumption: Aggregate and Cross Section," in Conference on Research in Income and Wealth, *Models of Income Determination, Studies in Income and Wealth*, vol. 28 (Princeton, 1964), pp. 127–28.

[23] Cf. p. 25 above.

Alternatively we can argue that the logic of (3.25) should lead us to rewrite (3.20) as

$$\frac{Z_{nt}}{p} = f(\bar{G}) + h(G_t - G^*),$$

from which it is clear that the deviation of Z_{nt}/p from its long-run value $f(\bar{G}) = Z_n^*/p$ cannot be considered an independent influence on G_t.

Note too that the chain of causation in the dynamic adjustment process of a more complicated model with bonds is not directly from an excess supply of money to the demand for consumption goods, but from this excess supply to the interest rate to the level of consumption; see above, especially p. 294, footnote 23.

[24] We might also note that under certain assumptions consumption function (3.22) can be transformed so as to reflect the "influence" of the deviation of Z_{nt} from Z_n^*. In particular, assume this function to have the form

$$(a) \qquad G_t = \alpha\left(\bar{G} + \frac{Z_{n,\,t-1}}{p}\right),$$

where α is a constant. This can then be transformed into

$$(b) \qquad \begin{aligned} G_t &= \alpha\left(\bar{G} + \frac{Z_n^*}{p}\right) + \alpha\left(\frac{Z_{n,\,t-1}}{p} - \frac{Z_n^*}{p}\right) \\ &= \bar{G} + \alpha\left(\frac{Z_{n,\,t-1}}{p} - \frac{Z_n^*}{p}\right). \end{aligned}$$

It is also clear from this example that we can describe the influence of real balances

Underlying these semantic points is the fundamental substantive one that actual behavior in our present model cannot be affected by the long-run equilibrium values of the variables. This can be seen most easily from the following counterexample: Assume that there is a change in tastes which causes a downward shift in that part of the Engel curve in Figure III-5 (p. 54) which is to the left of point C, so that the new curve intersects the 45° line at, say, point T'. This point then represents the new long-run equilibrium value of Z_n/p. It is, however, clear that the change in Z_n^*/p does not affect the individual's demand for real balances (and hence commodities) when his initial holdings of these balances are Ob—or any other quantity greater than Oc. This is simply a reflection of the basic fact already noted (pp. 435–36) that the individual's demand at any point is completely determined by his tastes and total wealth at that point.[25]

So much for the demand functions. Turning now to the determination of the long-run-equilibrium market price, we note that the analysis of Figure III-4 can also be presented in terms of a difference equation. Because of the complicated nature of this equation, its solution will not be attempted here. It is nevertheless clear that this equation (which determines the stability of the long-run-equilibrium price level) involves the short-run demand functions (3.20) or (3.22), and not the long-run functions (3.21) or (3.24).[26] Thus, for example, the reader can readily verify from Figure III-4 that convergence will take place if the Engel curve—which corresponds to equation (3.20)[27]—is linear with a less-than-unitary slope. This is the trivial case already referred to[28] in

---

on consumption either in terms of what I take it Mishan (*op. cit.*, pp. 107–8) would call the "asset-expenditure effect" [$\alpha \dfrac{Z_{n,t-1}}{p}$ in equation (a)], or in terms of what he would call the "cash-balance effect" [$\alpha \left(\dfrac{Z_{n,t-1}}{p} - \dfrac{Z_n^*}{p} \right)$ in equation (b)]—but not in terms of both simultaneously (cf. also p. 406, footnote 7 below). For reasons just explained, I myself feel that only the "asset-expenditure effect" is appropriate. A similar interpretation of Mishan's position can be given in terms of equation (23) on p. 227 above.

[25] Though the Engel curve in Figure III-5 has, for simplicity, been presented as a function of initial real balances, it is clear that it is actually a function of total wealth; see above, p. 31, footnote 28, and p. 421, footnote 15.

[26] Cf. p. 57 above, especially footnote 26.

[27] See footnote 25.

[28] Cf. p. 52, footnote 20 above.

which the price level remains unchanged during the adjustment process.

In concluding this section we emphasize once again[29] that the stationary-state functions (3.21) and (3.24) have no relevance to the consumption and money-demand functions of the constantly growing economies of the real world.[30] Correspondingly, it will be seen that the empirical studies described in Note M below specify functions related to the short-run functions (3.20) and (3.22).[31]

---

[29] See pp. 58–59 above, and especially the reference in footnote 32 to Liviatan, "On the Long-Run Theory of Consumption and Real Balances," *op. cit.*

[30] That this has not always been realized is clear from footnote 18 on p. 435 above.

[31] See especially the functions described on pp. 654–55 and 659–60.

4. Appendix to Chapter IV

a. THE DEMAND FUNCTIONS FOR COMMODITIES, BONDS, AND MONEY[1]

Consider the ath individual situated in the marketing period of the first week. In that period he decides on his excess demands for the current Monday and for $H - 1$ subsequent Mondays as well. The number H thus represents his economic horizon.

Let $\bar{Z}^a_{1s}$ ($s = 1, \dots, n - 2; a = 1, \dots, A$) represent the ath individual's initial endowment of the sth commodity in this first week. Similarly, let $\bar{Z}^a_{ks}$ ($k = 2, \dots, H$) represent the quantity of the sth commodity with which the individual knows he will be endowed in the kth week in the future. In the same way, Z^a_{1s} represents the amount the individual demands of the sth good in the current week, while Z^a_{ks} ($k = 2, \dots, H$) represents the amount he now plans to demand of the sth commodity in the kth week in the future. The amounts of excess demand planned for this and future weeks are then X^a_{hs}, where

$$(4.1) \qquad X^a_{hs} = Z^a_{hs} - \bar{Z}^a_{hs}$$

$$(a = 1, \dots, A; h = 1, \dots, H; s = 1, \dots, n - 2).$$

The price of the sth commodity is expected to be exactly the same in each and every week; as before, denote this price by p_s.

---

[1] Attached to Chapter IV:2–3.

The $(n-1)^{\text{th}}$ good is assumed to represent bonds. As will be recalled, these are obligations to pay one dollar one week from date of issue. Let $\bar{Z}^a_{n-1}$ be the given number of matured bonds—each of which will now be redeemed for one dollar—that the individual holds this Monday morning. These are to be contrasted with $Z^a_{1,n-1}$, the number of newly issued bonds he demands during the marketing period this Monday afternoon. By definition, these bonds constitute his initial holdings of the second week. Similarly, $Z^a_{k,n-1}$ $(k = 2, \ldots, H)$ represents the number of bonds which he now plans to demand in the kth week; and which, by definition, will constitute his initial, matured bond holdings of the $(k+1)^{\text{th}}$ week. In the same way, $\bar{Z}^a_n$ represents his initial money holdings in the first week; Z^a_{1n}, his amount of money demanded in the first week; and Z^a_{kn} $(k = 2, \ldots, H)$ the amount he plans to demand in the kth week. Again, by definition, Z^a_{kn} will constitute the initial money holdings of the $(k+1)^{\text{th}}$ week.

By definition, the excess demand for bonds $X^a_{h,n-1}$ $(h = 1, \ldots, H)$ is the same as the demand $Z^a_{h,n-1}$. The excess demand for money now planned for the first week is

(4.2)
$$X^a_{1n} = Z^a_{1n} - \bar{Z}^a_n,$$

and for the subsequent weeks,

(4.3)
$$X^a_{kn} = Z^a_{kn} - Z^a_{k-1,n} \qquad (k = 2, \ldots, H)$$

As shown in the text, the price of a bond p_{n-1} is related to the rate of interest r in the following way:

(4.4)
$$\frac{1 - p_{n-1}}{p_{n-1}} = r,$$

or

(4.5)
$$p_{n-1} = \frac{1}{1+r}.$$

This price, like any other one, is expected with certainty to be the same in future weeks as in the present one.[2] It follows that an individual who demands $Z^a_{h,n-1}$ $(h = 1, \ldots, H)$ bonds is planning to expend $Z^a_{h,n-1}/(1+r)$ dollars on the purchase of new (discounted) bonds in the

[2] Cf. p. 63.

h^{th} week, and to receive $Z^a_{h,\,n-1}$ dollars from the redemption of these bonds when they mature in the $(h + 1)^{\text{th}}$ week.

By assumption, the ath individual's excess-demand function for the sth commodity in the hth week can be written as

(4.6)
$$X^a_{hs} = F^a_{hs}\left(\frac{p_1}{p}, \ldots, \frac{p_{n-2}}{p}, r, \frac{\overline{Z}^a_{n-1}}{p} + \frac{\overline{Z}^a_n}{p} + \frac{\sum\limits_{s=1}^{n-2} p_s\overline{Z}^a_{1s}}{p}, \frac{\sum\limits_{s=1}^{n-2} p_s\overline{Z}^a_{2s}}{p}, \ldots, \frac{\sum\limits_{s=1}^{n-2} p_s\overline{Z}^a_{Hs}}{p}\right) - \overline{Z}^a_{hs}$$

$$(a = 1, \ldots, A; h = 1, \ldots, H; s = 1, \ldots, n - 2),$$

where the $H - 1$ last arguments of the function $F^a_{hs}(\;)$ represent the anticipated real incomes of future weeks. These anticipations too are held with certainty. As noted in the text (p. 66), all of the arguments in (4.6) which follow r can, under our present assumptions, be replaced by the single argument, wealth, inclusive of initial financial assets. For generality, however, this has not been done.

The demand—or excess-demand—function for *real* bond holdings in the hth week is

(4.7)
$$\frac{Z^a_{h,\,n-1}}{(1 + r)p} = F^a_{h,\,n-1}(\;) \qquad (h = 1, \ldots, H),$$

where the arguments of this function are the same as those of (4.6). By the budget restraint, the excess-demand function for *real* money holdings in the first week is then

(4.8)
$$\frac{X^a_{1n}}{p} = -\sum_{s=1}^{n-2} \frac{p_s}{p}[F^a_{1s}(\;) - \overline{Z}^a_{1s}] - \left[F^a_{1,\,n-1}(\;) - \frac{\overline{Z}^a_{n-1}}{p}\right].$$

Similarly, the presently planned excess-demand functions for subsequent weeks are

(4.9)
$$\frac{X^a_{kn}}{p} = -\sum_{s=1}^{n-2} \frac{p_s}{p}[F^a_{ks}(\;) - \overline{Z}^a_{ks}]$$
$$- [F^a_{k,\,n-1}(\;) - (1 + r)F^a_{k-1,\,n-1}(\;)]$$
$$(k = 2, \ldots, H).$$

The last bracketed term on the right-hand side of both (4.8) and (4.9) is the difference between the real value of the individual's planned expenditures on new (discounted) bonds on Monday afternoon of the hth week ($h = 1, \ldots , H$) and the real value of his planned receipts from the matured bonds which he holds on Monday morning of that week.

As can readily be seen, an equiproportionate increase in the p_s ($s = 1, \ldots , n - 2$), p, and $\overline{Z}_n^a$ leaves all arguments of (4.6) and (4.7) unaffected, except for $\overline{Z}_{n-1}^a/p$. If the individual in question is a creditor, his $\overline{Z}_{n-1}^a/p$ is positive, and this is reduced by the increase in p; hence he decreases his amounts demanded. If he is a debtor, his $\overline{Z}_{n-1}^a/p$ is negative, and this is (algebraically) increased by the increase in p; hence he increases his amounts demanded. In brief, we have here the real-indebtedness effect of the text.

The market excess-demand functions can be obtained by aggregating (4.6)–(4.9) over a. To simplify the notation, we shall make use of the fact that the present analysis is concerned with changes which leave the real incomes of all periods constant. Hence, for the purpose of our analysis, the influence of these incomes can be subsumed under the forms of the functions, which can be written as

$$(4.10) \quad X_{hs} = F_{hs}\left(\frac{p_1}{p}, \ldots , \frac{p_{n-2}}{p}, r, \frac{\overline{Z}_{n-1}^1}{p} + \frac{\overline{Z}_n^1}{p}, \ldots , \frac{\overline{Z}_{n-1}^A}{p} + \frac{\overline{Z}_n^A}{p}\right) - \overline{Z}_{hs}$$

$$(h = 1, \ldots , H; s = 1, \ldots , n - 2),$$

$$(4.11) \quad \frac{Z_{h, n-1}}{(1 + r)p} = F_{h, n-1}(\ \ ),$$

$$(4.12) \quad \frac{X_{1n}}{p} = -\sum_{s=1}^{n-2} \frac{p_s}{p}[F_{1s}(\ \ ) - \overline{Z}_{1s}] - F_{1, n-1}(\ \ ),$$

$$(4.13) \quad \frac{X_{kn}}{p} = -\sum_{s=1}^{n-2} \frac{p_s}{p}[F_{ks}(\ \ ) - \overline{Z}_{ks}]$$

$$- [F_{k, n-1}(\ \ ) - (1 + r)F_{k-1, n-1}(\ \ )]$$

$$(k = 2, \ldots , H).$$

These equations correspond to (4.6)–(4.9), respectively.

In aggregating (4.12) from (4.8) use has been made of the fact that the economy is a closed one, so that

$$(4.14) \qquad \sum_{a=1}^{A} \overline{Z}_{n-1}^{a} = 0.$$

That is, the aggregate amount of matured bonds *actually* held at the beginning of the first week must be zero. On the other hand, there is no reason why

$$(4.15) \qquad F_{h,\,n-1}(\quad) \equiv \sum_{a=1}^{A} F_{h,\,n-1}^{a}(\quad) \qquad (h = 1, \ldots, H)$$

must be zero. That is, there is no reason why the aggregate amount of bonds individuals *plan* to hold at a given set of prices during a given week must be zero. True, it will turn out that the individuals' plans will not be consistent with one another unless this amount is zero; unless, that is, they plan in the aggregate to lend as much as they plan to borrow. But of this the isolated individual formulating his plans is not and cannot be aware.

b. The System of Excess-Demand Equations. The Effect of a Change in the Quantity of Money. The Definition of "Neutral Money"[3]

From the preceding market excess-demand functions we can construct the corresponding market excess-demand equations for each and every week. However, by the assumption of the text, only those of the current week—that is, only those for $h = 1$—are relevant for the determination of current equilibrium prices and interest. Dropping the now unnecessary time index h, we write these excess-demand equations as

$$(4.16) \quad F_s\!\left(\frac{p_1}{p}, \ldots, \frac{p_{n-2}}{p}, r, \frac{\overline{Z}_{n-1}^1}{p} + \frac{\overline{Z}_n^1}{p}, \ldots, \frac{\overline{Z}_{n-1}^A}{p} + \frac{\overline{Z}_n^A}{p}\right) - \overline{Z}_s = 0$$

$$(s = 1, \ldots, n - 2),$$

$$(4.17) \quad F_{n-1}\!\left(\frac{p_1}{p}, \ldots, \frac{p_{n-2}}{p}, r, \frac{\overline{Z}_{n-1}^1}{p} + \frac{\overline{Z}_n^1}{p}, \ldots, \frac{\overline{Z}_{n-1}^A}{p} + \frac{\overline{Z}_n^A}{p}\right) = 0,$$

[3] Attached to Chapter IV:4.

(4.18)
$$\sum_{s=1}^{n-2} \frac{p_s}{p} [F_s(\quad) - \bar{Z}_s] + F_{n-1}(\quad) = 0,$$

(4.19)
$$\sum_{s=1}^{n-2} w_s \frac{p_s}{p} = 1.$$

Equation (4.19) defines the average price level p of the $n-2$ money prices p_s; it is analogous to (2.1). Equations (4.16), (4.17) and (4.18) relate, of course, to commodities, bonds, and money, respectively. We have, thus, $n+1$ equations in the n dependent variables p_s ($s = 1, \ldots, n-2$), p, and r. It is clear that any set of these variables which satisfies (4.16), (4.17), and (4.19) must also satisfy (4.18). Thus only n of these equations, at most, are independent.

Assume that for $\bar{Z}_{n-1}^a = \bar{Z}_{n-1}^{a0}$ and for $\bar{Z}_n^a = \bar{Z}_n^{a0}$ ($a = 1, \ldots, A$) the preceding system has the solution $p_s = p_s^0$ ($s = 1, \ldots, n-2$), $p = p^0$, and $r = r^0$. Consider now the solution for the same values of the $\bar{Z}_{n-1}^{a0}$, but for $\bar{Z}_n^a = t\bar{Z}_n^{a0}$—where t is a positive constant. That is, consider the effect of an equiproportionate increase in the initial money holdings of all individuals, their initial bond holdings being kept constant. By inspection of (4.16)–(4.19) one can readily see that at the prices $p_s = tp_s^0$, $p = tp^0$, and $r = r^0$, all arguments of the equations are the same as in the original equilibrium position except for the $\bar{Z}_{n-1}^a/p$. These now become $\bar{Z}_{n-1}^{a0}/tp^0$ instead of $\bar{Z}_{n-1}^{a0}/p^0$. Hence the functions on the left-hand sides of (4.16)–(4.18) need not have the same values as in the original equilibrium position; hence equations (4.16)–(4.18) need no longer be satisfied. That is, the proposed set of values will not generally be the new equilibrium set.

In contrast, consider the case where both $\bar{Z}_{n-1}^a = t\bar{Z}_{n-1}^{a0}$ and $\bar{Z}_n^a = t\bar{Z}_n^{a0}$. Here the set of values $p_s = tp_s^0$, $p = tp^0$, and $r = r^0$ clearly constitutes the new equilibrium solution. For with these new values each of the arguments of (4.16)–(4.18) has exactly the same value as in the original equilibrium position. Thus we conclude that an equiproportionate change in the initial holdings of both bonds and money causes an equiproportionate change in money prices and leaves the rate of interest unaffected.

c. The System of Excess-Demand Equations. The Effect of a Change
in the Quantity of Money. The Definition of "Neutral Money"
(Continued)[4]

Alternatively, we can proceed in the same manner as in Mathematical Appendix 3: d. In particular, the preceding paragraph deals with a change which does not affect the relative magnitudes of the $\bar{Z}_{n-1}^a$ and $\bar{Z}_n^a$ ($a = 1, \ldots, A$). Hence we can express each of these initial quantities as a fixed proportion of, say, the total quantity of money in the economy $\bar{Z}_n$. That is,

$$(4.20) \qquad\qquad \bar{Z}_{n-1}^a = \lambda_a \bar{Z}_n \qquad\qquad (a = 1, \ldots, A),$$

$$(4.21) \qquad\qquad \bar{Z}_n^a = \mu_a \bar{Z}_n,$$

where the λ_a and μ_a are given constants. Substituting from (4.20)–(4.21) into (4.16)–(4.17), reproducing (4.19), and dropping (4.18) as redundant, we obtain new functions which we write as

$$(4.22) \qquad G_s\left(\frac{p_1}{p}, \ldots, \frac{p_{n-2}}{p}, r, \frac{\bar{Z}_n}{p}\right) - \bar{Z}_s = 0 \quad (s = 1, \ldots, n-2),$$

$$(4.23) \qquad G_{n-1}\left(\frac{p_1}{p}, \ldots, \frac{p_{n-2}}{p}, r, \frac{\bar{Z}_n}{p}\right) = 0,$$

$$(4.24) \qquad\qquad \sum_{s=1}^{n-2} w_s \frac{p_s}{p} = 1.$$

Consider now (4.22)–(4.24) as n equations in the n variables p_s/p, r, and $\bar{Z}_n/p$. Solving the equations for these variables, we obtain

$$(4.25) \qquad\qquad \frac{p_s}{p} = \beta_s \qquad\qquad (s = 1, \ldots, n-2),$$

$$(4.26) \qquad\qquad r = \beta_{n-1},$$

$$(4.27) \qquad\qquad \frac{\bar{Z}_n}{p} = \beta_n,$$

where the β_i ($i = 1, \ldots, n$) are constants for any fixed set of w_s, $\bar{Z}_s^a$, λ_a, and μ_a. Revert now to the original designation of dependent variables.

---

[4] Attached to the last two paragraphs of Chapter IV:4.

Substituting from (4.27) into (4.25) and rewriting, we obtain

$$(4.28) \qquad p_s = \frac{\beta_s \bar{Z}_n}{\beta_n},$$

$$(4.29) \qquad r = \beta_{n-1},$$

$$(4.30) \qquad p = \frac{1}{\beta_n} \bar{Z}_n.$$

Equations (4.28) and (4.30)—as equations (3.17)–(3.18) under simpler circumstances—show the directly proportionate dependence of equilibrium money prices on the quantity of money in the economy. In the same way, equation (4.29) shows the rate of interest's independence of this quantity. Clearly, the validity of these conclusions is restricted to those cases in which the increase in money is brought about in the manner designated: that is, to cases of equiproportionate changes in the initial bond and money holdings of each individual, with every other independent variable (viz., tastes and the $\bar{Z}^a_{hs}$) being held constant.

In connection with the discussion of neutral money in the text, let us see what happens to the solution of equations (4.22)–(4.24) as $\bar{Z}_n$ approaches zero. Equation (4.28) shows that as this happens each of the individual p_s also approaches zero. But equation (4.25) shows that they do so in a way which preserves their ratios. In particular, we see from (4.25)–(4.26) that the limiting values of p_s/p and r remain β_s and β_{n-1}, respectively. In this sense, money, under the foregoing conditions, is neutral. We note finally from equation (4.27) that the quantity of real money balances $\bar{Z}_n/p$ also remains constant as $\bar{Z}_n$ approaches zero.

d. DEMAND CURVES AND MARKET-EQUILIBRIUM CURVES AGAIN[5]

From equation (4.12) we can obtain the demand function for current nominal money holdings, which we write as

$$(4.31) \quad Z_n = G(p_1, \ldots, p_{n-2}, p, r, \bar{Z}^1_{n-1}, \ldots, \bar{Z}^A_{n-1}, \bar{Z}^1_n, \ldots, \bar{Z}^A).$$

[5] Attached to Chapter XI:4.

In its aggregate form, this is assumed to have the form of equation (20) in Chapter IX: 5,

(4.32) $$M^d = pL\left(Y, r, \frac{M_0}{p}\right).$$

By varying r, keeping all other variables constant, we obtain from either of these functions the demand curve in Figure IX-6 (p. 222). Correspondingly, the slope of this curve equals the partial derivative of $G(\ )$ or $pL(\ )$ with respect to r. Figure IX-6 reflects the usual assumption that this slope is negative.

On the other hand, equation (4.29) presents a market-equilibrium function: it relates the equilibrium rate of interest to the given quantity of money in the economy, and shows it to be independent of this quantity. Clearly, a similar function can be obtained by solving the aggregated system (1)–(4) of Chapter X: 1 for the rate of interest. The line in Figure XI-4 is the graphical representation of this function, and hence a market-equilibrium curve. Its horizontality reflects the fact that the derivative of (4.29) with respect to $\bar{Z}_n$ is zero. This must obviously be true regardless of the negative derivatives of (4.31)—or (4.32)—with respect to r. In this way we again see the fundamental distinction between individual- and market-experiments— and the corresponding necessity of specifying the function whose derivative is being taken.[6]

Assume now that one of the independent variables of the analysis need not remain constant. Let it be represented by the introduction of a parameter α into the functions on the left-hand sides of (4.22)–(4.23). Then, when we solve (4.22)–(4.24) for the p_s/p, r, and $\bar{Z}_n/p$, we no longer obtain constants [as in (4.25)–(4.27)], but instead functions of α, say,

(4.33) $$\frac{p_s}{p} = W_s(\alpha) \qquad\qquad (s = 1, \dots, n-2),$$

(4.34) $$r = W_{n-1}(\alpha),$$

(4.35) $$\frac{\bar{Z}_n}{p} = W_n(\alpha).$$

That is, the equilibrium values of our variables now depend on the value

[6] Cf. above, Mathematical Appendix 1: a.

of α. Clearly, there is no necessary relation between the derivatives $W'_n(\alpha)$ and $W'_{n-1}(\alpha)$. In particular, there is no reason why a change in α which does not affect the equilibrium value of $\bar{Z}_n/p$ should not nevertheless affect the equilibrium value of r.

5. Special Appendix to Chapter V

THE PROBABILITY DISTRIBUTION GENERATED BY THE RANDOM PAYMENT
PROCESS[1]

by ARYEH DVORETZKY

Problem: In an urn there are N white and N black balls. They are drawn out "at random" one after the other without replacement. Let $w(n)$ and $b(n)$ denote, respectively, the number of white and black balls drawn among the first n. Find the distribution of $\max_{0 \leqslant n \leqslant 2N} [w(n) - b(n)]$; that is, find

$$p_k = Pr\left\{ \max_{0 \leqslant n \leqslant 2N} [w(n) - b(n)] = k \right\}$$

$$(k = 0, 1, \ldots, N).$$

* * * * *

This problem may be reformulated in the following manner: Let $\omega = (x_1, x_2, \ldots, x_{2N}) = [x_1(\omega), x_2(\omega), \ldots, x_{2N}(\omega)]$ denote a sequence of $2N$ terms, each of the terms being either $+1$ or -1. Consider the sample space formed of all 2^{2N} such sequences and the probability space formed by associating with each such sequence the same probability 2^{-2N}.

---

[1] Attached to Chapter V:2.

Put $S_n(\omega) = \sum_{i=1}^n x_i(\omega)$ and $M(\omega) = \max\limits_{0 \leqslant n \leqslant 2N} S_n(\omega)$. Then, in the notation of conditional probability,

(5.1) $$p_k = Pr\{M(\omega) = k \,|\, S_{2N}(\omega) = 0\}.$$

Putting $P_k = p_k + p_{k+1} + \cdots + p_N = \sum_{\nu=k}^N p_\nu$, we have

(5.2) $$P_k = Pr\{M(\omega) \geqslant k \,|\, S_{2N}(\omega) = 0\} = \frac{Pr\{A_k\}}{Pr\{S_{2N}(\omega) = 0\}},$$

where A_k $(k = 0, 1, \ldots, N)$ denotes the set of those sequences ω for which $M(\omega) \geqslant k$ and $S_{2N}(\omega) = 0$.

For every sequence ω in A_k there exists a unique integer $m = m(\omega)$, $0 \leqslant m < 2N$, for which $S_\nu(\omega) < k$ for $\nu < m$, $S_m(\omega) = k$, $S_{2N}(\omega) = 0$ [i.e., m is the smallest value for which $S_m(\omega) = k$]. Put now $y_\nu = x_\nu(\omega)$ for $1 \leqslant \nu \leqslant m$ and $y_\nu = -x_\nu(\omega)$ for $m < \nu \leqslant 2N$. Then $(y_1, y_2, \ldots, y_{2N})$ is also a sequence in our sample space, and it satisfies

$$
\begin{aligned}
y_1 + y_2 &+ \cdots + y_{2N} \\
&= \sum_{\nu=1}^m y_\nu + \sum_{\nu=m+1}^{2N} y_\nu \\
&= \sum_{\nu=1}^m x_\nu(\omega) - \sum_{\nu=m+1}^{2N} x_\nu(\omega) \\
&= \sum_{\nu=1}^m x_\nu(\omega) - \sum_{\nu=m+1}^{2N} x_\nu(\omega) + \left(\sum_{\nu=1}^m x_\nu(\omega) + \sum_{\nu=m+1}^{2N} x_\nu(\omega) \right) \\
&= 2 \sum_{\nu=1}^m x_\nu(\omega) = 2k.
\end{aligned}
$$

We have thus associated with every sequence ω in A_k a sequence ω' for which $S_{2N}(\omega') = 2k$. Moreover, if B_k denotes the set of sequences for which $S_{2N} = 2k$, we have established a one-to-one correspondence between the sequences in A_k and those in B_k. Thus both sets contain the same number of sequences, and hence $Pr\{A_k\} = Pr\{B_k\}$. Hence, by (5.2),

(5.3) $$P_k = \frac{Pr\{S_{2N}(\omega) = 2k\}}{Pr\{S_{2N}(\omega) = 0\}}.$$

Since $S_{2N}(\omega) = 2k$ means that there are $N + k$ terms in the sequence equal to $+1$ and $N - k$ equal to -1, we have $Pr\{S_{2N}(\omega) = 2k\} = \binom{2N}{N+k} 2^{-2N}$. Therefore, from (5.3),

(5.4) $$P_k = \frac{\binom{2N}{N+k}}{\binom{2N}{N}} = \frac{N!^2}{(N-k)!(N+k)!} \qquad (k = 0, 1, \ldots, N),$$

and

(5.5)
$$p_k = P_k - P_{k+1} = \frac{N!^2}{(N-k)!(N+k)!}\left[1 - \frac{N-k}{N+k+1}\right]$$
$$= \frac{(2k+1)\cdot N!^2}{(N-k)!(N+k+1)!}.$$

The quantities p_k and P_k above are functions of N as well as of k. Therefore, we shall denote them by $p_k^{(2N)}$ and $P_k^{(2N)}$, respectively, whenever wishing to study also their dependence on N.

From (5.5) we have

$$\frac{p_{k+1}^{(2N)}}{p_k^{(2N)}} = \frac{2k+3}{2k+1}\cdot\frac{N-k}{N+k+2} = \frac{2kN+3N-2k^2-3k}{2kN+N+2k^2+5k+2}.$$

Thus $p_{k+1} > p_k$ is equivalent to $2N > 4k^2 + 8k + 2$, or $N > 2(k+1)^2 - 1$, that is, to $k + 1 < \sqrt{(N+1)/2}$. Therefore $p_k^{(2N)}$ increases steadily as k increases up to the largest integer not exceeding $\sqrt{(N+1)/2}$, and as k increases further, $p_k^{(2N)}$ becomes a monotone decreasing function of k. (If $k_0 = \sqrt{(N+1)/2}$ is an integer, then there are two maxima: at $k = k_0$ and $k = k_0 - 1$.)

Applying Stirling's formula to (5.4), we obtain for $0 \leqslant k < N$

$$\log P_k^{(2N)} = (2N+1)\log N - (N-k+\tfrac{1}{2})\log(N-k)$$
$$- (N+k+\tfrac{1}{2})\log(N+k) + R$$
$$= -(N-k+\tfrac{1}{2})\log\left(1 - \frac{k}{N}\right)$$
$$- (N+k+\tfrac{1}{2})\log\left(1 + \frac{k}{N}\right) + R,$$

with the remainder term R satisfying $|R| < \dfrac{\text{const.}}{N-k}$. This yields

(5.6) $$\log P_k^{(2N)} \sim -\frac{k^2}{N}$$

as $N \to \infty$ while $k/N \to 0$. (The sign $\sim$ signifies that the ratio of the two sides tends to 1; k may also tend to infinity, but less rapidly than N.) If we put

(5.7) $$F_{2N}(\lambda) = Pr\{k \leqslant \lambda\sqrt{2N}\} = Pr\left\{\frac{k}{\sqrt{2N}} \leqslant \lambda\right\},$$

that is, if F_{2N} is the (cumulative) distribution function of $\dfrac{k}{\sqrt{2N}}$, we have from (5.6)

(5.8) $$\lim_{N \to \infty} F_{2N}(\lambda) = 1 - e^{-2\lambda^2}$$

for every $\lambda \geqslant 0$.

From (5.6) and (5.5) we have

(5.9) $$p_k^{(2N)} \sim \frac{2k+1}{N+k+1} e^{-k^2/N}.$$

Thus, if k and N tend to infinity so that $\dfrac{k}{\sqrt{2N}} \to \lambda$, we have

(5.10) $$\lim_{N \to \infty} \sqrt{2N} \cdot p_k^{(2N)} = 4\lambda e^{-2\lambda^2},$$

and the right side of this equation, which is equal to the derivative of the right side of (5.8), may be thought of as the asymptotic density of $k/\sqrt{2N}$. Using an estimate of the remainder in Stirling's formula, it is easy to obtain bounds for the difference of the two sides in (5.6) and (5.9), and hence also estimate the rate of approach to the limit in (5.8) and (5.10).

If for any q, $0 < q < 1$, we denote by $Q_q^{(2N)}$ the q percentile point of k; that is, if $Q_q^{(2N)}$ is the smallest integer m satisfying $p_0^{(2N)} + p_1^{(2N)} + \cdots + p_m^{(2N)} \geq q$, then according to (5.7) and (5.8),

$$(5.11) \qquad \lim_{N \to \infty} \frac{Q_q^{(2N)}}{\sqrt{2N}} = Q_q,$$

where Q_q is the positive root of $1 - e^{-2\lambda^2} = q$. Thus $Q_q^{(2N)} \sim Q_q \sqrt{2N}$; that is, though it increases with N, its rate of increase is much slower than that of N. Hence as N increases, $Q_q^{(2N)}/N$ generally decreases. Due to the discrete character of the integers, there may, however, occur occasional local exceptions to this rule. Nevertheless, we must always have for every positive integer $v > 1$ and $q > p_0^{(2N)} = 1/(N + 1)$

$$\frac{Q_q^{(2vN)}}{vN} < \frac{Q_q^{(2N)}}{N}.$$

This is an immediate consequence of the fact that for every positive integer k we have

$$(5.12) \qquad P_k^{(2N)} > P_{vk}^{(2vN)}.$$

To verify (5.12) we rewrite (5.4):

$$P_k^{(2N)} = \frac{N(N - 1) \cdots (N - k + 1)}{(N + k)(N + k - 1) \cdots (N + 1)}$$

$$= \prod_{m=1}^{k} \left(1 - \frac{k}{N + m} \right).$$

Then also

$$P_{vk}^{(2vN)} = \prod_{m=1}^{vk} \left(1 - \frac{vk}{vN + m} \right).$$

All the factors in these products are positive and smaller than 1, while the factors corresponding to $m = v, 2v, \ldots, kv$ of the last product are precisely equal to the factors corresponding to $m = 1, 2, \ldots, k$ (i.e., to all the factors) appearing in the expression for $P_k^{(2N)}$. This proves (5.12).

It may finally be remarked that the asymptotic result expressed by (5.8) remains valid under very general assumptions. Thus it is possible to prove the following:

Let $X_n (n = 1, 2, ...)$ be an infinite sequence of independent random variables satisfying $|X_n| \leqslant H < \infty$ $(n = 1, 2, ...)$ having mean zero and variance σ_n^2. Then if $\sum_{n=1}^{\infty} \sigma_n^2 = \infty$, we have, on putting $Y_n = X_1 + X_2 + \cdots + X_n$ and $s_n^2 = \sigma_1^2 + \sigma_2^2 + \cdots \sigma_n^2$,

$$\lim_{n \to \infty} Pr \left\{ \max_{0 \leqslant m \leqslant n} Y_m \leqslant \lambda s_n \,|\, Y_n < H \right\} = 1 - e^{-2\lambda^2}$$

for every $\lambda \geqslant 0$.

This, and indeed considerably more general results, follow from the fact that the stochastic process involved here approaches that of the Brownian motion $x(t)$, and the probability we are seeking approaches

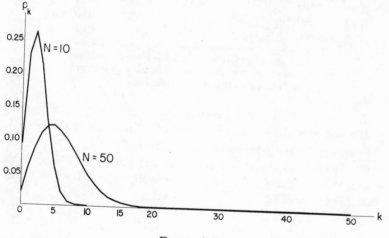

FIGURE A-5.

that of $Pr \left\{ \max_{0 \leqslant t \leqslant 1} x(t) \leqslant \lambda \,|\, x(1) = 0 \right\}$, which is easily computed to be $1 - e^{-2\lambda^2}$.[2]

Numerical Illustration:[3] Figure A-5 shows the exact distributions of k—as given by (5.5)—for $N = 10$ and $N = 50$. The ranges of these

---

[2] For a study of Brownian motion, see, e.g., P. Levy, *Processes stochastiques et mouvement Brownian* (Paris, 1948), or J. L. Doob, *Stochastic Processes* (New York, 1953).

[3] Figure A-5 and the Table of Percentile Values were prepared by Tsvi Ophir.

distributions are, of course, 0–10 and 0–50, respectively. The reader can verify that the asymptotic formula (5.10) gives a fair approximation of the former and an excellent one of the latter.

Table of Percentile Values

	90 Percent		99 Percent	
N	k	k/N	k	k/N
10†	4.8	0.48	6.8	0.68
50	10.7	0.21	15.2	0.30
100	15.2	0.15	21.5	0.21
500	33.9	0.07	48.0	0.10
1000	48.0	0.05	67.9	0.07

† As given by (5.4), $k = 4$ and $k = 6$ are the smallest integral values for which the cumulative probability $1 - P_k$ is at least .90 and .99, respectively.

We illustrate the use of the asymptotic formula (5.11) by computing from it the 90 and 99 percentile values of k for different values of N. The appropriate formulas are $k = 1.07\sqrt{2N}$ and $k = 1.52\sqrt{2N}$, respectively. These yield the values shown in the table above. This table ignores the fact that k, of course, can actually assume integral values only.

6. Appendix to Chapters V, VI, and VII

a. The Derivation of the Demand Functions from Utility Maximization[1]

For simplicity, assume prices to change equiproportionately and consider an individual whose economic horizon extends over three periods. Assume also that it is economically meaningful to attribute liquidity—and hence direct utility—to bonds as well as money.[2] Our individual thus maximizes the utility function[3]

$$(6.1) \qquad U = w\left(Z_1, \frac{B_1}{p}, \frac{M_1}{p}, Z_2, \frac{B_2}{p}, \frac{M_2}{p}, Z_3; \frac{M_0}{p}\right)$$

subject to the respective budget restraints of the three periods,

$$(6.2) \qquad pZ_1 + \frac{B_1}{1+r} + M_1 - B_0 - M_0 - p\bar{Z}_1 = 0,$$

$$(6.3) \qquad pZ_2 + \frac{B_2}{1+r} + M_2 - B_1 - M_1 - p\bar{Z}_2 = 0,$$

$$(6.4) \qquad pZ_3 \qquad\qquad - B_2 - M_2 - p\bar{Z}_3 = 0,$$

[1] Attached to Chapter V:3.

[2] Cf. p. 93, footnote 21. The problematic aspects of such an assumption are further discussed on pp. 464–65 below.

[3] On its form, see pp. 107 (footnote 36) and 410–11 above.

where the symbols are to be interpreted in accordance with the discussion on pp. 96–97 above. From this discussion it is also clear that the individual does not plan to hold financial assets at the end of the third week, so that such assets are not represented in either (6.1) or (6.4).[4]

Form now the expression

(6.5) $\qquad w(\quad) - \lambda_1[(6.2)] - \lambda_2[(6.3)] - \lambda_3[(6.4)]$,

where the λ_h ($h = 1, 2, 3$) are Lagrange multipliers. Differentiating with respect to Z_h, B_k, and M_k ($k = 1, 2$) then yields the following conditions for a maximum:

(6.6) $\qquad \dfrac{1}{p} \dfrac{\partial w(\quad)}{\partial Z_h} - \lambda_h = 0 \qquad\qquad (h = 1, 2, 3)$,

(6.7) $\qquad \dfrac{1}{p} \dfrac{\partial w(\quad)}{\partial \left(\dfrac{B_k}{p}\right)} - \dfrac{\lambda_k}{1 + r} + \lambda_{k+1} = 0 \qquad (k = 1, 2)$,

(6.8) $\qquad \dfrac{1}{p} \dfrac{\partial w(\quad)}{\partial \left(\dfrac{M_k}{p}\right)} - \lambda_k + \lambda_{k+1} = 0 \qquad (k = 1, 2)$.

Clearly, λ_h represents the marginal utility of a dollar's expenditure on commodities in the hth week. Thus equation (6.8) corresponds to equation (1) on p. 89, and equation (6.7) to equation (2) on p. 90, modified in accordance with equation (b) in footnote 21 on p. 93.

Eliminating the λ_h from these equations then yields

(6.9) $\qquad \dfrac{\dfrac{\partial w(\quad)}{\partial Z_k}}{\dfrac{\partial w(\quad)}{\partial \left(\dfrac{B_k}{p}\right)} + \dfrac{\partial w(\quad)}{\partial Z_{k+1}}} = 1 + r \qquad (k = 1, 2)$,

[4] For a more rigorous justification of this procedure (if such is needed) see my "Relative Prices, Say's Law, and the Demand for Money," *Econometrica*, XVI (1948), 140–42.

In order to see that the following results can be obtained for bonds which are perpetuities—and not only for those of one-week maturities considered here— compare the analysis in my "Further Considerations of the General Equilibrium Theory of Money," *op. cit.*, p. 188.

(6.10)
$$\frac{\dfrac{\partial w(\quad)}{\partial Z_k}}{\dfrac{\partial w(\quad)}{\partial\left(\dfrac{M_1}{p}\right)}+\dfrac{\partial w(\quad)}{\partial Z_{k+1}}}=1 \qquad (k=1,2).$$

In order to interpret the left-hand side of, say, (6.10), let us take the differential of (6.1) as of a given level of utility, assuming that only Z_k and M_k/p vary, and that the latter variation leads to a corresponding variation in Z_{k+1}. That is, consider a differential movement of Z_k, M_k/p, and Z_{k+1} along a given indifference hypersurface in accordance with the restriction $dZ_{k+1}=d(M_k/p)$.[5] This yields

(6.11)
$$\frac{\partial w(\quad)}{\partial Z_k}dZ_k+\left[\frac{\partial w(\quad)}{\partial\left(\dfrac{M_k}{p}\right)}+\frac{\partial w(\quad)}{\partial Z_{k+1}}\right]dZ_{k+1}=0.$$

Thus $-dZ_{k+1}/dZ_k$ (the marginal rate of substitution measured by this conceptual experiment) is represented by the left-hand side of (6.10). Accordingly, this equation corresponds to equation (7) on p. 93. Similarly, equation (6.9) corresponds to equation (8) there. It is also clear that the only effect on the foregoing analysis of dropping the assumption that bonds provide direct utility is that the first term in the denominator of (6.9) vanishes.[6]

We now consider (6.2)–(6.4) (divided through by p) and (6.9)–(6.10) as constituting seven equations in the seven dependent variables Z_h ($h=1,2,3$), B_k/p, and M_k/p ($k=1,2$), and in the independent variables r, $B_0/p+M_0/p+Z_1$, Z_2, and Z_3. Hence, assuming solvability, the dependent variables can be expressed as functions of the latter. Taking account of the fact that relative prices have been assumed

[5] Analytically, this involves taking the differential of (6.1) after substituting in it for Z_{k+1} from budget restraint (6.3) or (6.4), as the case may be. Cf. p. 92, footnote 20 above.

[6] The technical reason marginal conditions (6.9)–(6.10) differ in their form from those of the standard n-good case is that the optimum marginal rates of substitution in the latter describe the point of tangency between an n-dimensional indifference surface and an n-dimensional budget hyperplane. In the present case, however, the point of tangency is with a budget hyperplane of less than n dimensions. This will become clear from Section d below, especially p. 463, footnote 23.

constant in the present discussion (p. 89), we see that we have in this way derived demand functions of the type posited in (4.6)–(4.8) above.[7]

The extension of the foregoing argument to n periods is immediate.

b. THE DERIVATION OF THE DEMAND FUNCTIONS FROM REVEALED PREFERENCES[8]

Alternatively, we can derive demand functions (4.6)–(4.8) in accordance with Samuelson's method of revealed preferences.[9] Assume that at the given price level p^0 and interest rate r^0, and with the given initial endowments $\bar{Z}_h$ ($h = 1, 2, 3$), B_0, and M_0, the individual chooses the collection of Z_h^0, B_k^0, and M_k^0 ($k = 1, 2$). Since it is more convenient to carry out the analysis in terms of *real* bond and money holdings, we shall say that this collection consists of Z_h^0, $B_k^0/(1 + r^0)p^0$, and M_k^0/p^0, and shall denote it by "Collection Zero."

Assume now that we confront the individual with the same rate of interest and commodity endowments, but change other endowments and prices in the proportion t. That is, we confront him with the price level $p^* = tp^0$ and interest rate $r^* = r^0$, and with the endowments $\bar{Z}_h^* = \bar{Z}_h^0$, $B_0^* = tB_0$ and $M_0^* = tM_0$. Assume that under these conditions he chooses "Collection Star," consisting of Z_h^*, $B_k^*/(1 + r^*)p^*$,

---

[7] Except for the fact that M_0/p does not appear as a separate argument in these demand functions; cf. equation (6.1) and p. 107, footnote 36 above.

One point that might be noted is that if we were to examine now the planned excess demand for money for the Monday marketing period three weeks hence, we would necessarily discover a state of disequilibrium. For though the supply of money would still be $\bar{Z}_n$, the demand would be zero. For, by assumption, individuals do not plan now to hold any money at the end of the third week. But, as emphasized in the text (pp. 67 and 73–74), this potential disequilibrium is not permitted to manifest itself in the *tâtonnement* by which the excess-demand equations for current goods, (4.16)–(4.19), are solved. On the other hand, by the time we reach the "third" week, it will have become the "first" one. Hence individuals will then clearly have positive demands for money balances, so that a state of equilibrium can then be achieved.

Note finally that the commodity demand functions derived here do not have the form which is attributed to them by Mishan and which constitutes the basis of his contention that there are two effects connected with money holdings; see E. J. Mishan, "A Fallacy in the Interpretation of the Cash Balance Effect," *Economica*, XXV (1958), 106–18. Cf. also above, pp. 438–39, footnote 24.

[8] Attached to Chapter V:3, pp. 95–96.

[9] The following argument is adapted from Samuelson, *Foundations*, pp. 111–12. Its original form has been corrected in accordance with M. McManus' note "On

and M_k^*/p^*. We desire to show that Collection Zero is identical with Collection Star.

Let us rewrite budget restraints (6.2)–(6.4) as

$$(6.12) \qquad Z_1 + \frac{B_1}{(1 + r)p} \qquad + \frac{M_1}{p} \qquad = \frac{B_0}{p} + \frac{M_0}{p} + \bar{Z}_1,$$

$$(6.13) \qquad Z_2 + \frac{B_2}{(1 + r)p} - \frac{B_1}{p} + \frac{M_2}{p} - \frac{M_1}{p} = \qquad \bar{Z}_2,$$

$$(6.14) \qquad Z_3 \qquad\quad - \frac{B_2}{p} \qquad - \frac{M_2}{p} = \qquad \bar{Z}_3.$$

If to each of the variables in the foregoing restraints is attached the superscript "0" ("*"), then we have a description of the specific situation in which Collection Zero (Star) was chosen. Let us also assume that in any specific situation, one and only one collection is chosen—i.e., this collection is preferred to any other one that could have been purchased. Now the change described in the preceding paragraph does not affect either the prices of real goods or the real value of the endowments in (6.12)–(6.14). This means that under the price and endowment conditions that prevailed when Collection Zero was chosen, Collection Star could have been chosen; thus Collection Zero was preferred to Collection Star. But on the basis of the same reasoning, Collection Star was preferred to Collection Zero. Hence a contradiction. Hence these two collections must be identical. It follows that an equiproportionate change in money prices and in initial bond and money holdings, the rate of interest being held constant, has no effect on the amounts demanded of commodities, *real* bond holdings, and *real* money holdings.[10]

Patinkin's Use of Revealed Preference," *Southern Economic Journal*, XXIV (1957), 209–12.

[10] As McManus has emphasized (*ibid.*), we cannot carry out this argument except by simultaneously considering the budget restraints of all three weeks: for an individual cannot rationally choose his optimum collection in any one week without knowing his endowments over his entire economic horizon. This is also an immediate implication of Friedman's "permanent-income hypothesis" (*A Theory of the Consumption Function, op. cit.*, Chapters 2–3).

c. The Relationship to the Fisherine Analysis[11]

Let us now return to the utility analysis of Section *a* and consider its relationship to the Fisherine analysis, in which utility is maximized subject to a single wealth restraint. For generality, assume that there is a second bond—denoted by B'_k—whose price is $1/(1 + r')$. Assume that $r' < r$. Adding the term $B'_k/(1 + r')$ to the left-hand sides of (6.2) and (6.3); multiplying (6.3) thus modified by $1/(1 + r)$, and (6.4) by $1/(1+r)^2$; and adding the results to (6.2)—then yields

$$
\begin{aligned}
pZ_1 &+ \frac{1}{1 + r} \left\{ pZ_2 + \left[(r - r') \frac{B'_1}{1 + r'} + rM_1 \right] \right\} \\
(6.15) \quad &+ \frac{1}{(1 + r)^2} \left\{ pZ_3 + \left[(r - r') \frac{B'_2}{1 + r'} + rM_2 \right] \right\} \\
&= (B_0 + M_0 + p\bar{Z}_1) + \frac{p\bar{Z}_2}{1 + r} + \frac{p\bar{Z}_3}{(1 + r)^2} = pW_0.
\end{aligned}
$$

By a natural extension of the argument on p. 112, the expressions enclosed by square brackets in these restraints represent the imputed value (in terms of interest foregone) of the liquidity afforded by the "primed" bonds and by money.

Assume first that the "unprimed" bonds are not liquid, so that the individual's utility function is again represented by (6.1), with B_k replaced by B'_k. Maximization of (6.1) so modified subject to (6.2)–(6.4)[12] then yields (6.6)–(6.8)[13] and the two new equations

$$
(6.16) \qquad\qquad -\frac{\lambda_k}{1 + r} + \lambda_{k+1} = 0 \qquad\qquad (k = 1, 2).
$$

System (6.2)–(6.4), (6.6)–(6.8), and (6.16) then constitutes twelve equations in the twelve dependent variables Z_h, B_k/p, B'_k/p, M_k/p, and λ_h.

On the other hand, if in accordance with the Fisherine approach we maximize (6.1) subject to the over-all wealth restraint (6.15), we obtain

$$
(6.17) \qquad\qquad \frac{1}{p} \frac{\partial w(\ )}{\partial Z_h} - \frac{\lambda}{(1 + r)^{h-1}} = 0 \qquad\qquad (h = 1, 2, 3),
$$

---

[11] Attached to Chapter V:7.
[12] Modified so as to take account of expenditures on "primed" bonds as well.
[13] With B_k replaced by B'_k, and r by r'.

(6.18)
$$\frac{1}{p} \frac{\partial w(\ )}{\partial \left(\dfrac{B_k'}{p}\right)} - \lambda \frac{r - r'}{(1 + r)^k} \frac{1}{1 + r'} = 0 \qquad (k = 1, 2),$$

(6.19)
$$\frac{1}{p} \frac{\partial w(\ )}{\partial \left(\dfrac{M_k}{p}\right)} - \lambda \frac{r}{(1 + r)^k} = 0 \qquad (k = 1, 2),$$

where λ is the Lagrange multiplier. These together with (6.15) constitute eight equations in the eight dependent variables Z_h, B_k'/p, M_k/p, and λ, and in the two independent variables r and W_0. Hence, assuming solvability, the former can be expressed as functions of the latter. Note that the optimum values of B_k/p are then determined as residuals from budget restraints (6.2)–(6.3).[14]

It is left as an exercise for the reader to show that—by substituting from (6.16)—the system described two paragraphs above can be reduced to that of the preceding paragraph. Thus the equivalence of these two results is established.

This equivalence no longer obtains, however, if it is assumed that the "unprimed" bonds also provide utility. For then maximization in accordance with the Fisherine approach would yield the two additional —and economically implausible—equations

(6.20)
$$\frac{\partial w(\ )}{\partial \left(\dfrac{B_k}{p}\right)} = 0 \qquad (k = 1, 2).$$

This is the usual "free-good" result to be expected from assuming at one and the same time that (a) there is a utility-providing good and (b) the expenditures on this good are not reflected in the budget re-straint. Under the assumption of liquid bonds, then, the analysis can

[14] This essential feature of the Fisherine analysis is vitally dependent on the use of $1/(1 + r)$—and not $1/(1 + r')$—as the discount factor in (6.15). If the latter had been used, the resulting "wealth" restraint would have depended on the B_k instead of the B_k'. Correspondingly, since the B_k' appear in the utility function and hence in (6.17)–(6.19), the optimum holdings of neither the "primed" nor "unprimed" bonds could then be determined as residuals.

The economic interpretation of the necessity of using $1/(1 + r)$ as the discount factor is clear from the discussion on pp. 113–14 above. See also the geometrical presenta-tion in the next section of this Appendix, especially p. 465, footnote 18.

be validly carried out only by taking account of the budgetary implications of transactions in "unprimed" bonds; that is, only by means of system (6.2)–(6.4), (6.6)–(6.8), and (6.16).

Correspondingly, in the general case considered by this system, the two main conclusions of the Fisherine analysis—namely, that the optimum position is determined by the rate of interest and total wealth, and that the marginal rate of substitution of present for future consumption in this position equals $1 + r$—no longer obtain. In particular, equation (6.9) implies that this rate of substitution exceeds $1 + r$ by an amount that varies from individual to individual. To speak somewhat loosely, the liquidity of bonds acts like an increased interest rate to further decrease the attractiveness of present as compared with future consumption.[15]

Again, the necessity of taking explicit account of the weekly budget restraints (6.2)–(6.4) implies that the optimum position will generally be affected even by changes in $B_0 + M_0 + p\bar{Z}_1$, $p\bar{Z}_2$, and $p\bar{Z}_3$ which leave the sum of their discounted values invariant. The intuitive basis of this conclusion is also clear. For consider an individual with an income stream of fixed present value. The more this stream is concentrated in the present, the greater the bond holdings he can maintain while carrying out any given consumption plan, and hence the greater the liquidity he can enjoy. This increase in the individual's well-being must therefore affect his economic behavior.

Two final comments are in order. First, the invalidity of the Fisherine analysis stems not from the assumption *per se* that "unprimed" bonds provide utility, but from its implication within our model that there is then no asset which does not provide utility, and therefore no asset whose rate of return can properly be used to discount future income and consumption in deriving the Fisherine wealth restraint. Second, the foregoing discussion is predicated on the assumption that it is economically meaningful to attribute direct utility to all assets. But in addition to the specific problems raised by such an attribution within our model,[16] there is the more basic methodological question as to whether (from the viewpoint of the transactions motive which now concerns us)

---

[15] Similarly, the rate of interest now undervalues the absolute liquidity services of money balances: for it measures this liquidity relative to that of bonds—which under our present assumptions are also liquid.

[16] See p. 93, footnote 21.

"liquidity" should not be considered as a relative attribute, so that the least liquid asset is by definition one which does not provide any direct utility. If this is the case, the foregoing criticism of the Fisherine analysis is irrelevant.

d. The Relationship to the Fisherine Analysis (Continued)[17]

The argument of the preceding section can be instructively illustrated in terms of the somewhat simpler model analyzed in Chapter V:7. We note first that the existence of a direct utility for bonds obviously cannot affect the validity of wealth restraint (19) on p. 110, where the composite goods E_1 and E_2 are defined as on p. 112; for it cannot change the fact that the present value of all bond transactions over the individual's horizon is necessarily zero. This follows from the identity of the rate of interest at which newly issued bonds are discounted in the market and the rate at which the present value of their maturities is calculated. Hence the individual must satisfy the budget restraint represented by *FH* in Figure V-5, reproduced here for convenience as Figure A-6.

The difficulty arises, however, from the fact that movements along this line correspond to changes in the magnitude of bond holdings (p. 111). Consequently the direct utility of bonds causes such a movement to generate a shift of the entire indifference map. Hence the optimum combination of E_1 and E_2 cannot be determined in Fisherine manner by moving along this budget line until the highest point on an invariant indifference map is reached.[18]

We can, however, achieve a fuller understanding of the issues here by assuming that the marginal rate of substitution of E_1 for E_2 is

---

[17] Attached to Chapter V:7, especially pp. 113–14.

The argument of this section has benefited greatly from the criticisms and suggestions of the students in my monetary theory seminar at the Hebrew University in the fall of 1960.

[18] Indeed, the fact that the quantity of bonds necessarily changes with the level of E_2 makes it impossible even to define this composite good under our present assumption that bonds have utility; cf. p. 113, footnote 45. Note, however, that this particular difficulty disappears if we assume that money holdings are rented. This is the assumption on which the immediately following argument is based.

Note that the present paragraph also indicates the geometrical interpretation of the fact that the discount factor that must be used in the Fisherine case of the preceding section is $1/(1 + r)$ and not $1/(1 + r')$ (p. 463, footnote 14). For movements along a wealth line derived by discounting by $1/(1 + r')$ correspond to changes in the quantity of "primed" bonds and therefore generate shifts in the indifference map.

independent of bond holdings, so that the indifference map in Figure A-6 does remain invariant. Let us now start from point F on FH and begin to move southeast. This represents a simultaneous increase in the magnitude of bond holdings. Hence even though the indifference map remains the same, the level of utility to which each indifference curve corresponds increases accordingly. Consider now the point of tangency V. To speak somewhat loosely, a further infinitesimal movement southeast will now not affect the total utility which the individual

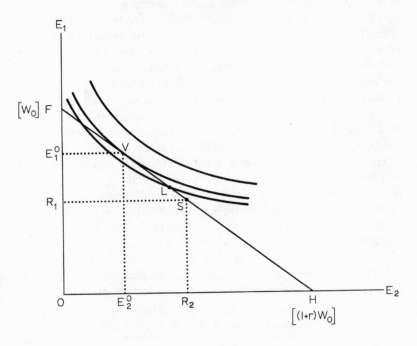

Figure A-6.

derives from E_1 and E_2; but it will increase his utility from bond holdings. Hence his optimum position must be rightwards of V, at (say) L.[19] In accordance with our preceding conclusion, the slope of the indifference curve at this point (the marginal rate of substitution of E_1 for E_2) is

[19] Note that this argument does not apply to the Fisherine case. Note, too, the last paragraph of the preceding footnote.

greater than the slope of the budget line $(1 + r)$—where in both cases the slope is taken with respect to the Y-axis.

This paradox of a seeming nontangential optimum position is immediately resolved by noting that point L actually does (and point V does not) correspond to a point of tangency in the relevant space in which our analysis is effectively being carried out.[20] This is the three-dimensional space containing indifference surfaces relating E_1, E_2, and B_1/p. Because we are dealing with a two-period case, the budget restriction in this space is represented not by a single plane (as in the ordinary one-period three-good case), but by a line in space defined by the intersection of the two planes corresponding to the weekly budget restraints (10) and (11) on p. 96, now rewritten as[21]

$$(6.21) \qquad E_1 + \frac{1}{1 + r} \frac{B_1}{p} = R_1$$

and

$$(6.22) \qquad E_2 - \frac{B_1}{p} = R_2 .$$

Alternatively—and more instructively for our present purpose—either of these restraints can be replaced by the wealth restraint

$$(6.23) \qquad E_1 + \frac{1}{1 + r} E_2 = W_0 ,$$

which, as we have seen (p. 113), is a linear combination of them.[22]

If, then, L in Figure A-6 is the individual's optimum position, it is so by virtue of its being the point of tangency between this budget line in space and a three-dimensional indifference surface.[23] Indeed, since

[20] I am indebted to Asher Shlain for this observation.

[21] The reader will recall that money balances are now assumed to be rented. This enables us to reduce what is essentially a four-dimensional problem (Z_1, Z_2, M_1/p, and B_1/p) to three. Cf. footnote 18 above.

[22] The set of attainable points in this three-dimensional space is the pyramid defined by (6.21)–(6.22)—rewritten as inequalities—and the additional restrictions that neither E_1 nor E_2 can be negative. The budget line in space is the only edge of this pyramid which does not lie in one of the coordinate planes. It passes through the point (R_1, R_2) in the E_1–E_2 coordinate plane; i.e., the plane corresponding to $B_1/p=0$.

[23] Cf. p. 459, footnote 6 above. In the present case, the left-hand sides of (6.9)–(6.10) describe the slopes of the line in space in the relevant directions.

it is now clear that Figure A-6 actually represents a cross-section plane of our three-dimensional indifference map at a given level of bond holdings (namely, the optimum level), it is also clear that L is the only point on this budget line which really lies in this plane. All the other points on FH merely represent the projection on this plane of the budget line in space. In particular, segment LH is the projection of that portion of this line which lies above the plane, and segment FL of that portion below. In any event, it is clear from (6.21)–(6.22) that the position of the budget line in space is dependent on the specific values of R_1 and R_2, with the consequences already described.[24]

We note finally that under the Fisherine assumption that bonds provide no direct utility, the indifference surfaces in E_1–E_2–B_1/p space are cylinders perpendicular to the E_1–E_2 coordinate plane. Now, the point of tangency between the budget line in space and the relevant indifference surface must lie in the plane defined by (6.23), which is also perpendicular to this coordinate plane. Hence the tangency between this wealth plane and the indifference surface is a straight line which is also perpendicular in this direction. Hence the E_1–E_2 coordinates of the point of tangency in space will remain invariant under any change in R_1 and R_2 which leaves the budget line in the same wealth plane; i.e., which leaves the discounted value of R_1 and R_2 constant. Only the B_1/p coordinate of the point of tangency will be affected by such a change. This is the graphical expression of the validity of the Fisherine analysis under the foregoing assumption.

e. THE MARGINAL UTILITY OF CASH BALANCES AND MARSHALL'S "MARGINAL UTILITY OF MONEY"[25]

Though it is fairly clear from the text—as well as from equations (6.6)–(6.8) above—it might be worthwhile elaborating on the distinction between the marginal utility of cash balances and Marshall's marginal utility of money, or the marginal utility of wealth, as we have called it.

[24] Cf. p. 464 above. Cf. also footnote 22.
[25] Attached to Chapter V:8.
The following is adapted from E. B. Wilson, "Notes on Utility Theory and Demand Equations," *Quarterly Journal of Economics*, LX (1945–46), 453–54.
For simplicity, the argument M_0/p in the utility—and hence demand—functions is ignored in what follows. Cf. equation (6.1) and p. 107, footnote 36 above.

For simplicity, consider again the Fisherine case of Chapter V: 7 in which the individual maximizes his utility

(6.24) $$U = u\left(Z_1, \frac{M_1}{p}, Z_2\right)$$

subject to

(6.25) $$pZ_1 + \frac{p}{1+r}\left[r\left(\frac{M_1}{p}\right) + Z_2\right] = pW,$$

to yield marginal conditions of the form (6.17) and (6.19), and thence demand functions of the form

(6.26) $$Z_1 = F(r, W),$$

(6.27) $$\frac{M_1}{p} = G(r, W),$$

(6.28) $$Z_2 = H(r, W).$$

Substituting into (6.24) then yields

(6.29) $$U = u[F(r, W), G(r, W), H(r, W)]$$
$$\equiv \phi(r, W).$$

The function $\phi(\ )$ relates the individual's utility from an optimum collection of goods to the independent variables which determine the composition of that collection. Let us now investigate the effect on this level of utility of an increase in W. That is, let us determine the partial derivative of $\phi(\ )$ with respect to W.

We note first that dividing budget restraint (6.25) through by p and then substituting in it from (6.26)–(6.28) yields the identity

(6.30) $$F(r, W) + \frac{1}{1+r}[rG(r, W) + H(r, W)] \equiv W.$$

Differentiating both sides of this identity with respect to W then yields

(6.31) $$\frac{\partial F(\ )}{\partial W} + \frac{r}{1+r}\frac{\partial G(\ )}{\partial W} + \frac{1}{1+r}\frac{\partial H(\ )}{\partial W} = 1.$$

This is a reflection of the simple fact that, by the budget restraint, any increase in wealth will be used up in a corresponding increase in expenditure on all three goods consumed by the individual.

Making use of (1.27), we now differentiate both sides of identity (6.29) to obtain

$$(6.32) \qquad \frac{\partial \phi(\ )}{\partial W} \equiv \frac{\partial u(\ )}{\partial Z_1} \frac{\partial F(\ )}{\partial W} + \frac{\partial u(\ )}{\partial \left(\frac{M_1}{p}\right)} \frac{\partial G(\ )}{\partial W} + \frac{\partial u(\ )}{\partial Z_2} \frac{\partial H(\ )}{\partial W}.$$

Substituting from (6.17) and (6.19) then yields

$$\frac{\partial \phi(\ )}{\partial W} = \lambda p \frac{\partial F(\ )}{\partial W} + \lambda p \frac{r}{1+r} \frac{\partial G(\ )}{\partial W} + \lambda p \frac{1}{1+r} \frac{\partial H(\ )}{\partial W}$$

$$(6.33) \qquad = \lambda p \left[\frac{\partial F(\ )}{\partial W} + \frac{r}{1+r} \frac{\partial G(\ )}{\partial W} + \frac{1}{1+r} \frac{\partial H(\ )}{\partial W} \right]$$

$$= \lambda p,$$

where use has been made of (6.31).

Clearly, $\lambda = \frac{1}{p} \frac{\partial \phi(r, W)}{\partial W}$ corresponds to Marshall's marginal utility of money.[26] It is, thus, conceptually distinct from the marginal utility of a dollar's worth of cash balances,

$$\frac{1}{p} \frac{\partial u\left(Z_1, \frac{M_1}{p}, Z_2\right)}{\partial \left(\frac{M_1}{p}\right)}.$$

Thus once again we see the importance—as brought out in Mathematical Appendix 1 : a—of specifying the function whose derivative is being taken.

f. THE PRECAUTIONARY DEMAND[27]

As already noted (p. 120, footnote 6, and pp. 123f., footnote 10), the (expected) utility function which lies behind our discussion of the

---

[26] *Principles*, pp. 838–39.
[27] Attached to Chapter VI:1.

precautionary motive is $U = F(E[Z_1], E[Z_2], \sigma(Z_2); \sigma(Z_1))$, which can be rewritten as

$$(6.34) \qquad U = F\left(E[Z_1,] E[Z_2,], \left|\frac{B_1}{p}\right| \sigma; \left|\frac{B_0}{p}\right| \sigma\right).$$

By assumption, the partial derivatives with respect to the first two arguments are positive, and with respect to the last two, negative. (Since the fourth argument is assumed constant in the present discussion, the partial derivative with respect to it does not actually concern us.)

In order to maximize $F(\ )$ subject to budget restraints (3) and (4) on p. 120,[28] we form the Lagrange sum

$$(6.35) \qquad \begin{aligned} F(\ ) &- \lambda_1\left(E[Z_1] + \frac{1}{1+r}\frac{B_1}{p} + \frac{M_1}{p} - R_1\right) \\ &- \lambda_2\left(E[Z_2] - R_2 - \frac{B_1}{p} - \frac{M_1}{p}\right), \end{aligned}$$

which is maximized with respect to $E[Z_1]$, $E[Z_2]$, B_1/p, and M_1/p. This yields the optimum conditions

$$(6.36) \qquad \frac{\dfrac{\partial F(\ )}{\partial(E[Z_1])}}{\dfrac{\partial F(\ )}{\partial(E[Z_2])} \pm \sigma\,\dfrac{\partial F(\ )}{\partial\left(\left|\dfrac{B_1}{p}\right|\sigma\right)}} = 1 + r,$$

$$(6.37) \qquad \frac{\dfrac{\partial F(\ )}{\partial(E[Z_1])}}{\dfrac{\partial F(\ )}{\partial(E[Z_2])}} = 1,$$

where the positive (negative) sign in the denominator of (6.36) holds for positive (negative) values of B_1/p. The left-hand side of (6.37) measures the marginal rate of substitution between present and future consumption on the assumption that the third argument in (6.34) remains constant: i.e., on the assumption that purchasing power is transferred from

---

[28] Clearly, restraints (5) and (6) on pp. 120f. are already reflected in the form in which the third and fourth arguments of $F(\ )$ appear. Cf. Mathematical Appendix 1:*d*.

present to future solely via money. On the other hand, the left-hand side of (6.36) measures this rate on the assumption that the transfer is made solely via bonds.[29] Thus equations (6.36)–(6.37) correspond respectively to (6.9)–(6.10) above.

g. COMMODITIES AS AN ASSET[30]

Let us now generalize the analysis of Section a to the case in which the price level is expected to change and commodity-inventories can be held. Let $(1 + s)^{h-1}p$ be the price of Z_h, and let Y_k $(k = 1, 2)$ represent the quantity of the composite commodity which is carried over from week k to week $k + 1$. There is no planned carryover for the end of the third week. The individual then maximizes his utility

$$(6.38) \quad U = U\left[Z_1, \frac{B_1}{(1+s)p}, \frac{M_1}{(1+s)p}, Z_2, \frac{B_2}{(1+s)^2p}, \frac{M_2}{(1+s)^2p}, Z_3; \frac{M_0}{p}\right]$$

subject to budget restraints

$$(6.39) \quad p(Z_1 + Y_1) + \frac{B_1}{1+r} + M_1$$
$$- B_0 - M_0 - p\bar{Z}_1 = 0,$$

---

[29] More rigorously (cf. p. 459 above), the differential of (6.34) along a given indifference hypersurface is

$$dU = \frac{\partial F(\ )}{\partial(E[Z_1])}\, d(E[Z_1]) + \frac{\partial F(\ )}{\partial(E[Z_2])}\, d(E[Z_2]) + \frac{\partial F(\ )}{\partial\left(\left|\frac{B_1}{p}\right|\sigma\right)}\, \frac{\partial\left(\left|\frac{B_1}{p}\right|\sigma\right)}{\partial\left(\left|\frac{B_1}{p}\right|\right)}\, d\left|\frac{B_1}{p}\right|$$

$$= \frac{\partial F(\ )}{\partial(E[Z_1])}\, d(E[Z_1]) + \frac{\partial F(\ )}{\partial(E[Z_2])}\, d(E[Z_2]) \pm \sigma \frac{\partial F(\ )}{\partial\left(\left|\frac{B_1}{p}\right|\sigma\right)}\, d\left(\frac{B_1}{p}\right) = 0.$$

If the transfer is made entirely via money, then $d(B_1/p) = 0$; if entirely via bonds, $d(B_1/p) = d(E[Z_2])$. Substituting these relations into the foregoing differential then yields the respective expressions for $-\dfrac{d(E[Z_1])}{d(E[Z_2])}$ just described.

[30] Attached to Chapter VI:3.

$$(1+s)\ p(Z_2 + Y_2) + \frac{B_2}{1+r} + M_2$$

(6.40)
$$- B_1 - M_1 - (1+s)p(Y_1 + \bar{Z}_2) = 0,$$

(6.41) $\quad (1+s)^2 p\, Z_3 \qquad - B_2 - M_2 - (1+s)^2 p(Y_2 + \bar{Z}_3) = 0.$

The utility function (6.38) shows that the individual values his bond and money holdings in terms of the prices of the week during which these holdings will constitute reserves. The foregoing maximization yields:

(6.42) $\qquad \dfrac{\partial U(\ )}{\partial Z_1} \quad - \lambda_1 p \qquad\qquad = 0,$

(6.43) $\qquad\qquad\qquad\qquad - \lambda_1 p \ + \lambda_2(1+s)p = 0,$

(6.44) $\quad \dfrac{1}{(1+s)p} \dfrac{\partial U(\ )}{\partial\left[\dfrac{B_1}{(1+s)p}\right]} - \dfrac{\lambda_1}{1+r} + \lambda_2 \qquad = 0,$

(6.45) $\quad \dfrac{1}{(1+s)p} \dfrac{\partial U(\ )}{\partial\left[\dfrac{M_1}{(1+s)p}\right]} - \lambda_1 \quad + \lambda_2 \qquad = 0,$

(6.46) $\qquad \dfrac{\partial U(\ )}{\partial Z_2} \quad - \lambda_2(1+s)p \qquad = 0,$

and so forth. Equation (6.43) is obtained from maximization with respect to Y_1. It is left as an exercise for the reader to derive equations (17)–(19) on p. 137 from the foregoing equations.

It is also readily evident that if there are anticipated price changes—but commodities cannot be carried over—then the Y_k disappear from budget restraints (6.38)–(6.40)—and with them equation (6.43). This, however, does not affect the remaining equations.

7. Appendix to Chapter VIII

a. Dichotomies of the Pricing Process[1]

The text distinguishes four types of dichotomies. These can be described in the following terms:

(i) The first dichotomy is implicit in the discussion of Mathematical Appendix 4:c. At the first stage of this dichotomy we consider the quantity of money, $\overline{Z}_n$, to be fixed but unknown, and solve equations (4.22)–(4.24) for the relative prices, rate of interest, and real value of cash balances, as in (4.25)–(4.27). At the second stage we add the equation specifying the quantity of money,

(7.1) $$\overline{Z}_n = \overline{Z}_n^0,$$

and thereby determine the money prices, as in (4.28)–(4.30).

(ii) The second dichotomy is also implicit in a preceding discussion. In particular, let us consider again our model (4.22)–(4.24) and apply to it the reasoning of Mathematical Appendix 3:a. In contradistinction to the preceding paragraph, however, $\overline{Z}_n$ is now assumed to be a known constant. On the other hand, we now drop the assumption that $p_n = 1$ and, accordingly, replace the argument $\overline{Z}_n/p$ of these equations by $p_n \overline{Z}_n/p$. It is then evident that the dependent variables p_i $(i = 1, \ldots, n)$

[1] Attached to Chapter VIII:3.

and p appear in system (4.22)–(4.24) so modified only in the form of the n ratios p_i/p. Hence the n equations of this system can at most be solved for

$$\frac{p_s}{p} = k_s \qquad (s = 1, \ldots, n-2),$$

(7.2)

$$r = k_{n-1}, \quad \text{and} \quad \frac{p_n}{p} = k_n,$$

where the k_i are constants. These solutions can then be rewritten as

(7.3) $$\frac{p_s}{p_n} = \frac{k_s}{k_n}, \quad r = k_{n-1}, \quad \text{and} \quad \frac{p}{p_n} = \frac{1}{k_n}.$$

Thus at this stage of the dichotomy we have already determined money prices p_s/p_n; but we have not yet determined accounting prices p_s. The second stage, then, consists of arbitrarily specifying the accounting price of any one of the commodities or of money. Thus, for example, we can add the equation

(7.4) $$p_n = t,$$

where t is a constant. Substituting this in (7.3), we then obtain the accounting prices of all other goods. The implications of the distinction between (7.4) and (7.1) have already been drawn in the text (pp. 173–74).

(iii) The third, and invalid, dichotomy begins by assuming that the excess-demand functions for commodities and bonds are independent of the absolute price level, so that the corresponding excess-demand equations can be written as

(7.5) $$D_s\left(\frac{p_1}{p}, \ldots, \frac{p_{n-2}}{p}, r\right) - \bar{Z}_s = 0 \qquad (s = 1, \ldots, n-2),$$

(7.6) $$D_{n-1}\left(\frac{p_1}{p}, \ldots, \frac{p_{n-2}}{p}, r\right) = 0,$$

where

(7.7) $$\sum_{s=1}^{n-2} w_s \frac{p_s}{p} = 1.$$

To these is added the excess-demand equation for money in, say, its Cambridge form,

(7.8) $$KpT - \bar{Z}_n = 0,$$

where $\bar{Z}_n$ and K are constants, and T is a function of the $\bar{Z}_s$ or $D_s(\ \ )$, or both.[2]

Choosing (7.6) as the equation to be "eliminated" by virtue of Walras' Law, we then dichotomize the pricing process in the following way: In the first stage we consider the subset of $n - 1$ equations (7.5) and (7.7). These depend only on—and therefore can determine—the equilibrium values of the $n - 1$ variables p_s/p and r. In the second stage we use these values to fix the value of T in (7.8). Since K and $\bar{Z}_n$ are constants, this equation can then determine the equilibrium value of the remaining variable p.

It can readily be shown that this dichotomy is internally inconsistent. For by the budget restraint we know that the excess-demand function for money must have the form

(7.9) $$-p\sum_{s=1}^{n-2} \frac{p_s}{p} [D_s(\ \ ) - \bar{Z}_s] - pD_{n-1}(\ \ ).$$

This implies that a doubling of money prices causes a doubling of the amount of excess demand for money. But the excess-demand function $KpT - \bar{Z}_n$ does not have this property. Thus the form of the monetary function implicit in the left-hand sides of (7.5)–(7.7) is inconsistent with the form explicit in the left-hand side of (7.8).

Nor can this dichotomy be saved by jettisoning the Cambridge equation. For let the excess-demand function for money be changed in such a way as to eliminate the preceding inconsistency. That is, let it explicitly assume the form (7.9). Equation (7.8) is accordingly replaced by

(7.10) $$\sum_{s=1}^{n-2} \frac{p_s}{p} [D_s(\ \ ) - \bar{Z}_s] + D_{n-1}(\ \ ) = 0.$$

[2] For generality, the dichotomy is stated here for the case of a model with bonds. If the reader prefers to work with the more familiar case of a model with only commodities and money, he need only consider the $(n - 1)^{\text{th}}$ good to be another commodity, replace r by p_{n-1}/p, and rewrite (7.6) as

$$D_{n-1}(\ \ ) - \bar{Z}_{n-1} = 0.$$

This does not affect the following argument in any significant way.

It is immediately seen that the dependent variables of this equation are precisely those of (7.5) and (7.7); in particular, the variable p appears only as the denominator of the price ratios p_s/p, and never by itself. Hence this equation cannot possibly determine the value of any variable not already determined by (7.5) and (7.7); and these equations, in turn, can at most determine the values of the only variables which appear in them—the p_s/p and r. Thus the assumption that demand depends only on relative prices implies that the value of p is indeterminate.

Our criticism of the foregoing dichotomy can thus be summarized in the following terms: With the quantity theory, its excess-demand *functions* are inconsistent. Without the quantity theory, its system of excess-demand *equations* is indeterminate.

We note finally that the inconsistency of the excess-demand functions can be stated alternatively in terms of the inconsistency of the system of dynamic market-adjustment equations which corresponds to static equations (7.5)–(7.8)—and whose properties are thus determined by those of the excess-demand functions.[3]

(iv) The fourth dichotomy—the "Keynesian case"—replaces (7.6) by

$$(7.11) \qquad D_{n-1}^* \left(\frac{p_1}{p}, \dots, \frac{p_{n-2}}{p}, r, \frac{\bar{Z}_n}{p} \right) = 0.$$

The form of the excess-demand function for money then becomes

$$(7.12) \qquad
\begin{aligned}
&-p \sum_{s=1}^{n-2} \frac{p_s}{p} \left[D_s \left(\frac{p_1}{p}, \dots, \frac{p_{n-2}}{p}, r \right) - \bar{Z}_s \right] \\
&\quad - p D_{n-1}^* \left(\frac{p_1}{p}, \dots, \frac{p_{n-2}}{p}, r, \frac{\bar{Z}_n}{p} \right).
\end{aligned}$$

This no longer implies that a doubling of prices doubles the amount of excess demand for money. On the other hand, it does imply that a doubling of prices *and* $\bar{Z}_n$ does do so. But this property is precisely that shared by the Cambridge function $KpT - \bar{Z}_n$.

Similarly, equation (7.10) is replaced by

$$(7.13) \qquad \sum_{s=1}^{n-2} \frac{p_s}{p} [D_s(\;\;) - \bar{Z}_s] + D_{n-1}^* \left(\frac{p_1}{p}, \dots, \frac{p_{n-2}}{p}, r, \frac{\bar{Z}_n}{p} \right) = 0.$$

[3] Cf. equations (3.5)–(3.7). Cf. also the graphical exposition on pp. 178f. above.

Here the variable p does appear by itself. Hence we can say that specification of the commodity equations (7.5) and (7.7) determines relative prices and the rate of interest, while specification of (7.13)—or (7.11)—then determines the absolute price level.

(v) As soon, however, as we leave the very special assumptions of this case, we generally cannot decompose the pricing process in this way. To be more specific, consider system (4.16)–(4.19). Use Walras' Law again to "eliminate" the bond equation—(4.17). Let us now assign an arbitrary value p^0 to the absolute price level. The subset (4.16) and (4.19) then constitutes $n - 1$ equations in the $n - 1$ variables $p_1/p^0, \ldots, p_{n-2}/p^0, r$. Hence we assume that it can determine a solution for these variables—say $(p_1/p^0)_0, \ldots, (p_{n-2}/p^0)_0, r_0$. Let us now insert these values into the money equation (4.18). This leaves only a single unknown variable in this equation—p. Hence (4.18) determines a value for this variable—say p^1. Clearly, there is no reason why p^0 and p^1 must be equal. Hence there is no reason why equations (4.16) and (4.19) must be satisfied by the set of values p^1 and $(p_1/p^0)_0, \ldots, (p_{n-2}/p^0)_0, r_0$. That is, there is no reason why $(p_1/p^0)_0, \ldots, (p_{n-2}/p^0)_0, r_0$ should be the equilibrium relative prices and rate of interest of the system (4.16)–(4.19) as a whole. Or, to put it the other way around, they will necessarily constitute these equilibrium values only if equations (4.16) are not affected by a change in the absolute price level from p^0 to p^1 which leaves relative prices constant—only, that is, if equations (4.16) are not affected by equiproportionate changes in the p_s and p. But this can be true only if these equations do not depend on the $\bar{Z}_{n-1}/p$ and $\bar{Z}_n/p$. And this, of course, is the "Keynesian case" of the preceding paragraph.

b. The Effects of a Shift in Liquidity Preference
(Change in K)[4]

For the purpose of analyzing a shift in liquidity preference we first define the "liquidity parameter" α^a. This is an index of the amount of liquidity convenience the ath individual derives from holding one dollar of real money balances: the higher this convenience, the higher α^a. This index can then be used to "deflate" the objective quantity of real balances $\bar{Z}_n^a/p$ in order to obtain its "subjective quantity" $\alpha^a \bar{Z}_n^a/p$. An

[4] Attached to Chapter VIII:5.

increase in α^a thus causes an increase in the subjective quantity of real balances, even though their objective quantity has not changed.

Let us now introduce this parameter into our system by modifying (4.16)–(4.19) in the following way:

$$(7.14) \qquad F_s\left(\frac{p_1}{p}, \ldots, \frac{p_{n-2}}{p}, r, \frac{\overline{Z}_{n-1}^1}{p} + \frac{\alpha^1 \overline{Z}_n^1}{p}, \ldots, \frac{\overline{Z}_{n-1}^A}{p} + \frac{\alpha^A \overline{Z}_n^A}{p}\right) - \overline{Z}_s = 0$$

$$(s = 1, \ldots, n-2),$$

$$(7.15) \qquad F_{n-1}\left(\frac{p_1}{p}, \ldots, \frac{p_{n-2}}{p}, r, \frac{\overline{Z}_{n-1}^1}{p} + \frac{\alpha^1 \overline{Z}_n^1}{p}, \ldots, \frac{\overline{Z}_{n-1}^A}{p} + \frac{\alpha^A \overline{Z}_n^A}{p}\right) = 0,$$

$$(7.16) \qquad -\sum_{s=1}^{n-2} \frac{p_s}{p} [F_s(\;\;) - \overline{Z}_s] - F_{n-1}(\;\;) = 0,$$

$$(7.17) \qquad \sum_{s=1}^{n-2} w_s \frac{p_s}{p} = 1.$$

A decrease in α^a thus decreases the arguments referring to real balances, and hence decreases the amounts demanded of commodities and bonds. From the left-hand side of (7.16)—which is, of course, the excess-demand function for real money holdings (4.12)—we then see that this causes an increase in the amount of money demanded. Thus a decrease in α^a is identified with an increase in liquidity preference.

It must now be emphasized that the α^a have been introduced into the foregoing functions in a very special way. In particular, consider the market for the first commodity. The "intensity" of an individual's increased liquidity preference with respect to this market is defined as being measured by the equiproportionate decrease in prices necessary to restore his subjective quantity of money to its original level with respect to its influence on this market. The preceding model assumes that this intensity is the same for each and every market. And it is this symmetry which defines a "neutral" shift in liquidity preference.

This case is to be contrasted with the one in which the ath individual is assumed to have a different liquidity parameter α_j^a $(j = 1, \ldots, n-1)$ for each and every market. Then his subjective quantities of money relevant to these markets $\alpha_j^a \overline{Z}_n^a / p$ are also different. Or, in other words, an increase in liquidity preference does not generally take place with the same intensity in each market. Or, in still other words, the extent of the price decline necessary to offset the effects of the increased liquidity preference on the individual's demand in one market is not generally the same as that necessary for another. Such a case will be analyzed in Mathematical Appendix 8 : c.

Our neutrality assumption clearly makes the problem of a shift in liquidity preference analytically equivalent to the already familiar problem of a change in the quantity of money. In particular, at the level of individual-experiments, the functions on the left-hand sides of (7.14)–(7.16) show that the excess amounts demanded of commodities, *real* bond holdings, and *real* money holdings are assumed to remain unaffected by an equiproportionate change in the p_s, $p_s \bar{Z}_{n-1}^a$, and α^a— all other independent variables being held constant. Correspondingly, at the level of market-experiments, equations (7.14)–(7.17) show that— provided there are neutral real-indebtedness effects—an equiproportionate change in the α^a causes an equiproportionate change in the equilibrium values of p_s and p, and leaves the equilibrium value of r invariant. The rigorous proof of this proposition obviously parallels that of Mathematical Appendix 4 : b for an equiproportionate change in the $\bar{Z}_n^a$.

c. The Effects of a Change in Initial Commodity Endowments (Change in T)[5]

From (4.6)–(4.8) write the market excess-demand equations for the current week in the form

$$(7.18) \quad Q_s \left(\frac{p_1}{p}, \ldots, \frac{p_{n-2}}{p}, r, \left| \frac{\bar{Z}_{n-1}^a}{p} + \frac{\bar{Z}_n^a}{p} \right|, \left| \frac{\sum_{s=1}^{n-2} p_s \bar{Z}_{hs}^a}{p} \right| \right) - \bar{Z}_s = 0$$

$$(s = 1, \ldots, n-2),$$

$$(7.19) \qquad\qquad Q_{n-1}(\ ) = 0,$$

$$(7.20) \qquad\qquad Q_n(\ ) - \bar{Z}_n = 0,$$

$$(7.21) \qquad\qquad \sum_{s=1}^{n-2} w_s \frac{p_s}{p} = 1,$$

---

[5] Attached to Chapter VIII : 6.

where $\left| \dfrac{\overline{Z}_{n-1}^a}{p} + \dfrac{\overline{Z}_n^a}{p} \right|$ and $\left| \dfrac{\sum\limits_{s=1}^{n-2} p_s \overline{Z}_{hs}^a}{p} \right|$ represent the respective arrays of the relevant arguments for all values of a and h. Clearly, (7.20) will be satisfied if the other equations are.

Assume that for $\overline{Z}_{hs}^a = \overline{Z}_{hs}^{a0}$ $(s = 1, \dots, n-2;\ a = 1, \dots, A;$ $h = 1, \dots, H)$ and $\overline{Z}_u^a = \overline{Z}_u^{a0}$ $(u = n-1, n)$ these equations have the solution $p_s = p_s^0$, $p = p^0$, $r = r^0$. Consider now the system of equations for $\overline{Z}_{hs}^a = t^0 \overline{Z}_{hs}^{a0}$ and for $\overline{Z}_u^a = \overline{Z}_u^{a0}$ $(u = n-1, n)$, where t^0 is a given positive constant. Take a trial solution of the form $p_s = k p_s^0$, $p = k p^0$, and $r = r^0$, where k is an unknown positive constant. Insert this into equation (7.18) for $s = 1$ to yield

$$(7.22) \quad Q_1 \left(\frac{p_1^0}{p^0}, \dots, \frac{p_{n-2}^0}{p^0}, r^0, \left| \frac{\overline{Z}_{n-1}^{a0}}{kp^0} + \frac{\overline{Z}_n^{a0}}{kp^0} \right|, \left| \frac{\sum\limits_{s=1}^{n-2} p_s^0 t^0 \overline{Z}_{hs}^{a0}}{p^0} \right| \right) - t^0 \overline{Z}_1^0 = 0.$$

This is a single equation in one unknown k. Assume that it has a solution $k = k^0$.

Clearly, just as we obtained an equation in k from (7.18) for $s = 1$, so can we obtain similar equations for $s = 2, \dots, n-2$, not to speak of the equation that can be obtained from (7.19). There is no reason why these additional equations should also be satisfied by $k = k^0$. In brief, the insertion of this trial solution into (7.18)–(7.19) gives us an overdetermined system of $n - 1$ independent equations in the single variable, k. This is clearly true even in the absence of a distribution effect.[6]

We note finally that even if all $n - 1$ equations should yield the same solution for k, there is no reason why this should be $k = 1/t^0$.

d. Say's Identity and a Barter Economy[7]

Let us denote by

$$(7.23) \qquad X_i(p_1, \dots, p_{n-2}, p, r) = 0 \qquad (i = 1, \dots, n)$$

---

[6] The reader should establish for himself that this line of reasoning does not lead to an overdeterminacy in the preceding section and in Mathematical Appendixes 3:*c* and 4:*b*. Cf. p. 192, footnote 62 above.

[7] Attached to Chapter VIII:7.

the market excess-demand equation for the ith good, where the $(n - 1)^{th}$ good is bonds, and the nth, money. According to Lange,[8] Say's Identity states

(7.24) $$\sum_{j=1}^{n-1} p_j X_j(p_1, \dots, p_{n-2}, p, r) \equiv 0,$$

or, what is more appropriate for our purposes,

(7.25)
$$X_{n-1}(p_1, \dots, p_{n-2}, p, r)$$
$$\equiv -(1 + r)\sum_{s=1}^{n-2} p_s X_s(p_1, \dots, p_{n-2}, p, r).$$

Alternatively, comparing (7.24) with (4.12), we can follow Lange and state Say's Identity as

(7.26) $$X_n(p_1, \dots, p_{n-2}, p, r) \equiv 0.$$

Consider now the first $n - 2$ equations of (7.23) together with the definition of p as given by (7.7). Take a specific value of $p = p^0$, and assume that for this value this system of $n - 1$ equations has a unique solution for the $n - 1$ variables p_s ($s = 1, \dots, n - 2$) and r. By (7.25), this solution together with $p = p^0$ must also satisfy (7.23) for $i = n - 1$. And, as is obvious from (7.26), it must also satisfy (7.23) for $i = n$. Hence this set of values must be an equilibrium one.

Take now any other value $p = p^1$. In general, the solution of (7.23) and (7.7) corresponding to this new value will differ from the preceding one. But by (7.25) this solution too must be an equilibrium one. Thus Say's Identity implies that money prices are indeterminate.[9] Hence this identity can meaningfully exist only in a barter economy. The absence of financial assets in such an economy then implies that the demand functions depend only on relative prices.

It should finally be noted that our line of reasoning here is that Say's Identity implies a barter economy and hence the homogeneity postulate. This is to be contrasted with Lange's accepted procedure of deducing

[8] "Say's Law ...," *op. cit.*, pp. 49–53. For generality, I have extended Lange's analysis to the case of an economy with bonds.

[9] In technical terms, the addition of Say's Identity to Walras' Law implies that there are only $n - 2$ independent equations in (7.23). Hence it can be assumed that these together with the remaining equation (7.7) do not suffice to determine the n variables p_s ($s = 1, \dots, n - 2$), p, and r.

this postulate directly from Say's Identity. According to Lange's argument, Say's Identity "excludes the use of cash balances for financing purchases of commodities";[10] or, alternatively, it precludes "the substitution of money for commodities."[11] Hence Say's Identity implies that "the quantity demanded of each commodity will depend only on relative commodity prices."[12]

This, however, is a *non sequitur*. For the constancy of money expenditures on commodities does not imply the absence of the real-balance effect. Thus, for example, a doubling of all prices might, through the real-balance effect, cause a halving of all quantities demanded, so that the total money expenditure on commodities remains constant. All we know from Say's Identity *per se* is that no matter how the real-balance effect might manifest itself, the functional dependence described by (7.24) makes it impossible for any change in prices to cause the amount of excess demand for money to depart from its zero value in (7.26).

[10] Lange, "Say's Law ...," *op. cit.*, p. 53; see also pp. 63–64.
[11] G. S. Becker and W. J. Baumol, "The Classical Monetary Theory ...," *Economica*, XIX (1952), 358.
[12] *Ibid.*

8. Appendix to Chapters X and XI

a. The Stability of the System as Analyzed in the Commodity and Bond Markets[1]

According to the assumptions made in the text, our dynamic analysis can be restricted to the bond and commodity markets. The equilibrium conditions for these markets are, respectively,

$$(8.1) \qquad B\left(Y_0, \frac{1}{r}, \frac{M}{p}\right) = 0,$$

$$(8.2) \qquad F\left(Y_0, r, \frac{M}{p}\right) - Y_0 = 0,$$

where M is a constant and

$$(8.3) \qquad B\left(Y_0, \frac{1}{r}, \frac{M}{p}\right) \equiv H\left(Y_0, \frac{1}{r}, \frac{M^H}{p}\right) - J\left(Y_0, \frac{1}{r}, \frac{M^F}{p}\right).$$

This identity makes use of the assumption that the distribution of money balances in the economy does not affect the equilibrium rate of interest. According to the discussion of Chapter IX, the partial derivatives of these functions are $B_1 \gtreqless 0$, $B_2 < 0$, $B_3 > 0$, $F_1 > 0$, $F_2 < 0$, and $F_3 > 0$, where the subscripts indicate the arguments with respect to which

[1] Attached to Chapter X:2.

differentiation is carried out. Since Y is assumed constant at Y_0, B_1 and F_1 play no role in the following analysis.

Consider now the general case in which the *tâtonnement* of the economy is described by the following dynamic equations:[2]

(8.4) $$\frac{dr}{dt} = -K_1 B\left(Y_0, \frac{1}{r}, \frac{M}{p}\right) - K_2\left[F\left(Y_0, r, \frac{M}{p}\right) - Y_0\right],$$

(8.5) $$\frac{dp}{dt} = K_3 B\left(Y_0, \frac{1}{r}, \frac{M}{p}\right) + K_4\left[F\left(Y_0, r, \frac{M}{p}\right) - Y_0\right],$$

where the K_j $(j = 1, \ldots, 4)$ are positive constants. By differentiating the functions $B(\ )$ and $F(\ )$, we obtain a linear approximation in the neighborhood of the equilibrium point,

(8.6) $$\frac{dr}{dt} = \left[\frac{K_1 B_2}{r_0^2} - K_2 F_2\right](r - r_0)$$
$$+ \left[\frac{K_1 B_3 M}{p_0^2} + \frac{K_2 F_3 M}{p_0^2}\right](p - p_0),$$

(8.7) $$\frac{dp}{dt} = \left[-\frac{K_3 B_2}{r_0^2} + K_4 F_2\right](r - r_0)$$
$$+ \left[-\frac{K_3 B_3 M}{p_0^2} - \frac{K_4 F_3 M}{p_0^2}\right](p - p_0).$$

Let

(8.8)
$$a = -\frac{B_2}{r_0^2} > 0, \qquad b = F_2 < 0,$$
$$c = -\frac{B_3 M}{p_0^2} < 0, \qquad d = -\frac{F_3 M}{p_0^2} < 0.$$

Then it can be shown that a method of successive approximation which proceeds according to the rules (8.4)–(8.5) will converge to the solution of equations (8.1)–(8.2) if the following characteristic equation in x,

(8.9) $$\begin{vmatrix} -K_1 a - K_2 b - x & -K_1 c - K_2 d \\ K_3 a + K_4 b & K_3 c + K_4 d - x \end{vmatrix} = 0$$

has roots whose real parts are negative.[3]

---

[2] On the following, cf. Mathematical Appendix 3:*b*. This makes it clear that what the following demonstrates is stability in the small, and not stability of the Walrasian *tâtonnement* in the large.

[3] As already indicated, this procedure is based on Samuelson, *Foundations*, pp.

Expanding (8.9), we obtain

(8.10) $$x^2 + gx + h = 0,$$

where

(8.11)
$$g = K_1 a + K_2 b - K_3 c - K_4 d,$$
$$h = -K_1 K_4 ad - K_2 K_3 bc + K_1 K_4 bc + K_2 K_3 ad.$$

It follows that the signs of both g and h are dependent on the relative magnitudes of the K_j and the partial derivatives. Hence the signs of the real parts of the solutions for x cannot be specified. Accordingly, the convergence of the system cannot be generally established.

Clearly, the smaller K_2 and K_3, the more likely that the signs of g and h will both be positive. In the extreme case where $K_2 = K_3 = 0$, this must definitely be so. By the quadratic formula for the solution of (8.10),

(8.12) $$x = \frac{-g \pm \sqrt{g^2 - 4h}}{2},$$

it then follows that the real parts of the roots of x must be negative. Hence in this case—which corresponds to that described by Figure X-2 of the text—the dynamic system must definitely converge to the equilibrium solution. Note that this conclusion holds even under the extreme Keynesian assumption $F_3(\quad) \equiv 0$.

b. The Stability of the System as Analyzed in
the Commodity and Money Markets[4]

Assume now that the analysis is carried out instead in terms of the commodity and money markets. Then (8.1) is replaced by

(8.13) $$L\left(Y_0, r, \frac{M}{p}\right) - \frac{M}{p} = 0,$$

---

269 ff. Cf. also Metzler, "Wealth, Saving, and the Rate of Interest," *op. cit.*, pp. 115–16.

Note one property of this system of successive approximation: If it converges, it must converge to a solution. This is a consequence of the assumption that the K_j are constant.

[4] Attached to Chapter XI:3 and p. 377.

where $L_1 > 0, L_2 < 0$, and $1 > L_3 > 0$. Under the Keynesian assumption that excess demand in the money market affects only the rate of interest, dynamic system (8.4)–(8.5) is then replaced by

(8.14)
$$\frac{dr}{dt} = Q_1 \left[L\left(Y_0, r, \frac{M}{p}\right) - \frac{M}{p} \right],$$

(8.15)
$$\frac{dp}{dt} = Q_2 \left[F\left(Y_0, r, \frac{M}{p}\right) - Y_0 \right],$$

where Q_1 and Q_2 are positive constants. Using the same procedure as in the preceding section, we can show that system (8.14)–(8.15) is stable if the following characteristic equation in x,

(8.16)
$$\begin{vmatrix} Q_1 L_2 - x & \dfrac{Q_1 M(1 - L_3)}{p^2} \\ Q_2 F_2 & \dfrac{-Q_2 M F_3}{p^2} - x \end{vmatrix} = 0,$$

has roots whose real parts are negative. Expanding, we obtain

(8.17)
$$x^2 + \left[\frac{Q_2 M F_3}{p^2} - Q_1 L_2 \right] x$$
$$+ \left[\frac{-Q_1 Q_2 M L_2 F_3}{p^2} - \frac{Q_1 Q_2 M F_2 (1 - L_3)}{p^2} \right] = 0.$$

By assumption as to the signs of the partial derivatives, both the coefficient of x and the constant term in the preceding equation are positive. Hence the real parts of its solutions are negative. Hence system (8.14)–(8.15) is stable. Once again this conclusion holds even in the extreme Keynesian case where $F_3( ) \equiv 0$.

Let us now denote the excess-demand function for money by[5]

(8.18)
$$X\left(Y, r, \frac{M}{p}\right) \equiv L\left(Y, r, \frac{M}{p}\right) - \frac{M}{p}.$$

The distinction emphasized in the text[6] is that between the identities

---

[5] Note that $X( )$ will depend on M/p even if $L( )$ does not.
[6] P. 264.

(in all the variables)

(8.19) $$X\left(Y, r, \frac{M}{p}\right) \equiv B\left(Y, r, \frac{M}{p}\right)$$

and

(8.20) $$X_3\left(Y, r, \frac{M}{p}\right) \equiv B_3\left(Y, r, \frac{M}{p}\right).$$

Equation (8.19) implies that *all* the partial derivatives are identical, and so is a much stronger restriction than (8.20). Note too that under the Keynesian assumption of $F_3(\ ) \equiv 0$, equation (8.20) follows directly from the budget restraint.[7]

c. The Effects of a Shift in Liquidity Preference as Analyzed in the Commodity and Bond Markets[8]

The analysis of a shift in liquidity preference follows the approach of Mathematical Appendix 7:*b*. If, as in the case analyzed there, this shift is neutral as between commodities and bonds, then the arguments M/p in (8.1)–(8.2) are replaced by $\mu M/p$—where μ is the liquidity parameter. It is then obvious by inspection that a change in μ causes the equilibrium price level in (8.1)–(8.2) to change in the same proportion and leaves the equilibrium rate of interest unaffected.

Let us now drop the assumption of neutrality and rewrite (8.1)–(8.2) as

(8.21)
$$F\left(Y_0, r, \frac{\alpha M}{p}\right) - Y_0 = 0$$

$$B\left(Y_0, \frac{1}{r}, \frac{\beta M}{p}\right) = 0,$$

where α and β are liquidity parameters. Clearly, an increase in liquidity preference need no longer affect the commodity and bond markets with the same intensity. That is, if we conduct an individual-experiment in which we increase liquidity preference, the price decline that will be found necessary to offset this increase in the commodity market need not be the same as that required in the bond market. Indeed, we can

---

[7] See p. 227, footnote 22.
[8] Attached to Chapter X:4.

think of an extreme case in which the increase in liquidity preference takes place only at the expense of commodities, so that no price decrease whatsoever is required to restore demand in the bond market. Such a case is represented in the left-hand sides of (8.21) by a decrease in α, with β remaining constant. At the other extreme we have the case of an increase in liquidity preference solely at the expense of bonds. This is represented by a decrease in β, with α remaining constant.

From these individual-experiments we can proceed to the corresponding market-experiments. In particular, consider the effect of an increase in liquidity preference on the equilibrium price level and rate of interest when this increase is solely at the expense of commodities. Holding β constant and differentiating (8.21) with respect to α, we obtain[9]

$$(8.22) \qquad F_2 \frac{\partial r}{\partial \alpha} - \frac{\alpha F_3 M}{p^2} \frac{\partial p}{\partial \alpha} = -\frac{F_3 M}{p},$$

$$(8.23) \qquad -\frac{B_2}{r^2} \frac{\partial r}{\partial \alpha} - \frac{\beta B_3 M}{p^2} \frac{\partial p}{\partial \alpha} = 0.$$

Let

$$(8.24) \qquad |D| = \begin{vmatrix} F_2 & -\dfrac{\alpha F_3 M}{p^2} \\[3mm] -\dfrac{B_2}{r^2} & -\dfrac{\beta B_3 M}{p^2} \end{vmatrix} = -\frac{\beta F_2 B_3 M}{p^2} - \frac{\alpha F_3 B_2 M}{p^2 r^2}.$$

[9] I must confess that I am not using here the more cumbersome notation advocated at such length in Mathematical Appendix 1:*a*. In terms of that discussion, we are assuming here that system (8.21) can be solved for the dependent variables r and p as (market-equilibrium) functions of the independent ones, α and β, to yield, say,

$$r = \phi(\alpha, \beta),$$

$$p = \psi(\alpha, \beta).$$

The symbols $\partial r/\partial \alpha$ and $\partial p/\partial \alpha$ then represent the respective partial derivatives of these functions with respect to α. In terms of our advocated notation, they are $\phi_1(\alpha, \beta)$ and $\psi_1(\alpha, \beta)$, respectively. Similarly, in (8.27)–(8.28) below, the symbols $\partial r/\partial \beta$ and $\partial p/\partial \beta$ represent, respectively, $\phi_2(\alpha, \beta)$ and $\psi_2(\alpha, \beta)$. For further details—and for an explanation of the whole procedure used in (8.22)–(8.28)—see the discussion of implicit differentiation in Mathematical Appendix 1:*c*.

The foregoing observations should also be applied, *mutatis mutandis*, to all subsequent cases in which we solve a system of equations for the derivatives of its dependent variables with respect to its independent ones.

By assumptions as to the signs of the partial derivatives, this must be positive. We now consider (8.22)–(8.23) as constituting a system of two equations in the two variables $\partial r/\partial \alpha$ and $\partial p/\partial \alpha$ and solve it by the use of determinants to yield

$$(8.25) \qquad \frac{\partial r}{\partial \alpha} = \frac{\begin{vmatrix} -\dfrac{F_3 M}{p} & -\dfrac{\alpha F_3 M}{p^2} \\[2ex] 0 & -\dfrac{\beta B_3 M}{p^2} \end{vmatrix}}{|D|} = \frac{\beta F_3 B_3 M^2}{p^3 |D|} > 0$$

and

$$(8.26) \qquad \frac{\partial p}{\partial \alpha} = \frac{\begin{vmatrix} F_2 & -\dfrac{F_3 M}{p} \\[2ex] -\dfrac{B_2}{r^2} & 0 \end{vmatrix}}{|D|} = \frac{-F_3 B_2 M}{r^2 p |D|} > 0.$$

In a similar way, if only β were to change while α remained constant, we would obtain

$$(8.27) \qquad \frac{\partial r}{\partial \beta} = \frac{-\alpha F_3 B_3 M^2}{p^3 |D|} < 0,$$

$$(8.28) \qquad \frac{\partial p}{\partial \beta} = \frac{-F_2 B_3 M}{p |D|} > 0.$$

d. The Effects of a Shift in Liquidity Preference as Analyzed in the Commodity and Money Markets[10]

These shifts in liquidity preference can be analyzed equivalently in terms of the commodity and money markets. Our equations are then

$$(8.29) \qquad F\left(Y_0, r, \frac{M}{p}, \lambda\right) - Y_0 = 0,$$

[10] Attached to Chapter XI:2.
For an explanation of the procedure used here—and, in particular, for the meaning of the derivatives $dr/d\lambda$ and $dp/d\lambda$ in (8.31)–(8.34)—see the preceding footnote.

$$(8.30) \qquad L\left(Y_0, r, \frac{M}{p}, \lambda\right) - \frac{M}{p} = 0,$$

where λ is the liquidity parameter. By assumption, $F_4 > 0$ and $L_4 < 0$. That is, a decrease in λ—already identified with an increase in liquidity preference—causes an increase in the amount of money demanded, and a decrease in the amount of commodities demanded.

Differentiating the foregoing system with respect to λ, we obtain

$$(8.31) \qquad F_2 \frac{dr}{d\lambda} - \frac{MF_3}{p^2} \frac{dp}{d\lambda} = -F_4,$$

$$(8.32) \qquad L_2 \frac{dr}{d\lambda} + \frac{M(1-L_3)}{p^2} \frac{dp}{d\lambda} = -L_4.$$

Solving, we obtain

$$(8.33) \qquad \frac{dr}{d\lambda} = \frac{\begin{vmatrix} -F_4 & \dfrac{-MF_3}{p^2} \\[2ex] -L_4 & \dfrac{M(1-L_3)}{p^2} \end{vmatrix}}{\Delta} = \frac{-MF_4(1-L_3) - MF_3L_4}{p^2\Delta}$$

and

$$(8.34) \qquad \frac{dp}{d\lambda} = \frac{\begin{vmatrix} F_2 & -F_4 \\ L_2 & -L_4 \end{vmatrix}}{\Delta} = \frac{-F_2L_4 + F_4L_2}{\Delta},$$

where

$$(8.35) \qquad \Delta = \begin{vmatrix} F_2 & \dfrac{-MF_3}{p^2} \\[2ex] L_2 & \dfrac{M(1-L_3)}{p^2} \end{vmatrix} = \frac{MF_2(1-L_3) + ML_2F_3}{p^2}.$$

By our assumptions as to the signs of the partial derivatives, Δ is negative, $dp/d\lambda$ is positive, and $dr/d\lambda$ is of indeterminate sign.

Let us now assume that the shift in liquidity preference is entirely at the expense of bonds. Then $F_4 = 0$. Hence $dr/d\lambda$ is negative—which agrees with (8.27).

Assume next that the shift is entirely at the expense of commodities. We first make use of this assumption and (8.29)–(8.30) to rewrite (8.18) as

(8.36)
$$L\left(Y_0, r, \frac{M}{p}, \lambda\right) - \frac{M}{p}$$
$$\equiv -\left[F\left(Y_0, r, \frac{M}{p}, \lambda\right) - Y_0\right] - B\left(Y_0, \frac{1}{r}, \frac{M}{p}\right),$$

Differentiating both sides of this identity partially with respect to λ, we obtain

(8.37) $L_4 = -F_4.$

That is, by the budget restraint, any increase in the demand for real money holdings must be exactly matched by a decrease in the demand for commodities. Substituting in (8.33), we then obtain

(8.38)
$$\frac{dr}{d\lambda} = \frac{-MF_4(1 - L_3 - F_3)}{p^2\Delta}.$$

By assumption, the marginal propensities to spend out of real balances on commodities, bonds, and money holdings, respectively, are all positive, and their sum is equal to unity. It follows that

(8.39) $0 < F_3 + L_3 < 1.$

Substituting in (8.38), we see that $dr/d\lambda$ is positive—which agrees with (8.25).

Consider finally the case in which the shift in liquidity preference is neutral as between commodities and bonds. Then, by Mathematical Appendix 7:b, the excess-demand functions for both commodities and *real* money holdings are not affected by equiproportionate changes in λ and p. That is, the left-hand sides of (8.29) and (8.30) are both homogeneous of degree zero in these variables. Applying Euler's theorem on homogeneous functions to these left-hand sides, respectively, we then obtain

(8.40)
$$\frac{-MF_3}{p} + \lambda F_4 = 0,$$

(8.41) $$\frac{M(1 - L_3)}{p} + \lambda L_4 = 0.$$

Substituting in (8.33), we see that under these conditions $dr/d\lambda = 0$.

e. The Effects of Shifts in the Propensities to Save and Invest[11]

Consider the system

(8.42) $$F\left(Y_0, r, \frac{M}{p}, \alpha\right) - Y_0 = 0,$$

(8.43) $$B\left(Y_0, \frac{1}{r}, \frac{M}{p}, \alpha\right) = 0,$$

where α is an as yet unspecified parameter. Differentiating this system with respect to α and solving by use of determinants, we obtain

(8.44) $$\frac{dr}{d\alpha} = \frac{M(F_4 B_3 - F_3 B_4)}{p^2 \Delta}$$

and

(8.45) $$\frac{dp}{d\alpha} = -\frac{B_4 F_2 + \dfrac{B_2 F_4}{r^2}}{\Delta},$$

where

(8.46) $$\Delta = -\frac{M}{p^2}\left(F_2 B_3 + \frac{F_3 B_2}{r^2}\right) > 0.$$

From the budget restraint we also have

(8.47) $$F_2 - \frac{B_2}{r^2} + L_2 = 0.$$

Let α represent the marginal productivity of capital. Then an increase in productivity stimulates investment activity; hence $F_4 > 0$. Now, if firms plan to finance this increased activity entirely by increasing their supply of bonds, then $B_4 = -F_4 < 0$. If, instead, the financing comes entirely out of their cash balances, then $B_4 = 0$. In both of these cases

[11] Attached to Chapter XI:5–6.

(though more so in the former) $dr/d\alpha$ is positive. Similarly, in both cases $dp/d\alpha$ is positive. In the former case this is established by substituting from (8.47) into (8.45). This result can also be obtained from (8.34). From this equation we also readily see that the increase in p is less when $L_4 = 0$ (i.e., $B_4 = -F_4$) than when $B_4 = 0$ (so that $L_4 < 0$).

Alternatively, let α be an index of the "tastes" for saving. Specifically, an increase in α represents an increased desire to save. Hence $F_4 < 0$. If all of these savings are directed to the bond market, then $B_4 = -F_4 > 0$; if to cash balances, then $B_4 = 0$. As the reader can readily establish, in both cases $dr/d\alpha$ and $dp/d\alpha$ are negative.

9. Appendix to Chapter XII

a. The Case of Money Illusion in the Supply Function of Labor[1]

The equilibrium condition in the labor market when there is money illusion on the supply side is represented by

$$(9.1) \qquad Q\left(\frac{w}{p}, K_0\right) - T(w) = 0.$$

In contrast with our preceding models, a change in the quantity of money now changes the real wage rate. Hence we can no longer conduct the analysis of such a change under the assumption that the levels of employment and real income are fixed at N_0 and Y_0, respectively. In particular, we must now write the equilibrium condition for the commodity market in the complete form implied by Chapter IX: 2–3,

$$(9.2) \qquad F\left\{\phi\left[Q\left(\frac{w}{p}, K_0\right)\right], r, \frac{M}{p}\right\} - \phi\left[Q\left(\frac{w}{p}, K_0\right)\right] = 0,$$

where $\phi[\ ]$ is the production function. Similarly, the bond equation

---

[1] Attached to Chapter XII:2.

Once again, the reader is referred to p. 489, footnote 9, for an explanation of the technique of differentiation used here.

becomes

(9.3) $$B\left\{\phi\left[Q\left(\frac{w}{p}, K_0\right)\right], \frac{1}{r}, \frac{M}{p}\right\} = 0.$$

By assumption, $Q_1 < 0$, $T' > 0$, $1 > F_1 > 0$, $F_2 < 0$, $F_3 > 0$, $\phi' > 0$, $B_1 = 0$, $B_2 < 0$, $B_3 > 0$. Differentiating (9.1)–(9.3) with respect to M, we then obtain

(9.4) $$\frac{dr}{dM} = -B_3 \cdot \frac{w}{p^3} T'\phi' Q_1 (F_1 - 1) \cdot \frac{1}{|A|}$$

and

(9.5) $$\frac{dp}{dM} = \left(\frac{Q_1}{p} - T'\right)\left(\frac{F_3}{p}\frac{B_2}{r^2} + \frac{F_2 B_3}{p}\right) \cdot \frac{1}{|A|},$$

where

(9.6) $$|A| = \left(\frac{Q_1}{p} - T'\right)\left(\frac{F_3 M B_2}{p^2 r^2} + \frac{F_2 M B_3}{p^2}\right)$$
$$- \frac{\phi' Q_1 (F_1 - 1)}{p} \cdot \frac{w}{p} T' \frac{B_2}{r^2}.$$

By our assumptions as to the signs of the partial derivatives, $|A| > 0$. Hence $dr/dM < 0$ and $dp/dM > 0$. It can also be readily shown that the derivative dw/dM must have the same sign as dp/dM. Substituting from (9.6) into (9.5), we can also see that $\frac{M}{p}\frac{dp}{dM} < 1$. All these results clearly depend on the assumption that changes in real national product have a neutral effect on the bond market; that is, $B_1 = 0$.

b. A Theorem on Samuelson's "Correspondence Principle"

The immediately following sections make repeated use of Samuelson's "correspondence principle."[2] The application of this principle will be simplified by first developing the following proposition:[3]

[2] *Foundations*, Chapter IX.
[3] Due to A. S. Amitsur. See the reference in my "Limitations of Samuelson's 'Correspondence Principle,'" *Metroeconomica*, IV (1952), 39, footnote 3.

Assume that the dynamic movements of a model are described by the system of differential equations

(9.7) $$\frac{dp_i}{dt} = \sum_{j=1}^{n} K_{ij} X_i(p_1, \ldots, p_n) \qquad (i = 1, \ldots, n),$$

where the $X_i(\ )$ are the excess-demand functions and the K_{ij} are constants. Define the matrices

(9.8) $$K = \begin{pmatrix} K_{11} & K_{12} & \cdots & K_{1n} \\ K_{21} & K_{22} & \cdots & K_{2n} \\ \multicolumn{4}{c}{\dotfill} \\ K_{n1} & K_{n2} & \cdots & K_{nn} \end{pmatrix}$$

and

(9.9) $$A = \begin{pmatrix} a_{11} & a_{12} & \cdots & a_{1n} \\ a_{21} & a_{22} & \cdots & a_{2n} \\ \multicolumn{4}{c}{\dotfill} \\ a_{n1} & a_{n2} & \cdots & a_{nn} \end{pmatrix},$$

where a_{ij} is the partial derivative of $X_i(\ )$ with respect to p_j, evaluated at the point of equilibrium. Then system (9.7) is stable if the characteristic equation

(9.10) $$|KA - zI| = 0$$

(where I is the identity matrix) yields roots for z whose real parts are all negative.[4]

Denote these roots by z_i. Then it follows from the properties of characteristic equations that

(9.11) $$\prod_{i=1}^{n} z_i = |KA|.$$

Assume that m of these roots are complex. These must occur in pairs of the type $x + iy$ and $x - iy$. Hence m must be even. Furthermore, the product of these m roots must be positive. Thus the sign of $|KA|$ must be the same as the sign of the product of the $n - m$ real roots. If the system is stable, this product—and hence $|KA| = |K||A|$—must therefore be positive for an even n, and negative for an odd one.

[4] Cf. Samuelson, *Foundations*, pp. 274–75. The discussion in Mathematical Appendix 3 : b above deals with the special case in which K is a diagonal matrix.

System (8.4)–(8.5) above provides an example of this proposition. It has been shown that if $K_2 = K_3 = 0$, this system must be stable. Under this assumption $|K|$ is a diagonal determinant equal to the negative quantity $-K_1K_4$. It follows from the preceding paragraph that $|A| = ad - bc$ must then be negative. From (8.8) we see that this is indeed so.

c. THE CASE OF DISTRIBUTION EFFECTS[5]

Let us now make use of the foregoing proposition to determine the properties of a system which provides for the influence of distribution effects. Let

$$(9.12) \qquad\qquad h = h(p)$$

be an index of the distribution effect which results from a price change. By the assumptions of the text we have

$$(9.13) \qquad\qquad B\left[Y_0, \frac{1}{r}, \frac{M}{p}, h(p)\right] = 0,$$

$$(9.14) \qquad\qquad F\left[Y_0, r, \frac{M}{p}, h(p)\right] - Y_0 = 0,$$

where $h'(\ ) > 0$, $B_4 > 0$, and $F_4 < 0$. Differentiating with respect to M, we obtain

$$(9.15) \qquad -\frac{B_2}{r^2}\frac{dr}{dM} + \left(-\frac{MB_3}{p^2} + B_4h'\right)\frac{dp}{dM} = -\frac{B_3}{p},$$

$$(9.16) \qquad F_2\frac{dr}{dM} + \left(-\frac{MF_3}{p^2} + F_4h'\right)\frac{dp}{dM} = -\frac{F_3}{p}.$$

Let

$$(9.17) \qquad |T| = \begin{vmatrix} -\dfrac{B_2}{r^2} & -\dfrac{MB_3}{p^2} + B_4h' \\[3ex] F_2 & -\dfrac{MF_3}{p^2} + F_4h' \end{vmatrix}.$$

[5] Attached to Chapter XII:3.

Solving (9.15)–(9.16), we then obtain

(9.18)
$$\frac{dr}{dM} = \frac{-B_3 F_4 h' + F_3 B_4 h'}{p|T|}$$

and

(9.19)
$$\frac{dp}{dM} = \frac{\dfrac{B_2 F_3}{r^2} + B_3 F_2}{p|T|}.$$

Knowledge of the signs of the partial derivatives of $B[\ \ ]$ and $F[\ \ ]$ alone does not suffice to determine the sign of $|T|$. Hence, in the absence of additional information, the signs of our comparative-statics derivatives dr/dM and dp/dM are also indeterminate.

Let us now form the dynamic counterpart of (9.13)–(9.14)

(9.20)
$$\frac{dr}{dt} = -K_5 B[\ \ ] - K_6 \{ F[\ \ ] - Y_0 \},$$

(9.21)
$$\frac{dp}{dt} = K_7 B[\ \ ] + K_8 \{ F[\ \ ] - Y_0 \},$$

where the K_j are all positive. Assume this system to be stable. The determinant $|K|$ of the preceding section is then equal to $-K_5 K_8 + K_6 K_7$. This can be positive, negative, or zero. Hence the sign of $|T|$—which corresponds to the $|A|$ of the preceding section—remains indeterminate even after we add the condition that the system must be stable. That is, dynamic analysis does not provide the necessary additional information about comparative-statics analysis: the "correspondence principle" does not work. If, however, we simplify our dynamic analysis and assume that excess demand in a given market affects only the price of that market, then $K_6 = K_7 = 0$, $|K| = -K_5 K_8$ is negative, and therefore (since there is an even number of equations) $|T|$ must also be negative. Thus under these assumptions the stability of the system implies that dr/dM must be negative and dp/dM positive.

The graphical analysis of this case in Figure XII-6 of the text presents BB as being positively sloped. Under our present assumptions, however, this is not necessarily true. In particular, a price rise now generates two opposing forces: on the one hand, it decreases the demand for bonds through the real-balance effect; on the other, it increases demand through the distribution effect. If, then, the latter force is sufficiently strong, the slope of *BB* might become negative.

There are now two possibilities: *BB* might cut *CC* either from above or from below. Consider first the latter possibility. As shown in Figure A-7, the curves intersect initially at the point (p_0, r_0). Let the quantity

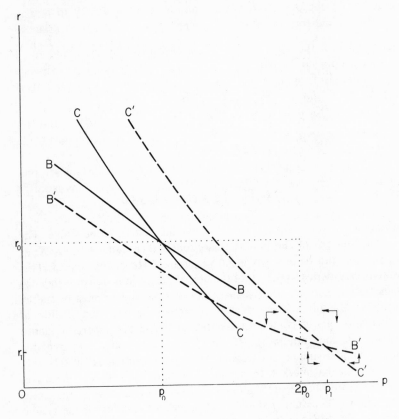

FIGURE A-7.

of money now double. Then, as explained in the text, *CC* shifts to the right. But, in contrast with the text, *BB* now shifts to the left: the increase in the quantity of money has created an excess demand in the bond market, and, at any given rate of interest, this excess—under our present assumptions—can be removed only by a price decrease. The intersection of $C'C'$ and $B'B'$ then determines the new equilibrium position (p_1, r_1). By construction, r_1 must be less than r_0.

It can readily be seen that in this case the negative slope of $B'B'$ does not interfere with the stability of the system. It is still true that at any point to the right of $C'C'$ there exists a state of excess supply of commodities driving prices down, while at any point above $B'B'$ there is an excess demand for bonds driving interest down. The arrows attached to the four representative points surrounding (p_1, r_1) in Figure A-7 show the operation of these market forces. At each of these points, at least one of the variables is moving in the direction of equilibrium.

Consider now the case in which BB cuts CC from above. This situation is represented in Figure A-8. Once again the increase in the quantity of money causes CC to shift to the right and BB to the left. This time, however, the intersection of $C'C'$ and $B'B'$ is necessarily at a higher rate of interest r_2.

It is this possibility which is precluded by our stability conditions. For, as can be seen from Figure A-8, whenever the economy is in the sectors represented by the points a and b, market forces press both variables away from their equilibrium values. Thus the system is unstable.

It is instructive to see how these geometrical restrictions are reflected in the stability condition $|T| < 0$. The curve BB is the graphical representation of equation (9.13); and CC, of (9.14). By the theory of implicit differentiation, we have

$$(9.22) \qquad \text{slope of } BB = -\frac{\dfrac{\partial B[\ ]}{\partial p}}{\dfrac{\partial B[\ ]}{\partial r}} = -\frac{\dfrac{-MB_3}{p^2} + B_4 h'}{\dfrac{-B_2}{r^2}}$$

and, since Y_0 in (9.14) is a constant,

$$(9.23) \qquad \text{slope of } CC = -\frac{\dfrac{\partial F[\ ]}{\partial p}}{\dfrac{\partial F[\ ]}{\partial r}} = -\frac{\dfrac{-MF_3}{p^2} + F_4 h'}{F_2}.$$

From the signs of the partial derivatives we know that (9.23) is always

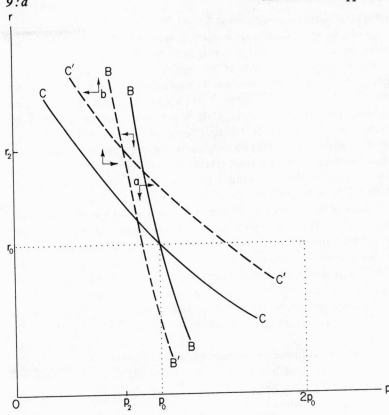

FIGURE A-8.

negative; while (9.22) is positive if and only if $\partial B[\quad]/\partial p$ is negative, and this, in turn, is negative if and only if B_4 is sufficiently small relative to B_3.

Let us now write our stability condition as

$$(9.24) \qquad |T| = \begin{vmatrix} \dfrac{\partial B[\quad]}{\partial r} & \dfrac{\partial B[\quad]}{\partial p} \\[2ex] \dfrac{\partial F[\quad]}{\partial r} & \dfrac{\partial F[\quad]}{\partial p} \end{vmatrix}$$

$$= \frac{\partial B[\quad]}{\partial r} \cdot \frac{\partial F[\quad]}{\partial p} - \frac{\partial B[\quad]}{\partial p} \cdot \frac{\partial F[\quad]}{\partial r} < 0,$$

where the partial derivatives are evaluated at the point of equilibrium. Transposing and dividing through, we then obtain

$$(9.25) \qquad -\frac{\dfrac{\partial F[\ ]}{\partial p}}{\dfrac{\partial F[\ ]}{\partial r}} < -\frac{\dfrac{\partial B[\ ]}{\partial p}}{\dfrac{\partial B[\ ]}{\partial r}}.$$

That is, under our simple dynamic assumptions, stability implies that at the point of equilibrium the slope of CC is less than that of BB. When the latter slope is positive, this is always satisfied; when negative, it is satisfied if and only if it cuts CC from below.

It should be emphasized again that these results flow from the over-simplified dynamic assumption that excess demand in one market affects only the price of that market. In the absence of this assumption, stability of the system will not necessarily imply that an increase in the quantity of money reduces interest.

d. THE CASE OF DISTRIBUTION EFFECTS (CONTINUED)[6]

These results can be obtained alternatively from the commodity and money markets. In particular, replace (9.13) by

$$(9.26) \qquad pL\left[Y_0, r, \frac{M}{p}, h(p)\right] - M = 0,$$

where $L_2 < 0$, $1 > L_3 > 0$, and, by assumption, $L_4 > 0$. Then instead of (9.15) we have

$$(9.27) \qquad L_2\frac{dr}{dM} + \left[\frac{M}{p^2}(1 - L_3) + L_4h'\right]\frac{dp}{dM} = -\frac{L_3}{p} + \frac{1}{p}.$$

Let

$$(9.28) \qquad |R| = \begin{vmatrix} L_2 & \dfrac{M}{p^2}(1 - L_3) + L_4h' \\[2ex] F_2 & -\dfrac{M}{p^2}F_3 + F_4h' \end{vmatrix} > 0.$$

---

[6] Attached to Chapter XII:3.

Solving (9.16) and (9.27), we obtain

(9.29) $$\frac{dr}{dM} = \frac{h'}{p|R|}\left[(1-L_3)F_4 + F_3L_4\right],$$

(9.30) $$\frac{dp}{dM} = -\frac{1}{p|R|}\left[L_2F_3 + (1-L_3)F_2\right].$$

Hence dp/dM must be positive. Consider now the sign of dr/dM. By assumption, the decreased demand for commodities caused by the distribution effect is used partly to supplement cash balances and partly to increase the demand for bonds. That is,

(9.31) $$F_4 + B_4 + L_4 = 0.$$

In addition we know that

(9.32) $$F_3 + B_3 + L_3 = 1.$$

Substituting from these equations into the numerator of (9.29) then yields

(9.33) $h'[(1-L_3)F_4 + F_3L_4] = h'[(F_3 + B_3)F_4 + F_3(-F_4 - B_4)]$

$$= h'(B_3F_4 - F_3B_4) < 0.$$

Hence dr/dM is negative.[7]

e. The Case of Government Debt and Open-Market Operations[8]

Let us now examine the influence of government debt and open-market operations. Rewrite equations (5) and (4) of the text (pp. 289f.) as

---

[7] The analysis of this section is actually more restricted than that of the preceding one. In particular, our assumption here that $0 < L_3 < 1$ implies that $\partial[L(\ ) - M/p]/\partial p$ is always positive—as is shown by the element in the first row, second column, of $|R|$ in (9.28); whereas the assumption of the preceding section that $\partial B[\ ]/\partial p$ might be positive implies—by the budget restraint (8.18), with the functions suitably modified—that L_3 might become greater than unity, so that $\partial[L(\ ) - M/p]/\partial p$ might become negative. This is the reason we can determine the sign of $|R|$ here without resort to the "correspondence principle." Cf. also the discussion of the excess-demand curve for real money holdings on pp. 419-20.

[8] Attached to Chapter XII: 4.

(9.34) $$B\left(Y_0, \frac{1}{r}, \frac{kV}{rp} + \frac{M}{p}\right) - \frac{kV}{rp} = 0,$$

(9.35) $$F\left(Y_0, r, \frac{kV}{rp} + \frac{M}{p}\right) - Y_0 = 0.$$

For convenience, the bars over the functional symbols have been dropped; it must, however, be remembered that the foregoing functions are different from those of the preceding section. By assumption, $0 \leqslant k \leqslant 1$, $0 < F_3 < 1$, and $0 < B_3 < 1$.

Consider first the case in which the quantity of money is increased in order to finance additional budgetary expenditures. Differentiating (9.34)–(9.35) with respect to M, holding V constant, we obtain

(9.36) $$\left[-\frac{B_2}{r^2} + \frac{(1 - B_3)kV}{r^2 p}\right] \frac{dr}{dM}$$
$$+ \left[\frac{kV}{rp^2}(1 - B_3) - \frac{B_3 M}{p^2}\right] \frac{dp}{dM} = -\frac{B_3}{p},$$

(9.37) $$\left(F_2 - \frac{F_3 kV}{r^2 p}\right) \frac{dr}{dM}$$
$$+ \left(-\frac{F_3 kV}{rp^2} - \frac{F_3 M}{p^2}\right) \frac{dp}{dM} = -\frac{F_3}{p}.$$

Let

(9.38) $$|W| = \begin{vmatrix} \dfrac{-B_2}{r^2} + \dfrac{(1 - B_3)kV}{r^2 p} & \dfrac{kV}{rp^2}(1 - B_3) - \dfrac{B_3 M}{p^2} \\[2ex] F_2 - \dfrac{F_3 kV}{r^2 p} & -\dfrac{F_3 kV}{rp^2} - \dfrac{F_3 M}{p^2} \end{vmatrix}.$$

We can then write our solutions of (9.36)–(9.37) as

(9.39) $$\frac{dr}{dM} = \frac{kF_3 V}{rp^3 |W|}$$

and

(9.40)
$$\frac{dp}{dM} = \frac{F_3\left[\dfrac{B_2}{r^2} - \dfrac{kV}{r^2 p}\right] + F_2 B_3}{p|W|}.$$

Using the same method as in Section *b* above, we can then show that under the simple dynamic hypothesis that an excess demand in a given market affects only the price of that market, stability of the system implies that $|W|$ is negative. Hence, for $0 < k \leqslant 1$, dr/dM is negative and dp/dM positive. Note that the degree to which r declines is directly proportionate to k and, indeed, becomes zero when the latter does.

Once again, these results can be interpreted graphically. In the commodity market the real-balance and real-indebtedness effects always reinforce each other; hence *CC* retains its negative slope. There is no such harmony of forces in the bond market. An increase in price decreases the demand for real bond holdings through the real-indebtedness and real-balance effects, but at the same time decreases the supply of real bond holdings. Only if the first effect is stronger than the second will the excess demand for bonds be negatively sloped with respect to the price level. This indeterminacy corresponds to the indeterminacy in the sign of the coefficient of dp/dM in (9.36)—which, of course, equals $\partial[B(\ ) - kV/rp]/\partial p$. On the other hand, $\partial[B(\ ) - kV/rp]/\partial r$—equal to the coefficient of dr/dM in (9.36)—must always be positive.

Thus a negative slope for *BB* can eventuate under exactly the same circumstances discussed above in connection with equations (9.22)–(9.23). Correspondingly, the graphical analysis of Figures A-7 and A-8 above can be applied directly to the present case too.

For the sake of completeness we also note the case—excluded by our present assumptions—in which $\partial[B(\ ) - kv/rp]/\partial r$ might be negative. Then the slope of *BB* can be negative either because both the numerator and denominator of (9.22) are positive—the only possibility which existed until now—or because both are negative. In the latter case stability can obtain only when *BB* cuts *CC* from above. Furthermore, an increase in the quantity of money shifts *BB* to the right; for the excess demand it generates is now eliminated by an increase in interest. There can also be the case in which the numerator of (9.22) is positive, while the denominator is negative, so that *BB* once again has a positive slope. Here an increase in the quantity of money shifts *BB* to the left and *CC* to the right, thus increasing interest. But this case is excluded by our stability condition. The reader can establish this by graphical analysis. Alternatively, he can readily see that if in (9.38) the elements in the first row of $|W|$ are negative and positive, respectively, then $|W|$ must be positive, violating our stability condition.

Let us now return to (9.34)–(9.35) and consider the case in which the change in *M* is the result of open-market operations. Here, by assumption, *V* is no longer constant. Specifically, letting *dM* represent the change in the quantity of money and *dV* the corresponding change in the number of bonds outstanding, we must have

$$(9.41) \qquad dM = -\frac{1}{r}\, dV.$$

That is, the increase in the quantity of money in circulation is equal to the amount expended on the purchase of bonds.

Differentiating (9.34)–(9.35) with respect to *M* again, but this time letting *V* vary in accordance with (9.41), we obtain a system of equations which is the same as (9.36)–(9.37), except that the right-hand sides of these equations are replaced by $-\dfrac{B_3}{p} - \dfrac{k(1 - B_3)}{p}$ and $-\dfrac{F_3}{p} + \dfrac{kF_3}{p}$, respectively. Solving, we obtain

$$(9.42) \qquad \frac{dr}{dM} = \frac{kF_3(V + rM)}{rp^3|W|} < 0,$$

$$(9.43) \qquad \frac{dp}{dM} = \frac{F_3(1 - k)\left[\dfrac{B_2}{r^2} - (1 - B_3)\dfrac{kV}{r^2 p}\right]}{p|W|}$$
$$+ \frac{\left(F_2 - \dfrac{F_3 kV}{r^2 p}\right)[B_3 + k(1 - B_3)]}{p|W|} > 0,$$

where once again the negative sign of $|W|$ is implied by the assumption of stability. Note that (9.42) is greater in absolute value than (9.39).

f. THE CASE OF GOVERNMENT DEBT AND OPEN-MARKET OPERATIONS (CONTINUED)[9]

Consider finally the case of a constant-purchasing-power bond. Equations (9.34) and (9.35) are then replaced by

$$(9.44) \qquad B\left(Y_0, \frac{1}{r}, \frac{kV}{r} + \frac{M}{p}\right) - \frac{kV}{r} = 0,$$

$$(9.45) \qquad F\left(Y_0, r, \frac{kV}{r} + \frac{M}{p}\right) - Y_0 = 0.$$

An increase in the quantity of money injected into the system through increased government budgetary expenditures clearly causes a proportionate increase in prices and leaves the rate of interest invariant. Consider now an increase injected through open-market operations. Here we must replace (9.41) by

$$(9.46) \qquad dM = -\frac{p}{r}\, dV.$$

That is, the quantity of money injected into the system by the purchase of a given number of bonds depends on the general price level as well as on the price of bonds. Differentiating (9.44)–(9.45) with respect to M, making use of (9.46), we obtain

$$(9.47) \qquad \left[-\frac{B_2}{r^2} + \frac{kV(1 - B_3)}{r^2}\right]\frac{dr}{dM} - \frac{B_3 M}{p^2}\frac{dp}{dM} = -\frac{B_3}{p} - \frac{k(1 - B_3)}{p},$$

$$(9.48) \qquad \left(F_2 - \frac{kVF_3}{r^2}\right)\frac{dr}{dM} - \frac{F_3 M}{p^2}\frac{dp}{dM} = -\frac{F_3}{p} + \frac{kF_3}{p}.$$

Let

$$(9.49) \qquad |X| = \begin{vmatrix} -\dfrac{B_2}{r^2} + \dfrac{kV(1 - B_3)}{r^2} & -\dfrac{B_3 M}{p^2} \\[2ex] F_2 - \dfrac{kVF_3}{r^2} & -\dfrac{F_3 M}{p^2} \end{vmatrix} < 0.$$

[9] Attached to Chapter XII:4.

Solving, we obtain

(9.50)
$$\frac{dr}{dM} = \frac{kF_3 M}{p^3 |X|} < 0,$$

(9.51)
$$\frac{dp}{dM} = \frac{F_3(1-k)\left[\dfrac{B_2}{r^2} - (1 - B_3)\dfrac{kV}{r^2}\right]}{p|X|}$$
$$+ \frac{\left(F_2 - \dfrac{F_3 kV}{r^2}\right)[B_3 + k(1 - B_3)]}{p|X|} > 0.$$

It should finally be emphasized that we have not been able to determine the signs of our comparative-statics derivatives in Sections *c* and *e* above except by using the information implied by the assumption that the system is stable under highly oversimplified dynamic conditions. Correspondingly, as soon as we consider more complicated—and, presumably, more realistic—conditions, the comparative-statics conclusions of the aforementioned sections need no longer hold. Thus our repeated use of the "correspondence principle" should not blind the reader to the fact that it is really an analytical tool of much narrower applicability than its name would lead us to believe.[10]

---

[10] Cf. the article cited in Section *b* above.

10. Appendix to Chapters XIII and XIV

a. The Effects of Monetary Changes Under the Assumption of Unemployment[1]

Let our system be represented by

$$(10.1) \qquad F\left(Y, r, \frac{kV}{rp} + \frac{M}{p}\right) - Y = 0,$$

$$(10.2) \qquad B\left(Y, \frac{1}{r}, \frac{kV}{rp} + \frac{M}{p}\right) - \frac{kV}{rp} = 0,$$

where p is now constant and Y variable, and where k has the same meaning as in Mathematical Appendix $9:e$ above. By assumption, $0 < F_1 < 1$ and $B_1 = 0$. Let this system operate according to the dynamic principles

$$(10.3) \qquad \frac{dY}{dt} = K_1[F(\ ) - Y],$$

$$(10.4) \qquad \frac{dr}{dt} = -K_2\left[B(\ ) - \frac{kV}{rp}\right],$$

[1] Attached to Chapter XIII:4.

For an explanation of the technique of differentiation used here, the reader is referred once again to p. 489, footnote 9.

where K_1 and K_2 are positive. Let

$$(10.5) \quad |A| = \begin{vmatrix} F_1 - 1 & F_2 - \dfrac{F_3 kV}{r^2 p} \\ 0 & -\dfrac{B_2}{r^2} - \dfrac{(B_3 - 1)kV}{r^2 p} \end{vmatrix} < 0.$$

The system is stable if the characteristic equation $|KA - xI| = 0$, or, more specifically,

$$(10.6) \quad [K_1(F_1 - 1) - x]\left[K_2\left(\frac{B_2}{r^2} + \frac{(B_3 - 1)kV}{r^2 p}\right) - x\right] = 0,$$

has roots whose real parts are negative. Inspection of this equation shows that this condition is met.

Consider now the effects of an increase in the quantity of money used to finance budgetary expenditures. Differentiating (10.1)–(10.2) with respect to M, the variable V being held constant, we obtain

$$(10.7) \quad \frac{dY}{dM} = \frac{F_3\left(\dfrac{B_2}{r^2} - \dfrac{kV}{r^2 p}\right) + F_2 B_3}{p|A|} > 0$$

and

$$(10.8) \quad \frac{dr}{dM} = \frac{(1 - F_1)B_3}{p|A|} < 0,$$

where we have once again made use of the assumption $B_1 = 0$.

In the case where the monetary increase goes to finance open-market purchases, we differentiate (10.1)–(10.2) with respect to M, letting V vary in accordance with (9.41), to obtain

$$(10.9) \quad \frac{dY}{dM} = \frac{F_3(1 - k)\left[\dfrac{B_2}{r^2} - \dfrac{(1 - B_3)kV}{r^2 p}\right]}{p|A|}$$

$$+ \frac{[B_3 + k(1 - B_3)]\left(F_2 - \dfrac{F_3 kV}{r^2 p}\right)}{p|A|} > 0$$

and

(10.10) $$\frac{dr}{dM} = \frac{(1 - F_1)[B_3 + k(1 - B_3)]}{p|A|} < 0.$$

The identity of the numerators of (10.7) and (9.40), on the one hand, and (10.9) and (9.43), on the other, is the mathematical counterpart of the familiar observation of "depression economics" that an increase in the quantity of money can expend itself either in increasing real output or in raising prices.

Alternatively, we can obtain these results from an analysis of the commodity and money markets. Replace (10.2) by

(10.11) $$L\left(Y, r, \frac{kV}{rp} + \frac{M}{p}\right) - \frac{M}{p} = 0,$$

where $L_3 > 0$; and (10.4) by

(10.12) $$\frac{dr}{dt} = K_3\left[L(\ ) - \frac{M}{p}\right],$$

where K_3 is positive. Let

(10.13) $$|B| = \begin{vmatrix} F_1 - 1 & F_2 - \dfrac{F_3 kV}{r^2 p} \\[2ex] L_1 & L_2 - \dfrac{L_3 kV}{r^2 p} \end{vmatrix} > 0.$$

The reader can then verify that the characteristic equation

(10.14) $$|KB - yI| = 0$$

has roots for y whose real parts are negative.

Consider now the case of a budgetary increase in the quantity of money. Here we differentiate (10.1) and (10.11) with respect to M, holding V constant, to obtain

(10.15) $$\frac{dY}{dM} = \frac{\begin{vmatrix} \dfrac{-F_3}{p} & F_2 - \dfrac{F_3 kV}{r^2 p} \\[2ex] \dfrac{1 - L_3}{p} & L_2 - \dfrac{L_3 kV}{r^2 p} \end{vmatrix}}{|B|} > 0$$

and

$$(10.16) \quad \frac{dr}{dM} = \frac{\begin{vmatrix} F_1 - 1 & \dfrac{-F_3}{p} \\[2ex] L_1 & \dfrac{1 - L_3}{p} \end{vmatrix}}{|B|}$$

$$= \frac{-(1 - F_1)(1 - L_3) + F_3 L_1}{p|B|}.$$

From budget restraint (23) on p. 227 and the assumption $B_1 = 0$, we have $F_1 + L_1 = 1$ and $F_3 + B_3 + L_3 = 1$, where all the derivatives are positive. Substituting these relationships in (10.16) then yields

$$(10.17) \quad \frac{dr}{dM} = \frac{-L_1 B_3}{p|B|} < 0.$$

Let us now examine the case of open-market operations. Once again we differentiate (10.1) and (10.11) with respect to M, but now we let V vary in accordance with (9.41). This yields

$$(10.18) \quad \frac{dY}{dM} = \frac{\begin{vmatrix} \dfrac{F_3}{p}(k - 1) & F_2 - \dfrac{F_3 k V}{r^2 p} \\[2ex] \dfrac{1 - (1 - k)L_3}{p} & L_2 - \dfrac{L_3 k V}{r^2 p} \end{vmatrix}}{|B|} > 0$$

and

$$(10.19) \quad \frac{dr}{dM} = \frac{\begin{vmatrix} F_1 - 1 & -F_3 + k F_3 \\ L_1 & 1 - L_3 + k L_3 \end{vmatrix}}{p|B|}$$

$$= \frac{\begin{vmatrix} F_1 - 1 & -F_3 \\ L_1 & 1 - L_3 \end{vmatrix}}{p|B|} + \frac{\begin{vmatrix} F_1 - 1 & k F_3 \\ L_1 & k L_3 \end{vmatrix}}{p|B|} < 0.$$

Comparing (10.19) with (10.16), we see that the fall in interest must be greater in the former case.

We note finally that by differentiating system (10.1)–(10.2) with respect to p, now assumed variable—while V and M are assumed constant instead—we obtain the derivatives dY/dp and dr/dp; these represent the operation of the real-balance effect described in the last paragraph of p. 334 above. The details of this derivation are left as an exercise for the reader.

b. A Variation of the "Liquidity Trap"[2]

Consider now the special case where any increase in the quantity of money is merely added to cash balances. That is, $L_3 = 1$. This implies $B_3 = F_3 = 0$. Substituting these values into (10.5) or (10.13), we see that the stability of the system is not thereby affected.

If, now, the quantity of money is increased to finance transfer payments, $dr/dM = dY/dM = 0$. This can be seen either from equations (10.7)–(10.8) or (10.15)–(10.16). On the other hand, in the case of open-market operations, the signs of the derivatives are not affected, as can be seen from either (10.9)–(10.10) or (10.18)–(10.19).

The reader can also establish that if there are no government bonds, then a decrease in p—M constant—will not affect either r or Y; i.e. $dr/dp = dY/dp = 0$. In terms of Figure XIII–3 (p. 332), the absence of a real-balance effect in the commodity and bond market will leave the relevant GG and PP curves invariant under the change in p. Nor will the MM curve shift: for the decline in p generates an increase in the demand for money (by means of the real-balance effect) which exactly equals the increase in supply; hence the money market will be in equilibrium at the same combinations of r and Y at which equilibrium prevailed before.[3]

In brief, under the foregoing assumption the real-balance effect is dissipated entirely in increasing the demand for money balances. However, as noted in the text (p. 338), this conclusion rests on the unreasonable assumption that the wealth effect in the form of the real-balance effect does not manifest itself similarly in all markets, but operates exclusively in the market for money.[4]

---

[2] Attached to pp. 338 and 352 (footnote 27).

[3] The argument in footnote 27 of p. 352 actually bears on those parts of the three curves which extend from r_1 and below. This, however, is all that is necessary to establish the existence of a "trap".

[4] The unreasonableness of this assumption is not mitigated by assuming (as does, e.g., Bailey, *op. cit.*, pp. 186–87) that money is a consumer's good.

11. On Stocks and Flows[1]

It is a commonplace that wealth is to income as a stock is to a flow—where the distinction between the latter two is that a stock is time-dimensionless, while a flow has the dimensions of $1/$time. The details of the wealth-income relationship are however more complicated than usually realized. Indeed, as indicated in the text,[2] they have been the source of some misunderstandings in the literature.

These misunderstandings have to do with the dimensional aspects of the wealth-income relationship. For convenience in dealing with this question, let us denote the dimensions of any expression $g(x)$ by $D[g(x)]$. Similarly, let $\$$ denote the dimensions of money and T the dimensions of time (which, in turn, is denoted as usual by t). We also make use of the fact that the dimensions of a product are the product of the dimensions.[3]

If the rate of flow of income over time is represented by the continuous functions $f(t)$—where, by definition, $D[f(t)] = \$/T$—and if in addition compounding is assumed to take place continuously, then wealth W_0

---

[1] Without wishing to burden them with responsibility for the emphasis and interpretation of this appendix, I would like to express my appreciation to Tsvi Ophir and Milton Friedman for their invaluable assistance on certain crucial points.

[2] See p. 19, footnote 15; pp. 377–78; and pp. 423f., footnote 16. For my own sins on this question, see p. 520, footnote 10 below.

[3] Cf. G. C. Evans, *Mathematical Introduction to Economics* (New York, 1930), Chapter 2.

can be defined as

$$(11.1) \qquad W_0 = \int_0^\infty \frac{f(t)dt}{e^{rt}},$$

where e^{rt} is the continuous-discount factor.[4] Since $D[r] = 1/T$ and $D[t] = T$, this factor is a pure number and thus time-dimensionless. Similarly, the numerator $f(t)dt$—the amount of income received during interval dt—is also time-dimensionless: for $D[f(t)dt] = D[f(t)]D[dt] = (\$/T)T = \$$.[5] Thus the right-hand side of (11.1) has the dimensions of money. Clearly, this is also the case for the left-hand side: for, in accordance with the usual definition of wealth, $D[W_0] = \$$.

From (11.1) we can also compute a constant rate of income-flow K, whose discounted value equals W_0. This is

$$(11.2) \qquad K = rW_0,$$

which clearly has the dimensions of money per unit of time.

Let us now turn to the definition of wealth in the case of period analysis. For simplicity, consider first the two-week Fisherine case of Chapter V:7. Here wealth is defined as

$$(11.3) \qquad W_0 = R_1 + \frac{R_2}{1 + r},$$

where R_1 and R_2 are the respective incomes of the first and second week, and r is the weekly rate of interest. From this formula it is clear that R_1 must have the same dimensions as W_0, which is a stock. By analogy, R_2 must then also have the dimensions of W_0; and this in turn implies that $1 + r$ is a pure number. Thus the requirements of dimensional consistency in (11.3) seem to lead to the paradoxical conclusion that both income and interest are time-dimensionless!

The solution to this paradox lies in realizing that (say) R_1 in (11.3) represents not a *rate* of income (e.g., a wage rate), but the *amount* of

---

[4] See Allen, *Mathematical Analysis for Economists, op. cit.*, pp. 232–34, 401–405.

[5] From certain mathematical viewpoints, dt can be considered only as the symbol of an operator; correspondingly, one can legitimately speak only of the dimensions of the right-hand side of (11.1) as a whole—and these dimensions are those of the sum which approaches it as a limit. Since, however, such a formulation does not affect the following conclusions, we have adopted the heuristically convenient device of treating dt as a separate variable with the same dimensions as t.

income received during the week (e.g., wage payments during the week); that is, R_1 corresponds not to $f(t)$ in equation (11.1), but to $f(t)dt$. Correspondingly, the time-dimensionlessness of R_1, just like that of $f(t)dt$, reflects the fact that this amount is not affected by changing the time-unit in which the interval is measured. In other words, the individual in equation (11.3) receives R_1 dollars in the first week and R_2 in the second—whether we call a week a week, or seven days, or 1/52 of a year. Similarly, the time-dimensionlessness of $1 + r$ represents the fact that the amount by which we must discount R_2 is not affected by saying that this income will be received "seven days hence" instead of "one week hence." Another point that should be emphasized is that the time-dimensionlessness of R_1 and R_2 is also reflected in the fact that these payments must be considered as if they were concentrated at *instants* of time: namely, the beginning of the first and second week, respectively; that is, those instants for which 1 and $1 + r$ are, respectively, the correct discount factors.

More rigorously, we must take account of the fact that the proper time dimensions in equation (11.3) are obscured by the tacit assumption that certain time periods are of unit length. In order to bring this out, let us place (11.3) within a somewhat broader context by assuming that R_1 and R_2 are the income payments respectively received at the beginning of the first and second "payment intervals," each assumed to be h time-units long. Similarly, let us define the "compounding interval"— assumed to be m time-units long—as that period of time after which the interest obligation is compounded. Finally, let us represent by F_1 and F_2 the *rates* of income flow which would conceptually have cumulated, respectively, to R_1 and R_2. That is,

$$(11.4) \qquad\qquad R_j = F_j h \qquad\qquad (j = 1, 2).$$

For simplicity, consider first the case in which the payment and compounding intervals are of equal length: that is, in which compounding takes place once each payment interval. Then the discounting formula corresponding to the foregoing assumptions is

$$(11.5) \qquad\qquad W_0 = \frac{F_1 h}{1} + \frac{F_2 h}{1 + mr},$$

where, by assumption, $h = m$. If in addition the payment (and compounding) interval is assumed to be one time-unit long, then (11.5) reduces in form to (11.3). Assume now that while the payment (and compounding) interval remains (say) a week, the time-unit is reduced to a day. This, of course, requires us to refer to a "week" as "seven days"; on the other hand, it clearly does not affect the value of either the numerators or denominators in (11.5): for the fact that the number associated with F_j will be reduced to one-seventh its former magnitude will be offset by the fact that the number associated with h will increase sevenfold—and a similar statement holds for r and m.[6] This time-dimensionlessness is, of course, a direct implication of the fact that $D[F_jh] = D[F_j]D[h] = (\$/T)T = \$$, and $D[mr] = D[m]D[r] = T(1/T) = 1$.

The foregoing discussion can be generalized to the case in which there are n equal payment intervals, assumed generally to differ in length from the compounding interval. If h/m is an integer greater than or equal to unity, wealth is then defined as

$$(11.6) \qquad W_0 = \sum_{i=1}^{n} \frac{F_i h}{(1 + mr)^{(h/m)i}},$$

where F_i is the conceptual rate of income flow during the ith interval, and where each of the actual income payments $F_i h$ is assumed to be made at the instant of time at the end of the interval.[7] We have already seen that the numerator of the right-hand expression is time-dimensionless and will now only note that F_i and h in this numerator obviously correspond respectively to $f(t)$ and dt in (11.1). We have also seen that $1 + mr$ is time-dimensionless, and this is clearly true for h/m as well. Hence it must also be true for the denominator in (11.6). In brief, since both the rate of discount *per compounding interval* and the relevant number of compounding intervals for any given income payment are unaffected by a change in the time-unit, so too is the discount factor that must be applied to any such payment.

---

[6] Note that if, say, $(1 + 0.1)$ is the discount factor when the time-unit is one week, then changing this time-unit to a day will *not* change the discount factor to $(1 + 0.1/7)^7$. For the change in the time-unit has not affected the length of the compounding interval, and, by definition, interest within this interval accumulates in a simple manner. Hence the relevant discount factor remains $[1 + 7(0.1/7)] = (1 + 0.1)$.

[7] Note that equations (11.3) and (11.5) assume payments to be made at the beginning of the respective intervals.

Equation (11.6) can also be modified so as to take account of the case in which h/m is not an integer. This, however, involves certain complications which need not concern us here.

Consider now the problem of determining a constant, perpetual income flow F whose present value equals W_0. This is obtained from (11.6) by setting $F_i = F$ $(i = 1, \ldots, n)$ and $n = \infty$ and solving the resulting equation for F. This yields the (conceptual) flow

$$(11.7) \qquad F = \frac{[(1 + mr)^{h/m} - 1]W_0}{h},$$

which clearly has the dimensions of $\$/T$. If $h = m$, this reduces to

$$(11.8) \qquad F = rW_0,$$

which is the counterpart of (11.2). Clearly, the corresponding constant income *payment* is

$$(11.9) \qquad R = Fh = (rW_0)h = (rh)W_0,$$

which is time-dimensionless.

The foregoing discussion has immediate implications both for some specific problems which have concerned us in earlier chapters, and for the more general problem of interpreting the relationship between wealth and income. To begin with the first set of problems, let us return for a moment to the one-week individual who concerned us in Chapter II and Mathematical Appendix 2: d. It is clear that no dimensional difficulties are involved in defining the wealth or total resources of that individual as the sum of his initial money holdings and week's income in the form of commodities.[8] That is, in the budget restraint of this individual, which is represented in equation (2.30) above as

$$(11.10) \qquad G + \frac{Z_n}{p} = \bar{G} + \frac{\bar{Z}_n}{p}$$

(where G and Z_n refer to commodities and money, respectively, and where the bars denote initial quantities), all of the terms are time-dimensionless. (For the same reason there is no dimensional difficulty— in the multiweek case of p. 96—in defining R_1 as $\bar{Z}_1 + B_0/p + M_0/p$.) From this it also follows that the properties of the demand for real balances expressed as a function of $\bar{G} + \bar{Z}_n/p$ are not affected by a change in the time-unit. This is true in particular for the intercept of this function with the Y-axis in Figure II-3.[9]

[8] See p. 19.
[9] See p. 31, footnote 28 above.

Note, however, that in analogy to equation (11.4) above, we can consider G and $\bar{G}$ in equation (11.10) as being respectively related to the consumption and income *flows* G' and $\bar{G}'$ in the following simple fashion:

$$(11.11) \qquad\qquad G = G'h, \quad \bar{G} = \bar{G}'h.$$

Substituting these into (11.10) and rearranging terms, we obtain

$$(11.12) \qquad\qquad \frac{Z_n}{p} - \frac{\bar{Z}_n}{p} = h\bar{G}' - hG'.$$

This is the excess demand for money considered as a stock. On the other hand, dividing through by h yields

$$(11.13) \qquad\qquad \frac{1}{h}\left(\frac{Z_n}{p} - \frac{\bar{Z}_n}{p}\right) = \bar{G}' - G'.$$

This is the excess demand for money considered as a flow. If $h = 1$ the number that would appear on the left-hand side of (11.12) would be the same as that on the left-hand side of (11.13); but the dimensions of these numbers would not be. A similar relationship would exist for the numbers corresponding to the right-hand sides. In any case, however, it is clear that (11.12) will be zero if and only if (11.13) is.[10]

This argument can be readily extended to the multiweek case on p. 96 above. If flows are represented by primed variables, the current excess demand for money in this case can be written either as a stock

$$(11.14) \qquad \frac{M_1}{p} - \frac{M_0}{p} = h\bar{Z}'_1 - hZ'_1 + \frac{B_0}{p} - \frac{1}{1+r}\frac{B_1}{p},$$

or as a flow

$$(11.15) \qquad \frac{1}{h}\left(\frac{M_1}{p} - \frac{M_0}{p}\right) = (\bar{Z}'_1 - Z'_1) + \frac{1}{h}\left(\frac{B_0}{p} - \frac{1}{1+r}\frac{B_1}{p}\right).$$

---

[10] Cf. p. 26 above.

This paragraph takes account of the criticism in R. W. Clower, "Stock and Flow Quantities: A Common Fallacy," *Economica*, XXVI (1959), 251–52. It also corrects other aspects of the argument which originally appeared in my "Indeterminacy of Absolute Prices in Classical Economic Theory," *Econometrica*, XVII (1949) Section 8; "Liquidity Preference and Loanable Funds: Stock and Flow Analysis," *Economica*, XXV (1958), 302–306, and XXVI (1959), 253–54; and pp. 25 (footnote 17) and 147 (footnote 16) of the first edition of this book.

Let us now turn to the more general implications of the foregoing argument for the wealth-income relationship. The usual discussion of this relationship seems to interpret the role of the rate of interest as that of converting an income flow (with dimensions $\$/T$) into a stock (with dimensions $\$$) by dividing this flow by the rate of interest (with dimensions $1/T$). If the income stream is a constant, perpetual one, this is indeed a valid interpretation—both when the stream is continuous [equation (11.2)] and when it is discrete [equation (11.8)]. If, however, the income stream is not a constant one, then the interpretation is not correct—and again there is no difference between the continuous [equation (11.1)] and discrete [equation (11.6)] cases. This in no way affects the fundamental distinction between a capital asset and the flow of services which it provides, or the parallel distinction between the source of an income flow and the flow itself. The only point is the essentially semantic one that in computing the value of this source we are actually applying time-dimensionless discount factors to a stream (or, if we prefer, time-sequence) of time-dimensionless income payments—where these payments refer to either infinitesimal or finite time intervals.[11]

On the other hand, it should be emphasized that there is a valid basis for our intuitive feeling that income payments are—and wealth is not—affected by a change in the "time-period." The relevant change, however, is not one in the time-unit, but one in the time-duration of the payment interval. This can be most easily seen in the case of the constant, perpetual income stream described by equations (11.8) and (11.9): a change in the time-unit leaves both R and W_0 unaffected; but a change in h, the time-unit being held constant, causes a proportionate change in R, while leaving W_0 invariant. Correspondingly, the accepted description of the distinction between W_0 and R as paralleling that between a "stock" and a "flow," should be understood as implicitly defining a "flow" not as a quantity whose dimensions are $1/T$, but as a quantity whose magnitude is directly proportional to h; similarly, the implicit definition of a "stock" is that of a quantity whose magnitude is independent of h. Clearly, such "stocks" and "flows" can be added together.

---

[11] A related semantic point is that the term "stock-flow model" should not be used to describe such models as that presented in Chapter III:7 above: for none of the variables in this model has the dimensions of $1/T$.

This contrast between income payments and wealth also holds—though only as an approximation—in the case of the finite income stream described by equation (11.6). The essential point here is that the counterpart of the change in h discussed in the preceding paragraph is an equiproportionate change in the frequency *and number* of income payments which leaves invariant their (conceptual) rates of flow and *un*discounted sum.[12]

The nature of the argument here is illustrated in Figure A-9. Let the stream of income payments in equation (11.6) be represented by the relevant rectangular areas under the step-function in this diagram:

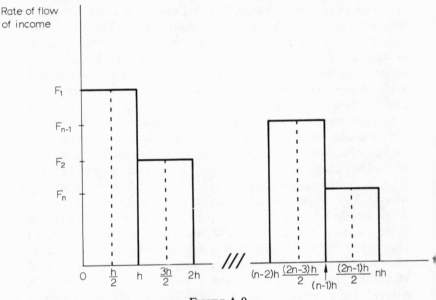

FIGURE A-9.

namely, the n rectangles corresponding to segments $(0, h)$, $(h, 2h)$, ... , $[(n - 1)h, nh]$ on the X-axis. Assume now that the (conceptual)

---

[12] If, however, the frequency is (say) increased while the number of payments is kept constant—which corresponds to decreasing h in equation (11.6) while keeping n constant—then the undiscounted sum of payments and the value of W_0 will obviously also decrease. In particular, as h approaches zero, so must W_0.

The failure to notice this fact is the major source of the misunderstanding discussed on pp. 423f., footnote 16 above.

rates and durations of income flow represented by the step-function remain unchanged, while the frequency and number of payments (and compoundings) are doubled. Then the stream of payments is now represented by the respective areas of the $2n$ rectangles corresponding to segments $\left(0, \frac{h}{2}\right), \left(\frac{h}{2}, h\right), \left(h, \frac{3h}{2}\right), ..., \left(\frac{2n-1}{2} h, nh\right)$. Clearly, each of these payments is half the corresponding original one. On the other hand, the measure of wealth is affected only to a relatively minor extent, as a result of the fact that slightly different discount factors are now being applied to the "same" income payments: i.e., payments which correspond to the same segments of the step-function in Figure A-9.

This argument can also be presented analytically in a somewhat more general form. In doing so, we shall for simplicity regard compounding as if it were taking place continuously, so that (11.6) is rewritten as

$$(11.16) \qquad W_0 = \sum_{i=1}^{n} \frac{F_i h}{e^{\rho h i}},$$

where ρ is chosen so as to satisfy the relationship

$$(11.17) \qquad e^{\rho} = (1 + mr)^{1/m}.$$

If the (conceptual) rates of flow of income F_i and their durations are left unchanged, while the frequency of payments is increased, say, k-fold, then the ith term in the summation of (11.16) is replaced by

$$(11.18) \qquad \sum_{j=1}^{k} \frac{F_i \dfrac{h}{k}}{e^{\rho h [(i-1) + j/k]}} \sim F_i \frac{h}{k} \sum_{j=1}^{k} \frac{1}{e^{\rho h i}} = \frac{F_i h}{e^{\rho h i}} \qquad (i = 1, ..., n).$$

This, then, is the proper sense in which it can be said that the measurement of wealth in (11.16) is unaffected by a change in the length of the payment interval.

Supplementary Notes

and

Studies in the Literature

Introduction

The purpose of this Supplement is to provide the detailed textual evidence necessary to support the interpretation and criticism of the literature presented in the text. In order to do this it has been necessary to present full-length studies of the monetary theories of Walras, Wicksell, and Cassel. The reader is, however, again warned that neither these studies nor, *a fortiori*, the less comprehensive notes on the other writers are intended to be read by themselves. Indeed, unless they are read together with the sections of the text to which they are explicitly attached, they are likely to appear as disjointed, captious criticisms of arbitrarily selected passages. The meaning of it all—the reasons for selecting the passages in question and the significance of the criticism leveled against them—can be understood only from the text itself.

To state this in somewhat more positive terms, the detailed studies of Notes B–K, together with their broader implications as developed, interpreted, and summarized in Chapters VIII: 1–4 and XV: 1–2, are intended to constitute a critical history of the general-equilibrium theory of money from its inception by Walras to its most recent statements by Keynes, Hicks, Leontief, Modigliani, and others. But it is a history largely written from a special viewpoint. In brief, our main interest is in the degree to which general-equilibrium theorists succeeded in their declared objective of integrating monetary theory with value theory.[1]

---

[1] It should be emphasized that this objective is one that characterized practically all economic theorists, and not just those of the general-equilibrium school. See the detailed examination of the literature in Marget, *Theory of Prices*, Vol. II, pp. 3–133.

Our criterion is a twofold one: first, the extent to which these theorists applied the formal apparatus of marginal-utility analysis to the theory of money; second—and far more important—the extent to which they consistently carried over their recognition of the real-balance effect to all phases of monetary and value theory.

As shown in the text, the critical points where we must test for such a recognition—or, rather, for its absence—are in the failure to present a stability analysis of the equilibrium absolute price level, in the assumption of a uniform unitary elasticity of demand for money, and in the invalid dichotomization of the pricing process. To the extent that it is relevant, each of the writers cited in the following notes will be subjected to this triple test. In many ways, the first of these tests is at once the simplest and the most revealing. And this explains why our history must begin with a thorough appreciation of the vital role of the *tâtonnement* in the general theoretical framework of Walras.

Note A. The Mechanism of the Quantity Theory in the Earlier Literature[1]

Examples of early expositions of the quantity theory which make it clear that an increase in the quantity of money raises prices through its prior effect in increasing demand are provided by Richard Cantillon,[2] Henry Thornton,[3] David Ricardo,[4] and John Stuart Mill.[5] On the other hand, it must be admitted that there were early exponents of the quantity theory who failed to provide any economic explanation of the effect of money on prices. Thus Montesquieu wrote:

If we compare the mass of gold and silver in the whole world with the quantity of merchandise therein contained, it is certain that every commodity or merchandise in particular may be compared to a certain portion of the entire mass of gold and silver. As the total of the one is to the total of the other, so part of the one will be to part of the other. Let us suppose that there is only one commodity or merchandise in the world, or only one to be purchased, and that

[1] Attached to Chapter VIII:1, especially p. 164.

[2] *Essay on the Nature of Trade* (1755), trans. and ed. H. Higgs (London, 1931), Part II, Chapters VI–VII, especially pp. 161 and 179.

[3] *An Enquiry into the Nature and Effects of the Paper Credit of Great Britain* (London, 1802), pp. 195 ff., 259–67.

[4] *The High Price of Bullion* (1810), in *The Works and Correspondence of David Ricardo*, ed. P. Sraffa (Cambridge, 1951), Vol. III, p. 91; *Reply to Mr. Bosanquet* (1811), *ibid.*, p. 217; *Notes on the Bullion Report and Evidence* (1810), *ibid.*, pp. 362–63; *Notes on Trotter* (1810), *ibid.*, p. 390, footnote 38.

[5] *Principles of Political Economy*, ed. W. J. Ashley (London, 1909), pp. 491–93, 496, 524. On this last page Mill writes: "Money acts upon prices in no other way than by being tendered in exchange for commodities."

this is divisible like money; a part of this merchandise will answer to a part of the mass of gold and silver; the half of the total of the one to the half of the total of the other; the tenth, the hundredth, the thousandth, part of the one to the tenth, the hundredth, the thousandth part of the other. ... the establishment of the price of things fundamentally depends on the proportion of the total of things to the total of signs.[6]

Similar passages appear in David Hume[7] and James Mill.[8] Even here, however, we should hesitate before concluding that these writers failed to see that an increase in the quantity of money raises prices only because it first increases demand. They may have instead considered this causal relationship to be too obvious for comment. Thus, for example, James Mill made it clear that he was aware of this relationship when he wrote:

The man who goes first to market with the augmented quantity of money, either raises the price of the commodities which he purchases, or he does not raise it.[9]

Another case in point is Ricardo. As against the purely mechanical exposition of the quantity theory in his *Principles*,[10] we have the other passages already cited that show that he fully understood the effect of an increase in the quantity of money in increasing demand.

We might finally observe—in connection with the discussion in Note G:2 below—that since, for the most part, classical value theory did not systematically discuss the problem of stability of equilibrium, no significance can be attached to the corresponding gap in its monetary theory. There are, however, exceptions. In particular, J. S. Mill is as open to criticism as any neoclassical economist for failing to include in his chapter on "The Value of Money as Dependent on Demand and Supply" a counterpart of the embryonic stability discussion of his earlier chapter on "Demand and Supply in their Relation to Value."[11]

---

[6] *The Spirit of the Laws*, trans. T. Nugent (New York, 1949), Vol. I, pp. 378–79.
[7] *Essays, Moral, Political, and Literary*, in *Philosophical Works* (Boston, 1854), Vol. III, pp. 313, 318, 334, 341–42.
[8] *Elements of Political Economy* (London, 1821), p. 95.
[9] *Ibid.*, p. 123.
[10] *Principles of Political Economy and Taxation*, ed. Sraffa, Chapter XXVII; see in particular p. 352.
[11] *Op. cit.*, Book III, Chapter II, §4, and Chapter VIII.

Note B. Walras' Theory of *Tâtonnement*[1]

Walras' theory of *tâtonnement* would seem to be one of his most imaginative and valuable contributions to economic analysis. This makes it all the more difficult to understand why it was neglected, misunderstood, and even disparaged for so many years.

There can be no mistaking the central role of this theory in Walras' argument. At each successive stage of this argument—beginning with an exchange economy, continuing with a simple production economy, and then going on to a production economy in which capital goods are transacted—Walras first shows how the additional complication he has just introduced does not affect the equality between the number of equations and the number of unknown prices. He then goes on to say: "In this way ... prices are determined mathematically. Now there remains only to show—and this is the essential point—that the problem

---

[1] Attached to Chapter III:3.

Except for its discussion of recontracting, this note was written substantially in its present form before the appearance of J. A. Schumpeter's authoritative critique of Walras in his *History of Economic Analysis* (New York, 1954), pp. 998–1026. On the main points of interpretation, as the reader will see, this note repeats Schumpeter's conclusions. There are, however, some significant differences which are duly pointed out.

Unless otherwise indicated, all references to Walras' *Eléments d'économie politique pure* are to the definitive edition (Paris, 1926) as translated and edited by W. Jaffé under the title *Elements of Pure Economics* (London, 1954). For convenience, this will be referred to henceforth as *Elements*.

of exchange for which we have just given a theoretical solution is the selfsame problem that is solved empirically on the market by the mechanism of free competition." At each stage Walras then follows this programmatic declaration with a clear and detailed description of the *tâtonnement* by which the market solves the system of equations relevant to his particular assumptions.[2] Indeed, the only stage of his argument at which he fails to provide such a detailed description is that which interests us most in this book: the stage at which he introduces the new good, fiat paper money, and the new price, the value of this money in terms of commodities.[3]

One question of importance for the history of doctrine is whether Walras made his theory of *tâtonnement* logically watertight by assuming the presence of recontracting.[4] If he did not make such an assumption, and if, accordingly, he visualized some purchases as being effected at the provisional prices "cried out," then he could not validly conclude that the *tâtonnement* necessarily brings the economy to that same set of prices yielded by a direct mathematical solution of the system of excess-demand equations. For, in the absence of recontract, the intermediary purchases which are carried out must affect the nature of the market excess-demand functions which determine the subsequent evolvement of the *tâtonnement*. In particular, the set of prices which prevails when the market is finally cleared depends on the time path of the *tâtonnement*

---

[2] The quotation is from *Elements*, pp. 162–63. Variations upon it—corresponding to the various stages of Walras' argument—appear on pp. 169, 241–42, and 282, respectively. The descriptions of the corresponding *tâtonnements* appear, accordingly, on pp. 169–72, 243–54 (which constitute Lesson 21), and 284–95 (which constitute Lesson 25), respectively.

It might be noted that Walras' theory of *tâtonnement* goes back to the very first edition (1874–77) of the *Eléments*; see *ibid.*, pp. 126–31, 251–57.

Goodwin (*op. cit.*, p. 5), basing himself on p. 106 of the *Elements*, says: "Walras disavowed in advance the use of this kind of market adjustment [i.e., the *tâtonnement*] as a practical device. ... He explicitly states that it is only a mathematical method of solution and not the practical one exemplified in the behavior of real markets." Actually, the passage on p. 106 says just the opposite—as do all the other passages just cited. Goodwin's statement must accordingly be rejected as a fundamental mis-interpretation of Walras' conceptual framework. Goodwin repeats this interpretation in his "Static and Dynamic Linear General Equilibrium Models" in *Input-Output Relations*, ed. The Netherlands Economic Institute (Leiden, 1953), pp. 59–60.

[3] See Note C:4 below.

[4] The term is, of course, Edgeworth's. See his *Mathematical Psychics* (London, 1881; reprinted 1953), pp. 17, 35 ff.; *Papers Relating to Political Economy* (London, 1925), Vol. II, pp. 311–12.

as a whole and will, therefore, not generally be the same for any two *tâtonnements*.

The general view of the contemporary literature has been that Walras did assume recontracting. Unfortunately, this view was until recently based on passages in the *Elements* which are—to say the least—not really explicit on the point in question.[5] Now, however, Jaffé and Schumpeter have independently supported this interpretation by citing the following apparently explicit passage, occurring in Walras' discussion of a production economy:

> [During the process of *tâtonnement*] ... entrepreneurs use *tickets* ["*bons*"] to represent the successive quantities of *products* which are first determined at random and then increased or decreased according as there is an excess of selling price over cost of production or vice versa, until selling price and cost are equal; and, on the other hand, ... landowners, workers and capitalists also use *tickets* to represent the successive quantities of *services* [which they offer] at prices first cried at random and then raised or lowered according as there is an excess of demand over offer or vice versa, until the two become equal.[6]

There can be no question that this passage describes a process of recontracting in which entrepreneurs and sellers of productive services merely note their offers to buy and sell on "tickets" and continuously revise these offers as the *tâtonnement* proceeds toward the equilibrium set of prices. But what can be questioned is whether Walras wrote this passage with full understanding of the analytical problem that called forth Edgeworth's device of recontracting. In particular, this problem exists for an exchange economy no less than for a production economy; yet Walras feels it necessary to introduce his tickets only in the latter case.

This distinction is made most clear in the sentences with which Walras precedes the foregoing passage. Here he writes:

[5] Cf. Kaldor, *op. cit.*, p. 126, who bases himself on *Elements*, pp. 169–70; and Hicks, *Value and Capital*, p. 128, who bases himself instead on *Elements*, pp. 83–84. It is worth noting that Hicks earlier considered this same passage to be "ambiguous," and gives no reason for his change of mind. ["Léon Walras," *Econometrica*, II (1934), 342, footnote 11.]

[6] *Elements*, ed. Jaffé, p. 242, italics and all but first set of brackets in translation. See Jaffé's illuminating explanation of the term "*bons*," *ibid.*, pp. 528–29, and note his statement that this device solves the "'problem of the path.'" On Schumpeter, see *History of Economic Analysis*, p. 1002.

... the process of *tâtonnement* in production entails a complication *which was not present* in the case of exchange. In exchange, [the total existing quantities of] commodities do not undergo any change. When a price is cried, and the effective demand and offer corresponding to this price are not equal, another price is cried for which there is another corresponding effective demand and offer. In production, productive services are transformed into products. After certain prices for services have been cried and certain quantities of products have been manufactured, if these prices and quantities are not the equilibrium prices and quantities, it will be necessary not only to cry new prices but also to manufacture revised quantities of products. In order to work out as rigorous a description of the process of *tâtonnement* in production as we did in exchange and yet take this additional circumstance into account, we have only to imagine, on the one hand, that entrepreneurs use *tickets* ...[7]

—and on into the preceding passage. It is also noteworthy that this passage does *not* make provision for consumers also to make use of tickets. Similarly, in the Preface to the fourth edition (1900) of the *Eléments*—in which the device of tickets was first used—Walras writes:

> In the theory of production, I no longer represented the preliminary *tâtonnement* toward equilibrium as it takes place effectively, but I assumed, instead, that it was done *by means of tickets* ["*sur bons*"] and then carried this fiction through the remainder of the book.[8]

All these passages make it clear that Walras was not fully aware of the logical necessity for recontracting. Instead, his reasoning seems to be that the *tâtonnement* in a production economy can affect the quantities of commodities produced for the market and hence their equilibrium prices, whereas in an exchange economy there is no danger of this since these quantities are fixed. There is no recognition of the fact that even in the latter economy the *tâtonnement* does not reach a unique set of prices unless recontracting takes place. Or, to put it in other words, Walras seems to forget that the given data of a production economy are not the quantities of commodities, but the quantities of productive services;[9] hence just as the *tâtonnement* does not affect the given data of

---

[7] *Elements*, p. 242, brackets in translation, but italics added. The term "groping" has been replaced by the original "*tâtonnement*."

[8] *Ibid.*, p. 37. First set of italics added, other italics and brackets in translation.
   In the second and third editions Walras made use of a somewhat different method of *tâtonnement*; see the relevant passage from these editions cited by Jaffé on pp. 582–83 of his edition.

[9] *Ibid.*, p. 238, line 4.

the exchange economy, so does it not affect those of the production economy. Hence there can be no difference between these two economies with respect to the logical necessity for assuming the existence of tickets in analyzing their workings.

Let us now assume recontract and turn to the problem of the convergence of the *tâtonnement*. Though recognizing the existence of this problem, Walras did not deal with it adequately. He realized that a *tâtonnement* on one price which brings it to equilibrium will generally, because of the interdependence of the system, disturb the equilibrium of other markets. But he argued that the direct pressure of excess demand in a given market definitely pushed its price toward its equilibrium level, while the changes in other prices "exerted indirect influences, some in the direction of equality and some in the opposite direction ... so that up to a certain point they cancelled each other out. Hence, the new system of prices ... is closer to equilibrium than the old system ... ; and it is only necessary to continue this process along the same lines for the system to move closer and closer to equilibrium."[10] The invalidity of this argument is sufficiently demonstrated by any of the divergent dynamic systems described in Mathematical Appendixes 3 and 9 above.

With the exception of Wicksell,[11] none of Walras' immediate successors carried the theory of *tâtonnement* beyond the point to which he himself had brought it. Writers such as Antonelli, Aupetit, and Osorio simply repeated his exposition.[12] Pareto, perhaps more than the others, realized the power and beauty of the theory.[13] He was also the only one who devoted attention to the problem of the convergence of the *tâtonnement*—though his attempt to show that this must always take place is actually invalid.[14] Fisher made no explicit reference to the

[10] *Ibid.*, p. 172. For similar passages, see pp. 251–53, 470.

[11] See Note E:1 below for a description of Wicksell's extension of the theory of *tâtonnement* (though without using the term) to the determination of the absolute price level.

[12] E. Antonelli, *Principes d'économie pure* (Paris, 1914); A. Aupetit, *Essai sur la théorie générale de la monnaie* (Paris, 1901); A. Osorio, *Théorie mathématique de l'échange*, trans. J. D'Almada (Paris, 1913).

[13] V. Pareto, *Cours d'économie politique* (Lausanne, 1896), Vol. I, pp. 24–25, 45–47, 61; *Manuel d'économie politique* (second ed.; Paris, 1927), pp. 232–34.

[14] This attempt is made in his *Cours*, Vol. I, p. 61, footnote 2. This footnote, with italics added, reads:

It would be desirable to demonstrate that, by these various adjustments,

process of *tâtonnement*; but he described the process implicitly—under ideal circumstances—through the hydrostatic mechanism which he used to illustrate his exposition.[15] On the other hand, Auspitz and Lieben,[16] Barone,[17] and Cassel[18] merely repeated Walras' demonstration of the equality between the number of equations and the number of unknown prices—without in any way indicating that one must also explain how the market solves these equations. And in this they set

---

the equilibrium position is always approached. For this it is observed that, *provided a sufficiently close value is taken*, these successive approximations approach closer and closer to the solution of the [market excess-demand] equations. ... We shall not develop this demonstration here, which would be useless for anyone not knowing mathematics, and which can be established very easily by anyone acquainted with the general theory of equations.

If this footnote refers to the successive approximations described in the text to which it is attached, then it is obviously wrong. For in his text Pareto clearly has in mind a Walrasian dynamic system like the one described in Mathematical Appendix 3:*b* above; and, as already emphasized, such a system need not converge to the equilibrium solution.

Pareto's error seems to have originated in the following way: In the note just cited he is tacitly considering the various systems of successive approximation (e.g., Newton's) which always converge to the solution of an equation, provided one starts with a value sufficiently close to this solution. That this is what Pareto had in mind is suggested by the phrase which has been italicized above. This conjecture is also supported by Pareto's reference to "the general theory of equations" at the end of his note. Thus Pareto was misled by his oversuggestive terminology into forgetting that the "successive approximations" provided by the normal operation of market forces are not necessarily those specified by the theory of equations; and that, consequently, the theorems of the latter may not be relevant to the analysis of the former.

I am indebted to my colleague of the Mathematics Department, Dr. Shmuel Agmon, for the foregoing interpretation of Pareto's footnote.

[15] Irving Fisher, *Mathematical Investigations in the Theory of Value and Prices* (1892; reprinted by the Yale University Press, 1925). The circumstances are ideal in that they must always lead to convergence. For a somewhat more explicit recognition of the process of *tâtonnement*, see *ibid.*, p. 55.

[16] R. Auspitz and R. Lieben, *Recherches sur la théorie du prix*, trans. L. Suret (Paris, 1914), Appendix IV. The original German work appeared in 1889.

[17] E. Barone, "The Ministry of Production in the Collectivist State," in *Collectivist Economic Planning*, ed. F. A. Hayek (London, 1935), pp. 247–51, 274. The original Italian article appeared in 1908.

[18] G. Cassel, *Theory of Social Economy*, trans. S. L. Barron (new rev. ed.; New York, 1932), Chapter IV. But in his *Nature and Necessity of Interest* (London, 1903), pp. 79–80, Cassel shows a full appreciation of the theory of *tâtonnement*—though without using the term, and without referring to Walras.

the pattern for the almost complete neglect of this fundamental question in the general-equilibrium literature of the interwar period.[19]

There can be no doubt that this neglect was abetted by the severe criticism to which the theory of *tâtonnement* was subjected by both economists and mathematicians. But in neither case have I succeeded in finding an understanding of the very real problem which Walras was trying to solve. Thus Edgeworth, in his oft-cited review of the second edition of Walras' *Eléments*, writes:

He diffuses over some thirty-five pages an idea which might have been adequately presented in a few paragraphs. For it is, after all, not a very good idea. What the author professes to demonstrate is the course which the higgling of the market takes—the path, as it were, by which the economic system works down to equilibrium. Now, as Jevons points out, the equations of exchange are of a statical, not a dynamical, character. They define a position of equilibrium, but they afford no information as to the path by which that point is reached. Prof. Walras' laboured lessons indicate *a* way, not *the* way of descent to equilibrium.[20]

Clearly, the third sentence of this citation is involved in a basic misconception; for Walras was primarily interested in describing, not the actual path to equilibrium, but the nature of the automatic forces which propel the economy along this path—be it what it may. Again, the penultimate sentence reveals a failure to realize that the *differences*

[19] Thus F. Divisia merely counts equations and unknowns [*Economique rationnelle* (Paris, 1927), Titre VI], and Hicks does the same (*Value and Capital*, Chapters IV, VIII, and XII, and their mathematical appendixes). The same is true for such standard works of the period as A. L. Bowley, *Mathematical Groundwork of Economics* (Oxford, 1924), pp. 20–22, 47–54; G. C. Evans, *Mathematical Introduction to Economics* (New York, 1930); and O. Weinberger, *Mathematische Volkswirtschafts-lehre* (Leipzig, 1930), pp. 94–106. H. L. Moore's *Synthetic Economics* (New York, 1929) is ambiguous. When counting equations, Moore makes no reference to the theory of *tâtonnement* (pp. 53, 100–106); but in other contexts he does (p. 152). The reader will also find it instructive to compare what E. H. Phelps Brown writes under the heading "The Solution of Equations and the Workings of the Market" with what Walras writes in similar contexts [*The Framework of the Pricing System* (London, 1936), pp. 83–90, 128–32].

A notable exception to this neglect is provided by O. Lange's stimulating use of the theory of *tâtonnement* to establish the feasibility of a socialist economy. See his *Economic Theory of Socialism* (Minneapolis, 1938), pp. 70–72, 89–90.

[20] *Nature*, XL (1889), 435, italics in original; cited by G. J. Stigler, *Production and Distribution Theories* (New York, 1941), p. 245. For Walras' reaction to the first sentence of the passage cited here, see *Elements*, p. 470.

See also Edgeworth's *Papers Relating to Political Economy*, Vol. II, p. 311.

between "statical" demand and supply functions can be used, as Walras did use them, to explain the motivating force of this movement. Finally, as Pareto pointed out, Walras' way may only be *a* way; but it is *the* way which represents the workings of economic phenomena.[21]

The mathematicians first criticized the facile assumption of many general-equilibrium economists[22] that equality between the number of equations and variables implies the existence of a unique solution, and then went on to demonstrate rigorously the conditions necessary for such uniqueness. Unfortunately, the foremost among them—Wald— implied that this demonstration with the "recondite methods of modern mathematics" was an *alternative* to Walras' theory of *tâtonnement*.[23] Neither Wald nor any of his contemporaries who proved the existence of a unique solution recognized that this theory dealt with a fundamental problem which they in their work ignored: namely, how did the *market* reach this solution?[24]

The reader may feel that the foregoing charge of neglect is too formalistic in its conception, and that discussions of the theory of *tâtonnement* can be found in the literature—though without use of the

[21] *Cours*, Vol. I, pp. 24–25.
It should also be clear that the attempts sometimes made to *contrast* Edgeworth's theory of recontracting with Walras' theory of *tâtonnement* are based on a fundamental misunderstanding. As emphasized above, the latter must be supplemented by the former in order to make it rigorous.

[22] But—as Jaffé has emphasized—not of Walras. Cf. *Elements*, pp. 108–9, 142, 200. In the last of these references Walras does, however, argue that multiple equilibria "are, in general, not possible" in the case of an economy with many commodities.

[23] A. Wald, "On Some Systems of Equations of Mathematical Economics," *Econometrica*, XIX (1951), 384–85 (trans. by O. Eckstein from the 1936 article). This is not to deny the validity of Wald's refutation of Walras' proof that the *tâtonnement* must converge; cf. above.
For an example of a writer who considers the possible existence of multiple solutions as constituting a refutation of the theory of *tâtonnement* itself, see G. Demaria, "Pareto," reprinted in *The Development of Economic Thought*, ed. H. W. Spiegel (New York, 1952), p. 639.

[24] In addition to the article by Wald just cited, see J. von Neumann, "A Model of General Economic Equilibrium," *Review of Economic Studies*, XIII (1945–46), 1–9 (trans. by O. Morgenstern from the 1938 article). See also the papers by K. Schlesinger and A. Wald in *Ergebnisse eines mathematischen Kolloquiums*, VI (1933–34), 10–20. Note in particular the concluding comment by K. Menger.
For a critical survey of this literature—as well as of the more recent contributions of K. J. Arrow, G. Debreu, and others—see R. E. Kuenne, *The Theory of General Economic Equilibrium* (Princeton, 1963) Chapter 9. See also Michio Morishima, "Existence of Solution to the Walrasian System of Capital Formation and Credit," *Zeitschrift für Nationalökonomie*, XX (1960), 238–43.

term and without reference to Walras.[25] In particular, he might claim that every discussion of the stability of equilibrium is *ipso facto* a discussion of the dynamics of a *tâtonnement*. But this is not so. First of all, there are certain stability discussions which are not even based on a dynamic analysis of the market; this, after all, is what Samuelson has so significantly and revealingly taught us about Hicks' discussion.[26] Second, even when these discussions are implicitly or explicitly based on such an analysis, it is not at all clear that the writers in question saw the analytical equivalence between the existence of stability, on the one hand, and the dynamic convergence of the *tâtonnement*, on the other. That is, it is not at all clear that they saw the equivalence between the statement "if the system is at its equilibrium position, then any arbitrary departure from this position generates dynamic market forces which bring it back," and the statement "no matter what the initial position from which the system starts, the dynamic workings of market forces bring it to its equilibrium position."

Only the slightest of nuances separates these two statements. Yet I would conjecture that an exhaustive study of the literature would show that this nuance generally blocked their full identification—and hence their full understanding. Before the reader rejects this conjecture as far-fetched, let him pause to consider the following thought-provoking facts: First, there is no evidence that Walras himself made this identification. He discusses stable and unstable equilibrium positions before he brings in his theory of *tâtonnement*;[27] conversely, once he brings in this theory, he never refers to this earlier discussion or even uses the term "stability."[28] Second, even Schumpeter, who at one point

---

[25] Cf. in this connection Pareto's comment that the "germ" of Walras' theory existed already in the familiar theoretical distinction between market and normal prices (*Cours*, Vol. I, p. 46, footnote).

[26] Samuelson, *Foundations*, p. 270. For Hicks' recognition of this criticism, see the second edition of *Value and Capital*, pp. 335–37.

[27] *Elements*, pp. 108–12. The first detailed presentation of the theory of *tâtonnement* appears on pp. 162 ff.; cf. above, footnote 2. True, on p. 106 there is a brief anticipation of this theory; but this makes it all the more significant that in his stability discussion a few pages later Walras does not refer back to it.

[28] This accords with yet another analytical characteristic of the *Elements*. Walras—like Marshall—never seems to have discussed unstable equilibrium except in a context of multiple equilibrium positions. In particular, the unstable position is almost always an intermediary one between two stable positions. There is no reference to the possibility that there may exist only one equilibrium position and that this may be unstable. Now, Walras recognizes the possibility of multiple equilibrium positions

explicitly identifies these two statements,[29] at other points implicitly distinguishes between them;[30] and—what is far more significant—at still other points mistakenly presents Hicks' nondynamic stability analysis as if it were relevant to Walras' dynamic theory of *tâtonnement*.[31] Finally, Samuelson himself—despite the fact that his path-breaking stability analysis is marked throughout by generous references to Walras—does not make explicit what seems to me to be the fundamental relation between his work and Walras': that his work ends the seventy-year analytical exile of Walras' theory of *tâtonnement*; that it constitutes the first significant development of this theory beyond Walras' pioneering presentation; that, in brief, it is the long-delayed, critical, and rigorous analysis of the necessary conditions under which Walras' *tâtonnement* will bring the economy to its equilibrium solution.[32]

---

only for the case of a two-commodity economy; he explicitly assumes it away for the case of a multicommodity one (*ibid.*, p. 200). At the same time, he develops his theory of *tâtonnement* only after he has already generalized the argument to such an economy. It is thus easy to imagine that this assumed impossibility of multiple equilibrium could have prevented Walras from thinking about his *tâtonnement* within the conceptual framework of his earlier discussion of stable and unstable equilibrium positions.

[29] *History of Economic Analysis*, p. 1002, footnote 8; p. 1007, footnote 22, first sentence. Note also that—as Schumpeter himself emphasizes—the distinction he later attempts to make is not relevant for our present discussion (*ibid.*, p. 1007, footnote 25).

[30] *Ibid.*, p. 1006, lines 7–10; p. 1008, bottom; p. 1014, lines 5–6.

[31] *Ibid.*, p. 1009, footnote 28; p. 1014, footnote 42.

[32] Samuelson, *Foundations*, Chapter IX—a slightly revised version of Samuelson's well-known 1941 *Econometrica* article.

As noted in Mathematical Appendix 3:*b*, however, Samuelson's work is restricted to stability in the small, whereas Walras' *tâtonnement* should be taken as referring to stability in the large. This latter question has been recently studied by Arrow, Block, and Hurwicz in their articles "On the Stability of the Competitive Equilibrium," *Econometrica*, XXVI (1958), 522–52 and XXVII (1959), 82–109. In the present context it is also interesting to note that these authors explicitly recognize the relationship of their work to Walras' *tâtonnement*; see in particular p. 106 of their 1959 article just cited.

The extensive literature which has grown up in recent years on the stability question has been usefully and critically surveyed by Takashi Negishi, "The Stability of a Competitive Economy: A Survey Article," *Econometrica*, XXX (1962), 635–69. See also p. 431, footnote 7 above for additional references.

Note C. Walras' Theory of Money[1]

1. INTRODUCTION

"But it is above all the theory of money which was entirely revised as a result of the studies on this question which I pursued from 1876 to 1899." With this prefatory remark to the definitive edition of his

[1] Attached to Chapters V:1 and VIII:1–3.

I am indebted to Professor William Jaffé for reading this study and giving me the benefit of his criticisms. These criticisms have convinced me that at least on one point I was not interpreting Walras properly (see p. 557, footnote 52). I have also noted some of the points of interpretation on which we have not been able to reach agreement.

This study is concerned primarily with Walras' pure theory of a fiat paper money. It makes only passing mention of his theory of a commodity-money, and completely leaves aside his theory of bimetallism. In brief, it attempts primarily to understand Lesson 29 and the first two sections of Lesson 30 in the definitive edition of the *Elements*.

The following bibliographical review provides the necessary background for this study: The first edition of Walras' *Eléments d'économie politique pure* appeared in two parts, in 1874 and 1877, respectively—with the first part including the chapters on monetary theory. This was followed by the *Théorie de la monnaie*, published originally in the *Revue scientifique* of April 10 and 17, 1886, and separately reprinted in that same year. The second and third editions of the *Eléments*—which are equivalent for our present purposes—then appeared in 1889 and 1896, respectively. In 1898 Walras revised and expanded his *Théorie de la monnaie*, added to it a "Note sur la 'Théorie de la quantité,'" and published it in his *Etudes d'économie politique appliquée*. On May 3, 1899, he read his memoir on "Equations de la circulation" before the Société Vaudoise des Sciences Naturelles. This was published the same year in the *Bulletin* of the Société (XXXV, 85–103). The new approach to monetary theory developed in

Eléments, Walras identified the major development that had taken place between the first and last editions of his basic work.[2]

Marget's well-known study makes it unnecessary to describe one phase of this development: the change from the transactions equation of the first edition to the cash-balance equation of the *Théorie de la monnaie* and later editions of the *Eléments*.[3] It is, however, clear that Walras considered as of at least equal importance the change that he introduced only in the last edition. In the words of the Preface to this edition:

In the first edition, this solution [of the problem of the value of money] was based on the concept of the "circulation to be cleared" ["*circulation à des-servir*"][4] which I had borrowed from the economists. Beginning with the second edition it was based on the concept of the "desired cash balance" ["*l'encaisse désirée*"],[5] of which I made use in my *Théorie de la monnaie*. However, in this second edition and in the third, as in the first, the equation

---

this memoir was then presented without significant change in the fourth and definitive editions of the *Eléments*, published in 1900 and 1926, respectively. For our purposes, these two editions are equivalent.

As indicated on p. 531, footnote 1, the abbreviation *Elements* will be used to designate Jaffé's translation of the definitive edition of the *Eléments* under the title *Elements of Pure Economics* (London, 1954).

[2] *Eléments d'économie politique pure (édition définitive)*, p. ix.

In the 1952 reprint of this edition (which is what I have used) the text reads "*qui a été entière-/ment modifiée*" (where the solidus indicates the end of a line). Professor Jaffé has pointed out to me the very interesting fact that in the fourth edition of the *Eléments* this clause appears in the much weaker form "*qui a été sensible-/ment modifiée*" and that in the definitive 1926 edition the space originally occupied by "*qui a été sensible-*" is just a blank. Therefore, Jaffé followed the fourth edition in his own translation.

Upon closer inspection, one can also see that the words "*été entière-*" have been inserted separately in the 1952 reprint of the definitive edition. Whether this change is one that was authorized by Walras or whether it was put in by a strange hand is something that we shall probably never know. But I cannot help feeling that it was authorized by Walras himself, correctly reevaluating the extent of the changes which he had made.

[3] A. W. Marget, "Léon Walras and the 'Cash-Balance Approach' to the Problem of the Value of Money," *Journal of Political Economy*, XXXIX (1931), 573–86.

However, for reasons made clear in the next section, I think it incorrect to identify Walras with the cash-balance *approach* in the accepted Cambridge sense of the term; for this reason I have referred here in the text only to the cash-balance *equation*.

[4] This is Jaffé's translation of the term (*op. cit.*, p. 38). Schumpeter translates it as "monetary requirements" of the economy (*History of Economic Analysis*, p. 1020). Cf. also Marget, "Léon Walras ... ," *op. cit.*, p. 575, footnote 14.

[5] This is again Jaffé's translation.

of the equality between the supply and the demand for money was always presented separately and empirically. In the present edition, it is deduced rationally from the budget restraint and from the equations of maximum utility [i.e., the marginal-utility conditions] at the same time as the equations of the equality between the supply and demand for circulating capital. In this way the *theory of circulation and of money*, like the *theories of exchange, of production, and of capitalization and credit*, comprises the positing and solving of a corresponding system of equations.[6]

The nature of Walras' distinction can be most easily appreciated by going back to the earlier works to which he refers. In the original version of the *Théorie de la monnaie* there had been no attempt to deduce the money equation from the principle of utility maximization. Instead, Walras had arbitrarily stated:

Without investigating the natural circumstances which may require land-owners, workers, capitalists, and entrepreneurs to hold, at a given moment, a cash balance of varying size in order to carry out purchases of varying sizes, we posit that, for simplicity, the value of this cash balance and of these purchases depends not only on the [objective] situation, but also on the character and habits of each individual. ... What must now be understood is that when a consumer or a producer requires to have in his possession a certain store [*provision*] of ... money, he is concerned not with the [nominal] quantity of this money—which as such is a matter of indifference to him—but solely with the quantity of other goods, commodities or services, that he will be able to obtain in exchange for his money. Let ... (A) then represent a commodity which is also the unit of account and the medium of exchange; let Q'_a be the existing quantity of this commodity; let α, β, γ, δ, ... represent the respective quantities of the commodities (A), (B), (C), (D), ... whose money value individuals require, at any given moment, to hold in the form of cash. The quantity of money Q''_a needed to satisfy these requirements is then

$$\alpha + \beta p_b + \gamma p_c + \delta p_d + \cdots$$

[6] *Eléments d'économie politique pure* (*édition définitive*), pp. ix–x, my own translation; Jaffé's translation of the last two sentences of this passage is incorrect.

I have translated Walras' "*équation d'échange*" as "budget restraint." This is the sense in which the term is used, *ibid.*, on pp. 251, 254, and 303. Note in particular the last reference, in which we find the same juxtaposition as in the Preface of "*l'équation de l'échange*" and "*les équations de satisfaction maxima.*" This parallelism is particularly significant in view of the fact that both the Preface and the material on p. 303 were newly written for the fourth edition. It explains why the term "*l'équation de l'échange*" is not used to describe the budget restraint in parts of the book carried over from earlier editions; cf., e.g., pp. 123 and 209–10.

[where p_b, p_c, p_d, ... are the respective prices of (B), (C), (D), ... in terms of (A)].[7]

As Marget has emphasized,[8] this demand function for money has precisely the same form as that presented in Keynes' familiar cash-balance equation $n = pk$.

It is readily seen that this passage deals only with the case of a money which also has normal commodity uses.[9] Correspondingly, the term "marginal utility of money" in the *Théorie de la monnaie* refers only to the utility of money as a commodity.[10] It must also be emphasized that Walras uses marginal-utility analysis in this work only *after* the preceding cash-balance equation is developed, and only for the purpose of demonstrating the validity of the quantity theory for a money which is also a commodity. Furthermore, this demonstration is restricted to the case where (1) the marginal utility of the money-commodity is inversely proportional to its quantity, and (2) the money value of the *encaisse désirée* is directly proportionate to the prices of other commodities.[11] We shall return to this point below.

The preceding passage is reproduced in the second and third editions of the *Eléments*—with one important change. Instead of referring to a commodity-money, it now refers to a fiat paper money.[12] Correspondingly, there is no resort to marginal-utility analysis at any point. In particular, the validity of the quantity theory is established directly from the cash-balance equation itself.[13] This absence

---

[7] *Théorie de la monnaie* (Paris, 1886), p. 13.

[8] "Léon Walras ... ," *op. cit.*, pp. 580 ff.

[9] Walras does, however, later discuss an economy in which both metallic and paper money exist (*Théorie de la monnaie*, p. 14). But note that in the version which appears in *Etudes d'économie politique appliquée* (Paris, 1898), this paper money becomes one against which a metallic reserve is held (pp. 98–100).

[10] Cf. also *ibid.*, p. 7, for a similar statement in an article written by Walras in 1884.

[11] *Théorie de la monnaie*, p. 13.

This second assumption actually contradicts Walras' cash-balance equation at the end of the preceding passage. In particular, it ignores the existence of the term α. Cf. footnote 14 below.

[12] The passage appears on pp. 377–78 of both editions. Another change in it—though one not significant for our present purposes—is that it generalizes the preceding demand function to include the *encaisse désirée* of producers and sellers of productive services, as well as of consumers.

[13] *Eléments* (2nd and 3rd eds.), p. 379.

of marginal-utility analysis also marks Walras' subsequent discussion of a commodity-money.[14]

Perhaps the most significant point added to these editions of the *Eléments* is the explicit relation between the *encaisse désirée* and the rate of interest. In Walras' own words:

> In a society where one holds money in cash from the moment when one receives it until the day when one gives it out in payment or lends it out, money renders few services, and those who hold it, producers or consumers, pointlessly lose [*perdent inutilement*] the interest on the capital which it represents.[15]

Furthermore, the cash-balance equation is solved in the market by a *tâtonnement* on the rate of interest.[16] We shall return to this question below.

There is no definite indication of the date on which Walras revised his *Théorie de la monnaie* for inclusion in his *Etudes d'économie politique appliquée* (1898). But it would seem to be sometime after the appearance of the third edition of the *Eléments* (1896). For the passage cited above from the original *Théorie de la monnaie*—which, as just pointed out, appears with few changes in this edition—is now extensively reformulated. In particular, considering again the case of a commodity (*A*) which also serves as money, Walras writes:

> When a landowner, worker, capitalist or entrepreneur desires to have in his possession, at a given moment, a certain store [*provision*] of ... money, it is evident that he is not concerned with the [nominal] quantity of this money, but only with the quantity of goods, commodities or services, *that he wants to buy with it*. In other words, the need one has for money is nothing but the need that one has for goods *that one will buy with this money*. This need is the need for storage [*besoin d'approvisionnement*];[17] it is satisfied at the cost of interest, and that is why the effective demand for money is a decreasing

---

[14] *Ibid.*, pp. 383–86.

Note that here Walras points out that the presence of the term *a* (which corresponds to the α of the *Théorie de la monnaie*) makes the monetary demand for money only *approximately* a rectangular hyperbola (p. 384). Cf. footnote 11 above.

[15] *Ibid.*, p. 382. Cf. also p. 380, lines 11–14.

[16] *Ibid.*, p. 381.

[17] This is Lange's translation. See his "Rate of Interest and the Optimum Propensity to Consume," *Economica*, V (1938), as reprinted in *Readings in Business Cycle Theory*, ed. G. Haberler (Philadelphia, 1944), p. 179, footnote 1.

The meaning of this phrase will be discussed in the next section.

function of the rate of interest. ... Let α, β, γ, δ, ... be the respective quantities of (A), (B), (C), (D), ... that consumers and producers *would like to buy at a given moment* in order to maintain their fixed and circulating capital at [a given interest] ... rate. Then the quantity of money

$$H_a = \alpha + \beta p_b + \gamma p_c + \delta p_d + \dots$$

would be the *encaisse désirée*.[18]

Finally, we point out that in the "Note sur la 'Théorie de la quantité' " appended to the revised version of the *Théorie de la monnaie*, Walras returns to the procedure of his original version and uses marginal-utility analysis to validate the quantity theory in the case of a money which is also a commodity.[19]

To summarize: In all his work before the fourth edition of the *Eléments*,[20] Walras merely posited his cash-balance equation on the basis of considerations which were extraneous to the main body of his argument. More specifically, in contrast with his analysis of every other good, Walras did not derive the demand function for money from utility maximization. Indeed, he made no use of marginal-utility analysis in his monetary theory except to deal with the case of a money which was also a commodity—and even here only *after* he had first posited the monetary equation. And in the second and third editions of the *Eléments* he did not even use it then.

2. THE CONCEPTUAL FRAMEWORK

Let us now see how all this was changed in the fourth edition. Here again Walras starts with the case of a fiat paper money. Now, however, for the first time, he analyzes the demand for such a money in terms of marginal utility. In particular, he speaks of the "service of storage" (*"service d'approvisionnement"*) which is provided by this money; describes the utility of these services in terms of ordinary utility functions; and derives the cash-balance equation from the maximization of these functions subject to the budget restraint.[21] This was the newly

---

[18] *Etudes d'économie politique appliquée*, pp. 94–95, italics added. Cf. also p. 154, line 5.

[19] *Ibid.*, pp. 153–58. This "Note" was definitely written between 1896 and 1898; see the reference to the former date in its first paragraph.

[20] Except, of course, for the memoir of 1899 referred to in footnote 1, p. 541 above.

[21] I was quite rightly taken to task a few years ago by W. Jaffé for carelessly

achieved integration of monetary theory and value theory which Walras acclaimed with such evident satisfaction in his Preface to this edition.[22]

Deferring the details of this derivation to the next section, let us first examine the crucial phrase "*service d'approvisionnement.*" What Walras seems to have had in mind—though we cannot be sure—is the following: The theories of exchange, production, and capital formation —Parts II–V of the *Elements*—are based on the provisional assumption that the economy is one of barter. Accordingly, its prices are all expressed in terms of one of the commodities, arbitrarily selected as the *numéraire*.[23] The equilibrium prices of this economy are then determined at the beginning of the period through a *tâtonnement* which makes use of tickets to enable recontract.[24] The production of the period is then carried out in accordance with these prices. At the end of the period entrepreneurs use the resulting produce to pay landowners, workers, and capitalists for the productive services they provided during the period. By the assumption of equilibrium, the total value of what entrepreneurs must pay is equal, and just equal, to the total value of what they have produced.

In Part VI of the *Elements* Walras drops the assumption that consumers—who are, of course, the sellers of productive services—must wait until the end of the production period to acquire commodities. Instead, once the *tâtonnement* is completed, he requires the sale of commodities to begin immediately. And this is what creates the need for consumers and producers to hold at the beginning of the period inventories of raw materials, finished commodities—and money. In Walras' own words:

Once equilibrium has been achieved in principle, upon completion of the preliminary *tâtonnement* by means of tickets, the actual transfer of services will begin immediately and will continue *in a given manner* during the whole period of time considered. The payment for these services, evaluated in *numéraire*, will be made in money *at fixed dates*. The delivery of the products

---

failing to see this in one of my earlier articles on this question. See his discussion in *Econometrica*, XIX (1951), 327.

[22] See the passages cited on pp. 541–43 above.

[23] The reader is reminded here of Marget's conclusive demonstration that Walras' "*numéraire*" is a concrete commodity and *not* an abstract unit of account ["Monetary Aspects of the Walrasian System," *Journal of Political Economy*, XLIII (1935), 172–79].

[24] Cf. Note B above, p. 533 in particular.

will also begin immediately and will continue *in a given manner* during the same period. And the payments for these products, evaluated in *numéraire*, will also be made in money *at fixed dates*. It is readily seen that the introduction of these conditions makes it necessary, first, so far as consumers are concerned, that they have on hand a fund of circulating or working capital consisting of: (1) certain quantities of final products ...; and (2) a certain quantity of cash on hand. ...

In a real operating economy, every consumer, whether landowner, labourer, or capitalist, has at every moment a fairly exact idea of: (1) what stocks of [final] products he ought to have for his convenience and (2) what cash balances he ought to have ... in order to replenish these stocks and make current purchases of consumers' goods and services for daily consumption while waiting to receive rents, wages, and interest payable *at fixed future dates*. ... There may be a small element of uncertainty which is due solely to the difficulty of foreseeing possible changes in the data of the problem. If, however, we suppose these data constant for a given period of time and if we suppose the prices of goods and services and also the dates of their purchase and sale to be known for the whole period, *there will be no occasion for uncertainty*.[25]

We note first that Walras has not really succeeded in providing a rationale for the holding of money. For, as the italicized phrases of the preceding passage show, the individuals of his economy know with certainty the exact amounts they must make and receive in payments, and the exact dates on which these payments must take place. Hence there is no reason why they should hold sterile cash balance during the intervening dates when they can instead hold interest-yielding assets. This, of course, is Hicks' well-known criticism of Walras.[26] But it is not at all a vital one. For, as Marget has pointed out, "even in a world in which everything were perfectly foreseen, a lack of synchronization between the receipt of income and its outlay would give rise to a need for cash-balances so long as there are not perfect facilities for the borrowing of money in anticipation of receipts and the investment of

---

[25] *Elements*, ed. Jaffé, pp. 316–17, with a few minor modifications and italics added. Cf. also *ibid.*, p. 242.

The foregoing interpretation of these paragraphs follows Schumpeter, *History of Economic Analysis*, p. 1021. It is also supported by A. Aupetit's exposition of Walras' monetary theory in his *Essai sur la théorie générale de la monnaie* (Paris, 1901), pp. 121–26.

[26] "Gleichgewicht und Konjunctur," *Zeitschrift für Nationalökonomie*, IV (1933), 446–48. Cf. also R. E. Kuenne, "Walras, Leontief, and the Interdependence of Economic Activities," *Quarterly Journal of Economics*, LXVIII (1954), 327–29.

money during the period elapsing between receipt and outlay."[27] The precise way in which such imperfections can be introduced into the analysis has been shown in Chapters V–VII, above.[28]

What is, however, of far greater significance is the clear evidence of the preceding passages that Walras was *not* an exponent of the cash-balance approach to monetary theory in the accepted sense of the term. For the essence of this approach is that the individual chooses to hold money as a *reserve* against possible discrepancies between payments and receipts, and against all sorts of other contingencies.[29] For Walras, however, the individual holds money, not out of choice, but out of necessity: he plans to buy a given quantity of goods; for some reason, though, he cannot buy it now but only at a fixed date in the future; consequently, he is compelled by the force of circumstances to hold his money in "storage" until then. At no point in the protracted development of his theory of the *encaisse désirée*—not in its first formulation in the *Théorie de la monnaie* in 1886, nor in its revision in the *Etudes d'économie politique appliquée* in 1898, nor in its definitive statement in the *Eléments* of 1900—does Walras even hint that he is thinking in terms of a monetary reserve.[30] Thus, although Walras must definitely be credited with having presented a cash-balance *equation*, he cannot be credited with having presented a cash-balance *theory*.[31]

An immediate corollary of the two preceding paragraphs is the conclusion that Walras does not succeed in providing a conceptual

[27] "Monetary Aspects of the Walrasian System," *op. cit.*, pp. 160–61.

[28] It should be emphasized that the approach of Chapters V and VI can be introduced into Walras' analysis without calling for a change in any other part of Walras' logical structure. On the other hand, because of its implications for the budget restraint, the penalty-cost approach of Chapter VII does require such changes.

[29] Cf., e g., the references to Marshall, Pigou, Lavington, Robertson, and Mises in Note D below, and to Wicksell in Note E:1.

[30] See the phrases italicized in the preceding passage and in the passage from *Etudes d'économie politique appliquée* cited on pp. 545–46.

This is the reason I find Lange's rendition of "*service d'approvisionnement*" as "service of storage" preferable to Jaffé's rendition as "service of availability" (*Elements*, p. 315). The latter carries with it too much of a connotation of "available as a reserve."

[31] This would seem to disagree with Marget's interpretation in his "Léon Walras and the 'Cash-Balance Approach' to the Problem of the Value of Money," *op. cit.* Note, however, that Marget does not discuss the question just emphasized in the text and concentrates primarily on the cash-balance equation as such. On the nature of this equation, see the passages from the *Théorie de la monnaie* cited in the preceding section.

framework which logically entitles him to introduce the *service d'appro-visionnement* of money into the utility function. Or, to put it the other way around, the conceptual framework which Walras does provide can actually explain the holding of money without such a procedure. As in Chapter VII above, the very structure of the economy makes the individual willing to maintain these holdings even though he derives no direct utility from them; for these holdings are necessary if the individual is to acquire an optimum collection of commodities.[32]

In sum, Walras was so anxious to force his monetary theory into the mold of his formal utility analysis that he paid insufficient attention to the details necessary to make this analysis economically meaningful. This impression can only be strengthened by his even more mechanical application of this analysis to the theory of saving. Here, as in the case of money, Walras announced in the Preface to the fourth edition of the *Eléments* that he would no longer simply posit behavior functions "empirically," but would instead derive them "rationally" from utility analysis. But he then proceeded to do this by defining a new good, the perpetuity; mechanically inserting this good into the utility function; and then maximizing the resulting function subject to the budget restraint. Once again there is not even an attempt to explain the economic meaning of such a utility function.[33, 34]

[32] Cf. pp. 146–47 above. Cf. also Kuenne, "Walras, Leontief, and the Interdependence of Economic Activities," p. 332, who makes much the same criticism of Walras.

[33] Clearly, it is possible to provide such an explanation. Thus, for example, perpetuities might be taken as representing the future commodities for which they can be exchanged [cf. Jaffé's "Léon Walras' Theory of Capital Accumulation," *Studies in Mathematical Economics and Econometrics* (Chicago, 1942), p. 44]. Indeed, in the second and third editions of *Eléments* (p. 271) Walras does say that in order to derive the savings function mathematically, it is necessary "to distinguish between *present* utility and *future* utility"; but this sentence disappears in the fourth edition. Jaffé tries to rationalize this by arguing that since Walras' theoretical structure is "a cross-section in time of the processes involving exchange, production, capital accumulation, and circulating media, it would have been irrelevant for Walras to include any function of a lapse of time explicitly" ("Léon Walras' Theory of Capital Accumulation," *op. cit.*, p. 43). But all this is irrelevant to our main point that in the fourth edition Walras does not feel it necessary to offer *any* economic explanation of his utility function and proceeds in a completely mechanical way.

Cf. *Elements*, ed. Jaffé, p. 45, footnote 2, and p. 275. Jaffé quotes the relevant passages from the second and third editions, *ibid.*, p. 587, and also cites some interesting correspondence on this point between Walras, on the one hand, and Bortkiewicz and Böhm-Bawerk, on the other.

[34] The deficiency in Walras' conceptual framework set forth in this section makes

3. THE UTILITY ANALYSIS

Leaving these problems behind, let us—for the sake of argument—accept Walras' insertion of the *service d'approvisionnement* into the utility function and see how his analysis proceeds from that point on. Let us also adapt this analysis to the case of an exchange economy. This does not affect the essentials of Walras' argument, yet does enable us to examine its validity under simplified circumstances. Clearly, whatever analytical difficulties we shall uncover under these circumstances will exist *a fortiori* in the more complicated ones actually considered by Walras.

Walras' point of departure is that an individual's demand for cash balances is a special case of his demand to hold inventories of goods, and that the *services d'approvisionnement* of these inventories are related to the goods themselves just as productive services are related to the capital goods which generate them. That is, inventories are circulating capital, to be analyzed in a manner completely analogous to that used for fixed capital. Hence if (A), (B), (C), ... are commodities and 1, p_b, p_c, ... their prices in terms of the *numéraire* (A), and if (A'), (B'), (C'), ... are these same commodities considered as circulating capital rendering a *service d'approvisionnement* "in the larders and cupboards of consumers," then the prices of these services are $p_{a'} = i$, $p_{b'} = p_b i$, $p_{c'} = p_c i$, ... (where i is the rate of interest) just as the net prices of ordinary productive services are equal to the value of the capital good rendering this service multiplied by the rate of interest.[35] Similarly, (U) is fiat paper money "having a price of its own [in terms of (A)] p_u, and a price for its *service d'approvisionnement* $p_{u'} = p_u i$."[36] Finally, there are the perpetuities (E), whose price in terms of (A) is $p_e = 1/i$. Walras

---

clear the dangers of relating Walras' H_α to the Cambridge K. In particular, it calls for a reexamination of Marget's view that Walras' *encaisse désirée* H_α indicates a full appreciation on his part of the problem of the velocity of circulation. ("Léon Walras ... ," *op. cit.*, pp. 590 ff.)

[35] *Elements*, ed. Jaffé, p. 319. This should be read against the background of *ibid.*, pp. 267–72. See also pp. 42–43.

[36] *Ibid.*, p. 320. See also p. 325, second paragraph. This distinction between the two prices of money is another point on which I erred grievously some years ago, and for which I was rightly criticized by Jaffé. Cf. above, p. 546, footnote 21.

It should be clear that p_u is analogous to the reciprocal of the absolute price level.

also makes use of the symbol (E'), but does *not* define $p_{e'}$, which, by analogy, should equal $p_e i = 1$.

For simplicity we shall omit Walras' analysis of the demand for (A'), (B'), ... and concentrate exclusively on his analysis of the demand for (U). Consider, then, an individual with certain initial endowments of goods, and, in particular, with the initial endowment of money q_u. Let his excess demands for the goods (A), (B), ... , (E) be represented by d_a, d_b, ... , d_e, respectively; and his excess supplies of productive services by o_t, o_p, o_k, ... The respective prices of these services are p_t, p_p, p_k, ... The individual's budget restraint is then

(1) $\quad o_t p_t + o_p p_p + o_k p_k + \cdots + o_u p_{u'} = d_a + d_b p_b + \cdots + d_e p_e,$

where the left-hand side gives us the income of the individual, and the right-hand side his expenditure.[37]

The individual's optimum values for o_t, o_p, o_k, ... , d_a, d_b, ... , d_e are assumed to be determined as in the earlier chapters on the theory of exchange, production, and capitalization. Walras turns, then, to the remaining variable, o_u, and states:

Finally, as regards money, let $r = \phi_\alpha(q)$, $r = \phi_\beta(q)$, ... , $r = \phi_\epsilon(q)$ be our individual's utility or want equations for the *services d'approvisionnement* of products (A'), (B'), ... and perpetual net income (E'), not *in kind*, but *in money*. The quantities α, β, ... , ε, positive or negative, of these services which he desires at the prices $p_{a'}$, $p_{b'}$ ... will be determined at one and the same time by the budget restraint and by the following equations of maximum satisfaction:

$$\begin{aligned}
\phi_\alpha(\alpha) &= p_{a'}\phi_a(d_a), \\
(2) \qquad \phi_\beta(\beta) &= p_{b'}\phi_a(d_a), \\
&\cdots\cdots\cdots\cdots\cdots \\
\phi_\epsilon(\varepsilon) &= p_{a'}\phi_a(d_a),
\end{aligned}$$

from which we obtain first, the quantities desired of the services (A'), (B'), ... , (E') [in the form of money][38]

---

[37] This is the first equation on p. 320 of the *Elements* (ed. Jaffé) with the terms representing circulating capital other than money omitted for simplicity. The term $o_u p_{u'}$ will be explained below.

This, and what follows, must be read against the background of Walras' earlier argument on pp. 237 ff., 274 ff., and 287 ff. of the *Elements*.

[38] The argument $p_{m'}$ related to circulating capital has been omitted from the following equations. See the preceding footnote.

$$\alpha = f_\alpha(p_t, p_p, p_k \ldots p_b, p_c, p_d \ldots p_{a'}, p_{b'}, \ldots p_{u'}, p_e),$$

(3) $\quad \beta = f_\beta(p_t, p_p, p_k \ldots p_b, p_c, p_d \ldots p_{a'}, p_{b'}, \ldots p_{u'}, p_e),$

$$\ldots\ldots\ldots\ldots\ldots\ldots\ldots\ldots\ldots\ldots\ldots\ldots\ldots\ldots\ldots\ldots\ldots\ldots$$

$$\varepsilon = f_\varepsilon(p_t, p_p, p_k \ldots p_b, p_c, p_d \ldots p_{a'}, p_{b'}, \ldots p_{u'}, p_e),$$

secondly, the value of these quantities expressed in terms of *numéraire*

(4) $\qquad\qquad \alpha p_{a'} + \beta p_{b'}, + \cdots + \varepsilon p_{a'},$

and finally the quantity of money effectively offered

(5) $\qquad\qquad o_u = q_u - \dfrac{\alpha p_{a'} + \beta p_{b'} + \cdots + \varepsilon p_{a'}}{p_{u'}}.$

In a similar manner we could derive the quantities effectively offered by the other individuals and, consequently, the total effective offer of money

(6) $\qquad\qquad O_u = Q_u - \dfrac{d_\alpha p_{a'} + d_\beta p_{b'} + \cdots + d_\varepsilon p_{a'}}{p_{u'}}$

[where O_u, Q_u, d_α, d_β, ... , d_ε are the respective aggregates over all individuals of o_u, q_u, α, β, ... , ε].

The value of all or part of the final products and perpetual net income *which individuals wish to purchase*, and which they desire to keep in their possession in the form of money [earmarked] for transactions or investment [purposes],[39] constitutes their *encaisse désirée*.[40]

[39] " *Monnaie de circulation ou d'épargne.*" I have followed Schumpeter's translation (*History of Economic Analysis*, p. 1000, footnote 5, and p. 1023, lines 6–8). Jaffé renders this expression as "cash or money savings."

[40] *Elements*, ed. Jaffé, pp. 320–21, with equation numbers and last set of italics added, and with the change in translation noted in the preceding footnote. I have also added all the bracketed expressions except the first, which is Jaffé's.

In the original version of this passage in the memoir on "Equations de la circulation" (*op. cit.*, pp. 90–91), Walras does not mention (E') and ε in the first paragraph, omits accordingly the last equations of (2) and (3) and the last term of (4), but nevertheless writes (5) and (6) in the form presented here, with the following additional explanation:

[In equations (5) and (6) $\varepsilon p_{a'}$ and $d_\varepsilon p_{a'}$ are the value in *numéraire* of the service of the money [earmarked] *for investment* [purposes] [*épargne*], individual or total, just as $\alpha p_{a'} + \beta p_{b'} + \cdots$ and $d_\alpha p_{a'} + d_\beta p_{b'} + \cdots$ are the value in *numéraire* of the service of the money [earmarked] *for transactions* [*purposes*], individual or total, and $\dfrac{\varepsilon p_{a'}}{p_{u'}}$ and $\dfrac{d_\varepsilon p_{a'}}{p_{u'}}$ are the equivalents in money (U) of the quantities ε and d_ε of *numéraire* (A), just as $\dfrac{\alpha p_{a'} + \beta p_{b'} + \cdots}{p_{u'}}$ and $\dfrac{d_\alpha p_{a'} + d_\beta p_{b'} + \cdots}{p_{u'}}$ are the equivalents in money (U) of the quantities

The phrase "*which individuals wish to purchase*"—which should be read together with the corresponding phrases of the revised *Théorie de la monnaie*[41]—reminds us that Walras conceives of the demand for money as being broken up into a differentiated mass whose component parts are conceptually earmarked for the respective quantities of commodities which the individual plans to buy.[42] Accordingly, Walras represents the utility of the *service d'approvisionnement* of money, not by a single

---

$\alpha, \beta, \ldots$ and $d_\alpha, d_\beta, \ldots$ of $(A'), (B'), \ldots$. In effect, individuals wish to have in their possession the value of all or part of the new capital [goods that they want to buy], fixed or circulating, just like the value of all or part of the consumers' goods that they want to buy, the sum total constituting their *encaisse désirée*.

It might also be noted that in this memoir the last argument in the functions on the right-hand side of (3) is written as i, instead of its reciprocal, p_e, which appears here in the *Elements*.

[41] Cf. above, pp. 545–46.

[42] Note, however, a curious asymmetry in Walras' procedure. Whereas $\alpha, \beta, \ldots$ are conceived as quantities of $(A'), (B'), \ldots$, ε is conceived not as a quantity of (E'), but of (A). This is clear from the passage of "Equations de la circulation" cited in footnote 40. Walras may have adopted this asymmetry in order to achieve a symmetrical form for his equations (2) and (4)–(6); for if ε is a quantity of (E'), the last equation of (2) must be written as

$$\phi_\varepsilon(\varepsilon) = \phi_a(d_a),$$

the last term of (4) as $+\varepsilon$, and, accordingly, the last terms in the numerators of the fractions in (5) and (6) as $+\varepsilon$ and $+d_\varepsilon$, respectively. That is, in each case the factor $p_{a'}$ which Walras now uses must be replaced by $p_{e'} = p_e i = 1$. See also the two paragraphs which follow now in the text.

I must, however, admit that as a result of Professor Jaffé's criticisms (see above, p. 541, footnote 1), I am not as sure as I originally was that Walras is guilty here of an asymmetry. Basing his argument especially on pp. 289–90 of the *Elements*, Jaffé has —in a personal letter—emphasized that Walras considers perpetuities, (E), only as an "imaginary" analytical construct (*ibid.*, p. 274) without "real" existence in his system. Correspondingly, individuals are assumed to use their savings to buy capital goods directly, and not perpetuities. (This is also borne out by the end of the passage from "Equations de la circulation" cited in footnote 40 above.) Hence, Jaffé argues, "(E') cannot properly be conceived as a quantity of money held available for the eventual purchase of such securities. This money is held in lieu of and available for the eventual purchase of real capital goods only; and all we can say is that the purchase of such real capital goods is tantamount to, but does not consist in, the purchase of as many units of the *imaginary* commodity (E) as there are units of the *numéraire* (A) which the capital goods will yield net of depreciation, etc."

The reason that I am not fully satisfied with this explanation is that if (E) is "real" enough to be treated like any other commodity with respect to having its own marginal-utility function and appearing in the budget restraint (*ibid.*, pp. 274–75), why should it not also be "real" enough to be treated like any other commodity with

function, but by a sequence of functions of these respective quantities. Note that in this way he also effectively expresses utility as a function of the *real*—as distinct from *nominal*—amount of money the individual holds. This is in keeping with his repeated emphasis that it is only with the former that the individual is concerned.[43]

Clearly, the whole purpose of Walras' rather complicated procedure is to reduce the problem of monetary theory to that of simply introducing into the ordinary theory of consumers' behavior some additional "commodities" (A'), (B'), ... with their respective prices $p_{a'}$, $p_{b'}$, ... Correspondingly, the optimum amounts of these "commodities" are determined by equations of exactly the same form as those presented for this theory in the earlier parts of the *Elements*. In particular, the "equations of maximum satisfaction" (2) show that the marginal utilities of the optimum quantities α, β, ... —like those of the optimum quantities of all other commodities—are proportionate to their respective prices, and that the factor of proportionality is the marginal utility of the *numéraire* (A).[44]

In fact, it seems to me that had not Walras adhered so unswervingly to the exact equational forms of his earlier exposition, he could have presented the optimum conditions of his monetary theory in a more persuasive and meaningful way. Specifically, let us rewrite (2) as

$$(7) \qquad \phi_\alpha(\alpha) = \frac{\phi_\beta(\beta)}{p_b} = \frac{\phi_\gamma(\gamma)}{p_c} = \cdots = i\phi_a(d_a).$$

Since all prices are in terms of (A), the reciprocal of p_b is the number of units of (B) that can be obtained for one unit of (A). The preceding equations thus state that a necessary condition for the maximization of utility is that the marginal utility of one unit of real balances held for purchasing power over (A) *equal* the marginal utility of one unit of real balances held for purchasing power over (B), etc., *equal* the common term $i\phi_a(d_a)$. Considering, first, all but the last of these equations, we

---

respect to having its own conceptual *service d'approvisionnement*? Why does Walras draw the line where he does?

It is hard to see how this question can be definitively settled. Fortunately, it is not important for the problems which interest us in this study.

[43] See the passages from the first and second editions of the *Théorie de la monnaie* cited on pp. 543–44 and 545–46 above.

[44] More generally, compare equations (1)–(3) here with the corresponding equations on p. 165, or pp. 238–39, or pp. 278–79 of the *Elements*.

see that, in the individual's optimum position, we can disregard all conceptual earmarkings and speak unambiguously of *the* marginal utility of real money balances. If we now note that $\phi_a(d_a)$ can be regarded as the marginal utility of one unit-of-(A)'s worth of expenditure, we then see that the last of equations (7) reduces to the simple statement that, in the individual's optimum position, the marginal utility of one unit-of-(A)'s worth of real balances must equal the marginal utility of i units-of-(A)'s worth of expenditure.[45] In this way Walras could have rigorously and precisely derived the general relationship between the demand for money and the rate of interest which he had emphasized in the second and third editions of the *Eléments* and in the revised version of the *Théorie de la monnaie*.[46]

Indeed, it is possible that Walras' failure to emphasize this relationship in the definitive edition of the *Elements*—it is adverted to only once, and even then not in his discussion of monetary theory proper[47] —may be connected with his failure to present his "equations of maximum satisfaction" in the form (7). On the other hand, Walras may have considered this relationship to be already expressed in his definition of the price of the *service d'approvisionnement* of money as $p_{u'} = p_u i$, and in his observation that, for money also the *numéraire*, this reduces to $p_{u'} = i$.[48]

Be that as it may, we note now that by dividing Walras' equation (4) through by i we obtain

$$(8) \qquad\qquad \alpha + \beta p_b + \cdots + \varepsilon.$$

This measures the total demand for real money balances in terms of the *numéraire* (A). Clearly, function (8) is the same cash-balance function which Walras first posited in his *Théorie de la monnaie* and then repeated in earlier editions of the *Eléments*.[49] And so Walras makes good his claim to have succeeded in deriving this function from the same utility analysis that he applies to all other problems in the theory of consumers' behavior.[50]

---

[45] Note that, except for its neglect of the time element, this is identical with equation (4) on p. 91 above.

[46] Cf. the passages cited on pp. 545–46 above.

[47] *Elements*, ed. Jaffé, p. 242, lines 7 to 5 from bottom.

[48] *Ibid.*, p. 320 (top).

[49] Cf. pp. 543–44 and 546 above.

[50] Cf. the passages from the Preface to the fourth edition of the *Elements* cited on pp. 542–43 above.

The real demand, (8), can be transformed into the nominal demand for units of paper money by dividing through by p_u—which is analogous, in the more familiar version of the cash-balance equation, to multiplying KT by the absolute price level, P. This is essentially what Walras does in his equation (5).[51] In particular, substituting $p_a i = p_{a'}$, $p_b i = p_{b'}, \ldots, p_u i = p_{u'}$, this reduces to

$$(9) \qquad o_u = q_u - \frac{\alpha + \beta p_b + \cdots + \varepsilon}{p_u}.$$

That is, o_u is the difference between the initial and optimum values of nominal money holdings. From the budget restraint (1) we can then infer that Walras conceives this difference as being invested in new capital goods to provide a yield equal to the rate of interest i, and, therefore, as contributing (in terms of *numéraire*) $o_u p_{u'}$ to the individual's income.[52]

Walras concludes this phase of his analysis by deriving from (6) the

[51] That this is his intention is even clearer from the passage in "Equations de la circulation" cited on p. 553, footnote 40, above.

[52] This is also the way I understand the terms in the budget restraint on p. 320 of the *Elements* which deal with circulating capital. These terms—which have for simplicity been omitted from our discussion (above, p. 552, footnote 37)—are $o_{a'} p_{a'} + o_{b'} p_{b'} + \cdots + q_m p_{m'}$. They would seem to represent the interest (in terms of *numéraire*) that can be earned by investing the value of the excess circulating capital $o_{a'}, o_{b'}, \ldots$ in new capital goods.

The sentence in the text to which this footnote is attached has also been changed as a result of the criticism by Professor Jaffé already noted above (p. 554, footnote 42). In its superseded version this sentence assumed the entire excess supply of money, o_u, to be invested—in Keynesian fashion—in the purchase of perpetuities. I am indebted to Jaffé for bringing this misinterpretation to my attention. [Cf., however, Kuenne's recent study of Walras, which argues—in a manner closer to the superseded sentence—that the term $o_u p_{u'}$ represents "the amount earned in current income by purchasing promissory notes" (*Theory of General Economic Equilibrium*, p. 317, footnote 52).]

Professor Jaffé informs me that he would now prefer to omit all mention of "securities" in his note 7 on pp. 542–43 of the *Elements*. Similarly, in the next to the last line of that note, he would now prefer to consider the source of the net income to be "new capital goods," and not "loans."

At the same time, I am unable to accept Jaffé's interpretation of $o_{b'} p_{b'}$ and, by implication, $o_u p_{u'}$, as given in his note 7; for Jaffé treats this as an income item even when this excess supply is used to purchase consumption goods.

It might also be pointed out that equations (8) and (9) in the text here are presented in Jaffé's (*ibid.*, pp. 543–44) and Kuenne's ("Walras, Leontief, and the Interdependence of Economic Activities," *op. cit.*, p. 335) interpretations of Walras' monetary theory as well.

market excess-supply equation for money

$$(10) \qquad Q_u - \frac{d_\alpha p_{a'} + d_\beta p_{b'} + \cdots + d_\varepsilon p_{a'}}{p_{u'}} = 0,$$

and demonstrating that the introduction of money into his model has not affected the equality between the number of equations and variables. Hence the problem is mathematically determinate.[53]

4. THE *Tâtonnement*

"Our next step is to pass from the theoretical solution which was formulated mathematically to the practical solution which is reached in the market."[54] With this standard formula[55] Walras opens his discussion of the *tâtonnement* by which an economy with paper money reaches the equilibrium solution of its system of market excess-demand equations—among which now appears (10). This is for us the most crucial—and, at the same time, most obscure—part of Walras' monetary theory.

Walras conducts this whole discussion against the explicit background of the detailed description of the *tâtonnement* presented in his earlier chapter on production and capital formation. He shows how, except for equation (10) above, all of the new equations introduced by his theory of circulation and money can be fitted into the various subsets of this earlier system of equations and solved together with them. In Walras' own words:

Only ... equation (10) expressing the equality between the demand and offer of (*U*) remain[s] outside [this solution].[56] Consequently, if a price $p'_{u'}$ is cried at random and is held fixed during the process of *tâtonnement* in production

---

[53] *Elements*, pp. 323–24.

The reader should recall that we are adapting Walras' analysis to an exchange economy. The foregoing equation is accordingly obtained from Walras' equation (10) (*ibid.*, p. 323) by setting the left-hand side identically equal to zero, and by substituting into the right-hand side from Walras' equation (9) on p. 321.

Clearly, just as equation (5) can be transformed into (9), so equation (10) can be transformed into

$$Q_u - \frac{d_\alpha p_a + d_\beta p_b + \cdots + d_\varepsilon p_a}{p_u} = 0.$$

[54] *Ibid.*, p. 325.
[55] See the beginning of Note B above.
[56] Jaffé's brackets.

and capital formation, we come to the last equation from which the equality between the price of the *numéraire* and unity is deducted at the same time as the equality between the demand and offer of the *numéraire*,[57] so that there remains only to solve ... [equation (10) above].[58] If we set[59]

(11) $$d_\alpha p_{a'} + d_\beta p_{b'} + \cdots + d_\varepsilon p_{a'} = H_\alpha,$$

then [equation (10)][60] becomes

(12) $$Q_u = \frac{H_\alpha}{p_{u'}}.$$

... if perchance

(13) $$Q_u p'_{u'} = H_\alpha,$$

the question [of the *tâtonnement*][60] would be completely settled. Generally, however, we find that

(14) $$Q_u p'_{u'} \gtrless H_\alpha,$$

and the problem is to determine how equality between the demand and offer of money is reached by a *tâtonnement* [involving an adjustment][60] in $p'_{u'}$.

On referring back to the various terms that enter into the composition of H_α, we perceive that they are not absolutely independent of $p_{u'}$, in view of the fact that $p_{u'}$ figures in the term $o_u p_{u'}$ of the budget restraint [(1)][60] which, together with the equations of maximum satisfaction [(2)],[60] enables us to deduce the quantities α, β, ... , ε for any one individual, and, consequently, the aggregate quantities d_α, d_β, ... , d_ε for all individuals together; but [we perceive][60] that, nevertheless, they do not depend upon it [$p_{u'}$][60] except very indirectly and very weakly.[61] That being the case, the equation of monetary

---

[57] This is essentially a statement of Walras' Law; the full meaning of this passage can be grasped only by reading it against the background of p. 294 of the *Elements*, section 259.

The reader must also remember that the *numéraire* referred to here is commodity (*A*), and *not* paper money (*U*).

[58] My own brackets.

[59] Once again, I am modifying this passage in a nonessential way in order to adapt it to an exchange economy.

[60] My own brackets.

The reader will recall that $p'_{u'}$ is the value of $p_{u'}$ arbitrarily chosen at the beginning of this passage and held fixed until now.

[61] This clause—which, as we shall see below, is crucial for a proper interpretation of Walras—appears in the original as "*mais que, toutefois, ils n'en dépendent que très indirectement et très faiblement.*" [*Eléments* (édition définitive), p. 311]. Jaffé renders this as a separate sentence which reads: "We must admit, however, that the dependence of these items on $p_{u'}$ is very indirect and very weak." This creates the misleading impression that Walras regards a "*strong* dependence" on $p_{u'}$ as the most favorable

circulation, when money is not a commodity, comes very close, in reality, to falling outside the system of equations of [general][62] economic equilibrium. If we first suppose [general][62] economic equilibrium to be established, then the equation of monetary circulation would be solved almost without any *tâtonnement*, simply by raising or lowering $p_{u'}$ according as[63] $Q_u \gtrless \dfrac{H_\alpha}{p'_{u'}}$ at price $p'_{u'}$ which had been cried at random. If, however,[64] this increase or decrease in $p_{u'}$ were to change H_α ever so slightly, it would only be necessary to continue the general process of *tâtonnement* in order to be sure of reaching equilibrium. This is what actually takes place in the money market.

Thus: *The price of the service of money is established through its rise or fall according as the* encaisse désirée *is greater or less than the quantity of money.*

There is, then, an equilibrium price $p_{u'}$; and if i is the equilibrium rate of net income, the unit quantity of money will be worth $p_u = \dfrac{p_{u'}}{i}$ .... Setting $H_\alpha = H_\alpha i$, we have

(15) $$Q_u = \frac{H_\alpha}{p_u} \text{.}^{65}$$

---

circumstance for the establishment of his theory, and that, therefore, a *"weak dependence"* is something that has to be somewhat grudgingly "admitted"—whereas, in point of fact, as the continuation of the passage shows, Walras regards this "weak dependence" as a most useful circumstance that enables him to simplify his analysis greatly. Indeed, he is happiest when he can assume that this dependence does not exist at all.

[62] Jaffé's brackets.

[63] Walras' inequality signs here should be reversed; for, say, an excess supply of money causes both bond and commodity prices in terms of (U) to rise, hence i and p_u to fall, and hence $p_{u'} = p_u i$ to fall *a fortiori*. (That Walras reads "$\gtrless$ " as "greater than or less than"—and not "less than or greater than"—can be seen from p. 172, line 7, and p. 245, lines 6–8—and the corresponding passages in the original.)

[64] As I understand it, in the preceding sentence Walras describes the *tâtonnement* as it would take place if H_α were completely independent of $p_{u'}$; whereas in the present sentence he relaxes this assumption to permit some degree of dependence.

[65] *Elements*, ed. Jaffé, pp. 325–27, with some minor changes to make the terminology of this translation consistent with that used elsewhere in this book—and with the major change in translation described in footnote 61. The equation numbers have again been added for convenience of reference. Italics in original.

It might be noted that Walras does not then deduce the quantity theory directly from equation (15)—as in the second and third editions of the *Eléments*—but reverts to the practice of his *Théorie de la monnaie* and deduces it from the application of a type of marginal-utility analysis to (15). (Cf. pp. 545–46 above and *Elements*, pp. 327–29.)

I do not understand the reason for Walras' reversion; nor do I fully understand the analysis itself. But it would take us too far from our main interests to pursue this question in detail.

This is the sum total of Walras' discussion of the *tâtonnement* by which the level of $p_{u'}$, and hence p_u, is determined. It shows that Walras is quite willing to assume that, with $p_{u'}$ arbitrarily fixed at the level $p'_{u'}$, a *tâtonnement* in the other markets first achieves equilibrium there; that, once this is accomplished, a *tâtonnement* in the money market then determines the equilibrium level of $p_{u'}$; *and that this latter* tâtonnement *can be carried out without reacting back and disturbing the equilibrium initially achieved in the other markets.* It fails to indicate any realization on the part of Walras that such a dichotomization of the pricing process contradicts the very conditions necessary for the existence of a monetary economy.

More specifically, assume that the economy as a whole is in equilibrium at a certain level of money prices. Let there now be an arbitrary change in $p_{u'}$, and let us assume that this does not react back on the other markets. Then these markets are still in equilibrium. Hence, by Walras' Law, so is the money market. Thus no market forces are created anywhere in the system to force $p_{u'}$ back to its original level. It follows that the equilibrium level of $p_{u'}$ is indeterminate. By the last paragraph of the passage just cited above, so, then, is the level of p_u. Thus if Walras' assumptions are carried to their extreme—and he certainly shows no objection in principle to having this done—they imply the indeterminacy of money prices, and hence the impossibility of all monetary theory.[66]

This basic inconsistency is itself the product of minor ones. Thus the crucial—though tacit—assumption of the third paragraph of the preceding passage is that the insensitivity of H_α to changes in $p_{u'}$ implies a corresponding absence of repercussions elsewhere in the system. But

---

[66] On this and the preceding paragraph, see pp. 182–83 and 176 above, respectively.

The statement in the preceding passage most revealing of Walras' state of mind is the one which reads: "... the equation of monetary circulation, when money is not a commodity, comes very close, in reality, to falling outside the system of equations of [general] economic equilibrium." I first cited this statement as evidence that Walras had dichotomized the pricing process invalidly in my "Indeterminacy of Absolute Prices in Classical Economic Theory," *Econometrica*, XVII (1949), 12. Unfortunately, I obscured the issue by confusing $p_{u'}$ and p_u (cf. above, pp. 547, footnote 36). At the same time, however, the exclusive concentration of my critics—and Walras' defenders—on this confusion has prevented them from seeing the real issue involved. Accordingly, their argument does not meet the criticism of Walras just explained in the text. Cf. Jaffé, *Elements*, p. 547, and Kuenne, "Walras, Leontief, and the Interdependence of Economic Activities," *op. cit.*, p. 330.

Schumpeter, on the other hand, attempts to explain away Walras' foregoing

this cannot be true. In particular, substituting equation (11) into (6), we obtain

$$\text{(16)} \qquad\qquad O_u = Q_u - \frac{H_\alpha}{p_{u'}}.$$

Clearly, the invariance of H_α with respect to changes in $p_{u'}$ does *not* imply any corresponding invariance of $O_u p_{u'}$. Hence a change in $p_{u'}$ will affect this term in budget restraint (1)—aggregated over all individuals—and thereby the state of demand in all markets of the economy.

There is, furthermore, a striking contrast between Walras' discussion of the *tâtonnement* here and in all preceding cases. In particular, his usual detailed and extended examination of the workings of the *tâtonnement* is significantly absent. Thus nowhere in the preceding passage does Walras describe the specific market mechanism through which any discrepancy between the supply and demand for money generates self-eliminating variations in $p_{u'}$. All he has to say on this crucial question is summed up in the non-committal formula that "the equation of monetary circulation would be solved ... simply by raising or lowering $p_{u'}$ according as $Q_u \gtrless H_\alpha/p'_{u'}$ at the price $p'_{u'}$ which has been cried out at random."[67]

Similarly, though Walras normally uses the device of arbitrarily holding one variable constant while completing a *tâtonnement* on the others, and then releasing the variable in question and completing a *tâtonnement* upon it, he always emphasizes that the variations generated by this second *tâtonnement* disturb the equilibrium initially achieved by the first one and require it to be recommenced; accordingly, he always proceeds next to describe in detail this recommenced *tâtonnement* and to prove that by continuing in this way the system will ultimately converge to its equilibrium position. Only in the preceding passage does he depart from this customary attempt at rigorous precision and rest with

---

statement as "an approximation to which the standards of rigorous analysis do not apply," made for the purpose of achieving "a simple form of the 'quantity theory'" (*History of Economic Analysis*, p. 1025). But this would seem to indicate that Schumpeter himself did not realize that, as just shown in the text, this "approximation" implies a denial of all monetary theory, and of the quantity theory in particular. the text. Cf. Jaffé, *Elements*, p. 547, and Kuenne, "Walras, Leontief, and the Interdependence of Economic Activities," *op. cit.*, p. 330.

See also p. 572, footnote 103 below for a discussion of Kuenne's recent contention that Walras should be interpreted as referring to the valid dichotomy on p. 180 above.

[67] I have left the inequality signs uncorrected; cf. above, p. 560, footnote 63.

the vague, general assurance that if variations "in $p_{u'}$ were to change H_α ever so slightly, it would only be necessary to continue the general process of *tâtonnement* in order to be sure of reaching equilibrium."[68]

At first sight, it seems possible to mitigate the force of the immediately foregoing criticisms[69] by assuming that by variations in $p_{u'}$ Walras has in mind variations in i; and that, accordingly, he restricts himself in the preceding passage to a bare reference to the *tâtonnement* because he has already presented a detailed description of it in his theory of capital formation (Lesson 25). Support for this contention comes from the fact that in the second and third editions of the *Eléments*—which also deal with the case of a paper money[70]—Walras explicitly identifies "*le marché du capital monnaie et le marché de la monnaie*" and states that "it is thus natural that the price cried out [during the *tâtonnement*] on the market for money be the rate of interest on money-capital."[71]

[68] In order to appreciate the full force of the contrast drawn in the two preceding paragraphs, the reader must compare for himself the extended discussions of Lessons 21 and 25 with the cryptic generalities of the preceding passage. Cf. also Note B above.

Of course, as shown above (p. 535), Walras' general attempt to prove the convergence of the *tâtonnement* is invalid. But this is an irrelevant consideration here.

[69] But not—it should be emphasized—that on the preceding page. This fundamental criticism of Walras is unaffected by the contention now to be presented.

[70] Cf. above, p. 544.

[71] *Eléments* (second and third editions), p. 381. Cf. the whole discussion there on pp. 379–83.

It should be emphasized—as Professor Jaffé has emphasized to me—that Walras is referring here to the market for *money-capital* (i.e., the market on which money is lent and borrowed for investment purposes) and *not* to the market for the sale and purchase of *capital goods*. But though conceptually distinct, these two markets are closely related in the Walrasian system: for the "rate of interest" determined in the former must always "tend to equality" with the uniform "rate of net income" determined in the latter. (This "rate of net income" is the ratio between the price of the service of a capital good—net of depreciation and insurance charges—and the price of the capital good itself; in equilibrium, this rate must obviously be the same for all capital goods.) (*Ibid.*, p. 381; cf. also *ibid.*, pp. 288–89, and *Elements*, ed. Jaffé, pp. 268–69 and 289–90.)

At the same time, it should also be emphasized that—in sharp contrast to Wicksell and Keynes of the *Treatise*—Walras makes little, if any, analytical use of the distinction between these two markets—and these two rates. Indeed, in the second and third editions of the *Eléments* he makes it clear that the market for money-capital "is only of practical and not theoretical interest" and that, accordingly, the analysis can concentrate exclusively on the market for capital goods (p. 289); and in the definitive edition he refers to the market for money-capital as a "superfoetation in theory" (ed. Jaffé, p. 290). Similarly, he uses the same symbol "i" to refer now to the rate of net income (*ibid.*, throughout Lessons 24 and 25) and now to the rate of interest (*ibid.*, p. 333, in the passage cited immediately below; cf. also the substitution on the

Additional support seems to come implicitly from a later discussion in the definitive edition of the *Elements* itself in which Walras deals with the case of a commodity-money—(*A*)—that is also *numéraire*. Since the price of (*A*) is thus by definition unity, the price of its *service d'approvisionnement* reduces to *i*. Correspondingly, Walras writes equation (12) above in the special form

(17) $$Q''_{a'} = \frac{H_\alpha}{i},$$

where $Q''_{a'}$ is the quantity of (*A*) used as money. If, now, there is an increase or decrease in $Q''_{a'}$,

> ... the rate of interest *i* will fall or rise in the money market, with the result that consumers will increase or decrease their *encaisse désirée*, since this is made up of quantities d_α, d_β, ... of (*A'*), (*B'*), ... which are decreasing functions of $p_{a'} = i$, $p_{b'} = p_b i$, ... and consequently of *i*. But, so long as the quantity of products does not increase, these movements can only result in a rise or fall in the prices p_b, ...[72] Entrepreneurs, on seeing this rise or fall in the prices of their products, will want to expand or contract their output, all the more so because the fall or rise in the rate of interest constitutes an

---

bottom of p. 332 and the reference to "interest charges" on the bottom of p. 242). Accordingly, I have sometimes used "*i*" in this double sense in the present discussion too.

I might finally add the opinion that Walras' whole attempt to identify the markets for money and money-capital in the second and third editions of the *Eléments* seems to be based on a serious confusion between the demand supply for money *balances* and the demand and supply for money *loans*; or, in our terminology, on a confusion between the market for *money* and the market for *bonds*. Nor do I feel that there is an adequate analysis in these editions of the relationship between the *tâtonnement* on the rate of interest in the market for money-capital and the *tâtonnement* on the rate of net income in the market for capital goods. Similarly, the role of the absolute price level and the way in which the equilibrium value of this level is determined on the market are not at all clear in the second and third editions—and in the definitive one too, if by variations in $p_{u'}$ Walras means variations in *i*. All this requires much more discussion than can be undertaken here.

[72] I do not understand Walras' reasoning here. True, an increase in the quantity of money depresses interest, thereby stimulates demand for (*B*), ..., and thereby causes p_b, ... to rise. But does it do so *because* the decrease in *i* causes the *encaisse désirée* to increase, or *in spite* of this? Would not the upward pressure on p_b be greater, the smaller the tendency to divert the increased quantity of money into cash balances?

A similarly puzzling passage appears in the second and third editions of the *Eléments* (p. 383) where a rise in interest is presented as decreasing the *encaisse désirée* and *thereby* the money prices of goods.

additional cause of profit or loss to them. In the end, however, all they will succeed in doing is to raise or lower the prices of the productive services the quantity of which has remained fixed (*ex hypothesi*). This rise or this fall will induce capitalists having more or less savings at their disposal to increase or decrease their demand for new capital goods; but since the aggregate quantity of capital goods still remains constant, the prices of these goods will merely rise or fall. Once the rise or fall in prices has permeated the entire system, the rate of interest will return to what it was [before the change in Q_a''].[73]

Persuasive as it might at first seem, this contention cannot stand up to a critical examination. First of all, if $p_{u'}$ denotes i, why does Walras say in the third paragraph of the first passage above[74] that the dependence of α, β, ... on $p_{u'}$ results only from the term $o_u p_{u'}$ in the budget restraint? Do not equations (3) show us that, completely aside from this term, α, β, ... depend on p_e, which is the reciprocal of the rate of interest? Indeed, do not these equations in their original form depend explicitly on *both* $p_{u'}$ *and* i?[75] Secondly, the last paragraph cited in the first passage definitely gives the impression that i has been determined independently of the *tâtonnement* on $p_{u'}$, and that therefore, once the equilibrium level of the latter is determined, the equilibrium value of p_u can be determined by dividing $p_{u'}$ by i.[76] Thirdly, if $p_{u'}$ denotes i, how can we reconcile the crucial dependence of d_α, d_β, ... on i in the second passage with Walras' desire to assume in the first passage that "the aggregate quantities d_α, d_β, ... do not depend upon

---

[73] *Elements*, p. 333; Jaffé's brackets.

It might be noted that this description of the way in which the rate of interest ultimately returns to its original level is an improvement over the unsupported statement of the second and third editions of the *Eléments* (p. 383) that it will do so. But, as compared with the analyses of other writers, it still leaves much to be desired. Cf. Note J below.

[74] For convenience I shall refer to the passage from the *Elements* cited on pp. 558–60 above as "the first passage" and to that just cited as "the second passage."

[75] "Equations de la circulation," *op. cit.*, p. 90; cf. above, p. 553, footnote 40.

[76] This impression emerges even more strongly from the exposition of Aupetit—who wrote under the immediate impact of Walras, and who adheres with only minor variations to the latter's presentation. After developing an equation which corresponds to (13) above, Aupetit writes:

> This equation, in which all terms but one are predetermined, determines $p_{u'}$—that is, the price of the service of money in terms of the *numéraire* [commodity (A)]. Knowing $p_{u'}$, we can then obtain the price of every commodity in terms of [paper money] (U) by multiplying their respective prices

it $[p_{u'}]$ except very indirectly and very weakly"? Finally, if the first passage is also concerned with a *tâtonnement* on *i*, why is not the argument of the second passage initially introduced there? For, as Walras' own presentation in the second and third editions of the *Eléments* shows, this argument is not restricted to the case of commodity-money, but is also applicable to that of fiat paper money.[77] [78]

All these considerations lead to the conclusion that by "*tâtonnement* on $p_{u'}$" in the first passage above, Walras could not have meant "*tâtonnement* on *i*." Instead, either he conceived of the *tâtonnement* as taking place on $p_{u'}$ as a whole; or, what seems more likely, he conceived of the *tâtonnement* as taking place on p_u, the reciprocal of the

---

in (*A*) by the price of (*A*) in terms of (*U*), that is by $i/p_{u'}$ [to yield]

$$p_{a,u} = \frac{i}{p_{u'}}, \qquad p_{b,u} = p_b \frac{i}{p_{u'}}, \qquad p_{c,u} = p_c \frac{i}{p_{u'}}, \; \dots \; .$$

From equation (13) and the preceding equations Aupetit then deduces the validity of the quantity theory of money. [*Essai sur la théorie générale de la monnaie* (Paris, 1901), p. 126, with notation changed to accord with Walras'.]

[77] Another point that might be mentioned here is that, for an exchange economy, the variable *i* does not appear explicitly in Walras' excess-demand equation for money; cf. p. 558, footnote 53, above. Note, however, that this is not so for the excess-demand equation which Walras actually analyzes on p. 326 of the *Elements*. Here, because of the assumption of a production economy, there is a term p_k which prevents all the *i*'s from canceling out. For this reason I do not think that this point is relevant to the present discussion.

[78] The outstanding interpreter of the first passage as dealing with a *tâtonnement* on the rate of interest *i* is Schumpeter (*History of Economic Analysis*, p. 1024), who has been followed on this by Kuenne ("Walras, Leontief, and the Interdependence of Economic Activities," *op. cit.*, p. 330, footnote 9). But neither one of these writers offers any textual evidence in support of this interpretation. And neither one sees any of the exegetical difficulties, just listed, which make such an interpretation untenable.

[Kuenne has recently commented upon this criticism and has described his reference to the rate of interest in the aforementioned footnote as a "loose" one. He also claims that "the body of the article spoke consistently of $p_{u'}$ as the term determined in the money market" (*Theory of General Economic Equilibrium*, p. 320, footnote 57).

Kuenne also states (*ibid.*) that on the page from Schumpeter's *History* here cited, Schumpeter "explicitly speaks of *i* instead of $p_{u'}$ only under the assumption that money is *numéraire* in which case they are identical." This, however, is besides the point: for the question at issue is the proper interpretation of the passage from Walras cited on pp. 558–60 above; and it is clear from the last four lines of p. 1024 of his *History* that Schumpeter interprets this passage (to which he refers explicitly) as dealing with "the influence of variations in the rate of interest."]

absolute price level, and—since he assumed the rate of interest to be already determined in the capital market[79]—represented the movements of this variable by the directly proportionate $p_{u'}$. In either case, the money market introduces a new variable into the analysis which, in accordance with the general Walrasian scheme, must be accorded a separate *tâtonnement*. It is also clear that this variable influences α, β, ... only through the term $o_u p_{u'}$ in the budget restraint. Finally, it is clear that the argument of the second passage deals with a problem that does not exist for Walras in the first one, and that he therefore has no reason to introduce this argument there. In particular, under the assumption of a commodity-money which is also *numéraire*, the analogue of p_u is identically unity. Hence, unlike the situation in the first passage, there can be no *tâtonnement* upon it. Hence the entire *tâtonnement* in this case must take place on i. And this is what Walras finds "remarkable": that even though the *tâtonnement* is so different from that of the first passage, the conclusion that an increase in the quantity of money decreases its value remains the same.[80]

Further, and perhaps conclusive, evidence that Walras thought of the *tâtonnement* in the first passage as proceeding on p_u is afforded by the case which Walras analyzes immediately after the second passage. Here he continues to consider a commodity-money, (A); but now he assumes that the *numéraire* is another commodity, (B). He then writes:

The curve representing the price of the monetized (A) in terms of another commodity (B) as a function of the quantity of (A) monetized closely approximates[81] a rectangular hyperbola ... . The equation of this curve is

$$(18) \qquad q = \frac{H}{p},$$

[where q is the quantity of (A) in monetary use and p is its price in terms of

[79] Cf. the preceding and next paragraph of the text.

[80] "What is most remarkable, in the case of a commodity which serves both as money and as *numéraire*, is the manner in which all prices rise and fall in terms of (A) in response to an increase or decrease in the *rareté* or value of this commodity in its monetary use when there is a decrease or increase in its quantity" (*Elements*, p. 333). After another sentence, this is followed by the second passage cited above.

[81] Walras does not refer again to this reservation and proceeds to present the curve as an *exact* rectangular hyperbola. The reservation itself is a carry-over from the parallel passage of the second and third editions of the *Eléments* (p. 384) which has already been discussed on p. 545, footnote 14 above.

(*B*) and] H is the *encaisse désirée* reckoned in terms of (*B*), *which*[82] *is assumed to be predetermined.*[83]

Now, H is the analogue of H_α in equation (15), and p is the analogue of p_u.[84] Thus the italicized phrase in the preceding passage would seem to imply that Walras considers H_α "to be predetermined"—that is, to remain unaffected by the *tâtonnement* in the money market.[85] But in the first passage Walras is also willing to assume that H_α remains unaffected by this *tâtonnement*.[86] Since $H_\alpha = H_\alpha i$, so that

$$(19) \qquad\qquad i = \frac{H_\alpha}{H_\alpha},$$

this means that i is also predetermined. Hence the *tâtonnement* must proceed on p_u. Alternatively, since

$$(20) \qquad\qquad \frac{H_\alpha}{p_{u'}} = \frac{1}{p_u}\left(\frac{H_\alpha}{i}\right) = \frac{1}{p_u}H_\alpha,$$

and since H_α is predetermined, the *tâtonnement* on $p_{u'}$ in

$$(21) \qquad\qquad Q_u = \frac{H_\alpha}{p_{u'}}$$

must be a *tâtonnement* on p_u.

At this point the reader may well ask: Why, then, does not Walras explicitly carry out the *tâtonnement* of the first passage on p_u? He must, however, remember that the presentation of the argument in terms of $p_{u'}$ is dictated by Walras' basic conception of the theory of money as a special case of the theory of circulating capital. This has been sufficiently emphasized in the preceding section.[87]

We might also digress for a moment to suggest that in the preceding passage Walras seems to regard the invariance of H with respect to p as a necessary condition for the validity of the quantity theory. A

---

[82] From the context it is clear that this refers to H.

[83] *Elements*, ed. Jaffé, p. 334, italics added.

[84] This is particularly clear from Walras' footnote on p. 334.

[85] For further support of this contention, see the discussion of Schlesinger on p. 569, footnote 94 below.

[86] See above, p. 560.

[87] See pp. 551 and 555. Walras' discussion in the Preface to the *Elements*, ed. Jaffé, pp. 42–43, is particularly illuminating on this point.

corresponding impression holds for his willingness—in the first passage cited above—to assume the invariance of H_α with respect to changes in $p_{u'}$.[88] Clearly, however, all that need be assumed for the validity of the theory is that H be invariant with respect to an equiproportionate change in p *and* in initial holdings of money. In brief, Walras seems to be guilty here of a confusion between a demand curve and a market-equilibrium curve.[89] More specifically, Walras' interpretation of his rectangular hyperbola seems to slip back and forth between these two different contexts. First, this hyperbola is a demand curve—it is a graphical representation of the excess-demand function (18),[90] and shifts to the right or left according as there is an increase or decrease in the *encaisse desiree*.[91] But then it is also a market-equilibrium curve—for it shows that, were it not for its nonmonetary use, the purchasing power of money would vary inversely with its quantity. Similarly, I cannot escape the impression that when Walras concludes the summary of his Preface with the statement that "the price of money, *qua* money [is] established as an inverse function of its quantity,"[92] it is equation (15) above he has in mind—and this despite the fact that it is developed as an excess-demand equation.

To return now to our main problem, we note that if Walras' first passage on the money market deals with a *tâtonnement* on p_u, the more serious the criticism to which it is open. For his willingness to assume that this *tâtonnement* can proceed "outside the system of equations of [general] economic equilibrium"[93] then constitutes a willingness to ignore the influence of variations in the absolute price level on the other markets. And so we are led to the highly probable conclusion that the invalid dichotomy was born together with general-equilibrium analysis —and had the same father.[94]

[88] This is definitely Schumpeter's view: "The main motive [of this assumed invariance] seems to have been a wish to gain possession of a simple form of 'quantity theory'" (*History of Economic Analysis*, p. 1025, footnote 71).

[89] Cf. above, Chapter VIII:2.

[90] Observe the notational symmetry between (18) and the excess-demand function (12).

[91] *Elements*, ed. Jaffé, p. 336 (bottom).

[92] *Ibid.*, p. 43.

[93] Above, p. 560.

[94] Cf. Chapter VIII:3 above.

Once again, the credibility of this conclusion is strengthened when we see how those who wrote in Walras' shadow approached the problem. Thus, in his monograph on the *Theorie der Geld- und Kreditwirtschaft* (Munich, 1914)—the relevant chapter of

5. Conclusions

Our study has shown that Walras' monetary theory was based on a mechanical application of the marginal-utility apparatus. At no point did Walras ever attempt to explain why money has utility. Nor did he ever recognize the fundamental nature of money in providing a reserve against contingencies. Correspondingly, he failed to clothe his elaborate mathematical framework with adequate economic meaning.

Furthermore, even in the definitive edition of the *Elements* Walras did not succeed in his proclaimed objective of presenting a finished and integrated theory of money. At a lower level of criticism, his theory has the minor inaccuracies[95] and rough edges[96] of an argument that has not

---

which has recently been translated under the title "Basic Principles of the Money Economy," *International Economic Papers*, No. 9 (1959), 20–38—Karl Schlesinger analyzes the details of various payment procedures, all of which yield an excess demand for money that is essentially Walras'

$$Q_u = \frac{H_\alpha}{p_u}$$

[cf. equation (15) above]. In each case he presents as a necessary precondition of his analysis the assumption that:

> Each economic unit makes its arrangements in such wise that cash reserves plus annual receipts just cover the year's prospective expenditures ... and that, on the assumption of a stationary economy, the cash balance at the end of the year is the same as at the beginning. The year's purchases and sales, and their order, are independent of the value of money [p_u] and are conditioned only by the economy's other data. Therefore the real balances and the amount of monetary purchasing power required for the transactions [H_α] can be determined without reference to p_u. [*Ibid.*, p. 26, bracketed expressions added; cf. also the similar statements on pp. 25 and 30.]

Since H_α is thus predetermined, and since Q_u is given to begin with, the foregoing equation depends upon only one unknown p_u, and can therefore determine its equilibrium value.

Thus Schlesinger seems to confuse the first, valid dichotomy (pp. 172–73 above) with the invalid one. It might also be noted that he rationalizes the assumption just quoted by stating that no one is "afraid of selling at lower prices so long as he can be sure of being able to use the proceeds for equally cheaper purchases" (*ibid.*, p. 23). The familiar ring of the "homogeneity postulate" is unmistakable.

We might in the context of this footnote also mention Pareto's statement that "the theory of money should come after the theory of general economic equilibrium" —so suggestive of the crucial passage from Walras' *Elements* cited on pp. 559–60 above (*Manuel d'économie politique*, p. 209).

[95] Cf. p. 560, footnote 63; pp. 561–62; and p. 564, footnote 72.
[96] Cf. p. 548, pp. 555–56, and p. 565, footnote 73.

been thought through to its logical end. At a higher level of criticism, his theory of money is not fully integrated with his theory of production and capital formation. This manifests itself in his failure to follow the basic pattern of this earlier theory in presenting a detailed and precise description of the *tâtonnement* in the money market. More important, the meager description that Walras does provide shows no recognition of the vital necessity—if money prices are to be determinate—for the existence of a mutual interdependence between this *tâtonnement* and that taking place in the other markets of the economy.[97] And this fundamental criticism holds even if it should be true that Walras was not guilty of the invalid dichotomy in the fullest sense of the term. Similarly, whether or not this dichotomy exists in Walras' theory, the fact remains that at no point does Walras even advert to the real-balance effect in the commodity market in his analysis of the determination of the absolute price level.[98]

Nevertheless, our evaluation of Walras' pioneering development of a general-equilibrium theory of money can only be enhanced when we see how little his immediate followers did to remedy these deficiencies in his analysis. Indeed, only two of them advanced this analysis beyond Walras' own formulation—though neither one of them did so with explicit reference to his work. The first was Wicksell, whose analysis of the *tâtonnement* in the money market will be discussed in Note E below. The second was Schlesinger, whose analysis of the conceptual framework which endows money holdings with utility will be discussed in Note D.[99] But for the rest, they had nothing to say. Pareto, Walras' intellectual successor, almost completely ignored his monetary theory.[100] Aupetit, though writing a monograph on the question, added but minor glosses to Walras' analysis. While popularizers of Walras—

[97] Cf. p. 562 above.

[98] All this should make clear why I find it impossible to accept Schumpeter's presentation of Walras' monetary theory as one fully integrated with his theory of production and capital formation (*History of Economic Analysis*, pp. 1020–21, 1025). A similar statement holds for Jaffé [*Econometrica*, XIX (1951), 327], Kuenne ("Walras, Leontief, and the Interdependence of Economic Activity," *op. cit.*, p.336), and Marget (*Theory of Prices*, Vol. II, p. 284, footnote 132).

[99] But, as just emphasized, Schlesinger was even more clearly in error than Walras in his analysis of the determination of the absolute price level.

[100] V. Pareto, *Cours d'économie politique* (Lausanne, 1896), Vol. I, pp. 163–299. Schumpeter considers Pareto to have "slid back rather than advanced in this particular field" (*History of Economic Analysis*, p. 1082). Marget is even more critical ("Léon Walras ... ," *op. cit.*, pp. 596–97; "Monetary Aspects ... ," *op. cit.*, pp. 152–54.)

such as Antonelli[101]—barely departed from the text he had set for them. All this was part of the uninterrupted neglect and distortion which Walras' monetary theory suffered at the hands of later writers.[102] [103]

[101] E. Antonelli, *Principes d'économie pure* (Paris, 1914), Chapter VI.

[102] The details of this neglect have, of course, been fully chronicled by Marget in his well-known "Léon Walras ... ," *op. cit.*, especially pp. 595 ff.

[103] A recent noteworthy contribution to the literature on Walras' theory of money has been R. E. Kuenne's detailed study in his *Theory of General Economic Equilibrium* (Princeton, 1963), Chapter 5, especially pp. 305–39. This study is the outgrowth of a series of articles by the author, all but one of which (see p. 548, footnote 26 above) appeared after the first edition of this book. Where Kuenne's study and the present one deal with the same problem, they are for the most part in agreement—the differences of interpretation being well within the standard error of observation of the difficult and frequently obscure text that Walras has left us (cf., e.g., p. 557, footnote 52 above). On one point, however—the possible presence of the invalid dichotomy in Walras' thinking as described in Section 4 above—the differences seem to be wider, though this too may in part reflect differences in emphasis (see *ibid.*, p. 337, lines 3–9, and p. 338, last paragraph).

Kuenne challenges the findings of Section 4 on the grounds that it neglects four pieces of evidence to the contrary (*ibid.*, pp. 337–38). It seems to me, however, that the irrelevance of the first, third, and fourth of these pieces is implicitly or explicitly shown in the respective discussions above of p. 559, footnote 61; p.168, lines 24–35 and p. 561, footnote 66, penultimate paragraph; and p. 168, lines 10–21.

Kuenne's main point, however—and the one which has not been discussed above— is that Walras' discussion should be interpreted as an instance of the valid dichotomy described on p. 180 above (*ibid.*, pp. 335–36, p. 337, lines 21–27, and p. 317, footnote 52, first paragraph). In support of this interpretation Kuenne cites the discussion at the bottom of p. 325 of the *Elements* in which Walras indicates that the equation for the *numéraire* is solved together with that for money. I do not, however, understand why Kuenne considers this as evidence that Walras was solving for equilibrium in the "promissory note market" (which for the present purpose corresponds to the crucial bond market in the dichotomy on p. 180 above) together with that for money. Indeed, it is clear from parallel passages in the *Elements* (cf., e.g., p. 294, §259) that this is not what Walras had in mind.

There is, however, a more basic point. Let us, for the sake of argument, accept Kuenne's contention that Walras did have in mind the valid dichotomy of p. 180 above. Now, Walras' model is one in which outside money exists [cf. *Elements*, p. 325, where Walras explains that his money (U) can take the form of "inconvertible paper francs"]. Hence, for reasons explained on p. 180 above (especially footnote 43), there is no justification for assuming that the influence of real balances [or, to use the phrase which Kuenne prefers, "nonhomogeneity" (*Theory*, p. 335,)] manifests itself in the bond, but not in the commodity, markets. In brief, even if valid, the dichotomy has no economic rationale within Walras' model.

From this it follows as a corollary that Walras is to be criticized in any event (as he has been on p. 571 above) for implying that changes in the absolute price level need not affect commodity demands in an outside-money economy. And the fact that this "homogeneity postulate" lies at the core of the invalid dichotomy is sufficient basis for our contention that the roots of this dichotomy are already to be found in his writings (see pp. 183 and 569 above).

Note D. The Marginal-Utility Theory

of Money after Walras[1]

The marginal-utility theory of money after Walras was the paralyzed victim of the "circularity" bogey. This bogey achieved its most imposing form at the hands of Helfferich.[2] Its intimidatory powers were further increased by Divisia's claim to have provided a mathematical proof that the utility function could not depend upon the amount of money.[3] And despite Marget's deft puncturing of its façade many

---

[1] Attached to Chapter V, Sections 1 and 8.

This note is intended only to highlight certain points. For a more general discussion of the literature on this question—including the circularity charge—cf. Marget, *The Theory of Prices*, Vols. I and II, consulting Subject Index under "Utility analysis and the cash-balance approach"; see, in particular, Vol. I, pp. 450 ff., 480 ff.; Vol. II, pp. 84 ff. See also H. S. Ellis, *German Monetary Theory: 1905–1933* (Cambridge, Mass., 1934), Chapters IV–V; and—for a defense of the charge—B. M. Anderson, *The Value of Money* (New York, 1917), Chapter V.

Ellis also refers to a monograph on this question by W. Hirsch entitled *Grenznutzentheorie und Geldwerttheorie unter besonderer Berücksichtigung der "österreichischen" Schule* (Jena, 1928). This monograph concludes that the circularity charge is valid and that marginal-utility analysis is therefore inapplicable to money (Ellis, *op. cit.*, p. 89).

[2] K. Helfferich, *Money*, trans. L. Infield (London, 1927), pp. 526–27.

[3] F. Divisia, *Economique rationnelle* (Paris, 1927), pp. 423–33. This proof obviously falls to the ground as soon as we drop its basic assumption that "utility of money" means the utility of the commodities which money can buy. See E. Fossati, "A Note About the Utility of Money," *Metroeconomica*, II (1950), 116–17, and *The Theory of General Static Equilibrium* (Oxford, 1957), pp. 223–24.

years ago,[4] it has continued to be accorded respectable consideration in the most recent literature.[5]

It seems quite likely that this bogey was also in back of the tendency —already noted by Marget[6]—of many writers formally to deny the applicability of marginal-utility analysis to money, while at the same time presenting a cash-balance approach, which by its very nature involves a comparison of choices and hence an analysis of utilities. Of particular interest are such writers as Wicksell,[7] Fisher,[8] and Keynes in his neoclassical days[9]—each of whom was at pains to state that "money as such has no utility except what is derived from its exchange-value, that is to say from the utility of the things which it can buy"— and each of whom then proceeded to base his analysis precisely on the advantage and convenience (utility) of holding money *as such*.[10] One cannot help being struck by the irony of the fact that these writers, who actually provided a conceptual framework which could have justified the formal application of utility analysis to money, did not do so; while Walras, who actually lacked this framework, did.[11]

It is even more ironical that Mises—who is known in the literature as *the* advocate of the application of marginal-utility analysis to money— should have made this application solely in terms of "the marginal utility of the goods for which the money can be exchanged,"[12] and not in

[4] *Theory of Prices*, Vol. I, p. 445, footnote 86. See also Samuelson, *Foundations* p.118.

[5] Cf., e.g., Schumpeter, *History of Economic Analysis*, pp. 1089–90.

[6] *Theory of Prices*, Vol. II, pp. 84–86, 92–93.

[7] *Lectures in Political Economy*, Vol. II, *Money*, trans. E. Classen (London, 1935), pp. 20, 130; *Interest and Prices*, pp. 18 and 29.

[8] *Purchasing Power of Money*, p. 32. Needless to say, Fisher was not a cash-balance theorist in the sense of determining the value of money by its demand and supply; but he implicitly explained the holding of money in the same terms used by this theory. Cf. *ibid.*, pp. 153–54. This is cited in full and discussed in Note F:1 below.

[9] J. M. Keynes, *A Tract on Monetary Reform* (London, 1923), p. 75. The following quotation in the text is from this reference. For a similar statement by an older member of Cambridge, see H. Sidgwick, *The Principles of Political Economy* (London, 1883), pp. 267–68. Cf. also M. Pantaleoni, *Pure Economics*, trans. T. B. Bruce (London, 1898), pp. 228–29; D. Kinley, *Money* (New York, 1904), p. 143. The latter, though, is somewhat ambiguous.

[10] On Wicksell and Fisher, see Notes E:1 and F:1 below, respectively. On Keynes, see *Tract on Monetary Reform*, p. 78.

[11] Cf. Note C:2 above, especially pp. 549–50.

[12] L. von Mises, *The Theory of Money and Credit*, trans. H. E. Batson (New, York, 1935), p. 109.

terms of the liquidity advantages of holding money that he described so clearly in other parts of his work.[13] As a result, Mises was forced to base his attempted escape from the circularity charge on a historical regression to the time when "the value of money is nothing other than the value of an object that is useful in some other way than as money."[14] Without going into the merits of this analytical construct, we need merely note that the argument of Chapter V:8 frees the marginal-utility theory of money from any logical dependence upon it. We might further note that this argument[15] also shows the incorrectness of Mises' contention that the quantity theory presupposes an inverse relationship between the quantity of money and its marginal utility.[16]

Walras' immediate followers made no mention of the circularity charge; but, for the most part—and as emphasized at the end of Note C above—neither did they develop his marginal-utility theory of money any further. Indeed, Pareto retrogressed on this point. For he used "marginal utility of money" to denote only "the utility of the money-commodity in its non-monetary uses or the utility of the money-income";[17] never the utility of the *service d'approvisionnement* of money.

---

[13] *Ibid.*, pp. 134–35, 147–48.

[14] *Ibid.*, p. 121. Hicks aptly describes Mises' theory as leading to the conclusion that "money is a ghost of gold." ["A Suggestion for Simplifying the Theory of Money," *Economica*, II (1935), as reprinted in *Readings in Monetary Theory*, p. 14.]

[15] See above, p. 95, footnote 25.

[16] Mises, *op. cit.*, pp. 141–42. It will be recalled that this contention also manifests itself at certain phases of Walras' work, and possibly even in the definitive edition of the *Elements* (cf. above, p. 544, and p. 560, footnote 65). Pareto, on the other hand, is definitely free of this confusion (*Cours*, Vol. I. p. 178, footnote).

[17] Marget, "Monetary Aspects ... ," *op. cit.*, pp. 152–54.

We might in this connection note that when Pareto deals with the case of a money which may not have utility for some individual, he becomes involved in an error. Thus he writes: "It may be that the possessor of a good ... derives no satisfaction from it; then we can say that he will *offer the entire quantity* at his disposal." But in the very next paragraph he fails to apply this principle correctly. For he states that for some individual money may have no utility, and therefore "he will use *the entire quantity that he receives* to procure [other] goods." If Pareto had applied his first statement correctly, he should have concluded: "and therefore he will use the entire quantity that he receives *plus his original stock* to procure other goods " (*Manuel*, p. 593, only first set of italics in original).

Even if we accept Pareto's second statement, this does not provide a determinate monetary theory. For to assume that every individual always holds on to his initial holdings of money is to become involved in the indeterminacy of Say's Identity. See above, Chapter VIII:7; see also Divisia, *op. cit.*, pp. 402–13 for an elaboration of Pareto's second statement, and a pointing out of this same indeterminacy.

As already noted (p. 571), the only one to improve on Walras' theory was Karl Schlesinger. And he suffered even more neglect than his predecessor.[18]

Unfortunately, space does not permit us to present the full-length study of Schlesinger's work that its highly stimulating originality clearly warrants. From the viewpoint of our present interests, this work is best regarded as dealing with the deficiencies in the conceptual framework of Walras' monetary theory. In particular, it remedies these deficiencies by providing a precise specification of the payment procedure that generates a demand for money.[19]

Schlesinger proceeds by a series of successively more complicated stages. In the final one he distinguishes between payments whose magnitudes and future due-dates are *fixed*, and those which are *uncertain*. The monetary demand generated by the first type of payments is determined without recourse to utility analysis. It is simply the maximum cumulative discrepancy between daily cash outflow and inflow that will be generated during the period in question by the *given* payment stream with which the individual is confronted. In other words, the very nature of this stream compels the individual to hold this amount of money at the beginning of the period if he is to avoid certain default. There is no room for the weighing of alternatives on his part.[20]

The element of alternative choices—and hence of utility analysis—enters only with respect to the uncertain payments.[21] If the individual did not hold a cash reserve against these payments, he would have to meet them by the forced sale of assets. And since future asset prices are uncertain, this involves the risk of loss. Hence it is rational for the individual to hold money instead of income-yielding assets; for the

---

[18] Marget, "Léon Walras ... ," *op. cit.*, p. 594.

[19] Cf. Note C:2 above.

Because Schlesinger does not refer to Walras in the main part of his analysis, Marget surmises that he "did not derive his inspiration directly from Walras at all" (*ibid.*, p. 595).This conclusion seems to me unjustified. Though it would have been better if Schlesinger had defined the precise relation of his work to Walras', the fact remains that he deals with a problem that Walras neglected. Hence the absence of explicit citations.

[20] Schlesinger, "Basic Principles of the Money Economy," *op. cit.*, pp. 26–28. Cf. p. 549 above.

[21] Unfortunately, this distinction is not the absolute one that it should be in Schlesinger's work. Thus on p. 27 he indicates that even the "fixed" payment stream may be modified by the individual's investing money in times of cash surplus, and disinvesting in times of deficit.

interest foregone on these holdings "is like a risk premium."[22] Denoting the real value of cash balances by r_v, Schlesinger represents the marginal utility of the insurance service which they thus provide by $f(r_v)$. He then states that the individual will not be in his optimum position unless $i = f(r_v)$, where i is the rate of interest.[23]

It can readily be seen that this optimum condition is incorrectly stated. The rate of interest does not have the dimensions of utility, and so cannot be equal to $f(r_v)$, which does. Instead of "i" Schlesinger should have written "the marginal utility of i dollars' worth of expenditure."[24] This, however, is a minor point.

Leaving this behind, we note that Schlesinger's analysis brings him finally to an excess-demand equation for money which he writes in the form

$$pF(Y) + p\Phi(r, Y) = M_0.$$

Here $F(Y)$ is the demand generated by the fixed payments, and $\Phi(r, Y)$ is that generated by the uncertain payments.[25] Schlesinger emphasizes that, because of the "law of large numbers," an increase in Y causes a less-than-proportionate increase in both of these functions.[26] Thus an expansion in his volume of transactions enables the individual to economize on the relative size of his cash balances. This, however, is true only if the increase in Y represents an increase in the *number* of transactions and not solely in their individual *magnitudes*. In the latter case the relative size of cash balances would remain the same.[27]

As the reader has undoubtedly noted, there is a remarkable similarity between the preceding excess-demand equation and Keynes'

$$L_1(Y) + L_2(r) = M_0.$$

Surely we do not read meaning into Schlesinger's analysis by saying that the first term in his equation reflects the transactions demand and

[22] *Ibid.*, p. 29.

[23] *Ibid.*, p. 30.

[24] Cf. equation (4), p. 91 above.

[25] This is Schlesinger's equation 4 (p. 31) with Q_u replaced by M_0, $1/p_u$ by p, i by r, and V—the real volume of transactions—by Y. The subscripts attached to the original functions have been dropped.

We might note here that Schlesinger indicates that the rate of interest also influences $F(\ )$, though he never introduces this rate explicitly into the function (*ibid.*, p. 27).

[26] *Ibid.*, pp. 24 (especially footnote 6), 28, and 30.

[27] *Ibid.*, p. 24. Cf. p. 87 above.

the second term the speculative demand. In particular, Schlesinger's $\Phi(r, Y)$—which reflects the risk entailed in holding assets—can properly be taken as a generalization of Keynes' speculative demand—which reflects the risk entailed in holding the specific asset, bonds. Indeed, the only fundamental difference between the two foregoing equations lies in the fact that Schlesinger premultiplies both of his demand components by p and thus frees his equation from the money illusion which is so significantly present in Keynes' equation (above, p. 278).

After Schlesinger, formal mathematical developments of a marginal-utility theory of money seem to have been restricted to Leser[28] and Samuelson.[29] The latter's analysis is presented as a modified version of Walras'. Actually, though, it improves the conceptual framework of Walras' analysis by presupposing the existence of certain unspecified "contingencies" and by then explaining the utility of money in terms of its availability to meet them.[30] Leser, on the other hand, makes no reference to Walras. But his work is similar to Walras' in its failure to explain what endows money with utility and in its conceptual earmarking of the money balance for the various commodities.[31] In particular, Leser's utility function is (in terms of the notation on pp. 403–404 above)

$$U = U\left(Z_1, \ldots, Z_{n-1}, \frac{Z_n}{p_1}, \ldots, \frac{Z_n}{p_{n-1}}\right),$$

which is one of the general forms of a function assumed to be homogeneous of degree zero in Z_n and the money prices. Leser then proceeds to his main (and somewhat neglected)contribution, which in part anticipates and in part even goes beyond the recent (and independently developed) analysis of the Slutzky equation corresponding to a utility function dependent on real money balances. Leser also distinguishes explicitly between the short-run and long-run effects of price and income

[28] C. E. V. Leser, "The Consumer's Demand for Money," *Econometrica*, XI (1943), 123–40.

[29] *Foundations*, pp. 117–22.

[30] *Ibid.*, p. 118. Cf. above, p. 549. This distinction between Samuelson and Walras was first emphasized by Kuenne, "Walras, Leontief, and the Interdependence of Economic Activities," *op. cit.*, p. 332, footnote 3.

[31] Leser, *op. cit.*, p. 124, Cf. above, p. 554. This earmarking is also assumed by Samuelson. On some of the broader implications of such a function, see pp. 410–11 above.

changes along the lines later made familiar by the work of Archibald and Lipsey.[32]

In one fundamental respect, however, Leser's development differs from—and is inferior to—Walras'. For it is effectively restricted to an unrealistic one-week-horizon case in which the cost of holding a dollar in real balances is (by assumption) a dollar's worth of commodities sacrificed for economic eternity.[33] Accordingly, Leser's monetary theory is one in which the rate of interest plays no role.

So much for the mathematical economists. We might now return to our ordinary cash-balance theorists and note that though—as empha-sized above—most of them were inhibited by fears of "circularity" from applying marginal-utility analysis to money, there were neverthe-less some who spoke explicitly of the marginal utility of money balances and who attempted to describe the optimum condition that it must satisfy. Thus, for example, Lavington is well known for his statement that:

Resources devoted to consumption supply an income of immediate satisfac-tion; those held as a stock of currency yield a return of convenience and security; those devoted to investment in the narrower sense of the term yield a return in the form of interest. In so far therefore as his judgment gives effect to his self-interest, the quantity of resources which he holds in the form of money will be such that the unit of resources which is just and only just worth while holding in this form yields him a return of convenience and security equal to the yield of satisfaction derived from the marginal unit spent on consumables, and equal also to the net rate of interest.[34]

Here, again, we have the same confusion already noted in the case of Schlesinger: "satisfaction" and "interest" do not have the same dimen-sions, and so cannot be compared. As Robertson has implied, this may be a mere slip of the pen.[35] But Robertson fails to see that the correction

[32] Cf. above, pp. 405 (footnote 4) and 434 (footnote 17).
An example of the aforementioned neglect is the absence of these last two sentences from the corresponding discussion of the first edition of this book.
[33] Cf. the optimum condition on which Leser concentrates exclusively, *ibid.*, p. 125. Compare with the equation on p. 90, footnote 18 above.
[34] F. Lavington, *The English Capital Market* (London, 1921), p. 30. This state-ment goes back to much less precise ones by A. Marshall, *Official Papers* (London, 1926), p. 268 (evidence before the Committee on Indian Currency, 1899, answer to question 11,759); and *Money Credit and Commerce* (London, 1923), p. 44. See also Pigou, *Essays in Applied Economics*, pp. 179–80, noting the reference to T. N. Carver.
[35] D. H. Robertson, *Essays in Monetary Theory* (London, 1940), p. 17, footnote 2. This reads: "Lavington had better, I think, have written 'measured also by'."

of this slip reveals an even more basic misconception. For Lavington's last sentence would then state that an optimum position obtains when the marginal utility of a dollar held in cash balances is equal at one and the same time to the marginal utility of *one* and *r* dollars' worth of commodities—where 100*r* per cent is the rate of interest. The nature of this misconception can best be seen against the background of Chapter V:3 above. In brief, Lavington confuses the subjective sacrifice of *permanently* adding a dollar to cash balances with that of adding it for only *one period*.[36]

A statement in the same vein as Lavington's—though without his error—can be found in Fisher:

> The most salable of all properties is, of course, money; and as Karl Menger pointed out, it is precisely this salability which makes it money. The *convenience* of surely being able, without any previous preparation, to dispose of it for any exchange, in other words, its *liquidity*, is itself a sufficient return upon the capital which a man seems to keep idle in money form. This liquidity of our cash balance takes the place of any rate of interest in the ordinary sense of the word. A man who keeps an average cash balance of $100, rather than put his money in a savings bank to yield him $5 a year, does so because of its liquidity. Its readiness for use at a moment's notice is, to him, worth at least $5 a year.[37]

The reader himself will have to explain how this striking passage can be made consistent with Fisher's observation referred to at the beginning of this note about "the fundamental peculiarity which money alone of all goods possesses,—the fact that it has no power to satisfy human wants except a power *to purchase* things which do have such power."[38]

[36] Compare the equation in footnote 18, p. 90 above with equation (4) on p. 91.

There is also an uncomfortable vagueness on this point in Robertson's *Money* (rev. ed.; London, 1948), p. 36.

[37] *The Theory of Interest* (New York, 1930), p. 216, italics in original. All but the last two sentences of this passage appear in a similar form in Fisher's earlier *Rate of Interest* (New York, 1907), p. 212. Cf. also the reference to the "waste of interest" in the *Purchasing Power of Money*, p. 152.

For a similar recognition by Wicksell of the dependence of the demand for money on the rate of interest, see *Interest and Prices*, p. 119; *Lectures*, Vol. II, p. 197.

[38] *Purchasing Power of Money*, p. 32, italics in original.

Nor do I think it possible to resolve this inconsistency by assuming that Fisher considered money to be a producer's good as in Chapter VII above; for in this case too money serves a function other than that of the mere purchase of commodities. The same comment holds for the references to Wicksell and Keynes cited on p. 574 above.

Note E. Wicksell's Monetary Theory

1. THE DETERMINATION OF THE ABSOLUTE PRICE LEVEL[1]

As already noted,[2] Wicksell denied the relevance of utility analysis for monetary theory. But despite this formal methodological declaration, he developed a cash-balance approach based implicitly on the services that money holdings as such provide. The striking passage in *Interest and Prices*[3] in which this is made clear is also the one which provides a description, unique in the literature, of the *tâtonnement* by which the absolute price level is determined. It reads:

Now let us suppose that for some reason or other commodity prices rise while the stock of money remains unchanged, or that the stock of money is diminished while prices remain temporarily unchanged. The cash balances will gradually appear to be *too small in relation to the new level of prices* (though in the first case they have not on the average altered in absolute amount. It is true that in this case I can rely on a higher level of receipts in the future. But meanwhile I run the risk of being unable to meet my obligations punctually, and at best I may easily be forced by shortage of ready money to forgo some purchase that would otherwise have been profitable.) I therefore seek to enlarge my balance. This can only be done—neglecting for the present the

[1] Attached to Chapter VIII:1.
[2] See beginning of Note D.
[3] London, 1936. Trans. R. F. Kahn from the original German of *Geldzins und Güterpreise* (1898).

581

possibility of borrowing, etc.—through a *reduction* in my *demand* for goods and services, or through an *increase* in the *supply* of my own commodity (forthcoming either earlier or at a lower price than would otherwise have been the case), or through both together. The same is true of all other owners and consumers of commodities. But in fact nobody will succeed in realizing the object at which each is aiming—to increase his cash balance; for the sum of individual cash balances is limited by the amount of the available stock of money, or rather is identical with it. On the other hand, the universal reduction in demand and increase in supply of commodities will necessarily bring about a continuous fall in all prices. This can only cease when prices have fallen to the level at which the cash balances are regarded as *adequate*. (In the first case prices will now have fallen to their original level.)[4]

Despite the vividness with which the real-balance effect is here described, there is another passage in Wicksell which indicates that even he might not have appreciated its full significance. This occurs in his defense of the quantity theory against Marx's criticism that the validity of the theory depends

... on the absurd hypothesis that commodities are without a price, and money without a value, when they first enter into circulation, and that, once in the circulation, an aliquot part of the medley of commodities is exchanged for an aliquot part of the heap of precious metals.[5]

The obvious answer to this criticism is that it is based on a fundamental misunderstanding of the equilibrating process: that commodities are always "with" a price and money always "with" a value, but that the dynamic workings of the real-balance effect assure that this price level—or this value—will not continue to prevail unless it is proportionate to the quantity of money. But Wicksell rests instead with the lame retort that Marx's cost-of-production theory must also start from the same "hypothesis" which he criticizes.[6]

---

[4] *Ibid.*, pp. 39–40, italics and parentheses in original.

See also in this context Wicksell's *Lectures on Political Economy*, Vol. II, *Money*, trans. E. Classen (London, 1935; the original Swedish edition appeared in 1906), pp. 142–43, 160–61. This will henceforth be referred to as *Lectures II*.

[5] K. Marx, *Capital*, trans. S. Moore and E. Aveling (Chicago, 1906), Vol. I, p. 139. Marx is referring here to Montesquieu's discussion cited in Note A above.

[6] *Lectures II*, pp. 147–48.

2. The Demand Curve for Money[7]

On the basis of the rectangular hyperbola which he draws in his *Lectures II*,[8] Wicksell is usually lumped together with Walras and economists of the Cambridge school as having maintained that the demand for money has uniform unitary elasticity.[9] Nevertheless, closer examination of Wicksell's discussion makes it quite clear that he intended his rectangular hyperbola to represent the market-equilibrium curve of Figure III-3 of the text, and not the demand curve of Figure III-1b.[10]

In particular, a reading of this discussion shows that Wicksell is not concerned with the "demand for money"—he does not even mention this term—but with the relationship between the quantity of money and its equilibrium exchange value. Wicksell emphasizes that money is like other goods in that an increase in its given supply decreases its value, but that it has the "special peculiarity" that this inverse dependence is necessarily a proportionate one. This is what he illustrates by the rectangular hyperbola mentioned above. The diagram in which this hyperbola is drawn—and in which it is contrasted with the corresponding curves for commodities—is reproduced here as Figure N-1. It is significant that the term "demand" does not appear in this diagram at all. It is also significant—and again just what our interpretation leads us to expect—that though the discussion on which this diagram is based makes use of "elasticity of demand" in the Marshallian sense,[11] Wicksell does *not* use this term to describe the properties of the rectangular hyperbola which he presents.

Further evidence in support of our interpretation is provided by a comparison of the foregoing diagram with the one presented by Wicksell in his theory of value. Here he analyzes the market for commodity *B* in terms of the diagram reproduced in Figure N-2, where *D* is expressly designated as the demand curve, and *S* as the supply.[12] In sharp distinction to Figure N-1, the price variable now appears on the horizontal axis. But this apparently mysterious reversal of axes is

[7] Attached to Chapter VIII:2.
[8] P. 142. See Figure N-1 below.
[9] Cf., e.g., Marget, *Theory of Prices*, Vol. II, p. 648.
[10] Cf. above, pp. 49 and 42.
[11] *Lectures II*, p. 141, line 9 from bottom.
[12] This is Wicksell's diagram in *Lectures I*, p. 56, with minor changes. Cf. also his earlier *Value Capital and Rent*, trans. S. H. Frowein (London, 1954), pp. 87–88.

precisely what the logic of Wicksell's argument—as it has been interpreted here—requires. For the demand and supply curves of Figure N-2
describe the outcome of a conceptual *individual*-experiment which takes
to price of the commodity as the *independent* variable; hence, in
accordance with mathematical custom, this variable appears on the
horizontal axis. But the market-equilibrium curves of Figure N-1
describe the outcome of a conceptual *market*-experiment which takes

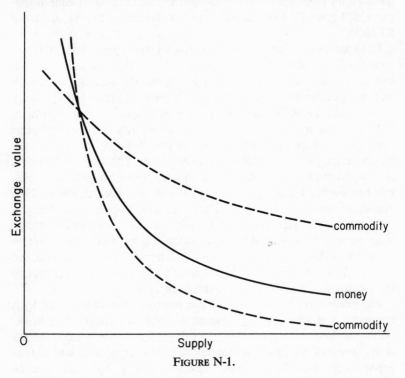

FIGURE N-1.

the price as the *dependent* variable; hence, in accordance with this
same custom, it now appears on the vertical axis. Thus the difference
between these two diagrams is not a chance one, but the systematic
reflection of their differing conceptual frameworks![13]

[13] It should be emphasized that, as Mr. Bent Hansen has kindly verified for me,
this distinction between the two diagrams characterizes all the Swedish editions of
Wicksell's *Lectures* as well.

We might finally note that though we can thus be sure that Wicksell does not intend the rectangular hyperbola of Figure N-1 as a demand curve for money, he at no point indicates what he does consider the form of this curve to be. On this very crucial question our information is sadly deficient.

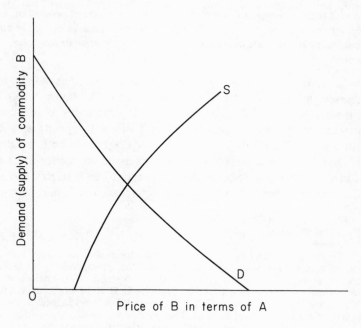

FIGURE N-2.

3. THE RELATIONSHIP BETWEEN RELATIVE PRICES AND MONEY PRICES[14]

Despite the fact that Wicksell devotes a complete chapter of his *Interest and Prices* to the question of "Relative Prices and Money

---

In this connection we should note that the rectangular hyperbola which Walras draws in his monetary theory appears in a diagram in which—just as in his earlier theory of exchange—price appears on the horizontal axis. See *Elements*, ed. Jaffé, comparing pp. 94–103 with p. 335. Cf. also above, p. 569.

[14] Attached to Chapter VIII:3.

Prices,"[15] he fails to make his view on this question completely clear. For one thing, he retains the same term "money prices" both when he considers money which is an abstract unit of account and when he considers money which is a concrete medium of exchange. This alone suffices to create serious exegetical pitfalls. Thus at one point in the chapter he writes:

The exchange of commodities in itself, and the conditions of production and consumption on which it depends, affect only exchange values or *relative* prices: they can exert *no direct influence whatever on the absolute level of money prices.*[16]

Similarly, in the *Lectures* we find: The quantities demanded "are expressed in [terms of] the $n-1$ ratios between the money prices of the n commodities."[17] Both passages provide what seems to be a clear statement of the invalid proposition that demand depends only on relative prices.[18] But this is actually not the case; for in both passages it is clear from the context that Wicksell is assuming money to be an abstract unit of account; hence the "price ratios" he is referring to are —in our terminology—the ratios of *accounting*, and not *money*, prices.[19]

[15] This is the title of Chapter III.

[16] *Ibid.*, p. 23, italics in original.

[17] *Lectures I*, p. 66.

[18] And this is the way I superficially interpreted these passages in my "Indeterminacy of Absolute Prices ... ," *op. cit.*, p. 12, footnote 5, and " Invalidity of Classical Monetary Theory," *Econometrica*, XIX (1951), 149, footnote 30. The nature of my error was made clear to me by a letter from Professor D. H. Robertson in the summer of 1951. It was also pointed out by G. S. Becker and W. J. Baumol, in their "Classical Monetary Theory: The Outcome of the Discussion," *Economica*, XIX (1952), 370.

It might be noted that this same error has been repeated more recently in G. L. S. Shackle's Foreword to Wicksell's *Value Capital and Rent*, p. 8. Here Shackle cites a passage from *Interest and Prices*, p. 39, which actually assumes that money does *not* function as a store of value—and uses it in an attempted interpretation of Wicksell's theory for a money which *is* a store of value. See the next footnote.

[19] " ... we shall now leave on one side the function that money fulfills as a store of value " (*Interest and Prices*, p. 23). From the context—and particularly from the discussion when this assumption is dropped later on p. 39—it is clear that by this assumption Wicksell meant that money is equivalent to an abstract unit of account. See also *ibid.*, p. 24.

"These prices may also be regarded as expressed ... in terms of a measure of value, such as money, which takes no part in the real exchange" (*Lectures I*, p. 66). " ... goods are only exchanged for goods (so that money, if it is used at all, functions in a merely formal manner)" (*ibid.*, p. 67). In his discussion on these pages Wicksell

Thus his statements are completely unobjectionable.[20]

A little later in this chapter Wicksell does, however, refer to the case of a money which has concrete existence and which can therefore act as a "store of value." But even here he leaves his position uncomfortably obscure. In particular, he writes:

... one thing is certain: money prices, as opposed to relative prices, can never be governed by the conditions of the commodity market itself (or of the production of goods); it is rather in the relations of this market to the *money market*, in the widest sense of the term, that it is necessary to search for the causes that regulate money prices.[21]

The implication here is unmistakable that relative prices *can be* " governed by the conditions of the commodity market itself." But there is no way of knowing if this ambiguous phrase refers to the "conditions" of equilibrium in the commodity market itself—in which case it is an expression of the invalid dichotomy—or to the "conditions" of the initial given quantities in this market—in which case it is not.[22]

4. THE "CUMULATIVE PROCESS"[23]

A correct appreciation of the place of the "cumulative process" in Wicksell's monetary theory must start from the understanding that Wicksell always regarded himself as an adherent of the quantity theory and as one of its loyal defenders against critics.[24] At the same time, however, he consistently opposed mechanical formulations of this theory and emphasized the importance of rationalizing it in economic

---

clearly demonstrates—to use our terminology—the determinacy of money prices and indeterminacy of accounting prices.

[20] See p. 22 above.

[21] *Interest and Prices*, p. 24, italics in original. See also the equally obscure observation on p. 94 that "relative prices are the only things that really matter so far as production and consumption are concerned."

[22] In this case it is an expression of the first—and valid—dichotomy described in Chapter VIII: 3 above.

[23] Attached to Chapter X: 3 (end), and XV: 1.

In addition to the references to *Interest and Prices* and *Lectures II* given in this section, the reader might also find it profitable to consult Wicksell's "Influence of the Rate of Interest on Prices," *Economic Journal*, XVII (1907), 213–19.

[24] *Interest and Prices*, Chapters IV–V; *Lectures II*, pp. 141–75.

terms. This, indeed, was his explicit purpose in writing the vivid passage cited in full on pp. 581–82 above. It must also be stressed that the "money" which Wicksell associated with the quantity theory was the metallic currency which served as legal tender and as the ultimate reserves of the banking system. In particular, he did *not* include in it demand deposits. Instead, he regarded the expansion of demand deposits as an increase in the "virtual velocity" of the metallic bank reserves, enabling them to carry out a larger volume of payments.[25]

It is against this background that Wicksell defined his major analytical task: One of the "weakness[es] of the Quantity Theory ... [is that it] assumes an almost completely individualistic system of holding cash balances," whereas such balances have been "replaced in practice by a kind of collective holding of balances, arising out of the acceptance by banks of deposits."[26] In particular, an increase in the quantity of metallic money in a modern economy goes primarily to supplement bank reserves, and not private cash balances. Hence there exists no direct real-balance effect to drive prices upwards. It is therefore necessary to supplement the traditional quantity theory with an explanation of how an increase in bank reserves ultimately brings about an increase in prices. And this is the role of the "cumulative process."[27][28]

---

[25] *Interest and Prices*, pp. 59–62; *Lectures II*, pp. 67–70, 168–69.

[26] *Interest and Prices*, p. 41.

[27] In addition to the references in the three preceding footnotes, see *Interest and Prices*, pp. vii, xxiii–xxiv, 79–80, 101; *Lectures II*, p. 160.

That Wicksell was an advocate of the quantity theory has been duly emphasized by Marget in his *Theory of Prices*, Vol. I, Chapters VI–X. In particular, Marget takes Ohlin to task for implying the contrary in his Introduction to the English translation of *Interest and Prices* (p. xiv; cf. Marget, *Theory of Prices*, p. 184, footnote 73, and p. 221, footnote 43).

In this connection Wicksell seems to have suffered more from his "introducers" than from his critics. Thus in his Foreword to Wicksell's *Value Capital and Rent*, Shackle returns to Ohlin's implication that Wicksell was an opponent of the quantity theory (*ibid.*, pp. 8–9). Shackle bases himself primarily on Wicksell's statement that the validity of the quantity theory depends on the "flimsy" assumption that the "velocity of circulation of money" remains unchanged (*Interest and Prices*, p. 42). But, as is clear from what has just been explained in the text, this is simply a misunderstanding of Wicksell's usage of "velocity." In particular, Wicksell meant nothing more damaging to the quantity theory by this statement than did Fisher when he made the equation of exchange depend on M' as well as M. Cf. also *Interest and Prices*, pp. 61–62.

[28] The remainder of the present study reproduces with minor changes the contents of my "Wicksell's 'Cumulative Process,' " *op. cit.*, pp. 836–44.

The details of this process can best be seen by following through Wicksell's analysis of what is in many ways his "standard case." Assume a gold-standard world, and consider one particular economy, A, which does not produce gold. Start off from a position of equilibrium. Assume now that this equilibrium is disturbed by the discovery of new gold fields in economy B. Wicksell now distinguishes between two effects of the discovery of gold, both of which tend to increase prices in the non-gold-producing country, A. First, there is a direct effect due to the increased demand of B for the goods of A. This causes a price increase in A without any change in the interest rate.[29] If the gold were to be kept entirely in the hands of private individuals in A, there would be no further effects. If, however, some of the gold is transferred directly to A's banks by foreign capitalists, or is deposited there by the public of A, then there is an additional effect.

The banks, finding themselves with excess reserves, will desire to expand their loans. In order to attract borrowers, they will reduce the bank rate. This will have two consequences: "in the first place saving will be discouraged and for that reason there will be an increased demand for goods and services for present consumption. In the second place [since the real rate—the marginal efficiency of capital—depends only on real factors,[30] which have not changed] the profit opportunities of entrepreneurs will thus be increased." Hence they will increase their bank borrowings. The new demand deposits that will thus be placed at their disposal[31] will enable them to increase their "demand for goods and services, as well as for raw materials already in the market for future production.... Owing to the increased income thus accruing to the workers, land-owners, and the owners of raw materials, etc., the prices of consumption goods will begin to rise, the more so as the factors of production previously available are now withdrawn for the purposes of future production. Equilibrium in the market for goods and services

[29] *Lectures II*, pp. 197–98, 215–16.

[30] *Lectures II*, pp. 190–91, 199; *Interest and Prices*, pp. xxvi, 106, Chapter IX.

[31] Throughout his analysis it is clear that Wicksell assumes an expansion in bank credit to be a fundamental intermediate step of the process. For detailed textual evidence, see Marget, *Theory of Prices*, Vol. I, pp. 183 ff. Marget refers to *Interest and Prices*, pp. xxiv, 27, 76, 82 (footnote), 83 f., 85, 101, 105, 110, 135, 144, 152, 190; and to *Lectures II*, p. 197.

Wicksell's failure to make this assumption even more explicit is another reflection of the already emphasized fact that he did *not* consider demand deposits as constituting part of the money supply proper.

will therefore be disturbed. As against an increased demand in two directions there will be an unchanged or even diminished supply [since we are assuming full employment], which must result in an increase in wages (rent) and, directly or indirectly, in prices."[32] Again, it must be emphasized that "only in so far as new gold is deposited in the banks in the form of 'capital', i.e., without being drawn out in cheques and notes soon after, can it give rise to a lowering of interest rates and in that way affect prices."[33]

The resulting price increase is, to use Wicksell's term, "cumulative"; that is, a *given* discrepancy between the bank rate[34] and the real rate will, *if maintained indefinitely*, bring about a *continuous*, and not merely a *given*, increase in prices. In other words, after the initial increase in prices, "a further rise in prices [does not] require a further fall in the rate of interest." It must be emphasized that by "cumulative process" Wicksell does *not* mean a self-generating one, that is, one which carries within itself all the elements necessary for its own perpetuation. Specifically, as we have just seen, even if the discrepancy between real and market rates were to be maintained during subsequent periods, prices could not continue to rise unless bank credit continued to expand. Nor does Wicksell mean that the process continues because it generates expectations of further price rises. For he assumes that entrepreneurs generally anticipate future prices to be the same as present ones. He does recognize that this assumption is not always true. But, as we shall soon see, he makes it clear that he considers the case of elastic

[32] *Lectures II*, pp. 194–95; cf. also *Interest and Prices*, pp. 87 ff. The assumption of full employment is explicitly made on p. 195 of the former reference.

In his *Interest and Prices* Wicksell considers only the indirect effect, and so insists that no change in prices can take place without a prior change in the interest rate. In *Lectures II* Wicksell not only modifies this stand by introducing the direct effect, but goes as far as to relegate the indirect effect to secondary importance, stating that "contrary to Ricardo's view, [it] does not happen as a rule" (*Lectures II*, p. 215). (Cf. also the passage from Wicksell's Preface to the first Swedish edition of *Lectures II* cited by Ohlin in his Introduction to *Interest and Prices*, pp. xv–xvi. This Preface is omitted from the English translation.)

In the light of Viner's study of the treatment accorded to the direct and indirect effects in the classical literature, it is interesting to note that Wicksell attributes his earlier view to the classical school [*ibid.*; Jacob Viner, *Studies in the Theory of International Trade* (New York, 1937), pp. 394–403].

[33] *Lectures II*, p. 215.

[34] In what follows, this term is used interchangeably with "market rate," since, in Wicksell's system, this is initially set by the banks.

price expectations to be a special one, outside his main field of investigation.[35]

The question then arises: Are there any forces which bring the cumulative process to an end? Do there exist any "limits ... which restrict the power of the banks" to maintain indefinitely a rate lower than the real one?[36] Taking account of the effect of higher prices on the reserves of the banks, Wicksell answers this question in the affirmative. First of all, the high prices will cause an external drain, forcing the banks to raise their rate. But this is not a sufficient answer; for if other countries are expanding at the same rate, this influence will not be operative.[37]

Wicksell then introduces the fundamental restrictive element in this process: If the banks maintain their rate below the real one, the resulting expansion of bank loans will ultimately bring about an internal drain. For "when there are no [bank] notes of small denomination and where metallic money is used in business, then on this assumption [of a continuous rise in commodity prices] the increased demand for gold for internal business would soon empty the bank's vaults." Hence, in order to protect their reserves, the banks must raise their rates. In this way, "the two rates of interest ... reach *ultimate* equality, but only after, and as a result of, a previous movement of prices."[38][39] When this equality is reached, there will be no further incentive for entrepreneurs to increase their borrowings from the banks. Throughout this process of adjustment the marginal efficiency of capital—that is, the real rate of interest—remains unchanged: for the prices of productive services and investment goods rise in the same proportion as the anticipated

[35] The quotation in this paragraph is from *Interest and Prices*, pp. 93–94.

Supporting evidence for the second half of this paragraph will be found in the references cited in footnote 32 above; *Interest and Prices*, p. 95; and *Lectures II*, pp. 185 and 196, Cf. also the discussion below of the "divergent case."

[36] *Interest and Prices*, pp. 111 ff.

[37] *Lectures II*, p. 189; *Interest and Prices, pp.* 78, 113.

[38] An implicit assumption of the analysis is that there is no rationing of credit. Cf. Marget, *Theory of Prices*, Vol. I, pp. 223 ff.

[39] The two citations in the text are from *Lectures II*, p. 189, and *Interest and Prices*, p. 135, respectively. Italics in original. There will also be an internal drain into industrial use; cf. *Interest and Prices*, p. 113; *Lectures II*, pp. 124–25.

For other passages dealing with the process described in the text, cf. the following: *Lectures II*, pp. 90, 124–26, 164, 179, 186, 194, 196, 198, 201–202, 204; *Interest and Prices*, pp. xxvi–xxvii, 113–17. Cf. also the passage from *Interest and Prices*, pp. 108–11, cited on p. 368 above.

prices of the goods they produce. Thus the system is brought to a new equilibrium position: one in which the market rate of interest is the same as it was before the disturbance, but prices are, and remain, at a higher level.[40]

Thus the operation of a cumulative process does not imply that the system is unstable, and that, after the initial disturbance, it continuously moves away from an equilibrium position. On the contrary, through its effects on bank reserves, the cumulative process in Wicksell's analysis plays the role of the fundamental equilibrating mechanism forcing the banks to eliminate any discrepancy between the rate they set and the real rate, and thus restoring equilibrium to the loan market.

Underlying the preceding analysis is a simple hypothesis about the dynamic behavior of the market rate. Wicksell assumes that "banks never alter their interest rates unless they are induced to do so by the force of outside circumstances. They raise the rate when their gold stocks are threatened with depletion, or their current obligations are so great that their disparity in relation to their gold holdings is regarded as dangerous, or, still more, where both of these things occur together, as is often the case."[41] This passage makes it clear that Wicksell considers a decrease in absolute reserves and an increase in deposits as being two distinct phenomena, even though each causes a decline in the reserve ratio. In fact, the general tenor of Wicksell's presentation is that banks are much more sensitive to the former than they are to the latter. This interpretation is supported by some explicit passages.[42] But,

[40] *Lectures II*, pp. 198–99. Cf. also *Interest and Prices*, p. 95.

In the first reference Wicksell discusses the possibility that the process of adjustment will also affect the real rate through "forced savings." This will be discussed further in Note J.

[41] *Lectures II*, p. 204.

[42] Thus the second passage referred to in footnote 39 above goes on to say: "Prices constitute, so to speak, a spiral spring which serves to transmit the power between the natural and the money rates of interest; but the spring must first be sufficiently stretched or compressed. In a pure cash economy, the spring is short and rigid; it becomes longer and more elastic in accordance with the stage of development of the system of credit and banking." (*Interest and Prices*, pp. 135–36.)

There is a similar passage some twenty-five pages before: " ... it is clear that in an elastic monetary system where there is only a small reaction against an alteration in prices [i.e., a small internal drain], a fairly constant difference between the two rates of interest could be maintained for a long time, and the effect on prices might be considerable." (*Ibid.*, p. 110.)

Unless Wicksell is assuming the difference in sensitivity just described, it is hard

most important of all, it is a necessary dynamic assumption of Wicksell's system as presented above. For if bankers were guided, not by their *absolute* reserves, but solely by their reserve *ratio*, then they would raise their rates and slow up the expansion of their loans as soon as their reserve ratio declined. In this way the cumulative process could *conceivably* be brought to an end without an internal drain; correspondingly, the movement of prices would not be the *necessary* intermediate step of the argument that it is in Wicksell's presentation.

This exclusive concentration on the level of absolute reserves also explains why Wicksell does not incorporate into his analysis another equilibrating mechanism: namely, as prices rise, the demand for loans at any given rate of interest increases, since entrepreneurs need more money to carry out their projects. Ordinarily, one would say that this would tend to raise the rate of interest. But if we accept Wicksell's assumption that bankers change the rate only in response to changes in their absolute reserves, this increase in demand cannot directly affect the rate. Consequently, this influence is never even mentioned in Wicksell's analysis.[43]

Wicksell emphasizes that it takes time for this equilibrating process to work. Indeed, it is the lag in the adjustment of the market rate to the real rate which enables him to explain the fact that historically rising prices and rising interest rates go together. Wicksell stresses that it is not the level of the market rate which counts, but its relation to the real rate. If the market rate is only slowly moving up toward equality with the real rate, then throughout the period of adjustment the expansion of bank loans is continuing, and with it the increase of prices. Hence the data do not contradict his theory.[44]

Wicksell also recognizes that if the price increase continues for some time, the assumption that anticipated prices are the same as present ones may have to be dropped. "The upward movement of prices will in some measure 'create its own draught.' When prices have been rising steadily for some time, entrepreneurs will begin to reckon on the basis not merely of the prices already attained, but of a further rise in

---

to see why there should be the difference he indicates between a cash and credit economy.

[43] Compare this with the passages from Hume, Thornton, Ricardo, and Mill cited in Note J below.

[44] *Interest and Prices*, pp. 107, 167–68; *Lectures II*, pp. 205–7.

prices." In such an event, "to put an immediate stop to any further rise in prices, it would not be sufficient for the banks to restore the rate of interest to its original level." Wicksell's position here seems to be that even in this case the system will return to equilibrium, but that the return will be a spiraling one. That is, the market rate will first rise above the real rate, and then, as the anticipated price rises fail to materialize, it will fall back to equality with it. He does admit that in the case of a speculative fever there may be "no limit to the rise in prices." But he gives scant attention to this possibility, and explicitly declares that it is outside his main field of interest.[45]

On the basis of the preceding exposition it is also quite easy to see the conditions under which the divergent case—in which prices continue to rise indefinitely—can occur. Two situations must be distinguished: If there is a banking system operating with required gold reserves, "the condition on which the banks could maintain a rate of interest permanently below the real rate would therefore be an incessant flow to them of new gold, and under such circumstances commodity prices would also rise continuously."[46]

If, however, there is a Wicksellian "ideal bank" or "pure credit" system,[47] no such condition is necessary. In this system no one desires to use gold; all money is in the form of demand deposits and bank notes. Hence banks have no need to maintain any gold reserves, are never in any danger of an internal drain, and are thus free to set and maintain indefinitely any market rate they choose. If this rate is less than the real one, bank credit and demand deposits will expand. By increasing the quantity of money in this way, the banks can bring about any specified price level by maintaining a discrepancy between the market and real rates until the desired price level is reached, and then equalizing the rates at that point.[48]

It is within the preceding context that we must understand the frequently quoted passage in which Wicksell writes:

[45] *Interest and Prices*, pp. 96–98. In his *Lectures II*, Wicksell devotes only five lines to this subject (p. 207).

[46] *Lectures II*, p. 198.

[47] Described in *Lectures II*, pp. 84–91; *Interest and Prices*, pp. 68 ff.

[48] Cf. the references on p. 589, footnote 31, and p. 591, footnote 39. It might also be noted that in his Preface to *Interest and Prices* (p. xxvi), Wicksell restricts the conclusion that the market and real rates must be equalized to the "monetary system of actual fact." Cf. also *ibid.*, p. 80, and especially pp. 110–11. Cf. also the discussion which now follows of Wicksell's passage, *ibid.*, pp. 100–101.

It should now be clear that, in so far as our hypothetical conclusions are in accordance with reality, the movement and equilibrium of actual money prices represent a fundamentally different phenomenon, *above all in a fully developed credit system*, from those of *relative* prices. The latter might perhaps be compared with a mechanical system which satisfies the conditions of *stable* equilibrium, for instance a pendulum. Every movement away from the position of equilibrium sets forces into operation—on a scale that increases with the extent of the movement—which tend to restore the system to its original position, and actually succeed in doing so, though some oscillations may intervene.

The analogous picture for *money* prices should rather be some easily movable object, such as a cylinder, which rests on a horizontal plane in so-called *neutral* equilibrium. The plane is somewhat rough, and a certain force is required to set the price-cylinder in motion and to keep it in motion. But so long as this force—the raising or lowering of the rate of interest—remains in operation, the cylinder continues to move in the same direction. Indeed, it will, after a time, start "rolling": the motion is an accelerated one up to a certain point, and it continues for a time even when the force has ceased to operate. Once the cylinder has come to rest, there is no tendency for it to be restored to its original position. It simply remains where it is so long as no opposite forces come into operation to push it back.

It is, of course, clear that such forces can never be entirely absent, no matter how developed the credit system may be, if a precious metal or some other material substance serves as a monetary basis. The simple quantity theory is no longer adequate to deal with the nature of these reactions and with the manner of their operation. It is this question which we shall shortly be considering.[49]

It would be a serious misunderstanding of Wicksell's analysis to interpret this passage as making an absolute distinction between the two types of equilibria.[50] Such an interpretation is directly refuted by the demonstration above that Wicksell uses the cumulative process as an equilibrating mechanism bringing the system to *one definite level of money prices*. But even aside from this fundamental objection, the internal evidence of this passage, as well as of its counterpart in *Lectures II*, shows that Wicksell is not making a general distinction, but is restricting his analysis (as he must, to be consistent) to the case of a pure credit economy.

[49] *Interest and Prices*, pp. 100–101. All but the first italics are in the original.
[50] This is the interpretation given by G. Myrdal [*Monetary Equilibrium* (London, 1939), pp. 35–36] and P. N. Rosenstein-Rodan ["The Coördination of the General Theories of Money and Price," *Economica*, III (1936), 275–76].

This evidence is unmistakable. There is, in the first place, the first italicized phrase of the passage.[51] Secondly, in the corresponding passage in *Lectures II*[52] the statement that the equilibrium of money prices is only a neutral one is explicitly restricted to the case of "a monetary system of unlimited elasticity"—an alternative term Wicksell uses to describe his pure credit system.[53] Finally, the concluding paragraph of the above-quoted passage removes any doubt that might remain. In fact, this concluding paragraph (which is the last one of Chapter VII) clearly sets the stage—and gives the cue—for the analysis of the equilibrating cumulative process which Wicksell goes on to describe in Chapter VIII.[54]

Thus, when read with the qualification upon which he himself insists, Wicksell's dramatic contrast reduces to a commonplace. When, in addition, we recall that throughout this process of moving from one point of "neutral" equilibrium to another the volume of demand deposits is continuously changing,[55] it is immediately apparent that, under corresponding conditions, even relative prices would be in "neutral equilibrium"! For what Wicksell is essentially saying is that the level of money prices is indeterminate as long as the quantity of money is not fixed, and that continuous changes in the quantity of money will cause continuous changes in the "price" (value) of money relative to other commodities. But the same statement can be made for the relative price of potatoes—if the quantity of potatoes in the market is continuously changing. Conversely, the equilibrium of money prices can be just as stable as that of relative prices—provided that in each case the initial quantities remain unchanged.

Indeed, one cannot read the foregoing passage without feeling that the emphasis which Wicksell places upon it is simply a reflection of his failure to include demand deposits in his definition of the money supply.

[51] Not italicized in the original.

[52] *Lectures II*, p. 197.

[53] In support of this interpretation of "unlimited elasticity," cf. *Lectures II*, p. 194, lines 6–15; *Interest and Prices*, pp. 110, 135.

[54] On this whole discussion, cf. the references in footnote 48 on p. 594.

Though Rosenstein-Rodan quotes from the passage cited here in support of his interpretation, he significantly omits both the first italicized phrase and the final paragraph (*op. cit.*, p. 275, footnote 2).

Note how the last paragraph of this passage bears out the interpretation of Wicksell's relation to the quantity theory emphasized at the beginning of this section.

[55] Cf. above, p. 589, footnote 31.

Accordingly, one cannot help feeling that had he worked with a modern definition of "money," he would never have written this passage in the first place.[56]

---

[56] For the broader implications of the cumulative process as a simultaneous *tâtonnement* in the commodity and bond (bank-loan) markets, see Chapter XV:1 above.

Note F. Newcomb, Fisher, and the Transactions Approach to the Quantity Theory

1. The Real-Balance Effect[1]

Newcomb's work is of particular interest to us because of his emphasis on the fact that changes in the quantity of money affect prices only through their prior effect on the demand for commodities.[2] Indeed, he explicitly writes this demand as a function of the quantity of money. Furthermore, the form of his function is such that it is unaffected by an equiproportionate change in the price level *and* in the quantity of money![3] Nevertheless, it would be a mistake to accept all this as definite recognition of the real-balance effect. For nowhere in his argument does Newcomb bring in that crucial intermediate stage where the monetary increase makes individuals feel that their cash balances are larger than needed so that they can expand their purchases accordingly.[4]

[1] Attached to Chapter VIII:1.

[2] S. Newcomb, *Principles of Political Economy* (New York, 1885), pp. 315–58 (especially pp. 342–44 and 351–55) and pp. 380–84.

[3] *Ibid.*, equation (b) on p. 354, and the discussion leading up to it. The equation is $D = N \cdot F/P$—where D is the amount of commodities demanded, N a constant, F the "flow of currency," and P the price level. On p. 323 we find F defined as $V \cdot R$—where V is the volume of currency and R its velocity of circulation.

[4] Contrast this with the corresponding passages from Wicksell (Note E:1 above) and Fisher (next paragraph).

That is, Newcomb fails to distinguish sufficiently, if at all, between money considered as an income or expenditure flow, and money considered as a reserve balance.[5]

Though drawing his inspiration from Newcomb,[6] Fisher greatly improved his predecessor's exposition of this point. In particular, the following passage clearly reveals Fisher's understanding of each component of the tripartite quantity-theory thesis,[7] and of the real-balance effect in particular:

Suppose, for a moment, that a doubling in the currency in circulation should not at once raise prices, but should halve the velocities instead; such a result would evidently upset for each individual the adjustment which he had made of cash on hand. Prices being unchanged, he now has double the amount of money and deposits which his convenience had taught him to keep on hand. He will then try to get rid of the surplus money and deposits by buying goods. But as somebody else must be found to take the money off his hands, its mere transfer will not diminish the amount in the community. It will simply increase somebody else's surplus. Everybody has money on his hands beyond what experience and convenience have shown to be necessary. Everybody will want to exchange this relatively useless extra money for goods, and the desire so to do must surely drive up the price of goods. No one can deny that the effect of every one's desiring to spend more money will be to raise prices. Obviously this tendency will continue until there is found another adjustment of quantities [of money] to expenditures, and the V's are the same as originally. That is, if there is no change in the quantities sold (the Q's), the only possible effect of doubling M and M' will be a doubling of the p's; for we have just seen that the V's cannot be permanently reduced without causing people to have surplus money and deposits, and there cannot be surplus money and deposits without a desire to spend it, and there cannot be a desire to spend it without a rise in prices. In short, the only way to get rid of a plethora of money is to raise prices to correspond.[8, 9]

[5] Cf. Newcomb, *op. cit.*, pp. 218–19, 351–55, 380–87. Note also that the formula in footnote 3 above depends on the "flow of currency." Cf. also the beginning of Note A above.

[6] See the dedication page in the *Purchasing Power of Money* (New York, 1911).

[7] Above, pp. 163–64.

[8] *Ibid.*, pp. 153–54. The bracketed expression "of money" is inserted on the basis of the following passage two pages earlier: "He adjusts this time of turnover [i.e., V] by adjusting his average quantity of pocket money, or till money, to suit his expenditures [*ibid.*, p. 152]."

[9] For a similar passage, see Fisher's *Elementary Principles of Economics* (New York, 1912), pp. 242–47.

2. The Question of Stability Analysis[10]

Clearly, there is a type of stability analysis in the preceding passage. But I am troubled by the fact that Fisher presents it within a comparative-statics framework, and not (as in the stability analysis of his value theory[11]) within a static one. Consequently, I wonder if Fisher would have applied the foregoing argument to show (like Wicksell) that if the p's fall while M remains constant, the p's will be forced up again. This would be an unjustified quibble—were it not for the evidence of the literature that just such an incomplete recognition of the real-balance effect has repeatedly manifested itself.[12]

3. The Relationship Between the Monetary Equation and the Commodity Equations[13]

The contention of Chapter VIII:3 that Fisher failed to understand the proper relationship between the monetary equation and the commodity equations is based primarily on the following passage from the *Purchasing Power of Money*, reproduced together with its crucial footnote:

[It is a] ... fallacious idea that the price level cannot be determined by other factors in the equation of exchange because it is already determined by other causes, usually alluded to as "supply and demand." This vague phrase has covered multitudes of sins of slothful analysts in economics. Those who place such implicit reliance on the competency of supply and demand to fix prices, irrespective of the quantity of money, deposits, velocity, and trade, will have their confidence rudely shaken if they will follow the reasoning as to price causation of separate articles. They will find that there are always just one *too few equations* to determine the unknown quantities [i.e., money prices] involved.* The equation of exchange is needed in each case to supplement the equations of supply and demand.

* Cf. Irving Fisher, " Mathematical Investigations in the Theory of Value and Prices," *Transactions of the Connecticut Academy of Arts and Science*, Vol. IX, 1892, p. 62.[14]

---

10 Attached to Chapter VIII:1.

11 *Elementary Principles*, pp. 266–67.

12 Cf. Notes G:2 and I:3 below. Cf. also pp. 538–39 above.

13 Attached to Chapter VIII:3.

14 Pp. 174–75, italics in original. Part of this passage has already been cited in the text, p. 184. The work cited in Fisher's footnote was reprinted in New Haven, 1925. All references are to this reprint.

It would take us too far afield to insert here a complete statement of price-determining principles. But the compatibility of the equation of exchange with the equations which have to deal with prices individually may be brought home to the reader sufficiently for our present purposes by emphasizing the distinction between (1) individual prices relatively to each other and (2) the price *level.* The equation of exchange determines the latter (the price level) only, and the latter only is the subject of this book. It will not help, but only hinder the reader to mix with the discussion of price levels the principles determining individual prices relatively to each other.

Admittedly, this passage does not *explicitly* say that the commodity demand and supply equations by themselves determine relative prices. But it certainly is hard to see what other meaning it could have. At any rate, it is clear that Fisher conceived the special role of the equation of exchange to be the determination of the absolute price level. It is also clear—and this is what has already been noted in the text—that Fisher was confused as to the nature of the various prices. For if we check the reference he cites in the footnote we will see that the equation added there is the definitional $p_n = 1$, serving to determine *accounting* prices, and not the equation of exchange, serving to determine *money* prices![15] In other words, Fisher confused the valid dichotomy between money and accounting prices with the invalid one between relative and money prices.

At first sight, the following passage offers corroborating evidence for this contention:

The demand for sugar is not only relative to the price of sugar, but also to the general level of other things. Not only is the demand for sugar at ten cents a pound greater than the demand at twenty cents a pound (at a given level of prices of other things), but the demand at twenty cents *at a high level of prices* is greater than the demand at twenty cents *at a low level of prices.* In fact if the price level is doubled, the demand at twenty cents a pound will be as great as the demand was before at ten cents a pound, assuming that the doubling applies likewise to wages and incomes generally.[16]

Here is a seemingly unambiguous statement that demand is unaffected by a doubling of all prices.[17] Nevertheless, the evidence is not conclusive;

[15] Cf. also the equation added on p. 59 of the *Mathematical Investigations in the Theory of Value and Prices.*

[16] *Purchasing Power of Money,* pp. 176–77, italics in original.

[17] Indeed, this is the way I understood it until W. J. Baumol (in a letter written in the spring of 1953) suggested the possibility set out in the next sentence.

for Fisher may tacitly be assuming that this doubling of prices is accompanied by a doubling of money holdings, so that there is no real-balance effect. That this is not a far-fetched possibility is suggested by the parallel discussion in his *Elementary Principles of Economics*, which begins with the explicit assumption "that we change our monetary unit so that what is now fifty cents should be called a dollar."[18] On the other hand, this discussion in no way indicates that Fisher was aware of the crucial importance of this accompanying increase in the quantity of money. This is particularly noticeable in his subsequent statement that "if previously people were willing to take [a certain quantity of sugar] ... at one price, they are now willing to take it at double that price, because this double price means in purchasing power exactly the same thing as the original price."[19] The equally necessary "and because their initial nominal money holdings have also doubled" is significantly absent.

Actually, the *Elementary Principles of Economics* provides just as convincing proof as the *Purchasing Power of Money* that Fisher was guilty of the invalid dichotomy. Chapter XV of the former—in which the passages just cited appear—is essentially an elaboration of the two passages from the latter cited earlier in this section. The reader must study this Chapter XV for himself and see if he can leave it with any other impression than that of the invalid dichotomy. It should particularly be emphasized that the final, summarizing paragraph of this chapter is the source of the revealing passage cited in full at the end of Chapter VIII: 3 above.[20]

[18] *Elementary Principles*, p. 274.

[19] *Ibid.*, p. 275.

[20] Note also how this chapter constantly develops the theme that "individual prices, such, for instance, as the price of sugar, presuppose a price level" (*ibid.*, p. 258).

It might finally be noted that A. G. Hart also interprets Fisher's *Elementary Principles* this way—though without realizing that the dichotomy is invalid. Cf. his *Money, Debt, and Economic Activity* (2nd ed.; New York, 1953), p. 144, footnote 4.

Note G. Marshall, Pigou, and the Cambridge Cash-Balance Approach to the Quantity Theory

1. THE REAL-BALANCE EFFECT[1]

The Cambridge cash-balance tradition begins, of course, with Marshall[2] and continues with Pigou,[3] Keynes,[4] and Robertson.[5]

[1] Attached to Chapter VIII:1.

[2] A. Marshall, *Money Credit and Commerce* (London, 1923), pp. 43–50, 282–84. As Marshall emphasized, the crucial parts of this analysis are reproduced from his testimony before the Gold and Silver Commission (1887–88) and the Indian Currency Committee (1899). This is reprinted in *Official Papers by Alfred Marshall* (London, 1926), pp. 34–38, 51–52, 267–69. For the dating of Marshall's development of monetary theory even further back, to the 1870's, see J. M. Keynes, "Alfred Marshall, 1842–1924," in *Memorials of Alfred Marshall*, ed. A. C. Pigou (London, 1925), pp. 27–30.

For the real-balance effect, see *Money Credit and Commerce*, bottom of p. 43; *Official Papers*, p. 52. On the other hand, it might be noted that in his *Economics of Industry* (London, 1881), Marshall analyzes the consequences of a general decline of prices without making any mention of this effect [Book III, Chapter I, §5; as reprinted in *Readings in Business Cycles and National Income*, ed. A. H. Hansen and R. V. Clemence (New York, 1953), p. 102].

[3] A. C. Pigou, "The Value of Money," *Quarterly Journal of Economics*, XXXII (1917–18), reprinted in *Readings in Monetary Theory*, ed. F. A. Lutz and L. W. Mints (Philadelphia, 1951), pp. 162–83. This appears in a revised form under the title "The Exchange Value of Legal Tender Money," *Essays in Applied Economics* (London, 1923), pp. 174–98.

For the real-balance effect, see "Value of Money," *op. cit.*, pp. 166–67.

[4] J. M. Keynes, *Tract on Monetary Reform* (London, 1923), pp. 74–79.

For the real-balance effect, see bottom of p. 75. For the terming of Fisher's theory as "artificial," see bottom of p. 78. Cf. also Keynes' review of Fisher's *Purchasing Power of Money*, in *Economic Journal*, XXI (1911), 394–96.

[5] D. H. Robertson, *Money* (rev. ed.; London, 1948), pp. 27–40, 180–81. For the

None of these writers provides as vivid or systematic a picture of the real-balance effect as do Wicksell[6] and Fisher.[7] Nevertheless, they do at various points indicate their recognition of this effect.[8]

2. THE ABSENCE OF STABILITY ANALYSIS[9]

One of the central motivations of the Cambridge cash-balance approach is the desire to integrate monetary theory and value theory. Thus Marshall goes out of his way to show how the value of money can be determined by the use of ordinary demand and supply curves.[10] Pigou systematically organizes his analysis of the "Value of Money"[11] under the successive section headings "The Demand for Legal Tender Money," "The Supply of Legal Tender Money," and "Demand and Supply." And Robertson stresses that his book on *Money* is "the second volume of a series [namely, Cambridge Economic Handbooks]. Its connection with its predecessor—Mr. Henderson's *Supply and Demand*—is to be found in the emphasis laid on the theory of money as a special case of the general theory of value."[12]

It is the contrast it affords with this obvious desire that lends crucial significance to the failure of Cambridge economists to carry over to their monetary theory the stability analysis of their value theory. Thus Marshall's graphical analysis of international trade in Appendix J of *Money Credit and Commerce* has a detailed discussion of stability conditions,[13] but his graphical analysis of the determination of the value of money in Appendix C is void of even an allusion to such a discussion. This omission must also be contrasted with Marshall's well-known discussions of stability conditions in his ordinary theory of value.[14]

---

real-balance effect, see *ibid.*, p. 36, lines 20–21; see also *Banking Policy and the Price Level* (New York, 1949, originally published 1926), pp. 47–50, 59–60.

[6] Above, Note E:1.

[7] Above, Note F:1.

[8] See the specific references in the preceding footnotes.

[9] Attached to Chapter VIII:1.

[10] *Money Credit and Commerce*, Appendix C. Note too how Keynes emphasizes that Marshall taught "the quantity theory of money as a part of the general theory of value" ("Alfred Marshall, 1842–1924," *op. cit.*, p. 29).

[11] *Op. cit.*

[12] *Money*, p. xii. Robertson returns to this theme on p. 30.

[13] See especially p. 341. Cf. also his *Pure Theory of Foreign Trade* (reprinted London, 1930), Chapter II.

[14] *Principles*, pp. 345–46, 806–7. Cf. also his *Pure Theory of Domestic Values* (reprinted London, 1930), pp. 11–14.

The same asymmetry characterizes Pigou—who refers to the latter discussions in their appropriate contexts,[15] but who makes no attempt to apply them to monetary theory. Similarly instructive is the absence of stability analysis in Robertson's *Money*[16] as compared with its presence in Henderson's *Supply and Demand.*[17]

It is particularly interesting to see how this asymmetry is perpetuated in the early textbooks which drew their inspiration from Marshall. Thus both J. S. Nicholson[18] and S. Chapman [19] present simple stability discussions in their value-theory chapters[20] and omit such discussions in their monetary-theory ones.[21] But at the same time, Chapman concludes his discussion of the quantity theory by emphasizing that "the reader will now perceive that the theory of money fits into the ordinary theory of the determination of the value of things by demand and supply"![22]

3. The Unitary Elasticity of Demand for Money[23]

In the well-known Appendix C to his *Money Credit and Commerce*, Marshall presents a diagram, reproduced here as Figure N-3, in which the demand curve for gold in its monetary use is represented by the

[15] *Economics of Welfare* (fourth ed.; London, 1932), pp. 794–801; *Economics of Stationary States* (London, 1935), p. 39.

[16] Pp. 27–38.

[17] (Rev. ed.; London, 1932), Chapter II, especially bottom of p. 23.

[18] *Principles of Political Economy* (London: Vol. I, 1893; Vol. II, 1897; Vol. III, 1901). On the debt to Marshall, see the Preface to Vol. I.

[19] *Outlines of Political Economy* (2nd ed.; London, 1917). On Marshall, see once again the Preface.

[20] Nicholson, in Vol. II, pp. 38–39; Chapman, on pp. 168–72.

[21] Nicholson, in Vol. II, pp. 118–22; Chapman, on pp. 211–17. It might be noted that neither does any such discussion appear in Nicholson's *Treatise on Money* (London, 1888).

[22] *Op. cit.*, p. 215. Among modern cash-balance expositions, Chandler's (*op. cit.*, pp. 549–50) seems to be the only one with a stability analysis.

We might note that David Barbour does present the beginnings of a stability analysis when he asks what happens if "all prices and wages ... are increased five-fold." His argument—which is not very complete—is, however, carried out entirely in terms of the effect of such a price rise in generating an internal drain and thereby reducing bank reserves; the effect on the real value of individual cash reserves is completely ignored. It should also be emphasized that Barbour's thinking on monetary theory does not show any Marshallian influence. [*The Standard of Value* (London, 1912), p. 37; see also pp. 38–40, 44.]

[23] Attached to Chapter VIII:2.

rectangular hyperbola *dd'*. Similarly, "supply is ... shown by a vertical straight line [*BS*] representing a given aggregate stock of gold."[24] If gold has only monetary uses, its equilibrium value is then determined by the intersection of *dd'* and *BS* at *A*. If, however, it also has non-monetary uses, its equilibrium value is determined by the intersection of *DD'* with *BS*—where *DD'* represents the composite demand curve for both types of uses. In his classic essay on the "Value of Money," Pigou essentially restricts himself to the monetary demand, refines and elaborates Marshall's discussion considerably, but also emphasizes that the demand curve for money has the form of a rectangular hyperbola and is therefore of uniform unitary elasticity.[25]

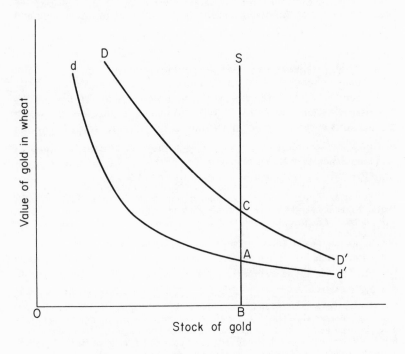

FIGURE N-3.

[24] *Money Credit and Commerce*, p. 283.
[25] "Value of Money," *op. cit.*, p. 165; "The Exchange Value of Legal Tender Money," *op. cit.*, p. 176, lines 16–18; p. 190.

It must be emphasized that, unlike Wicksell,[26] Marshall and Pigou are definitely referring to a demand curve and *not* a market-equilibrium curve.[27] Correspondingly, they are definitely using "unitary elasticity of demand for money" in the ordinary Marshallian sense of elasticity. That this is the intended usage can be seen from the fact that the only distinction Marshall draws in Appendix C between his rectangular hyperbola and any other demand curve is that the former refers to a stock and not a flow.[28] It can be seen even more explicitly from the footnote at the end of the Appendix, in which Marshall refers the reader to the specific demand and supply curves of the *Principles* for an extension of his analysis to more complicated cases. This footnote concludes with the observation that even in these cases "the representative currency-demand curve for gold would be a rectangular hyperbola."

The case of Pigou is also clear. In what other than the usual Marshallian sense can we understand the passage in which he writes that "when the supply of legal-tender money varies in a given measure, the resultant change in the value of money will be less, the more elastic is the demand. Since, however, the demand for money always has an elasticity equal to unity, this proposition has no practical implications."[29] To this can be added the equally revealing passage cited at the beginning of Chapter VIII:2 above.

As has, however, been noted in the text,[30] if the assumptions of Marshall's ordinary demand curve are transferred to his money demand curve, then the latter should indeed be represented by the rectangular hyperbola of Figure II-1b. I hesitate, however, to make such a transfer because it has implications at odds with other characteristics of Marshall's analysis. In particular, the whole point of Marshall's approach is to organize the forces which determine the equilibrium price into two categories—demand and supply—which, ideally, are mutually exclusive. Now, the distinguishing feature of the demand curve in Figure II-1b is that it depends on the *supply* of money. Surely this interdependence of demand and supply—so unusual for Marshall— would have been explicitly pointed out by him. This consideration is

[26] Above, Note E:2.
[27] Cf. pp. 48–50 above.
[28] *Money Credit and Commerce*, p. 282.
[29] "The Exchange Value of Legal Tender Money," *op. cit.*, p. 190.
[30] Pp. 170–71.

even more telling with reference to Pigou. For though he does point out that "the demand schedule and the supply schedule for money are not strictly independent of one another," he does not base this observation on the grounds referred to in Figure II-1b.[31]

Marshall and Pigou made the phrase "unitary elasticity of demand for money" a standard fixture of the literature on monetary theory.[32] This phrase is, however, used indiscriminately to refer now to a demand curve, now to a market-equilibrium curve, and now to both at the same time. Thus Chapman writes:

... if the quantity of commodities remains fixed, an increase of money causes depreciation of money and a decrease of money appreciation of money. The latter proposition is sometimes expressed quantitatively in technical language by saying that the *elasticity of demand for money is unity* (see pp. 42–44).[33]

This by itself is a perfect description of the market-equilibrium rectangular hyperbola in Figure III-3; but the pages to which Chapman refers at the end of the passage provide an explanation of the elasticity of demand of a Marshallian demand curve! Similarly, Taussig writes:

Hence when there is twice as much money, the same number of commodities will be offered for the money, and prices will be twice as high as before. In other words, using a phrase already explained, the elasticity of demand for money is unity.[34]

Once again, though the first sentence describes a market-equilibrium curve, the only context in which Taussig has "already explained" the phrase "elasticity of demand" is in connection with a Marshallian demand curve.[35] Finally, we can consider the example of Cannan, who, for the most part, uses "unitary elasticity of demand" in the

[31] "Value of Money," *op. cit.*, p. 181.

[32] But, as Marget has emphasized, Walras had earlier presented a graphical analysis in all essentials identical with Marshall's Figure J. See "Léon Walras ... ," *op. cit.*, pp. 578–79. Cf. also above, pp. 567–68.

[33] *Op. cit.*, pp. 217–18, italics and page references in original.

[34] F. W. Taussig, *Principles of Economics* (4th ed., rev.; New York, 1939), Vol. I, p. 252.

[35] *Ibid.*, pp. 126–30.

Note also that subsequently, on p. 252, Taussig writes:

Herein the position of money is unique. As regards the immense majority of commodities, demand is elastic in some cases, inelastic in others, but rarely so balanced that the same sum is always spent on any one.

Here again he seems to be using elasticity in the Marshallian sense.

Marshallian sense,[36] but who also argues in the market-equilibrium sense that this elasticity may be less than unity because the expectations generated by a rising price level might cause it to rise more than in proportion to the quantity of money.[37] [38]

It might finally be noted that descriptions of the demand curve for money as having unitary elasticity in the Marshallian sense have continued to characterize the more recent literature—as the examples of Samuelson,[39] Chandler,[40] and Hart[41] show.

4. THE RELATIONSHIP BETWEEN MONETARY THEORY AND VALUE THEORY[42]

To the best of my knowledge, the only discussion by Cambridge economists of the relationship between monetary theory and value theory that is relevant to our present inquiry occurs at the beginning of Pigou's essay on the "Value of Money." Here Pigou writes:

For the present purpose [of determining the value of money] it is convenient to adopt a plan similar to that employed by Dr. Marshall in his unpublished paper on the "Pure Theory of Foreign Trade," which has been reproduced in Professor Pantaleoni's *Pure Economics*, and to assume that the value of all commodities other than money in terms of one another *is determined independently of the value of money*. On this assumption, the value of any combination of commodities in general can be cited in terms of any single commodity. The aggregate of all commodities is represented by so many bushels of wheat; and the value of money by the number of bushels of wheat which a unit of it will purchase. This value is governed, like the value of everything else, by the general conditions of demand and supply. An investigation of

---

[36] E. Cannan, "The Application of the Theoretical Apparatus of Supply and Demand to Units of Currency," *Economic Journal*, XXXI (1921), reprinted in *Readings in Monetary Theory*, p. 10. See also his *Money: Its Connexion with Rising and Falling Prices* (4th ed., rev.; London, 1923), pp. 66–70.

[37] *Ibid.*, pp. 69–71; "The Application ... ," *op. cit.*, pp. 10–12.

[38] Though not as explicit as Chapman and Taussig, Keynes' discussion in his *Tract on Monetary Reform* (pp. 75–77) seems to me to be involved in their same confusion between demand curves and market-equilibrium curves. There is also some hint of this confusion in Marshall's *Money Credit and Commerce*, p. 45.

[39] *Foundations of Economic Analysis*, p. 121. Cf. also his *Economics: An Introductory Analysis* (2nd ed.; New York, 1951), p. 346 (bottom).

[40] *Op. cit.*, pp. 549–50.

[41] *Op. cit.*, p. 197.

[42] Attached to Chapter VIII:3.

the causes upon which the value of money depends means, therefore, just as it would do if we were concerned with lead or tobacco, a detailed analysis of these two groups of forces. To this analysis, therefore, we may at once proceed.[43]

The crucial question is the meaning of the phrase which has been italicized. If this means "determined independently *by value theory,*" then Pigou is clearly involved in the false dichotomy discussed at length in Chapter VIII:3. But what else can the phrase mean? It cannot refer to the determination of relative prices that takes place in the first stage of the first dichotomy of Chapter VIII:3.[44] For in this stage the forms of the demand functions are already known, and, in particular, their dependence on the amount of real balances already specified; hence one of the major tasks Pigou sets himself (viz., the determination of the demand for money) is already accomplished. Furthermore, as emphasized in the text, this first stage constitutes all of economic analysis; all that remains is the arbitrary specification of the quantity of money. This is hardly the fitting point of departure for an essay whose purpose is to show how demand-and-supply analysis can be applied to the problem of money.

Further light on this question is cast by the passage in Marshall to which Pigou seems to be referring. This passage reads as follows:

> The pure theory of foreign trade ... is based upon the hypothesis that two countries, say England and Germany, carry on trade with each other but only with each other. ... *It is assumed that the pure theory of domestic values has provided the means of measuring the value in England of all the various wares exported by England in terms of any one of them.* Suppose cloth of a definite quality to be one of them; then the value, in England, of all the wares which England exports may be expressed as that of a certain number of yards of cloth. So the value in Germany of all the wares which Germany exports may be expressed as that of, say, a certain number of yards of linen.[45]

The parallels between this passage and Pigou's are quite clear. Hence, if Pigou is "adopting" Marshall's plan, he is assuming that "the value of all commodities other than money in terms of one another" has been "independently determined" by the "pure theory of domestic values." But this is the essence of the invalid dichotomy.[46]

[43] "Value of Money," *op. cit.*, pp. 163–64, italics added.
[44] Cf. p. 173.
[45] A. Marshall, *The Pure Theory of Foreign Trade*, p. 1, italics added.
[46] Cf. p. 183 above.

Note H. Monetary Aspects
of the Casselian System

Cassel's familiar version of the Walrasian system[1] is of particular interest to us because of its oft-quoted conclusion that the system of equations can determine prices "only up to a multiplicative factor" and that it is the function of monetary theory to provide this missing factor.[2] In order to understand the meaning of this conclusion in Cassel's system, we must first unravel the implicit assumptions on which the system is based. This is the purpose of the present study. As with Walras above, we can restrict the discussion to the case of a simple exchange economy.

Cassel presents his system in Book I of his work. This location is of critical significance. For Cassel repeatedly emphasizes that the prevailing assumption of Book I is that money exists only as an abstract unit of account.[3] Correspondingly, the prices to which he refers throughout this book—and throughout the well-known Chapter IV, in particular—are, in our terminology, accounting prices.

Let us now examine Cassel's system in detail. For convenience we shall denote his abstract unit of account by the "guinea." Assume that

---

[1] G. Cassel, *The Theory of Social Economy*, trans. S. L. Barron (new rev. ed.; New York, 1932), Chapter IV. As Wicksell has emphasized, despite the obvious indebtedness of his work to Walras', Cassel does not cite him even once (*Lectures I*, p. 225).

[2] *Theory of Social Economy*, p. 155.

[3] Cf. the following two passages, occurring in Book I: "In the following theoretical inquiries into the exchange economy in general, we shall regard money merely in its

there is a simple exchange economy[4] with n commodities, the respective accounting—that is, guinea—prices of which are denoted by $p_1 \ldots , p_n$. Each consumer in this economy is given an initial credit of a fixed number of guineas which he is free to spend as he chooses during the period.[5] Let the demand functions of this economy be represented by[6]

(1)

$$D_1 = F_1(p_1, \ldots , p_n),$$
$$D_2 = F_2(p_1, \ldots , p_n),$$
$$\ldots\ldots\ldots\ldots\ldots\ldots\ldots\ldots$$
$$D_n = F_n(p_1, \ldots , p_n),$$

---

use as a common scale of reckoning in all economic valuations. This does not mean that the eventual actual use of a material commodity as a medium of exchange has no special economic significance. Such a significance there is, but the study of it belongs to the special theory of money, and must be deferred to Book III." (*Ibid.*, pp. 46–47.)

"Money shall, as we said, be introduced only as a scale of reckoning. ... We may assume money calculations to be merely bookkeeping, and payments in money as so many book entries. For the moment we will ignore the existence of a material commodity used as money. The question of how the scale of reckoning is itself decided upon—how prices are fixed in concrete figures—must be left open until we consider it in the special theory of money." (*Ibid.*, p. 50.)

For similar passages, see p. 383, last paragraph before new section (for the meaning of "price-scale" in this paragraph, see *ibid.*, p. 374); and p. 440, lines 3–4.

These passages make it clear that on this one point Wicksell's criticism of Cassel in his *Lectures I* (p. 224) is not valid. For Wicksell interprets Cassel as dealing with a unit of account which is also a commodity. Note, however, that Wicksell later grudgingly indicates that Cassel may have had in mind an abstract unit of account and seems to concede that in such a case Cassel's argument is logically intact (*ibid.*, p. 225, lines 5–7).

Similarly, the fact that Bent Hansen disregards the preceding passages suffices to invalidate the interpretation of Cassel which he presents in his "Role of Money in the Classical Economic Interdependence System—Patinkin vs. Cassel [in Danish], *Ekonomisk Tidskrift*, LIV (1952), 100–120. These passages are also ignored in H. Dickson's criticism in the same volume (pp. 152–59) and Hansen's reply to him (pp. 226–27). See also footnote 5 below.

I am indebted to Hansen for providing me with a typescript of R. S. Stedman's English translation of his article.

[4] In order to avoid possible confusion, it might be noted that our use of this term does not correspond to Cassel's. He uses it to describe an economy in which production may also take place (*Theory of Social Economy*, pp. 42 ff.).

[5] "We first assume that the quantity of money which every consumer expends on the satisfaction of his wants in the period under consideration is fixed in advance." (*Ibid.*, p. 138.)

Lest we think that the phrase "quantity of money" refers to a money which physically exists as a medium of exchange, and thus indicates a dropping of the general assumption of Book I that money is only an abstract unit of account, we

Let "the [given] quantities of goods available to consumers in a particular period"[7] be represented by S_i. Our equilibrium conditions are then[8]

(2)
$$F_1(p_1, \ldots, p_n) = S_1,$$
$$F_2(p_1, \ldots, p_n) = S_2,$$
$$\ldots\ldots\ldots\ldots\ldots\ldots\ldots\ldots$$
$$F_n(p_1, \ldots, p_n) = S_n.$$

Cassel then concludes: "This series of equations contains n equations for determining the n unknown prices; which is, in general, sufficient for determining the n unknown quantities. In the present case, where the money expenditure of consumers is given beforehand, prices too are obviously fixed at their absolute level."[9]

The first thing that strikes our attention in this passage is the apparent failure to take account of the equational dependence dictated by Walras' Law. But a closer investigation of Cassel's system shows that actually no such dependence exists! This is a consequence of the crucial assumption that the amounts individuals can spend are fixed beforehand and are therefore independent of the amounts of commodities supplied on the market. That is, these supplies appear, as it were, from some exogenous source, so that their sale does not generate income for consumers. It is the severing of this customary link which invalidates

---

should note how Cassel describes this assumption at every later point: "In the present case, where the money expenditure of consumers is given beforehand ..." (*ibid.*, p. 140); "Our main assumptions were that the sums of money to be spent by consumers are fixed beforehand, ..." (pp. 148–49); "We first assumed, as we said, that the sum of money which every consumer expends for the satisfaction of his wants in the unit period is fixed in advance" (p. 150); "... on the assumption that the aggregate payments of consumers were given" (p. 151); "This condition was fulfilled so long as the total expenditure of the consumer, reckoned in money terms, was taken for granted" (p. 155).

Each of these passages bears out the interpretation presented here in the text. Each also shows us how we should understand the parallel passages in the nonmathematical version of Cassel's argument on pp. 64 (lines 1–6), 73 (lines 8–6 from bottom), and 76 (lines 18–22).

It is on the passage from p. 140 that Hansen—mistakenly, in my judgment—justifies his procedure of ignoring Cassel's general proclamation of the role of money in his Book I (Hansen, *op. cit.*, p. 108).

[6] The following reproduces Cassel's system (1), *Theory of Social Economy*, p. 139.
[7] *Ibid.*, p. 138. See also p. 141, lines 4–7.
[8] The following reproduces Cassel's system (2), *ibid.*, p. 140.
[9] *Ibid.*, p. 140.

Walras' Law and thereby validates Cassel's otherwise unacceptable procedure.

We can see this most clearly through the following reformulation of Cassel's argument: Let each individual maximize his utility, subject to the restraint of the fixed number of guineas he can spend. Let I_0 represent the total amount of guinea-credits made available in the economy as a whole. Then it can be readily shown that, in the absence of distribution effects, the demand functions in (1) above have the form

$$D_1 = G_1\left(\frac{p_1}{p_n}, \dots, \frac{p_{n-1}}{p_n}, \frac{I_0}{p_n}\right),$$

$$\dots\dots\dots\dots\dots\dots\dots\dots\dots\dots\dots\dots$$

$$(3) \quad D_{n-1} = G_{n-1}\left(\frac{p_1}{p_n}, \dots, \frac{p_{n-1}}{p_n}, \frac{I_0}{p_n}\right),$$

$$D_n = G_n\left(\frac{p_1}{p_n}, \dots, \frac{p_{n-1}}{p_n}, \frac{I_0}{p_n}\right) \equiv \frac{I_0}{p_n} - \sum_{j=1}^{n-1} \frac{p_j}{p_n} G_j\left(\frac{p_1}{p_n}, \dots, \frac{p_{n-1}}{p_n}, \frac{I_0}{p_n}\right).$$

For simplicity, we have deflated all prices by p_n; we could just as well have taken any other price. We have also made use of the budget restraint

$$(4) \quad \sum_{i=1}^{n} p_i D_i = I_0$$

to rewrite the demand function for the nth commodity as indicated.[10]

Our equilibrium conditions (2) then become

$$G_1\left(\frac{p_1}{p_n}, \dots, \frac{p_{n-1}}{p_n}, \frac{I_0}{p_n}\right) = S_1,$$

$$\dots\dots\dots\dots\dots\dots\dots\dots\dots\dots\dots\dots\dots\dots\dots$$

$$(5) \quad G_{n-1}\left(\frac{p_1}{p_n}, \dots, \frac{p_{n-1}}{p_n}, \frac{I_0}{p_n}\right) = S_{n-1},$$

$$\frac{I_0}{p_n} - \sum_{j=1}^{n-1} \frac{p_j}{p_n} G_j\left(\frac{p_1}{p_n}, \dots, \frac{p_{n-1}}{p_n}, \frac{I_0}{p_n}\right) = S_n,$$

[10] That Cassel was aware that his demand functions depended on I_0, but that he omitted this because of its constancy, is indicated by his statement on p. 152, lines 8–9.

where the S_i are constants. Because of the argument I_0/p_n, the p_i do *not* appear solely as ratios. Hence, as Cassel states, the preceding system is one of n equations in the n individual prices p_i.

Let us now see if this system possesses the usual equational dependence of general-equilibrium systems. Assume that the set of prices $p_1^0, \ldots, p_n^0$ satisfy the first $n - 1$ of these equilibrium equations. This set will also satisfy the last equation if and only if

(6) $$I_0 - \sum_{j=1}^{n-1} p_j^0 S_j = S_n.$$

But, in general, there is no reason to suppose that this will be the case. That is, the last equation of (5) also adds a restriction on the prices. Walras' Law does not hold![11]

There can be no doubt that Cassel was fully aware of the nature of his assumptions. Thus, after completing his discussion of the preceding case, and in the way of passing on to more complicated ones, he wrote:

The assumption that the money expenditure of consumers on the purchase of finished goods for satisfying their wants is fixed in advance must now be dropped. The money payments of a consumer are clearly determined by his income. ...

The income of the individual is, however, determined by the prices of the factors of production which he sells in the course of the productive process. The various incomes of the members of the exchange economy are thus determined by the pricing process, and neither these incomes nor the payments made with them should therefore be regarded as magnitudes, fixed in advance, in the pricing problem. Not until we regard income, too, as one of the unknowns in the pricing problem are we in a position to deal with the pricing problem in a way which accurately reflects our exchange economy, shows that consumers are at the same time producers, and indicates how much of the final product the individual producer is in a position to acquire in exchange for his productive labour. The pricing problem, thus given a general application, contains in itself the problem of economic distribution.[12]

[11] For a simple numerical example of the preceding system, see E. H. Phelps Brown, *The Framework of the Pricing System* (London, 1936), pp. 80–83. The assumptions of this example effectively reduce money to a pure unit of account (*ibid.*, pp. 43–45).

[12] *Theory of Social Economy*, pp. 150–51.

To translate these passages into a form appropriate for an exchange economy in our sense of the term, replace "factors of production" in the first sentence of the

Under the new assumption that consumers' incomes are generated by their sales of initial quantities of commodities,[13] budget restraint (4) is replaced by

$$(7) \qquad \sum_{i=1}^{n} p_i D_i = \sum_{i=1}^{n} p_i S_i ;$$

and Cassel's demand equations (1) now assume the familiar form[14]

$$D_1 = H_1\left(\frac{p_1}{p_n}, \ldots, \frac{p_{n-1}}{p_n}\right),$$

....

$$(8) \quad D_{n-1} = H_{n-1}\left(\frac{p_1}{p_n}, \ldots, \frac{p_{n-1}}{p_n}\right),$$

$$D_n = H_n\left(\frac{p_1}{p_n}, \ldots, \frac{p_{n-1}}{p_n}\right) \equiv S_n + \sum_{j=1}^{n-1} \frac{p_j}{p_n}\left[S_j - H_j\left(\frac{p_1}{p_n}, \ldots, \frac{p_{n-1}}{p_n}\right)\right].$$

In contrast with the demand functions (3), these depend solely on the ratios of the prices. And, just as our interpretation leads us to expect, this is precisely the property which Cassel now—*and for the first time*—ascribes to his demand functions.[15]

The equilibrium conditions corresponding to the foregoing demand

---

second paragraph cited by "initial quantities of commodities." Analytically, nothing is thereby changed.

[13] See the preceding footnote.

[14] Cf. Mathematical Appendix 2:*e*.

[15] As I read it, Cassel's argument proceeds as follows: In the paragraph beginning on the bottom of p. 151 he explains that as a result of the new assumptions set out in the long citation above, "the content of equations [(1)] ... is now changed" since they "no longer include the total payments which we previously assumed to be given as constants." The argument is then interrupted by the paragraph beginning So far ..." on p. 152 and is not taken up again until the paragraph beginning "It is clear ..." on p. 154. In this paragraph Cassel then says that the demand functions depend only on the ratios of the prices of the productive services. Translated into terms of an exchange economy in our sense of the term, this means that they depend on the ratios of the accounting prices of commodities. This is the basis for the interpretation in the text here.

functions have the form[16]

$$H_1\left(\frac{p_1}{p_n}, \ldots, \frac{p_{n-1}}{p_n}\right) = S_1,$$

$$\ldots\ldots\ldots\ldots\ldots\ldots\ldots\ldots\ldots\ldots\ldots\ldots$$

(9)

$$H_{n-1}\left(\frac{p_1}{p_n}, \ldots, \frac{p_{n-1}}{p_n}\right) = S_{n-1},$$

$$\sum_{j=1}^{n-1} \frac{p_j}{p_n}\left[S_j - H_j\left(\frac{p_1}{p_n}, \ldots, \frac{p_{n-1}}{p_n}\right)\right] = 0.$$

We note, first, that the reintroduction of the supply-income nexus has revalidated Walras' Law: any set of prices satisfying the first $n - 1$ equations must clearly also satisfy the nth. We note second—in the words of the oft-quoted statement with which Cassel concludes his discussion and to which we referred at the beginning of this study—that

... the system of equations is indeterminate, in that it determines the prices in question only up to a multiplicative factor; or, as it is popularly expressed, determines only the relative and not the absolute prices. In order to obtain the absolute prices, a new condition must be introduced; for example, the price of a commodity or of a group of commodities must be given. This condition was fulfilled so long as the total expenditure of the consumer, reckoned in money terms, was taken for granted. In the general pricing problem, a multiplicative factor of all prices remains undetermined. The determination of this factor, and, consequently, the final solution of the pricing problem, belongs to the theory of money.[17]

This brings us to our main point. For if the foregoing interpretation is correct, what Cassel has established is the indeterminacy of *accounting* prices. He is, then, quite right in saying that this indeterminacy can be removed by specifying "the price of a commodity or of a group of

[16] Note that the following system is equivalent to that of Mathematical Appendix 3:*a.*

[17] *Ibid.*, p. 155.

Phelps Brown (*op. cit.*, pp. 142–46) overlooks the fact that the introduction of the supply-income nexus renders his system indeterminate. This can be seen most easily by noting that the replacement of the two budget restraints on the bottom of p. 212 by those on the bottom of p. 144 leaves the resulting system on pp. 212–13 dependent only on the ratios of prices.

commodities." He is, however, quite wrong in implying that this is what is done by "the theory of money." For, on the one hand, the specification of accounting prices is a purely arbitrary act, completely outside the realm of economic analysis; while, on the other, the theory of money is concerned with *money* and not *accounting* prices. Thus Cassel, like Fisher, is guilty of confusing these fundamentally distinct prices.[18]

As a corollary to the preceding confusion, Cassel seems also to have confused the valid dichotomy between money and accounting prices with the invalid one between relative and money prices. In particular, because of his failure to realize the crucial analytical distinction between money which is only an abstract unit of account and money which is also a concrete medium of exchange, Cassel carries over intact his analysis of Book I (which, as already emphasized, assumes an abstract money) to Book III (which assumes a concrete one). Accordingly, he continues to refer in Book III to this earlier analysis and to imply that his commodity equations of Book I are valid also for a money economy; that these equations determine only relative, and not money, prices; and that this indeterminacy is removed by adding to these equations the cash-balance equation, $PTR = M$, where R is the equivalent of the Cambridge K. This interpretation—and its attribution to Cassel of the invalid dichotomy—is borne out by the juxtaposition of the passage from Book I of the *Theory of Social Economy* just cited and the following two passages from Book III:

> For theoretical economics, our analysis of money has a special significance. Just as the fixing of prices is a primary practical need of every system of exchange, so also must the fundamental treatment of the theory of exchange be carried through as an analysis of the determination of prices. It has been shown in the first two Books of this work that such a theory can be worked out as a theory of the determination of prices *without it being necessary for special attention to be devoted to the part played by the existing means of payment*. The analysis of the origin of the monetary system shows that this

[18] The reader will find it convenient to read this paragraph against the background of Chapters III:2–3 and VIII:3. See especially pp. 173–74. On Fisher, see beginning of Note F:3.

It should be clear that my criticism of Cassel is not the fruitless terminological one that the foregoing statement uses "absolute prices" to denote what I call "accounting prices," but the substantive one that the last sentence of this statement describes the determination of accounting prices—be they called what they may—in an incorrect way.

role, by its very conception, is distinct from the part played by the price-scale. For the purposes of theoretical treatment, it is natural that the part played by the means of payment, and especially its significance for the price-scale, should be made the object of a special inquiry. This gives us the task of Book III.[19]

When the demand for money is given, equilibrium requires the demand for money to be equal to the total quantity of money present M—that is, that $PTR = M$. This equation suffices to determine the unknown—the general price-level.[20]

Further support for this interpretation comes from Cassel's discussion in his *Fundamental Thoughts in Economics*,[21] in which he refers to the discussion in his *Theory of Social Economy*[22] and writes:

True, there remains the important question: How is the unit of money fixed, what determines its purchasing power, and how can the stability of this unit be guaranteed? These questions cannot be answered at the outset of our study of economics. They must necessarily be deferred to a later exposition of the theory of money. However, our discussion has already shown what is the essential task of this theory: the theory of money has to clear up how the purchasing power of an abstract unit of money is determined.

In our first exposition of the general economic theory we must simply postulate a unit of money as fixed and invariable. If we do that we are able to construct a theory of prices, and the result of this theory is that, in a state of equilibrium, the prices of all goods are determined. However, as they are determined in a unit which is itself left undetermined, it is clear that the prices of goods can only be determined, in the general theory, relatively to one another.[23] This means that the prices of goods are determined except for a

[19] *Theory of Social Economy*, p. 383, with italics added. Much the same passage appears in the earlier edition of Cassel's work translated by J. McCabe (New York, 1924), p. 356. Indeed, I suspect that the original German versions are identical.

Note that Cassel uses "theory of the determination of prices" to mean "theory of the determination *of relative commodity prices.*" This is important for an understanding of some of the passages quoted below.

[20] *Theory of Social Economy*, trans. S. L. Barron, p. 457. Much the same passage appears in the earlier McCabe translation (New York, 1924), p. 432.

For similar passages in the Barron translation, see p. 456, paragraph beginning "If we wish ... ," and p. 458, lines 6–8.

[21] London, 1925.

[22] Trans. McCabe.

[23] Note again how by "general economic theory" Cassel means "general theory *of the determination of relative commodity prices.*"

Note too how this paragraph up to this point—and particularly its first sentence—fits in with the statement of the invalid dichotomy given on pp. 182–83 above.

multiplicative factor which rests undetermined. This degree of undetermined-ness can be removed by fixing absolutely one price. As soon as this is done, all prices are fixed at their absolute level. To explain how this absolute fixation of prices is possible is just the special task of the theory of money, and this is, therefore, a question which must be passed by in an exposition of the general economic theory. When we come later to the theory of money, it will show itself to be a great advantage to have the objects of this theory thus definitely fixed beforehand. The exposition here given of the role of the scarcity of the means of payment with regard to fixation of absolute price already determines the main lines on which the whole theory of money has to proceed.[24]

The place of the theory of money in the general economic theory is, accord-ing to what I have said, determined by the nature of the solution of the general problem of price-setting outlined in these lectures.[25] We have postulated a monetary unit in which we can reckon all prices, and we have found that prices reckoned in this unit are determined *by our system of equations* except for a multiplicative factor. This degree of undeterminedness can only be removed by fixing the unit in which prices are reckoned. To show how this is done is the task of the theory of money.[26]

The following passage from Cassel's *On Quantitative Thinking in Economics*[27]—which also takes the *Theory of Social Economy* as its frame of reference—is likewise revealing:

In my representation of the equilibrium theory of prices a monetary system is postulated, and the question of how the monetary unit itself is fixed is left to be treated in a separate theory of money. The central task of this theory is to show how the unit of money may be fixed by a suitable restriction of the supply of means of payment. Thus the general price-problem is divided into two problems: first a problem of how *relative* prices are determined; secondly, a problem of how the *general level* of prices is fixed. This separation of the two different sides of the general price-problem is a *first* characteristic of my treatment of this problem. I believe that it is so natural, and has such great scientific and educational advantage, that it is hardly possible to do without it.[28]

[24] *Fundamental Thoughts in Economics*, pp. 61–63.

[25] Once again, by "general economic theory" and "general problem of price-setting" Cassel is referring to relative commodity prices; see footnote 23 above.

[26] *Ibid.*, p. 123, italics added.

[27] Oxford, 1935.

[28] *Ibid.*, p. 154, italics in original.

For additional support of the foregoing interpretation, see Cassel's earlier discus-sion in his *Nature and Necessity of Interest* (London, 1903), pp. 70–71 and 158–60, noting in particular the statement on p. 70 that "it has been thought necessary to

We note finally that in his monetary theory Cassel implies the existence of a demand curve for money which is of uniform unitary elasticity. Specifically, he states that "the demand for money, in conditions which otherwise are equal, is proportional to the general price-level."[29] As in the case of Marshall and Pigou,[30] it is clear from the context that Cassel is referring here to a demand curve, and not a market-equilibrium curve.[31]

---

make a separate theory of value: such a theory should explain the relative values of commodities, *irrespective of any common measure of value or medium of exchange*" (italics added).

See also the following passage from Cassel's "Rate of Interest, the Bank Rate, and the Stabilization of Prices," *Quarterly Journal of Economics*, XLII (1927–28), as reprinted in *Readings in Monetary Theory*, p. 319, noting again the explicit sense in which Cassel uses the term "general economic theory":

> When we postulate an abstract unit in which all prices are reckoned, we are able to study all problems concerning relative prices; that is we can master the whole domain usually comprised under the heading of general economic theory. There remains, however, one essential question to be solved. The question is, how the unit itself is determined, or, in other words, how the absolute height of prices is fixed. This question forms the object of the theory of money, and its solution is in fact the only essential task of this theory.

In the paragraph before this passage, Cassel refers to his *Theory of Social Economy*.

On the other hand, it should be pointed out that at another point in his writing Cassel provides what might be taken to be an expression of the valid first dichotomy of Chapter VIII:3. In particular, he states that "the equilibrium system of equations can only determine *relative* prices. The *absolute* height of prices is a monetary question, depending as it does on the supply of means of payment." ["Keynes' 'General Theory,'" *International Labour Review*, XXXVI (1937), 439, italics in original.]

[29] *Theory of Social Economy*, p. 456.

[30] Above, Note G:3.

[31] Bent Hansen has informed me that the material referred to in footnotes 20 and 29 above does not appear in the second revised Swedish edition (1938) of Cassel's work. More specifically, all the material in the Barron translation from p. 455 (line 2 from bottom) to the end of §50 on p. 459 is omitted from this Swedish edition. I am unable to judge the significance of this fact.

Note I. Dichotomies of the Pricing Process

1. THE FIRST VALID DICHOTOMY[1]

I have not succeeded in finding an example spelled out in detail of the valid dichotomy between money and relative prices. It should, however, be clear from the text that it is implicit in any of the frequent statements in the literature that a change in the quantity of money causes a proportionate change in prices. The reason these statements fall just a shade below being full expressions of the dichotomy is that they usually do not explicitly add the obvious and undoubtedly recognized implication that relative prices—and real balances—remain unaffected. In some cases, however, the invariance of relative prices is made explicit —as the following passage from McCulloch shows:

But though the quantity of money in circulation determines the *price* of commodities, or their value estimated in money, it does not exercise the smallest influence over the quantity of other commodities for which any one in particular will exchange.[2]

[1] Attached to Chapter VIII: 3, especially pp. 172–73.
The nature of this dichotomy and its misleading similarities to the invalid third dichotomy were described in my " Further Considerations of the General Equilibrium Theory of Money," *op. cit.*, Section 5. See also my " Indeterminacy of Absolute Prices," *op. cit.*, p. 23.
[2] J. R. McCulloch, *The Principles of Political Economy* (4th ed.; Edinburgh, 1849), p. 217, italics in original.

We have also the following passage from Davenport:

The level of general prices, therefore, is unimportant to the trader. If what he sells changes in price, this does not matter so long as what he buys correspondingly changes. *The real and essential relations of goods to goods are finally in no wise complicated by the situation of prices in general or by the volume of media.* So elastic is the demand for media that indefinite increases in its volume may be absorbed through a general rise of prices.[3]

This passage is of particular interest in that it illustrates one of the pitfalls of textual interpretation on the point in question. Specifically, the first sentence by itself seems to say that demand must remain unaffected by a proportionate change in prices; but subsequent sentences show that Davenport is here considering a change in prices accompanied by a corresponding change in the quantity of money, so that no real-balance effect exists. But, as in the case of Fisher,[4] there is no evidence that Davenport was aware of the critical importance of this additional assumption.

Passages similar to McCulloch's can be found in James Mill,[5] Barbour,[6] Hawtrey,[7] and Cassel.[8]

2. THE SECOND VALID DICHOTOMY[9]

There are many examples of the valid dichotomy between money and accounting prices.[10] In all of them the presentation is like that of Mathematical Appendix 7: a(ii) above. Thus see, for example,

[3] H. J. Davenport, *The Economics of Enterprise* (New York, 1913), p. 273, italics added.

[4] See the penultimate paragraph of Note F: 3 above.

[5] *Op. cit.*, p. 121.

[6] *Op. cit.*, pp. 41, 44.

[7] *Currency and Credit*, pp. 35–36. Note that Hawtrey's assumed "unit of value" is not an abstract one in our sense of the term, but corresponds instead to a fiat paper money. Its "abstractness" for Hawtrey lies in its existence only as an account in the bank. But since these accounts constitute hoards of purchasing power, they "exist" in exactly the same sense that paper money does [*ibid.*, pp. 3, 5, 7, 14 ("In the first place ..."), and 33].

[8] Cf. p. 620, footnote 28 above. As emphasized there, however, Cassel was confused on this point.

[9] Attached to Chapter VIII: 3, especially pp. 173–74.

[10] For an early example of a precisely drawn distinction between accounting and money prices, see A. Cournot, *Mathematical Principles of the Theory of Wealth* (1838), trans. N. T. Bacon (New York, 1929), p. 27. Cournot, however, has no discussion of the dichotomy.

Wicksell,[11] Fisher,[12] Bowley,[13] and Cassel.[14] The last of these inspired similar statements by other members of the Swedish school such as Ohlin,[15] Lindahl,[16] and Lundberg.[17]

3. The Third and Invalid Dichotomy[18]

The preceding notes have presented the varying degrees of evidence that leads one to suspect that the original exponents of general-equilibrium analysis—Walras,[19] Fisher,[20] and Cassel[21]—were themselves already involved in the invalid dichotomy. Regardless of the conclusiveness of this evidence, this much is clear: none of these writers —nor even Wicksell[22]—explicitly and precisely defined the correct relationship that exists between the commodity equations and the money equation. Thus if they were not the advocates of the invalid dichotomy, they were certainly not its opponents.

When we turn to later writers, all doubts disappear. Here we find explicit presentations of the invalid dichotomy in all its details. The first such presentation—to my knowledge—was due to Divisia. This writer considered an economy consisting only of commodities and money. He then took it upon himself to fill the "lacuna" in Pareto's theory of price determination (he ignored Walras) and did so by clearly stating that the commodity equations, which independently determine relative prices, must be "complemented" by the monetary equation, which then determines the absolute price level.[23] This invalid description

[11] *Lectures I*, pp. 66–67; cf. above, Note E: 3. See also his *Value Capital and Rent*, pp. 79–80, 91–92.

[12] *Mathematical Investigations in the Theory of Value and Prices*, pp. 58–62.

[13] A. L. Bowley, *The Mathematical Groundwork of Economics* (Oxford, 1924), p.52.

[14] As interpreted in Note H above, especially pp. 617–18.

[15] B. Ohlin, *Interregional and International Trade* (Cambridge, Mass., 1933), p. 556.

[16] E. Lindahl, *Studies in the Theory of Money and Capital* (London, 1939), pp. 282–83.

[17] E. Lundberg, *Studies in the Theory of Economic Expansion* (Stockholm, 1937), pp. 6–7.

[18] Attached to Chapter VIII: 3, especially p. 175, footnote 33.

[19] Note C: 4 (end). See also the discussion of Schlesinger and the reference to Pareto on p. 570, footnote 94.

[20] Note F: 3.

[21] Note H, pp. 618–20.

[22] Note E: 3. Cf. also the discussion of Pigou in Note G: 4.

[23] F. Divisia, *Economique rationnelle* (Paris, 1927), pp. 402, 413–15. His argument is

of the relationship between monetary and value theory acquired the status of undisputed, received doctrine in its repeated endorsements and restatements at the hands of such writers as Marget,[24] Rosenstein-Rodan,[25] Myrdal,[26] Lange,[27] Modigliani,[28] Schneider,[29] Hickman,[30] and Hart.[31, 32] This status was reinforced by the acceptance of the invalid dichotomy's central proposition by Leontief,[33] Haberler,[34] Marschak,[35] Samuelson,[36] Tinbergen,[37] and Boulding[38]—all of whom

---

essentially the one presented in Mathematical Appendix 7 : a(iii)—with the $(n-1)^{\text{th}}$ good treated as a commodity (see *ibid.*, p. 334, footnote 2).

[24] *Theory of Prices*, Vol. II, p. 284, footnote 132, where Marget endorses Divisia's treatment as "superior to that of Pareto" and "in all essentials identical" with that of Walras.

[25] *Op. cit.*, pp. 257–58.

[26] *Op. cit.*, pp. 11–12.

[27] "Say's Law ... ," *op. cit.*, pp. 64–65. True, Lange does object here to the dichotomy—but only because he adds to it the assumption of Say's Identity. When however, he drops this assumption, he explicitly concedes to Modigliani that the dichotomy is valid (Modigliani, "Liquidity Preference," *op. cit.*, p. 217, footnote 35).

It might also be noted that in Appendix 4 to his *Price Flexibility and Employment* (Bloomington, Ind., 1945), Lange presents a model which, despite the fact that it includes bonds, is involved in exactly the same type of indeterminacy as that shown to hold for the invalid dichotomy. The reason for this is that Lange in effect applies the homogeneity postulate to the bond equation as well as to the commodity equations. That is, his explicit assumptions imply that the former too is independent of real balances. Hence an equiproportionate departure of prices from an initial set of equilibrium values does not disturb equilibrium in the bond market either. Hence the absolute level of money prices is indeterminate. (For the details of this argument, cf. above, pp. 180–81.)

The puzzling thing is that even though Lange himself proves this indeterminacy in the Appendix to his book (p. 102), he makes no mention of it in the text proper! This leads to all sorts of internal inconsistencies in his argument. Thus on p. 14 of the text he argues that an equiproportionate decrease in prices may well cause a decrease in the *real* excess demand for money; while on p. 100 of the Appendix he proves that the excess-demand function for *nominal* money holdings is homogeneous of degree one in the prices—so that an equiproportionate change in prices can *never* affect the real value of these holdings.

[28] "Liquidity Preference," *op. cit.*, Section 13. The title of this section is "The Logical Consistency of the Quantity Theory of Money and the Dichotomy of Monetary and Real Economics." In the penultimate paragraph of this section Modigliani writes: "The necessary condition for money to be neutral is that the $n-1$ 'real' demand and supply equations be homogeneous of order zero ...." This is the mathematical term for dependence solely on relative prices. It should also be noted that money is "neutral" for Modigliani if and only if the quantity theory holds. (Cf. above, p. 175, footnote 34.)

[Modigliani has revised his position in the light of the foregoing criticism and as indicated above (p. 180, footnote 43 and p. 298, footnote 29) now validly presents the dichotomy in terms of a pure inside-money economy. It might, however, be noted that Modigliani's statement that neither the dichotomy nor neutrality holds in an economy with both inside and outside money ("Monetary Mechanism," *op. cit.*, p. 87) fails to take account of the fact that in general these two quantities of money are related, so that the neutrality of money can (under certain assumptions) be preserved even in this case (cf. above, pp. 299–300 and 308).

It might also be noted that the empirical work which Modigliani (together with Albert Ando) has recently done on consumption centers on a function which does not satisfy the homogeneity condition just cited from his "Liquidity Preference" article. For, as pointed out on pp. 659–60 below, this function depends effectively upon total nonhuman wealth, including real financial assets; hence, like the consumption function in this book, it will be affected even by a change in the absolute price level which leaves relative prices invariant.

[29] E. Schneider, *Pricing and Equilibrium*, trans. T. W. Hutchison (London, 1952), pp. 290–307, especially pp. 304–6; cited in F. H. Hahn's review of the book in *Economic Journal*, LXIII (1953), 409.

The following passage from Schneider is particularly instructive:

> We have introduced money as a means of payment *after* the equilibrium price relations were determined, simply for the purpose of giving an absolute level to the prices, and in order to determine the multiplicative factor left indeterminate in equations (10), (11), and (12). [These are essentially the excess-demand equations for commodities.] The quantity equation was, as it were, fitted on subsequently as an appendix to the "essential" equations (10), (11), and (12). It is important to emphasize that the equilibrium relative prices are completely independent of the monetary resources of the system. They result from equations (10), (11), and (12), which have nothing to do with monetary factors. [*Op. cit.*, p. 306, italics in original.]

[30] W. Braddock Hickman, "The Determinacy of Absolute Prices in Classical Economic Theory," *Econometrica*, XVIII (1950), 9–20.

[31] *Op. cit.*, p. 144, especially footnote 4.

[32] In my "Dichotomies of the Pricing Process in Economic Theory" [*Economica*, XXI (1954), 124], I also referred to Hicks' *Value and Capital* as providing a statement of the invalid dichotomy. This has been changed here because his case is not as clear-cut as those of the other writers just listed. In particular, if we abstract from the possible case of Walras (cf. p. 572, footnote 103 above), Hicks provides the only instance that I have been able to find of a writer who—prior to the dichotomy discussion of the last fifteen years—presents the dichotomy for an economy in which there are bonds as well as commodities (*ibid.*, pp. 158–59). On the other hand, it should be emphasized that there is nothing to indicate that Hicks had in mind the valid form of the dichotomy presented on p. 180 above. Indeed, by his failure to point out the crucial role that the bond market can play in his dichotomy, and by entitling his discussion "The traditional dichotomy between 'real' and 'monetary' economics" (*ibid.*, p. ix, heading for Section 5 of Chapter XII), Hicks clearly implies that he draws no significant distinction between his version of the dichotomy and the more familiar one presented by the other writers just listed. Similarly, his failure to offer any criticism of this more familiar dichotomy would seem to indicate that he sees no basic objection to it.

[33] W. W. Leontief, "The Fundamental Assumption of Mr. Keynes' Monetary Theory of Unemployment," *Quarterly Journal of Economics*, LI (1936–37), 192. Here

he italicizes the "homogeneity postulate": "*The quantity of any service or any commodity demanded or supplied by a firm or an individual remains unchanged if all the prices upon which it (directly) depends increase or decrease exactly in the same proportion.*"

Leontief then states:

> The significance of this theorem for the analysis of monetary influences within the framework of our economic system has been mentioned often enough. It is best expressed by the well-known hypothetical "experiment" of doubling overnight the cash holdings of all business enterprises and households. Ricardo used this device to show that the prices of all commodities and services will undergo under this condition a proportionally equal change, and the quantities produced, traded and consumed by all individual firms and households will remain exactly the same as before. *His conclusion is obviously based upon the homogeneity postulate.* [*Ibid.*, p. 193, italics added.]

The italicized sentence shows that Leontief considers the homogeneity postulate to be a necessary condition for the quantity theory (cf. above, p. 175, footnote 34). Leontief then argues that the distinguishing feature of Keynes' *General Theory of Employment, Interest, and Money* is the repudiation of this postulate. This context thus makes it clear that Leontief is talking about a money economy and is referring to money prices.

The passage from Leontief cited on p. 185, footnote 51 above occurs in his "Interrelation of Prices, Output, Savings, and Investment," *Review of Economic Statistics*, XIX (1937), 116. To this passage is appended a footnote referring the reader to the *Q. J. E.* article just cited. This footnote refers to the article as a whole; but there can be no doubt from the context that it is specifically related to the homogeneity postulate —and this is the way I have interpreted it in the text.

This postulate has continued to appear in Leontief's writings. See in particular his reaffirmation of it in his comment on my 1949 *Econometrica* article in the same journal, XVIII (1950), 21–24. Indeed, this postulate still forms one of the basic ones on which Leontief develops the "theoretical scheme" in back of his input-output analysis in the second edition of his *Structure of American Economy, 1919–1939* (2nd ed., enlarged; New York, 1951), Part II, p. 46 in particular. This fact lends even greater strength to T. C. Koopman's observation—made on other grounds—that the "designation 'general equilibrium analysis' for [Leontief's] ... model ... is inappropriate." This, however, does not affect the validity of Leontief's statistical analysis as such. See "Papers and Proceedings," *American Economic Review*, XXXIX (1949), 234.

[34] G. Haberler, *Prosperity and Depression* (3rd ed.; Geneva, 1941), p. 460, footnote 1, where Haberler reproduces Leontief's homogeneity postulate and identifies it with absence of "money illusion." It is particularly interesting to contrast this with the central role Haberler assigns to the real-balance effect elsewhere in his book; see *ibid.*, pp. 242, 389, 403, 491–503.

[35] J. Marschak, "Money Illusion and Demand Analysis," *Review of Economic Statistics*, XXV (1943), 40.

[36] In his analysis of the demand functions of a money economy Samuelson writes: "These equations are homogeneous of order zero in all prices and income just as in the usual case of demand" (*Foundations*, p. 121). Earlier Samuelson indicates that prices are not necessarily measured in terms of an abstract unit of account (p. 119, lines 8–7 from bottom; p. 120, lines 3–8). Note also Samuelson's reference to Marschak's article mentioned above.

stated or implied that the commodity equations depend only on relative, and not absolute, prices (i.e., the "homogeneity postulate"). Indeed, as emphasized in the text (p. 187), the willingness of most of these writers to denote the dependence of commodity demand upon the absolute price level by the term "money illusion"[39] is itself evidence of the failure to fully understand the real-balance effect.

*   *   *   *   *

Since the above was written, extended attempts to justify the invalid dichotomy have been made by Valavanis,[40] Archibald and Lipsey,[41]

The specific passage from Samuelson cited on p. 184, footnote 48 above occurs in his "Note on the Pure Theory of Consumer's Behavior," *Economica*, V (1938), 63. It is reproduced here in full—again, with one of those revealing footnotes:

> *Postulate II.* We further assume that the consumer's behavior is independent of the units in which prices are expressed. More specifically, if we multiply all prices and income by the same positive quantity, the amounts taken will remain the same.*
>
> ---
>
> * This homogeneity assumption has been challenged by Mr. Keynes with respect to a different problem. For the pure theory of consumer's behavior it is probably without objection. In any case it is always implicitly made.

From the context of Postulate II it is clear that Samuelson has accounting prices in mind. This is implied by the fact that the prices of his n goods are written $p_1, \ldots, p_n$, and we never find one of these prices set equal to unity. Now, the footnote is obviously an implicit reference to Leontief's article on Keynes cited in footnote 33 above. Thus Samuelson identifies his postulate, which can be true only for *accounting* prices, with Leontief's homogeneity postulate, which is stated for *money* prices.

[37] J. Tinbergen, *Econometrics* (Philadelphia, 1951), p. 20. The crucial passage here reads: "... the so-called 'money-illusion,' through which the absolute value of the prices have an independent significance for ... [the buyer]."

[38] K. E. Boulding, "Welfare Economics," in *Survey of Contemporary Economics: Vol. II*, ed. B. F. Haley (Homewood, Ill., 1952), pp. 28–29.

[39] This term seems to have been used first by Irving Fisher, though in a completely different sense. For him it denoted "the failure to perceive that the dollar, or any other unit of money, expands or shrinks in value," and the corollary tendency to speak as if the prices of commodities all happened to rise or fall at the same time by coincidence. See his *Money Illusion* (New York, 1928), p. 4.

[40] S. Valavanis, "A Denial of Patinkin's Contradiction," *Kyklos*, VII (1955), 351–68.

Valavanis' argument has been endorsed by E. Schneider, "Patinkin über Geld und Güterpreise," in *Festskrift til Frederik Zeuthen* (Copenhagen, 1958), pp. 324–25 (especially footnote 23); R. Musgrave, *Theory of Public Finance* (New York, 1959), pp. 427–28; and G. Ackley, *Macroeconomic Theory* (New York, 1961), pp. 120–23.

[41] "Monetary and Value Theory: A Critique of Lange and Patinkin," *Review of Economic Studies*, XXVI (1958), 9–17.

In contrast with the other writers cited here, Archibald and Lipsey do recognize

and Encarnación.[42] All of these are minor variations on Hickman's 1950 demonstration[43]—which was not at all in question[44]—that the system of static equilibrium equations specified by the invalid dichotomy can be consistent in the sense of having a formal mathematical solution.[45] None of them, accordingly, were of any relevance to the dichotomy issue as it existed at the time they were written. This has been sufficiently explained above.[46]

---

that the dichotomized model they advocate has the property that "out of equilibrium [it] does not make economic sense" (*ibid.*, p. 16); however, as Baumol has already pointed out ("Monetary and Value Theory," *op. cit.*, p. 30), they fail to see that it was essentially for this reason that the traditional dichotomy had been rejected. This failure also marks Archibald and Lipsey's more recent "Monetary and Value Theory: Further Comment," *Review of Economic Studies*, XXVIII (1960), 50–51.

[42] J. Encarnación, "Consistency Between Say's Identity and the Cambridge Equation," *Economic Journal*, LXVIII (1958), 827–30.

[43] *Op. cit.*, pp. 14–15.

[44] See my explicit concession to Hickman on this point in "The Invalidity of Classical Monetary Theory," *Econometrica*, XIX (1951), 141, especially footnote 17.

[45] A common feature of these attempts is the assumption of Say's Identity. The fact, however, that this identity does not eliminate the inconsistency which concerns us has already been explained in my 1951 *Econometrica* article (*ibid.*, p. 138; see also p. 141) and in my subsequent "Dichotomies of the Pricing Process in Economic Theory," *Economica*, XXI (1954), 113–14. (For a graphical presentation, see above, p. 176, footnote 41.) Accordingly, Say's Identity was not mentioned in the criticism of the invalid dichotomy which was presented in the first edition of this book [pp. 108–9 and 334–35; reproduced above on p. 178 (lines 6–27) and in Mathematical Appendix 7: a(iii) (except for the last paragraph), respectively]. Similarly, this criticism—which is a summary and refinement of that which appeared in the two articles just cited—makes no mention of the question of the existence of a solution for the system of static excess-demand equations.

All of these attempts also make use of the obscure contention—stemming again from Hickman—that money, alone of all goods, must have two equations (termed by Valavanis the "mirror image" and "technological restriction," respectively) to describe its behavior. This is criticized in greater detail in my "Invalidity of Classical Monetary Theory," *op. cit.*, p. 142, footnote 18. See also Karl Brunner, "Inconsistency and Indeterminacy in Classical Economics," *Econometrica*, XIX (1951), 169–71 (especially footnote 24), and Lindbeck, "Den Klassiska 'Dichotomien,'" *op. cit.*, pp. 35–39.

[46] Pp. 176–77, especially footnote 38.

Note J. The Classical and Neoclassical Theory of Money and Interest[1]

The passages on which the interpretation of the text is based—and to whose authors specific references are made—are to be found in Hume,[2] Thornton,[3] Ricardo,[4] Mill,[5] Sidgwick,[6] Marshall,[7] Pigou,[8] Giffen,[9] Wicksell,[10] and Fisher.[11] The reader will also find it instructive to

[1] Attached to Chapter XV:1.
On this note, cf. J. W. Angell, *The Theory of International Prices* (Cambridge, Mass., 1926), Chapter V; F. A. Hayek, *Prices and Production* (2nd ed.; London, 1935), Lecture I.

[2] *Op. cit.*, p. 336.

[3] *Op. cit.*, pp. 261–62, 287–91.

[4] *Principles*, pp. 363–64; *High Price of Bullion, Works and Correspondence*, ed. Sraffa, Vol. III, p. 91.

[5] *Principles*, Book III, Chapter XXIII.

[6] *Op. cit.*, pp. 265, 279–94.

[7] *Principles*, pp. 520–21, 533–34; *Money Credit and Commerce*, pp. 73, 255–57. See also Marshall's testimony before the Gold and Silver Commission (1887) and the Indian Currency Committee (1899) as reprinted in *Official Papers by Alfred Marshall*, pp. 40–52, 127–31, 158, 270, 274, 307.

[8] A. C. Pigou, *Industrial Fluctuations* (2nd ed.; London, 1929), pp. 275–77.

[9] R. Giffen, *Essays in Finance*, second series (New York, 1886), pp. 37–88, especially pp. 47–51.

[10] See the detailed discussion in Note E:4 above.

[11] *The Rate of Interest*, pp. 8–9; *Elementary Principles of Economics*, 356–57; *The Theory of Interest*, p. 47.

consult Cantillon,[12] Jevons,[13] Bagehot,[14] Palgrave,[15] Walras,[16] Keynes,[17] and Hawtrey.[18]

The following passages show the readiness of classical and neo-classical economists to recognize the permanent influence of a monetary change on the rate of interest in the case of "forced savings."[19] Thus Mill concludes his analysis of this case with the observation:

> In any supposable case, however, the issue of paper money by bankers increases the proportion of the whole capital of the country which is destined to be lent. The rate of interest must therefore fall, until some of the lenders give over lending, or until the increase of borrowers absorbs the whole.[20]

In the same vein, Nicholson, after arguing that the rate of interest remains invariant under a change in the monetary unit, writes:

> But although this general position with the assumptions made is theoretically sound, it is easy to show that the transition from one level of prices to another may have an effect on the rate of interest.
>
> In the example just taken the real burden of all fixed charges would be exactly one-twentieth of what it was before the depreciation of the standard. ... And generally, so far as all old debts with fixed charges are concerned, the proportion of the national income absorbed by them would be so much less,

[12] *Op. cit.*, pp. 119, 215. Cantillon emphasizes that the rate of interest is determined by "the proportionate number of Lenders and Borrowers."

[13] W. S. Jevons, *Investigations in Currency and Finance* (London, 1884), pp. 31–32.

[14] W. Bagehot, *Lombard Street* [originally published 1873 (new ed.; London, 1915), pp. 112–13].

[15] R. H. Inglis Palgrave, *Bank Rate in England, France, and Germany, 1844–78* (London, 1880), pp. 139–41. Cf. also the article on "Interest, Theory of," in *Palgrave's Dictionary of Political Economy* (new ed.; London, 1923), Vol. II, p. 428.

[16] *Elements*, ed. Jaffé, p. 333; cf. p. 565, footnote 73 above.

[17] In his review of Fisher's *Purchasing Power of Money, Economic Journal*, XXI (1911), 395.

[18] Independently of Wicksell, and in a somewhat different context, Hawtrey emphasizes the effect of the internal drain caused by a price increase on the discount policy of banks. Indeed, this is the crucial element of his monetary theory of the trade cycle. See, for example, his "Trade Cycle" (1926), reprinted in *Readings in Business Cycle Theory*, ed. G. Haberler (Philadelphia, 1944), especially pp. 341–45.

[19] For the history of this doctrine, see Hayek, *Prices and Production*, pp. 18–22, and in particular the citation from Malthus on p. 32: "A Note on the Development of the Doctrine of 'Forced Saving,'" *Quarterly Journal of Economics*, XLVII (1932–33), 123–33; Jacob Viner, *Studies in the Theory of International Trade* (New York, 1937), pp. 187–97.

[20] *Essays on Some Unsettled Questions of Political Economy* (reprinted London, 1948), p. 118.

and as a consequence there would be so much more available for fresh investment. In other words, the extinction of so much debt would leave more to be lent, and if the demand did not increase proportionately, the rate of interest must fall.[21]

Similarly, Wicksell, after describing how an inflow of gold temporarily lowers the market rate but ultimately brings about higher prices at an unchanged rate of interest, writes:

The objection has been raised to the whole of the above reasoning that a lowering of the loan rate must also depress the real rate. ... This possibility certainly cannot be entirely rejected. *Ceteris paribus* a lowering of the real rate unconditionally demands new real capital, i.e., increased saving. But this would certainly occur, even if involuntarily, owing to the fact that higher prices would compel a restriction of consumption on the part of those people who had fixed money incomes. ...[22]

As a final example we have the following citation from Pigou:

When bankers create more credit for business men, they make, in their interest, subject to the explanations given in that chapter, a forced levy of real things from the public, thus increasing the stream of new capital available for them, and causing a fall in the real rate of interest on long and short loans alike. It is true, in short, that the bankers' rate for money is bound by a mechanical tie to the real rate of interest on long loans: but it is not true that this real rate is determined by conditions wholly outside bankers' control.[23, 24]

As an indication of the unjustified rigidity with which the classical theory of interest is today interpreted, we might finally note that both

---

[21] *Principles of Political Economy*, Vol. II, p. 232.

[22] Wicksell, *Lectures II*, pp. 198–99; cf. Note E:4 above, especially p. 592, footnote 40.

Wicksell does not identify the source of the "objection" with which he begins this passage. He might have been thinking of Cassel, who states just this in his *Theory of Social Economy*, trans. J. McCabe (London, 1923), p. 479, footnote. Unfortunately, I have not been able to check the earlier editions of Wicksell's *Lectures* in order to determine when this passage first appears. (Cassel's statement was cited by Robertson; see footnote 25 below.)

[23] *Industrial Fluctuations*, p. 277. (Cited by Metzler; see footnote 25 below.)

[24] For another example similar to the preceding ones, see Mises, *op. cit.*, Part III, Chapter V, especially pp. 347–48.

Metzler, the critic of this theory, and Robertson, its defender, are at one in regarding the proposition that the rate of interest can be permanently affected by forced savings as constituting a noteworthy deviation from the classical view.[25]

[25] In particular, Metzler cites the foregoing passage from Pigou as evidence that "his ideas concerning the interest rate were somewhat nonclassical even before ... his *Employment and Equilibrium*" ("Wealth, Saving, and the Rate of Interest," *op. cit.*, p. 95, footnote 7); while Robertson cites Cassel's criticism of Wicksell's earlier position that the real rate remains unchanged throughout the cumulative process as "an exception" to the view of "classical or neo-classical writers" that "the rate of interest can sensibly be regarded as in the long run invariant to changes in the supply of money." Robertson also adds that "Keynes in his *Treatise* days (Vol. I, p. 198) rather unexpectedly sided on this issue with Wicksell's [original view]." ["More Notes on the Rate of Interest," *Review of Economic Studies*, XXI (1953–54), 137.]

Note K. Keynes' *General Theory*

1. THE REAL-BALANCE EFFECT[1]

There are several passages in the *General Theory* which clearly reflect Keynes' implicit assumption that the real-balance effect does not directly influence the commodity market. In particular, when Keynes, in his Chapter XIX, turns to a detailed analysis of the "repercussions" of a wage and price decline on the propensity to consume and on the marginal efficiency of capital, he ignores the real-balance effect this decline generates.[2] Instead he concludes:

> It is, therefore, on the effect of a falling wage- and price-level *on the demand for money* that those who believe in the self-adjusting quality of the economic system must rest the weight of their argument; though I am not aware that they have done so. If the quantity of money is itself a function of the wage- and price-level, there is indeed, nothing to hope in this direction. But if the quantity of money is virtually fixed, it is evident that its quantity in terms of wage-units can be indefinitely increased by a sufficient reduction in money wages. ...[3]

---

[1] Attached to pp. 180; 188, point (8); 241–42; and 297–98.

[2] *General Theory*, pp. 261–66. Similarly, at an earlier point Keynes observes that "no reason has been given why a change in the quantity of money should affect either the investment demand-schedule or the readiness to save out of a given income" (*ibid.*, p. 182). True, this comment occurs when Keynes is projecting himself into the classical position, and so may be cited out of context; on the other hand, it clearly implies that Keynes himself has "no reason" to give for such an effect.

[3] *Ibid.*, p. 266, italics added.

Thus a wage and price decline is analytically equivalent to an increase in the quantity of money; hence, argues Keynes, it is like the latter in influencing effective demand only through its prior influence on the rate of interest.[4] Similarly, Keynes repeatedly emphasizes that the alternative to holding money is to hold bonds, and that any excess supply of the former is diverted to purchasing the latter.[5] There is never any indication that it may also be diverted to purchasing commodities.

Nor do I believe it possible or advisable to accept the recently made suggestion[6] to rationalize Keynes' omission of the real-balance effect from the commodity market (as well as all other markets) on the grounds that he was restricting his analysis to a pure inside-money economy (cf. pp. 297–98 above). For the argument of the *General Theory* definitely refers to an economy in which outside money also exists.[7] Furthermore, the *General Theory* surely assumes the existence of government bonds; hence this alone should have required taking account of the fact that a price decline generates a real-balance effect in the broad sense of a real-financial-asset effect (p. 290 above). But over and above these fine exegetical points is the broad interpretive one that we do no service to Keynes by attempting to free him of the foregoing criticism at the cost of needlessly restricting the relevance of his unemployment analysis to the unrealistic case of an economy with neither outside money nor government bonds. This is clear from the discussion above (pp. 336–39).

In sum, the model of the *General Theory* has both inside and outside money and should accordingly have provided for a wealth effect in the form of a real-balance effect in all markets. Its failure to do so is, however, of particular significance for the commodity market; for, in contrast with the situation in the bond and money markets (see above, pp. 297–98, 299–300, and 307–308), it is only through this effect that demand in this market can be directly affected by changes in the

---

[4] *Ibid.*, p. 266. Note also Keynes' later statement that "the primary effect of a change in the quantity of money on the quantity of effective demand is through its influence on the rate of interest" (*ibid.*, p. 298).

[5] *General Theory*, pp. 84, 168–69, 171–72, 199–202, 205–6.

[6] See Johnson, "Monetary Theory and Policy," *op. cit.*, p. 343.

[7] Thus on p. 200 of the *General Theory* Keynes assumes that "M consists of gold coins" or, alternatively, that "changes in M are due to the Government printing money wherewith to meet its current expenditure." Note also the references on p. 230 of the *General Theory* to an "inconvertible managed currency" and to a "gold-standard currency" (cf. pp. 299–300 above).

absolute price level. For this reason our criticism of Keynesian economics on this score [pp. 242, 264–65 (footnote 6), 324–25, *et passim*] has concentrated exclusively on the commodity market.

It is interesting to speculate on the train of reasoning which caused Keynes to ignore the real-balance effect. It seems likely that he did recognize the influence of wealth on consumption (or rather savings), but thought of this influence only in terms of nonmonetary assets. Correspondingly in his main discussion of the short-run consumption function—where, by assumption, the stock of nonmonetary assets is fixed[8]—he did not even consider the possible influence of wealth.[9] On the other hand—and this is precisely what our interpretation leads us to expect—as soon as Keynes discussed a period long enough for noticeable capital growth, he immediately recognized that the resulting increase in wealth causes a decrease in the propensity to save.[10] But this, unfortunately, did not bring him to realize that an analogous influence could exist even in the short run, provided one took account of *monetary* assets as well as *nonmonetary* ones (cf. p. 19 above).

The intellectual atmosphere which characterized the advent of Keynesian economics was hardly conducive to correcting this error. For in those first exciting days of analyzing aggregate demand in terms of the *flows* of consumption and investment, it was distinctly old-fashioned to explore the influence on this demand of the *stock* of money. Thus despite the fact that Haberler in 1939 had already begun to draw the implications of the real-balance effect for Keynesian economics,[11] and that Pigou in 1943 had devoted to it a major article,[12] the formulators of Keynesian models continued to ignore this effect in their

[8] *Ibid.*, p. 245.

[9] *Ibid.*, Chapter VIII, especially pp. 91–95.

[10] *Ibid.*, p. 218, second paragraph.

[11] *Prosperity and Depression* (3rd ed., 1941), pp. 242, 389, and 403. These pages appear unchanged from the 1939 edition. In the 1941 edition Haberler enlarged and elaborated on this earlier discussion (*ibid.*, pp. 491–503). Note also the reference on p. 499 to T. de Scitovsky, "Capital Accumulation, Employment and Price Rigidity," *Review of Economic Studies*, VIII (1940–41), 71–72.

It should, however, be recalled that even Haberler failed to see the full implications of this effect; cf. Note I: 3.

[12] A. C. Pigou, "The Classical Stationary State," *Economic Journal*, LIII (1943), 343–51. See also his earlier *Employment and Equilibrium* (London, 1941), pp. 126–29 [cited by G. Ackley, "The Wealth-Saving Relationship," *Journal of Political Economy*, LIX (1951), 154, footnote 1]; and his later "Economic Progress in a Stable Environment," *Economica*, XIV (1947), reprinted in *Readings in Monetary Theory*, pp. 241–51.

consumption functions until the obvious pressures of postwar excess liquidity made it impossible to do so any longer. And even then they did not always see the equilibrating role played by a price increase—and the negative real-balance effect which it generates—in bringing to an end the pressures of an inflationary gap.[13]

2. THE THEORY OF INTEREST[14]

On page 199 of the *General Theory*, Keynes writes his liquidity-preference equation in the by-now familiar form

$$M = M_1 + M_2 = L_1(Y) + L_2(r).$$

The proper interpretation of this equation turns on the crucial question as to the units in which M and Y are measured. If they are real units, the equation is free of money illusion, and the interpretation of Chapter XIII : 4 applies.[15] If they are nominal units, the equation reflects money illusion in the speculative demand, and the interpretation of Chapter XII : 1 applies.[16]

[13] Cf. Chapter X : 3, especially p. 238.

See, for example, the distinctly Keynesian analysis of the report on *Inflationary and Deflationary Tendencies, 1946–48*, prepared by the United Nations Department of Economic Affairs (New York, 1949). Here the damping effect of a price rise is restricted to its effect on the distribution of income (*ibid.*, p. 7). Similarly, Bent Hansen's monograph on the *Theory of Inflation* (London, 1951) completely overlooks the negative real-balance effect in the commodity market; cf. especially pp. 133–35. See also Erik Lundberg, *Business Cycles and Economic Policy* (London, 1957), pp. 125–26. Lundberg may, however, have been tacitly assuming that the quantity of money is continuously increased with the price level; cf. *ibid.*, p. 144. Cf. also P. A. Samuelson, *Economics: An Introductory Analysis* (5th ed.; New York, 1961), pp. 275–77, especially p. 276, footnote 1.

Another revealing example is provided by Milton Friedman, who overlooked the equilibrating role of the real-balance effect in his "Discussion of the Inflationary Gap," *American Economic Review*, XXXII (1942), 314–20, and who subsequently explicitly corrected this omission; see his revision of this article in *Essays in Positive Economics* (Chicago, 1953), especially pp. 253–57.

To the best of my knowledge, the first explicit account of the role of the real-balance effect in eliminating an inflationary gap was given by E. M. Bernstein, "Latent Inflation: Problems and Policies," *International Monetary Fund: Staff Papers*, I (1950), 1–16. This role is, of course, implicit in the passage from Wicksell cited in full in Note E : 1 above.

[14] Attached to Chapter XV : 2, and to Chapters XII : 1 and XIII : 4.

[15] Note that in this event Keynes would be making the neoclassical assumption of uniform unitary elasticity of demand for money.

[16] We are assuming here that an increase in Y causes a proportionate increase in

Unfortunately, the discussion in which the foregoing equation is imbedded is ambiguous on this point. But if we go on a few pages we find the following revealing passage:

> In a static society or in a society in which for any other reason no one feels any uncertainty about the future rates of interest, the Liquidity Function L_2, or the propensity to hoard (as we might term it), will always be zero in equilibrium. Hence in equilibrium $M_2 = 0$ and $M = M_1$; so that any change in M will cause the rate of interest to fluctuate until income reaches a level at which the change in M_1 is equal to the supposed change in M. Now $M_1 V = Y$, where V is the income-velocity of money as defined above and Y is the aggregate income. Thus if it is practicable to measure the quantity, O, and the price, P, of current output, we have $Y = OP$, and therefore, $MV = OP$; which is much the same as the Quantity Theory of Money in its traditional form.[17]

The equating of Y to OP in this passage clearly implies that the former is measured in nominal units. The equating of $M_1 V$ to Y then implies that M_1, too, is measured in these units. Hence, if this usage is extended to the earlier discussion on page 199, the liquidity-preference equation there is clearly involved in a money illusion.

Further evidence that Keynes conceived of his liquidity-preference equation in nominal terms is provided by the following passage:

> It may illustrate the argument to point out that, if the liquidity-preferences due to the transactions-motive and the precautionary-motive are assumed to absorb a quantity of cash which is not very sensitive to changes in the rate of

---

the transactions-precautionary demand, so that *this* demand is not affected by money illusion. That this assumption accords with Keynes' is indicated by the passage from the *General Theory*, pp. 171–72, cited below. Cf. also the following passage from a later article: "So far as the active circulation [i.e., transactions and precautionary balances] is concerned, it is sufficiently correct as a first approximation to regard the demand for money as proportionate to the effective demand, i.e., to the level of money income." This is a first approximation only because the active demand "is also to some extent a function of the rate of interest"—a factor obviously ignored in the liquidity-preference equation cited here. This passage would also seem to indicate that Y in this equation should be understood as money income. ["The Theory of the Rate of Interest," in *Lessons of Monetary Experience: Essays in Honor of Irving Fisher* (1937), reprinted in *Readings in the Theory of Income Distribution*, ed. W. Fellner and B. F. Haley (Philadelphia, 1946), pp. 421–22.]

[17] *General Theory*, pp. 208–9.

It might be incidentally noted that Keynes' argument here is incorrect. For, as the analysis of Chapter XI:1 above shows, the condition $L_2 = 0$ is *not* necessary for the validity of the quantity theory.

interest as such and apart from its reactions on the level of income, so that the total quantity of money, less this quantity, is available for satisfying liquidity-preferences due to the speculative-motive, the rate of interest and the price of bonds have to be fixed at the level at which the desire on the part of certain individuals to hold cash (because at that level they feel "bearish" of the future of bonds) is exactly equal to the amount of cash available for the speculative-motive. Thus each increase in the quantity of money must raise the price of bonds sufficiently to exceed the expectations of some "bull" and so influence him to sell his bond for cash and join the "bear" brigade. If, however, there is a negligible demand for cash from the speculative-motive except for a short transitional interval, an increase in the quantity of money will have to lower the rate of interest almost forthwith, in whatever degree is necessary to raise employment *and the wage-unit* sufficiently to cause the additional cash to be absorbed by the transactions-motive and the precautionary-motive.

As a rule, we can suppose that the schedule of liquidity-preference relating the quantity of money to the rate of interest is given by a smooth curve which shows the rate of interest falling as the quantity of money is increased. For there are several different causes all leading towards this result.

In the first place, as the rate of interest falls, it is likely, *cet. par.*, that more money will be absorbed by liquidity-preferences due to the transactions-motive. For if the fall in the rate of interest increases the national income, the amount of money which it is convenient to keep for transactions will be increased more or less proportionately to the increase in income; whilst, at the same time, the cost of the convenience of plenty of ready cash in terms of loss of interest will be diminished. *Unless we measure liquidity-preference terms of wage-units rather than of money* (which is convenient in some contexts), similar results follow if the increased employment ensuing on a fall in the rate of interest leads to *an increase of wages, i.e. to an increase in the money value of the wage-unit.* In the second place, every fall in the rate of interest may, as we have just seen, increase the quantity of cash which certain individuals will wish to hold because their views as to the future of the rate of interest differ from the market views.[18]

The first italicized clause of the last paragraph clearly indicates that in general Keynes does *not* measure liquidity preference in the real terms of wage-units.[19]

[18] *General Theory*, pp. 171–72, italics added.

[19] Note, however, the ambiguous passage earlier in his discussion in which Keynes states that "an individual's liquidity-preference is given by a schedule of the amounts of his resources, valued in terms of money or of wage-units, which he will wish to retain in the form of money in different sets of circumstances" (*ibid.*, p. 166).

As noted in the text, the money-illusion interpretation receives convincing support from Keynes' significant failure to ever indicate that the nominal speculative demand is sensitive to changes in the price level.[20] In particular, Keynes' discussion of the foregoing equation on pages 200–201 is void of any such recognition. Nor is it likely that this merely indicates the assumed presence of absolute wage and price rigidity. For in this discussion Keynes assumes Y to increase as a result of an increase in M; and in general—and even under the assumption of unemployment—Keynes assumes that increases in the level of employment (and hence real income) generate increases in the wage-unit.[21]

Any remaining doubts about the validity of this interpretation are removed by the structure of Keynes' argument in the passage just quoted—a passage which closely parallels that of pages 200–201. The phrases italicized in the first and last paragraphs of this passage show that Keynes is taking into consideration a possible rise in the wage-unit. Yet though Keynes indicates the implications of this rise for the transactions and precautionary demands, he does not do so for the speculative demand. This omission is particularly significant in the last paragraph, where—as shown by the last sentence—Keynes is assuming the existence of a speculative demand which is not negligible.

The same significant omission also characterizes Keynes' observation at a later point that "a reduction of the wage-unit will release cash from its other uses for the satisfaction of the liquidity-motive." It is clear from the context that by "liquidity-motive" Keynes means "speculative motive." Yet there is no recognition of the fact that just as a reduction of the wage-unit can reduce the demand for cash for "other uses," so too can it reduce the demand for speculative uses.[22]

---

[20] Above, p. 373.

[21] *General Theory*, pp. 249, 251, 301.

[22] *Ibid.*, p. 232 (top). For a similar passage, see p. 298, lines 11–5 from bottom, noting that by "schedule of liquidity-preference" Keynes has in mind only the schedule of the speculative demand. For another instance in which this term is used in this narrow sense, see p. 168. This is one of the pitfalls in interpreting Keynes' monetary theory: "liquidity-preference" can mean either the total, $L_1(Y) + L_2(r)$, or just $L_2(r)$ by itself. The reader must in each case determine the intended meaning from the context.

All of the foregoing passages show us how we should understand the less specific passages in the *General Theory* in which Keynes merely indicates that a fall in the wage-unit increases the real value of money balances and thereby decreases interest (cf., e.g., pp. 253, 266–67). Here, too, the intention is that the decrease in the

Consider finally the passage in which Keynes writes:

> If the reader still finds himself perplexed [by the proposition that an increase in the desire to save will not reduce interest], let him ask himself why, the quantity of money being unchanged, a fresh act of saving should diminish the sum which it is desired to keep in liquid form at the existing rate of interest.[23]

It is clear from the context that by "the sum ... " Keynes is referring to the speculative demand. The answer, then, to Keynes' question is that this "sum" will diminish because of the effect of "the fresh act of saving" in decreasing aggregate demand for commodities and hence prices.[24] But this is an answer which Keynes—significantly enough—does not give.

The only passage seemingly at variance with the foregoing interpretation of Keynes occurs in his Appendix to Chapter XIV. Here Keynes cites in full Ricardo's discussion of the rate of interest[25] and then states:

> (1) If Ricardo had been content to present his argument solely as applying to any given quantity of money created by the monetary authority, it would still have been correct on the assumption of flexible money-wages. (2) If, that is to say, Ricardo had argued that it would make no permanent alteration to the rate of interest whether the quantity of money was fixed by the monetary authority at ten millions or at a hundred millions, his conclusion would hold. (3) But if by the policy of the monetary authority we mean the terms on which it will increase or decrease the quantity of money, i.e., the rate of interest at which it will, either by a change in the volume of discounts or by open-market operations, increase or decrease its assets—which is what Ricardo expressly does mean in the above quotation—then it is not the case either that the policy of the monetary authority is nugatory or that only one policy is compatible with long-period equilibrium; (4) though in the extreme case where money-wages are assumed to fall without limit in face of involuntary unemployment through a futile competition for employment between the unemployed labourers, there will, it is true, be only two possible long-period

---

wage-unit decreases the amount of money needed for transactions and precautionary motives, and hence increases the residual amount available for the speculative motive. That is, there is no intention in these passages that the speculative demand is also decreased by the fall in the wage-unit.

[23] *Ibid.*, p. 213.
[24] Cf. above, pp. 254–55 and 270.
[25] *Principles*, ed. Sraffa, *op. cit.*, p. 363.

positions—full employment and the level of employment corresponding to the rate of interest at which liquidity-preference becomes absolute (in the event of this being less than full employment). (5) Assuming flexible money-wages, the quantity of money as such is, indeed, nugatory in the long period; (6) but the terms on which the monetary authority will change the quantity of money enters as a real determinant into the economic scheme.[26]

At first sight, Keynes' concession to Ricardo in the second sentence seems to contradict the assumption of money illusion in the speculative demand, for under this assumption changes in the quantity of money can permanently alter the rate of interest, even with perfectly flexible money wages.[27] But we must note that this passage as it now stands also contradicts Keynes' own later insistence that the validity of the quantity theory depends on the assumption that the speculative demand is zero.[28] This leads me to suspect that in the preceding passage Keynes is tacitly assuming that there is no speculative demand. If this is true, both contradictions disappear simultaneously.[29]

We might finally note that Keynes' agreement with Leontief that his differences with classical monetary theory flow from a denial of the homogeneity postulate[30] cannot be taken as evidence that Keynes was aware of his money-illusion assumption in our sense of the term. For, as has been sufficiently emphasized in the text, the denial of Leontief's homogeneity postulate does not imply money illusion in this sense.[31] Even aside from this, it is not at all clear what Keynes had in mind when he agreed with Leontief. For he supports this agreement with an immediate reference to his paper on the "Theory of the Rate of Interest"[32] where—as far as I can see—this postulate plays no role.

[26] *General Theory*, p. 191. The statements have been numbered for convenience of reference. The fifth one has already been cited on p. 374, footnote 22.

[27] Cf. Chapter XII:1.

[28] See the passage from pp. 208–209 cited at the beginning of this section. Note that Keynes again emphasizes the importance of this assumption for classical theory in his "Theory of the Rate of Interest," *op. cit.*, pp. 423–24.

[29] Another obscure point in this passage is the nature of the distinction which Keynes has in mind in his second and third—and fifth and sixth—statements. Without at all being sure, I think it is related to the distinction made in the text between an increase in the quantity of money generated by a gratuitous distribution of new money by the government, and one generated by open-market purchases (Chapter XII:4).

[30] "General Theory of Employment," *Quarterly Journal of Economics*, LI (1936–37), 209.

[31] Chapter VIII:3.

[32] *Op. cit.*

3. THE THEORY OF UNEMPLOYMENT[33]

Clearly, Keynes recognized the importance of wage rigidities in the real world.[34] Nevertheless, as emphasized in the text, these rigidities do not constitute a logically necessary part of his theory of unemployment. Indeed, such an interpretation stands in direct contradiction to Keynes' Chapter XIX, the very title of which is "Changes in Money-Wages." This chapter—which forms the climax of Keynes' argument —applies the analytical apparatus of the *General Theory* to a detailed examination of the implications of downward wage flexibility and concludes that:

> There is, therefore, no ground for the belief that a flexible wage policy is capable of maintaining a state of continuous full employment;—any more than for the belief that an open-market monetary policy is capable, unaided, of achieving this result. The economic system cannot be made self-adjusting along these lines.[35]

Thus wage rigidities in this chapter are not an *assumption* of the analysis, but the *policy conclusion* which Keynes reaches after investigating the results to be expected from wage flexibility.[36]

All, then, that Keynes means by the statement that the system may settle down to a position of "unemployment equilibrium" is that the automatic workings of the system will *not* restore the system to a position of *full-employment equilibrium*. He does *not* mean "equilibrium" in the usual sense of the term that nothing tends to change in the system. All that is strictly in equilibrium is the level—or, possibly, only the

---

[33] Attached to Chapter XIII:1 (especially pp. 314–15) and Chapter XIV:1 (especially pp. 339–40).

[34] Cf., e.g., *General Theory*, pp. 232–33, 303.

[35] *Ibid.*, p. 267.

In this context one might also cite in full the passage from p. 378 referred to on p. 339 above:

> Furthermore, it seems unlikely that the influence of banking policy on the rate of interest will be sufficient by itself to determine an optimum rate of investment. I conceive, therefore, that a somewhat comprehensive socialisation of investment will prove the only means of securing an approximation to full employment; though this need not exclude all manner of compromises and of devices by which public authority will co-operate with private initiative.

[36] See the final section of this chapter, *ibid.*, pp. 269–71.

fact—of unemployment; but there is no equilibrium of the money wage rate.[37]

This is admittedly loose—and hence undesirable—usage of a term which has a precise, accepted meaning. We should recognize it as such and criticize it as such. But we should not permit it to involve us in a futile and irrelevant debate on whether there can or cannot be a coexistence of "unemployment equilibrium" and "flexible wages." For, as emphasized in the text, if these terms are understood in their usual sense, such a coexistence is by definition impossible. But, as also emphasized in the text, this has no bearing whatsoever on Keynes' central thesis: namely, that a full-employment policy based on the downward flexibility of money wages is not a practicable one.[38]

---

[37] Evidence of this usage is provided by the long passage from the *General Theory*, p. 191, cited at the end of the preceding section. Here, in the fourth statement, Keynes speaks of a "long-period position" of less-than-full employment—even though in this position "money-wages are assumed to fall without limit in face of involuntary unemployment."

Cf. also the following passage from p. 253:

> ... if competition between unemployed workers always led to a very great reduction of the money-wage, there would be a violent instability in the price-level. Moreover, there might be no position of stable equilibrium except in conditions consistent with full employment; since the wage-unit might have to fall without limit until it reached a point where the effect of the abundance of money in terms of the wage-unit on the rate of interest was sufficient to restore a level of full employment. At no other point could there be a resting-place.

Here Keynes is using "equilibrium" in the strict sense of the term. For a similar passage see pp. 303–304.

[38] Above, pp. 315 and 339.

Note L. On Say's Law[1]

Though the text has shown that Say's Identity is not a logically necessary component of the classical position,[2] there still remains the question as to whether Say, Ricardo, Mill—both senior and junior—and other deniers of the possibility of a "general glut" did or did not think in terms of this identity.

In support of Keynes'[3] and Lange's[4] contention that they did so think, one can cite the following passage from Say:

It is worth while to remark, that a product is no sooner created, than it, *from that instant*, affords a market for other products to the full extent of its own value. When the producer has put the finishing hand to his product, he is most anxious to sell it immediately, lest its value should diminish in his hands. Nor is he less anxious to dispose of the money he may get for it; for the value of money is also perishable. But the only way of getting rid of money is in the purchase of some product or other. Thus the mere circumstance of the creation of one product immediately opens a vent for other products.[5]

---

[1] Attached to Chapter XIV:4–5.

[2] For an earlier exposition and emphasis on this proposition, see my "Involuntary Unemployment and the Keynesian Supply Function," *Economic Journal*, LIX (1949), 378.

[3] *General Theory*, pp. 18–21, 25–26.

[4] "Say's Law: A Restatement and Criticism," *op. cit.*, pp. 52–53.

[5] J. B. Say, *A Treatise on Political Economy*, trans. C. R. Prinsep from the fourth French edition (Philadelphia, 1834), pp. 138–39; italics added from original French of third edition, *Traité d'économie politique* (Paris, 1817), p. 145.

Similarly, Ricardo observes:

Whoever is possessed of a commodity is necessarily a demander, either he wishes to consume the commodity himself, and then no purchaser is wanted; or he wishes to sell it, and purchase some other thing with the money, which shall either be consumed by him, or be made instrumental to future production.[6]

And in the same vein James Mill writes:

... no man wants money but in order to lay it out, either in articles of productive, or articles of unproductive consumption.[7]

On the other hand, the standard passage from J. S. Mill which Keynes cites in support of his identity interpretation definitely does *not* carry the meaning that Keynes—and later writers—have attached to it. This passage reads:

... what it is which constitutes the means of payment for commodities ... is simply commodities. Each person's means of paying for the productions of other people consists of those which he himself possesses. All sellers are inevitably and *ex vi termini* buyers. Could we suddenly double the productive powers of the country, we should double the supply of commodities in every market; but we should, by the same stroke, double the purchasing power. Everybody would bring a double demand as well as supply: everybody would be able to buy twice as much, because everyone would have twice as much to offer in exchange.[8]

In order to see how this passage has been torn out of context, we must first note its place in the chapter in which it appears. In the first section

---

The force of this evidence is, however, diminished by the fact that one page earlier Say presents the weaker statement that "even when money is obtained with a view to hoard or bury it, the *ultimate* object is always to employ it in a purchase of some kind" (*Treatise*, p. 137, footnote, italics added).

[6] *Notes on Malthus, Works*, ed. Sraffa, Vol. II, p. 305.

[7] *Elements of Political Economy* (London, 1821), pp. 191–92.

[8] J. S. Mill, *Principles*, Book III, Chapter XIV, Section 2, pp. 557–58. Cited in full—with minor modifications—by Keynes as an example of the "classical doctrine" that "the whole of the costs of production must necessarily be spent in the aggregate, directly or indirectly, on purchasing the product" (*General Theory*, p. 18).

I hasten to add that on an occasion when I cited this passage myself, I "clarified" its meaning by adding the words "and, presumably, would" in brackets after the "everybody would be able to" of its last sentence. ("Involuntary Unemployment and the Keynesian Supply Function," *op. cit.*, p. 377.) The distortion thereby introduced is clear from what follows immediately.

of this chapter Mill refers to the overproduction thesis of Malthus, Chalmers, and Sismondi. He then begins the second section with the following paragraph:

When these writers speak of the supply of commodities as outrunning the demand, it is not clear which of the two elements of demand they have in view—the desire to possess, or the means of purchase; whether their meaning is that there are, in such cases, more consumable products in existence than the public desires to consume, or merely more than it is able to pay for. In this uncertainty, it is necessary to examine both suppositions.[9]

Mill then devotes the remainder of this second section to the second "supposition" and shows that the "supply of commodities in general cannot exceed the power of purchase."[10] Finally he returns in the third section to the first "supposition" and argues that "the supply of commodities in general never does exceed the inclination to consume."[11]

Now, the passage which Keynes cites occurs in the second section of Mill's chapter. Hence it cannot refer to the *willingness* to consume— as Keynes would have it—but to the *power* to consume. Indeed, when read within the context that Mill specifies, this passage expresses nothing more objectionable than the innocuous "national income equals national product" identity of contemporary social accounting!

As against the foregoing interpretation of Keynes and Lange, we have the recent interpretation of Becker and Baumol[12] and Schumpeter[13]— all of whom maintain that Say's Law was not intended as an identity; that classical economists had reference only to the long-run ability of the economy to absorb any increase in output; and that this is attested by their explicit recognition of the possibility of short-run over supply in the market.[14]

---

[9] *Principles*, p. 557.

[10] This is the heading of Section 2 as listed in the Table of Contents, *ibid.*, p. xliii.

[11] Heading for Section 3, *ibid.*, p. xliv.

[12] *Op. cit.*, pp. 360–61, 371–74.

[13] *History of Economic Analysis*, pp. 615–25.

See also G. J. Stigler, "Sraffa's *Ricardo*," *American Economic Review*, XLIII (1953), 591–99.

[14] Indeed, Schumpeter—following A. P. Lerner—argues that Say's Law simply states that an increase in production generates a corresponding increase in income and hence an increase in aggregate demand (*History of Economic Analysis*, pp. 617, 623–24).

Evidence for this long-run interpretation of Say's Law—and, consequently, for viewing it as dealing with the question of secular stagnation as contrasted with that of cyclical depression—is provided by the fact that Ricardo, for example, discusses it in his Chapter XXI, entitled "Effects of Accumulation on Profits and Interest."[15] Similarly, Malthus criticizes this law in Chapter VII of his *Principles* ("On the Immediate Causes of the Progress of Wealth") under the subheading "Of Accumulation, or the Saving from Revenue to add to Capital, considered as a Stimulus to the Increase of Wealth."[16] On the other hand, Ricardo clearly recognizes the short-run "distress" that can be generated by "Sudden Changes in the Channels of Trade."[17] We might also note Ricardo's observation to Malthus:

It appears to me that one great cause of our difference in opinion, on the subjects which we have so often discussed, is that you have always in your mind the immediate and temporary effects of particular changes—whereas I put these immediate and temporary effects quite aside, and fix my whole attention on the permanent state of things which will result from them.[18]

This distinction between the temporary "excess of all commodities above the money demand" which characterizes a "commercial crisis" and the "permanent decline in the circumstances of producers, for want of markets" contemplated by opponents of Say's Law is made most explicitly by J. S. Mill.[19] It should also be noted that Mill returns to the problem of Say's Law in Book IV (entitled "Influence of the Progress of Society on Production and Distribution"), Chapter IV (entitled "Of the Tendency of Profits to a Minimum"), and emphasizes

---

[15] *Principles, Works.*

[16] T. R. Malthus, *Principles of Political Economy* (1st ed.) as abridged in Ricardo, *Works*, ed. Sraffa, Vol. II, pp. 300–301. The same is true of the second edition (Tokyo, 1936 reprint), pp. 309, 314.

[17] *Principles*, title of Chapter XIX.

[18] Letter to Malthus, *Works*, Vol. VII, p. 120.

Note that though Malthus begins his reply to this letter by stating his agreement with this observation, he goes on to say that

... a still more specific and fundamental cause of our difference [is that] ... you seem to think that the wants and tastes of mankind are always ready for the supply; while I am most decidedly of opinion that few things are more difficult, than to inspire new tastes and wants, particularly out of old materials. [*Ibid.*, p. 122.]

[19] *Principles*, p. 561.

that the real difficulty generated by an increasing amount of capital "would not consist in any want of a market," but in the fact that it is "impossible ... to employ this capital without submitting to a rapid reduction of the rate of profit."[20] All this emphasizes the long-run context in which Mill viewed the problem of overproduction.

It is also significant that in his famous Chapter XV "On Markets," Say adduces evidence in support of his thesis from the fact "that there should now be bought and sold in France five or six times as many commodities, as in the miserable reign of Charles VI [1380–1422]."[21] Again, in his *Letters to Malthus*, Say argues that the enactment of the Elizabethan Poor Laws proves that "*there was* no employ in a country which since then has been able to furnish enough for a double and triple number of laborers."[22] Here is the same line of reasoning with which modern-day opponents of the "stagnation thesis" attempt to refute it by, say, citing Kuznets' data on the growth in per capita national product of the United States by more than three and a half times during the eighty-year period ending in 1948.[23]

Even if we accept this secular interpretation of Say's Law—and the evidence in favor of it is convincing—we must again emphasize that classical economists failed to specify the market mechanism which makes this law valid.[24] In particular, they did not think in terms of the

[20] *Ibid.*, p. 732. Mill had already made this clear on pp. 561–62.

[21] *Treatise*, p. 137.

[22] (London, 1821; reprinted 1936), pp. 4–5, italics in original.

[23] S. Kuznets, "Long-Term Changes in the National Income of the United States of America since 1870," *Income & Wealth of the United States: Trends and Structure*, ed. S. Kuznets, Income and Wealth Series II (Cambridge, 1952), p. 55.

[24] Cf. end of Chapter XIV:5 above.

There are, indeed, hints here and there of an equilibrating mechanism, but these are never developed into a systematic theory. Thus Say writes that "excessive saving ... carries its remedy along with it. Where the capitals become too abundant, the interest which the capitalists derive from them become too low to balance the privations they impose upon themselves by their savings" (*Letters to Malthus*, p. 37). For a similar statement, see also Ricardo, *Notes on Malthus*, *Works*, ed. Sraffa, Vol. II, p. 309, note (199). Ricardo also emphasizes his view that low profits can only mean high wages so that laborers will consume whatever capitalists do not (*ibid.*, pp. 308, 311). For a similar statement, see J. S. Mill, *Principles*, pp. 66–68, 732.

[25] See Becker and Baumol, *op. cit.*, pp. 360–61, 374. These authors denote the process described in Chapter XIV:5 by the term "Say's Equality" and claim to find it presented in J. S. Mill, *Essays on Some Unsettled Questions of Political Economy*, pp. 67–74.

In these pages Mill does clearly provide a vivid picture of the temporary stagnation that would be generated if, for some reason, people "liked better to possess

automatic price and interest variations analyzed in Chapter XIV:5. There would be no need to stress this here had not the contrary recently been implied.[25,26]

money than any other commodity" (p. 72). But he does not explain why the stagnation is only temporary, and he certainly does not say—or even imply—that the positive real-balance effect of a declining price level plays any role in the recovery. All he does say on this subject is contained in the following cryptic paragraph:

> It is true that this state [of stagnation] can be only temporary, and must even be succeeded by a reaction of corresponding violence, since those who have sold without buying will certainly buy at last, and there will then be more buyers than sellers. But although the general over-supply is of necessity only temporary, this is no more than may be said of every partial over-supply. An overstocked state of the market is always temporary, and is generally followed by a more than common briskness of demand [p. 71].

The present discussion should thus make it clear that "Say's Equality" is a completely misleading term. More specifically, though passages can be—and have been—cited to show that classical economists might have thought in terms of the "Identity," none have been cited that would justify the attempt to associate them with the "Equality."

[26] At first sight it seems tempting to describe the statement that the system must always be brought to a condition of full-employment equilibrium by

(a) $$\sum_{j=1}^{n-1} p_j D_j = \sum_{j=1}^{n-1} p_j S_j,$$

to be contrasted with the statement of Say's Identity (cf. Mathematical Appendix 7:*d*)

(b) $$\sum_{j=1}^{n-1} p_j D_j \equiv \sum_{j=1}^{n-1} p_j S_j,$$

where p_j is the price of the jth commodity, D_j its quantity demanded, and S_j its quantity supplied. And this, indeed, is what Schumpeter does (*History of Economic Analysis*, p. 619). Actually, however, condition (a) says much less than what is said by Chapter XIV:4–5 and by the earlier article cited above (p. 645, footnote 2). The point of departure of these latter interpretations is that equilibrium means full employment, so that the essence of the classical position is that the system of equilibrium conditions

(c) $$D_j(p_1, \dots, p_{n-1}) = S_j(p_1, \dots, p_{n-1}) \qquad (j = 1, \dots, n-1)$$

always has a solution. An immediate implication of this statement is then the much weaker statement (a).

Note M. Empirical Investigations

of the Real-Balance Effect[1]

As already noted in the text, the role of the real-balance effect in the postwar inflationary experience of various Western countries has been described by A. J. Brown.[2] A somewhat less conclusive picture has been given by J. G. Gurley in his analysis of postwar European monetary reforms.[3] Similarly, while conceding that liquid assets may have affected consumer spending in the U.S. immediately after the war, Morris Cohen contends that they had no significant effect in the period 1947–51.[4] On the other hand, my own studies of the Israel economy would seem to indicate the importance of the real-balance effect in the inflationary process of that country.[5]

More systematic evidence on the real-balance effect is available from econometric studies of the demand functions for money and commodities, respectively.[6] In the former category are the studies by

---

[1] Attached to p. 21, footnote 17; p. 289, footnote 15; p. 340, footnote 11; *et passim.*

[2] *The Great Inflation, op. cit.*, Chapter X, especially pp. 236–37.

[3] "Excess Liquidity and European Monetary Reforms, 1944–1952," *American Economic Review*, XLIII (1953), 76–100.

[4] "Liquid Assets and the Consumption Function," *Review of Economics and Statistics*, XXXVI (1954), 202–11.

[5] "Monetary and Price Developments in Israel: 1949–1953," *Scripta Hierosolymitana*, III (1955), especially pp. 30, 40–41; *The Israel Economy: The First Decade* (Jerusalem, 1959), pp. 109–111.

[6] As emphasized above (e.g., p. 242), the assumption of outside money implies

H. F. Lydall,[7] M. Bronfenbrenner and T. Mayer,[8] and A. H. Meltzer[9]—all of whom use liquid assets or wealth inclusive of financial assets as one of the independent variables explaining the demand for money. Far more intensive work has, however, been done on the commodity market, and particularly on the consumption function.[10] The relevant studies of this function have been based on cross-section data, as well as on time series. Among the cross-section studies is the one by Lawrence R. Klein (based on the U.S. Survey of Consumer Finances for 1949), which found a significant negative correlation between liquid assets and savings.[11] Less conclusive results were obtained by Malcolm R. Fisher in his analysis of the U.K. 1953 savings survey.[12] Similarly, Sten Thore did not find any significant influence of wealth (including liquid assets) on savings in his analysis of the 1957 Swedish savings survey.[13]

By far the greater part of the evidence, is, however, available from the time-series studies. Some of these are exclusively of the consumption

---

that the real-balance effect should manifest itself throughout the economy—and in a similar fashion in all markets except that for bonds (see pp. 68–69).

[7] "Income, Assets, and the Demand for Money," *Review of Economics and Statistics*, XL (1958), 3–4, 6–7.

[8] "Liquidity Functions in the American Economy," *Econometrica*, XXVIII (1960), 817–18.

[9] "The Demand for Money: The Evidence from the Time Series," *Journal of Political Economy*, LXXI (1963), 224–25.

[10] The investment function has been excluded from the present survey because of the much less firm state of our knowledge about it. See, however, Robert Eisner and Robert H. Strotz, "Determinants of Business Investment," in Commission on Money and Credit, *Impacts of Monetary Policy* (Englewood Cliffs, N.J., 1963), pp. 156–65; note also the bibliography provided *ibid.*, p. 332 (item C:2). Of particular relevance is Edwin Kuh and John R. Meyer, "Investment, Liquidity, and Monetary Policy," *ibid.*, pp. 339–474.

[11] L. R. Klein, "Statistical Estimation of Economic Relations from Survey Data," in *Contributions of Survey Methods to Economics*, ed. L. R. Klein (New York, 1954), pp. 207–11. See also his "Assets, Debts, and Economic Behavior," in Conference on Research in Income and Wealth, *Studies in Income and Wealth*, Vol. 14 (New York, 1951), pp. 207–27.

[12] "Exploration in Savings Behaviour," *Bulletin of the Oxford University Institute of Statistics*, XVIII (1956), 240–45.

In his discussion of this analysis, Milton Friedman suggested that liquid assets were a proxy for permanent income ["Savings and the Balance Sheet," *Bulletin of the Oxford University Institute of Statistics*, XIX (1957), 129–34]. It will, however, be shown below (pp. 658–59) that this alternative hypothesis does not imply that consumption is not affected by real balances.

[13] *Household Saving and the Price Level* (Stockholm, 1961), p. 70. Thore, however, attributes this finding in part to specification errors of his model; *ibid.*, pp. 73–76.

function, while others estimate it as one component of an econometric model of the economy as a whole. The studies also differ among themselves with respect to the period covered, the nature of the data (annual or quarterly), the definition of real balances (or, more to the point, net financial assets), the specification of the type of function and of the other variables contained in it, and the method of estimation.

The findings of these studies (all of which refer to the United States) are summarized in Table A.[14] Of most significance to us is the last column, which compares the studies on the basis of their implied estimates of the elasticity of real consumption with respect to the price level, η_p. Under the assumption of linearity this is

$$(1) \qquad \eta_p = -\alpha \frac{(M/p)}{C},$$

where α is the coefficient of real balances M/p, and C is real consumption. Thus the value of η_p is clearly dependent on the relative volume of financial assets in the economy. In accordance with usual practice, the elasticities of Table A are evaluated at the mean values of M/p and C in the time series on which the respective studies are based. For the most part, it turns out that the ratio of these mean values is close to unity, so that the estimates of η_p are not too different from those of α. Note too that η_p is the negative of the elasticity of real consumption with respect to real financial assets.[15]

[14] Two other studies which have yielded a statistically significant real-balance effect—but which do not fit into the framework of the table—are Raymond W. Goldsmith, "Experiments with the Saving Function," in R. W. Goldsmith *et al.*, *A Study of Saving in the United States* (Princeton, 1956), Vol. III, pp. 410–12; and L. E. Gallaway and P. E. Smith, "Real Balances and the Permanent Income Hypothesis," *Quarterly Journal of Economics*, LXXV (1961), 302–13. See also the study by Crockett referred to on p. 436, footnote 22 above. The articles by Ta-Chung Liu and Charles Schotta, Jr.(which specifies a savings function with money illusion) appeared too late to be included in Table A; see Bibliography.

The studies of Hamburger, Ando and Modigliani, and Arena are discussed separately below.

[15] Specifically, if the consumption function is

$$C = f\left(Y, X, \frac{M}{p}\right),$$

where Y represents real disposable income and X other variables, then

$$\eta_p = \frac{\partial f(\ )}{\partial p} \cdot \frac{p}{C} = -\alpha \frac{M}{p^2} \cdot \frac{p}{C} = -\alpha \frac{(M/p)}{C}$$

(cont. on p. 654)

With the exception of the first and fourth studies described in Table A, the coefficient of real balances is highly significant: in practically all cases, at least three times the standard error. There is, however, considerable and puzzling variation in the results—particularly when account is taken of the long-run estimates of α and η_p. Contrary to the views of several of the investigators,[16] there does not seem to be a systematic tendency for postwar data to yield higher estimates of α than prewar data. Thus the Christ and Morishima-Saito[17][18] estimates are much higher than those of Klein-Goldberger and Fox—even though the latter are more heavily weighted with postwar observations. This, however, is not conclusive. A proper test of the foregoing views should be based on a comparison of the results obtained by using the same method of estimation and the same equation for both prewar and postwar data. The same is true, *mutatis mutandis*, of the impression created by the table that estimates of α derived from quarterly data are higher than those from annual ones—particularly when account is taken of the long-run values.

Zellner attempts to explain this difference on the grounds that "the effects of a change in liquid assets may be exhausted *within* the period of a year; therefore the full effects of such a change do not show up when annual data are employed." He also suggests that "in testing the

---

and

$$\eta_{M/p} = \frac{\partial f(\ )}{\partial (M/p)} \cdot \frac{(M/p)}{C} = \alpha \frac{(M/p)}{C}.$$

See above, pp. 420–21, equations (2.36) and (2.39), for a corresponding proposition on the demand function for real balances.

[16] See Christ, "Test of an Econometric Model," *op. cit.*, pp. 59–60; Zellner, *op. cit.*, p. 565.

[17] I find the Morishima-Saito estimates problematic on two grounds: first, the use of national instead of disposable income (see footnote *m* to Table A); and second, the duplication between Y and K (see footnote 28 below).

[18] Morishima and Saito rightly emphasize that—due to the interdependence of the system—the influence of a change in the quantity of money (assumed to be exogenous) on one of the endogenous variables is not measured by α, but by a multiplier solved out from the system as a whole (cf. Mathematical Appendix 1:*b*, above). Thus they estimate that the "impact elasticity-multiplier of the amount of money on national product" (that is, the percentage change in national product caused—during the first year after its occurrence—by a 1 per cent change in the quantity of money) in their model is 0.442 (*op. cit.*, p. 143). This is to be compared with their estimate of 0.215 for $\eta_{M/p}$.

hypothesis that the size of liquid asset holdings affects consumption expenditures (including expenditures on durables), it may be the case that the estimated coefficient of liquid assets reflects not only the influence of liquid assets on consumption (defined to include only depreciation on durables) but also consumers' substitution of durable assets for liquid assets. If this is the case, a problem of identification exists."[19]

On the other hand, Griliches *et al.* argue quite convincingly that their quarterly estimates of the long-run value of α are much too high to be plausible. Thus the results for 1952–60[20] imply that "an increase of one billion dollars in the *stock* of consumer liquid assets would lead to an indefinite *permanent* increase of half a billion dollars in the *annual rate* of consumption expenditures." Accordingly these authors suggest "*either* that liquid assets are a proxy for permanent income[21] *or* that they 'work' because they vary largely in response to transitory changes in consumption which are themselves negatively serially correlated."[22]

In the absence of additional information, it is impossible to judge the validity of these conjectures. I would, however, now like to emphasize that none of the studies presented in Table A really tests the real-balance effect in the manner implied in this book—and this for two reasons. First, they define real balances as liquid assets, and not as net financial assets of fixed money value (i.e., assets whose real value is affected by an equiproportionate change in commodity prices).[23] Second, and far more important, they give the impression that it is real balances *per se* which influence consumption, instead of real balances as a component of total wealth. As has constantly been emphasized above,[24] it is this

---

[19] Zellner, *op. cit.*, p. 565; italics in original.

The problem of identification noted by Zellner could in part be overcome by analyzing the function for nondurable consumption alone; this would require us also to eliminate that part of money balances being held for the purchase of durables.

[20] See line 10 of table. The long-run estimate of α in this equation (to which reference is made in the quotation which follows) is $\frac{1}{1 - 0.259} \cdot 0.367 = 0.495$.

[21] See once again the discussion on pp. 658–59 below.

[22] Griliches *et al.*, *op. cit.*, p. 496, italics in original.

For other discussions of Zellner's results—as well as further aspects of the liquid-asset question—see G. Ackley, *Macroeconomic Theory* (New York, 1961), pp. 274–82; Daniel B. Suits, "The Determinants of Consumer Expenditure: A Review of Present Knowledge," in Commission on Money and Credit, *Impacts of Monetary Policy* (Englewood Cliffs, N.J., 1963), pp. 29–35, 41–43.

[23] See p. 290 above.

[24] See pp. 19, 200–201, and 405ff.

Investigator	Period covered	Nature of data	Method of estimation[b]	Definition of real balances[c]	1
1. Klein	1921–41	Annual, per capita	RF	M_1	78
2. Christ	1921–47[g]	Annual, aggregate	DLS	M_1	3.80
3. Christ	1921–47[g]	Annual, aggregate	DLS	M_1	7.07
4. Klein and Goldberger	1929–50[g]	Annual, aggregate	LI	M_2	−34.5 (7.7)
5. Klein and Goldberger	1929–52[g]	Annual, aggregate	LI	M_2	−22.26 (9.66)
6. Fox	1929–52[g]	Annual, aggregate	DLS	M_2	−21.06
7. Zellner	1947–55[k]	Quarterly, aggregate	DLS	M_2	−18.96
8. Zellner	1947–55[k]	Quarterly, aggregate	DLS	M_2	−21.91
9. Griliches et al.	1947–55[l]	Quarterly, aggregate	DLS	M_2	−24.7
10. Griliches et al.	1952–60	Quarterly, aggregate	DLS	M_2	−9.6
11. Griliches et al.	1947–60[k]	Quarterly, aggregate	DLS	M_2	−13.1
12. Morishima and Saito	1902–52	Annual, per capita of population aged 15 and over	TSLS	M_1	−0.27

NOTES:

[a] – means variable not in equation. Number in parentheses under coefficient represents standard error.

[b] DLS = direct least squares
  RF = reduced form
  LI = limited information
  TSLS = two-stage least squares

[c] M_1 = total deposits (demand and time) adjusted, and currency outside banks: beginning of period.
  M_2 = nonbusiness holding of currency, demand and time deposits, savings-and-loan-association shares, and U.S. Government securities, at beginning of period. Exact definition may vary slightly from study to study.

[d] Figure in parentheses represents "long-run elasticity," obtained by multiplying coefficient of M/p by $1/(1 − a)$—where a is the coefficient of C_{-1} in any equation in which it appears. This is the same procedure as is used for obtaining the long-run value of the other coefficients (say, of Y) in such equations. See Marc Nerlove, "Distributed Lags and Estimation of Long-Run Supply and Demand Elasticities: Theoretical Considerations," *Journal of Farm Economics*, XL (1958), 309; see also Klein and Goldberger, *op. cit.*, pp. 62–63.

[e] Not significant.

[f] Not computed because coefficient of real balances not significant.

[g] Excluding 1942–45.

[h] Disposable income was decomposed into wage income, nonwage nonfarm income, and farm income—the coefficients of which were 0.62 (±0.04), 0.46 (±0.03), and 0.39 (±0.025), respectively.

		Coefficients of: [a]					
Y (real disposable income)	Y_{-1}	C_{-1} (real consumption lagged)	N (population)	t (time)	K (tangible capital)	M/p (real balances)	Estimate[a] of η_p
0.58	0.13	–	–	–	–	0.06[e]	f
0.512 (0.06)	–	0.214 (0.09)	–	−0.21 (0.10)	–	0.208 (0.06)	−0.19 (−0.26)
0.583 (0.06)	–	–	–	−0.27 (0.10)	–	0.297 (0.04)	−0.27
h	–	0.23 (0.05)	0.36 (0.08)	–	–	0.024[e] (0.02)	f
i	–	0.26 (0.075)	0.26 (0.10)	–	–	0.072 (0.025)	−0.06 (−0.10)
j	–	0.21 (0.07)	0.25 (0.10)	–	–	0.063 (0.023)	−0.05 (−0.08)
0.375 (0.110)	–	0.489 (0.160)	–	–	–	0.219 (0.067)	−0.21 (−0.43)
0.708 (0.021)	–	–	–	–	–	0.368 (0.054)	−0.36
0.576 (0.113)	–	0.228 (0.150)	–	–	–	0.319 (0.070)	−0.27 (−0.41)
0.445 (0.113)	–	0.259 (0.120)	–	–	–	0.367 (0.108)	−0.30 (−0.50)
0.539 (0.077)	–	0.265 (0.102)	–	–	–	0.258 (0.044)	−0.21 (−0.35)
0.571[m] (0.051)	–	–	–	–	0.512 (0.118)	0.215 (0.032)	−0.215

[i] Disposable income decomposed as in preceding footnote, with respective coefficients of 0.55 ($\pm$0.06), 0.41 ($\pm$0.05), and 0.34 ($\pm$0.04).

[j] Disposable income decomposed as in footnote h, with respective coefficients of 0.62 ($\pm$0.06), 0.46 ($\pm$0.04), and 0.39 ($\pm$0.04).

[k] Excluding 1950 III and 1951 I.

[l] Excluding 1950 III and 1951 I. Differs from Zellner's estimates because of revisions in data.

[m] Data refer to net national income.

SOURCES:
Line 1. L. R. Klein, *Economic Fluctuations in the United States, 1921–1941* (New York, 1950), pp. 80–85, 142.
Lines 2–3. Carl Christ, "A Test of an Econometric Model for the United States, 1921–1947," in Universities-National Bureau Committee for Economic Research, *Conference on Business Cycles* (New York, 1951), pp. 59–60, 70, 74–75, 85, 90, 97–98.
Lines 4–5. L. R. Klein and A. S. Goldberger, *An Econometric Model of the United States, 1929–1952* (Amsterdam, 1955), pp. 51, 64–66, 90, 123, 130–31.
Line 6. Karl A. Fox, "Econometric Models of the United States," *Journal of Political Economy*, LXIV (1956), 135.
Lines 7–8. Arnold Zellner, "The Short-Run Consumption Function," *Econometrica*, XXV (1957), 560, equations (2) and (4).
Lines 9–11. Z. Griliches, G. S. Maddala, R. Lucas, and N. Wallace, "Notes on Estimated Aggregate Quarterly Consumption Functions," *Econometrica*, XXX (1962), 495.
Line 12. Michio Morishima and Mitsuo Saito, "A Dynamic Analysis of the American Economy, 1902–1952," *International Economic Review*, V (1964), 129. The estimated equation is linear in the logarithms.

latter formulation which is implied by our analysis. Correspondingly, the relevant consumption function is

$$(2) \qquad C = g\left(\frac{W}{p}, X\right) \equiv g\left(\frac{W_N}{p} + \frac{M}{p}, X\right),$$

where W is the money value of total nonhuman wealth, W_N is its nonmonetary component, M is its monetary component (net financial assets), and X represents human wealth and all other variables.[25] As a linear approximation we then have

$$(3) \qquad C = \gamma + \alpha\left(\frac{W_N}{p} + \frac{M}{p}\right) + \delta X.$$

Though we shall not make use of it in the following form, it should be noted that this equation can also be written as

$$(4) \qquad C = \gamma + \beta r\left(\frac{W_N}{p} + \frac{M}{p}\right) + \delta X,$$

where r is the average rate of return on capital, and β is the marginal propensity to consume out of permanent income from nonhuman wealth, defined as $Y_P = r\left(\frac{W_N}{p} + \frac{M}{p}\right)$. Thus permanent income in a monetary economy includes the imputed income from money balances.[26] Correspondingly, the value of Y_P—and hence the level of consumption—is affected by an equiproportionate change in prices.

---

[25] One could, of course, argue that disposable income in the equations described in Table A (the last equation excluded) is a proxy for nonmonetary wealth, so that these equations are after all of the desired form [see equation (4) below; see also p. 200 above]. It does, nevertheless, seem to me desirable in empirical work to use the wealth variable explicitly—to the extent that data are available. The reason for this proviso will become clear in a moment.

It should also be noted that some investigators indicated that they were using real balances as a proxy for total wealth or net worth (see e.g., Klein and Goldberger, *op. cit.*, p. 8; M. R. Fisher, *op. cit.*, p. 241; Zellner, *op. cit.*, p. 565).

[26] At first sight, this procedure would seem to create difficulties in connection with the budget restraint: for *imputed* income cannot be used to finance *actual* consumption expenditures. The answer, of course, is that this income is used to "finance" the corresponding imputed consumption of the services of money balances—which is *not* included in *C*. There are, however, certain difficulties here which have been mentioned on p. 112, footnote 44 above.

In brief, a proper specification of the permanent-income hypothesis must take account of the real-balance effect.

A comparison of (3) and (4) shows that $\alpha = \beta r$. Setting $r = 0.06$ and $\beta = 0.70$, Thomas Mayer has used this fact to estimate α as 0.042.[27] We need not, however, limit ourselves to such a priori approximations. For in recent years there has been increasing interest in empirical consumption functions of the form presented in equation (3)—though for reasons which have nothing to do with the real-balance effect, and which stem instead from a fundamental reconsideration of the theory of consumption. In any event, there are now several estimates of equations of this type that can be exploited for our purposes.

One of the first such estimates was made by William Hamburger in 1955.[28] The value of this interesting study is, however, impaired by the inadequacy of the data then available. The situation was radically improved as a result of the monumental work of Raymond Goldsmith and his colleagues,[29] which has made possible the more recent studies of Ando and Modigliani (on the period 1929–59, excluding 1941–46)[30] and Arena (on the period 1901–58).[31]

Both of these studies use as their wealth variable the net worth of the household sector as estimated by Goldsmith (see item W in Sources to Table B on p. 662); this variable thus includes net financial assets. The Ando-Modigliani function is expressed in terms of money variables and has the form

$$(5) \qquad (pC) = \alpha(W_N + M) + \beta(pY_L) + \delta(pZ),$$

[27] "The Empirical Significance of the Real Balance Effect," *Quarterly Journal of Economics*, LXXXIII (1959), 280–82. Actually, Mayer contends that the estimate of α depends on whether the change in p is expected to be permanent or temporary. I have, however, explained on pp. 143–44 above why I do not believe this distinction to be well-taken.

[28] "The Relation of Consumption to Wealth and the Wage Rate," *Econometrica*, XXIII (1955), 1–17.

[29] Raymond W. Goldsmith, *A Study of Saving in the United States*, 3 vols. (Princeton, 1955); Raymond W. Goldsmith, Robert E. Lipsey and Morris Mendelson, *Studies in the National Balance Sheet of the United States*, 2 vols. (Princeton, 1963).

[30] Albert Ando and Franco Modigliani, "The 'Life Cycle' Hypothesis of Saving," *American Economic Review*, LIII (1963), 55–84; LIV (1964), 111–13. The results cited here are the revised ones of the 1964 publication.

[31] John J. Arena, "The Wealth Effect and Consumption: A Statistical Inquiry," *Yale Economic Essays*, III (1963), 251–303; this is summarized in Arena's "Capital Gains and the 'Life Cycle' Hypothesis of Saving," *American Economic Review*, LIV (1964), 107–110.

where Z represents other variables, and pY_L money income from labor. By dividing through by p this is seen to be of the same form as (3), except for the absence of a constant term.[32] Arena provides estimates of an equation whose variables are expressed alternatively in money and real values. In both cases the equation is assumed to have a constant term—which in the case of the equation expressed in money values implies the existence of money illusion. Furthermore, Arena's income variable is total disposable income—which means that there is duplication between the property income included in this variable and the capitalized value of this income reflected in the wealth variable. It is, of course, this duplication which Ando and Modigliani's use of Y_L is designed to avoid.[33]

The investigators present results for several alternative equations.[34] The estimates of α are always positive (mostly in the range 0.04–0.08) and highly significant. This corresponds to an average value of η_p in the period 1947–58 which ranges from -0.05 to -0.10. A similar range obtains for the years 1934 and 1940. It is, however, noteworthy that the range for 1930 is -0.03 to -0.07, which is a reflection of the relatively smaller volume of net financial assets which existed in the economy in that critical year.[35]

These estimates of α can be interpreted as being in accord with the hypothesis presented in this book. It is, however, desirable to subject

[32] From the statistical viewpoint, of course, the two equations are not identical [even with the constant term deleted from (3)], and will lead to different estimates of the parameters. This follows from the fact that the respective random variables of these equations [which have been omitted from equations (3) and (6)] are not the same.

[33] A similar objection can be made to the Morishima-Saito equation described in line 12 of Table A above.

Another instance of duplication in Arena's estimates occurs in his attempt to test the influence of liquid assets on consumption. Arena shows that the coefficient of this variable is not significant when it appears in addition to the wealth variable in the consumption function ("The Wealth Effect and Consumption," *op. cit.*, p. 279). But he overlooks the fact that liquid assets are already included in his wealth variable, so that the proper interpretation of this result is that liquid assets do not influence consumption over and above their influence as a component of total wealth. Cf. the discussion which follows.

[34] The reference to Arena's results is restricted to those of his equations which are free of money illusion; see his "Wealth Effect and Consumption," *op. cit.*, Table 5, p. 302.

[35] These estimates are obtained by multiplying the values of α by the (average) ratio of M to pC in Table B on p. 662.

this hypothesis to more discriminating tests which would determine (a) if the explanatory power of an equation with monetary and nonmonetary wealth is significantly greater than that of an equation with nonmonetary wealth alone, and (b) if the influence of monetary wealth on consumption is significantly different from that of nonmonetary wealth. Unfortunately, the data necessary for these tests are available only for the postwar years 1947–58, and for the three prewar years 1930, 1934, and 1940 (see Table B). These data have nevertheless been used to provide least-squares estimates of the alternative equations

(6)
$$C = \gamma + \alpha_1 \frac{W_N}{p} + \beta Y_L$$

and

(7)
$$C = \gamma + \alpha_1 \frac{W_N}{p} + \alpha_2 \frac{M}{p} + \beta Y_L,$$

in order to see if the addition of monetary wealth as a variable in equation (7) causes a significant increase in R^2 as compared with equation (6), and if in equation (7) the estimate of α_1 is significantly different from that of α_2.[36]

The results of these estimates are summarized in Table C, where Part I refers to the postwar years alone and Part II to the same period with the addition of the three prewar years. The values of R^2 in all equations are very high. Nevertheless, there is in each part of the table a significant (at the 0.05 level) improvement in R^2 as we move from equation (6) to (7).[37, 38] On the other hand, no such uniform picture emerges of the difference between α_1 and α_2. For the observations inclusive of the three prewar years, the difference is significant at the 0.05 level; it is, however, not significant for the postwar years alone. For

----

[36] I am indebted to Nissan Liviatan for guidance and advice in all that is connected with the preparation and interpretation of these estimates. The calculations themselves were carried out by Miss Susanne Freund under his direction.

I am also grateful to Zvi Griliches for helpful discussions of several points.

[37] The test of significance of the increase in R^2 caused by adding a variable is equivalent to the test of significance of the coefficient of that variable; see D. A. S. Fraser, *Statistics: An Introduction* (New York, 1958), pp. 296–304. The conclusion of the text thus follows from the significance of α_2 in equations (7) of Table C.

[38] It should also be noted that, for the postwar years, α_1 in equation (6) is not significantly different from zero at the 0.05 level, but that it does become significant in equation (7).

TABLE B. Data and Sources
(Billions of current dollars)

	pC	pY_L	W	M	W_N	p
			beginning of year			
1930	71.85	58.17	489.51	63.36	426.15	71.4
1934	53.30	43.38	335.23	78.31	256.92	57.2
1940	70.90	62.09	411.86	96.12	315.74	59.9
1947	156.79	143.17	803.21	263.87	539.34	95.5
1948	169.93	157.41	890.42	268.04	622.38	102.8
1949	172.86	159.95	941.28	268.17	673.11	101.8
1950	182.92	174.61	953.34	269.46	683.88	102.8
1951	201.89	190.00	1064.12	265.56	798.56	111.0
1952	213.63	202.22	1151.28	274.93	876.35	113.5
1953	224.19	216.01	1196.92	284.19	912.73	114.4
1954	231.34	218.91	1225.48	293.92	931.56	114.8
1955	245.11	234.48	1318.64	302.00	1016.64	114.5
1956	261.70	250.56	1427.33	304.28	1123.05	116.2
1957	277.76	263.23	1514.73	315.46	1199.27	120.2
1958	289.50	269.10	1555.97	327.86	1228.11	123.5

SOURCES

pC — consumption excluding consumer durables, and including depreciation thereon: Albert Ando and E. Cary Brown, "Lags in Fiscal Policy," in Commission on Money and Credit, *Stabilization Policies* (Englewood Cliffs, N.J., 1963), p. 150, Appendix Table I-A1, item C^2.

pY — labor income after taxes on cash basis: *ibid.*, item Y^2.

W — net worth of the household sector: Raymond Goldsmith, Robert E. Lipsey, and Morris Mendelson, *Studies in the National Balance Sheet of the United States* (Princeton, 1963), Vol. 2; defined as the item 'equities' aggregated from Tables III-1 (nonfarm households), III-2 (nonfarm unincorporated business), and III-3 (agriculture), for 1947–58; and from Tables III-1d, III-2a and III-3b for 1930, 1934 and 1940. (In source, data are presented as of end of year.)

M — net financial assets of fixed money value: *ibid.*, calculated from the following items in the source:

II. *Intangible assets*
1. Currency and demand deposits
2. Other bank deposits and shares
3. Life insurance reserves, private
4. Pension and retirement funds, private
5. Pension and insurance funds, government
10. Other loan.
11. Mortgages, nonfarm

12. Mortgages, farm
13. Securities, U.S. Government
14. Securities, state and local
15. Securities, other bonds and notes
18. Equity in mutual financial organizations
20. Other intangible assets

less III. *Liabilities*
6. Consumer debt
7. Trade debt
8. Loans on securities

9. Bank loans, n.e.c.
10. Other loans
11. Mortgages

This is the same as intangible assets (excluding securities, preferred stock; securities, common stock; and equity in other business) *less* liabilities.

W_N — W *less* M.

p — annual average consumer price index (BLS) (1947–49 = 100): all years except 1958 from U.S. Bureau of the Census, *Historical Statistics of the United States, Colonial Times to 1957* (Washington 1960), p. 125, Series E-113. 1958 from *Federal Reserve Bulletin*, June 1964, p. 776, converted to the 1947–49 base.

Table C. Estimates of the Consumption Function

	1	W_N/p (α_1)	M/p (α_2)	W/p (α)	Y_L (β)	R^2	$s_{\alpha_1-\alpha_2}$
			Coefficients of: [a]				
I 1947–58							
(6)	28.3	0.057 (0.040)	–	–	0.665 (0.235)	0.989	–
(7)	−7.9	0.083 (0.031)	0.170 (0.058)	–	0.512 (0.181)	0.994	0.058
(8)	15.1	–	–	0.094 (0.032)	0.447 (0.188)	0.993	–
II 1930, 1934, 1940, 1947–58							
(6)	16.6	0.021 (0.009)	–	–	0.880 (0.034)	0.997	–
(7)	−4.4	0.084 (0.018)	0.160 (0.044)	–	0.501 (0.105)	0.999	0.027
(8)	10.5	–	–	0.041 (0.013)	0.769 (0.567)	0.998	–

[a] – means variable not in equation or not relevant.
The number in parentheses below each coefficient is the standard error.

these years, then, we are justified in specifying our consumption function as

$$(8) \qquad C = \gamma + \alpha\left(\frac{W_N}{p} + \frac{M}{p}\right) + \beta Y_L,$$

where the coefficients of W_N/p and M/p have been constrained to be equal.[39, 40] The corresponding estimate is presented in Table C. For the sake of completeness, however, the table also records the estimate based on the data including the prewar observations.

Due to the fewness of observations, these results can be considered only as illustrative. A more thorough analysis would have to give

[39] Except for the constant term, this equation is of the Ando-Modigliani type.
[40] Note that the test of significance of the null hypothesis $\alpha_1 - \alpha_2 = 0$ is also a test of the null hypothesis that there is no improvement in R^2 as we move from the constrained-regression equation (8) to (7). For equation (7) can be written as

$$C = \gamma + \alpha_1\left(\frac{W_N}{p} + \frac{M}{p}\right) + (\alpha_2 - \alpha_1)\frac{M}{p} + \beta Y_L,$$

which differs from (8) only by the additional variable M/p. Hence the proposition of footnote 37 can be applied.

attention to the relatively low estimates of β which characterize most of the equations in the table; to the fact that, in Part II of the table, α in equation (8) is lower than both α_1 and α_2 in equation (7), of which α is theoretically an average; and to the question of serial correlation and other problems of statistical estimation.[41] Such an analysis would also have to consider the possibility that the estimate of α_2 in equation (7) is biased upward because of the fact that consumers accumulate liquid assets in anticipation of making purchases of durable consumers' goods.[42]

There are other basic questions which have not been dealt with here. Thus it would be desirable to carry out a direct test of the hypothesis that consumers are free of money illusion: i.e., that they react in the same manner to (say) an increase in real financial assets brought about by a monetary increase and to one brought about by a price decline. Again, the question may be raised as to whether the proper measure of wealth is the net worth of consumers, or the total wealth of the private sector: for the ultimate holders of this wealth are households. This alternative measure also leads us to define the net financial assets of households not as in Table B, but as the net fixed-money-value debt of the government to the private sector. This definition is actually more in accord with the approach of this book.[43] It also confronts us explicitly with the problem discussed on p. 289 above of the proper discount factor to apply to government interest-bearing debt held by the private sector—a problem which tends to be overlooked when wealth is defined as the net worth of households.[44]

[41] In their study, Ando and Modigliani do suggest ways of dealing with the first and last problems (*op. cit.*, pp. 60–73).

[42] This is the possibility raised by Zellner; see pp. 656–57 above. Note that the fact that our consumption series excludes durables does not preclude this possibility; see footnote 19 above.

[43] Cf. p. 290 above. This definition is also closer to the definition of real balances presented in the revised version of my "Price Flexibility and Full Employment," *Readings in Monetary Theory*, Table 1, p. 275. It is also the one used by Meltzer in his "Demand for Money," *op. cit.*, pp. 224–25; cf. also Meltzer's discussion of various definitions of wealth, *ibid.*, pp. 228–31.

[44] Because it presents estimates of reduced-form equations only, the study by Friedman and Meiselman on "The Relative Stability of Monetary Velocity and the Investment Multiplier in the United States, 1847–1958" (*op. cit.*) has been excluded from the survey of consumption functions presented in this note. It should, however be noted that Friedman and Meiselman's interpretation of their findings in terms of the predominance of "monetary" (as distinct from "credit") effects (*ibid.* pp. 215–20) is in part an alternative statement of the hypothesis that there exists a real-balance effect in the commodity markets.

Note N. Notes to the Prefaces

1. FIRST EDITION

The critical articles referred to in the Preface are, in chronological order:

Herbert Stein, "Price Flexibility and Full Employment: Comment," *American Economic Review*, XXXIX (1949), 725–26.

This note corrected an error in my "Price Flexibility and Full Employment" in the same journal, XXXVIII (1948), 543–64. I commented upon it in *ibid.*, XXXIX (1949), 726–28.

W. Braddock Hickman, "The Determinacy of Absolute Prices in Classical Economic Theory," *Econometrica*, XVIII (1950), 9–20.

Wassily Leontief, "The Consistency of the Classical Theory of Money and Prices," *Econometrica*, XVIII (1950), 21–24.

Cecil G. Phipps, "A Note on Patinkin's 'Relative Prices,'" *Econometrica*, XVIII (1950), 25–26.

These three articles were criticisms of my "Relative Prices, Say's Law, and the Demand for Money," *Econometrica*, XVI (1948), 135–54, and "The Indeterminacy of Absolute Prices in Classical Economic Theory," *ibid.*, XVII (1949), 1–27. They were replied to in my "Invalidity of Classical Monetary Theory," *ibid.*, XIX (1951), 134–51. They were also discussed in Karl Brunner, "Inconsistency and Indeterminacy in Classical Economics," on pp. 152–73 of the same volume, and in

Yukichi Kurimura, "On the Dichotomy in the Theory of Price," *Metroeconomica*, III (1951), 117–34.

F. H. Hahn, "The General Equilibrium Theory of Money—A Comment," *Review of Economic Studies*, XIX (1951–52), 179–85.
This was a well-taken criticism of my "Reconsideration of the General Equilibrium Theory of Money," *Review of Economic Studies*, XVIII (1950–51), 42–61. It was discussed—and the argument changed so as to deal with it—in my "Further Considerations of the General Equilibrium Theory of Money," *ibid.*, XIX (1951–52), 186–95.

Gary S. Becker and William J. Baumol, "The Classical Monetary Theory: The Outcome of the Discussion," *Economica*, XIX (1952), 355–76.
Replied to in my "Dichotomies of the Pricing Process in Economic Theory," *Economica*, XXI (1954), 113–28. This reply also provides a systematic survey of the entire preceding debate. I should also add that at the time of writing it I had not yet seen the significance of the absence of stability analysis in neoclassical monetary theory, nor had I completed my study of Walras and his immediate successors. This is the reason the refutation of Becker and Baumol's position implicit in Chapter VIII:1–4 (and particularly on pp. 186–88) is so much more categorical than my original reply.[1]

*   *   *   *   *

I might also take advantage of this note to refer briefly to F. J. de Jong's "Supply Functions in Keynesian Economics," *Economic Journal*, LXIV (1954), 3–24. This is partly given over to a criticism of my "Involuntary Unemployment and the Keynesian Supply Function" in the same journal, LIX (1949), 360–83. However, de Jong's criticisms on p. 7 of his article are irrelevant to the general argument presented on pp. 368–70, 378–81 of my article. (It is, of course, this general argument which is the basis of that in Chapters XIII–XIV above.) Similarly, de

---

[1] The Becker-Baumol article has recently been reprinted with a "Postscript" which noticeably reduces the degree of disagreement between us [see *Essays in Economic Thought: Aristotle to Marshall*, ed. J. J. Spengler and W. R. Allen (Chicago, 1960), pp. 766–67]. There nevertheless remain significant differences of opinion—as is evident from a comparison of the summary of the issues provided by this postscript with that provided in Chapter VIII:4 above.

Jong's contention that Keynes uses an aggregate supply function identical in conception with the one presented in my 1949 article cannot be maintained (cf. de Jong, *op. cit.*, Propositions II, XI, XII, and, especially, XIV). In particular, Keynes' use of an "aggregate supply function" on pp. 26–27 of the *General Theory* (on which de Jong primarily relies) cannot be interpreted in this way. This is immediately evident from Keynes' statement that under Say's Identity his (Keynes') "aggregate supply function" coincides with his "aggregate demand function"; whereas, as is shown by Figure 8 of my original article (or in Figure XIV-6 above), this is definitely not true for our function.

As a result of other considerations, however, I have in this book modified my original graphical representation of the aggregate supply curve. In particular, it is no longer represented as being dependent on Y (a point about which I always felt uncomfortable—"Involuntary Unemployment ... ," *op. cit.*, p. 366); nor is it depicted as being a horizontal line. Both of these changes are really in accordance with the general model presented in the original article (*ibid.*, pp. 378–81).

2. SECOND EDITION

As already indicated in the Preface, by far the most important of the many revisions made in this book is that of Chapters V–VII. In particular, Sections 1, 2, 3, and 8 of Chapter V provide a thorough-going revision of the utility theory of money presented in Chapters V–VII of the original edition. In carrying out this revision I have deleted the discussion of the one-week-horizon case originally presented in Chapter V; for as was already implied in the first edition of this book (pp. 17 and 47; see the corresponding passages on pp. 14 and 61, above), the assumption of this case—that an individual plans to carry over cash balances to a period for which he makes no other plans—is of questionable economic meaning (see, however, p. 148, footnote 6 above). The most important change here has, however, been the broadening of the concept of "marginal rate of substitution" as it relates to money holdings—or, for that matter, any other asset. This broadening has enabled a simple economic interpretation of the mathematics that lie behind the discussion of Chapter VI:2–3 of the first edition—and a consequent replacing of the basically incorrect descriptions of the optimum position which appear there. The remaining part of Chapter V of the present edition—consisting of Sections 4-7—is new. It presents the argument graphically in terms of a Fisherine analysis generalized to an individual making an optimum two-period plan for money holdings as well as consumption.

Chapter VI:1-2 then makes the necessary modifications (some of which are far-reaching) in this Fisherine framework so as to provide a reformulation and generalization of the Markowitz-Tobin analysis of the optimum portfolio under conditions of uncertainty. This analysis is also interpreted as supplying an alternative rationale of the assumption that money has utility: an assumption whose formulation in the first edition—reproduced essentially unchanged in Chapter V above (pp. 79-80) —has sometimes been considered unduly vague. Chapter VII, on the other hand, shows that this assumption (which, in the original edition, was the only one considered as a possible basis for a microeconomic theory of money) is actually not a methodologically necessary one, and that even if money does not provide the utility of a consumer's good, it can nevertheless be demanded for its "indirect utility" as a producer's good in accordance with the inventory approach of Baumol and Tobin. This approach, too, is reformulated and embedded within a Fisherine framework. The same is true of the analysis in Chapter VI:3-4 of the effect of anticipated changes in the price level on the individual's optimum pattern of consumption and money holding.

The other major instances of new or rewritten material in the text —involving for the most part whole sections within chapters—can be briefly described as follows: correction and simplification of the analysis of the demand curve for money, as well as its reinterpretation as an Engel curve (Chapter II:5); graphical representation of the stability and comparative-statics properties of a simple money economy (pp. 41-42, 44); reformulation and reinterpretation of the Archibald-Lipsey long-run-equilibrium analysis (Chapter III:7); further attenuation of the criticism of the neoclassical rectangular-hyperbola demand curve for money (pp 170-71); elaboration (if not over-elaboration) of the inconsistency of the traditional dichotomy [pp. 176 (line 28)-179 (line 9)]; recapitulation of the over-all critique of neoclassical monetary theory (Chapter VIII:4); modification of the discussion of the demand curve for money (pp. 225-26); provision of a truly general-equilibrium analysis of the static and dynamic functioning of a full-employment economy, replacing and in part correcting the original analysis of the commodity and money (or bond) markets alone (Chapter XI: 2–3, 5); a complete rewriting and further expansion of the original quite inadequate analysis of open-market operations, functioning of the banking system, and the influence of expectations, taking as its point of departure the work of Gurley and Shaw and others[2] (Chapter XII: 4–7); provision of a truly general-equilibrium analysis of money under conditions of unemployment (pp. 333–34); correction and expansion of the analysis of the role of the real-balance effect in a secular growth process (Chapter XIV: 5).

Three further changes of a more general nature should be mentioned. The first one—which appears throughout this book—is the emphasis on the interpretation of the real-balance effect as a manifestation of the wealth effect. Though this was the way in which this effect was conceived in the first edition (see, *e.g.*, pp. 27, 126, and 205), this fact was not systematically and consistently integrated into the analysis. One misleading aspect of this failure has already been noted on p. 20, footnote 16. Another one is that the demand functions of Chapter XII: 4 and of the Mathematical Appendixes were originally written as dependent upon the individual components of wealth, and not on their sum—though the latter relationship was adverted to on p. 314 of the first edition (see, however, above, p. 107, footnote 36, and p. 460, footnote 7).

The second such change—which also manifests itself at various points in the book—has to do with Gurley and Shaw's fruitful distinction between outside and inside money. The implications of this distinction for the dichotomy discussion are explained on p. 180 (footnote 43), pp. 297–98, *et passim*. On the other hand—for reasons that should be clear from the discussion on pp. 299–301—I now consider this distinction to be less far-reaching in its consequences for the neutrality-of-money issue than I once did (see also pp. 297 and 307–308).

The last change relates to the criticism of Keynesian interest theory. It is now clear to me (and should really have always been clear) that a shift in liquidity preference in this theory connotes a shift only between money and bonds, and not commodities—a fact now made explicit in Chapter X:4. For the same reason it is now clear to me that the original summary of the criticism of Keynesian interest theory in Chapter XV:2

---

[2] I regret that I have been unable to take into consideration the interesting analysis of these and other issues in George Horwich, *Money, Capital and Prices*, (Homewood, Ill., 1964)—a work which appeared when the present book was already in proof.

is somewhat unfair, and this has therefore been modified. On the other hand, the force of this modified criticism is greater as a result of the demonstration in the new Chapter VI: 1–2 (especially pp. 125–26) that the argument of this book holds also for the speculative motive.

It is also worth noting one discussion which has been carried over virtually intact from the first edition: namely, the discussion of involuntary unemployment in Chapter XIII. This intactness reflects, not my satisfaction with this discussion, but rather my inability to revise it so as to deal with the logical difficulty described on p. 323, footnote 9. This difficulty has been the concern of some recent writers (see the articles by Cross and Williamson and by Gogerty and Winston listed in the Bibliography), but I do not feel that the solutions they propose are satisfactory. Thus, for example, Cross and Williamson present a *tâtonnement* under conditions of unemployment which differs from the one described in Chapter XIII: 2–3 by virtue of their assumption that the excess inventories generated by the initial decline in demand cause the price level to fall and hence the real wage rate to rise, so that firms decrease the amount of labor they demand in accordance with their demand curve. This, however, implies that the existence of involuntary unemployment depends upon the continued existence of excess inventories—an implication which, it seems to me, runs counter to the facts.

The foregoing changes in the text have been accompanied by corresponding changes in the Mathematical Appendix, leading in some cases to the complete rewriting or addition of material. This is true for the rigorous analysis of the real-balance effect in terms of the Slutzky wealth effect (Appendix 2: b); the description of the short-run demand functions (Appendix 2: d) and of their relation to the long-run ones (Appendix 3: e); and the utility analysis of the demand for money (Appendix 6). There has also been added an entirely new section devoted to a graphical analysis of the composite-good theorem, which is now used at so many points in the text to simplify the argument (Appendix 2: c). Similarly, there has been added an explication of the proper relationship between stocks and flows (Appendix 11).

On the other hand, aside from the attenuation of the criticism of the neoclassical demand curve for money, the further discussion of the invalid dichotomy, and the reconsideration of the critique of Keynesian interest theory—the changes in the text have had little impact on the Supplementary Notes and Studies in the Literature. Nor have I attempted to take account of the work in doctrinal history which has appeared since the first edition of this book (though I have—on p. 572—commented briefly on one aspect of Kuenne's recent interpretation of Walras). Correspondingly, with a few exceptions (primarily, those referred to implicitly in the first sentence of this paragraph—*viz.*, Notes G:3, I:3, and, to a much lesser extent, K:2), these Notes have been left in their original form. Note M is, however, new—though it did have some modest beginnings in the references which appeared on p. 22, footnote 12 of the first edition. As indicated in the Preface, this Note reflects the generally increased concern of the present edition with the empirical aspects of the analysis.

Bibliography
and
Indexes

Bibliography of Works Cited[1]

Ackley, G., "The Wealth-Saving Relationship," *Journal of Political Economy*, LIX (1951), 154–61.

——, *Macroeconomic Theory*, New York, 1961.

Allen, R. G. D., *Mathematical Analysis for Economists*, London, 1938.

Anderson, B. M., *The Value of Money*, New York, 1917.

Ando, A., and Brown, E. Cary, "Lags in Fiscal Policy," in Commission on Money and Credit, *Stabilization Policies*, Englewood Cliffs, N.J., 1963, pp. 97–164.

——, and Modigliani, F., "The 'Life Cycle' Hypothesis of Saving: Aggregate Implications and Tests," *American Economic Review*, LIII (1963), 55–84; LIV (1964), 111–13.

Angell, J. W., *The Theory of International Prices*, Cambridge, Mass., 1926.

Antonelli, E., *Principes d'économie pure*, Paris, 1914.

Archibald, G. C., and Lipsey, R. G., "Monetary and Value Theory: A Critique of Lange and Patinkin," *Review of Economic Studies*, XXVI (1958), 1–22.

—— and ——, "Monetary and Value Theory: Further Comment," *Review of Economic Studies*, XXVIII (1960), 50–56.

Arena, J. J., "The Wealth Effect and Consumption: A Statistical Inquiry," *Yale Economic Essays*, III (1963), 251–303.

—— "Capital Gains and the 'Life Cycle' Hypothesis of Saving," *American Economic Review*, LIV (1964), 107–10.

---

[1] Excludes certain works of a purely mathematical nature cited only in the Mathematical Appendix.

Arrow, K. J., "Homogeneous Systems in Mathematical Economics: A Comment," *Econometrica*, XVIII (1950), 60–62.

—— and Hurwicz, L., "On the Stability of the Competitive Equilibrium I," *Econometrica*, XXVI (1958), 522–52.

——, Block, H. D., and Hurwicz, L., "On the Stability of the Competitive Equilibrium II," *Econometrica*, XXVII (1959), 82–109.

——, and Hurwicz, L., "Competitive Stability under Weak Gross Substitutability: Nonlinear Price Adjustment and Adaptive Expectations," *International Economic Review*, III (1962), 233–55.

——, Karlin, S., and Scarf, H., *Studies in the Mathematical Theory of Inventory and Production*, Stanford, 1958.

——, and Nerlove, M., "A Note on Expectations and Stability," *Econometrica*, XXVI (1958), 297–305.

Aupetit, A., *Essai sur la théorie générale de la monnaie*, Paris, 1901.

Auspitz, R., and Lieben, R., *Recherches sur la théorie du prix*, trans. L. Suret, Paris, 1914.

Bagehot, W., *Lombard Street* (1873), new ed., London, 1915.

Bailey, Martin J., *National Income and the Price Level*, New York, 1962.

Ball, R. J., and Bodkin, R., "The Real Balance Effect and Orthodox Demand Theory: A Critique of Archibald and Lipsey," *Review of Economic Studies*, XXVIII (1960), 44–49.

——, and Drake, P. S., "The Relationship Between Aggregate Consumption and Wealth," *International Economic Review*, V (1964), 63–81.

Barbour, D., *The Standard of Value*, London, 1912.

Barone, E., "The Ministry of Production in the Collectivist State," in *Collectivist Economic Planning*, ed. F. A. Hayek, London, 1935, pp. 245–90.

Baumol, W. J., "The Transactions Demand for Cash: An Inventory Theoretic Approach," *Quarterly Journal of Economics*, LXVI (1952), 545–56.

——, *Economic Dynamics*, 2nd ed., New York, 1959.

——, "Monetary and Value Theory: Comments," *Review of Economic Studies*, XXVIII (1960), 29–31.

——, "Stocks, Flows, and Monetary Theory," *Quarterly Journal of Economics*, LXXVI (1962), 46–56.

Bear, D. V. T., "The Relationship of Saving to the Rate of Interest, Real Income, and Expected Future Prices," *Review of Economics and Statistics*, XLIII (1961), 27–35.

Becker, G. S., and Baumol, W. J., "The Classical Monetary Theory: The Outcome of the Discussion," *Economica*, XIX (1952), 355–76.

—— and ——, Postscript to "The Classical Monetary Theory: The Outcome of the Discussion," in *Essays in Economic Thought: Aristotle*

to *Marshall*, ed. J. J. Spengler and W. R. Allen, Chicago, 1960, pp. 766–67.

Bernstein, E. M., "Latent Inflation: Problems and Policies," *International Monetary Fund: Staff Papers*, I (1950), 1–16.

Bieri, H. G., "Der Streit um die 'klassische Dichotomie,'" *Schweizerische Zeitschrift für Volkswirtschaft und Statistik*, II (1963), 172–81.

Boulding, K. E., *Economic Analysis*, rev. ed., New York, 1948.

———, "Welfare Economics," in *Survey of Contemporary Economics: Vol. II*, ed. B. F. Haley, Homewood, Ill., 1952, pp. 1–38.

Bowley, A. L., *The Mathematical Groundwork of Economics*, Oxford, 1924.

Bronfenbrenner, M., and Mayer, T., "Liquidity Functions in the American Economy," *Econometrica*, XXVIII (1960), 810–34.

——— and ———, "Rejoinder to Professor Eisner," *Econometrica*, XXXI (1963), 539–44.

Brown, A. J., "Interest, Prices and the Demand Schedule for Idle Money," *Oxford Economic Papers*, II (1939), 46–69.

———, *The Great Inflation: 1939–1951*, London, 1955.

Brown, E. H. P., *The Framework of the Pricing System*, London, 1936.

Brunner, K., "Inconsistency and Indeterminacy in Classical Economics," *Econometrica*, XIX (1951), 152–73.

———, "A Schema for the Supply Theory of Money," *International Economic Review*, II (1961), 79–109.

Bushaw, D. W., and Clower, R. W., *Introduction to Mathematical Economics*, Homewood, Ill., 1957.

Cagan, P., "The Monetary Dynamics of Hyperinflation," in *Studies in the Quantity Theory of Money*, ed. M. Friedman, Chicago, 1956, pp. 25–117.

———, "The Demand for Currency Relative to the Total Money Supply," *Journal of Political Economy*, LXVI (1958), 303–28.

Cannan, E., "The Application of the Theoretical Apparatus of Supply and Demand to Units of Currency," *Economic Journal*, XXXI (1921), as reprinted in *Readings in Monetary Theory*, ed. F. A. Lutz and L. W. Mints, Philadelphia, 1951, pp. 3–12.

———, *Money: Its Connexion with Rising and Falling Prices*, 4th ed., revised, London, 1923.

Cantillon, R., *Essay on the Nature of Trade*, (1755), trans. and ed. H. Higgs, London, 1931.

Cassel, G., *The Nature and Necessity of Interest*, London, 1903.

———, *Fundamental Thoughts in Economics*, London, 1925.

———, "The Rate of Interest, the Bank Rate, and the Stabilization of Prices," *Quarterly Journal of Economics*, XLII (1927–28), as reprinted in *Readings*

in Monetary Theory, ed. F. A. Lutz and L. W. Mints, Philadelphia, 1951, pp. 319–33.

———, *The Theory of Social Economy*, new rev. ed., trans. S. L. Barron, New York, 1932. (Trans. J. McCabe, New York, 1924.)

———, *On Quantitative Thinking in Economics*, Oxford, 1935.

———, "Keynes' 'General Theory'" *International Labour Review*, XXXVI (1937), 437–45.

Chandler, L. V., *Economics of Money and Banking*, rev. ed., New York, 1953.

Chapman, S., *Outlines of Political Economy*, 2nd ed., London, 1917.

Christ, C., "A Test of an Econometric Model for the United States, 1921–1947," in Universities-National Bureau Committee for Economic Research, *Conference on Business Cycles*, New York, 1951, pp. 35–107.

———, "Patinkin on Money, Interest, and Prices," *Journal of Political Economy*, LXV (1957), 347–54.

Cipolla, C. M., *Money, Prices, and Civilization in the Mediterranean World: Fifth to Seventeenth Century*, Princeton, 1956.

Clower, R. W., "Stock and Flow Quantities: A Common Fallacy," *Economica*, XXVI (1959), 251–52.

———, and Burstein, M. L., "On the Invariance of Demand for Cash and Other Assets," *Review of Economic Studies*, XXVIII (1960), 32–36.

Cohen, M., "Liquid Assets and the Consumption Function," *Review of Economics and Statistics*, XXXVI (1954), 202–11.

Cohen, M. R., and Nagel, E., *An Introduction to Logic and the Scientific Method*, New York, 1934.

Collery, A., "Note on the Saving-Wealth Relation and the Rate of Interest," *Journal of Political Economy*, LXVIII (1960), 509–10.

Cournot, A., *The Mathematical Principles of the Theory of Wealth* (1838), trans. N. T. Bacon, New York, 1929.

Crockett, J., "Income and Asset Effects on Consumption: Aggregate and Cross Section," in Conference on Research in Income and Wealth, *Models of Income Determination, Studies in Income and Wealth*, Vol. 28, Princeton, 1964, pp. 97–132.

Cross, J. G., and Williamson, J., "Patinkin on Unemployment Disequilibrium," *Journal of Political Economy*, LXX (1962), 76–81.

Davenport, H. J., *The Economics of Enterprise*, New York, 1913.

Demaria, G., "Pareto," as reprinted in *The Development of Economic Thought*, ed. H. W. Spiegel, New York, 1952, pp. 629–51.

Dickson, H., "Remarks on B. Hansen's Essay on Cassel and Patinkin" (in Swedish), *Ekonomisk Tidskrift*, LIV (1952), 152–59.

Divisia, F., *Economique rationnelle*, Paris, 1927.

Bibliography of Works Cited

Edgeworth, F. Y., *Mathematical Psychics* (1881), reprinted New York, 1953.

——, review of L. Walras' *Elements d'économie politique pure*, 2nd ed., in *Nature*, XL (1889), 434–36.

——, *Papers Relating to Political Economy*, 3 vols., London, 1925.

Eisner, R., "Another Look at Liquidity Preference," *Econometrica*, XXXI (1963), 531–38, 550.

——, and Strotz, R. H., "Determinants of Business Investment," in Commission on Money and Credit, *Impacts of Monetary Policy*, Englewood Cliffs, N.J., 1963, pp. 60–338.

Ellis, H. S., *German Monetary Theory: 1905–1933*, Cambridge, Mass., 1934.

Encarnación, J., "Consistency Between Say's Identity and the Cambridge Equation," *Economic Journal*, LXVIII (1958), 827–30.

Enthoven, A. C., "Monetary Disequilibrium and the Dynamics of Inflation," *Economic Journal*, LXVI (1956), 256–70.

Evans, G. C., *Mathematical Introduction to Economics*, New York, 1930.

Fellner, W., *Trends and Cycles in Economic Activity*, New York, 1956.

Ferber, R., "Research on Household Behavior," *American Economic Review*, LII (1962), 19–63.

Finch, D., "Purchasing Power Guarantees for Deferred Payment," *International Monetary Fund: Staff Papers*, V (1956), 1–22.

Fisher, I., *Mathematical Investigations in the Theory of Value and Prices* (1892), reprinted Yale University Press, 1925.

——, *The Rate of Interest*, New York, 1907.

——, *The Purchasing Power of Money*, New York, 1911; new and rev. ed., 1913.

——, *Elementary Principles of Economics*, New York, 1912.

——, *The Money Illusion*, New York, 1928.

——, *The Theory of Interest*, New York, 1930.

Fisher, M. R., "Exploration in Savings Behavior," *Bulletin of the Oxford University Institute of Statistics*, XVIII (1956), 201–78.

Fossati, Eraldo, "A Note About the Utility of Money," *Metroeconomica*, II (1950), 112–20.

——, *The Theory of General Static Equilibrium*, Oxford, 1957.

Fox, K. A., "Econometric Models of the United States," *Journal of Political Economy*, LXIV (1956), 128–42.

Friedman, M., "Discussion of the Inflationary Gap," *American Economic Review*, XXXII (1942), 314–20; reprinted in a revised form in *Essays in Positive Economics*, Chicago, 1953, pp. 251–62.

——, "The Marshallian Demand Curve," *Journal of Political Economy*, LVII (1949), as reprinted in *Essays in Positive Economics*, Chicago, 1953, pp. 47–99.

———, "The Quantity Theory of Money—A Restatement," in *Studies in the Quantity Theory of Money*, ed. M. Friedman, Chicago, 1956, pp. 3–21.

———, *A Theory of the Consumption Function*, Princeton, 1957.

———, "Savings and the Balance Sheet," *Bulletin of the Oxford University Institute of Statistics*, XIX (1957), 125–36.

———, and Meiselman, D., "The Relative Stability of Monetary Velocity and the Investment Multiplier in the United States, 1847–1958," in Commission on Money and Credit, *Stabilization Policies*, Englewood Cliffs, N.J., 1963, pp. 165–268.

———, and Savage, L. J., "The Utility Analysis of Choices Involving Risk," *Journal of Political Economy*, LVI (1948), as reprinted in *Readings in Price Theory*, ed. G. J. Stigler and K. E. Boulding, Chicago, 1952, pp. 57–96.

Gallaway, L. E., and Smith, P. E., "Real Balances and the Permanent Income Hypothesis," *Quarterly Journal of Economics*, LXXV (1961), 302–13.

Giffen, R., *Essays in Finance*, second series, New York, 1886.

Gilbert, J. C., "The Demand for Money: The Development of an Economic Concept," *Journal of Political Economy*, LXI (1953), 144–59.

Gogerty, D. C., and Winston, G. C., "Patinkin, Perfect Competition, and Unemployment Disequilibria," *Review of Economic Studies*, XXXI (1964), 121–26.

Goldberger, A. S., *Impact Multipliers and Dynamic Properties of the Klein-Goldberger Model*, Amsterdam, 1959.

Goldsmith, R. W., *et al.*, *A Study of Saving in the United States*, 3 vols., Princeton, 1955, 1956.

———, Lipsey, R. E., and Mendelson, M., *Studies in the National Balance Sheet of the United States*, 2 vols., Princeton, 1963.

Goodwin, R. M., "Iteration, Automatic Computers, and Economic Dynamics," *Metroeconomica*, III (1951), 1–7.

———, "Static and Dynamic Linear General Equilibrium Models," *Input-Output Relations*, ed. The Netherlands Economic Institute, Leiden, 1953, pp. 54–87.

Graham, F. D., *Exchange, Prices, and Production in Hyper-Inflation: Germany 1920–23*, Princeton, 1930.

Griliches, Z., Maddala, G. S., Lucas, R., and Wallace, N., "Notes on Estimated Aggregate Quarterly Consumption Functions," *Econometrica*, XXX (1962), 491–500.

Gurley, J. G., "Excess Liquidity and European Monetary Reforms, 1944–1952," *American Economic Review*, XLIII (1953), 76–100.

———, and Shaw, E. S., *Money in a Theory of Finance*, Washington, D.C., 1960.

Bibliography of Works Cited

Haavelmo, Trygve, "The Probability Approach in Econometrics," *Econometrica*, XII, Supplement (1944).

Haberler, G., *Prosperity and Depression*, 3rd ed., Geneva, 1941.

———, "The Pigou Effect Once More," *Journal of Political Economy*, LX (1952), 240–46.

Hahn, F. H., "The General Equilibrium Theory of Money—A Comment," *Review of Economic Studies*, XIX (1951–52), 179–85.

———, "The Patinkin Controversy," *Review of Economic Studies*, XXVIII (1960), 37–43.

Haley, B. F., "Value and Distribution," in *Survey of Contemporary Economics*, ed. H. S. Ellis, Philadelphia, 1948, pp. 1–48.

Hamburger, W., "The Relation of Consumption to Wealth and the Wage Rate," *Econometrica*, XXIII (1955), 1–17.

Hansen, A. H., "The Pigouvian Effect," *Journal of Political Economy*, LIX (1951), 535–36.

———, *A Guide to Keynes*, New York, 1953.

Hansen, B., *A Study in the Theory of Inflation*, London, 1951.

———, "The Role of Money in the Classical Economic Interdependence System—Patinkin vs. Cassel" (in Danish), *Ekonomisk Tidskrift*, LIV (1952), 100–120.

Harberger, A. C., "The Dynamics of Inflation in Chile," in C. Christ, *et al.*, *Measurement in Economics: Studies in Mathematical Economics and Econometrics in Memory of Yehuda Grunfeld*, Stanford, 1963, pp. 219–50.

Hart, A. G., *Money, Debt, and Economic Activity*, 2nd ed., New York, 1953.

Hawtrey, R. G., "The Trade Cycle," *De Economist* (1926), as reprinted in *Readings in Business Cycle Theory*, ed. G. Haberler, Philadelphia, 1944, pp. 330–49.

———, *Currency and Credit*, 3rd ed., London, 1927.

Hayek, F. A., "A Note on the Development of the Doctrine of 'Forced Saving,'" *Quarterly Journal of Economics*, XLVII (1932–33), 123–33.

———, *Prices and Production*, 2nd ed., London, 1935.

Hegeland, H., *The Quantity Theory of Money*, Göteberg, 1951.

Helfferich, K., *Money*, trans. L. Infield, London, 1927.

Henderson, H. D., *Supply and Demand*, rev. ed., London, 1932.

Hickman, W. B., "The Determinacy of Absolute Prices in Classical Economic Theory," *Econometrica*, XVIII (1950), 9–20.

Hicks, J. R., "Gleichgewicht und Konjunctur," *Zeitschrift für Nationalökonomie*, IV (1933), 441–55.

———, "Léon Walras," *Econometrica*, II (1934), 338–48.

———, "A Suggestion for Simplifying the Theory of Money," *Economica*,

II (1935), as reprinted in *Readings in Monetary Theory*, ed. F. A. Lutz and L. W. Mints, Philadelphia, 1951, pp. 13–32.

————, "Mr. Keynes and the 'Classics,'" *Econometrica*, V (1937), as reprinted in *Readings in the Theory of Income Distribution*, ed. W. Fellner and B. F. Haley, Philadelphia, 1946, pp. 461–76.

————, *Value and Capital*, Oxford, 1939; 2nd ed., 1946.

————, *A Contribution to the Theory of the Trade Cycle*, Oxford, 1950.

————, "A Rehabilitation of 'Classical' Economics?," *Economic Journal*, LXVII (1957), 278–289.

Hirshleifer, J., "On the Theory of Optimal Investment Decision," *Journal of Political Economy*, LXVI (1958), 329–52.

Hume, D., *Philosophical Works*, 4 vols., Boston, 1854.

Jaffé, W., "Léon Walras' Theory of Capital Accumulation," *Studies in Mathematical Economics and Econometrics*, ed. O. Lange, *et al.*, Chicago, 1942, pp. 37–48.

————, "Walrasiana: The *Elements* and its Critics," *Econometrica*, XIX (1951), 327–28.

James, E., *Problèmes monétaires d'aujourd'hui*, Paris, 1963.

Jevons, W. S., *Investigations in Currency and Finance*, London, 1884.

Johansen, L., "The Role of the Banking System in a Macro-Economic Model," *Statsökonomisk Tidskrift* (1956), as translated in *International Economic Papers*, No. 8 (1958), 91–110.

Johnson, H. G., "The General Theory after Twenty-Five Years," *American Economic Review: Papers and Proceedings*, LI (1961), 1–17.

————, "Monetary Theory and Policy," *American Economic Review*, LII (1962), 335–84.

Kahn, R. F., "Some Notes on Liquidity Preference," *The Manchester School of Economics and Social Studies*, XXII (1954), 229–57.

Kaldor, N., "A Classificatory Note on the Determinateness of Equilibrium," *Review of Economic Studies*, I (1933–34), 122–36.

Kalecki, M., "Professor Pigou on the 'Classical Stationary State'—A Comment," *Economic Journal*, LIV (1944), 131–32.

Kennedy, C. M., "Monetary Policy," *The British Economy: 1945–1950*, ed. G. D. N. Worswick and P. H. Ady, Oxford, 1952, pp. 188–207.

Keynes, J. M., Review of I. Fisher's, *The Purchasing Power of Money* in *Economic Journal*, XXI (1911), 393–98.

————, *A Tract on Monetary Reform*, London, 1923.

————, "Alfred Marshall, 1842–1924," *Memorials of Alfred Marshall*, ed. A. C. Pigou, London, 1925, pp. 1–65.

————, *A Treatise on Money*, 2 vols., London, 1930.

————, *The General Theory of Employment, Interest and Money*, New York, 1936.

————, "The General Theory of Employment," *Quarterly Journal of Economics*, LI (1936–37), 209–23.

————, "The Theory of the Rate of Interest," in *Lessons of Monetary Experience: Essays in Honor of Irving Fisher* (1937), as reprinted in *Readings in the Theory of Income Distribution*, ed. W. Fellner and B. F. Haley, Philadelphia, 1946, pp. 418–24.

————, "Alternative Theories of the Rate of Interest," *Economic Journal*, XLVII (1937), 241–52.

Kinley, D., *Money*, New York, 1904.

Klein, L. R., *The Keynesian Revolution*, New York, 1947.

————, *Economic Fluctuations in the United States, 1921–1941*, New York, 1950.

————, "Assets, Debts, and Economic Behavior," in Conference on Research in Income and Wealth, *Studies in Income and Wealth*, Vol. 14, New York, 1951, pp. 195–227.

————, *Econometrics*, Evanston, Ill., 1953.

————, "Statistical Estimation of Economic Relations from Survey Data," in *Contributions of Survey Methods to Economics*, ed. L. R. Klein, New York, 1954, pp. 189–240.

————, "Stocks and Flows in the Theory of Interest," in *The Theory of Interest Rates*, ed. F. H. Hahn and F. Brechling, London, 1965.

————, *et al.*, "Stock and Flow Analysis in Economics," *Econometrica*, XVIII (1950), 236–52.

————, and Goldberger, A. S., *An Econometric Model of the United States, 1929–1952*, Amsterdam, 1955.

Knight, F. H., *The Ethics of Competition*, New York, 1935.

Kuenne, R. E., "Walras, Leontief, and the Interdependence of Economic Activities," *Quarterly Journal of Economics*, LXVIII (1954), 323–54.

————, *The Theory of General Economic Equilibrium*, Princeton, 1963.

Kuh, E., and Meyer, J. R., "Investment, Liquidity, and Monetary Policy," in Commission on Money and Credit, *Impacts of Monetary Policy*, Englewood Cliffs, N. J., 1963, pp. 339–474.

Kurimura, Y., "On the Dichotomy in the Theory of Price," *Metroeconomica*, III (1951), 117–34.

Kuznets, S., *National Income and Its Composition, 1919–1938*, New York, 1941.

————, "Long-Term Changes in the National Income of the United States of America since 1870," *Income and Wealth of the United States: Trends and Structure*, ed. S. Kuznets, International Association for Research in

Income and Wealth, Income and Wealth Series II, Cambridge, 1952, pp. 29–241.

———, *Economic Change*, New York, 1953.

Lange, O., *On the Economic Theory of Socialism*, Minneapolis, 1938.

———, "Rate of Interest and the Optimum Propensity to Consume," *Economica*, V (1938), as reprinted in *Readings in Business Cycle Theory*, ed. G. Haberler, Philadelphia, 1944, pp. 169–92.

———, "Say's Law: A Restatement and Criticism," in *Studies in Mathematical Economics and Econometrics*, ed. O. Lange, *et al.*, Chicago, 1942, pp. 49–68.

———, *Price Flexibility and Employment*, Bloomington, Ind., 1945.

Lavington, F., *The English Capital Market*, London, 1921.

Leontief, W. W., "Composite Commodities and the Problem of Index Numbers," *Econometrica*, IV (1936), 39–59.

———, "The Fundamental Assumption of Mr. Keynes' Monetary Theory of Unemployment," *Quarterly Journal of Economics*, LI (1936–37), 192–97.

———, "Interrelation of Prices, Output, Savings, and Investment," *Review of Economic Statistics*, XIX (1937), 109–32.

———, "Postulates: Keynes' *General Theory* and the Classicists," *The New Economics*, ed. S. E. Harris, New York, 1948, pp. 232–42.

———, "The Consistency of the Classical Theory of Money and Prices," *Econometrica*, XVIII (1950), 21–24.

———, *Structure of American Economy, 1919–39*, 2nd ed., enlarged, New York, 1951.

———, "Theoretical Note on Time-Preference, Productivity of Capital, Stagnation and Economic Growth," *American Economic Review*, XLVIII (1958), 105–111.

Lerner, A. P., "On Generalizing the General Theory," *American Economic Review*, L (1960), 121–43.

Leser, C. E. V., "The Consumer's Demand for Money," *Econometrica*, XI (1943), 123–40.

Lindahl, E., *Studies in the Theory of Money and Capital*, London, 1939.

Lindbeck, A., "Den Klassiska 'Dichotomien,'" *Ekonomisk Tidskrift*, LXIII (1961), 24–46.

———, *A Study in Monetary Analysis*, Stockholm, 1963.

Liu, Ta-Chung, "An Exploratory Quarterly Econometric Model of Effective Demand in the Postwar U.S. Economy," *Econometrica*, XXXI (1963), 301–48.

Liviatan, N., "On the Long-Run Theory of Consumption and Real Balances," *Oxford Economic Papers*, XVII (1965).

———, "Multiperiod Future Consumption as an Aggregate," forthcoming.

Bibliography of Works Cited

——, and Patinkin, D., "On the Economic Theory of Price Indexes," *Economic Development and Cultural Change*, IX (1961), 502–36.

Lloyd, C., "The Real-Balance Effect: *Sine Qua* What?," *Oxford Economic Papers*, XIV (1962), 267–74.

——, "The Real-Balance Effect and the Slutzky Equation," *Journal of Political Economy*, LXXII (1964), 295–99.

Lundberg, E., *Studies in the Theory of Economic Expansion*, Stockholm, 1937.

——, *Business Cycles and Economic Policy*, London, 1957.

Lydall, H. F., "Income, Assets, and the Demand for Money," *Review of Economics and Statistics*, XL (1958), 1–14.

Makower, H., and Marschak, J., "Assets, Prices and Monetary Theory," *Economica*, V (1938), as reprinted in *Readings in Price Theory*, ed. K. Boulding and G. J. Stigler, Philadelphia, 1952, pp. 283–310.

Malthus, T. R., *Principles of Political Economy*, 1st ed., as abridged in Ricardo, *Works*, ed. Sraffa, Vol. II; 2nd ed., reprinted Tokyo, 1936.

Manne, A. S., *Economic Analysis for Business Decisions*, New York, 1961.

Marchal, J., "La restauration de la théorie quantitative de la monnaie par Don Patinkin et ses limites," *Revue d'économie politique*, LXIX (1959), 877–920.

Marget, A. W., "Léon Walras and the 'Cash Balance Approach' to the Problem of the Value of Money," *Journal of Political Economy*, XXXIX (1931), 569–600.

——, "Monetary Aspects of the Walrasian System," *Journal of Political Economy*, XLIII (1935), 145–86.

——, *The Theory of Prices*, New York: Vol. I, 1938; Vol. II, 1942.

Markowitz, H., "Portfolio Selection," *Journal of Finance*, VII (1952), 77–91.

——, *Portfolio Selection*, New York, 1959.

Marschak, J., "Money and the Theory of Assets," *Econometrica*, VI (1938), 311–25.

——, "Money Illusion and Demand Analysis," *Review of Economic Statistics*, XXV (1943), 40–48.

——, "The Rationale of Money Demand and of 'Money Illusion,'" *Metroeconomica*, II (1950), 71–100.

——, "Economic Measurements for Policy and Prediction," *Studies in Econometric Method*, ed. W. C. Hood and T. C. Koopmans, New York, 1953, pp. 1–26.

Marshall, A., *Pure Theory of Foreign Trade*, reprinted London, 1930.

——, *Pure Theory of Domestic Values*, reprinted London, 1930.

——, *Principles of Economics*, 8th ed., London, 1920.

——, *Money, Credit and Commerce*, London, 1923.

————, *Official Papers*, London, 1926.

Marshall, A., and M. P., *Economics of Industry* (1881), excerpt as reprinted in *Readings in Business Cycles and National Income*, ed. A. H. Hansen and R. V. Clemence, New York, 1953, pp. 96–103.

Marty, A. L., "Gurley and Shaw on Money in a Theory of Finance," *Journal of Political Economy*, LXIX (1961), 56–62.

Marx, K., *Capital*, trans. S. Moore and E. Aveling, 3 vols., Chicago, 1906–09.

Mayer, T., "The Empirical Significance of the Real Balance Effect," *Quarterly Journal of Economics*, LXXIII (1959), 275–91.

McCulloch, J. R., *The Principles of Political Economy*, 4th ed., Edinburgh, 1849.

McKean, R. N., "Liquidity and a National Balance Sheet," *Journal of Political Economy*, LVII (1949), as reprinted in *Readings in Monetary Theory*, ed. F. A. Lutz and L. W. Mints, Philadelphia, 1951, pp. 63–88.

McManus, M., "On Patinkin's Use of Revealed Preference," *Southern Economic Journal*, XXIV (1957), 209–12.

Meinich, P., "Money Illusion and the Real Balance Effect," *Statsøkonomisk Tidsskrift*, LXXVIII (1964), 8–33.

Meltzer, A. H., "The Demand for Money: The Evidence from the Time Series," *Journal of Political Economy*, LXXI (1963), 219–46.

————, "Yet Another Look at the Low Level Liquidity Trap," *Econometrica*, XXXI (1963), 545–49.

Metzler, L. A., "Business Cycles and the Modern Theory of Employment," *American Economic Review*, XXXVI (1946), 278–91.

————, "Wealth, Saving, and the Rate of Interest," *Journal of Political Economy*, LIX (1951), 93–116.

Michaely, M., "Relative-Prices and Income-Absorption Approaches to Devaluation: A Partial Reconciliation," *American Economic Review*, L (1960), 144–47.

Mill, J., *Elements of Political Economy*, London, 1821.

Mill, J. S., *Essays on Some Unsettled Questions of Political Economy* (1844), reprinted London, 1948.

————, *Principles of Political Economy*, ed. W. J. Ashley, London, 1909.

Mincer, J., "Market Prices, Opportunity Costs, and Income Effects," in Carl Christ *et al.*, *Measurement in Economics: Studies in Mathematical Economics and Econometrics in Memory of Yehuda Grunfeld*, Stanford, 1963, pp. 67–82.

Mints, L. W., *A History of Banking Theory*, Chicago, 1945.

————, *Monetary Policy for a Competitive Society*, New York, 1950.

Mises, L. von, *The Theory of Money and Credit*, trans. H. E. Batson, New York, 1935.

Bibliography of Works Cited

Mishan, E. J., "A Fallacy in the Interpretation of the Cash Balance Effect," *Economica*, XXV (1958), 106–18.

Modigliani, F., "Liquidity Preference and the Theory of Interest and Money," *Econometrica*, XII (1944), as reprinted in *Readings in Monetary Theory*, ed. F. A. Lutz and L. W. Mints, Philadelphia, 1951, pp. 186–239.

———, Postscript to "Liquidity Preference and the Theory of Interest and Money," in *The Critics of Keynesian Economics*, ed. H. Hazlitt, Princeton, 1960, pp. 183–84.

———, "The Monetary Mechanism and Its Interaction with Real Phenomena," *Review of Economics and Statistics*, XLV (1963), Supplement, pp. 79–107.

———, "Some Empirical Tests of Monetary Management and of Rules versus Discretion," *Journal of Political Economy*, LXXII (1964), 211–45.

Montesquieu, C. de, *The Spirit of the Laws*, trans. T. Nugent, 2 vols. in 1, New York, 1949.

Moore, H. L., *Synthetic Economics*, New York, 1929.

Morag, A., "Deflationary Effects of Outlay and Income Taxes," *Journal of Political Economy*, LXVII (1959), 266–74.

Morishima, Michio, "Existence of Solution to the Walrasian System of Capital Formation and Credit," *Zeitschrift für Nationalökonomie*, XX (1960), 238–43.

———, and Saito, Mitsuo, "A Dynamic Analysis of the American Economy, 1902–1952," *International Economic Review*, V (1964), 125–64.

Mosak, J. L., "On the Interpretation of the Fundamental Equation of Value Theory," in *Studies in Mathematical Economics and Econometrics*, ed. O. Lange, *et al.*, Chicago, 1942, pp. 69–74.

Mundell, R. A., "The Public Debt, Corporate Income Taxes, and the Rate of Interest," *Journal of Political Economy*, LXVIII (1960), 622–26.

Musgrave, R., *Theory of Public Finance*, New York, 1959.

Myrdal, G., *Monetary Equilibrium*, London, 1939.

Negishi, T., "The Stability of Competitive Economy: A Survey Article," *Econometrica*, XXX (1962), 635–69.

Nerlove, Marc, "Distributed Lags and Estimation of Long-Run Supply and Demand Elasticities: Theoretical Considerations," *Journal of Farm Economics*, XL (1958), 301–11.

Neumann, J. von, "A Model of General Economic Equilibrium," *Review of Economic Studies*, XIII (1945–46), 1–9.

Nevin, E., *The Mechanism of Cheap Money*, Cardiff, 1955.

Newcomb, S., *Principles of Political Economy*, New York, 1885.

Nicholson, J. S., *A Treatise on Money*, London, 1888.

———, *Principles of Political Economy*, London: Vol. I, 1893; Vol. II, 1897; Vol. III, 1901.

Ohlin, B., *Interregional and International Trade*, Cambridge, Mass., 1933.
———, "Alternative Theories of the Rate of Interest," *Economic Journal*, XLVII (1937), 423–27.
Osorio, A., *Théorie mathématique de l'échange*, trans. J. D'Almada, Paris, 1913.

Paish, F. W., "Cheap Money Policy," *Economica*, XIV (1947), 167–79.
Palgrave, R. H., *Bank Rate in England, France, and Germany, 1844–78*, London, 1880.
Palgrave's Dictionary of Political Economy, new ed., London, 1923, article "Interest, Theory of."
Pantaleoni, M., *Pure Economics*, trans. T. B. Bruce, London, 1898.
Pareto, V., *Cours d'économie politique*, 2 vols., Lausanne, 1896–97.
———, *Manuel d'économie politique*, 2nd ed., Paris, 1927.
Patinkin, D., "Relative Prices, Say's Law, and the Demand for Money," *Econometrica*, XVI (1948), 135–54.
———, "Price Flexibility and Full Employment," *American Economic Review*, XXXVIII (1948), 543–64; ibid., XXXIX (1949), 726–28; reprinted with revisions in *Readings in Monetary Theory*, ed. F. A. Lutz and L. W. Mints, Philadelphia, 1951, pp. 252–83.
———, "The Indeterminacy of Absolute Prices in Classical Economic Theory," *Econometrica*, XVII (1949), 1–27.
———, "Involuntary Unemployment and the Keynesian Supply Function," *Economic Journal*, LIX (1949), 360–83.
———, "A Reconsideration of the General Equilibrium Theory of Money," *Review of Economic Studies*, XVIII (1950–51), 42–61.
———, "The Invalidity of Classical Monetary Theory," *Econometrica*, XIX (1951), 134–51.
———, "Further Considerations of the General Equilibrium Theory of Money," *Review of Economic Studies*, XIX (1951–52), 186–95.
———, "The Limitations of Samuelson's 'Correspondence Principle,'" *Metroeconomica*, IV (1952), 37–43.
———, "Wicksell's Cumulative Process," *Economic Journal*, LXII (1952), 835–47.
———, "Dichotomies of the Pricing Process in Economic Theory," *Economica*, XXI (1954), 113–28.
———, "Keynesian Economics and the Quantity Theory," in *Post-Keynesian Economics*, ed. K. K. Kurihara, New Brunswick, N.J., 1954, pp. 123–52.

Bibliography of Works Cited

————, "Monetary and Price Developments in Israel: 1949–1953," *Scripta Hierosolymitana*, III (1955), 20–52.

————, "Secular Price Movements and Economic Development: Some Theoretical Aspects," in *The Challenge of Development*, ed. A. Bonné, Jerusalem, 1958, pp. 27–40.

————, "Liquidity Preference and Loanable Funds: Stock and Flow Analysis," *Economica*, XXV (1958), 300–18; XXVI (1959), 253–55.

————, *The Israel Economy: The First Decade*, Jerusalem, 1959.

————, "Keynesian Economics Rehabilitated: A Rejoinder to Professor Hicks," *Economic Journal*, LXIX (1959), 582–87.

————, "Financial Intermediaries and the Logical Structure of Monetary Theory," *American Economic Review*, LI (1961), 95–116.

————, "Demand Curves and Consumer's Surplus," in Carl Christ, *et al.*, *Measurement in Economics: Studies in Mathematical Economics and Econometrics in Memory of Yehuda Grunfeld*, Stanford, 1963, pp. 83–112.

————, "An Indirect-Utility Approach to the Theory of Money, Assets, and Savings," in *The Theory of Interest Rates*, ed. F. H. Hahn and F. Brechling, London, 1965, pp. 52–79.

Phillips, A. W., "A Simple Model of Employment, Money and Prices in a Growing Economy," *Economica*, XXVIII (1961), 360–70.

Phipps, C. G., "A Note on Patinkin's 'Relative Prices,'" *Econometrica*, XVIII (1950), 25–26.

Pigou, A. C., "The Value of Money," *Quarterly Journal of Economics*, XXXII (1917–18), as reprinted in *Readings in Monetary Theory*, ed. F. A. Lutz and L. W. Mints, Philadelphia, 1951, pp. 162–83.

————, "The Exchange Value of Legal Tender Money," *Essays in Applied Economics*, London, 1923, pp. 174–98.

————, *Industrial Fluctuations*, 2nd ed., London, 1929.

————, *Economics of Welfare*, 4th ed., London, 1932.

————, *Economics of Stationary States*, London, 1935.

————, *Employment and Equilibrium*, London, 1941.

————, "The Classical Stationary State," *Economic Journal*, LIII (1943), 343–51.

————, "Economic Progress in a Stable Environment," *Economica*, XIV (1947), as reprinted in *Readings in Monetary Theory*, ed. F. A. Lutz and L. W. Mints, Philadelphia, 1951, pp. 241–51.

Power, J. H., "Price Expectations, Money Illusion, and the Real-Balance Effect," *Journal of Political Economy*, LXVII (1959), 131–43.

Ricardo, D., *Works and Correspondence*, ed. P. Sraffa, 9 vols, Cambridge, 1951–52.

Robertson, D. H., *Banking Policy and the Price Level*, London, 1926.

——, *Essays in Monetary Theory*, London, 1940.

——, *Money*, rev. ed., London, 1948.

——, "More Notes on the Rate of Interest," *Review of Economic Studies*, XXI (1953–54), 136–41.

Robinson, Joan, "The Rate of Interest," *Econometrica*, XIX (1951), 92–111.

——, *The Rate of Interest*, London, 1952.

Robson, P., "Index-Linked Bonds," *Review of Economic Studies*, XXVIII (1960), 57–68.

Rosenstein-Rodan, P. N., "The Coördination of the General Theories of Money and Price," *Economica*, III (1936), 257–80.

Samuelson, P. A., "A Note on the Pure Theory of Consumer's Behavior," *Economica*, V (1938), 61–71.

——, *Foundations of Economic Analysis*, Cambridge, Mass., 1947.

——, "The Simple Mathematics of Income Determination," in *Income, Employment and Public Policy: Essays in Honor of Alvin H. Hansen*, New York, 1948, pp. 133–55.

——, *Economics: An Introductory Analysis*, 2nd ed., New York, 1951; 5th ed., New York, 1961.

——, "Consumption Theorems in Terms of Overcompensation rather than Indifference Comparisons," *Economica*, XX (1953), 1–9.

Say, J. B., *Traité d'économie Politique*, 3rd ed., Paris, 1817.

——, *Letters to Malthus* (1821), reprinted London, 1936.

——, *A Treatise on Political Economy*, trans. C. R. Prinsep from the 4th French ed., Philadelphia, 1834.

Sayers, R. S., "British and American Experience in the Early Post-War Years," *Quarterly Journal of Economics*, LXIII (1949), as reprinted in *Central Banking After Bagehot*, Oxford, 1957, pp. 20–34.

Schlesinger, K., *Theorie der Geld- und Kreditwirtschaft*, Munich, 1914.

——, "Basic Principles of the Money Economy," *International Economic Papers*, No. 9 (1959), 20–38 [a translation of Chapter 3 of the preceding].

——, "Über die Produktionsgleichungen der ökonomischen Wertlehre," *Ergebnisse eines mathematischen Kolloquiums*, VI (1933–34), 10–11.

Schotta, C., Jr., "The Real Balance Effect in the U.S., 1947–63," *Journal of Finance*, XIX (1964), 619–30.

Schneider, E., *Pricing and Equilibrium*, trans. T. W. Hutchison, London, 1952.

——, "Patinkin über Geld und Güterpreise," in *Festskrift til Frederik Zeuthen*, Copenhagen, 1958, pp. 315–31.

Schultze, C. L., *Recent Inflation in the United States*, Washington, D.C., 1959. (Study Paper No. 1 of the Joint Economic Committee, Congress of the U.S.).

Bibliography of Works Cited

Schumpeter, J. A., "Money and the Social Product," *Archiv für Sozialwissenschaft und Sozialpolitik*, XLIV (1917/18), as translated in *International Economic Papers*, No. 6 (1956), 148–211.

———, *Theory of Economic Development*, Cambridge, 1934.

———, *History of Economic Analysis*, New York, 1954.

Scitovsky, T., "Capital Accumulation, Employment and Price Rigidity," *Review of Economic Studies*, VIII (1940–41), 69–88.

Shackle, G. L. S., "Interest Rates and the Pace of Investment," *Economic Journal*, LVI (1946), 1–17.

———, "The Nature of Interest Rates," *Oxford Economic Papers*, New Series, I (1949) as reprinted in *Uncertainty in Economics*, Cambridge, 1955, pp. 105–27.

———, "Recent Theories Concerning the Nature and Role of Interest," *Economic Journal*, LXXI (1961), 209–54.

Shaw, E. S., *Money, Income, and Monetary Policy*, Chicago, 1950.

Shephard, R. W., *Cost and Production Functions*, Princeton, 1953.

Sidgwick, H., *The Principles of Political Economy*, London, 1883.

Simons, H. C., *Economic Policy for a Free Society*, Chicago, 1948.

Spiro, A., "Wealth and the Consumption Function," *Journal of Political Economy*, LXX (1962), 339–54.

Spraos, J., "An Engel-Type Curve for Cash," *Manchester School of Economics and Social Studies*, XXV (1957), 183–89.

Stein, Herbert, "Price Flexibility and Full Employment: Comment," *American Economic Review*, XXXIX (1949), 725–26.

Stigler, G. J., *Production and Distribution Theories*, New York, 1941.

———, *Theory of Price*, rev. ed., New York, 1952.

———, "Sraffa's *Ricardo*," *American Economic Review*, XLIII (1953), 586–99.

Suits, D. B., "The Determinants of Consumer Expenditure: A Review of Present Knowledge," in Commission on Money and Credit, *Impacts of Monetary Policy*, Englewood Cliffs, N.J., 1963, pp. 1–59.

Suppes, P., *Introduction to Logic*, Princeton, 1957.

Taussig, F. W., *Principles of Economics*, 2 vols., 4th ed., revised, New York, 1939.

Thore, S., *Household Saving and the Price Level*, Stockholm, 1961.

Thornton, H., *An Enquiry into the Nature and Effects of the Paper Credit of Great Britain*, London, 1802.

Tinbergen, J., *Econometrics*, Philadelphia, 1951.

Tobin, J., "Liquidity Preference and Monetary Policy," *Review of Economic Statistics*, XXIX (1947), 124–31.

———, "A Dynamic Aggregative Model," *Journal of Political Economy*, LXIII (1955), 103–15.

——, "The Interest Elasticity of Transactions Demand for Cash," *Review of Economics and Statistics*, XXXVIII (1956), 241–47.

——, "Liquidity Preference as Behavior Toward Risk," *Review of Economic Studies*, XXV (1958), 65–86.

United Nations Department of Economic Affairs, *Inflationary and Deflationary Tendencies, 1946–48*, New York, 1949.

Valavanis, S., "A Denial of Patinkin's Contradiction," *Kyklos*, VII (1955), 351–66.

Viner, J., *Studies in the Theory of International Trade*, New York, 1937.

Wald, A., "Uber die eindeutige positive Lösbarkeit der neuen Produktionsgleichungen," *Ergebnisse eines mathematischen Kolloquiums*, VI (1933–34), 12–20.

——, "On Some Systems of Equations of Mathematical Economics," *Econometrica*, XIX (1951), 368–403.

Walras, L., *Eléments d'économie politique pure*, Lausanne: 1st ed., 1874–77 (issued in two consecutively paginated volumes); 2nd ed., 1889; 3rd ed., 1896; 4th ed., 1900; definitive ed., 1926.

——, *Théorie de la monnaie*, Paris, 1886.

——, *Etudes d'économie politique appliquée*, Paris, 1898.

——, "Equations de la circulation," *Bulletin de la Société Vaudoise des Sciences Naturelles*, XXXV (1899), 85–103.

——, *Elements of Pure Economics*, trans. and ed. W. Jaffé, London, 1954.

Weinberger, O., *Mathematische Volkswirtschaftslehre*, Leipzig, 1930.

Whitin, T. M., *The Theory of Inventory Management*, 2nd ed., Princeton, 1957.

Wicksell, K., *Value Capital and Rent*, trans. S. H. Frowein, London, 1954.

——, *Interest and Prices*, trans. R. F. Kahn, London, 1936.

——, *Lectures on Political Economy*, (Vol. I, *General Theory*; Vol. II, *Money*), trans. E. Classen, London, 1934–5.

——, "The Influence of the Rate of Interest on Prices," *Economic Journal*, XVII (1907), 213–19.

Wilson, E. B., "Notes on Utility Theory and Demand Equations," *Quarterly Journal of Economics*, LX (1945–46), 453–60.

Wold, H., *Demand Analysis*, Stockholm, 1952.

Wonnacott, P., "Neutral Money in Patinkin's Money, Interest and Prices," *Review of Economic Studies*, XXVI (1958), 70–71.

Zellner, A., "A Short-Run Consumption Function," *Econometrica*, XXV (1957), 552–67.

Index of Names

693

Index of Names

Hicks, J.R., xxi, 77 n., 369 n., 575 n., 627; and complementarity, 108 n., 416; and composite-good theorem, 411–416; and convexity of indifference curve, 152 n., 415 n.; and demand for money, 349 n., 352 n.; and dichotomies, 175 n., 626 n.; and dynamic analysis, 51 n., 67 n., 539, 540; and employment theory, 330 n., 331 n., 333 n., 353 n.; and equilibrium concepts, 51 n.; and income effect, *see* and wealth effect; and interest theory, 80 n., 81 n., 109–110, 213 n., 330 n., 331 n., 333 n., 336 n., 349 n., 376; and "liquidity trap," 349 n., 353 n.; and "marginal utility of money," 115 n.; and real-balance effect, 353 n.; and multi-period analysis, 61 n., 67 n.; and substitution effect, 20 n., 152 n., 405 n., 408 n., 415 n.; and *tâtonnement*, 533 n., 537 n.; and theory of consumer's behavior, 3, 5 n., 19, 152 n., 411–417; and Walras' Law, 377 n.; and Walras' monetary theory, 548; and wealth effect, 20 n., 405 n., 408–409
Hirsch, W., 573 n.
Hirshleifer, J., 132 n.
Horwich, G., 669
Hume, D., 366, 369, 530, 593 n., 630
Hurwicz, L., xx, 39 n., 42 n., 312 n., 431 n., 540 n.

Indian Currency Committee, 603 n., 630 n.

Jaffé, W., xxi; and dichotomy in Walras, 559 n., 561 n., 562 n.; 571 n.; and multiple equilibria in Walras, 538 n.; and Walras' capital theory, 550 n., 554 n., 563 n.; and Walras' monetary theory, 541 n., 542 n., 543 n., 546 n., 549 n., 551 n., 553 n., 554 n., 557 n., 559 n., 563 n.; and Walras' *tâtonnement*, 533, 534 n.
James, E., 312 n.
Jevons, W.S., 370 n., 537, 630, 631
Johansen, L., 301 n.
Johnson, H.G., 29 n., 223 n., 378 n.; on demand curve for money, 31 n., 349 n., 423 n., 434 n.; on inside-outside-money models, 298 n.; on invalid dichotomy, 177 n.; on Keynes' speculative demand, 118 n., 126 n.; on Keynes' theory of unemployment, 635 n.; on real-balance effect, 289 n., 635 n.; on stocks and flows, 20 n., 423 n.
Jong, F.J. de, 666–667
Jorgenson, D., xvii, 126 n., 416 n.

Kahn, R.F., 81 n., 352 n.
Kaldor, N., 40 n., 533
Kalecki, M., 296 n.
Kennedy, C.M., 355 n.
Keynes, J.M., xxi, 163 n., 527, 604 n.; and demand curve for money, 222–223; and employment theory, 324–325, 335–343, 365, 643–644; and full-

Keynes, J.M. (*Continued*) employment policy, 336, 339–340; and "homogeneity postulate," 627 n., 628 n., 642; and interest theory, 81 n., 109–110, 253–254, 257, 278–281, 329–330, 366, 370 n., 372–375, 380, 633 n., 637–642, 670; and "liquidity trap," 349–354; and minimum interest rate, 69, 215, 221, 349–354; and multiplier, 343–348; as neoclassical economist, 167, 544, 563 n., 574, 580 n., 603, 609 n., 630, 631 n.; and portfolio approach to monetary theory, 81 n.; and pure inside-money model, 339 n., 635; and quantity theory, 257, 369, 370 n., 638 n.; and real-balance effect in bond market, 352 n., 635; and real-balance effect in commodity market, 180, 241–242, 339 n., 634–637; and real-balance effect in money market, 254, 352 n., 635; and real wage rate, 324 n., 341 n.; and Say's Identity, 193, 355–357, 367 n., 645–647; and Schlesinger, 577–578; and shift in liquidity preference, 248, 334, 669; and speculative demand for money, 118 n., 253–255, 257, 278–281, 638–641; and stocks and flows, 165, 188, 636–637; and supply function for commodities, 325, 358, 667; and "unemployment equilibrium," 315, 643–644; and wage and price flexibility, 337 n.; and Walras, 372, 557 n.
Kinley, D., 574 n.
Klein, L.R., 346 n., 392 n.; on empirical estimates of real-balance effect, 652–658 *passim*; on Keynesian theory of employment, 336 n.; on stocks and flows, 376 n., 378 n.
Knight, F.H., 314 n.
Koopmans, T.C., 627
Kuenne, R.E., 180 n., 538 n., 548 n., 550 n., 557 n., 561 n., 562 n., 566 n., 571 n., 572 n., 578 n., 670
Kuh, E., 652 n.
Kurimura, Y., 665
Kuznets, S., 161 n., 649

Lange, O., 336 n., 341 n.; and dichotomies, 174, 175 n., 181 n., 625; and Say's Identity, 193, 194 n., 195 n., 482–483, 645, 647; and *tâtonnement*, 537 n.; and Walras, 545 n., 549 n.; and Walras' Law, 36 n.
Latané, H., 223 n.
Lavington, F., 372, 549 n., 579
Leontief, W.W., 96 n., 527, 665; on composite good, 411, 412 n.; on "homogeneity postulate" and invalid dichotomy, 174 n., 175 n., 184 n., 185 n., 625–628 *passim*; on Keynesian economics, 373 n., 642
Lerner, A.P., 327 n., 377 n., 647 n.,
Leser, C.E.V., 55 n., 405 n., 408 n., 411, 434 n., 582
Levhari, D., xvii

695

Index of Names

Pareto, V., 3; and dichotomy, 570 n., 625 n.; and marginal utility of money, 575; and monetary theory, 571, 624; and *tâtonnement*, 535, 536 n., 538, 539 n.

Patinkin, D., 12 n., 37 n., 118 n., 136 n., 147 n., 171 n., 188 n., 258 n., 295 n., 333 n., 353 n., 410 n., 412 n., 416 n., 458 n., 520 n., 626 n., 629 n., 651 n., 664 n., 665, 666, 667

Phillips, A.W., 363 n.

Phipps, C., 665

Pigou, A.C., 579 n., 621; and banking system, 299 n.; and cash-balance approach, *see* and quantity theory; and determinants of K, 18 n.; and "forced savings," 371, 632, 633 n.; and interest theory, 366, 370 n., 630; and invalid dichotomy, 174, 175 n., 183, 609–610, 624 n.; and meaning of T, 170 n.; and quantity theory, 15 n., 163, 166 n., 167, 299 n., 549 n.; and real-balance effect, 19 n., 364 n., 603, 636; and stability analysis, 604, 605; and unitary elasticity of demand for money, 169, 606–608

Power, J.H., 144 n.

Ricardo, D., 627 n.; cited by Keynes, 641–642; and interest theory, 239–241, 366, 367, 369, 590 n., 593 n., 630, 641–642; and quantity theory, 58 n., 164, 239–241, 529, 530; and "Say's Law," 365 n., 645, 646, 648, 649 n.

Robertson, D.H., 586 n.; and interest theory, 367 n., 579, 632, 633 n.; and quantity theory, 167, 549 n., 603; and stability analysis in money market, 604–605, and threefold margin, 94 n.

Robinson, J., 81 n., 352 n., 355 n.

Robson, P., 292 n.

Rosenstein-Rodan, P.N., 175 n., 595 n., 596 n., 625

Saito, M., 340 n., 654, 655, 656, 660

Samuelson, P.A., xxi, 110 n., 268 n., 387 n., 609; and "correspondence principle," 386, 496–498, 509; and demand curve for money, 609; and dynamic analysis, 39 n., 67 n., 235 n., 429–430, 485 n., 539–540; and "homogeneity postulate," 175 n., 184 n., 625, 627 n., 628 n.; and index numbers, 412 n.; and interest theory, 110 n.; and real-balance effect, 637 n.; and revealed preferences, 96 n., 460–461; and utility analysis of money, 411, 574 n., 578

Savage, L.J., 119 n.

Say, J.B., 365 n.; 645, 646 n., 649

Sayers, R.S., 355 n.

Schlesinger, K., and invalid dichotomy, 568 n., 569–570 n., 624 n.; and Keynesian interest theory, 372 n., 577–578; and marginal-utility theory of money, 571, 576–577, 579; and nature of demand for money, 81 n., 148 n.,

Schlesinger, K. (*Continued*)
576–577; and penalty costs, 148 n.; and probability analysis of money, 87 n., 88 n., 576–577; and solubility of system, 37 n., 538 n.

Schneider, E., 174, 175 n., 625, 626, 628 n.

Schotta, C., Jr., 653 n.

Schultze, C.L., 310 n.

Schumpeter, J.A., 571 n., 574 n.; and "forced savings," 59 n., 164 n.; and "Say's Law," 647, 650 n.; and *tâtonnement*, 531 n., 533, 539–540; and Walras' monetary theory, 542 n., 548 n., 553 n., 561 n., 566 n., 569 n., 571 n.

Scitovsky, T., 636 n.

Selden, R.T., 223 n.

Shackle, G.L.S., 81 n., 336 n., 378 n., 586 n., 588 n.

Shaw, E.S., 64 n.
See also Gurley, J.G., and Shaw, E.S.

Shephard, R.W., 416 n.

Sheshinsky, E., xvii

Shlain, A., xvii, 467 n.

Sidgwick, H., 366, 574 n., 630

Simons, H.C., 340 n.

Sismondi, J.C.L.S. de, 365, 647

Slutzky, E., 3, 10 n., 141, 405 n., 406, 408

Smith, P. E., 653 n.

Somers, H.M., 376 n.

Spiro, A., 20 n., 201 n.

Spraos, J., 29 n.

Stein, H., xxi, 665

Stigler, G.J., 11 n., 537 n., 647 n.

Strotz, R.H., 652 n.

Suits, D.B., 657 n.

Suppes, P., 177 n.

Taussig, F.W., 608, 609

Thore, S., 652

Thornton, H., 164, 366, 367, 369, 370 n., 529, 593, 630

Tinbergen, J., 175 n., 625, 628 n.

Tobin, J., xvi; on consumption function, 19 n.; on growth models, 363 n.; on inventory approach to demand for money, 147 n., 148 n.; on Keynes' speculative demand for money, 118 n., 126 n.; on "liquidity trap," 223 n., 350 n.; on portfolio approach to demand for money, 81 n., 119 n., 123 n., 126 n., 156 n., 226 n.

Uzawa, H., 431 n.

Valavanis, S., 628, 629 n.

Viner, J., 58 n., 292 n., 309 n., 590 n., 631 n.

Wald, A., 37 n., 405 n., 538

Wallace, N., 655 n.

Walras, L., 81 n., 527, 573, 583, 611, 624, 666, 670; and cash-balance equation, 163, 543–544; and cash-balance theory, 163 n., 549; and demand curve for money, 567–568, 608 n.; followers of,

Index of Subjects*

* Discussions in the Mathematical Appendix and Supplementary Notes to which cross-references are given in the text are for the most part not listed again in this Index.

699

Index of Subjects

Dimensions, time, *see* Time dimensions

Discounting of future, 63–64, 112 n.
See also Time preference

Disequilibrium, and dynamic analysis, 234–235; and unemployment theory, 323, 328, 337–338

Disinflation, 310 n.

Disposable income, 208

Distribution effects, assumed absent, 200, 207; and government bonds, 292; implications of, 285–289; neutral, 74; and unemployment, 336–337

Diversification of portfolio, 149 n., 301

Dynamic analysis, 34, 39, 44–45, 230–236, 258, 263, 273, 310–312, 331–333, 335, 539; and comparative statics, 287 n.; deficiencies of in classical monetary theory, 530; deficiencies of in neoclassical monetary theory, 167–169, 186; and general-equilibrium analysis, 260–263; in growth models, 361–362; not affected by choice of market, 261–262; oversimplified assumptions of, 235–236; and unemployment, 323, 325–328
See also "Correspondence principle"

Dynamic system, 178, 260–262, 429–430, 477, 485, 487, 510

Economies of scale, in lending and borrowing, 301; and money reserves, 87, 155–156, 158, 192: absent from precautionary motive, 125: role in growth model, 363

Efficient portfolio, 125

Elasticity of demand, for money, 27–30, 424; and money illusion, 23
See also Unitary elasticity of demand for money

Elimination of dependent equation, 37, 428

Employment policy, Keynesian, 336–337, 339

Employment policy, neoclassical, 335–336, 340

Employment theory, Keynesian, ignores commodity supply curve, 325, 339, 344, 358, 666–667; ignores real-balance effect, 325, 353; interpretation of, 337–339; and Keynesian interest theory, 375; and labor supply curve, 341–342; and "liquidity trap," 353; and minimum interest rate, 349–355; oversimplified form of, 324–325, 339, 357; and rigidities, 340–342; and Say's Identity, 355–358
See also "Diagonal-cross" diagram

Employment theory, neoclassical, 336, 340; independent of Say's Identity, 355–357, 360

"*Encaisse désirée*," 542, 544, 545

Endogenous variables, *see* Dependent variables

Endowment, initial, analogy to income, 9, 61; analogy to wealth, 19; defined for barter economy, 6; defined for money economy, 13, 17, 19; defined for multi-

Endowment (*Continued*)
period economy, 61; effects of change in, 191–192

Engel curve, 416; for money, 30–31

Equations, dependent, 37, 73, 194

Equations and variables, counting of, 36–37, 73–74, 228–229, 536–537; equality in number, 37

Equation of exchange, 163, 184

Equilibrium, defined, 11, 35; and full employment, 315; long-run, defined, 50, 51 n.: dynamics of, 51–56: distribution of real balances in, 53: not present in Keynesian or growth models, 58–59; multiplicity of, 45, 539 n.; short-run defined, 50, 51 n.; stability of, 38–39, 539 n.

Euler's theorem, 492

Excess capacity, 321, 325; defined, 6–7; for money, 24

Excess-demand curve, defined and generated, 7–8; market, relation of to individual curves, 10, 31–33; relation to excess-demand function, 10

Excess-demand function, *see* Bonds, excess-demand function for; Commodities, excess-demand function for; Money, excess-demand function for

Excess output, 321

Excess payment due, defined, 84

Excess supply, defined, 7; of commodities, 321

Exchange economy, defined, 4; not restrictive assumption, 76

Exogenous variables, *see* Independent variables

Expectations, certain, 61, 67, 80, 200, 257–258; destabilizing, 310–312, 337; in growth models, 361; static and dynamic, 80 n.; uncertain, *see* Uncertainty; and unemployment, 337

Expected-utility hypothesis, 118–119

External drain, 591

Financial-asset effect, 290, 307, 311, 317

Financial assets, net, definition of, 289–290, 295–296, 299, 307, 654 n., 662 n., 664; in postwar period, 21, 656

Financial embarrassment, 79

Financial intermediaries, 301–302

Financing of investment, 271–272

Fisherine analysis, generalized to money economy, 96, 110–114, 128–136; and infinite horizon, 96 n.; and liquidity of bonds, 113–114
See also Time preference; Wealth restraint, Fisherine

Flexibility, wage and price, 275; and monetary theory, 328–334; and unemployment, 315, 323–324, 327, 337

Flight from cash, 145

Flow, *see* Stocks and flows

"Flow equilibrium" *vs* "Stock equilibrium," 51 n.

Flow of funds, 201–202

"Forced savings," 59, 164, 285–287, 371

Index of Subjects